JAMES HOGG

# Contributions to
# Blackwood's Edinburgh Magazine

## Volume 1: 1817–1828

THE STIRLING / SOUTH CAROLINA RESEARCH EDITION OF
THE COLLECTED WORKS OF JAMES HOGG
GENERAL EDITORS – DOUGLAS S. MACK AND GILLIAN HUGHES

THE STIRLING / SOUTH CAROLINA RESEARCH EDITION OF
# THE COLLECTED WORKS OF JAMES HOGG
GENERAL EDITORS – DOUGLAS S. MACK AND GILLIAN HUGHES

Volumes are numbered in the order of their publication in
the Stirling / South Carolina Research Edition

JAMES HOGG

# Contributions to Blackwood's Edinburgh Magazine

## Volume 1: 1817–1828

Edited by
Thomas C. Richardson

EDINBURGH UNIVERSITY PRESS
2008

© Edinburgh University Press, 2008

Edinburgh University Press
22 George Square
Edinburgh
EH8 9LF

Typeset at the University of Stirling and in Manchester
Printed by Antony Rowe Ltd, Chippenham, Wiltshire

ISBN 978 0 7486 2488 1

A CIP record for this book is available
from the British Library

The Stirling / South Carolina Research Edition of

# The Collected Works of James Hogg

## Advisory Board

## The Aims of the Edition

James Hogg lived from 1770 till 1835. He was regarded by his contemporaries as one of the leading writers of the day, but the nature
of his fame was influenced by the fact that, as a young man, he had
been a self-educated shepherd. The second edition (1813) of his poem
*The Queen's Wake* contains an 'Advertisement' which begins as
follows.

> THE *Publisher having been favoured with letters from gentlemen in vari-*
> *ous parts of the United Kingdom respecting the Author of the* QUEEN'S
> WAKE, *and most of them expressing doubts of his being a Scotch Shepherd,*

> *he takes this opportunity of assuring the public, that* THE QUEEN'S WAKE
> *is really and truly the production of* JAMES HOGG, *a* common Shep-
> herd, *bred among the mountains of Ettrick Forest, who went to service
> when only seven years of age; and since that period has never received any
> education whatever.*

His contemporaries tended to regard the Scotch Shepherd as a man
of powerful and original talent, but it was felt that his lack of education caused his work to be marred by frequent failures in discretion,
in expression, and in knowledge of the world. Worst of all was Hogg's
lack of what was called 'delicacy', a failing which caused him to deal
in his writings with subjects (such as prostitution) which were felt to
be unsuitable for mention in polite literature.

A posthumous collected edition of Hogg was published in the late
1830s. As was perhaps natural in the circumstances, the publishers
(Blackie & Son of Glasgow) took pains to smooth away what they
took to be the rough edges of Hogg's writing, and to remove his
numerous 'indelicacies'. This process was taken even further in the
1860s, when the Rev. Thomas Thomson prepared a revised edition
of Hogg's *Works* for publication by Blackie. These Blackie editions
present a comparatively bland and lifeless version of Hogg's writings. It was in this version that Hogg was read by the Victorians, and
he gradually came to be regarded as a minor figure, of no great
importance or interest.

Hogg is thus a major writer whose true stature was not recognised in his own lifetime because his social origins led to his being
smothered in genteel condescension; and whose true stature was
obscured after his death, because of a lack of adequate editions. The
poet Douglas Dunn wrote of Hogg in the *Glasgow Herald* in September 1988: 'I can't help but think that in almost any other country of
Europe a complete, modern edition of a comparable author would
have been available long ago'. The Stirling / South Carolina Edition
of James Hogg seeks to fill the gap identified by Douglas Dunn.
When completed the edition will run to thirty-four volumes; and it
will cover Hogg's prose, his poetry, and his plays.

### General Editors' Acknowledgements

The research for the volumes of the Stirling / South Carolina Edition of James Hogg has been sustained by funding and other support generously made available by the University of Stirling and by
the University of South Carolina. Valuable grants or donations have

also been received from the Carnegie Trust for the Universities of Scotland, from the Arts amd Humanities Research Council, from the Association for Scottish Literary Studies, and from the James Hogg Society. The work of the Edition could not have been carried on without the support of these bodies.

Dr Gillian Hughes was General Editor for the present volume, and her work during the earlier stages of its preparation was made possible by a major research grant awarded by the Arts and Humanities Research Board to the Stirling/South Carolina Research Edition of the Collected Works of James Hogg.

## Volume Editor's Acknowledgements

This volume has been completed with the gracious assistance and support of many people and institutions. First and foremost I want to thank Gillian Hughes, the General Editor for this volume, who has been a model editor in every way throughout the lengthy process of completing this edition. Gill has freely shared her vast knowledge of Hogg's life and works, she has been meticulous in her attention to the details of the text, and she has always been prompt and thorough in response to my questions and in completing her editorial duties. A special note of thanks also goes to Douglas Mack, who invited me to edit the present edition and who has been exceedingly generous with his exceptional knowledge of Hogg. Both Gill and Douglas have provided information and suggestions far beyond the specific acknowledgements in the annotations to the texts. There are also several Hogg scholars to whom I am indebted for their previous research on matters related to Hogg and *Blackwood's Edinburgh Magazine*, especially to Peter Garside and David Groves, as well as J. H. Alexander, Ian Campbell, Janette Currie, Hans de Groot, Ian Duncan, and Robin MacLachan. Richard Jackson has provided valuable assistance with questions about Hogg's music. Duncan Macmillan has graciously provided information about Scottish artists in Hogg's time. I am also grateful to the Canadian author, Alice Munro, for talking with me about her family connections with the Hoggs and Laidlaws.

The present edition includes works published from Hogg's manuscripts held in several libraries. I wish to thank these libraries for permission to quote from and edit for publication manuscripts in their care: the Alexander Turnbull Library of the National Library of New Zealand, Wellington; the Beinecke Rare Book and Manuscript Library, Yale University; the British Library; the Mitchell Library, Cultural and Leisure Services, Glasgow City Council; Special Collections, the University of Otago Library, Dunedin, New Zealand; and the Trustees of the National Library of Scotland. I appreciate the assistance of the members of staff of these libraries, who without exception have attended to my requests with friendliness and the utmost professionalism.

Many people presently and formerly at Mississippi University for Women have been responsible for supporting me with research time and travel grants, as well as tending to my administrative duties in my absence: President Claudia Limbert, Sheila Adams, Tina Blackwell, Pat Donat, Sam Gingerich, Sandra Jordan, Dorothy Kerzel, Carol Morgan, Bridget Pieschel, and Lisa Powers. This project could not have been completed without the friendly assistance of Gail Gunter, Interim Director of the Fant Memorial Library and Interlibrary Loan Librarian. I also appreciate the assistance of Mississippi University for Women students: Jennifer Berryman, Lauren Dodd, Stephanie Evers, Moriah Mozingo, Laura Vernon, and Leigh Porciau. I want to acknowledge the Faculty Research Committee for a generous research grant to consult the Hogg manuscripts in the Beinecke Rare Book and Manuscript Library, Yale University. I also want to acknowledge the MUW administration and the Mississippi Board of Trustees of State Institutions of Higher Learning for granting me a sabbatical that enabled me to complete this volume.

Finally, I want to express my appreciation to my family for their support and assistance: my son, Thomas; my daughter, Cameron; and Cameron's husband, Cader Howard. I am deeply grateful to my wife, Emma, who has provided valuable advice along the way and, above all, who has encouraged my work and who has been exceptionally patient with me as I have frequently travelled away from home to be able to complete this project.

Thomas C. Richardson,
Mississippi University for Women

# Contents

Contributions to *Blackwood's Edinburgh Magazine* for 1817–1828

# Introduction

## 1. Hogg and the Beginning of *Blackwood's Edinburgh Magazine*

In the 'Memoir of the Life of James Hogg' that prefaces the third edition of *The Mountain Bard* (1821), James Hogg writes: 'I had the honour of being the beginner, and almost sole instigator of that celebrated work, BLACKWOOD'S MAGAZINE'.[1] Although Hogg perhaps exaggerates his role in the establishment of *Blackwood's Edinburgh Magazine* (from April through September 1817 William Blackwood's magazine was published as the *Edinburgh Monthly Magazine*), Hogg clearly was instrumental in the success and notoriety of Blackwood's periodical venture. Furthermore, Hogg's relationships—for good or for ill—with Blackwood and the magazine's major contributors were central both to his literary career and his personal life. Hogg published a story and a poem in the first issue of *Blackwood's Edinburgh Magazine* (*Edinburgh Monthly Magazine*), and from April 1817 until April 1835, just months before his death, Hogg contributed more than one hundred works to *Blackwood's* and wrote perhaps another forty pieces for the magazine that were not published there.[2] His contributions to *Blackwood's* showcase the diversity of his talent and his achievement as a writer; his published works include a variety of songs and lyric poetry, narrative and dramatic poetry, sketches of rural and farming life, review essays, ballads, short stories, satirical pieces, and even a 'screed' on politics.

*Blackwood's Edinburgh Magazine* was founded in 1817 by the Edinburgh bookseller and publisher, William Blackwood. Blackwood set up business as a bookseller on South Bridge in Edinburgh in 1804, after having learned the trade as an apprentice for Bell & Bradfute in Edinburgh and then as an employee of Mundell in Glasgow and Cuthill in London. In 1810 Blackwood expanded his business to include publishing. Blackwood's trade increased significantly in both scope and reputation in 1811 when he became the Edinburgh agent for the well-established and influential London publisher, John Murray, and the business was extended further in 1813 when Blackwood established ties with James and John Ballantyne, Walter Scott's printers. In what was considered a bold move at the time, Blackwood relocated his premises in 1816 from the Old Town of Edinburgh to the New Town, moving to 17 Princes

Street. It was from here that he launched his 'Maga'[3] into the periodical competition of Edinburgh. Blackwood had been encouraged to pursue this new enterprise by the review and magazine successes of his Edinburgh bookselling and publishing rival, Archibald Constable (publisher of the *Edinburgh Review* and *Scots Magazine*), as well as his London publishing ally, John Murray (publisher of the *Quarterly Review*). Blackwood's political leanings, like Murray's, were Tory, and Blackwood in part sought to establish a Tory voice in Scotland, like Murray's in London, to counter the Whig tendencies of Constable's *Edinburgh Review*. Blackwood also expected to compete favourably in the more-diverse 'magazine' market, again targeting Archibald Constable and capitalising on the declining interest in his long-standing *Scots Magazine*.[4]

James Hogg's business relationship with William Blackwood had begun in 1814 with the failure of George Goldie's publishing firm—almost three years before Blackwood's first issue of his first magazine. Goldie was the publisher of Hogg's successful book-length poem, *The Queen's Wake* (1813), but by 1814, in the midst of the general economic malaise resulting from the Napoleonic wars, Goldie found himself in financial difficulties. Hogg had wanted to publish the third edition of *The Queen's Wake* with Archibald Constable, whose financial position at the time was much more stable than Goldie's, but Goldie insisted on his right to publish the work. In July 1814 Goldie published the third edition; by early September Goldie had declared bankruptcy and sales of his titles had ceased. Had Goldie permitted Constable to publish the third edition of *The Queen's Wake*, there might have been a different history between Hogg and Blackwood. As it turned out, though, Blackwood was appointed one of the trustees for Goldie's firm; on 28 October 1814, Hogg wrote to Blackwood to seek relief from the restrictions on the sale of *The Queen's Wake* and to offer a plan for disposition of the inventory. Hogg was pleased with the manner in which the trustees handled his predicament with the Goldie firm, as he writes in the 1832 version of his 'Memoir': 'Mr. Blackwood sold the copies for me on commission, and ultimately paid me more than double of what I was to have received from Goldie. For this I was indebted to the consideration and kindness of the trustees'.[5] A year later Blackwood and Murray published Hogg's *Pilgrims of the Sun* (1815) and followed that with *Mador of the Moor* in 1816. By the time a plan for *Blackwood's Edinburgh Magazine* (*Edinburgh Monthly Magazine*) was conceived, then, Hogg was well established with William Blackwood's publishing house and had begun a personal friendship with Blackwood that lasted—although not without some bitter disputes—until nearly the end of their lives.[6]

Hogg claimed that he had been interested in establishing a new magazine from the time that he had concluded his own short-lived periodical, *The Spy*, which ran from September 1810 until August 1811. Several years after *The Spy*, Hogg enlisted his friend Thomas Pringle to join in his projected new periodical enterprise. Pringle had been employed at the Register House in Edinburgh since 1808. As a poet Pringle had developed friendships with both Hogg and Walter Scott, and he contributed 'Epistle to Mr R– S * * * *' to Hogg's collection of parodies of contemporary poets, *The Poetic Mirror* (1816). Pringle was a willing partner in Hogg's magazine proposal, and when Hogg took the idea to William Blackwood to enquire of Blackwood's interest, he found that Blackwood—independent of Hogg and Pringle— was already exploring the magazine market potential:

> [Pringle and I] agreed to join our efforts, and try to set it a-going; but, as I declined the editorship on account of residing mostly on my farm at a distance from town, it became a puzzling question who was the best qualified among our friends for that undertaking. We at length fixed on Mr. Gray as the fittest person for a principal department, and I went and mentioned the plan to Mr. Blackwood, who, to my astonishment, I found had likewise long been cherishing a plan of the same kind. He said he knew nothing about Pringle, and always had his eye on me as a principal assistant; but he would not begin the undertaking until he saw he could do it with effect. Finding him, however, disposed to encourage such a work, Pringle, at my suggestion, made out a plan in writing, with a list of his supporters, and sent it in a letter to me. I inclosed it in another, and sent it to Mr. Blackwood; and not long after that period Pringle and he came to an arrangement about commencing the work, while I was in the country.[7]

One of the 'arrangements' that Pringle apparently made with Blackwood was to hire James Cleghorn as co-editor. Cleghorn, a farmer from Berwickshire, moved to Edinburgh in 1811 to edit Archibald Constable's *Farmer's Magazine* (to which Hogg was a contributor). Hogg had little respect for Cleghorn's editorial abilities, so Hogg distanced himself from the management of *Blackwood's*: 'from the time I heard that Pringle had taken in Cleghorn as a partner I declined all connexion with it, farther than as an occasional contributor. I told him the connexion would not likely last for a year, and insisted that he should break it at once; but to this proposal he would in nowise listen'.[8] Indeed, it was only six months later that the *Edinburgh Monthly Magazine* met the fate that Hogg claimed he had predicted. Pringle and Cleghorn proved to be mediocre, even disinterested, editors. Blackwood was dissatisfied with their work almost from the start; he was unhappy with sales and increasingly had to take on editorial responsibilities himself. Pringle and Cleghorn, on the other hand, complained of Blackwood's editorial interference. Although Blackwood seemed to expect the *Edinburgh Monthly Magazine* to be competitive in both the review and miscellany markets, he did not take the business steps necessary to make it so; in particular, Blackwood's expectation of unpaid contributions from authors made the process of securing works for publication difficult, at best, and nearly impossible for the editors or Blackwood to attract the calibre of authors generally writing for the *Edinburgh Review* and to whom the *Review* was providing liberal compensation.[9] Hogg was called to Edinburgh by Blackwood in the summer of 1817 to attempt a resolution of the differences between the publisher and his editors, but, as Hogg writes, his success was only temporary: 'A reconciliation was effected at that time, and I returned again into the country. Soon, however, I heard that the flames of controversy, and proud opposition, had broken out between the parties with greater fury than ever; and, shortly after, that they had finally separated, and the two champions gone over and enlisted under the banners of Mr. Constable, having left Mr. Blackwood to shift for himself'.[10] Blackwood notified Pringle and Cleghorn that he would cease publication of the magazine in September after only six issues. As Hogg notes, Pringle and Cleghorn signed on with Archibald Constable to edit the *Scots Magazine*, which Constable renamed the *Edinburgh Magazine and Literary Miscellany*. Blackwood, too, changed the name of his publication to *Blackwood's Edinburgh Magazine* and renewed his magazine venture in October 1817 with a bold editorial focus, a commitment to competitive compensation of authors, and a small team of talented, energetic, and sometimes controversial writers, led by John Wilson and John Gibson Lockhart.[11]

James Hogg, too, played a significant role, although to a large extent inadvertently, in establishing the new direction of *Blackwood's Edinburgh Magazine*. In spite of Hogg's claims of responsibility for establishing 'Maga' and of intimacy with Blackwood, Hogg had been kept in the dark about Blackwood's plans for the new magazine. Hogg wrote to Blackwood on 12 August 1817: 'I regret much that you have told me so little of your plan; if the name is to change who is to be Editor &c.'[12] Hogg's publications in the early numbers of the

*Edinburgh Monthly Magazine* in general fit the pedestrian character of the Pringle-Cleghorn editorship and, as might be expected for uncompensated work, primarily were works that had been written for or previously published in a different market. Hogg contributed a three-part series, 'Tales and Anecdotes of the Pastoral Life', to the first three issues of the magazine. These sketches of a country wedding probably had been written for a book-length collection of stories and sketches for which Hogg had sought a publisher as early as 1813.[13] Hogg's 'Verses' celebrating the allied 'Victory over the French' in 1814 (pp. 5–6) had been published in an Edinburgh newspaper in 1814 in a report on the occasion for which the poem was written. 'A Last Adieu' (pp. 18–19), a poem on the death of the poet's mother, Margaret Laidlaw Hogg, apparently had been written within weeks after her death in 1813. Only the 'Shakespeare Club of Alloa' (pp. 14–18) seems to have been written specifically for *Blackwood's*, although the verses that are part of this article were written for another occasion. However, Hogg was committed to the success of Blackwood's magazine, and in his letter of 12 August 1817 Hogg wrote to Blackwood to express his concern about the impact of the editorial conflict on the magazine and his confidence in Blackwood's ultimate triumph: 'I am greatly concerned about your Magazine but I have some dependence on your spirit not to let it drop or relax till your literary friends gather again about you'.[14] A month later (24 September 1817) Hogg wrote to Blackwood again to offer his encouragement and support in the magazine competition that had developed between Blackwood and Constable as a consequence of the actions of Pringle and Cleghorn. Hogg, who also had a business relationship with Constable, speculated that 'both the miscellanies will turn out good, there is no excellence without emulation'. Hogg argued that Constable would have the early advantage since he had 'a number of *great guns* about him which perhaps may be induced to fire off a shot at first but who will disdain to continue writing for a two shilling Magazine'. Blackwood should have the long-term advantage, however, given the record of Pringle and Cleghorn and provided Blackwood pay his authors well and strictly maintain their anonymity. Hogg continues to pledge his support: 'You may be sure of my best efforts [...] *the redoubted Ettrick Shepherd* is on your side'. Hogg also told Blackwood that he found the Blackwood-Constable controversy a fit subject for his pen: 'I am highly amused at this terrible trial of strength that is commencing between you and Constable and have a great mind to write something original on the occassion'.[15] What Hogg wrote was 'Translation of an Ancient Chaldee

Manuscript, *Supposed to have been written by Daniel*' (pp. 26–44), which Blackwood published anonymously and in a greatly-enlarged form in the October 1817 number of *Blackwood's Edinburgh Magazine* and which became the defining piece for William Blackwood's new magazine and for much of James Hogg's relationship with it.

## 2. The Chaldee Shepherd

'Translation of an Ancient Chaldee Manuscript' is a satirical sketch, written in the style of the Authorised Version of the Bible, about the publishing rivalry between Archibald Constable and William Blackwood, with a special focus on the controversy surrounding Blackwood's beginning of the *Edinburgh Monthly Magazine* and his difficulties with Pringle and Cleghorn. Hogg must have written the 'Chaldee' on 24 September 1817, the day he informed Blackwood he was considering writing something 'original', for on 25 September Hogg wrote to Blackwood again, enclosing the 'Chaldee': 'Please read over this beautiful allegory of mine with the editor of the Magazine and cause him to add a short history of its preservation in the archives of Rome or somewhere and by whom it came to be noticed and translated into our language'.[16] The 'editor' added the explanatory introduction as Hogg requested, but 'he' also added much more: the published work was four times as long as Hogg's original. The 'editor' who revised and enlarged Hogg's original work turned out to be a trinity of John Gibson Lockhart, John Wilson, and William Blackwood himself. Lockhart tells the story of the final composition of the 'Chaldee' in a letter to his friend, Jonathan Christie, in January 1818:

> The history of it is this: Hogg, the Ettrick Shepherd, sent up an attack on Constable the bookseller, respecting some private dealings of his with Blackwood. Wilson and I liked the idea of introducing the whole panorama of the town in that sort of dialect. We drank punch one night from eight till eight in the morning, Blackwood being by with anecdotes, and the result is before you.[17]

The 'result' of the night's drinking and talking was a transformation of Hogg's original clever, playful, and focused satire of forty-six scripture-like verses into a much more thorough catalogue (181 verses) of the writers, but the 'Chaldee' also became a work that was in places mean spirited, in poor taste, 'obnoxious' (according to Blackwood himself), and libellous (according to at least one of the satire's victims).[18]

Blackwood sent Hogg a proof of the new version of the 'Chaldee'. In acknowledging the proof, Hogg wrote to Blackwood that he was generally pleased with the additional material, although he was concerned about the chapter that contained the most offensive characterisations: 'I have laughed at least as heartily at the continuation of *Daniel* as you did at the original the conciet is excellent indeed I see that mine was quite an imperfect thing without some description of the forces on the other side–the third chapter however is very faulty–the characters are made too plain and the language of scripture compleatly departed from. I have remedied that in proof in a great measure but alas it is out of time!'[19] Hogg was 'out of time' as he thought; the magazine was published the next day, 20 October 1817. However, Hogg's revisions to the proof were not so extensive as to have made a significant difference to the public response to the work.[20] In the same letter to Blackwood Hogg wrote: 'As it is it will create great interest I am certain of its popularity as well as of its being blamed'.[21] Hogg's judgment proved correct on both points. The 'Chaldee' created such a stir that the October 1817 issue of the magazine sold quickly and a second edition was called for; however, because the 'Chaldee' was so controversial–and because Blackwood was facing legal difficulties as a consequence of it–the 'Chaldee' was omitted from the second edition. Thomas Carlyle effectively summarises the 'great interest' created by the 'Chaldee' in a letter to Robert Mitchell, 19 November 1817. Carlyle is critical of the October 1817 number of *Blackwood's* in general; the issue contained other vituperative articles, such as the first of a series of attacks on the 'Cockney School of Poetry'. For Carlyle, though, the 'Chaldee' was the worst of the magazine's distasteful assaults on personal dignity:

> The greater part of it is full of gall: but the most venomous article is the 'translation of a Chaldee manuscript' said to be found in the library of Paris–It is written in the phrase of the Scriptures–[and gives] an allegorical account of the origin & end of the late Edin*r* magazine–greatly to the [dis]paragement of Constable & the Editors–Most of the Authors of Edin*r* are characterised with great acrimony–under the likeness of birds & beasts & creeping things–Blackwood is like to be beleaguered with prosecutions for it–two are already raised against him. Replies in the shape of 'explanations,' 'letters to Drs M'Crie and Thomson' have been put forth–more are promised–and doubtless, rejoinders are in a state of preparation. Whatever may become of Blackwood or his

antagonists—the 'reading' or rather the talking 'public' is greatly beholden to the Author. He has kept its jaws moving these four weeks—and the sport is not finished yet—[22]

According to R. P. Gillies, the 'talking public' consisted of nearly the whole of Edinburgh: 'Every one talked of it, from the wise and learned judges on the bench, who gave their decisions in defence of "the beasts," down to shopkeepers and other people who had never read a new book till then'.[23] Clearly 'sport' or 'joke' was all that Hogg had intended when he sent Blackwood the original 'Chaldee', and he anticipated merely a response in kind, as he writes in his 'Memoir': 'All that I expected was a little retaliation of the same kind in the opposing magazine; and when I received letter after letter, informing me what a dreadful flame it had raised in Edinburgh, I could not be brought to believe that it was not a joke'.[24] Indeed, had Hogg's 'Chaldee' been published as he had written it, the public reaction likely would have more nearly matched his expectations, although almost certainly with some criticism of the imitation of the biblical style. However, the introduction of direct insults to personalities by Wilson, Lockhart, and Blackwood changed the character of the work dramatically and, as Hogg notes, created much to 'blame'. The 'writing public' as well as the 'talking public' were kept busy. Part of the 'sport' of the 'Chaldee' was to try to guess the identity of the satire's subjects and, as Gillies notes, 'copies of the original number were handed about with manuscript notes, identifying the principal characters, and high prices were occasionally offered for a copy which the fortunate possessor had read and could dispense with'.[25] More serious responses included a series of pamphlets from James Grahame under the pseudonym 'Calvinus', as well as a lawsuit from John Graham Dalyell. James Grahame's pamphlets denounced the blasphemies of the 'Chaldee': 'Abstract from this performance its profanity and impiety, and it is "a tale told by an ideot;" but, with these qualities, it is an outrage on religion, committed by a madman'.[26] John Graham Dalyell sued Blackwood for £5000 over his characterisation in the 'Chaldee': 'His face was like unto the face of an ape, and he chattered continually, and his nether parts were uncomely. Nevertheless his thighs were hairy, and the hair was as the shining of a sattin raiment, and he skipped with the branch of a tree in his hand, and he chewed a snail between his teeth [...] he was born of his mother before yet the months were fulfilled, and the substance of a living thing is not in him' (p. 40). Blackwood settled Dalyell's suit for £230.[27]

Blackwood, who must have expected such negative reactions, was probably most concerned about the opinion of Walter Scott, who is presented in the 'Chaldee' as a supporter of both Constable and Blackwood, because Blackwood did not want to lose the favour of Scotland's most influential literary figure. Blackwood wrote to Scott, acknowledging the shortcomings of the work but disingenuously blaming his independent editor: 'I anxiously hope you will not be displeased with the Chaldee MS. There will be various opinions as to the propriety of publishing this. The editor took his own way & I cannot interfere with him'.[28] Scott was amused at the 'Chaldee', but he was concerned about the personal criticisms, many of which he considered unfair. Scott wrote to Blackwood in November 1817: 'The article [...] possesses a great deal of satirical humour, but the prudence of publishing it may be seriously questioned. Edinburgh is rather too narrow for satire so markedly personal, and there are certainly several individuals who, from their character and situation, have reason to resent having been so roughly treated'.[29] Scott would not withdraw his support of the magazine based on this article alone, but if the magazine were to 'continue to be a receptacle for articles, however able, composed in the same tone, I could not, consistently with my feelings of what is due to the literary society of Edinburgh, continue my permanent assistance. The field for fair pleasantry is wide enough without enlarging it at the expense of exciting, and not unjustly, feelings of personal and private resentment'.[30] Blackwood also wrote to William Laidlaw to explain his position on the 'Chaldee', no doubt expecting that Laidlaw would encourage Scott's continued support. Blackwood writes that he had been

> much occupied by disagreeable discussions, in consequence of the hue and cry attempted to be raised by Constable and his adherents against me on account of the article entitled Chaldee MSS. No one can regret more than I do that this article appeared. After I saw it in proof, I did everything I could to prevent it, and at last succeeded in getting the Editor to leave it out. In the course of a day, however, he changed his mind, and determined that it should be in. I was therefore placed in a terrible dilemma; and as I must have stopped the Magazine if I did not allow the Editor to have his own way, I was obliged to submit. I was in hopes it would have been laughed over as a cruel joke enough, but that it would soon have been forgot, there is so much excellent matter in the Magazine to redeem it.[31]

When the game did not go as Hogg expected, Hogg sought to

distance himself as much as possible from the publication, at least for a time. Hogg, too, wrote to William Laidlaw, on 28 October 1817, barely a week after the magazine was published, but with a greater sense of urgency than Blackwood displayed: 'For the love of God open not your mouth about the Chaldee M. S. All is combustion there have been meetings and proposals and an express has arrived from Edin to me this morning. Deny all knowledge else they say I am ruined if it can by any means be attached—Let all be silence'.[32] Hogg also wrote to Blackwood on the same day:

> I cannot tell you how much I think of the Magazine it is so interesting and spirited throughout it is safe—But I have had an express from Edin. to day telling me of a dreadful irruption about a certain article and the imminent danger the author is in should he be discovered I care not much for the whole crew of them but as it is I think it as well to keep out of the way for a little until the indignation be a little overpast lest I should be inveigled in my drinking parties or by designing men to intimate more than I should do.[33]

In spite of Hogg's initial fear of personal retribution, Hogg was not touched by John Graham Dalyell's suit or by the stinging responses that charged the authors with insults to human dignity and even with blasphemy. When the 'dreadful irruption' of public outrage had subsided, and perhaps emboldened by his escape from the consequences of his earlier instigations, Hogg wrote 'a long continuation' of the 'Chaldee', in the same biblical style, taking as his subjects 'the painters, poets, lawyers, booksellers, magistrates, and ministers of Edinburgh'.[34] When Blackwood declined to publish the 'continuation', Hogg considered publishing the complete 'Chaldee' as a pamphlet and under his own name, which was only prevented by the 'energy' and 'sharp remonstrances' of John Wilson, Walter Scott, and Hogg's friend, John Grieve.[35] Hogg, who clearly was taken with this style of writing, over several years wrote additional works that incorporated the style and/or themes of the 'Chaldee'—none of which Blackwood published. Hogg wrote a piece in the 'Chaldee' style entitled 'The Boar' (pp. 44–47), probably in early 1818, and in 'The Boar' he addresses the consequences of the 'Chaldee' for Constable, as well as the tension that had developed between Hogg and Blackwood's 'editor'. In July 1818 Hogg wrote to Blackwood about another satirical sketch, 'John Paterson's Mare', which, though not written in the 'Chaldee' style, like the 'Chaldee' addresses the competition between Constable and Blackwood. Hogg considered

'John Paterson's Mare' in the same class of work as the 'Chaldee': 'I think it will be next to the Chaldee in popularity as it is fully as ingenious'.[36] Part of Hogg's lengthy note to 'Johnnie Cope' in the Second Series of *The Jacobite Relics of Scotland* (1821) includes a two-chapter 'curious Chaldee Manuscript, intituled, "The Chronicles of Charles the Young Man"', supposedly dating from the time of the events it describes in 1745.[37] In Hogg's novel *The Three Perils of Man* (1822), 'The Friar's Tale' in the second volume is told in 'Chaldee'-style verses.[38] Several years later Hogg wrote a satire of the church in the 'Chaldee' style; the work apparently was intended for the *Edinburgh Literary Journal*, although it was never published.[39] Even in the early 1830s Hogg was planning another big 'Chaldee'-like scandalous splash, this time taking Whig politics as his subject. Hogg wrote to John Lockhart on 24 February 1832: 'I likewise want from you a list of all the heros of the Whigs with their public and private characters with every thing that is ludicrous bad or whimsical about each of them and if you will give me these I'll lock myself up and let you see a Manuscript that shall have some effect'.[40] Hogg's 'Whig Chaldee' apparently never materialised.

Blackwood was not interested in additional satires from Hogg on the state of publishing in Edinburgh. Blackwood had written to his London agents, Baldwin, Cradock, and Joy, on 6 November 1817, in response to their concern over their liability for Maga's attacks on Leigh Hunt, promising there was no need to worry about the propriety of future articles: 'I regret as much as you do the personalities in the Magazine but I could not get the Editor to alter them. This business has however been a good lesson to him, and you may rest assured we will not again need to be under any fears as to what he will insert in the future Numbers'.[41] Although for a time the Maga writers toned down their 'obnoxiousness', they did not eliminate altogether the attacks on personalities. Over the next few years Hogg himself on several occasions was the target rather than the instigator of Maga's objectionable writing. Ultimately, the 'combustion' that burned Hogg was not the public reaction to the 'Chaldee', but the public portrayal of Hogg by his literary associates at *Blackwood's Edinburgh Magazine*. Hogg's authorship of the 'Chaldee' would become a source of derision even among Hogg's literary friends, as Hogg notes in his 'Memoir': 'Certain of my literary associates call me *The Chaldee Shepherd*, and pretend to sneer at my assumption of being the author of that celebrated article. Certes they have long ago persuaded the country that I was not'.[42] The 'Chaldee Manuscript', then, was as pivotal a publication in establishing Hogg's public personality after 1817 as it was in establishing the new *Blackwood's Edinburgh Magazine*, and the 'Chaldee' shadowed Hogg's literary career in and out of *Blackwood's*. Hogg relinquished some authorial independence with the magazine's managers with the 'Chaldee', but eventually Hogg achieved a great deal of notoriety that largely worked to his advantage, although as 'The Chaldee Shepherd' he felt compelled to prove his authorship over and over again. Finally, it gave Hogg a theme to pursue (perhaps *ad nauseam*) for the rest of his periodical career, sometimes stirring 'a great tumult' of which he 'wist not what it was' (p. 44).

*Blackwood's Edinburgh Magazine* had been revitalised with the October 1817 number, which was under a new 'editor'. With the launch of William Blackwood's new magazine came also the beginning of a new dynamic between Hogg and the house of Blackwood—a love-hate relationship that Hogg could neither be entirely satisfied with nor abandon altogether. Blackwood's new editor was largely responsible for Hogg's duality of experience with *Blackwood's*. Blackwood had offered to the Baldwin firm the same (untruthful) excuse for the indiscretions of the October 1817 issue that he had offered to Scott: that he had no control over his editor. The editor was never identified, however, and the editor's identity was kept a deliberate puzzle. The editor is introduced by Blackwood, Lockhart, and Wilson in the published version of the 'Chaldee Manuscript' as 'a man clothed in dark garments, having a veil upon his head; and there was a rod in his hand'. The man in the veil encouraged 'Ebony' and promised to deliver him from his 'distresses' and to ensure that he would be beyond the reach of his adversaries. Ebony was heartened by the 'boldness' of the veiled man and thus gave him charge of Maga: 'Do thou as it seemeth unto thee; as thou sayest even so will I do'. The veiled man provided Ebony with a list of 'mighty creatures' to call for assistance, and the creatures came to Ebony's aid: 'And the man with the veil stood by, but there was a cloud about him, neither could they which came see him, nor tell who it was that compelled their coming' (p. 36). The question of the editor's identity added to both the mystery and the controversy of Blackwood's new magazine, and the controversy, especially, continued long after the October 1817 number.[43]

After William Blackwood's disappointment with Pringle and Cleghorn, it is not surprising that Blackwood wanted to be more firmly in control of his magazine; he could not afford a second failed start. Blackwood's editorial ploy gave him the pretence of distance from the magazine's scandalous operations. The fact that Blackwood did not name a person specifically to the position of editor meant that he was able to blame the editor for the magazine's indiscretions and, to some degree, minimise criticism of himself and deflect criticism from John Wilson and John Lockhart, his closest editorial associates. It is clear now (and was assumed then) that in the early numbers Blackwood shared responsibilities with Wilson and Lockhart to select material for the magazine and to conduct correspondence with contributors; the early editorship was a group effort, although John Wilson was the dominant voice.[44] A major portion of the writing for the early issues was also done by Wilson and Lockhart. Wilson and Lockhart were perfectly suited to Blackwood's editorial needs; they had the education, ability, and vision to put *Blackwood's Edinburgh Magazine* on a competitive footing with Constable's periodicals. Both Wilson and Lockhart had classical educations from Glasgow and Oxford universities. Both had studied law in Edinburgh, and both men were excellent writers. Both men were capable of being bold, witty, playful, direct, ironical, and even extreme. Both were also solid Tories, which suited Blackwood's political ideology. Just as importantly for the success of *Blackwood's*, however, both men were engaged with the authors and ideologies that came to define the Romantic age. What Wilson and Lockhart added to William Blackwood in the management of *Blackwood's Edinburgh Magazine* was a clearly Romantic vision of culture; they understood and contributed to the 'spirit of the age'. The new editorial vision, together with attractive compensation for the contributors, soon set *Blackwood's* at the forefront of the literary magazines of the day.

John Lockhart, through the voice of his fictional persona, Peter Morris, in *Peter's Letters to His Kinsfolk*, reflects on the beginnings of *Blackwood's Edinburgh Magazine* nearly two years after its establishment and offers insights into the ideological success of Maga that surpassed Blackwood's political vision for his magazine. Lockhart notes that the timing of the magazine's appearance was 'happily chosen, just when the decline of that intense and overmastering interest, formerly attracted to the Edinburgh Review' was beginning to be 'felt' and 'acknowledged'.[45] If William Blackwood had not seized the moment, someone else necessarily would have, Lockhart's Morris argues; the time of the *Edinburgh Review*'s dominant political and philosophical ideologies had passed. Morris writes that '[Wastle] regards the Scotch philosophers of the present day, and among, or above the rest, Mr Jeffrey and the Edinburgh Reviewers, as the legitimate progeny of the sceptical philosophers of the last age'.[46] Morris continues:

The system of political opinions, inculcated in the Edinburgh
Review, is, in like manner, as I honestly think, admirably
fitted to go hand in hand with a system of scepticism; but
entirely irreconcilable with the notion of any fervent love and
attachment for a religion, which is, above all things, the religion
of feeling. The politicians of this Review are men of great
shrewdness and sagacity, and many of them are men of much
honesty; but it is impossible to suppose for a moment, that
they are men either of very high or of very beautiful feeling.[47]

The contrasting ideologies of the *Edinburgh Review* and *Blackwood's
Edinburgh Magazine* are effectively summed up in Morris's criticisms
of Jeffrey and the *Review* for their negative treatment of Burns and
Wordsworth and their failure to acknowledge the significance of
contemporary literature. Morris, in discussing Wordsworth, defines
one of the essential ideas of Romanticism: 'The delight which is
conferred by vivid descriptions of stranger events and stronger
impulses than we ourselves experience, is adapted for all men, and
is an universal delight. That part of our nature, to which they address
themselves, not only exists in every man originally, but has its
existence fostered and cherished by the incidents of every life'.[48] It is
clear, then, why Hogg as a writer was such a good fit for *Blackwood's*.

When the veil around the editorship finally was lifted, the editor,
appropriately, was discovered to be a fictitious old man with
rheumatism, 'Christopher North', but a fictitious character written
most frequently by John Wilson. Although Lockhart was heavily
involved with Maga, there is no doubt that Wilson was the primary
force behind the new magazine and exerted considerable control
and influence over the magazine and its contents. On 20 October
1817, the day the new *Blackwood's Edinburgh Magazine* was published,
Blackwood wrote to Wilson, sending him 'the first complete copy I
have of the Magazine' because the success of the Magazine is 'wholly
indebted' to Wilson.[49] Even before the appearance of the October
1817 number, Charles Kirkpatrick Sharpe had learned of Wilson's
role in the second incarnation of Blackwood's magazine but had
predicted disaster because of it. Blackwood and Sharpe had fallen
out over the publication of an edition of James Kirkton's *Secret and
True History of the Church of Scotland*, but had since mended their
relationship. Sharpe wrote to Robert Surtees, in a letter postmarked
1 October 1817, ironically before he was to see himself parodied by
the new editor in the 'Chaldee Manuscript':

Blackwood and I have in some sort made up matters—but

this will not long continue, I guess; Wilson, the Palm and Plague man, is now the editor of his Magazine, which of course must soon fall, or fall into other hands—the worthy in question being as shifting as the northern lights, and stark mad to boot—Constable drives on in triumph, with new Editors and a new title page—for my part, as both of these Magazines are staft with vulgar antediluvian Whiggery, I cannot endure them—but I give Constable some trifles, because he gives me many better things—[50]

James Hogg had a different view of Wilson's connection to the magazine, as he wrote to Blackwood in August 1817, also before the defining new issue of Maga: 'Wilsons papers, though not perfect, have a masterly cast about them; a little custom would make him the best periodical writer of the age keep hold of him'.[51] Hogg underscored his confidence in Wilson again, writing to Blackwood just two months later: 'I have great dependance on Wilson's powers do not you see with what spirit the fellow writes whether it be to laud to blame or to mock the worst fault about him is that he lets his imagination run away with him if he leans to one side at all he leans too much he either praises or blames in the extreme'.[52] There were times in the coming months and years when Hogg was the subject of Wilson's extremes and when Hogg must have regretted his recommendations of Wilson, although Hogg should not have been altogether surprised at Wilson's editorial antics and hurtful caprices. Hogg met Wilson several years before *Blackwood's*, probably in early 1813, and they immediately struck up a warm friendship. They spent a great deal of time together when Hogg was in Edinburgh, and Hogg visited Wilson at his home in the Lake District in September 1814, where they 'had a Queen's Wake every wet day—a fair set-to who should write the best poem between breakfast and dinner'.[53] However, in 1815 Hogg considered himself betrayed by Wilson when Wilson disparaged Hogg's poem *The Field of Waterloo* to the point that Blackwood would not publish it. Hogg was driven 'into an ungovernable rage' by this and sent Wilson a letter, 'a tickler. There was scarcely an abusive epithet in our language that I did not call him by'. Hogg's letter was a 'source of amusement' to Wilson; Wilson apologised to Hogg, which endeared him to Hogg even more.[54] However, this would not be the last of Wilson's efforts to undermine Hogg and his literature.

## 3. 'A Wing of Wauchope's Moor-hen'

The new 'editor' had an immediate impact on *Blackwood's Edinburgh*

*Magazine* and on Hogg's relationship with it. In sending the 'Chaldee Manuscript' to William Blackwood, Hogg had requested specific editorial additions to his work, although he received much more than he asked for from Wilson, Lockhart, and Blackwood. Over time, the editor took or allowed more and more liberties with Hogg's writing and his personality, including signing Hogg's name to works by Wilson, Lockhart, and D. M. Moir—without Hogg's permission— and ascribing behaviour and comments to Hogg that were inventions of the editor. The editor had specific ideas for Hogg's role with the new *Blackwood's*, however. In addition to the 'Chaldee Manuscript', Hogg submitted two elegiac poems for publication in the October 1817 issue, 'Extempore Song' (pp. 24–25) and 'Elegy' (pp. 25–26), both of which had been written on the occasion of the death of an unidentified child. 'Extempore Song' was not published in *Blackwood's*. 'Elegy', which had been published previously in *The Spy*, was published with advice to Hogg from the editor of *Blackwood's* about the kind of poetry Hogg should write and an admonition to Hogg to write within the limits of a narrowly-prescribed role. The editor's suggestions include a verse model, signed 'Wilson'—presumably John Wilson—that was intended as a guide for Hogg in determining his role in *Blackwood's*. The editor requests that Hogg occasionally submit songs to Maga—a genre in which Hogg rivals Burns, he writes—as well as pastoral works, like 'Kilmeny' from *The Queen's Wake*, 'peopled [...] with the aërial creatures whom he loves' and suited to 'his habits and his native genius'. Such public advice seems unnecessary if, in fact, Wilson intended to offer friendly advice or to request of Hogg works in the style of some of Hogg's previous successes; after all, Hogg and Wilson had known each other for several years and a personal communication would have been appropriate. Rather, it seems that Wilson instead pronounces judgment publicly on Hogg's abilities as a poet and sends a message that Hogg is only a peasant poet who is not to be admitted fully into the society of the Edinburgh literati. Wilson's verse example also, in part, parodies the kinds of poetry for which Hogg had established a reputation and perhaps is exacting some poetic revenge for Hogg's parodies of Wilson's poetry that Hogg had written for *The Poetic Mirror* (1816).[55] The editor/Wilson over the years would frequently make fun of Hogg's reputation as a poet or his poor book sales by a mocking comparison with Burns, Byron, or Wordsworth, or by a sarcastic proclamation that people of his time were simply not prepared to recognise Hogg's genius.[56]

On the whole, and perhaps ironically, Wilson seems to see the Romantic character of Hogg and his works as a limiting factor for

Hogg's relationship with the Edinburgh-based *Blackwood's Edinburgh Magazine*. On the other hand, Lockhart frequently finds himself in a position of being an apologist for Hogg and of balancing Wilson's scornful attitude towards Hogg's peasant-poet role with a more-positive assessment of his literary achievements. Part of what Lockhart accomplishes in his discussion of *Blackwood's Edinburgh Magazine* in *Peter's Letters to His Kinsfolk* is to make a public acknowledgement of the faults of the early numbers of the magazine, in particular the attacks on Coleridge and Playfair.[57] In the attacks on personalities, Lockhart's Morris writes, the magazine's conductors, especially Wilson and Lockhart, violated their own principles and damaged their reputations: 'They stained, in plain language, the beginning of their career with the sins of many wanton and malicious personal satires, not immediately subservient to the inculcation of any particular set of principles whatever, and in their necessary and ultimate tendencies quite hostile to the noble and generous set of principles, religious and political, as well as literary, of which these persons had professed themselves to be the champions'.[58] Lockhart also offers what amounts to an apology to Hogg in a glowing acknowledgement of Hogg as the successor to Burns. Lockhart does this in the context of Morris's report of the Burns Dinner, and he puts the tribute in Wilson's mouth in the form of a toast to Hogg. Morris writes that Wilson's 'eloquence' was inspired by his feelings for Hogg:

> His theme was indeed the very best that the occasion could have thrown in his way; for what homage could be so appropriate, or so grateful to the Manes of Burns, as that which sought to attain its object by welcoming and honouring the only worthy successor of his genius? I wish I could recall for your delight any portion of those glowing words in which this enthusiastic speaker strove to embody his own ideas— and indeed those of his audience—concerning the high and holy connection which exists between the dead and the living peasant—both "sprung from the very bosom of the people," both identifying themselves in all things with the spirit of their station, and endeavouring to ennoble themselves only by elevating it. It was thus, indeed, that a national assembly might most effectually do honour to a national poet. This was the true spirit for a commemoration of Robert Burns.[59]

There was nothing of Hogg's in the November 1817 issue, although Hogg had sent Blackwood 'two long articles' on 28 October:[60] one,

an article on sheep, was not published, and the other, probably the
'Letter to Charles Kirkpatrick Sharpe, Esq. on his Original Mode of
Editing Church History' (pp. 47–54), appeared in the December
1817 number and is one of only two review essays that Hogg was
permitted to write for *Blackwood's*. Hogg had hoped to have a role as
a reviewer in Maga, as he wrote to Blackwood on 19 October 1817:
'I'll wager I will write some reviews for the Magazine that shall
astonish Jeffery himself. I would fain bespeak Rob. Roy if not engaged
you have never yet given me a valuable or original work to review'.[61]
It is not clear why Blackwood did not permit Hogg to write reviews
for Maga. Blackwood undoubtedly was concerned about Hogg's
occasional lapses in judgment, but it is more likely that Blackwood
and/or Wilson did not consider that Hogg had the breadth of
knowledge to write a proper review, that his review topics must be
restricted to Hogg's narrow experience and educational background.
Although there is a Romantic rather than an Enlightenment tone to
*Blackwood's*, still there was an intellectual reputation to consider if
Maga's reviews were to compete with those of the *Edinburgh Review*.

Hogg's 'Letter to Sharpe' is a review of Sharpe's edition of James
Kirkton's *The Secret and True History of the Church of Scotland*. Kirkton
(d. 1699) was a Covenanting minister who wrote first-hand about
the struggles of the Church of Scotland in the seventeenth century.
Sharpe, a Tory and member of the Church of England, held views
that differed widely from those expressed in Kirkton's history, and
his annotations to Kirkton's text, according to Hogg, were an effort
to undermine Kirkton's narrative rather than provide historically-
objective explanations. Hogg grew up hearing stories of the
Covenanters who had inhabited the land where he lived and worked,
and at the time of the review he was engaged in completing his
sympathetic Covenanting novel, *The Brownie of Bodsbeck*, for publication
by Blackwood. Hogg thought Sharpe's portrayal of the Covenanters
was unfairly negative (as he did of Walter Scott in his novel, *Old
Mortality*)[62] and Sharpe's editorial methods biased and deceptive. As
Peter Garside has argued, Sharpe's edition of Kirkton provides the
same kind of contrasting voices, as well as a similar editor-subject
bias, later found in Hogg's novel, *The Private Memoirs and Confessions of
a Justified Sinner*.[63] Hogg also uses the device of a second critical voice
within the review. Although the review is not signed by Hogg and
he was not implicated in the authorship, he still puts much of his
harshest criticism in the mouth of a 'revered and worthy old friend
of mine' (p. 51), whom Hogg apparently invented to provide some
critical distance from his own authorial voice. Given Hogg's

familiarity with the history of the Covenanters, especially as evidenced in his own fiction, and given the history of Sharpe and Blackwood's relationship, Sharpe's edition of Kirkton was a safe topic for a review essay from Hogg; there was nothing for Blackwood to lose.

Hogg's second review essay appeared in the February 1823 number of *Blackwood's*. The article, 'The Honourable Captain Napier and Ettrick Forest' (pp. 96–137), reviewed William John Napier's book, *A Treatise on Practical Store-Farming, As Applicable to the Mountainous Region of Etterick Forest* (1822).[64] Again, given Hogg's history as a shepherd-farmer in Ettrick and Yarrow, as well as his own published accounts of farming in Napier's part of the country, Hogg was the right person, in terms of his knowledge of the subject, to write this review. However, he was not able to publish this essay without first taking the unusual step of getting the approval of the author whose book was being reviewed. Given Napier's position of power and influence in Ettrick and Yarrow, it is possible that Hogg himself sought Napier's blessing on the review to avoid offending him, especially in terms of the personal information and the fun at the Captain's expense. The manuscript version of the review includes a joke on Mrs Napier, as well as mention of Hogg's continuing grudge against Napier for his having taken away Hogg's sailing privileges on St Mary's Loch; both of these passages were omitted from the published version. It seems more likely, though, that given Hogg's fondness for literary sport, Blackwood was not entirely confident in Hogg's ability to write the review with due deference to Captain–soon to be Lord–Napier, and that Blackwood required him to get Napier's approval of the review before he would publish it. In either case, working with Napier proved frustrating to Hogg. Hogg wrote to Blackwood that Napier was 'so very capricious and thin skinned' that Hogg almost gave up on the article: 'he has revised it twice, and after spending the day and a part of the night here with me' he finally authorised publication.[65] Hogg also took Napier to task for being so 'thin skinned' in the public arena, especially as it concerns the magazine makers: 'Before you be half the time before the public that I have been you will be better innured to such jokes If you think the reviewers and magazine makers have not a right to bring every circumstance of a man's life that is publicly known and any way connected with his work forward you are in a confounded mistake, and that you will find'.[66] Hogg had learned his advice to Napier the hard way, through his own experience with *Blackwood's Edinburgh Magazine* from 1817 through 1822.

In the months following the 'Letter to Sharpe', Hogg published very little in *Blackwood's*: two poems (January and April 1818; pp. 55–56, 70–72) from his *Selection of German Hebrew Melodies* that had been published in London [1817] as a music collection, a sketch about his dog Sirrah (March 1818; pp. 61–69), and a playful 'occasional' sonnet to John Carnegie (April 1818; p. 70). Hogg had also submitted to Blackwood two works that were not published: an essay on his own volume of parodies, *The Poetic Mirror* (pp. 56–57), and two poems parodying Leigh Hunt's poetry, the 'New Poetic Mirror' (pp. 57–61). In February 1818 there was another turn in Hogg's relationship with *Blackwood's Edinburgh Magazine*. Maga published the first of a series of letters from 'Timothy Tickler' addressed to various literary figures. Timothy Tickler was a fictitious persona generally associated with Robert Sym, an Edinburgh lawyer and uncle of John Wilson, although Sym apparently rarely, if ever, wrote under the Tickler name. The first two Tickler letters, in February and March, were addressed to Hogg and were written by Wilson in response to a series of articles on Hogg's life by Hogg's friend, James Gray, that appeared in the January, February, and March 1818 issues of Constable's *Edinburgh Magazine*.[67] Gray's articles present Hogg as a 'self-taught genius' and provide a detailed history of Hogg's family and the circumstances of nature that 'kindled his genius into activity, and developed the extraordinary powers of his mind'.[68] Wilson responds to Gray's celebratory account of Hogg's character, upbringing, and poetical talents by denigrating Hogg in almost every point. In the Tickler letters Wilson introduces themes that he is to take up again and again: Hogg's lack of formal education, his inability to read the classical literature in the original languages, his career as shepherd, his social standing, his appearance and dress, and his fondness for 'many a glass of whisky'.[69]

Although Hogg apparently had seen the manuscripts of the Tickler letters, he was incensed that they were published without his permission and, he believed, that they had been altered since he had seen them. In the summer of 1818 Hogg wrote a reply, 'Letter to Timothy Tickler' (pp. 72–77), in which he responds to the criticisms and insults levelled at him by Wilson; the reply was not published.[70] He probably accurately captured Wilson's motives for writing the Tickler letters: 'In the first place you saw that it was an attempt to place me in a light that you could not endure; for tho' always in a jocular manner, you have uniformly set yourself against every thing that had a tendency to raise my poetical character. In the second place you saw that the critical letters themselves were the best, and most original things in Constable's Magazine' (p. 74). Hogg also indicates that he has given up writing for 'that outrageous Magazine in Prince-street' (p. 77). Wilson's Tickler letters might also have been the fuel for other works that Hogg wrote during this time, although Hogg was sensing a more general turn against him throughout 1818, as he wrote later in the year: 'I begin to feel a cold side to a work which holds such an avowed one to me'.[71] Hogg was puzzled by and disenchanted with his circle of friends at Blackwood's, and he was at a loss to explain his treatment by them. His tale, 'The Hunt of Eildon', seems to have been written in part as a light-hearted search for an explanation. 'The Hunt of Eildon' was published by Blackwood in *The Brownie of Bodsbeck; And Other Tales*, which came out in May 1818. The story is about a shepherd, Croudy, who was transformed one night into a 'huge bristly boar'. He was terrified on seeing his condition and tried to escape from it: 'It is well known what a ridiculous figure a hog makes at any time when frightened, and exerting itself to escape from the supposed danger [...]. Consider, then, what it would be to see one in such a fright as this poor beast was, and trying to escape from himself; running grunting over hill and dale, hanging out his tongue with fatigue, and always carrying the object of his terror with him'.[72] Croudy is changed back into a shepherd just before the butcher slaughters him. Croudy believes that Pery, the lover of Gale, another shepherd, is a witch and responsible for Croudy's enchantment. Pery is convicted of witchcraft and sentenced to death. While Pery and Gale are together the night before her scheduled execution, they are granted their wish to be transformed into two beautiful birds, 'moorfowl, light of heart, and elated with joy'.[73] And thus they are delivered from prison. But the story does not end there:

> When the jailor related what had happened, it may well be conceived what consternation prevailed over the whole country. The two moor-fowl were soon discovered on a wild hill in Tiviotdale, where they have remained ever since, until last year, that Wauchope shot the hen. He suspected what he had done, and was extremely sorry, but kept the secret to himself. On viewing the beauty of the bird, however, he said to himself,—'I believe I have liked women as well as any man, but not so well as to eat them; however, I'll play a trick upon some, and see its effect.' Accordingly he sent the moor-hen to a friend of his in Edinburgh, at whose table she was divided among a circle of friends and eaten, on the 20th of October 1817, and that was the final end of poor Pery, the Maid of Eildon. The effect on these gentlemen has been prodigious— the whole structure of their minds and feelings has undergone

xxxiv          INTRODUCTION

a complete change, and that grievously to the worse; and even their outward forms, on a near inspection, appear to be altered considerably. This change is so notorious as to have become proverbial all over the New Town of Edinburgh. When any one is in a querulous or peevish humour, they say,—'He has got a wing of Wauchope's moor-hen.'[74]

Of course the '20th of October, 1817' was the publication date of the first number of the new *Blackwood's Edinburgh Magazine*, which contained the 'Chaldee Manuscript' and which was under a new editor who expressed a new attitude towards Hogg. It made as much sense to Hogg as anything to explain the change of attitude of his friends by 'it must have been something they ate'.

The image from 'The Hunt of Eildon' of a ludicrous and terrible figure of a distressed boar is taken up again in an unpublished piece entitled 'The Boar', which was written in the biblical style of the 'Chaldee Manuscript'. The date of composition of 'The Boar' is uncertain, but it probably was written in 1818 during this time of growing tensions between Hogg and the Blackwoodians, especially John Wilson. Writing to Blackwood in June 1818, Hogg complains of Wilson's rejection of his submissions and also of Wilson's patronising attitude towards him: 'I have not been writing any new thing for the Magazine I know W. will not let in any thing of mine. he will perhaps tell me as he did lately "This would *perhaps* do for the Mentor. If you like I shall *try* to get it in there" After the rejection The old Soldier's tale I cannot think of any prose article just now that would possibly gain admittance, in the present taste of the editors'.[75] A month later he writes Blackwood again, weary of his treatment by Wilson (and perhaps Lockhart): 'I have been quizzed too much by your chaps already I will not so easily take again. I am writing for another Magazine with all my birr and intend having most excellent sport with it as the editors will not understand what one sentence of my celebrated allegories mean, till they bring the whole terror of Edin aristocracy on them'.[76] Although Hogg complains that Wilson will not publish his works in *Blackwood's*, Wilson and Blackwood both apparently still became angry with him for writing for someone else. They also seemed to be concerned that he might be writing an anti-Blackwood 'Chaldee'. Hogg writes Blackwood again on 21 July, disgusted with the house of Blackwood but acknowledging that he could not stay angry with the 'two devils':

Does it ever enter into your stupid head that I would write any thing against your work and my old friends. It would only be on consultation and a certainty that it would be advantageous to all parties if I did. At any rate I never accused you of quizzing me and I hope I never shall have occassion as for the two devils the thing is implanted in their very natures and I must bear it though I believe they have banished me their too much loved society it may make me angry for an hour or two at a time but shall never make me admire or love them the less.[77]

'The Boar' recalls the havoc wreaked on his adversaries, Constable and his associates, by the 'Boar of Lebanon' with the 'Chaldee Manuscript' and suggests that Ebony could suffer similar consequences as a result of the Boar's treatment by Blackwood and Wilson if the Boar changes sides and directs his anger towards Ebony, the leopard, and the scorpion. 'The Boar' is also critical of the tendency of Wilson (the leopard) to betray those who trust him:

And when all the people beheld the boar of Lebanon and how he fought, lo! their spirits were moved within them with laughter.

For he went forth into the host of the enemy in fury and in great wrath and he contended with them and cursed them and he smote certain of them and plucked off their hair, and they remained not but went and tarried at Jericho until their beards were grown.

And the wounds that he gave were unseemly for he cared not though he took forth their bowels in disorder trampling on them; and many there were who engaged him that were compelled to go over unto those of the circumcision.

But behold while the battle yet raged he came unto a place where dung had been laid upon the face of the ground but the men of the city had carried it forth in waggons to the field.

And he began with the snout of his nose to dig and to grovel in the soil where the abomination had lain in former days and his length of tail was twisted as a serpent twisteth herself before she spring upon the adversary.

And the man in the veil was grieviously offended and the leopard was moved with indignation for his heart is decietful more than the hearts of other beasts and he hath a sting in his tail wherewith he woundeth whom he listeth even though they put their trust in him. (p. 44)

Hogg did not publish anything in *Blackwood's* for a full year, from

April 1818 to April 1819, and only four times from April 1818 until December 1822: twice in 1819, once in 1820, and once in 1821. Maga did publish 'Verses Addressed to the Right. Hon. Lady Anne Scott of Buccleuch' in October 1818, but these dedicatory verses from *The Brownie of Bodsbeck* were published from the novel in lieu of a review and were not submitted for publication by Hogg. Although Hogg had little to do with Maga during this four-year period, he was not cut off from business with William Blackwood. Hogg completed *The Brownie of Bodsbeck; And Other Tales*, which Blackwood published in two volumes in 1818. Much of Hogg's time was taken up with collecting and preparing for publication the *Jacobite Relics*; the two 'series' of *Relics* were also published by Blackwood, the first appearing in 1819 and the second in 1821. In the April and May 1819 issues of *Blackwood's Edinburgh Magazine*, Hogg published a two-part piece on 'Storms', the first two numbers of a new series, 'The Shepherd's Calendar', which he published in irregular instalments through April 1828. 'The Shepherd's Calendar' stories thematically followed the 'Tales and Anecdotes of Pastoral Life' that had appeared in the first three numbers of *Blackwood's* (then the *Edinburgh Monthly Magazine*). At the conclusion of the third 'Tales and Anecdotes' story in the June 1817 issue, Hogg had indicated that the series would be continued. 'The Shepherd's Calendar' technically was not the promised continuation of the earlier series, but the stories built on the topics that were introduced in 'Tales and Anecdotes', although they generally exhibit a more mature style and in some cases represent some of his most sophisticated works of short fiction.[78] As Douglas Mack points out, the 'Shepherd's Calendar' stories present 'a resonant and convincing portrait of the life and spirit of a particular society'.[79] Hogg was a storehouse of these rural tales; they were easy for him to tell, and as William Laidlaw said of Hogg's dog stories, he could 'write them as fast as the A, B, C'.[80] Hogg published a total of fourteen stories under the 'The Shepherd's Calendar' title, so the stories represented an important facet of his life with *Blackwood's*. The stories were well-suited to magazine publication, and William Blackwood seemed to welcome them as interesting stories about an important way of life for a country that was predominantly rural and agricultural. The success of the stories for Hogg in *Blackwood's* probably came from the editor's regard for these kinds of sketches as fulfilling the role that had been set out for him in October 1817, but the stories also fit the Romantic character of Maga. Douglas Mack argues that Hogg accomplished much more than preserving the traditions of rural Scotland: 'These articles in *Blackwood's* are in fact much more than a pleasant exercise in nostalgia for a fast-fading rural way of life. Rather, they become a celebration of the worth to be found in the values of Ettrick, and a sophisticated subversion of some of the assumptions of Enlightenment Edinburgh'.[81]

After 'Storms' Hogg did not publish again in *Blackwood's* until March 1820, although in the meantime there were several works published in Maga in Hogg's name. The August and September 1819 issues of *Blackwood's* were primarily devoted to a fictitious hunting expedition, 'Christopher in the Tent'. The characters on this expedition were largely fictitious as well, including (but not limited to) the 'Editor' of *Blackwood's*; Peter Morris, the fictional persona of John Lockhart's *Peter's Letters to His Kinsfolk*, that had just been published by Blackwood in July; William Wastle, Morris's Edinburgh connection and a pseudonym used by Lockhart in *Blackwood's*; Timothy Tickler; the Irishman Odoherty, largely associated with William Maginn; Kempferhausen, associated with R. P. Gillies; and the Ettrick Shepherd. John Wilson had written to Hogg at the request, he claimed, of the 'Editor of Blackwood's Magazine' to ask him to write some poems on a 'Fairy' subject for the September 1819 'Tent' issue; Wilson gave Hogg specific directions for the poems: 'Now, suppose a troup of Fairies all to alight on the flag staff of the Tent, & to sing to, or address in any way you chuse the contributors as they are all lying asleep at night. First one Fairy may speak & then another—and they should all be invited into the Tent and sip a little whisky—& then their departure should be described sailing away over the hills'.[82] In the same letter Wilson also suggested a poem on 'The Praise of Whisky', and further added: 'I should like to hear from you—two or three lines or so—"The Lament of an old Heath-Cock" is a good subject for you—As you know the Editor always inserts your articles I hope you will send him several'. Wilson continues his insistence on a very narrowly-defined role for Hogg in Maga, and he is surely being intentionally ironic about accepting Hogg's 'articles'. Hogg apparently did not send Wilson any of the requested material, although on 29 October 1819, a frustrated Hogg wrote to Blackwood that he had written Wilson to provide some information about 'localities' for Wilson's 'Tent', although the letter at some point was 'lost':

> I wrote a long letter to Wilson on the subject of *the tent* though not a communication it might be called a letter of localities that he might have availed himself of them. To my great regret that letter was lost But really I have been so much mortified by the refusal of all my pieces that I cannot bear to think of

writing for the Magazine now. And though I always praise it above all other periodical works and wish it with all my heart every success yet would I rather sit down and write for the shabbiest work in the kingdom where every thing I write is revered. Indeed I have always felt that to whatever I gave my deserved admission I might have disgraced myself but my name now should not be a disgrace to any literary work.[83]

Hogg's frustration went beyond the refusal of his works for Maga. In the 'Tent' episodes, Hogg is given a fictitious role to play, and because he was presented under his own, widely-recognised pen name, the reader might not necessarily have made a distinction between the 'Shepherd' of the 'Tent' and the Shepherd of Ettrick. Hogg continues in the letter of 29 October to let Blackwood know that there are problems with his characterisation in this episode. Even though he is not offended by it, he claims, there are others who consider that his character has been compromised in the public's eyes. It was a subtle hint about Hogg's concerns over his role in Maga that both Blackwood and the editor chose to ignore:

I find that all my friends without exception think that the editors have dealt cavalierly with me in the tent scenes and that their representation is meant to injure my literary character throughout I have judged as impartially of the thing as I can and I do not see it. I think it is excellent sport and very good natured sport beside. I might pretend to be angry. I could easily do that; but the truth is I am not. I do not see that the contrast between such a blundering ignorant good natured fellow and his poetry can have aught but a good effect. I only wish the quiz on my worthy friend Dr. Russel had been left out as I am universally blamed for it here and it is likely to cherish a good deal of ill-will here among friends that were formerly so happy together.[84]

Hogg did not write any poetry for the 'Tent' episodes, but there are three poems in these two issues attributed to him by the author of the 'Tent'. These were not the only works that appeared in his name but without his knowledge during this period of scarce activity by him in Maga. There were sonnets signed with Hogg's name in the March 1818 and January 1820 issues. Lockhart's 'Letter from the Ettrick Shepherd, Enclosing a Fragment of the Mad Banker' also appeared in the January 1820 number. In October 1820 Lockhart published in *Blackwood's* his 'Letter from James Hogg to his Reviewer', a response to the review of Hogg's first volume of *Jacobite Relics* that had appeared in the *Edinburgh Review* for August 1820.[85] Hogg was baffled by the behaviour of Wilson and Lockhart, as he wrote to John Aitken: 'What a hand of me these Magazine rascals are making Lockhart was here at the very time and even on the very day that [TEAR] letter to the reviewer is dated. What strange fellows they are'.[86] Hogg eventually lost patience with Blackwood for the freedoms with his name used by Blackwood and his authors, both in signing his name to their works and in turning his personality into a fictional character. Hogg expressed both his frustration and his embarrassment to Margaret Phillips, to whom he was engaged, in a letter dated 14 February 1820:

> Your health is drunk every night, given by one friend or another, for our mutual attachment is blown over the whole kingdom and you will perhaps see that Blackwood's Magazine-mongers have been making game of it. They have likewise attached my name to several of their grovelling productions, but not a line in that work has been wrote by me for the last nine months. I have no connection with it; but as my funds are mostly in Blackwoods hands and as he has so much in his power regarding the success of my works I am obliged for my own interest to keep on fair terms there knowing they can do me no harm.[87]

Although Hogg secured a promise from Blackwood that nothing would appear in Maga again without his having seen it,[88] he clearly felt trapped by Blackwood and his magazine's controlling writers. Hogg enjoyed the friendship of Wilson, Lockhart, Blackwood, and others; he enjoyed access to the most important Edinburgh literary circles; and he relied heavily on Blackwood for most of his publishing opportunities and income. Hogg's relationship with *Blackwood's* was also complicated by his relationship with William Blackwood the book publisher. Therefore, he felt that he had no choice but to accept the abuse handed out by Maga's 'devils', and Wilson in particular, and brush it off as merely 'good natured sport'. Hogg would soon discover, though, that Wilson was capable of much worse.

In between Lockhart's 'letters from Hogg' in *Blackwood's*, Hogg published his own 'Letter'; the only work by him to appear in *Blackwood's* in 1820 is 'Letter from the Ettrick Shepherd, Enclosing a Letter from James Laidlaw' (pp. 78–82) in the March 1820 number. James Laidlaw, Hogg's cousin, had emigrated to Canada in 1818. Laidlaw had written to his son, Robert, about their new life in Canada; Robert and his brother, William, had remained in Scotland, but their father wanted them to join the rest of the family. Hogg published Laidlaw's letter, along with an introductory letter that provided some amusing—but unflattering—anecdotes about Laidlaw. Laidlaw's letter was authentic, and the letter was published without Laidlaw's permission or knowledge. Ironically, given Hogg's own issues with his treatment by Blackwood, part of his intent was to make fun of Laidlaw's limited education and knowledge of the world. Hogg insisted the editor publish the letter as is, including Laidlaw's unique spelling system. As might be expected, publication of the letter angered Laidlaw when he finally learned of it—as it surely would have angered Hogg had he been in Laidlaw's situation.

In 1821, Hogg again published only one work in Maga. 'Account of a Coronation-Dinner' (pp. 83–93) appeared in the second part of the August number. The work was written in the form of a letter from a Glasgow merchant, 'John M'Indoe', to a Glasgow manufacturer, 'William M'Ilhose'. The 'Coronation-Dinner' sketch describes a fictitious dinner of the Dilletanti Society in Edinburgh celebrating the coronation of King George IV on 19 July 1821. M'Indoe attends this 'private' dinner instead of the 'great public dinner' because of the Glaswegians' interest in the '*men of genius*' (p. 83) of Edinburgh. The sketch is a light-hearted depiction of the dinners of the Dilletanti Society, with Hogg perhaps following the model of the Burns Dinner described by Peter Morris in Lockhart's *Peter's Letters to His Kinsfolk*,[89] although the character descriptions are anonymous as in Hogg's own 'Chaldee Manuscript'. The 'Coronation-Dinner' sketch is perfectly suited to *Blackwood's* and is in keeping with Hogg's fondness for literary sport. Yet, given what was at stake for Hogg, it is curious that he wrote this sketch at this particular time. Sir Walter Scott had invited Hogg to accompany him to London to attend the coronation and to write about it in order to earn some money to ease his financial difficulties. Scott also had begun an effort to secure a pension for Hogg from the new Royal Society of Literature. Hogg declined Scott's invitation to go to London, pleading the necessity of attending the St Boswell's Fair to stock his farm. When it was clear that the trip to London was not possible for Hogg to manage, Lockhart encouraged him to write 'a real grand song for the Kings coronation dinner *here*' as a means of impressing the Royal Society.[90] Hogg could not manage the Edinburgh dinner either. Although Hogg suggests within the 'Coronation-Dinner' that he had 'written more loyal and national songs than any bard now living' (p. 92), there is actually nothing in 'Account of a Coronation-Dinner' for the general reader to link him directly to the sketch or to the patriotic bard. Ironically, Hogg later (in 1830) would blame his characterisation in the *Noctes Ambrosianæ* for his failure to be granted an annual stipend from the Royal Society of Literature.[91] It is unfortunate—and puzzling—that Hogg did not follow through on his prospects with the Society when both Walter Scott and John Lockhart were working on his behalf in conjunction with the coronation of King George IV, which took place eight months before the beginning of the *Noctes*.

Hogg published 'Account of a Coronation-Dinner' in a time of unsettledness with Blackwood. Hogg had been engaged in a dispute with Blackwood over £50, and he was also concerned about George Goldie's published response to Hogg's 'Memoir' in the third edition of *The Mountain Bard*.[92] Hogg was trusting in Blackwood, Hogg's 'firmest and best friend', for an appropriate resolution to his difficulties, and he reminded Blackwood in a letter of 19/20 August 1821 of their agreement regarding publications by or about Hogg: 'I have a written promise from you most absolutely given that my name should never once be mentioned nor alluded to in your work without my own consent'.[93] It is only a matter of days, however, before Hogg is again betrayed in the pages of Maga. In the same issue with 'Account of a Coronation-Dinner', *Blackwood's* published a review of Hogg's *Mountain Bard* 'Memoir'.[94] The review, written by John Wilson, is in the form of a letter to Christopher North 'From an Old Friend with a New Face'. The 'new face' of this old friend was ugly. The article is a blistering attack on Hogg, in style and focus similar to the Tickler letters of 1818, which also had as their subject a life of Hogg; however, the review is much more severe and more pointedly vicious. The letter writer claims he is so disgusted with Hogg's 'Memoir' that he has been completely put off pork. He asks: 'Pray, who wishes to know any thing about his life? Who, indeed, cares a single farthing whether he be at this blessed moment dead or alive?' The writer finds it 'sickening' to 'hear Hogg and Burns spoken of in the same year, and written of in the same volume'. He calls Hogg's periodical *The Spy* 'truly a sickening concern'. He is critical of Hogg's lack of education: 'He could not write, he says, till he was upwards of twenty years of age. This I deny. He cannot write now'. Wilson dismisses Hogg's life as 'one continued bungle'. Yet, he continues, 'the self-conceit of the man is incredible'. Further, in an extended discussion he dismisses Hogg's authorship of the 'Chaldee Manuscript': 'Why, no more did he write the Chaldee Manuscript than the five books of Moses'. He attacks Hogg's claim that he turned down the editorship of *Blackwood's*: 'This happened the same year that he declined the offer of the governor-generalship of India, and a seat in the cabinet.

[...] Ebony is no blockhead; and who but a supreme blockhead would make Hogg an editor!' Importantly, too, Wilson makes it clear that Hogg has no place in the Edinburgh literary circles; he 'is liker a swineherd in the Canongate, than a shepherd in Ettrick Forest'. He portrays Hogg as a 'monster' in Edinburgh, reminiscent of Frankenstein's creature, whose appearance frightens off all who behold him. Hogg leaves Ettrick, Wilson writes, and 'comes jogging into Edinburgh' to find a publisher for his works, but

> not one will bite. No wonder. Only picture to yourself a stout
> country lout, with a bushel of hair on his shoulders that had
> not been raked for months, enveloped in a coarse plaid
> impregnated with tobacco, with a prodigious mouthful of
> immeasurable tusks, and a dialect that set all conjecture at
> defiance, lumbering suddenly in upon the elegant retirement
> of Mr Miller's back-shop, or the dim seclusion of Mr John
> Ogle! Were these worthies to be blamed if they fainted upon
> the spot, or run out yelling into the street past the monster,
> or, in desperation, flung themselves into safety from a back
> window over ten stories?[95]

Wilson then proceeds to denigrate Hogg's works. The article concludes with an editorial note from 'North' that attempts to soften the article by proclaiming it a good-humoured piece, possibly written by Hogg, that will elicit laughter from no one 'more freely than the Shepherd himself'. This afterword no doubt was insisted on by Blackwood in anticipation of public sentiment going against him— not to mention that of Hogg.

The response was as expected. James Ballantyne, Blackwood's printer, threatened to quit working for Blackwood if he printed the article.[96] D. M. Moir wrote to Blackwood on 23 August: 'The Epistle on Hogg quite puzzles me it is a capital specimen of the Timothy Tickler tribe; but if Hogg swallows it without wry faces he must be possessed of imperturbable good nature. I hope there is some understanding with him about it'.[97] There was no prior understanding with Hogg, however, although there seems to have been a *mis*understanding between Hogg and Blackwood. Apparently Blackwood had shown Hogg part of the article in advance. When Hogg saw the article in slips, he had assumed that the article was by George Goldie and that Blackwood had conspired with Goldie, as Hogg wrote, 'to crush me to pieces in all respects at once'.[98] Perhaps Hogg thought that his reminder to Blackwood of his promise not to publish on Hogg without his consent, as well as his appeal to his friendship with Blackwood, would be enough to prevent him from publishing the article. Blackwood went forward with publication, and in spite of Hogg's fondness for literary sport, he could not accept this extreme attack. Wilson's review of Hogg's 'Memoir' went far beyond the bounds of decency or of Hogg's sense of fun or his willingness to suffer abuse in order to continue his place in the company of the Ebony writers. Hogg was also too much of an insider with Maga for the excuse of 'my editor took his own way' to work with him. Hogg wrote to Blackwood on 4 September 1821, after having finally read the article in Maga:

> Well sir you have now put the crown on all the injurious abuse that I have suffered from you for these three years and a half, and that in despite of your word of honour which no miserable pretext can justify. If I have ever done ought either to you or your correspondents to deserve this it was unintentional. For my own part I would have regarded this wanton attack as I did all the rest of the ribaldry and mockery that has been so liberally vomited forth on me from your shop but there are other feelings now beside my own that I am bound to respect, and on these the blows that you inflict wound deeper and smart with more poignancy, nor can any palliatives that I can use heal them. [...] If you really had it in your power to have repressed this piece of beastly depravity and did not do it I must consider you as worse than the worst assassin out of hell.[99]

Hogg went on to request the name of the author of the article in order to appease his anger and settle this issue. Blackwood refused to disclose the author, and on 17 October Hogg wrote to Blackwood threatening legal action:

> I am extremely sorry to advert to your behaviour to me in another point which has driven me to the only means of redress left to me as a christian. In less than two months you will recieve a citation for the publication of falshoods [sic] tending to injure me as a man, and an author; and for forging my name together with a charge of damages that will astonish you, as it has already done myself. Even though you saw me in an unbridled passion you ought to have given me the satisfaction I asked which would have saved a great deal of trouble and expense to us both. I soon found it out; and if aught on earth could have mitigated the injury done me, it would have been a frank avowal of the friend's name who in

his rash and thoughtless manner wrote it; in whose heart I never before at least believed that any malice or evil intent dwelt; but highly as I before esteemed him I never will forgive him, especially for not at once acknowledging it to me. You will have found by this time that the opinion of the world is grieveously against you for your unmerited abuse of me but it is quite needless to dispute a point which others must now judge for us.[100]

In the end Hogg did not take legal action against Blackwood, but neither did he publish in *Blackwood's* for the next sixteen months. Robert Cadell was quick to take advantage of Hogg's situation, flattering the writer's ego, expressing his abhorrence at Hogg's treatment in Maga, and encouraging him to continue to write for the *Edinburgh Magazine*: 'We are particularly obliged by your articles, and hope you will keep your promise to continue—any from you must be good—and find a place—and I think I may add no very great danger of your being abominably abused—furthermore you shall have as high remuneration as E. M. can afford to give you'.[101] On 3 October Hogg wrote to John Grieve, telling Grieve that he had accepted Cadell's 'proffered friendship' and would write for him: 'He says after establishing their Mag. (by the Chaldee I suppose) they have done all in their power to ruin me.'[102] In spite of his intense anger with Blackwood, Hogg, interestingly, also tells Grieve that he does not understand the outrage that the article had sparked from so many people: 'I have been assailed from all quarters with letters on the treatment of Blackwood. There is surely something in it worse than I can see for it appears to me to be a joke an even down quiz without much ill meaning but written in a beastly stile'. Perhaps Hogg's comments to Grieve served as a face-saving device with an old friend, for it was just two weeks later that Hogg threatened Blackwood with legal action. Hogg's conflicted feelings over his relationship with Blackwood and Wilson are evident in his letter to Grieve; these conflicted feelings would typify his relationship with Maga for the rest of his life, even in his times of magazine prosperity.

## 4. The *Noctes* Shepherd

After the 'Coronation-Dinner' sketch in August 1821, Hogg did not publish again in *Blackwood's* until December 1822; however, Hogg resumed a business relationship with William Blackwood several months earlier. Blackwood published in book form Hogg's dramatic work, *The Royal Jubilee* (1822), to coincide with King George IV's visit to Edinburgh in August 1822, and *The Royal Jubilee* was reviewed in the September 1822 special number of *Blackwood's* commemorating the King's visit. Hogg also sent Blackwood two articles for Maga, although he could not have had a serious expectation that Blackwood would accept them. On 11 April 1822 Hogg sent Blackwood 'Hints to Reviewers', a satire on the *Edinburgh Review* that had been turned down by the *Edinburgh Magazine* 'on the score of sheer terror';[103] Blackwood also declined to publish this work. On 14 June 1822 Hogg sent Blackwood a revised version of 'John Paterson's Mare'. Hogg intended this article—another sketch of the publishing rivalry between Constable and Blackwood—as an overture of reconciliation with Blackwood: 'I send you the accompanying article merely as a token that I have foregiven all that is past and that I wish all byganes to be byganes between us for ever that had any tendency to dislike. I cannot bear to live in terms of utter estrangement with a man from whom I experienced so many repeated kindnesses and obligations'.[104] Since he had earlier written Blackwood about the story (July 1818), Hogg had revised it considerably, he said, but Blackwood was not interested even in the revised version. Blackwood was glad to receive the sketch from Hogg as a good-will gesture towards renewal of their Maga relationship. Blackwood wrote a polite letter to Hogg rejecting the story but welcoming him back as a contributor. Blackwood was not interested in opening up old, sore subjects again: 'the whole affair about these poor creatures Pringle & Cleghorn is entirely forgotten, and it would be like slaughtering the long ago dead & buried'.[105] Furthermore, Blackwood did not think it was appropriate for Hogg to attack Constable, who was ill and who also had just published Hogg's *Poetical Works* in four volumes. Perhaps Hogg was naïve enough to believe that Blackwood would actually publish the sketch. Perhaps he thought that his act of reconciliation might also serve the dual purpose of needling Blackwood a little as well. What was finally published in *Blackwood's* for December 1822 was 'The Women Folk' (p. 95), a song that had been published three years earlier in *No. of the Border Garland*.[106] The *Blackwood's* publication included the music for Hogg's melody line, and the song is sung by the 'Hogg' character in a new series within Maga, the *Noctes Ambrosianæ*.

The *Noctes Ambrosianæ* is a series of fictitious conversations among a group of both real and imaginary characters set primarily in William Ambrose's Tavern in Gabriel's Road (later in Picardy Place), Edinburgh.[107] The *Noctes* began in the March 1822 issue of *Blackwood's* and extended to seventy-one parts that appeared frequently, but not on a regular schedule, through February 1835. John Wilson was the

primary writer for the series, but John Lockhart was also a major
contributor, as was (to a lesser extent) William Maginn. It was
commonplace for a *Noctes* to have been written collaboratively, though,
and the conversations regularly dropped in songs and poetry by
other authors, especially James Hogg. Although the *Noctes*
conversations are works of fiction, and many of them written far
distant from Ambrose's Tavern, nonetheless there were numerous
occasions that saw the *Blackwood's* writers in fact gathered for long
evenings of drinking and convivial conversation. Indeed, the new
*Blackwood's Edinburgh Magazine* could be said to have grown out of
the first real night at Ambrose's (at least figuratively): the night
Lockhart, Wilson, and Blackwood 'drank punch from eight till eight'
and interlarded Hogg's 'Chaldee Manuscript' with a great deal of
'deevilry'. The conversations cover a wide range of topics of
contemporary interest, including new works of literature, the major
political issues of the day, other current events, articles in the
newspapers and magazines, and public personalities; the topics of
conversation are sometimes more trivial, such as fox hunting, food,
tigers, deer and boar, and the singing of Edinburgh ladies. A favourite
subject of the *Noctes* characters is Tory superiority over the Whigs,
especially as that superiority is manifest in the publishing industry
of the time. The diverse cast of characters and the dialogic form
make the *Noctes* an ideal forum for presenting the 'spirit of the age'.
As J. H. Alexander has written, the *Noctes* 'may be regarded as an
outstanding example of second generation Romantic genius,
comparable in many ways with Byron's *Don Juan* in its outrageousness,
its variety, its virtuoso improvisatory quality, its exploratory and
subversive aspect, its allusiveness, and its vast entertainment value'.[108]

The series was immensely popular with the *Blackwood's* readership.
Thomas Carlyle was an avid reader of the *Noctes*, and in his
'reminiscence' of 'Christopher North', written in the spring of 1868,
Carlyle reflects on what the *Noctes* had meant to him, although he
also expresses his regrets that Wilson had used so much energy and
talent on such a shallow project: 'Those wild *Noctes Ambrosianae* of his
were uniformly a great entertainment to me; admirable flashes of
broad strong insight, genially triumphant sarcasm, humour and satire;
beautiful bits of poetic delineation, wild tones of piety and melody:
but all imbedded in such an element of drunken semi-frenzy,—sad to
me to think they were *lost*, jewels thrown into a sea of conflagration,
inextricably inextricable, there!'[109] Henry Cockburn, whose
periodical associations were primarily with Francis Jeffrey and the
*Edinburgh Review*, also lauded the *Noctes* in *Memorials of His Time*:

no periodical publication that I know of can boast of so extraordinary a series of jovial dramatic fiction. [...] There is not so curious and original a work in the English or Scotch languages. It is a most singular and delightful outpouring of criticism, politics, and descriptions of feeling, character, and scenery, of verse and prose, and maudlin eloquence, and especially of wild fun. [...] And its Scotch is the best Scotch that has been written in modern times. I am really sorry for the poor one-tongued Englishman, by whom, because the Ettrick Shepherd uses the sweetest and most expressive of living languages, the homely humour, the sensibility, the descriptive power, the eloquence, and the strong joyous hilarity of that animated rustic can never be felt'.[110]

Most of the major characters in the *Noctes* were well-established personae from earlier issues of *Blackwood's*, especially the fictitious adventures in the 'Tent' issues of August and September 1819, where Christopher North first references 'our monthly dinner at Ambrose's'.[111] There are many characters that appear in the *Noctes* issues over the years, but the primary recurring characters, especially in the early numbers, are 'North', 'Tickler', 'Odoherty', and 'James Hogg'—also known as 'the Ettrick Shepherd' or simply 'Shepherd'. The first three characters are commonly, but loosely, associated with John Wilson, Robert Sym, and William Maginn, and their pseudonyms are limited to their fictitious roles in *Blackwood's*. Although other characters, such as Lord Byron and Thomas De Quincey (the English Opium-Eater), make fictitious 'guest appearances' in the *Noctes* under their real names, it is only Hogg who appears as himself regularly throughout the series. Hogg does not appear in every *Noctes*, nor does every *Noctes* use Hogg as a subject, but, as Henry Cockburn suggests, the character of James Hogg/the Ettrick Shepherd was central to the success and appeal of the *Noctes* series. The *Noctes* writers understood this as well, for the 'Shepherd' is made to ask in the January 1828 number, either sincerely or with irony: 'What's a Noctes withouten the Shepherd?'[112] This point was made more evident after a break between Hogg and Blackwood in the early 1830s when the *Noctes* ceased publication for eighteen months.

Even though Hogg does not appear as a character in the *Noctes* until his return to Maga in December 1822, he is a frequent topic of conversation in the early *Noctes* issues. In the first number of the *Noctes*, March 1822, Wilson seems to extend to Hogg a public offer of reconciliation and apology for the 'beastly depravity' of his review of Hogg's 'Memoir', although the offer is not altogether unqualified. The apology comes from the fictitious Odoherty, who claims that he was the author of the article; however, the apology does not come until Wilson reminds the reader (with a touch of irony) once again who Hogg really is, what he does for a living, and what business should take him to Edinburgh:

> *Odoherty.* Does he never come to Edinburgh now?
> *Editor.* Oh yes, now and then he is to be seen, about five in the morning, selling sheep in the Grassmarket. I am told he is a capital manager about his farm, and getting rich apace.
> *Odoherty.* I am glad to hear it. I'm sorry I wrote that article on his life. It was too severe, perhaps.
> *Editor.* Never mind; 'tis quite forgotten. He is now giving out that he wrote it himself.
> *Odoherty.* It was a devilish good article. He could not have written three lines of it.
> *Editor.* No, no, but neither could you have written three lines of Kilmeny, no, nor one line of his dedication to Lady Anne Scott. Hogg's a true genius in his own style. Just compare him with any of the others of the same sort; compare him with Clare for a moment. Upon my word, Hogg appears to me to be one of the most wonderful creatures in the world, taking all things together. I wish he would send me more articles than he does, and take more pains with them.[113]

The praise of Hogg is short-lived, though. In April 1822 Hogg gets a brief mention as the 'Shepherd of Chaldea', and in May he is referred to as *'the Learned Pig'*. For five years *Blackwood's* had been publishing articles attacking Leigh Hunt and the 'Cockney' poets, but in the July 1822 *Noctes* the Byron character is made to say that Leigh Hunt is 'worth fifty Hoggs'.[114]

When the Hogg character makes his first appearance in the *Noctes*, then, he has already been set up to appear as James Hogg the author. Hogg's pen name, the Ettrick Shepherd, had long been used by Hogg to sign his own works and was immediately recognisable by the reading public as James Hogg. There was good reason, therefore, for the 'Hogg' character—and later the 'Shepherd'—to be thought of in terms of James Hogg himself. It was clear, too, that Maga's new series would embrace the method that made the new *Blackwood's Edinburgh Magazine* an instant success in October 1817—the literature of personality—and this often to Hogg's detriment. The Hogg character speaks to the personality issue in the June 1823 *Noctes*. Mullion has suggested sending Hogg as an ambassador to the Duke of Burgundy, to which Hogg responds: 'I wish, doctor, ye would let Hogg alane.– What for are ye aye harling me intil your havers, by the lug and the horn?–I dinna like it. [...] It's no decent to be aye meddling wi' folks' personalities. I'm sure by this time the whole set o' you might hae mair sense. Ye ken what ye hae gotten by your personalities'.[115] J. H. Alexander has rightly observed that 'the Hogg/Shepherd is a good deal closer to certain central aspects of James Hogg than has generally been recognised–that a credible James Hogg may be discerned in the *Noctes*, which were after all written by those who knew him well, both sober and in his cups, in situations formal and informal'.[116] The truth of Alexander's observation also had a negative side for Hogg; the writers who knew him well sometimes turned that knowledge into a self-mocking or self-parodying voice in the character of the *Noctes* Shepherd. Hogg occasionally complained to Blackwood about the characterisation of the fictional 'Shepherd' in the *Noctes*, which, he was convinced, had damaged his literary career and cost him a great deal of money. He writes in his 'Memoir' about Blackwood and his *Magazine*: 'That Magazine of his, which owes its rise principally to myself, has often put words and sentiments into my mouth of which I have been greatly ashamed, and which have given much pain to my family and relations, and many of those after a solemn written promise that such freedoms should never be repeated'.[117] On 6 April 1830 Hogg wrote to Blackwood about the price he had paid personally and professionally for his portrayal in Maga, especially in the *Noctes*:

> I know and have been sensible these many years that you are my sincere friend else I would not have submitted to the thousand vulgarities and absurdities with which I am characterised in Maga. It has ruined my literary character altogether, so completely that I am told by many London correspondents that no work of mine will ever sell again or likely ever be published again. Among other bad things it has deprived me of £100 a year by fairly keeping me out of the Royal Lit. society. Every churchman voted against me on the ground of my dissipation as described in the *Noctes* and neither denied by myself nor any friend publicly. This is a fact which I have attested by some of your own friends, as well as mine.[118]

John Lockhart later defended Hogg to the Royal Society of Literature in an article in the *Quarterly Review* for January 1831: 'a more worthy, modest, sober and loyal man does not exist in his Majesty's dominions than this distinguished poet, whom some of his waggish friends have taken up the absurd fancy of exhibiting in print as a sort of boozing buffoon'.[119] The 'boozing buffoon' characterisation caught the attention of Wilson, and the March 1831 *Noctes* has North and the Shepherd take issue with Lockhart's criticism of Hogg's role in the *Noctes*.[120] Unfortunately, the expression 'boozing buffoon' is clever enough to have survived over time and is now the epithet most commonly associated with the Ettrick Shepherd of the *Noctes*.

Hogg's love of 'speerits' is a significant facet of Hogg's personality in the *Noctes*, though. The appearance of the Hogg character in December 1822 coincides with the introduction of an imbibing Hogg. When called upon by Odoherty to sing 'The Women Folk', Hogg requests additional time for additional drink: 'I canna sing yet, Captain: just bear wi' me till I've had another tumbler or twa—that's a good fellow, now—I'll gie ye sangs anew or the morn's morning'.[121] Hogg's fondness for 'the bowl' is both portrayed and discussed over much of the life of the *Noctes*. In the September 1825 *Noctes* Hogg sings a song to the tune of 'Auld Lang Syne' about the value of the 'glass and bowl' for 'knittin' soul to soul' (p. 180). Of course Hogg had already been introduced to the public as the drinking shepherd, if not a 'boozing buffoon', in Wilson's first letter of Timothy Tickler in February 1818.[122] Furthermore, John Lockhart, in *Peter's Letters*, after the glowing tribute to Hogg at the Burns Dinner, also connects Hogg with Burns in their fondness for strong drink: Hogg 'long before I came into his neighbourhood, had finished the bottle of port allowed by our traiteur, and was deep in a huge jug of whisky toddy—in the manufacture of which he is supposed to excel almost as much as Burns did—and in its consumption too, although happily in rather a more moderate degree'.[123] In the July 1826 number of the *Noctes* Tickler feels compelled to defend Hogg's sobriety: 'I never saw you the worse of liquor in my life, James'.[124] And in the April 1827 number the Shepherd complains that the participants in the 'meetings' at Ambroses are being abused by the 'water-drinkers' for 'preferrin' speerits' and that the Shepherd has 'come in for the chief part of the abuse':

> Confound their backbiting malignity! Is there a steadier hand than that in a' Scotland?—see how the liquid quivers to the brim, and not a drop overflowing—Is my nose red? my broo blotched? my een red and rheumy? my shanks shrunk? my knees, do they totter? or does my voice come from my heart in a crinkly cough, as if the lungs were rotten? Bring ony ane

INTRODUCTION

o' the base water-drinkers here, and set him doon afore me, and let us discuss ony subject he likes, and see whase head's the clearest, and whase tongue wags wi' maist unfaulterin' freedom![125]

J. H. Alexander describes Lockhart's defence of Hogg as a 'boozing buffoon' as 'more than slightly over the top';[126] the same could be said of Wilson's defences of Hogg in the *Noctes*, especially as those defences are voiced by the Hogg character himself. The subject of Hogg's alcohol consumption is only one example of how the *Noctes* calls public attention to a less-than-noble aspect of Hogg's character, or 'personality', only to have that character trait denied and/or defended by the *Noctes* circle. Frequently Wilson writes a *Noctes* that by the tone and character of its defence serves to undermine its apparent positive purpose; there is no doubt that Wilson intended such a subterfuge.

The *Noctes* conversations provide Wilson with an opportunity to persist in goading Hogg with Wilson's favourite Hogg topics, especially his authorship of the 'Chaldee Manuscript' and his rank among the poets. For example, in the opening number of the *Noctes*, when Odoherty mentions 'Hogg's Chaldee', the Editor replies, picking up again the question of Hogg's authorship from Wilson's review of Hogg's 'Memoir' from the year before: '*Hogg's* Chaldee!—good'.[127] On the other hand, the March 1824 number of the *Noctes* does not deny Hogg's authorship; rather, it wrongly links him to the more damning parts of the 'Chaldee'. Odoherty provides a preview of Hogg's poem in progress, *Queen Hynde*. Hogg is not present for the night's conversation, so North suggests he is working on his epic (which Odoherty corrects to 'He-pig') poem, *Queen Hynde*. Odoherty volunteers to recite the beginning of the poem which, he claims, like the 'Æneid or Madoc', is 'to open with a recapitulation of all his works'. Odoherty says he will quote the opening of *Queen Hynde*:

> Come listen to my lay, for I am he
> Who wrote Kilmeny's wild and wondrous song,
> Likewise the famous Essay upon Sheep,
> And Mador of the Moor; and then, unlike
> Those men who fling their pearls before the Hog,
> I, Hogg, did fling my Perils before men. [...]
> But still more famous for the glorious work,
> Which I, 'neath mask of oriental sage,
> Wrote and concocted in auspicious hour—
> THE CHALDEE MANUSCRIPT—which, with a voice

Of thundering sound, fulmined o'er Edinburg,
Shook the old Calton from its granite base,
Made Arthur's Seat toss up its lion head,
And snuff the wind in wonder; while around,
Eastward and westward, northward, southward, all
The ungodly, struck with awe and ominous dread
Of the great ruin thence impending o'er them,
Fled frighted, leaving house and home behind,
In shameful rout—or, grovelling prostrate, shew'd
Their nether parts uncomely—[128]

Here Tickler interrupts and says: 'I think you may stop there'. It is Odoherty who is Hogg's antagonist here, as he commonly is in the *Noctes* and, ironically, it is North who is Hogg's defender and who will 'not permit Hogg to be quizzed'. Of course it was Wilson, along with Lockhart and Blackwood, who wrote the 'Chaldee' section referencing the 'nether parts'—not Hogg.

Another aspect of Hogg's 'personality' in the *Noctes* is as a writer with an ego of consequence and who is obsessed with his reputation as a poet and how he ranks among the great poets of his own time. This trait, too, has developed out of Wilson's earlier writings about Hogg. In the June 1824 *Noctes*, for example, after the death of Byron in April, the characters discuss Byron's greatness as a poet. Tickler says: 'I think the name of Byron will then be ranked as the third name of one great æra of the imaginative literature of England'. Hogg asks, hopefully: 'After Sir Walter and me?' But Tickler intends Scott and Wordsworth, not Hogg.[129] In the January 1825 *Noctes*, written by Lockhart, the characters conduct a conversational review of *Queen Hynde*, which had just been published in December. North comments:

There are many things in it as absurd as possible—some real monstrosities of stuff—but on the whole, this, sir, is James Hogg's masterpiece, and that is saying something, I guess. There is a more sustained vigour and force over the whole strain than he ever could hit before; and though, perhaps, there is nothing quite so charming as my Bonny Kilmeny, that was but a ballad by itself—while here, sir, we have a real workmanlike poem—a production regularly planned, and powerfully executed. Sir, James Hogg will go down as one of the true worthies of this age.[130]

In the next *Noctes* (March 1825), written by Wilson, Wilson makes fun of the poor sales of *Queen Hynde*, as well as Hogg's standing and popularity as a poet: 'second only to Byron', says North. The

Shepherd himself says: 'Me and Wordsworth are aboon the age we
live in—it's no worthy o' us; but wait a whyleock—wait only for a
thousand years, or thereabouts, Mr North, and you'll see who will
have speeled to the tap o' the tree'.[131] And in a lengthy soliloquy that
opens the January 1828 number, the Shepherd comments on 'the
moral world, which belangs to men o' genius like Me and Burns'.[132]

Wilson understood well Hogg's frustration with his sometimes
insulting, sometimes abusive, portrayal of Hogg's character as a
person and as an author in the *Noctes*, as well as in Wilson's essays
on Hogg that had appeared over several years. Wilson would have
heard Hogg's justified rants often enough from Hogg himself, and
Blackwood also would have conveyed Hogg's anger to Wilson.
Wilson allows Hogg to voice that anger from time to time in the
*Noctes*. Perhaps this is intended by Wilson as a way to let Hogg vent
his anger publicly, although it is just as likely Wilson's way of
controlling his voice. Wilson is also flaunting his ability to get under
Hogg's skin. For example, in the November 1826 number the
Shepherd is permitted to underscore his frustrations with his works
being rejected by Wilson, as well as his manuscripts not being
returned:

> *Shepherd.* Or suppose that some shepherd, more silly than
> his sheep, that roams in yon glen where Yarrow frae still St
> Mary's Loch rowes wimplin to join the Ettrick, should lay
> down his cruick, and aneath the shadow o' a rock, or a ruin,
> indite a bit tale, in verse or prose, or in something between
> the twa, wi' here and there aiblins a touch o' nature—what is
> ower ower aften the fate o' his unpretendin' contribution, Mr
> North? A cauld glint o' the ee—a curl o' the lip—a humph o'
> the voice—a shake o' the head—and then, but the warld, wicked
> as it is, could never believe it, a wave o' your haun', and
> instantly, and for evermore, is it swallowed up by the jaws of
> the Baalam-box, greedy as the grave, and hungry as Hades.
> Ca' ye that friendship—ca' ye that respec'—ca' ye that sae muckle
> as the common humanity due to ane anither, frae a' men o'
> woman born, but which you, sir,—na, dinna frown and gnaw
> your lip—hae ower aften forgotten to show even to me, the
> Ettrick Shepherd, and the author of the Queen's Wake?[133]

Certainly this could have been written by Hogg at almost any point
in his relationship with Wilson and the *Blackwood's* writers. Wilson
could not let go of Hogg's 'Memoir' in *The Mountain Bard*, which
Wilson had savaged in *Blackwood's* in August 1821. After having

attacked Hogg in the review of the 'Memoir' for Hogg's claim he had originally been offered the editorship of *Blackwood's Edinburgh Magazine*, as a further insult Wilson names Hogg 'Editor' in February 1826 since North is getting old, 'rather doited–crabbed to the contributors';[134] this perhaps also refers back to Hogg's addressing North in 'A Scots Mummy' (August 1823; pp. 139–43) as 'ye auld crusty, crippled, crabbit, editor body' (p. 142).

Like almost everything about Hogg's relationship with *Blackwood's*, though, the *Noctes Ambrosianæ* proved to be a mixed opportunity for Hogg. If Hogg's personality became a source of ridicule on the one hand, on the other hand the fictitious Hogg/Shepherd character was a favourite among the Maga readers, which kept his name before the public and stimulated an interest in the 'real' Hogg. The series provided a source of easy income for Hogg; the *Noctes* format afforded an ideal forum for publishing his songs, for there was no necessity for his songs to have any bearing on the subject of the discussions in any particular issue. In the convivial setting where 'the bowl' was regularly passed, it was only necessary for one character to exclaim, 'James, give us a song', to establish a context for a song. From December 1822 through the end of 1828 (the concluding date for the present volume), Hogg published twenty-two titles in the *Noctes*— more than forty per cent of the titles published by Hogg in *Blackwood's* from 1822 through 1828. All nine of Hogg's works in *Blackwood's* in 1826 were songs that were sung by the Shepherd or Hogg character in the *Noctes*. Furthermore, half of Hogg's *Noctes* works had been published first elsewhere, so his *Noctes* publications were effortlessly achieved. Hogg's reputation as a songwriter, especially, was enhanced by work in the *Noctes*. Five songs were published with the music; three of these songs had been published in *No. of the Border Garland* [1819] and included original tunes by Hogg.[135] On 11 August 1827 Hogg wrote to Blackwood: 'I am perswaded that some things in Maga have operated singularly to my advantage for the applications for contributions from my *highly gifted pen* have of late increased to a most laughable and puzzling extent. Three came with your letter last night all from music publishers in London'.[136] Hogg's presence in the *Noctes* as both character and author certainly played a large role in his increased attention in the literary marketplace.

The *Noctes* works also highlight the breadth of Hogg's song subjects: there are courting and love songs, such as 'When the Kye Comes Hame' (p. 138), 'The Brakens Wi' Me' (pp. 181–82), 'My Bonny Mary' (pp. 190–92), and 'I'll No Wake Wi' Annie' (pp. 312–13); humorous songs about the dark side of the human character, such as 'The Great Muckle Village of Balmaquhapple' (pp. 188–89), 'Tam Nelson' (pp. 254–55), 'Meg o' Marley' (pp. 189–90), and 'The Laird o' Lamington' (pp. 164–65); and serious topical verse, such as 'There's Some Souls 'ill Yammer and Cheep' (p. 256) and 'Hymn to the Devil' (pp. 159–62). Hogg published several occasional songs as well, which are among his most successful pieces in the *Noctes.* 'I Lookit East–I Lookit West' (pp. 253–54) had been written in 1815 at the request of John Galt for the dinner instituting the Royal Caledonian Society in London, an organisation whose primary purpose was to provide support and education for children of Scottish military personnel. 'I Lookit East–I Lookit West' praises the generosity and kindness of those who have tended to the needs of children and the indigent:

> And weel I ken that Heaven will bless
> The heart that issued the decree,
> The widow and the fatherless
> Can never pray and slighted be. (p. 254)

Hogg wrote 'Songs for the Duke of Buccleuch's Birth day' (pp. 183–88) for the nineteenth birthday of Walter, the fifth Duke of Buccleuch. Walter was the son of Charles, the fourth Duke, who had granted Hogg the lease of the Altrive farm in 1815. 'Rejoice Ye Wan and Wilder'd Glens' (pp. 185–86) and 'Wat o' Buccleuch' (pp. 186–88)) celebrate the historical significance of the Buccleuch family as protectors and benefactors of the Borders and welcome Walter into his place as leader of that distinguished family. The songs also challenge Walter to accept the responsibilities of his position and live up to the tradition of leadership that he has inherited:

> O young Buccleuch O kind Buccleuch
>   What thousand hearts yearn o'er thee
> What thousand hopes await thy smile
>   And prostrate lie before thee
> Be thou thy Border's pride and boast
>   Like sires renowned in story
> And thou shalt never want an host
>   For country king and glory. (p. 186)

'The Stuarts of Appin' (pp. 348–50) is also an occasional song, written to be sung at a dinner in honour of the appointment of David Stewart of Garth as governor of St Lucia in 1828. The song laments the fall of the Stuarts, as well as a number of Highland clans, in the Jacobite risings of the early eighteenth century. Hogg poignantly yet forcefully conveys both the nobility of the clans and the tragic loss in the aftermath of the Jacobite defeat.

Hogg also wrote satirical songs for the *Noctes* to attack the Whigs and Blackwood's publishing rivals. In 'In Embro Town' (pp. 313–14), for example, the *Blackwood's* writers hold court in Ambrose's 'spence', led by the fictitious Maga editor, 'Christopher North', who has 'gien a' the Whigs in the land a threshin''. The court decrees that 'the Whigs are neerdoweels, great and sma'': 'The Whigs are found out, and in siccan a rout, | That their hurdies are scantily worth a threshin''. In the same *Noctes*, 'Chalk! Chalk!' (p. 314) attacks the Cockneys again, but the song especially targets the London publisher, Henry Colburn, who published several popular 'silver fork' novels in the 1820s. Colburn had a business interest in several periodicals, and the song suggests that Colburn was guilty of 'puffing' his fiction in his periodicals. 'Chalk! Chalk!' continues the critical sparring between Colburn and Blackwood that had begun nearly a decade earlier and that had been carried out both in the publishers' works and in their personal correspondence. John Lockhart, the author of the *Noctes* in which 'Chalk! Chalk!' appears, very likely also had a hand in this song.

Perhaps the most effective, delightful, and enduring triumph of Hogg's satirical songs in the *Noctes* is 'If E'er You Would Be a Brave Fellow' (pp. 162–63), which Hogg had written to celebrate the occasions that were the basis for the *Noctes*. This song was actually sung by Hogg one night at a gathering of the *Blackwood's* group at Ambrose's Tavern. The song playfully addresses the competition between the Whigs of the *Edinburgh Review* (designated as 'the Blue and the Yellow' from the colours of its cover) and the Tories of *Blackwood's Edinburgh Magazine* (whose title page included an engraving of George Buchanan). The song opens:

> If e'er you would be a brave fellow, young man,
> Beware of the Blue and the Yellow, young man;
>   If ye wud be strang,
>   And wish to write lang,
> Come join in the lads that get mellow, young man.
> Like the crack o' a squib that has fa'en on, young man,
> Compared wi' the roar o' a cannon, young man,
>   So is the Whig's blow
>   To the pith that's below
> The beard o' auld Geordie Buchanan, young man.
>                                        (pp. 162–63)

The song addresses the ineptness of the Whig authors ('Like auld maidens, fash'd wi' the vapours') and the weakness of their argued positions ('he'll never fight weel, | As lang as he dads wi' a docken'). The song concludes with a toast to the King and his loyal Tory supporters and a wish for execution by hanging for the opposition:

> May he dance cutty-mun,
> Wi' his neb to the sun,
> And his doup to the General Director, young man. (p. 163)

The song was published in the March 1825 *Noctes*, untitled, and to no fanfare within the context of the *Noctes* dialogue. However, when Hogg published the song in his 1831 collection of *Songs*, there it was entitled 'The Noctes Sang', in honour of the occasion for which it was written. Hogg also provided the background to the song for the *Songs* publication. In his introduction to the poem in *Songs*, Hogg notes that it was written in Edinburgh one day for singing in Ambrose's at night 'on a particular occasion, when a number of foreign literary gentlemen were to be of the party. I did not sing it till late at night, when we were all beginning to get merry; and the effect on the party was like electricity. It was encored I know not how oft, and Mr Gillies ruffed and screamed out so loud in approbation, that he fell from his chair, and brought an American gentleman down with him'.[137]

When Hogg was in Edinburgh he would often join his *Blackwood's* companions for the conviviality of a night at Ambrose's, but he was never permitted to join the authorship of the *Noctes* in Maga. He once sent a 'complete' *Noctes* to Blackwood, but it was not used;[138] Hogg wrote a *Noctes* dialogue to introduce his two 'Songs for the Duke of Buccleuch's Birth day', but Wilson did not publish it with the songs. Hogg also sent Blackwood several songs to be included in a special 'Balloon' *Noctes*, to be written by Wilson, in which the characters would travel over Scotland in a hot-air balloon (pp. 346–48). Wilson never wrote the *Noctes*, and when Hogg wanted to publish his own balloon story in *Blackwood's* to include his songs, he was not permitted to do so.[139] Wilson jealousy guarded his territory, sometimes irrationally so. Towards the end of the *Noctes* series, in 1834, Hogg tried his hand at a *Noctes* again, and he wrote to Alexander Blackwood a telling commentary on the distinctive achievement of Wilson's *Noctes*, especially the voice of the 'Shepherd' character. Hogg's comment underscores the extent to which Hogg had become a fictional character, but it also seems to suggest that the lines had blurred even for Hogg between the Shepherd of Ettrick and the Shepherd of the *Noctes*: 'I have been trying my hand on a *Noctes* for these two or three days but Wilson has not seen it as yet I fear it will be all to re-write. I *cannot* imitate him and what is far more extraordinary I cannot imitate myself'.[140]

Hogg's personality was central to the *Noctes*, and Hogg was a perfect target for the literary and critical browbeating of the *Noctes* authors: too dependent on Blackwood for his literary life and too powerless to fight back in any significant way. Lacking formal education, he could be made to look humorously ignorant and naïve; as an author of some success but limited influence and focus (as defined by the editor of *Blackwood's*), he could be made to look humorously arrogant about his place in the history of literature; as a shepherd from the isolation of Ettrick, he could be made to speak humorously or blunderingly about the issues and ideas of the time; and as a man who enjoyed good talk and good punch with his friends at Ambrose's Tavern, he could be made into a 'boozing buffoon'. Additionally, 'Hogg' or 'The Shepherd' always sings James Hogg's songs within the *Noctes*, so the voice of the character merges with the voice of the author. It requires little suspension of disbelief for the reader to get from the Ettrick Shepherd to the *Noctes* Shepherd and vice versa. There is no doubt that Hogg benefited from the *Noctes* as an outlet for his songs and as a means of marketing his works and his name. There is also no doubt that Hogg was often embarrassed by his voice in the *Noctes* and frustrated by the negative comments on his works from the mouths of the *Noctes* characters. Although it is not likely that Hogg's portrayal in the *Noctes* in itself cost Hogg a pension from the Royal Society of Literature, ultimately, though, Hogg saw the *Noctes* as the culmination of his frustrations with Blackwood and the *Blackwood's* writers, as he wrote in his 'Reminiscences of Former Days':

> I soon found out that the coterie of my literary associates had made it up to act on O'Dogherty's principle, never to deny a thing that they had *not* written, and never to acknowledge one that they *had*. On which I determined that, in future, I would sign my name or designation to every thing I published, that I might be answerable to the world only for my own offences. But as soon as the rascals perceived this, they signed my name as fast as I did. Then they contrived the incomparable "Noctes Ambrosianæ," for the sole purpose of putting all the sentiments into the Shepherd's mouth, which they durst not avowedly say themselves, and those too often applying to my best friends. The generality of mankind have always used me ill till I came to London.[141]

## 5. The Justified Author

Although Hogg was never permitted to write the fictions of the *Noctes* for Maga, he wrote extensively about the magazine culture in Edinburgh. The 'Chaldee' and related works, 'The Hunt of Eildon', and 'If E'er You Would Be a Brave Fellow' have been discussed previously. Hogg's dramatic poem, 'Examination of the School of Southside' (pp. 146–52), appeared in the December 1824 issue of *Blackwood's*. 'Examination of the School of Southside' is a parody of Wordsworth's poetry in the tradition of Hogg's *Poetic Mirror* poems, but the poem is also a satire on Maga, especially targeting the character of Timothy Tickler, whose residence is Southside. When questioned by the minister as school examiner, the schoolmaster, to the minister's dismay, seems more interested in science and mathematics than religious instruction. The minister also examines two students, both of whom are 'Ticklers'. Although the Girl is able to tell the minister what he wants to hear, the Boy creates a scandal. He responds to the Catechism question, 'who made thee', with 'my parents' (p. 148), and he goes on to pronounce 'Mr Tickler' the 'worthiest man in the parish' (p. 150). The incensed minister also asks the Boy which is 'the best book in the world', and he replies, 'Blackwood's Magazine' (p. 149). The Boy defends *Blackwood's* as

> The greatest bulwark in our native land,
> Around its holy faith, its sacred rights,
> Its principles of loyalty and truth,
> And all that cherishes content and peace
> Among a bold, a free, and happy people. (p. 149)

The minister concludes that the Boy is destined for a hanging, 'opposite our good friend David's corner' (p. 149). In August 1830 Hogg published two poems, 'When Bawdrons, Wi' Her Mousin' Paw' and 'Maga at No. 45', about Blackwood's relocation of his publishing business from 17 Princes Street to 45 George Street.[142] 'Maga at No. 45' humourously elevates the significance of the move to the rank of other major '45' events in Scottish history, such as the Scottish army's defeat of the English at Ancrum Moor in 1545 and the Jacobite rising of 1745. 'When Bawdrons, Wi' Her Mousin' Paw' is a prophecy of the Shepherd's wearing a crown in the 'gran' Saloon' of Blackwood's new premises. The song echoes 'The Hunt of Eildon' in imagining the transformation of a 'Big Boar' into a man; Hogg fantasises that with the move he will achieve the literary status among the *Blackwood's* writers that he believed he had deserved from the beginning of Maga.

The best known and perhaps most complex of Hogg's fictions involving the Blackwoodians occurs in the second 'Editor's Narrative' of his novel, *The Private Memoirs and Confessions of a Justified Sinner* (1824). Hogg wrote to Blackwood on 7 August 1823, enclosing 'for Maga the particulars of a curious incident that has excited great interest here'.[143] Hogg's article, 'A Scots Mummy' (pp. 139–43), tells the story of the unusual preservation in the Yarrow peat of the body of a young man who had committed suicide. The story is in the form of a letter to Christopher North from James Hogg and opens with Hogg's reminding North of the conversation between the two that had led to the article. The introductory dialogue picks up on some of the *Noctes* themes. North wants from Hogg a story about 'the grand phenomena of nature' coming from Hogg's exceptional eye 'for discerning the goings on of the mighty elements'. Hogg believes that North must be making his request out of his drunken condition, but he does not want to question North for fear of angering the quick-tempered North/Wilson: 'I maunna pretend no to understand him, for fear he get intil a rage'. North then advises Hogg to 'look less at lambs and rams [...] and more at the grand phenomena of nature' and, recalling the Hogg character's fondness for drink, further advises Hogg to 'drink less out of the toddy-jug, shepherd, and more at the perennial spring' (p. 139). Hogg concludes the sketch with the offer of a proof of the authenticity of the preservative qualities of peat by suggesting that North conduct the experiment on himself: 'If you should think of trying the experiment on yourself, you have nothing more to do than hang yourself in a hay rope [...] and leave orders that you are to be buried in a wild height, and I will venture to predict, that though you repose there for ages an inmate of your mossy cell, of the cloud, and the storm, you shall set up your head at the last day as fresh as a moor-cock' (p. 143). No doubt there were many occasions when Hogg would have wished that North, hence John Wilson, would hang himself.

Hogg's traditional story of the preserved body of a suicide became part of the life story of the fictitious Robert Wringhim, the 'sinner' of Hogg's *Confessions*, and Hogg integrated 'A Scots Mummy'—without the magazine-specific context—into the second 'Editor's Narrative' in the novel.[144] The Editor uses Hogg's 'letter' from *Blackwood's* to support the incredible story of Robert Wringhim that the Editor had just told. The Editor notes the 'stamp of authenticity' in Hogg's letter, but he doubts the story's truth because it is in *Blackwood's Edinburgh Magazine*: 'so often had I been hoaxed by the ingenious fancies displayed in that Magazine, that when this relation met my eye, I did not believe it'. The Editor decides to investigate the story himself and to that end consults his 'townsman and fellow collegian, Mr. L–t of C–d' (presumably John Lockhart of Chiefswood), who claims not to doubt the story, but also acknowledges that 'Hogg has imposed as ingenious lies on the public ere now'.[145] The Editor and L–t meet Hogg at the Thirlestane Fair, but Hogg declines to accompany them on their quest 'to houk up hunder-year-auld banes'. The Editor engages another shepherd as a guide, who said of Hogg's *Blackwood's* letter that there was 'hardly a bit o't correct'.[146]

Hogg engages in some self-deprecating humour in the second 'Editor's Narrative' of *Confessions*, but this fun at his own expense serves to provide a 'stamp of authenticity' to the Blackwoodian, *Noctes*-like, setting of this part of the novel and establishes the foundation for a more significant achievement here. In the second 'Editor's Narrative', Hogg identifies himself as a major player in the sport of *Blackwood's Edinburgh Magazine*. Given the introduction of 'Mr. L–t' into the novel, it is also likely that to his own mind, if not to the reader's, Hogg associated the character of the 'Editor' with John Wilson. The Editor is an outsider to the world of the Ettrick Shepherd. Furthermore, the Editor's attention to the details of the suicide, especially the negative ones, seems to interfere with his understanding of the person himself and perhaps says more about the character of the Editor than of the Editor's subject. For example, when the Editor and his companions dig up the grave of the suicide, the Editor provides a detailed description of what was found in the grave, down to the dung in the hollow of the shoe: 'There was one thing I could not help remarking, that in the inside of one of the shoes there was a layer of cow's dung, about one eighth of an inch thick, and in the hollow of the sole fully one fourth of an inch. It was firm, green, and fresh; and proved that he had been working in a byre'.[147] The Shepherd in the second 'Editor's Narrative', suspicious of the Editor's motives, declines to participate in the Editor's jaunt. As in Hogg's real events leading up to 'Account of a Coronation-Dinner', Hogg underscores the primacy of farming for Hogg, truly the Ettrick *Shepherd*, and pleads the excuse of his business at the Thirlestane Fair for declining the invitation. In an important gesture for Hogg the author, the fictional Shepherd of the 'Editor's Narrative' turns his back on the Editor and, for a moment, Hogg symbolically rejects the shallow– even hurtful–exploits of the Maga 'editor', his *Noctes,* and his insults to personalities.

After 'A Scots Mummy' there was a break of six months before the publication of Hogg's next work, a new instalment of 'The Shepherd's Calendar' in February 1824. Apparently there are no extant letters from Hogg to Blackwood between August 1823 and January 1824 (when he sends Blackwood the new number of 'The Shepherd's Calendar') to suggest a reason for the break. Presumably Hogg was working on his novel, *Confessions of a Justified Sinner*, during this period, as well as additional instalments of 'The Shepherd's Calendar'. Hogg undoubtedly was also angry about a scathing review by Wilson of Hogg's most recent novel, *The Three Perils of Woman*, in the October 1823 number of *Blackwood's*.[148] There were only four works by Hogg in *Blackwood's* for 1824—two instalments of 'The Shepherd's Calendar', 'Examination of the School of Southside', and 'The Left-Handed Fiddler' (pp. 144–46), an amusing poem comparing the left-handed fiddler with other perversities and anomalies in nature, such as Edward Irving's misreading the Bible, or Francis Jeffrey's breaking into a dance in the middle of his speech in a jury trial. Another poem that appeared in the December 1824 issue, 'New Christmas Carol', was signed with Hogg's name but was written by D. M. Moir.[149]

Following Byron's death in April 1824, Blackwood and Lockhart encouraged Hogg to prepare his correspondence with Byron for publication. Unfortunately, Hogg could not find his letters from Byron, which greatly distressed him, both for the personal loss and for the potential loss of a publishing opportunity. Hogg thought that the Byron correspondence would be especially well suited to the *Noctes*.[150] When Hogg could not find his letters, it seems that Blackwood encouraged him to reconstruct the correspondence, as he wrote to Hogg on 4 December 1824: 'You should give the letters as near as you possibly can recollect them'.[151] Hogg got as far as reproducing one letter each of Byron's and his own, and Blackwood had the correspondence typeset in proof pages. But Blackwood and Lockhart had second thoughts. They were undoubtedly concerned about copyright issues, but they probably also were concerned about what Hogg meant when he said that the letters 'would create a considerable sensation';[152] therefore, the letters were never published.

From 1823 through 1828 (the end date of this first volume of *Contributions to Blackwood's Edinburgh Magazine*), though, Hogg published steadily in *Blackwood's*, and, indeed, Hogg's contributions to *Blackwood's* saw a remarkable increase. For the first six years of *Blackwood's Edinburgh Magazine*, 1817–1822, Hogg published nineteen titles in the magazine; for the next six years, 1823–1828, Hogg published an astonishing fifty titles in Maga. Predictably, during this period of literary prosperity with *Blackwood's* Hogg was not always happy with

Blackwood and Wilson—he often complained about the failure to return the manuscripts of works not published in *Blackwood's* and of Blackwood's objections to his textual improprieties—but he also credits his successful relationship with Maga at this time for the increased demand for his works in other publications. Hogg's happier association with *Blackwood's* can in part be explained by his staying close to the role defined for him early on: forty per cent of his works were songs in the *Noctes* and nearly twenty-five per cent more were 'Shepherd's Calendar' stories. Clearly, though, Hogg's contributions had increased in scope as well as number, and by the end of 1825 Hogg seems to have achieved a solid place among the literary writers in *Blackwood's*. There are a number of factors that contributed to Hogg's rise in Maga during these years. John Lockhart left Edinburgh in December 1825 to edit the *Quarterly Review* in London; Wilson probably had more need of Hogg's friendship after Lockhart's departure. Wilson probably also felt less threatened by Hogg as a writer. Wilson himself had achieved substantial recognition for his work in *Blackwood's*, and by 1825 Wilson had also established himself as a writer of fiction—a genre in which Hogg had excelled, although Wilson had refused to acknowledge Hogg's achievements. Blackwood also seemed to take a greater hand in decisions about Hogg's work for the magazine. D. M. Moir, known as 'Delta' (Δ) in Maga, frequently was called upon by Blackwood to read manuscripts for the magazine and to make recommendations concerning publication; correspondence between Moir and Blackwood suggests that Blackwood often relied on Moir rather than Wilson for recommendations on Hogg's work. There is no doubt, too, that increased opportunities for Hogg to publish in the annuals, as well as a large number of new magazines, contributed to Hogg's increased success with *Blackwood's*. Given the possessiveness of Blackwood and Wilson, they would have wanted to keep Hogg as 'their' writer. Hogg was also critical to the success of the *Noctes*, so maintaining a satisfactory relationship with him was important for continuing the popularity of that series.

Hogg published ten works in *Blackwood's* throughout 1825, using a variety of forms and subjects, including five songs in the *Noctes* and an instalment of 'The Shepherd's Calendar'. In January 1825 *Blackwood's* published 'The Grousome Caryl', the first poem in Maga in Hogg's 'ancient stile', and the first of what became a series of longer poems that would be collected and published in book form by Blackwood as *A Queer Book* (1832).[153] From January 1825 to April 1831, Hogg published sixteen poems in *Blackwood's* that comprised the majority of the poems in *A Queer Book*. Like the stories of *The Shepherd's Calendar*, the poems of *A Queer Book* on the surface, at least, met the Blackwoodian expectations for the 'author of *The Queen's Wake*': the poems had a ballad-like quality and generally focused on Border landscapes, history, and traditions. Also like *The Shepherd's Calendar* stories, the *Queer Book* poems are much more complex than their settings might suggest. Many of the poems address the more sensitive political, religious, and social issues of the time, and as Peter Garside has noted, Blackwood was inclined to give Hogg more latitude than usual in the poems in which he used his invented 'ancient stile' (although not all of the *Queer Book* poems used this style).[154] Garside describes Hogg's ancient style as 'a combination of ballad phraseology, the rhetoric of the late medieval Scottish "makars", such as Robert Henryson, and more modern idiomatic expression'.[155] Hogg had used this style as early as 1813 in portions of *The Queen's Wake*, and although Blackwood reminded Hogg—perhaps out of concern for not being thought a dupe—that 'at no period whatever was the Scots language so written', he did not reject Hogg's use of this invented language for these poems in Maga.[156] There was one *Blackwood's* poem in this style, 'Ane Pastorale of the Rocke' (December 1827; pp. 283–98), that was not included in *A Queer Book* and thus is included in the present edition. 'Ane Pastorale of the Rocke' is a satirical fable about the competition for supremacy between an eagle and a raven, who seem to represent, respectively, Tories and Whigs. Although the poem concludes with a direct attack on the Whigs, asserting with Samuel Johnson that Satan was the first Whig,[157] both parties come under attack in the poem. The poem addresses the political climate in Great Britain during the debates about Catholic Emancipation and the Corn Laws; both issues were widely discussed in *Blackwood's* in 1827. These major political issues were complicated by the controversy surrounding the appointment of George Canning, a liberal Tory, as Prime Minister in April 1827 after Lord Liverpool's resignation. Prominent Tory leaders resigned rather than serve under Canning, which led to Canning's appointment of several Whig leaders to his government. Hogg's poem captures the general political disarray of this period.

In July 1825 Hogg published 'Some Passages in the Life of Colonel Cloud' (pp. 166–80), a delightful, playful story about a Hogg-persona's travelling companion, a young man from humble circumstances who invented exaggerated personal accomplishments and family importance. The piece was intended in part as a satire on James Browne, then editor of Constable's *Edinburgh Magazine*, and the story relates the adventures of the narrator and 'Cloud' on a journey to the Highlands. The story describes places actually visited by Hogg, including details of a tour that Hogg took in 1816, the year in which the story is set. As David Groves has pointed out, the story of Cloud's delusions and confused identities is suggestive of Hogg's *Confessions of a Justified Sinner*, and perhaps Browne is in some ways a model for Gil-Martin.[158] Although Hogg's story ended on a note of affection, Browne eventually had the last word with a pointed response to Hogg's 'Memoir' that introduced *Altrive Tales* (1832)— *The "Life" of the Ettrick Shepherd Anatomized*[159]—reminiscent of Wilson's review in *Blackwood's* of an earlier version of the 'Memoir'. Hogg had originally intended 'Some Passages in the Life of Colonel Cloud' to be part of a series of sketches, *Lives of Eminent Men*, that he had envisioned publishing in Maga and then as a book-length collection. Blackwood sent the first three stories to D. M. Moir for Moir's review and publication recommendation. Although Moir liked 'Colonel Cloud', he found the other two stories, 'Some Remarkable Passages in the Life of an Edinburgh Baillie' and 'The Adventures of Colonel Peter Aston', completely unsatisfactory. In an undated letter to Blackwood, Moir criticises the stories in terms similar to the attacks on Hogg's prose in the *Noctes*: 'there is no attempt at digesting of story or incident, no plot, no elaboration, no style in the writing; and all is just a pouring forth, sometimes clear, sometimes muddy as it may chance [...] finery or coarseness present themselves just as they may turn up [...] his benignant feelings are wantonly broken in upon, either by a careless recklessness, or an incoherent want of taste'.[160] Moir recommended against publication of the stories, both in Maga and as part of a book-length collection. Blackwood followed Moir's advice. Eventually Hogg revised the stories and published them in *Tales of the Wars of Montrose* (1835), but without the 'Colonel Cloud' story.[161]

Although all of Hogg's Maga publications in 1826 were *Noctes* songs, he wrote other works for Maga that were rejected by Blackwood—most notably, three pastoral dramas, 'Dramas of Simple Life'.[162] Hogg wrote to Blackwood in September 1826 that he wanted to publish the dramas in a series of separate numbers of *Blackwood's*.[163] Blackwood rejected the first drama as not 'worthy' of Hogg; perhaps Blackwood did not think the quality of the piece was up to Hogg's usual standard, but he certainly did not like the dark, violent ending or the sexual innuendos. Blackwood was willing to publish the second 'Drama' provided Hogg added a scene to the ending, although Blackwood also objected to the 'coarseness' of the work.[164] Hogg refused to allow the second drama to be published without the first, so he withdrew it from consideration. Off and on until early 1828 Hogg renewed his efforts to have Blackwood publish the dramas, but again was unsuccessful. Finally Hogg revised the first drama into the story 'Katie Cheyne', which was intended for Allan Cunningham's annual, *The Anniversary*, but ended up in *Sharpe's London Magazine* for August 1829.[165] The second drama was greatly enlarged and became 'The Bush aboon Traquair', which was first published posthumously in Hogg's *Tales and Sketches* (1836–37). Apparently there is no extant evidence to suggest that Hogg ever wrote the third drama that he had originally proposed to Blackwood. Blackwood would also reject other substantial works by Hogg in 1827 and 1828. He turned down a story of 'Polar curiosities' that Hogg claimed to have extracted from John Harris's *Navigantium Atque Itinerantium Bibliotheca*; this work apparently became 'The Surpassing Adventures of Allan Gordon', which was also published posthumously in *Tales and Sketches* (1836–37). Hogg's 'Remarkable Egyptian Story', which was sent to Blackwood in February 1828, was published in *Fraser's Magazine* in February 1833.

In 1827 Hogg published five instalments of 'The Shepherd's Calendar', an 'Ode' (pp. 257–59) on the death of Lord Byron that apparently had been written soon after Byron's death in 1824, 'Ane Pastorale of the Rocke' and another 'ancient stile' poem, and a short story. His story, 'The Marvellous Doctor' (pp. 262–83), was published in the September 1827 number, although he had sent the story to William Blackwood in May. 'The Marvellous Doctor' is the story of a herb doctor who had developed a potion that would enable the possessor to control completely the behaviour of anyone to whom it was administered. Hogg within the story claims to have heard the tale from the doctor himself when the doctor had stayed with Hogg's family. Hogg often insisted on the truth of his stories, but in this case the framing device of a 'true' context was especially important, given the sexual suggestiveness of the subject. However, the story also has political undertones; the story is set largely in Spain in the second half of the eighteenth century, and Hogg seems to imply that Spain's rulers must have been under a spell to align with France against England in the Seven Years War. The unusually long time between Hogg's submission of the manuscript and the story's appearance in *Blackwood's* is accounted for by William Blackwood's assessment that the story was 'too strong for delicate folks to tolerate'.[166] At Hogg's suggestion Blackwood sent the story to Hogg's nephew, Robert Hogg, who could be relied upon to 'obliterate any appearance of indelicacy'.[167] Robert cut out three of the five 'adventures', leaving a story acceptable to Blackwood, although D. M. Moir thought the revised story still contained 'much to fault'.[168] Hogg frequently clashed with Blackwood on matters of propriety, which frustrated Hogg by the delay in publication or the rejection of works altogether, or if the works were published, he sometimes thought them 'quite ruined' by Robert's pruning.[169] In December 1825 Blackwood deleted a verse in Hogg's song 'The Brakens Wi' Me' because he could not reach Hogg in time to revise the song, as he wrote to Hogg: 'for a country lass to talk of her lover *drawing on her at sight*, is either most unnatural for what can she know about drawing bills?—or it is what whose who accuse you of coarseness could call not decent'.[170] Of course Blackwood himself was usually Hogg's greatest 'accuser' of 'coarseness'. In September 1826 Blackwood again complained of 'coarseness' in the second of Hogg's 'Dramas of Simple Life'.[171] The work still was not published in January 1828, when Hogg sent the work to Robert for editing: 'The Pastoral drama is in Roberts hands for you but he suspects you will object to some small part of it on the *old score*. May the deil take the indelicacy of both your mind and his!'[172]

Within the time frame of the present volume, Hogg's most productive year in terms of number of titles published in *Blackwood's* was 1828; thirteen titles appeared in nine separate issues: six songs were included in the *Noctes*, there were three instalments of 'The Shepherd's Calendar', as well as two poems that became part of *A Queer Book*. Hogg also published two short stories in 1828. The first, 'Trials of Temper' (pp. 299–312), appeared in January 1828 and is a comic tale of romance and mistaken identity. The story concludes with a poetic 'Moralitas' (which Blackwood called 'one of the prettiest pieces' Hogg ever wrote),[173] suggesting that Hogg intended the story to be a modern-day fable comparable to the poetic fables of Robert Henryson. The second story, 'A Strange Secret' (June 1828; pp. 315–45), is a serious tale set in the Highlands in the early years of the nineteenth century, when Britain was threatened with invasion by Napoleon, but the story also develops historical associations with the aftermath of the 1745 Jacobite rebellion. The plot of the story focuses on the disappearance of the son of the sister of an Earl and heir to a Protestant title, and the quest to find the child, thought to be under the care of the Catholic clergy. The story in *Blackwood's* concludes with the suggestion that the story is to be continued, but that continuation never appeared in Maga. 'A Strange Secret' was reprinted in Hogg's two-volume collection of tales, *The Shepherd's Calendar*, published by Blackwood in 1829. *The Shepherd's Calendar* version includes a lengthy continuation that may have been edited by Robert Hogg for this purpose from another of Hogg's unpublished works and perhaps without Hogg's prior knowledge.[174]

In spite of his publishing success in Maga, Hogg was often irritated with Blackwood because, he claimed, Blackwood rejected too many of his works and then would not return his manuscripts in a timely manner–or at all. Hogg wrote to Blackwood on 8 October 1828: 'You being the only publisher I claim as a friend I like to give you the first offer of every thing I think will suit you but I care not now how many you reject for there are plenty of demands on me provided you return the M. S. S. but I am most peremptory about this for I have no duplicate of one of them'.[175] It was not always true that Hogg did not keep copies of his submitted manuscripts, but if Blackwood did not return the works Hogg was unable to send them to other periodicals for consideration. Blackwood and Wilson seemed jealous of Hogg's successes outside Maga at this time, and it is likely that Blackwood retained Hogg's manuscripts as a means of controlling his access to other publication outlets. At one point Hogg complained to Blackwood: 'I see no right you or the nearest friend has to intermeddle with my bargains with other men. If it is a maxim with the trade to monopolise every authors whole works whom they once befriend or publish a book for, and that no other man must take a share on any conditions they ought all to be damned to hell'.[176]

In Hogg's novel *The Private Memoirs and Confessions of a Justified Sinner*, Robert Wringhim opens his 'Memoirs' with a summary evaluation of his life: 'My life has been a life of trouble and turmoil; of change and vicissitude; of anger and exultation; of sorrow and of vengeance. My sorrows have all been for a slighted gospel, and my vengeance has been wreaked on its adversaries'.[177] If one were to substitute 'literature' for 'gospel' in Wringhim's second sentence, the terms of Wringhim's judgment of his life might well describe Hogg's life with *Blackwood's Edinburgh Magazine* and its major supporters. Maga gave Hogg some of his highest and lowest moments as a writer. There was exaltation, certainly, but also a great deal of turmoil, vicissitude, and anger, as well as sorrow for a slighted literature; occasionally there was even some satisfying vengeance wreaked on Hogg's adversaries. The correspondence between Hogg and Blackwood repeatedly reflects Hogg's conflicted feelings. On the one hand, for example, Hogg is angered by Wilson's 'beastly depravity' and 'rash and thoughtless' literary behaviour; on the other hand, Hogg praises Wilson as the heart and soul of *Blackwood's Edinburgh Magazine*: 'There is one master spirit pervades it. It is to all other periodicals like a proffessor's gig going like lightening through a train of coal and dung carts'.[178] Hogg recognised the curious relationship he had with Wilson, as he wrote to Blackwood: 'I have a strange indefinable sensation with regard to [Wilson], made up of a mixture of terror admiration and jealousy just such a sentiment as one deil might be supposed to have of another'.[179] At one point Hogg writes that he is 'mortified by the refusal of all my pieces', and at another time he writes that his publications in *Blackwood's* 'have operated singularly to my advantage' and have increased his opportunities to publish in other magazines. Often Hogg's correspondence with William Blackwood sings Blackwood's praises and acknowledges his generosity and friendship; at other times he writes to Blackwood that 'I am almost ruing the day that I ever saw you'[180] and that Blackwood is 'worse than the worst assassin out of hell'. In a letter to John Wilson in 1833, Hogg reflects on his twenty-year business relationship and friendship with William Blackwood: 'I have recieved many marked kindnesses from Blackwood as well as many insults and just as these predominate in my mind I have the kindest affection for him or the bitterest ill-will. [...] He has many times grieved me [...] but then on the other hand for the space of twenty years whenever he saw me in a difficulty he was always the first man to step forward and relieve me. He never in his life refused to relieve me'.[181]

There were many reasons for which Hogg valued his connection with the *Blackwood's* group and for which he was willing to endure some abuse and humiliation. Hogg genuinely liked Blackwood, Wilson, and Lockhart; he valued their friendship and respected their talents. Hogg also valued the associations with the Edinburgh literary establishment that the connection with the Blackwoodians afforded him. Hogg enjoyed the steady income that came from the periods of his regular periodical contributions, and the exposure in Maga extended his reputation as a writer, both within Great Britain and internationally. *Blackwood's Edinburgh Magazine* was published in North America, and Hogg's works were often extracted from *Blackwood's* and reprinted in newspapers and periodicals in the United States and Canada. Taken as a whole, Hogg's relationship with William Blackwood and Maga represents the heart of Hogg's literary life, and the advantages for Hogg clearly predominate.

Hogg's publications in *Blackwood's* for 1829 through 1835 are included in the second volume of the Stirling / South Carolina edition of Hogg's *Contributions to Blackwood's Edinburgh Magazine*, and the Introduction to that volume discusses the works published there. The flush times for Hogg with *Blackwood's* would continue for another three years, through 1831, before there would be another lengthy, painful break between Hogg and Blackwood. Hogg would continue to have greater scope in the material that Blackwood would publish. After the remarkable story, 'The Brownie of the Black Haggs' (October 1828), there would be no more instalments of 'The Shepherd's Calendar' in Maga. However, the poems that would become *A Queer Book* would continue to be published frequently through April 1831. Hogg would also publish additional, lengthy narrative poems, such as 'The Raid of the Kers' and 'Lyttil Pynkie', that would add a new dimension to Hogg's Maga works. The number of Hogg's songs in the *Noctes* would diminish, but there would also be a significant increase in the publication of Hogg's prose fiction, including such important stories as 'Some Remarkable Passages in the Remarkable Life of the Baron St Gio', 'A Horrible Instance of the Effects of Clanship', and 'The Mysterious Bride'. These changes in the balance of Hogg's contributions to *Blackwood's* are indications of Hogg's continued liberation from his earlier stereotyped role in Maga and his greater acceptance as a mature artist. Hogg's publications in *Blackwood's* during this period have received relatively little critical attention, but these works represent some of the best and most important of his magazine contributions.

## 6. The Present Edition

The present edition of Hogg's contributions to *Blackwood's Edinburgh Magazine* includes all works from *Blackwood's* for which Hogg's authorship can be established with reasonable certainty except for certain works that were collected from *Blackwood's* in Hogg's lifetime for publication in book form in *The Shepherd's Calendar* (1829) and *A Queer Book* (1832); these two collections have been published previously as separate volumes in the Stirling/South Carolina Research Edition of the Collected Works of James Hogg, and items included in the relevant S/SC volumes are omitted from the present edition to avoid unnecessary publication duplication. A complete list of Hogg's publications in *Blackwood's Edinburgh Magazine* is included in the present edition in Appendix C.

In an effort to present a full picture of Hogg's connection with Maga, and in keeping with the practice of the S/SC edition to provide appropriate and efficient placement of previously-unpublished texts, the present edition includes several works that Hogg intended for publication in *Blackwood's* but that either were never published in Hogg's lifetime or were never published in the versions in which

they were intended for *Blackwood's*. Additionally, because there are
such substantial and important differences between the manuscript
and published versions of 'Translation of an Ancient Chaldee
Manuscript' and 'The Honourable Captain Napier and Ettrick Forest',
the present edition includes both versions as representing distinct
texts. A fragment of a manuscript that might represent Hogg's
unpublished continuation of the 'Chaldee Manuscript' is published
in Appendix A. For the reader's convenience Appendix B provides
the song tunes identified in Hogg's *Blackwood's* texts, and Appendix
C also lists works Hogg submitted for publication in *Blackwood's* but
which were never published there.

Unless otherwise indicated in the notes to the texts, the *Blackwood's*
printed texts serve as the copy texts for those works published in
*Blackwood's*, and the manuscripts serve as the copy texts for previously-
unpublished works. The present edition follows Hogg's idiosyncratic
spelling and punctuation from the manuscripts except that end
punctuation has been added to the prose works where Hogg normally
would have expected the printer to add such punctuation. The notes
to the texts discuss the publication history of each work.

The works in the present edition are organised chronologically
according to the publication date in *Blackwood's*. The works are
grouped under headings that cover a full year (two volumes) of
*Blackwood's* issues. *Blackwood's Edinburgh Magazine* (*Edinburgh Monthly
Magazine*) was published monthly beginning in April 1817, and each
volume covered six months. This system of volume numbering was
adjusted in 1821, with volume ten beginning with a second part of
the August double issue and ending in December 1821 rather than
March 1822. Beginning with the January 1822 number, the volumes
ran from January through June and July through December; thus,
two volumes were published in one calendar year. Works published
in the present edition from manuscripts or other sources are included
within the publication chronology based on the best available
evidence for dating the texts. (Exceptionally, there is only one Hogg
*Blackwood's* publication in the present edition for the period April
1820 through December 1821; therefore, for publication convenience,
this grouping covers four volumes instead of two.)

Finally, meticulous efforts were made to verify Hogg's authorship
of works in *Blackwood's Edinburgh Magazine*. It is difficult, however, to
be completely confident of Hogg's authorship in some cases: the
publisher's records are incomplete, works were published
anonymously or pseudonymously, other writers signed Hogg's name
to their own material, and occasionally works were written jointly.

The notes to the texts include relevant evidence of Hogg's authorship; Appendix C provides a list of works attributed to Hogg in *Blackwood's Edinburgh Magazine* but for which the evidence of authorship points away from Hogg.

## Notes

1   James Hogg, *The Mountain Bard*, 3rd edn (Edinburgh: Oliver & Boyd, 1821), p. lxiii. See also *The Mountain Bard* volume of the Stirling/ South Carolina Research Edition of the Collected Works of James Hogg (hereafter S/SC Edition), ed. by Suzanne Gilbert (S/SC, 2007), p. 224.

2   Appendix C in the present edition (pp. 377–88) provides a complete list of Hogg's publications in *Blackwood's Edinburgh Magazine*, as well as a list of works intended for *Blackwood's*, 1817–28, but which were not published there.

3   F. D. Tredrey tells the story of the origin of the 'Maga' nickname for *Blackwood's Edinburgh Magazine*: 'When Blackwood had proudly taken home the first number of his Magazine, he is said to have presented it to his wife with the words, "There's ma Maga-zine." His Doric pronunciation of the first syllables appealed to his associates, and the Magazine became "Maga" to all its friends'. See F. D. Tredrey, *The House of Blackwood 1804–1954* (Edinburgh: Blackwood, 1954), p. 51.

4   Henry Cockburn, in *Memorials of His Time* (Edinburgh: Adam and Charles Black, 1856), wrote that 'our only monthly periodical work was the dotard *Scots Magazine*, which now lived, or rather tried to live, upon its antiquity alone' and that in establishing his magazine Blackwood took advantage of 'an opening for a new adventure' (p. 313). For additional information about the history of William Blackwood's publishing firm and the beginning of *Blackwood's Edinburgh Magazine*, see Mrs Oliphant, *Annals of a Publishing House: William Blackwood and His Sons*, 2 vols (Edinburgh: Blackwood, 1897); F. D. Tredrey, *The House of Blackwood 1804–1954* (Edinburgh: Blackwood, 1954); David Finkelstein, *The House of Blackwood: Author-Publisher Relations in the Victorian Era* (University Park: The Pennsylvania State University Press, 2002); Philip Flynn, 'Beginning *Blackwood's*: The Right Mix of *Dulce* and *Utile*', *Victorian Periodicals Review*, 39 (Summer 2006), 136–157; and *Blackwood's Magazine, 1817–25: Selections from Maga's Infancy*, ed. by Nicholas Mason and others, 6 vols (London: Pickering & Chatto, 2006).

5   See 'Memoir of the Author's Life' and 'Reminiscences of Former Days' in *Altrive Tales*, ed. by Gillian Hughes (S/SC, 2003) (hereafter *Memoir*), p. 32. Hogg's letter to Blackwood of 28 October 1814 is published in *The Collected Letters of James Hogg: Volume 1 1800–1819*, ed. by Gillian Hughes, assoc. eds Douglas S. Mack, Robin MacLachlan, and Elaine Petrie (S/SC, 2004) (hereafter *Letters 1*), pp. 217–18. For further discussion of the publishing history of the third edition of *The Queen's Wake*, see Douglas Mack's Introduction to the S/SC Edition of *The Queen's Wake* (S/SC, 2004), pp. lx–lxv.

6   For more on Hogg's relationship with William Blackwood, see Gillian
    Hughes, *James Hogg: A Life* (Edinburgh: Edinburgh University Press,
    2007).
7   *Memoir*, ed. Hughes, p. 43.
8   *Memoir*, ed. Hughes, p. 43.
9   On 23 July 1817 William Blackwood wrote to his London publishers,
    Baldwin, Cradock, and Joy: 'I have been much disappointed in my
    Editors who have done little in the way of writing or procuring
    contributions. Ever since the work began I have had myself almost
    the whole burden of procuring contributions which by great exertions
    I got from my own friends, while at the same time I had it not in my
    power to pay for them, as by our agreement the Editors were to
    furnish me with the whole of the materials for which and their
    Editorial labours they were to receive half of the profits of the work'
    (National Library of Scotland (hereafter NLS), MS 30,001, fol. 49).
    See also Oliphant, *Annals of a Publishing House*, I, 98–100.
10  *Memoir*, ed. Hughes, p. 44.
11  Mrs Grant of Laggan writes in 1819 that *Blackwood's Edinburgh Magazine*
    'not only abounds in attic salt, but in that pungent pepper by mortals
    styled personality. It is supported by a club of young wits, many of
    whom are well known to me; who, I hope, in some measure fear
    God, but certainly do not regard man'. Anne MacVicar Grant, *Memoir
    and Correspondence*, ed. by J. P. Grant, 3 vols (London: Longman, 1845),
    II, 209. Although Blackwood changed the name of his magazine after
    six issues, he did not change the numbering of the volumes. The first
    number of *Blackwood's Edinburgh Magazine* began with volume 2 to
    indicate that *Blackwood's* was a continuation of the *Edinburgh Monthly
    Magazine*.
12  *Letters 1*, ed. Hughes, p. 295.
13  The 'Tales and Anecdotes' stories are published in the present edition
    at pp. 1–5, 6–14, and 19–24; please see the notes to 'Tales and
    Anecdotes of the Pastoral Life. No. I' (pp. 391–93) for information
    about the history of these stories. Hereafter page references to the
    present edition are cited within the text; please also see the notes to
    individual works for additional information.
14  *Letters 1*, ed. Hughes, p. 295.
15  *Letters 1*, ed. Hughes, pp. 300–01.
16  *Letters 1*, ed. Hughes, p. 303.
17  Quoted in Andrew Lang, *The Life and Letters of John Gibson Lockhart*, 2
    vols (London: John C. Nimmo, 1897), I, 157.
18  William Blackwood wrote to Baldwin, Cradock, and Joy on 6
    November 1817: 'You must be aware that I myself have no controul
    over the measures of my Editor, yet had I been aware of the obnoxious
    nature of certain passages in this Paper I should certainly have
    endeavoured to have prevented its appearance in any publication to
    which my name is affixed'. Blackwood also noted that the 'Editor'
    altered the 'obnoxious phrases' in the second edition of this number
    (NLS, MS 30,001, fols 66–67). John Grahame Dalyell sued Blackwood
    for £5000 for libel over his portrayal in the 'Chaldee' manuscript;
    the suit was settled for £230. The present edition also includes the

published version of the 'Chaldee Manuscript' as revised by Lockhart, Wilson, and Blackwood (pp. 30–44).

19 *Letters 1*, ed. Hughes, p. 304.

20 Hogg's revised proof is preserved in the British Library, shelfmark C. 60. k. 4. Hogg's revisions are addressed in the notes to the published version of the 'Chaldee Manuscript'.

21 *Letters 1*, ed. Hughes, p. 304.

22 *The Collected Letters of Thomas and Jane Welsh Carlyle*, ed. by Charles Richard Sanders and others, 34 vols (Durham: Duke University Press, 1970–2007), I, 114.

23 R. P. Gillies, *Memoirs of a Literary Veteran*, 3 vols (London: Richard Bentley, 1851), II, 234.

24 *Memoir*, ed. Hughes, p. 45.

25 Gillies, *Memoirs of a Literary Veteran*, II, 235.

26 Calvinus [James Grahame], *Two Letters to the Rev. Dr Thomas M'Crie and the Rev. Mr Andrew Thomson, on the Parody of Scripture, Lately Published in Blackwood's Edinburgh Magazine* (Edinburgh: John Fairbairn, 1817), p. 8.

27 For the 'Summons of Damages' against Blackwood by Dalyell and the manuscript 'Discharge of Dalyell to Blackwood' see NLS, MS 4807, fols 48–51.

28 NLS, MS 30,304, pp. 2–3.

29 *The Letters of Sir Walter Scott*, ed. by H. J. C. Grierson, 12 vols (London: Constable, 1932–37), V, 6.

30 Scott, *Letters*, ed. Grierson, V, 6–7.

31 Quoted in Oliphant, *Annals of a Publishing House*, I, 150–51.

32 *Letters 1*, ed. Hughes, p. 308.

33 *Letters 1*, ed. Hughes, p. 307.

34 *Memoir*, ed. Hughes, p. 45. A fragment of Hogg's manuscript that probably is this 'continuation' is preserved in the University of Otago Library and is published in Appendix A in the present edition, pp. 352–60.

35 *Memoir*, ed. Hughes, p. 45.

36 James Hogg to William Blackwood, 14 June 1822, in *The Collected Letters of James Hogg: Volume 2 1820–1831*, ed. by Gillian Hughes, assoc. eds Douglas S. Mack, Robin MacLachlan, and Elaine Petrie (S/SC, 2006) (hereafter *Letters 2*), p. 164.

37 See James Hogg, *The Jacobite Relics of Scotland. Second Series*, ed. by Murray G. H. Pittock (S/SC, 2003), pp. 330–35 (p. 330).

38 See James Hogg, *The Three Perils of Man; or, War, Women, and Witchcraft*. 3 vols (London: Longman, Hurst, Rees, Orme, and Brown, 1822), II, 158–81.

39 A proof of Hogg's church satire, entitled 'A Chaldee Manuscript', is preserved in the National Library of Scotland, shelfmark RB. 1. 128. A note on the proof by 'AB' indicates that the 'article was intended for the Edin. Literary Journal of June 27th 1829, but was not inserted'. Hogg's manuscript of this work is preserved in the Alexander Turnbull Library, Wellington: James Hogg Collection (Item 7). MS-Papers-0042-01.

40 NLS, MS 924, no. 85.

41 NLS, MS 30,001, fols 68–69.

42 *Memoir*, ed. Hughes, p. 44.

43 John Scott, editor of the *London Magazine*, insulted Lockhart's integrity and accused Lockhart of being the editor of *Blackwood's*. Following a series of abusive written exchanges, John Scott and Lockhart's friend, Jonathan Christie, fought a duel at Chalk Farm on 16 February 1821. Scott was killed by Christie in the duel. For a full account of this conflict, see Patrick O'Leary, *Regency Editor: Life of John Scott* (Aberdeen: Aberdeen University Press, 1983).

44 For further discussion of *Blackwood's* 'editor', see Maurice Milne, 'The "Veiled Editor" Unveiled: William Blackwood and His Magazine', *Publishing History*, 16 (1984), 87–103.

45 John Lockhart, *Peter's Letters to His Kinsfolk*, '3rd' edn, 3 vols (Edinburgh: Blackwood; London: Cadell and Davies, 1819), II, 204.

46 Lockhart, *Peter's Letters*, II, [128]. Note: p. 128 in this edition is incorrectly numbered '228'.

47 Lockhart, *Peter's Letters*, II, 136–37.

48 Lockhart, *Peters Letters*, I, 126.

49 NLS, MS 30,304, p. 1.

50 NLS, MS 9309, fols 22–23.

51 *Letters 1*, ed. Hughes, p. 295.

52 *Letters 1*, ed. Hughes, p. 305.

53 James Hogg, *Songs, by the Ettrick Shepherd* (Edinburgh: Blackwood, 1831), p. 117.

54 *Memoir*, ed. Hughes, p. 49.

55 See 'The Morning Star, or the Steam-boat of Alloa', 'Hymn to the Moon', and 'The Stranded Ship' in *The Poetic Mirror, or The Living Bards of Britain* (Edinburgh: Ballantyne; London: Longman, 1816).

56 For example, see 'Familiar Epistles to Christopher North, *From an Old Friend with a New Face*', *Blackwood's Edinburgh Magazine*, 10 (August 1821), 43–52 (p. 44). See also pp. li–liii in the Introduction to the present edition.

57 See Lockhart, *Peter's Letters*, II, 212–21.

58 Lockhart, *Peter's Letters*, II, 212–13.

59 Lockhart, *Peter's Letters*, I, 133.

60 *Letters 1*, ed. Hughes, p. 307.

61 *Letters 1*, ed. Hughes, p. 305.

62 See James Hogg, *Anecdotes of Scott*, ed. by Jill Rubenstein (S/SC, 1999), pp. 22, 50–51.

63 See Peter Garside's Introduction to the S/SC Edition of *The Private Memoirs and Confessions of a Justified Sinner*, ed. by P. D. Garside, afterword by Ian Campbell (S/SC, 2001), pp. xxxvi–xxxviii.

64 Because there are substantial differences between Hogg's manuscript and the printed text of 'The Honourable Captain Napier and Ettrick Forest', the present edition includes both Hogg's manuscript version (pp. 96–114) and the *Blackwood's* version (pp. 114–37).

65 *Letters 2*, ed. Hughes, p. 179.

66 *Letters 2*, ed. Hughes, p. 177.

67 'Life and Writings of James Hogg', *Edinburgh Magazine* 2 (January, February, March 1818), 35–40, 122–29, 215–23.

68 'Life and Writings of James Hogg', *Edinburgh Magazine*, 2 (January 1818), 37, 36.

69 'Letter to Mr James Hogg', *Blackwood's Edinburgh Magazine*, 2 (February 1818), 501–04 (p. 503).

70 See 'Letter from James Hogg to Timothy Ticker', pp. 72–77 in the present edition, and notes. The 'Letter' in the present edition is published as Hogg had edited it. The complete draft text of Hogg's 'Letter to Tickler', including Hogg's deleted portions, is edited by Gillian Hughes and published in *Letters 1*, pp. 366–75.

71 *Letters 1*, ed. Hughes, p. 383.

72 James Hogg, 'The Hunt of Eildon', *The Brownie of Bodsbeck; And Other Tales*, 2 vols (Edinburgh: Blackwood, 1818), II, 229–346 (pp. 263–64).

73 Hogg, *Brownie of Bodsbeck*, II, 336.

74 Hogg, *Brownie of Bodsbeck*, II, 338–39.

75 *Letters 1*, ed. Hughes, p. 356.

76 *Letters 1*, ed. Hughes, p. 363.

77 *Letters 1*, ed. Hughes, p. 365.

78 To avoid unnecessary publication duplication in the S/SC Edition, stories from *Blackwood's Edinburgh Magazine* that are published in the S/SC Edition of *The Shepherd's Calendar* are not reprinted in the present edition. See James Hogg, *The Shepherd's Calendar*, ed. by Douglas S. Mack (S/SC, 1995).

79 Hogg, *The Shepherd's Calendar*, ed. Mack, p. xix.

80 William Laidlaw to William Blackwood, NLS, MS 4003, fols 125–26.

81 Hogg, *The Shepherd's Calendar*, ed. Mack, p. xii.

82 NLS, Acc. 12,431.

83 *Letters 1*, ed. Hughes, p. 421.

84 *Letters 1*, ed. Hughes, p. 421. The authors of 'The Tent' issue of *Blackwood's* sent Constable and a group of his writers on a pilgrimage to the Kirk of Shotts. Among those lampooned in this episode was Hogg's friend, James Gray, author of the articles on Hogg's life in the January–March 1818 issues of the *Edinburgh Magazine*. See *Blackwood's Edinburgh Magazine*, 5 (September 1819), 671–81.

85 For the citations of works published in Hogg's name in *Blackwood's Edinburgh Magazine*, see Appendix C in the present edition, pp. 381–83.

86 *Letters 2*, ed. Hughes, p. 54.

87 *Letters 2*, ed. Hughes, p. 7.

88 William Blackwood wrote to Hogg on 2 December 1820: 'All I can now say is this, that whatever be the consequence, there shall nothing appear in the Magazine of or concerning you, but what you yourself shall previously see' (NLS, MS 30,002, fols 16–17).

89 See Lockhart, *Peter's Letters*, I, 110–47

90 NLS, MS 2245, fols 58–59.

91 Hogg to William Blackwood, 6 April 1830, in *Letters 2*, ed. Hughes, p. 378.

92 See Peter Garside, 'James Hogg's Fifty Pounds', *Studies in Hogg and his World*, 1 (1990), 128–32; and Gillian Hughes, *James Hogg: A Life*, pp. 177–78. See also George Goldie's pamphlet, *A Letter to a Friend in*

*London* (Edinburgh, 1821).

93 *Letters 2*, ed. Hughes, p. 105.

94 See 'Familiar Epistles to Christopher North, *From an Old Friend with a New Face*', *Blackwood's Edinburgh Magazine*, 10 (August 1821), 43–52.

95 'Familiar Epistles to Christopher North', *Blackwood's*, 10 (August 1821), 44–45.

96 Mrs Oliphant quotes the correspondence between James Ballantyne and William Blackwood. Ballantyne wrote to Blackwood:

> Do you really mean to insert that most clever but most indecently scurrilous attack upon Hogg? For my own part, I do not stand up for Hogg's conduct; but such language as is applied to him appears to me absolutely unwarrantable, and *in your Magazine* peculiarly and shockingly offensive.
>
> You will do as you think best certainly; but I must at once say that if it goes in I must withdraw, in all subsequent numbers, from the concern. How much I shall regret this on many accounts I need not say; but I cannot allow such an article to appear with even my implied approbation attached to it. It is hard, you may think, that an editor should be fettered by his printer; but I cannot help this. The printer must not be made to encounter what he considers to be a disgrace.

Blackwood replied:

> The article on Hogg is to be very much altered indeed, else you may depend upon it that *I* could not allow it to appear. But really of this you must permit me to be judge, for, disagreeable and unpleasant as it would be for us to part, I cannot submit to be told what *I must not insert* in the Magazine. My character and interest are at stake, and you may depend upon it that nothing will appear in the Magazine but what it will be both for my credit and interest to publish, and, of course, for you to print.

(Quoted in Oliphant, *Annals of a Publishing House*, I, 338–39).

97 D. M. Moir to William Blackwood, 23 August 1821, NLS, MS 4007, fols 194–95.

98 *Letters 2*, ed. Hughes, p. 105.

99 *Letters 2*, ed. Hughes, p. 109.

100 *Letters 2*, ed. Hughes, p. 120.

101 NLS, MS 791, p. 210. Cadell's letter is dated 27 September 1821.

102 *Letters 2*, ed. Hughes, pp. 114, 113.

103 *Letters 2*, ed. Hughes, p. 159.

104 *Letters 2*, ed. Hughes, p. 164.

105 NLS, MS 30,305, pp. 341–44, quoted in *Letters 2*, ed. Hughes, p. 164.

106 See *No. of the Border Garland* (Edinburgh: Nathaniel Gow and Son, [1819]), pp. 6–7.

107 Much has been written about Hogg's role in the *Noctes*. For further discussion, see J. H. Alexander, 'Hogg in the *Noctes Ambrosianæ*', *Studies in Hogg and his World*, 4 (1993), 37–47; J. H. Alexander, '*Blackwood's*: Magazine as Romantic Form', *Wordsworth Circle*, 15 (1984), 57–68; *The Tavern Sages: Selections from the Noctes Ambrosianae*, ed. by J. H. Alexander (Aberdeen: Association for Scottish Literary Studies, 1992); Gillian Hughes, *James Hogg: A Life* (Edinburgh: Edinburgh University Press,

2007); Karl Miller, *Electric Shepherd: A Likeness of James Hogg* (London: Faber and Faber, 2003); Mark Parker, *Literary Magazines and British Romanticism* (Cambridge: Cambridge University Press, 2000); Alan Lang Strout, 'The *Noctes Ambrosianæ* and James Hogg', *Review of English Studies*, 13 (1937), 46–63; 177–89.

108 See J. H. Alexander's Introduction to *The Tavern Sages*, p. xii.
109 Thomas Carlyle, 'Christopher North', *Reminiscences*, ed. by Charles Eliot Norton, intro. by Ian Campbell (London: Dent, 1972), p. 378.
110 Cockburn, *Memorials of His Time*, p. 318.
111 'The True and Authentic Account of the Twelfth of August', *Blackwood's Edinburgh Magazine*, 5 (August 1819), 597–613* [mispaged] (p. 597).
112 *Noctes Ambrosianæ No. XXXV, Blackwood's Edinburgh Magazine (BEM)*, 23 (January 1828), 112–36 (p. 121).
113 *Noctes Ambrosianæ No. I, BEM*, 11 (March 1822), 369–*71 (p. *361).
114 *Noctes Ambrosianæ No. II, BEM*, 11 (April 1822), 475–89 (p. 482); *Noctes Ambrosianæ No. III, BEM*, 11 (May 1822), 601–18 (p. 605); *Noctes Ambrosianæ No. IV, BEM*, 12 (July 1822), 100–14 (p. 102).
115 *Noctes Ambrosianæ No. IX, BEM*, 13 (June 1823), 716–23 (p. 719).
116 Alexander, 'Hogg in the *Noctes Ambrosianæ*', p. 42.
117 *Memoir*, ed. Hughes, p. 59.
118 *Letters 2*, ed. Hughes, p. 378.
119 'Southey's Lives of Uneducated Poets', *Quarterly Review*, 44 (January 1831), 52–82 (p. 82).
120 See *Noctes Ambrosianæ No. LV, BEM*, 29 (March 1831), 535–71.
121 *Noctes Ambrosianæ No. VI, BEM*, 12 (December 1822), 695–709 (p. 697).
122 See 'Letter to Mr James Hogg', *Blackwood's Edinburgh Magazine*, 2 (February 1818), 501–04 (pp. 503–04).
123 Lockhart, *Peter's Letters*, I, 135–36.
124 *Noctes Ambrosianæ No. XXVII, BEM*, 20 (July 1826), 90–109 (p. 91).
125 *Noctes Ambrosianæ No. XXXII, BEM*, 21 (April 1827), 473–89 (p. 475).
126 Alexander, 'Hogg in the *Noctes Ambrosianæ*', p. 39.
127 *Noctes Ambrosianæ No. I, BEM*, 11 (March 1822), 369–*71 (p. 371).
128 *Noctes Ambrosianæ No. XIII, BEM*, 15 (March 1824), 358–66 (pp. 359–60).
129 *Noctes Ambrosianæ No. XV, BEM*, 15 (June 1824), 706–24 (p. 712).
130 *Noctes Ambrosianæ No. XVIII, BEM*, 17 (January 1825), 114–30 (p. 127).
131 *Noctes Ambrosianæ No. XIX, BEM*, 17 (March 1825), 366–86 (pp. 366–67).
132 *Noctes Ambrosianæ No. XXXV, BEM*, 23 (January 1828), 112–36 (p. 112).
133 *Noctes Ambrosianæ No. XXIX, BEM*, 20 (November 1826), 770–92 (pp. 784–85).
134 *Noctes Ambrosianæ No. XXIV, BEM*, 19 (February 1826), 211–27 (p. 214).
135 The songs in the *Noctes* from *No. of the Border Garland* are 'I'll No Wake Wi' Annie' (pp. 2–3), 'The Women Folk' (pp. 6–7), and 'The Laird o' Lamington' (pp. 18–19).
136 *Letters 2*, ed. Hughes, p. 276.
137 Hogg, *Songs*, p. 28.
138 See Hogg to William Blackwood, 19 March 1826, *Letters 2*, ed. Hughes, p. 243.

139 Hogg eventually published his balloon story with songs as 'Dr David Dale's Account of a Grand Aerial Voyage', *Edinburgh Literary Journal*, 23 January 1830, pp. 50–54.

140 Hogg to Alexander Blackwood, 3 July 1834, NLS, MS 4039, fols 31–32.

141 *Memoir*, ed. Hughes, p. 74.

142 'When Bawdrons, Wi' Her Mousin' Paw' and 'Maga at No. 45' were sung by the 'Shepherd' character in *Noctes Ambrosianæ No. LI, Blackwood's Edinburgh Magazine*, 28 (August 1830), 383–436 (pp. 385, 422–23).

143 *Letters 2*, ed. Hughes, p. 193.

144 See Hogg, *Confessions of a Justified Sinner*, ed. Garside, pp. 165–69.

145 Hogg, *Confessions of a Justified Sinner*, ed Garside, p. 169.

146 Hogg, *Confessions of a Justified Sinner*, ed. Garside, p. 170.

147 Hogg, *Confessions of a Justified Sinner*, ed. Garside, p. 172.

148 See 'Hogg's Three Perils of Woman', *Blackwood's Edinburgh Magazine*, 14 (October 1823), 427–37.

149 Moir included 'New Christmas Carol' in his manuscript list of works in *Blackwood's Edinburgh Magazine*. See NLS, Acc. 9856, no. 25. See also David Groves, 'James Hogg and the "New Christmas Carol": A Misattribution', *Notes and Queries*, 46 (December 1999), 474.

150 See Hogg to William Blackwood, 28 June 1824, *Letters 2*, ed. Hughes, p. 203.

151 NLS, MS 2245, fols 84–85.

152 *Letters 2*, ed. Hughes, p. 222.

153 To avoid unnecessary publication duplication in the S/SC Edition, poems from *Blackwood's Edinburgh Magazine* that are published in the S/SC Edition of *A Queer Book* are not reprinted in the present edition. See James Hogg, *A Queer Book*, ed. by P. D. Garside (S/SC, 1995).

154 See Peter Garside's Introduction to *A Queer Book*, ed. Garside, pp. xiv–xxi.

155 Hogg, *A Queer Book*, ed. Garside, p. xv.

156 William Blackwood to Hogg, 22 January 1825, NLS, MS 30,308, p. 43.

157 See James Boswell, *Boswell's Life of Johnson*, ed. by George Birkbeck Hill, rev. L. F. Powell, 6 vols (Oxford: Clarendon Press, 1946), III, 326.

158 David Groves, 'The Genesis of "Gil-Martin": James Hogg, "Colonel Cloud", and "The Madman in the *Mercury*"', *Notes and Queries*, 52 (December 2005), 467–69.

159 [James Browne], *The "Life" of the Ettrick Shepherd Anatomized; in a series of strictures on the Autobiography of James Hogg*, by An Old Dissector (Edinburgh: William Hunter, 1832).

160 NLS, MS 4724, fols 253–54.

161 For a full discussion of the publication history of these rejected stories, see Gillian Hughes's Introduction to James Hogg, *Tales of the Wars of Montrose*, ed. by Gillian Hughes (S/SC, 1996).

162 Manuscripts of the first two 'Dramas of Simple Life' have been preserved, and the works are published in the present edition: 'A Pastoral Love Scene' (pp. 193–209) and 'Dramas of Simple Life No. II' (pp. 209–53).

163 *Letters 2*, ed. Hughes, pp. 250–51.
164 William Blackwood to Hogg, 23 September 1826, NLS, MS 30,309, pp. 385–87.
165 See 'Katie Cheyne' and notes in James Hogg, *Contributions to Annuals and Gift-Books*, ed. by Janette Currie and Gillian Hughes (S/SC, 2006), pp. 108–19, 307–09.
166 William Blackwood to Hogg, NLS, MS 30,310, pp. 128A–30.
167 Hogg to William Blackwood, *Letters 2*, ed. Hughes, p. 266.
168 D. M. Moir to William Blackwood, NLS, MS 4020, fols 35–36.
169 Hogg to William Blackwood, 10 March 1829, *Letters 2*, ed. Hughes, p. 328.
170 NLS, MS 30,308, p. 161.
171 See note 164.
172 Hogg to William Blackwood, 5 January 1828, *Letters 2*, ed. Hughes, p. 282.
173 NLS, MS 2245, fols 110–11.
174 See the introductory note to 'A Strange Secret' in the present edition, pp. 548–50.
175 *Letters 2*, ed. Hughes, pp. 308–09.
176 *Letters 2*, ed. Hughes, p. 59.
177 Hogg, *Confessions of a Justified Sinner*, ed. Garside, p. 67.
178 Hogg to William Blackwood, 5 July 1827, *Letters 2*, ed. Hughes, p. 272.
179 Hogg to William Blackwood, 25 January 1825, *Letters 2*, ed. Hughes, p. 222.
180 Hogg to William Blackwood, 20 November 1820, *Letters 2*, ed. Hughes, p. 60.
181 NLS, MS 2530, fols 3–4. The letter is dated 16 March 1833.

# Tales and Anecdotes
## of the Pastoral Life

### No. I

Mr Editor,

Last autumn, while I was staying a few weeks with my friend Mr Grumple, minister of the extensive and celebrated parish of *Woolenhorn*, an incident occurred which hath afforded me a great deal of amusement; and as I think it may divert some of your readers, I shall, without further preface, begin the relation.

We had just finished a wearisome debate on the rights of teind, and the claims which every clergyman of the established church of Scotland has for a grass glebe; the china cups were already arranged, and the savoury teapot stood basking on the ledge of the grate, when the servant-maid entered, and told Mr Grumple that there was one at the door who wanted him.

We immediately heard a debate in the passage,—the parson pressing his guest to *come ben*, which the other stoutly resisted, declaring aloud that "it was a' nonsense thegither, for he was eneuch to fley a' the grand folk out o' the room, an' set the kivering o' the floor a-swoomin." The parlour door was however thrown open, and, to my astonishment, the first guests who presented themselves were two strong honest-looking colleys, or shepherd's dogs, that came bouncing and capering into the room, with a great deal of seeming satisfaction. Their master was shortly after ushered in. He was a tall athletic figure, with a black beard, and dark raven hair hanging over his brow; wore clouted shoes, shod with iron, and faced up with copper; and there was altogether something in his appearance the most homely and uncouth of any exterior I had ever seen.

"This," said the minister, "is Peter Plash, a parishioner of mine, who has brought me in an excellent salmon, and wants a good office at my hand, he says, in return."–"The bit fish is naething, man," said Peter, sleeking down the hair on his brow; "I wish he had been better for your sake—but gin ye had seen the sport that we had wi' him at Pool-Midnight, ye wad hae leughen till ye had burstit." Here the shepherd, observing his two dogs seated comfortably on the hearth-rug, and deeming it an instance of high presumption and very bad manners, broke out with—"Ay, Whitefoot, lad! an' ye're for being a gentleman too! My certy, man, but ye're no blate!—I'm ill eneuch, to be sure, to come into a grand room this way, but yet I wadna set up my impudent nose an' my muckle rough brisket afore the lowe, an' tak a' the fire to mysel—Get aff wi' ye, sir! An' you too, Trimmy, ye limmer! what's your business here?"—So saying, he attempted, with the fringe of his plaid, to drive them out; but they only ran about the room, eyeing their master with astonishment and concern. They had never, it seemed, been wont to be separated from him either by night or by day, and they could not understand why they should be driven from the parlour, or how they had not as good a right to be there as he. Of course, neither threats nor blows could make them leave him; and it being a scene of life quite new to me, and of which I was resolved to profit as much as possible, at my intercession matters were made up, and the two canine associates were suffered to remain where they were. They were soon seated, one on each side of their master, clinging fondly to his feet, and licking the wet from his dripping trowsers.

Having observed that, when the shepherd entered, he had begun to speak with great zest about the sport they had in killing the salmon, I again brought on the subject, and made him describe the diversion to me.—"O man!" said he, and then indulged in a hearty laugh—(*man* was always the term he used in addressing either of us—*sir* seemed to be no word in his vocabulary)—"O man, I wish ye had been there! I'll lay a plack ye wad hae said ye never saw sic sport sin' ever ye war born. We gat twall fish a'thegither the-day, an' sair broostals we had wi' some o' them; but a' was naething to the killin o' that ane at Pool-Midnight. Geordie Otterson, Mathew Ford, an' me, war a' owre the lugs after him. But ye's hear:—When I cam on to the craigs at the weil o' Pool-Midnight, the sun was shinin bright, the wind was lown, an' wi' the pirl* being away, the pool was as clear as crystal. I soon saw by the bells coming up, that there was a fish in the auld hauld; an' I keeks an' I glimes about, till, faith! I sees his blue murt fin. My teeth were a' waterin to be in him, but I kend the shank o' my waster† wasna half length. Sae I cries to Geordie, 'Geordie,' says I, 'aigh man! here's a great chap just lyin steeping like a aik clog.' Off comes Geordie, shaugle shauglin a' his pith; for the creature's that greedy o' fish, he wad venture his very saul for them. I kend brawly what wad be the upshot. 'Now,' says I, 'Geordie, man yoursel for this ae time. Aigh, man! he is a terrible ane for size—See, yonder he's lying.' The sun was shinin sae clear that the deepness o' the pool was a great

*Ripple
†Fishspear

cheat. Geordie bait his lip for perfect eagerness, an' his een war stelled in his head–he thought he had him safe i' the pat; but whenever he put the grains o' the leister into the water, I could speak nae mair, I kend sae weel what was comin; for I kend the depth to an inch.–Weel, he airches an' he vizies for a good while, an' at length made a push down at him wi' his whole might. Tut!–the leister didna gang to the grund by an ell–an' Geordie gaed into the deepest part o' Pool-Midnight wi' his head foremost! My sennins turned as suple as a dockan, an' I just fell down i' the bit wi' lauchin–ye might hae bund me wi' a strae. He wad hae drowned for aught that I could do; for when I saw his heels flinging up aboon the water as he had been dancin a hornpipe, I lost a' power thegither; but Mathew Ford harled him into the shallow wi' his leister.

"Weel, after that we cloddit the pool wi' great stanes, an' aff went the fish down the gullots, shinin like a rainbow. Then he ran, and he ran! an' it was wha to be first in him. Geordie got the first chance, an' I thought it was a' owre; but just when he thought he was sure o' him, down cam Mathew full drive, smashed his grains out through Geordie's and gart him miss. It was my chance next; an' I took him neatly through the gills, though he gaed as fast as a shell-drake.

"But the sport grew aye better.–Geordie was sae mad at Mathew for taigling him, an' garring him tine the fish (for he's a greedy dirt), that they had gane to grips in a moment; an' when I lookit back, they war just fightin like twae tarriers in the mids o' the water. The witters o' the twa leisters were fankit in ane anither, an' they couldna get them sindrie, else there had been a vast o' blude shed; but they were knevillin, an' tryin to drown ane anither a' that they could; an' if they hadna been clean fore-foughen they wad hae done't; for they were aye gaun out o' sight an' comin howdin up again. Yet after a', when I gaed back to redd them, they were sae inveterate that they wadna part till I was forced to haud them down through the water and drown them baith."

"But I hope you have not indeed drowned the men," said I. "Ou na, only keepit them down till I took the power fairly frae them–till the bullers gae owre coming up; then I carried them to different sides o' the water, an' laid them down agroof wi' their heads at the inwith; an' after gluthering an' spurring a wee while, they cam to again. We dinna count muckle o' a bit drowning match, us fishers. I wish I could get Geordie as weel doukit ilka day; it wad tak the smeddum frae him–for, O, he is a greedy thing! But I fear it will be a while or I see sic glorious sport again."

Mr Grumple remarked, that he thought, by his account, it could not be very good sport to all parties; and that, though he always encouraged these vigorous and healthful exercises among his parishioners, yet he regretted that they could so seldom be concluded in perfect good humour.

"They're nae the waur o' a wee bit splore," said Peter; "they wad turn unco milk-an'-water things, an' dee away a'thegither wantin a broolzie. Ye might as weel think to keep a ale-vat working wantin barm."

"But, Peter, I hope you have not been breaking the laws of the country by your sport to-day?"

"Na, troth hae we no, man—close-time disna come in till the day after the morn; but atween you an' me, close-time's nae ill time for us. It merely ties up the grit folk's hands, an' thraws a' the sport into our's thegither. Na, na, we's never complain o' close-time; if it warena for it there wad few fish fa' to poor folk's share."

This was a light in which I had never viewed the laws of the fishing association before; but as this honest hind spoke from experience, I have no doubt that the statement is founded in truth, and that the sole effect of close-time, in all the branches of the principal river, is merely to tie up the hands of every respectable man, and throw the fishing into the hands of poachers. He told me, that in all the rivers of the extensive parish of *Woolenhorn*, the fish generally run up during one flood, and went away the next; and as the gentlemen and farmers of those parts had no interest in the preservation of the breeding salmon themselves, nor cared a farthing about the fishing associations in the great river, whom they viewed as monopolizers of that to which they had no right, the fish were wholly abandoned to the poachers, who generally contrived, by burning lights at the shallows, and spearing the fish by night, and netting the pools, to annihilate every shoal that came up. This is, however, a subject that would require an essay by itself.

Our conversation turned on various matters connected with the country; and I soon found, that though this hind had something in his manner and address the most uncultivated I had ever seen, yet his conceptions of such matters as came within the sphere of his knowledge were pertinent and just. He sung old songs, told us strange stories of witches and apparitions, and related many anecdotes of the pastoral life, which I think extremely curious, and wholly unknown to the literary part of the community. But at every observation that he made, he took care to sleek down his black hair over his brow, as if it were of the utmost consequence to his making a respectable appearance, that it should be equally spread, and as close pressed down as possible. When desired to join us in drinking tea, he said "it was a' nonsense thegither, for he hadna the least occasion;" and when pressed to take bread, he persisted in the declaration that "it was great nonsense." He loved to talk of sheep, of dogs, and of *the lasses*, as he called them; and conversed with his dogs in the same manner as he did with any of the other guests; nor did the former ever seem to misunderstand him, unless in his unprecedented and illiberal attempt to expel them from the company.–"Whitefoot! haud aff the woman's coat-tails, ye blockhead! Deil hae me gin ye hae the mense of a miller's horse, man." Whitefoot instantly obeyed.– "Trimmy! come back aff the fire, dame! Ye're sae wat, ye raise a reek like a cottar wife's lum–come back, ye limmer!" Trimmy went behind his chair.

It came out at last that his business with Mr Grumple that day was to request of him to go over to *Stridekirton* on the Friday following, and unite him, Peter Plash, in holy wedlock with his sweetheart and only joe, Jean Windlestrae; and he said, if I "would accompany the minister, and take share of a haggis wi' them, I wad see some good lasses, and some good sport too, which was far better." You may be sure I accepted of the invitation with great cordiality, nor had I any cause to repent it. I have, since that time, had many conversations with Peter, of which I have taken notes; but the description of a country wedding, together with the natural history of the Scottish sheep, the shepherd's dog, and some account of the country lasses, I must reserve for future communications.                    H.

# Verses

*Recited by the Author, in a Party of his Countrymen, on the Day that the News arrived of our final Victory over the French*

> Now, Britain, let thy cliffs o' snaw
>     Look prouder o'er the merled main!
> The bastard Eagle bears awa,
>     And ne'er shall ee thy shores again.
>
> Bang up thy banners red an' riven!                    5
>     The day's thy ain–the prize is won!
> Weel may thy lions brow the heaven,
>     An' turn their gray beards to the sun.

Lang hae I bragged o' thine an' thee,
  Even when thy back was at the wa';          10
An' thou my proudest sang sall be,
  As lang as I hae breath to draw.

Gae hang the coofs wha boded wae,
  An' cauldness o'er thy efforts threw,
Lauding the fellest, sternest fae,          15
  Frae hell's black porch that ever flew.

O he might conquer idiot kings,
  These bars in nature's onward plan;
But fool is he the yoke that flings
  O'er the unshackled soul of man.          20

'Tis like a cobweb o'er the breast,
  That binds the giant while asleep,
Or curtain hung upon the east,
  The day-light from the world to keep!

Come, jaw your glasses to the brim!          25
  Gar in the air your bonnets flee!
"Our gude auld king!" I'll drink to him,
  As lang as I hae drink to pree.

This to the arms that well upbore
  The Rose and Shamrock blooming still—          30
An' here's the burly plant of yore,
  "*The Thristle o' the Norlan' hill!*"

Auld Scotland!—land o' hearts the wale!
  Hard thou has fought, and bravely won:
Lang may thy lions paw the gale,          35
  `And turn their dewlaps to the sun!
                                        H.

# Tales and Anecdotes
# of the Pastoral Life
### No. II

THE wedding-day at length arrived; and as the bridegroom had
charged us to be there at an early hour, we set out on horseback,

immediately after breakfast, for the remote hamlet of Stridekirtin. We found no regular path, but our way lay through a country which it is impossible to view without soothing emotions. The streams are numerous, clear as crystal, and wind along the glens in many fantastic and irregular curves. The mountains are green to the tops, very high, and form many beautiful soft and shaded outlines. They are, besides, literally speckled with snowy flocks, which, as we passed, were feeding or resting with such appearance of undisturbed repose, that the heart naturally found itself an involuntary sharer in the pastoral tranquillity that pervaded all around.

My good friend, Mr Grumple, could give me no information regarding the names of the romantic glens and mountains that came within our view; he, however, knew who were the proprietors of the land, who the tenants, what rent and stipend each of them paid, and whose teinds were unexhausted; this seemed to be the sum and substance of his knowledge concerning the life, character, and manners, of his rural parishioners, save that he could sometimes adduce circumstantial evidence that such and such farmers had made money of their land, and that others had made very little or none.

This district, over which he presides in an ecclesiastical capacity, forms an extensive portion of the Arcadia of Britain. It was likewise, in some late ages, noted for its zeal in the duties of religion, as well as for a thirst after the acquirement of knowledge concerning its doctrines; but under the tuition of such a pastor as my relative appears to be, it is no wonder that practical religion should be losing ground from year to year, and scepticism, the natural consequence of laxity in religious duties, gaining ground in proportion.

It may be deemed, perhaps, rather indecorous, to indulge in such reflections respecting any individual who has the honour to be ranked as a member of a body so generally respectable as our Scottish Clergy, and who, at the same time, maintains a fair *worldly* character; but in a general discussion—in any thing that relates to the common weal of mankind; all such inferior considerations must be laid aside. And the more I consider the simplicity of the people of whom I am now writing—the scenes among which they have been bred—and their lonely and sequestered habits of life, where the workings and phenomena of nature alone appear to attract the eye or engage the attention,—the more I am convinced that the temperament of their minds would naturally dispose them to devotional feelings. If they were but taught to read their Bibles, and only saw uniformly in the ministers of religion that sanctity of character by which the profession ought ever to be distinguished, these people would naturally be such as every well-wisher to the human race would desire a scattered peasantry to be. But when the most decided variance between example and precept is forced on their observation, what should we, or what can we, expect? Men must see, hear, feel, and judge accordingly. And certainly in no other instance is a patron so responsible to his sovereign, his country, and his God, as in the choice he makes of spiritual pastors.

These were some of the reflections that occupied my mind as I traversed this beautiful pastoral country with its morose teacher, and from these I was at length happily aroused by the appearance of the cottage, or shepherd's steading, to which we were bound. It was situated in a little valley in the bottom of a wild glen, or *hope*, as it is there called. It stood all alone; but besides the dwelling-house, there was a little byre that held the two cows and their young,—a good stack of hay, another of peats,—a sheep-house, and two homely gardens; and the place had altogether something of a snug, comfortable appearance. Though this is only an individual picture, I am told it may be viewed as a general one of almost every shepherd's dwelling in the south of Scotland; and it is only such pictures that, in the course of these tales, I mean to present to the public.

A number of the young shepherds and country-lasses had already arrived, impatient for the approaching wedding; others were coming down the green hills in mixed parties all around, leading one another, and skipping with the agility of lambs. They were all walking barefooted and barelegged, male and female—the men were dressed much in the ordinary way, only that the texture of their clothes was somewhat coarse, and the women had black beavers, white gowns, and "green coats kilted to the knee." When they came near the house they went into little sequestered hollows, the men and women apart, "pat on their hose an' shoon, and made themsels a' trig an' witching," and then came and joined the group with a joy that could not be restrained by walking,—they run to mix with their youthful associates.

Still as they arrived, we saw, on our approach, that they drew up in two rows on the green, and soon found that it was a contest at leaping. The shepherds were stripped to the shirt and drawers, and exerting themselves in turn with all their might, while their sweethearts and sisters were looking on with no small share of interest.

We received a kind and hospitable welcome from honest Peter and his father, who was a sagacious-looking old carle, with a broad bonnet and gray locks; but the contest on the green still continuing, I went and joined the circle, delighted to see a pastime so appropriate to the shepherd's life. I was utterly astonished at the agility which the fellows displayed.

They took a short race of about twelve or fourteen paces, which they denominated the *ramrace*, and then rose from the footing-place with such a bound as if they had been going to mount and fly into the air. The crooked guise in which they flew shewed great art—the knees were doubled upward—the body bent forward—and the head thrown somewhat back; so that they alighted on their heels with the greatest ease and safety, their joints being loosened in such a manner that not one of them was straight. If they fell backward on the ground, the leap was not accounted fair. Several of the antagonists took the ramrace with a staff in their hand, which they left at the footing-place as they rose. This I thought unfair, but none of their opponents objected to the custom. I measured the distance, and found that two of them had actually leapt twenty-two feet, on a level plain, at one bound. This may appear extraordinary to those who never witnessed such an exercise, but it is a fact of which I can adduce sufficient proof.

Being delighted as well as astonished at seeing those feats of agility, I took Peter aside, and asked him if I might offer prizes for some other exercises. "Hout na," said Peter; "ye'll affront them; let them just alane; they hae eneuch o' incitement e'now, an' rather owre muckle atween you an' me; forbye the brag o' the thing—as lang as the lasses stand and look at them, they'll ply atween death an' life." What Peter said was true,—instead of getting weary of their sports, their ardour seemed to increase; and always as soon as the superiority of any individual in one particular exercise was manifest, another was instantly resorted to; so that ere long there was one party engaged in wrestling, one in throwing the stone, and another at hop-step-and-leap, all at one and the same time.

This last seems to be rather the favourite amusement. It consists of three succeeding bounds, all with the same race; and as the exertion is greater, and of longer continuance, they can judge with more precision the exact capability of the several competitors. I measured the ground, and found the greatest distance effected in this way to be forty-six feet. I am informed, that whenever two or three young shepherds are gathered together, at fold or bught, moor or market, at all times and seasons, Sunday's excepted, one or more of these athletic exercises is uniformly resorted to; and certainly, in a class where hardiness and agility are so requisite, they can never be too much encouraged.

But now all these favourite sports were terminated at once by a loud cry of "Hurra! the broose! the broose!" Not knowing what *the broose* meant, I looked all around with great precipitation, but for some time could see nothing but hills. At length, however, by marking the direction in which the rest looked, I perceived, at a considerable distance down the glen, five horsemen coming at full speed on a determined race, although on such a road, as I believe, a race was never before contested. It was that by which we had lately come, and the only one that led to the house from all the four quarters of the world. For some time it crossed "the crooks of the burn," as they called them; that is, it kept straight up the bottom of the glen, and crossed the burn at every turning. Of course every time that the group crossed this stream, they were for a moment involved in a cloud of spray that almost hid them from view, and the frequent recurrence of this rendered the effect highly comic.

Still, however, they kept apparently close together, till at length the path left the bottom of the narrow valley, and came round the sloping base of a hill that was all interspersed with drains and small irregularities of surface; this producing no abatement of exertion or speed; horses and men were soon foundering, plunging, and tumbling about in all directions. If this was amusing to view, it was still more so to hear the observations of the delighted group that stood round me and beheld it. "Ha, ha, ha! yonder's ane aff! Gude faith! yon's Jock o' the Meer-Cleuch; he has gotten an ill-faur'd flaip.– Holloa! yonder gaes another, down through a lair to the een-holes! Weel done, Aedie o' Aberlosk! Hie till him, Tousy, outher now or never! Lay on, ye deevil, an' hing by the mane! Hurray!"

The women were by this time screaming, and the men literally jumping and clapping their hands for joy at the deray that was going on; and there was one little elderly-looking man whom I could not help noting; he had fallen down on the ground in a convulsion of laughter, and was spurring and laying on it with both hands and feet. One, whom they denominated Davie Scott o' the Ramseycleuch-burn, amid the bay of dogs and the shouts of men and women, got first to the bridegroom's door, and of course was acknowledged to have won the *broose*; but the attention was soon wholly turned from him to those behind. The man whose horse had sunk in the bog, perceiving that all chance of extricating it again on the instant was out of the question, lost not a moment, but sprung to his feet—threw off his clothes, hat, and shoes, all at one brush—and ran towards the goal with all his might. Jock o' the Meer-Cleuch, who was still a good way farther back, and crippled besides with his fall, perceiving this, mounted again—whipped on furiously, and would soon have overhied his pedestrian adversary; but the shepherds are bad horsemen, and, moreover, Jock's horse, which belonged to Gideon of Kirkhope, was unacquainted with the sheep-drains, and terrified at them; consequently, by making a sudden jerk backwards when he should have leapt across one of them, and when Jock supposed that he was just going to do so, he threw his rider a second time. The shouts of laughter were again renewed, and every one was calling out, "Now for the mell! Now for the mell! Deil tak the hindmost now!" These sounds reached Jock's ears; he lost no time in making a last effort, but flew at his horse again—remounted him—and, by urging him to a desperate effort, actually got a-head of his adversary just when within ten yards of the door, and thus escaped the disgrace of *winning the mell.*

I was afterwards told, that in former ages it was the custom on the Border, when the victor in the race was presented with the prize of honour, the one who came in last was, at the same time, presented with a mallet or large wooden hammer, called a *mell* in the dialect of the country, and that then the rest of the competitors stood in need to be near at hand, and instantly to force the *mell* from him, else he was at liberty to knock as many of them down with it as he could. The mell has now, for many years, been only a nominal prize; but there is often more sport about the gaining of it than the principal one. There was another occurrence which added greatly to the animation of this, which I had not time before fully to relate. About the time when the two unfortunate wights were unhorsed in the bog, those who still kept on were met and attacked, open mouth, by at least twenty frolicsome collies, that seemed fully as intent on sport as their masters. These bit the hind-legs of the horses, snapped at their noses, and raised such an outrage of barking, that the poor animals, forespent as they were, were constrained to lay themselves out almost beyond power. Nor did the fray cease when the race was won. Encouraged by the noise and clamour which then arose about the gaining of the mell, the staunch collies continued the attack, and hunted the racers round and round the houses with great speed, while the horses were all the time wheeling and flinging most furiously, and their riders, in desperation, vociferating and cursing their assailants.

All the guests now crowded together, and much humour and blunt wit passed about the gaining of the broose. Each of the competitors had his difficulties and cross accidents to relate; and each affirmed, that if it had not been such and such hindrances, he would have gained the broose to a certainty. Davie Scott o' the Ramseycleuch-burn, however, assured them, that "he was aye hauding in his yaud wi' the left hand, and gin he had liket to gie her out her head, she wad hae gallopit amaist a third faster."–"That may be," said Aedie o' Aberlosk, "but I hae come better on than I expectit wi' my Cameronian naig. I never saw him streek himsel sae afore–I dare say he thought that Davie was auld Clavers mounted on Hornie. Poor fallow!" continued he, patting him, "he has a good deal o' anti-prelatic dourness in him; but I see he has some spirit, for a' that. I bought him for a powney, but he's turned out a beast."

I next overheard one proposing to the man who left his horse, and exerted himself so manfully on foot, to go and pull his horse out of the quagmire. "Na, na," said he, "let him stick yonder a while, to learn him mair sense than to gang intill an open well-ee and gar ane get a mell. I saw the gate I was gawn, but I couldna swee him aff; sae I just thought o' Jenny Blythe, and plunged in. I kend weel some-thing was to happen, for I met her first this morning, the ill-hued carlin: but I had need to haud my tongue!–Gudeman, let us see a drap whisky." He was presented with a glass. "Come, here's Jenny Blythe," said Andrew, and drank it off.–"I wad be nae the waur o' a wee drap too," said Aberlosk, taking a glass of whisky in his hand, and looking stedfastly through it; "I think I see Jock the elder here," said he; "ay, it's just him–come, here's *the five kirks o' Eskdale.*" He drank it off. "Gudeman, that's naething but a *Tam-Park* of a glass: if ye'll fill it again, I'll gie a toast ye never heard afore. This is *Bailey's Dictionary,*" said Aedie, and drank it off again.–"But, when a' your daffin's owre, Aedie," said John, "what hae ye made o' our young friend?"–"Ou! she's safe eneuch," returned he; "the best-man and John the elder are wi' her."

On looking round the corner of the house, we now perceived that the bride and her two attendants were close at hand. They came at a *quick canter.* She managed her horse well, kept her saddle with great ease, and seemed an elegant sprightly girl, of twenty-four or there-abouts. Every cap was instantly waved in the air, and the bride was saluted with three hearty cheers. Old John, well aware of what it behoved him to do, threw off his broad bonnet, and took the bride respectfully from her horse–kissed and welcomed her home. "Ye're welcome hame till us, Jeany, my bonny woman," said he; "may God bless ye, an' mak ye just as good an' as happy as I wish ye." It was a beautiful and affecting sight, to see him leading her toward the home that was now to be her own. He held her hand in both his–the wind waved his long gray locks–his features were lengthened consider-ably the wrong way, and I could perceive a tear glistening on his furrowed cheek.

All seemed to know exactly the parts they had to act; but every thing came on me like magic, and quite by surprise. The bride now stopped short on the threshold, while the old man broke a triangular cake of short-bread over her head, the pieces of which he threw about among the young people. These scrambled for them with great violence and eagerness; and indeed they seemed always to be most in their element when any thing that required strength or activity was presented. For my part, I could not comprehend what the sudden convulsion meant, (for in a moment the crowd was moving like a whirlpool, and tumbling over one another in half dozens) till a little girl, escaping from the vortex, informed me that "they war battling wha first to get a haud o' the bride's bunn." I was still in the dark, till at length I saw the successful candidates presenting their favourites with small pieces of this mystical cake. One beautiful maid, with light locks, blue eyes, and cheeks like the vernal rose, came nimbly up to me, called me familiarly by my name, looked at me with perfect seriousness, and without even a smile on her innocent face, asked me *if I was married.* I could scarcely contain my gravity, while I took her by the hand, and answered in the negative.–"An' hae ye no gotten a piece o' the bride's cake?"–"Indeed, my dear, I am sorry I have not."–"O, that's a great shame, that ye hae nae gotten a wee bit! I canna bide to see a stranger guided that gate. Here, sir, I'll gie ye the tae half o' mine, it will ser' us baith; an' I wad rather want mysel than sae civil a gentleman that's a stranger should want."

So saying, she took a small piece of cake from her lap, and parted it with me, at the same time rolling each of the pieces carefully up in a leaf of an old halfpenny ballad; but the whole of her demeanour shewed the utmost seriousness, and of how much import she judged this trivial crumb to be. "Now," continued she, "ye maun lay this aneath your head, sir, when ye gang to your bed, and ye'll dream about the woman ye are to get for your wife. Ye'll just think ye see her plainly an' bodily afore your een; an' ye'll be sae weel acquainted wi' her, that ye'll ken her again when ye see her, if it war amang a thousand. It's a queer thing, but it's perfectly true; sae ye maun *mind no to forget.*"

I promised the most punctual observance of all that she enjoined, and added, that I was sure I would dream of the lovely giver; that indeed I would be sorry were I to dream of any other, as I deemed it impossible to dream of so much innocence and beauty.–"*Now mind no to forget,*" rejoined she, and skipped lightly away to join her youthful associates.

As soon as the bride was led into the house, old Nelly, the

bridegroom's mother went aside to see the beast on which her daughter-in-law had been brought home; and perceiving that it was a mare, she fell a-crying and wringing her hands.—I inquired, with some alarm, what was the matter.—"O dear, sir," returned she, "it's for the poor bairnies that'll yet hae to dree this unlucky mischance—Laike-a-day, poor waefu' brats! they'll no lie in a dry bed for a dozen o' years to come!"

"Hout! haud your tongue, Nelly," said the best man, "the thing's but a freat a'thegither. But really we couldna help it: the factor's naig wantit a fore-fit shoe, an' was beckin like a water-craw. If I had ridden five miles to the smiddy wi' him, it is ten to ane but Jock Anderson wad hae been drunk, an' then we wadna hae gotten the bride hame afore twall o'clock at night; sae I thought it was better to let them tak their chance than spoil sae muckle good sport, an' I e'en set her on Wattie Bryden's pownie. The factor has behaved very ill about it, the muckle stottin gowk! If I had durst, I wad hae gien him a deevil of a thrashin; but he says, 'Faith it's—that—yes, indeed—that—he will send them—yes, faith—it's even a—*a new tikabed* every year.'"

The ceremony of the marriage next ensued; but as there was nothing peculiar about it (except that it took place in the bridegroom's house, and not at the bride's former home, which was out of the parson's reach); and as it was, besides, the dullest part of that day's exercise, I shall not say much about it, only that every thing was done decently and in order. But I have run on so long with this Number, that I fear I must postpone the foot-race, the dinner discourse, and final winding up of the wedding, till a future opportunity.                                                                    H.

# Shakspeare Club of Alloa

Mr EDITOR,

YOUR readers must have remarked in the newspapers, for some years bygone, accounts of an yearly festival in memory of Shakspeare, held at a place called ALLOA, situated, I believe, somewhere on the banks of the Forth; a town which I think I have once or twice heard mentioned, though on what account I do not at present recollect, if it was not in consequence of this very club, or a famous STEAM BOAT, on a new plan, that was there constructed.

Curious to learn how the anniversary of Shakspeare first came to be celebrated in such a remote corner of our country, I have made every inquiry I could anent it, in order to lay the account before your readers; but to very little purpose. I have been told that this poetic union had its origin about sixteen years ago, and was first set on foot in opposition to a *Musical Club*–(it must be an extraordinary place this Alloa)–which was established there at the same time. The latter, however, like its own enchanting strains, died away, and has left no trace behind; but the poetical brotherhood continued stedfast, flourished, gained ground, and promises to be permanent. The members have a hall, a library, and a store of wines, spirits, &c. To this store or cellar every one of them has a key, and is at liberty to treat his friends from it to any extent he pleases, without check or control. There is something extremely liberal and unreserved in this, and were we members of this club, we would certainly prefer this privilege to any literary one that can possibly be attached to it.

The festival this year, I am told, lasted *eight days complete;* and my informer assures me, that (*saving* on the 23d, the anniversary of their patron's birth) during all that time every man of them went sober to his bed. I believe the gentlemen thought so, which was much the same as if it had really been the case. Their principal amusements are songs, recitations, literary toasts, and eulogiums; and the meeting, it appears, was greatly enlivened this year by the attendance of a Mr Stevenson, a young professional singer, whose powers of voice promise the highest excellence yet attained in Scottish song. I have likewise been so far fortunate as to procure the sole copy of a poetical address delivered by the President, on his health being drank, which gives a better definition of the club than any thing I could possibly have obtained. It would surely be a great treat to your readers, could you procure some of their *eulogiums* literally as delivered, that we might see what kind of ideas the people of that outlandish place entertain about poets and poetry in general. The following appears to be somewhat in the style of the Poet Laureate.

> Brethren, know you the import of this meeting?
> This festival, in which from year to year
> We feel a deeper interest?–List to me.
> I have a word to say–one kindly meant
> As a remembrancer of days gone by,                          5
> And bond of future time–Here have we met
> These many fleeting years; each in his place;
> Have seen the self same friendly faces greet us
> With kindred joy, and that gray bust of him,
> Our patron bard, with flowers and laurels crowned.          10
> There is a charm in this–a something blent
> With the best genial feelings of the heart;

Each one will own it. Turn we to the past:
Survey th' events and changes that have been
In lands and nations round us, since we first                    15
Joined in poetic unity. That view
Is fraught with tints so grand, so wonderful,
That Time's old annals, though engraved with steel,
And cast in blood, no parallel unfold.–
In these we had our share–we took a part                        20
With arm, but more with heart. With sullen eye
We saw the vessels waning from our port;
Our native Forth, that wont to be a scene
Of speckled beauty with the shifting sail,
The veering pennon, and the creaking barge.                     25
Deep-loaded to the wale, with fraughtage rich,
Heaved on in glassy silence,–tide on tide,
And wave on wave lashed idly on our strand.
Sore altered were the times!–We bore it all,
Determined, by our country and our King                         30
To stand, whate'er the issue.–When the scene
Look'd more than usual dark–when empires fell
Prostrate as by enchantment–and the threat
Of stern invasion sounded in our ears,
We looked up to the Ochils–and our minds                        35
Dwelt on the impervious Grampian glens beyond,
As on a last retreat–for we had sworn
That Bancho's old unalienable line
Should there find shelter–'mid a land and race
By man ne'er conquered, should a sore extreme                   40
Urge the expedient.–In this hall the while
Constant we met–weekly and yearly met,
And in the pages of our Bard revered,
Our canonized Shakspeare, learned to scan
And estimate the sanguine springs that moved                    45
The world's commotion.–There we saw defined
The workings of ambition–the deceit
Of courts and conclaves–traced the latent source
Of human crimes and human miseries:
His is the Book of Nature!–Now the days                         50
Of tumult are o'erpast.–Our crested helms
In heaps lie piled–our broad Hungarian blades,
Which erst with martial sound on stirrup rung,
Cumbering the thigh, or gleaming in the air

Like bending meteors–like a canopy     55
Of trembling silver:–all are laid aside!
Piled in the armoury, rusting in the sheath!
There let them lie.–O! may the gloomy fiend
Of home commotion never force the hands
Of brethren to resume them! Times indeed     60
Are changed with us!–The sailor's song is hushed,
Pale discontent sits on the Labourer's brow;
Blest be the Ruler's heart who condescends
Some slight indulgence at this trying hour,
Nor like the Prince of Israel, who despised     65
The old men's counsel, threats a heavier yoke.
Changes must happen–but in silence still
We wait the issue, with a firm resolve
To cherish order. In our manual there–
Our bond of union broadly is defined     70
The mob's enormities; for reason, faith,
Nor prudence govern there.–All this, when viewed
With retrospective glance, gives to this day,
And to this social bond, no common share
Of interest and regard. Nay, more, my friends,     75
Ourselves are changed in feature and in frame
Since first we met.–Then light of heart we were,
Ardent and full of hope, and wedded all
To the aspirings of the heaven-born muse.
But years have altered us!–Sedateness now     80
Is settled on each brow.–Friends have departed,
And families sprung around us.–Thus our joys,
Our loves, and feelings, like ourselves, are changed,
Softened to sadness–mellowed to a calm
Which youth and passion ruffle may no more!     85
How different all our views, our hopes, and fears,
From those we knew on that auspicious day
We took the name we bear–the greatest name
The world e'er listed.–Kingdoms may decay,
And Empires totter, change succeed to change,     90
But here no change presents–uncoped with still
Stands our immortal Shakspeare–he whose birth
This day we celebrate.–O! be this day
For ever sacred to his memory–
And long may we, my Brethren, though divided     95
To the four winds of heaven, meet again,

Happy and free, on this returning day.
And when the spare and silvery locks of age
Wave o'er the wrinkled brow and faded eye,
Memento of a change that is to be;                100
May we survey this day and all behind
Without regret, and to the future look
With calm composure and unshaken hope.

No 5, DEVON STREET
*May* 1817.


# A Last Adieu

ADIEU, my loved parent, the trial is o'er,
The veil o'er thy couch of forgetfulness spread;
Thy kind heart shall grieve for my follies no more,
Nor the suppliant tear for thy wanderer be shed.

Long over thy head has the tempest blown fell,      5
But riches, unknown, were unvalued by thee;
In the wild wast thou born, in the wild didst thou dwell,
The pupil of Nature, benevolent and free;

And never, in all her uncultured domain,
Was nourished a spirit more genial and kind;      10
Chill poverty could not thy ardour restrain,
Nor cloud thy gay smile, or the glow of thy mind.

When winter-wreaths lay round our cottage so small,
When fancy was ardent, and feeling was strong,
O how I would long for the gloaming to fall,      15
To sit by thy knee and attend to thy song!

The song of the field where the warrior bled;
The garland of blossom dishonoured too soon;
The elves of the green-wood, the ghosts of the dead,
And fairies that journeyed by light of the moon.      20

I loved thee, my parent—my highest desire
Was 'neath independence to shield thy gray head;
But fortune denied it—extinguished the fire—
And, now thou art gone, my ambition is fled.

I loved thee!–and now thou art laid in thy grave,                25
Thy memory I'll cherish, while memory is mine;
And the boon that my tongue aye from Heaven shall crave,
Shall be the last blessing that hung upon thine.

Though over thy ashes no tombstone is seen,
The place shall be hallowed when ages are past;             30
No monument tells, 'mid the wilderness green,
Where the minstreless lies of the Border the last.

But over that grave will the lover of song,
And the lover of goodness, stand silent and sigh;
And the fays of the wild will thy requiem prolong,           35
And shed on thy coverlet dews of the sky:

And there, from the rue and the rose's perfume,
His dew-web of dawn shall the gossamer won;
And there shall the daisy and violet bloom,
And I'll water them all with the tears of a son.                40

Adieu, my loved parent! the trial is past–
Again thy loved bosom my dwelling may be;
And long as the name of thy darling shall last,
All due be the song and the honour to thee!

                                                           H.

# Tales and Anecdotes
# of the Pastoral Life

## No. III

As soon as the marriage ceremony was over, all the company shook
hands with the young couple, and wished them every kind of joy and
felicity. The rusticity of their benisons amused me, and there were
several of them that I have never to this day been able to comprehend. As for instance,–one wished them "thumpin luck and fat
weans;" another, "a bien rannle-bauks, and tight thack and rape o'er
their heads;" a third gave them "a routh aumrie and a close nieve;"
and the lasses wished them "as mony hinny moons as the family had
fingers an' taes." I took notes of these at the time, and many more,
and set them down precisely as they were spoken; all of them have

doubtless meanings attached to them, but these are perhaps the least mystical.

I expected now that we should go quietly to our dinner; but instead of that, they again rushed rapidly away towards the green, crying out, "Now for the broose! now for the broose!"–"The people are unquestionably mad," said I to one that stood beside me; "are they really going to run their horses again among such ravines and bogs as these? they must be dissuaded from it." The man informed me that the race was now to be on foot; that there were always two races–the first on horseback for the bride's napkin, and the second on foot for the bridegroom's spurs. I asked him how it came that they had thus altered the order of things in the appropriation of the prizes, for that the spurs would be the fittest for the riders, as the napkin would for the runners. He admitted this, but could adduce no reason why it was otherwise, save that "it was the gude auld gate, and it would be a pity to alter it." He likewise informed me, that it was customary for some to run on the bride's part, and some on the bridegroom's; and that it was looked on as a great honour to the country, or connexions of either party, to bear the broose away from the other. Accordingly, on our way to the race-ground, the bridegroom was recruiting hard for runners on his part, and, by the time we reached the starting-place, had gained the consent of five. One now asked the *best-man* why he was not recruiting in behalf of the bride. "Never mind," said he; "do ye strip an' mak ready–I'll find them on the bride's part that will do a' the turn." It was instantly rumoured around, that he had brought one all the way from Liddesdale to carry the prize away on the bride's part, and that he was the best runner on all the Border side. The runners, that were all so brisk of late, were now struck dumb; and I marked them going one by one, eyeing the stranger with a jealous curiosity, and measuring him with their eyes from head to foot.–No, not one of them would venture to take the field against him!–"they war only jokin'– they never intendit to rin–they war just jaunderin wi' the bridegroom for fun."–"Come, fling aff your claes, Hobby, an' let them see that ye're ready for them," said the best-man. The stranger obeyed–he was a tall, slender, and handsome youth, with brown hair, prominent features, and a ruddy complexion.–"Come, lads," said the best man, "Hobby canna stand wanting his claes; if nane of ye are ready to start with him in twa minutes, he shall rin the course himsel, and then I think the folk o' this country are shamed for ever."–"No sae fast," said a little funny-looking fellow, who instantly began to strip off his stockings and shoes; "no sae fast, lad; he may won, but he sanna won untried." A committee was instantly formed apart, where it was soon agreed, that all the good runners there should, with one accord, start against this stranger; for that, "if naebody ran but Tam the tailor, they wad be a' shamed thegither, for Tam wad never come within a stane-clod o' him."—"Hout, ay—that's something like yoursels, callants," said old John; "try him—he's but a saft feckless-like chiel; I think ye needna be sae feared for him."—"It is a' ye ken," said another; "do nae ye see that he's lingit like a grew—and he'll rin like ane;—they say he rins faster than a horse can gallop." "I'll try him on my Cameronian whenever he likes," said Aberlosk; "him that beats a Cameronian has but another to beat."

In half a minute after this, seven athletic youths were standing in a row stripped, and panting for the race; and I could note, by the paleness of their faces, how anxious they were about the result—all save Aedie o' Aberlosk, on whom the whisky had made some impression, and who seemed only intent on making fun. At the distance of 500 yards there was a man placed, whom they denominated *the stoop*, and who had his hat raised on the end of his staff, lest another might be mistaken for him. Around this *stoop* they were to run, and return to the starting-place, making in all a heat of only 1000 yards, which I was told is the customary length of a race all over that country. They took all hold of one another's hands—the best-man adjusted the line in which they stood, and then gave the word as follows, with considerable pauses between: *Once—twice—thrice,*—and off they flew like lightning, in the most beautiful style I ever beheld. The ground was rough and unequal, but there was no restraint or management practised; every one set out on full speed from the very first. The Borderer took the lead, and had soon distanced them a considerable space—all save Aberlosk, who kept close at his side, straining and twisting his face in a most tremendous manner; at length he got rather before him, but it was an over-stretch—Aedie fell flat on his face, nor did he offer to rise, but lay still on the spot, puffing and swearing against the champion of Liddesdale.

Hobby cleared the *stoop* first by about twenty yards;—the rest turned in such a group that I could not discern in what order, but they were all obliged to turn it to the right, or what they called "sun-ways-about," on pain of losing the race. The generality of the "weddingers" were now quite silent, and looked very blank when they saw this stranger still keeping so far a-head. Aberlosk tried to make them all fall one by one, by creeping in before them as they passed; and at length laid hold of the hindmost by the foot, and brought him down.

By this time two of the Borderer's acquaintances had run down the green to meet him, and encourage him on. "Weel done, Hobby!" they were shouting: "Weel done, Hobby! Liddesdale for ever!–Let them lick at that!–Let the benty-necks crack now!–Weel done, Hobby!"–I really felt as much interested about the issue, at this time, as it was possible for any of the adverse parties to be. The enthusiasm seemed contagious; for though I knew not one side from the other, yet was I running among the rest, and shouting as they did. A sort of half-animated murmur now began to spread, and gained ground every moment. A little gruff Cossack-looking peasant came running near with a peculiar wildness in his looks, and accosted one of the men that were cheering Hobby. "Dinna be just sae loud an' ye like, Willie Beattie; dinna mak nae mair din than just what's needfu'. Will o' Bellendine! haud till him, sir, or it's day wi' us! Hie, Will, if ever ye ran i' your life!–By Jehu, sir, ye're winning every third step!– He has him *dead!* he has him *dead!*" The murmur, which had increased like the rushing of many waters, now terminated in a frantic shout. Hobby had strained too hard at first, in order to turn the stoop before Aberlosk, who never intended turning it at all–the other youth was indeed fast gaining on him, and I saw his lips growing pale, and his knees plaiting as if unable to bear his weight–his breath was quite exhausted, and though within twenty yards of the stoop, Will began to shoulder by him. So anxious was Hobby now to keep his ground, that his body pressed onward faster than his feet could keep up with it, and his face, in consequence, came deliberately against the earth–he could not be said to fall, for he just run on till he could get no farther for something that stopped him. Will o' Bellendine won the broose amid clamours of applause, which he seemed fully to appreciate–the rest were over Hobby in a moment; and if it had not been for the wayward freaks of Aberlosk, this redoubted champion would fairly have won the mell.

The lad that Aedie overthrew, in the midst of his career, was very angry with him on account of the outrage–but Aedie cared for no man's anger. "The man's mad," said he; "wad ye attempt to strive wi' the champion of Liddesdale?–Hout, hout! haud your tongue; ye're muckle better as ye are. I sall tak the half o' the mell wi' ye."

On our return to the house, I was anxious to learn something of Aedie, who seemed to be a very singular character. Upon applying to a farmer of his acquaintance, I was told a number of curious and extravagant stories of him, one or two of which I shall insert here, as I profess to be giving anecdotes of the country life.

He once quarrelled with another farmer on the highway, who, getting into a furious rage, rode at Aedie to knock him down. Aedie, who was on foot, fled with all his might to the top of a large dunghill for shelter, where, getting hold of a graip (a three-pronged fork used in agriculture), he attacked his adversary with such an overflow of dung, that his horse took fright, and in spite of all he could do, run clear off with him, and left Aedie master of the field. The farmer, in high wrath, sent him a challenge to fight with pistols, in a place called Selkith Hope, early in the morning. This is an extremely wild, steep, and narrow glen. Aedie attended, but kept high up on the hill; and when his enemy reached the narrowest part of the Hope, began the attack by rolling great stones at him down from the mountain. Nothing could be more appalling than this–the farmer and his horse were both alike terrified, and, as Aedie expressed it, "he set them baith back the gate they cam, as their heads had been a lowe."

Another time, in that same Hope of Selkith, he met a stranger, whom he mistook for another man called Jamie Sword; and because the man denied that he was Jamie Sword, Aedie fastened a quarrel on him, insisting on him either being Jamie Sword, or giving some proofs to the contrary. It was very impudent in him, he said, to give any man the lie, when he could produce no evidence of his being wrong. The man gave him his word that he was not Jamie Sword. "O, but that's naething," said Aedie, "I give you my word that you are, and I think my word's as good as yours ony day." Finally, he told the man, that if he would not acknowledge that he was wrong, and confess that he was Jamie Sword, he would fight him.–He did so, and got himself severely thrashed.

The following is a copy of a letter, written by Aedie to a great personage, dated Aberlosk, May 27th, 1806.*

*"To George the Third, London.*
DEAR SIR,–I went thirty miles on foot yesterday to pay your taxes, and, after all, the bodies would not take them, saying, that I was too late, and that they must now be recovered, with expenses, by regular course of law. I thought if your Majesty was like me, money would never come wrong to you, although it were a few days too late; so I enclose you £27 in notes, and half-a-guinea, which is the amount of what they charge me for last year, and fourpence halfpenny over. You must send me a

---

* In case our readers should imagine that this curious epistle is a mere coinage of our facetious correspondent, we are enabled, from undoubted authority, to assure them, that both Aedie and his letter are faithful transcripts from real and *existing originals.*                                                                 EDITOR.

receipt when the coach comes back, else they will not believe that I have paid you.

Direct to the care of Andrew Wilson, butcher in Hawick.
I am, dear sir, your most humble servant,

A*** B****.

To the King.

P. S.–This way of taxing the farmers will never do; you will see the upshot."

It has been reported over all that country, that this letter reached its destination, and that a receipt was returned in due course of post; but the truth is (and for the joke's sake, it is a great pity it should have been so), that the singularity of the address caused some friends to open the letter, and return it, with the money, to the owner; but not before they had taken a copy of it, from which the above is exactly transcribed.
H.

*(To be continued.)*

# Extempore Song

I downa laugh, I downa sing,
  Tho' the wine flows round fu' merrily;
Tho' mony a bonny ee smiles round
  An' ilk ane is turned on me.
I was the blithest of you a'                                      5
  The last time I sat in this ring
But there's a blank at my right hand
  That checks the tongue that fain wad sing

O let me sit in listless mood!
  I'll be as cheerfu' as I may:                                  10
I knew not when I took my seat
  That my sweet flowret was away
Fresh as the ruddy dawn of day
  Was the young cheek that ance I kiss'd
Wild as the laverock's matin lay                                 15
  The song of love that I did list

And I have clasp'd a slender waist
  And press'd a hand that press'd again
The time–the place–the words that past
  This heart maun evermair retain                    20
My days of bliss are on the wing
  My hopes, of love, and fame to share;
Then dinna bid your minstrel sing,
  Whose thoughts are gane, he kens nae where!
                                        J. HOGG

# Elegy

FAIR was thy blossom, tender flower,
  That opened like the rose in May,
Though nursed beneath the chilly shower
  Of fell regret for love's decay!

How oft thy mother heaved the sigh                    5
  O'er wreathes of honour early shorn,
Before thy sweet and guiltless eye
  Had opened on the dawn of morn!

How oft above thy lowly bed,
  When all in silence slumbered low,                  10
The fond and filial tear was shed,
  Thou child of love, of shame, and woe!

Her wronged, but gentle bosom burned
  With joy thy opening bloom to see,
The only breast that o'er thee yearned,               15
  The only heart that cared for thee.

Oft her young eye, with tear-drops bright,
  Pleaded with Heaven for her sweet child,
When faded dreams of past delight
  O'er recollection wandered wild.                    20

Fair was thy blossom, bonny flower,
  Fair as the softest wreath of spring,
When late I saw thee seek the bower
  In peace thy morning hymn to sing!

Thy little feet across the lawn              25
     Scarce from the primrose pressed the dew,
I thought the Spirit of the dawn
     Before me to the greenwood flew.

Even then the shaft was on the wing,
     Thy spotless soul from earth to sever;       30
A tear of pity wet the string
     That twang'd and sealed thy doom forever.

I saw thee late the emblem fair
     Of beauty, innocence, and truth,
Stand tiptoe on the verge of air,           35
     'Twixt childhood and unstable youth:

But now I see thee stretched at rest,
     To break that rest shall wake no morrow;
Pale as the grave-flower on thy breast!
     Poor child of love, of shame, and sorrow!     40

May thy long sleep be sound and sweet,
     Thy visions fraught with bliss to be;
And long the daisy, emblem meet,
     Shall shed its earliest tear o'er thee.

J. HOGG.

Translation of an Ancient
# Chaldee Manuscript
*Supposed to have been written by Daniel*

*[Manuscript version]*

And I saw in my dream, and behold one like the messenger of a king
came toward me from the east, and he took me up and carried me
into the midst of the great city that looketh toward the north, and
toward the east, and ruleth over every people, and kindred, and tongue
that handle the pen of the writer.

And he said unto me take heed what thou seest for great things
shall come of it, the moving of a straw shall be as the whirlwind, and
the shaking of a reed as the great tempest.

And I looked, and behold a man clothed in plain apparrel stood
in the door of his house; and I saw his name and the number of his
name; and his name was as it had been the colour of ebony, and his

number was the number of a maiden, when the days of the years of her virginity have expired.

And I turned mine eyes, and behold two beasts came from the lands of the borders of the south, and when I saw them I wondered with great admiration.

The one beast was like a lamb, and the other like a bear; and they had wings in their heads; their faces also were like the faces of men, the joints of their legs like the polished cedars of Lebanon, and their feet like the feet of horses preparing to go forth to battle; and then they arose, and they came onward over the face of the earth, and they touched not the ground as they went.

And they came unto the man who was clothed in plain apparrel and stood in the door of his house.

And they said unto him, give us of thy wealth that we may eat and live, and thou shalt enjoy the fruits of our labours for a time, times or half a time.

And he answered and said unto them what will you do unto me whereunto I may employ you?

And the one said I will teach the people of thy land to till and to sow; to reap the harvest, and gather the sheaves into the barn; to feed their flocks, and enrich themselves with the wool.

And the other said I will teach the children of thy people to know and discern betwixt right and wrong, the good and the evil, and in all things that relate to learning, and knowledge, and understanding.

And they proffered unto him a book; and they said unto him take thou this, and give us a sum of money that we may eat and drink that our souls may live.

And we will put words into the book that shall astonish the children of thy people; and it shall be a light to thy feet and a lamp unto thy path; it shall also bring bread to thy houshold and a portion to thy maidens.

And the man hearkened to their voice; and he took the book and gave them a piece of money, and they went away rejoicing in heart, and I heard a great noise as if it had been the noise of many chariots, and of horsemen horsing on their horse.*

But after many days they put no words into the book; and the man was astonied, and waxed wroth; and he said unto them what is this that you have done unto me, and how shall I answer those to whom I am engaged? And they said what is that unto us? see thou to that.

---

* singular as the formation of this sentence may appear it could not otherwise be literally translated into our language

And the man wist not what to do, and he called together the friends of his youth, and all those on whose wisdom he could rely and he pressed them, and they put words into the book, and it went forth abroad, and all the world wondered after the book, and after the two beasts that had put such amazing words into the book.

And in those days, and at that time, there lived also a man who was *Crafty* in counsel and cunning in all manner of working; and the man was an upright and a just man, one that feared God and eschewed evil; and he never was accused before any judge of fraud, or of perjury, or deceit; for the man was honourable among the children of men.

And I beheld the man and he was comely and well-favoured, and he had a notable horn in his forehead with which he ruled the nations.

And I saw the horn that it had eyes, and a mouth speaking great things, and it magnified itself even to the prince of the host, and it cast down the truth to the ground, and it practised and prospered.

And when the man saw the book, and beheld the things that were in the book he was troubled in spirit and much cast down.

And he said unto himself why stand I idle here and why do not I bestir myself? lo! this book shall become a devouring sword in the hand of mine adversary, and with it will he root up or loosen the horn that is in my forehead, and the hope of my gains shall perish from the face of the earth.

And he hated the book, and the two beasts that had put such words into the book, for he judged according to the reports of men; nevertheless the man was *Crafty* in counsel, and more cunning than his fellows.

And he said unto the two beasts, come ye and put your trust under the shadow of my wings, and we will destroy the man whose name is as ebony, and his book.

And I will overturn, overturn, overturn, it; and I will tear it in pieces, and cast it out like dung upon the face of the earth.

And we will tread him down as the dust of the streets, and trample him under our feet; and we will break him to pieces and grind him to powder and cast him into the brook Kidron.

And I will make of you a great name; and I will place you next to the horn that is in my forehead, and it shall be a shelter to you in the day of great adversity; and it shall defend you from the horn of the unicorn, and from the might of the bulls of Bashan.

And you shall be watchers, and a guard unto it, from the emmet, and the spider, and the toad after his kind.

And from the mole that walketh in darkness; and from the blow-fly after his kind, and the maggot after his kind.

And by these means you shall wax very great, for the things that are low shall be exalted.

And the two beasts gave ear unto him, and they came over unto him, and bowed down before him with their faces to the earth; and his heart was lifted up, and I saw them marshalling their hosts for the battle.

But when the tidings of these things came to the man who was clothed in plain apparrel, he was sore dismayed, and his countenance fell.

And it repented him that he had taken the book or sent it forth abroad; and he said I have been sore decieved and betrayed; but I will of myself yield up the book, and burn it with fire, and give its ashes to the winds of heaven.

But certain sons of Belial that were there present said unto him. Why art thou dismayed? and why is thy countenance fallen?

Go to now; gird up thy loins like a man, and call unto thee thy friends, and the men of thine houshold, and thou shalt behold and see that they that are for thee are more and mightier than those that be against thee.

And when the man whose name was as ebony, and whose number was the number of a maiden when the days of the years of her virginity have expired, heard this saying he turned about.

And he took from under his girdle a gem of curious workmanship of silver, made by the hands of a cunning artificier, and overlaid within with pure gold; and he took from thence something in colour like unto the dust of the earth or the ashes that remain of a furnace, and he snuffed it up like the east wind, and returned the gem again into its place.

And he opened his mouth, and he said unto them, as thou hast spoken so shall it be done.

Woe unto all them that take part with the man who is *Crafty* in counsel, and with the two beasts!

For I will arise, and increase my strength, and come upon them like the locust of the desert, to abolish, and overwhelm, and to destroy, and to pass over.

And he called unto him the beautiful leopard from the valley of the palm trees, whose going forth was comely as the grey-hound, and his eyes like the lightening of flame.

And he called the curlew and the falcon from among the birds that fly in the firmament of heaven; the fiery lynx also that lurked behind the white cottage on the mountains and his fellow the dark wolf that delighted in the times of ancient days.

And he brought down the great wild boar from the forest of Lebanon, and he roused up his sluggish spirit, and I saw him whetting his dreadful tusks for the battle.

And the griffon came with the bond of the testimony of contention between his teeth; and I saw him standing over the body of one that had been buried long in the grave, defending it from all around, that he might devour up the carcass himself.

And the slow-hound and the beagle after their kind, and the hyena that raiseth up and gnaweth the bones of the dead, with all the beasts of the field more than could be numbered, they were so many.

And the hosts drew near; and the city was moved; and my spirit failed within me, and I was sore afraid, and I turned to escape away.

And the man said unto me cry. And I said what shall I cry for the day of vengeance and retribution is come upon all those that ruled the nations with a rod of iron?

And I fled into an inner chamber to hide myself, and I heard a great tumult but I knew not what it was.


# Translation from an Ancient
# Chaldee Manuscript

[THE present age seems destined to witness the recovery of many admirable pieces of writing, which had been supposed to be lost for ever. The Eruditi of Milan are not the only persons who have to boast of being the instruments of these resuscitations. We have been favoured with the following translation of a Chaldee MS. which is preserved in the great Library of Paris (Salle 2d, No 53, B.A.M.M.), by a gentleman whose attainments in Oriental Learning are well known to the public. It is said that the celebrated Silvester De Sacy is at present occupied with a publication of the original. It will be prefaced by an Inquiry into the Age when it was written, and the name of the writer.]

## CHAPTER I

1 AND I saw in my dream, and behold one like the messenger of a King came toward me from the east, and he took me up and carried me into the midst of the great city that looketh toward the north and toward the east, and ruleth over every people, and kindred, and tongue, that handle the pen of the writer.

2 And he said unto me, Take heed what thou seest, for great things shall come of it,—the moving of a straw shall be as the whirlwind, and the shaking of a reed as the great tempest.

3 And I looked, and behold a man clothed in plain apparel stood in the door of his house: and I saw his name, and the number of his name; and his name was as it had been the colour of ebony, and his number was the number of a maiden, when the days of the years of her virginity have expired.

4 And I turned mine eyes, and behold two beasts came from the land of the borders of the South; and when I saw them I wondered with great admiration.

5 The one beast was like unto a lamb, and the other like unto a bear; and they had wings on their heads; their faces also were like the faces of men, the joints of their legs like the polished cedars of Lebanon, and their feet like the feet of horses preparing to go forth to battle: and they arose and they came onward over the face of the earth, and they touched not the ground as they went.

6 And they came unto the man who was clothed in plain apparel, and stood in the door of his house.

7 And they said unto him, Give us of thy wealth, that we may eat and live, and thou shalt enjoy the fruits of our labours for a time, times, or half a time.

8 And he answered and said unto them, What will you do unto me whereunto I may employ you?

9 And the one said, I will teach the people of thy land to till and to sow; to reap the harvest and gather the sheaves into the barn; to feed their flocks, and enrich themselves with the wool.

10 And the other said, I will teach the children of thy people to know and discern betwixt right and wrong, the good and the evil, and in all things that relate to learning, and knowledge, and understanding.

11 And they proffered unto him a Book; and they said unto him, Take thou this, and give us a piece of money, that we may eat and drink that our souls may live.

12 And we will put words into the Book that shall astonish the children of thy people; and it shall be a light unto thy feet, and a lamp unto thy path; it shall also bring bread to thy household, and a portion to thy maidens.

13 And the man hearkened to their voice, and he took the Book and gave them a piece of money, and they went away rejoicing in heart. And I heard a great noise, as if it had been the noise of many chariots, and of horsemen horsing upon their horses.

14 But after many days they put no words into the Book, and the man was astonied and waxed wroth, and he said unto them, What is this that you have done unto me, and how shall I answer those to whom I am engaged? And they said, What is this unto us? see thou to that.

15 And the man wist not what for to do; and he called together the friends of his youth, and all those whose heart was as his heart, and he entreated them, and they put words into the Book, and it went forth abroad, and all the world wondered after the Book, and after the two beasts that had put such amazing words into the Book.

16 ¶ Now in those days, there lived also a man who was crafty in counsel, and cunning in all manner of working:

17 And I beheld the man, and he was comely and well-favoured, and he had a notable horn in his forehead wherewith he ruled the nations.

18 And I saw the horn, that it had eyes, and a mouth speaking great things, and it magnified itself even to the Prince of the Host, and it cast down the truth to the ground, and it grew and prospered.

19 And when this man saw the Book, and beheld the things that were in the Book, he was troubled in spirit, and much cast down.

20 And he said unto himself, Why stand I idle here, and why do I not bestir myself? Lo! this Book shall become a devouring sword in the hand of mine adversary, and with it will he root up or loosen the horn that is in my forehead, and the hope of my gains shall perish from the face of the earth.

21 And he hated the Book, and the two beasts that had put words into the Book, for he judged according to the reports of men; nevertheless, the man was crafty in counsel, and more cunning than his fellows.

22 And he said unto the two beasts, Come ye and put your trust under the shadow of my wings, and we will destroy the man whose name is as ebony, and his Book.

23 And I will tear it in pieces, and cast it out like dung upon the face of the earth.

24 And we will tread him down as the dust of the streets, and trample him under our feet; and we will break him to pieces, and grind him to powder, and cast him into the brook Kedron.

25 And I will make of you a great name; and I will place you next to the horn that is in my forehead, and it shall be a shelter to you in the day of great adversity; and it shall defend you from the horn of the unicorn, and from the might of the Bulls of Bashan.

26 And you shall be watchers and a guard unto it from the emmet

and the spider, and the toad after his kind.

27 And from the mole that walketh in darkness, and from the blow-fly after his kind, and the canker-worm after his kind, and the maggot after his kind.

28 And by these means you shall wax very great, for the things that are low shall be exalted.

29 And the two beasts gave ear unto him; and they came over unto him, and bowed down before him with their faces to the earth.

30 ¶ But when the tidings of these things came to the man who was clothed in plain apparel, he was sore dismayed, and his countenance fell.

31 And it repented him that he had taken the Book, or sent it forth abroad: and he said, I have been sore deceived and betrayed; but I will of myself yield up the Book, and burn it with fire, and give its ashes to the winds of heaven.

32 But certain that were there present said unto him, Why art thou dismayed? and why is thy countenance fallen? Go to now; gird up thy loins like a man, and call unto thee thy friends, and the men of thine household, and thou shalt behold and see that they that are for thee are more and mightier than those that be against thee.

33 And when the man whose name was as ebony, and whose number was the number of a maiden when the days of the years of her virginity have expired, heard this saying, he turned about;

34 And he took from under his girdle a gem of curious workmanship of silver, made by the hand of a cunning artificer, and overlaid within with pure gold; and he took from thence something in colour like unto the dust of the earth, or the ashes that remain of a furnace, and he snuffed it up like the east wind, and returned the gem again into its place.

35 Whereupon he opened his mouth, and he said unto them, As thou hast spoken, so shall it be done.

36 Woe unto all them that take part with the man who is crafty in counsel, and with the two beasts!

37 For I will arise and increase my strength, and come upon them like the locust of the desert, to abolish and overwhelm, and to destroy, and to pass over.

38 So he called together the wise men of the city, both from the Old City and from the city which is on this side of the valley, even the New City, which looketh towards the north; and the wise men came.

39 And, lo! there stood before him an aged man, whose hair was white as snow, and in whose hand there was a mirror, wherein passed

to and fro the images of the ancient days.

40 And he said, Behold, I am stricken in years, mine eyes are dim. What will ye that I do unto you? Seek ye them that are young.

41 And all the young men that were there lifted up their voice and said, We have sat at thy feet all the days of the years which we have lived upon the earth; and that which we know is thine, and our learning is thine; and as thou sayest, even so will we do.

42 And he said unto them, Do ye what is meet in this thing, and let not our friend be discomfited, neither let the man which is crafty rejoice, nor the two beasts.

43 And when he had said this, he arose and went away; and all the young men arose up, and humbled themselves before him when he went away.

44 Then spake the man clothed in plain apparel to the great magician who dwelleth in the old fastness, hard by the river Jordan, which is by the Border. And the magician opened his mouth, and said, Lo! my heart wisheth thy good, and let the thing prosper which is in thy hands to do it.

45 But thou seest that my hands are full of working, and my labour is great. For lo I have to feed all the people of my land, and none knoweth whence his food cometh, but each man openeth his mouth, and my hand filleth it with pleasant things.

46 Moreover, thine adversary also is of my familiars.

47 The land is before thee, draw thou up thy hosts for the battle in the place of Princes, over against thine adversary, which hath his station near the mount of the Proclamation; quit ye as men, and let favour be shewn unto him which is most valiant.

48 Yet be thou silent, peradventure will I help thee some little.

49 So he made request also unto a wise man which had come out of Joppa, where the ships are, one that had sojourned in far countries, whose wisdom is great above all the children of the east, one which teacheth the sons of the honourable men, and speaketh wonderful things in the schools of the learned men.

50 One which speaketh of trees and of beasts, and of fowl and of creeping things, and of fishes, from the great Leviathan that is in the deep sea even unto the small muscle which dwelleth in the shell of the rock,

51 Moreover, of all manner of precious stones, and of the ancient mountains, and of the moving of the great waters.

52 One which had been led before the Chief Priests, and lauded of them for smiting a worshipper of Fire in the land, which being interpreted, signifieth bread.

53 And he said, Behold, here is a round stone, set thou that in a ring, and put the ring upon thy finger, and behold while the ring is upon thy finger, thou shalt have no fear of the man which is crafty, neither of the two beasts.

54 Then the man spake to a wise man which had a light in his hand and a crown of pearls upon his head, and he said, Behold I will brew a sharp poison for the man which is crafty and his two beasts. Wait ye till I come. So he arose also and went his way.

55 Also to a wise young man, which is learned in the law, even as his father was learned, and who lifteth up his voice in the courts of the treasury of our Lord the King, with his fellow, who is one of the sons of the Prophets.

56 He spake also to a learned man who sendeth all the King's messengers to the four corners of the great city, each man clothed in scarlet, and bearing a bundle of letters, touching the affairs of men, in his right hand.

57 He spake also unto a sweet singer, who is cunning to play upon all stringed instruments, who weareth a charm upon his bosom, even a stone, whereon is engraved ancient writing. And he framed songs, and waxed very wroth against the horn which is in the forehead of the man which is crafty.

58 Also to one who had been a physician in his youth, and who had dwelt with the keeper of the gates of the wise men.

59 But he was now a dealer in wine and oil, and in the fishes which are taken in the nets of the people of the west.

60 Also in strong drink.

61 Then sent he for one cunning in sharp instruments and edged tools, even in razors; but he had taken unto himself a wife, and could not come.

62 But behold, while they were yet speaking, they heard a voice of one screeching at the gate, and the voice was a sharp voice, even like the voice of the unclean bird which buildeth its nest in the corner of the temple, and defileth the holy places.

63 But they opened not the door, neither answered they a word to the voice of its screaming. So the unclean thing flew away, neither could they find any trace of its going.

64 And there was a silence in the assembly. And behold, when they began to speak, they were too many, neither could the man know what was the meaning of their counsel, for they spake together, and the voice of their speaking was mingled.

65 So the man was sore perplexed, and he wist not what for to do.

## CHAPTER II

1 Now, behold, as soon as they were gone, he sat down in his inner chamber, which looketh toward the street of Oman, and the road of Gabriel, as thou goest up into the land of Ambrose, and the man leaned with his face upon his hand.

2 And while he was yet musing, there stood before him a man clothed in dark garments, having a veil upon his head; and there was a rod in his hand.

3 And he said, Arise, let not thine heart be discouraged, neither let it be afraid.

4 Behold, if thou wilt listen unto me, I will deliver thee out of all thy distresses, neither shall any be able to touch a hair of thy head.

5 And when the man heard the voice of his speaking, behold there was in his voice courage, and in his counsel boldness. And he said unto him, Do thou as it seemeth unto thee; as thou sayest even so will I do.

6 And the man who had come in answered and said, Behold I will call mighty creatures which will comfort thee, and destroy the power of thy adversary, and will devour the two beasts.

7 So he gave unto the man in plain apparel a tablet, containing the names of those upon whom he should call. And when he called they came; and whomsoever he asked he came.

8 And the man with the veil stood by, but there was a cloud about him, neither could they which came see him, nor tell who it was that compelled their coming.

9 And they came in the likeness of living things, but I knew not who they were which came.

10 And the first which came was after the likeness of the beautiful leopard, from the valley of the palm trees, whose going forth was comely as the grey-hound, and his eyes like the lightning of fiery flame.

11 And the second was the lynx that lurketh behind the white cottage on the mountains.

12 There came also, from a far country, the scorpion, which delighteth to sting the faces of men, that he might sting sorely the countenance of the man which is crafty, and of the two beasts.

13 Also the great wild boar from the forest of Lebanon, and he roused up his spirit, and I saw him whetting his dreadful tusks for the battle.

14 And the griffin came with a roll of the names of those whose blood had been shed between his teeth: and I saw him standing over the body of one that had been buried long in the grave, defending it

from all men; and behold there were none which durst come near him.

15 Also the black eagle of the desert, whose cry is as the sound of an unknown tongue, which flieth over the ruins of the ancient cities, and hath his dwelling among the tombs of the wise men.

16 Also the stork which buildeth upon the house-top, and devoureth all manner of unclean things, and all beetles, and all manner of flies, and much worms.

17 And the hyæna that escheweth the light, and cometh forth at the evening tide to raise up and gnaw the bones of the dead, and is as a riddle unto the vain man.

18 And the beagle and the slow-hound after their kind, and all the beasts of the field, more than could be numbered, they were so many.

19 ¶ And when they were all gathered together, the man which was clothed in plain apparel looked round about, and his heart was right merry when he saw the mighty creatures which had come in unto him, and heard the tumult of their voices, and the noise of the flapping of their wings.

20 And he lifted up his voice, and shouted with a great shout, and said, Behold, I am increased greatly, and I will do terrible things to the man who is crafty and to his two beasts.

21 And he sent away a swift messenger for a physician, which healeth all manner of bruises, and wounds, and putrifying sores, lest that he should go for to heal up the wounds of the man which is crafty, or of his two beasts.

22 (Now this physician was a mild man, neither was there any gall within him, yet he went not.)

## Chapter III

1 And while these things were yet doing, I heard a great rushing, and the sound as of a mighty wind: and I looked over the valley into the old city, and there was a tumult over against the mount of Proclamation.

2 For when tidings of these things came to the man which was crafty, his heart died within him, and he waxed sore afraid.

3 And he said unto himself, What is this? Behold, mine adversary is very mighty, neither can I go forth to fight him: for whom have I save myself only, and my two beasts?

4 And while he was yet speaking, the two beasts stood before him.

5 And the beast which was like unto a bear said, Behold, it is yet

harvest, and how can I leave my corn which is in the fields? If I go forth to make war upon the man whose name is as ebony, the Philistines will come into my farm, and carry away all the full sheaves which are ready.

6 And the beast which was like unto a lamb answered and said, Lo! my legs are weary, and the Egyptians which were wont for to carry me are clean gone; and wherewithal shall I go forth to make war upon the man whose name is as ebony?

7 Nevertheless will I put a sweet song against him into thy Book.

8 But the man which was crafty answered and said, Unprofitable generation! ye have given unto me a horn which is empty, and a horse which hath no feet. If ye go not forth to fight with mine adversary, deliver me up the meat which I have given unto you, and the penny which ye have of me, that I may hire others who will fight with the man whose name is as ebony.

9 And the beasts spake not at all, neither answered they him one word.

10 But as they sat before him, the beast which was like unto a bear took courage; and he opened his mouth and said,

11 O man, thou hast fed me heretofore, and whatever entereth within my lips is thine. Why now should we fall out about this thing?

12 Call unto thee thy counsellors, the spirits, and the wise men, and the magicians, if haply they may advise thee touching the man whose name is as ebony, and the creatures which are within his gates. Whatsoever they say, that shall be done.

13 Yet the man was not pleased, neither was his countenance lightened: nevertheless, he did even as the beast said.

14 So he called unto him a familiar spirit, unto whom he had sold himself.

15 But the spirit was a wicked spirit and a cruel: so he answered and said, Lo, have not I put great might into the horn which is in thy forehead? What more said I ever that I would do unto thee? Thy soul is in my hands: do as thou listest in this thing.

16 But the man entreated him sorely, yet he listened not: for he had great fear of the vision of the man who was clothed in dark garments, and who had a veil upon his head;

17 (For he was of the seed of those which have command over the devils.)

18 And while the beasts were yet looking, lo, he was not;

19 For even in the twinkling of an eye he was present in the courts of the palace, to tempt the souls of the chief priests, and the scribes, and all those which administer the law for the king, and to deliver

some malefactors which he loved out of their hand.

20 ¶ Then the man called with a loud voice on some other spirits, in whom he put his trust.

21 And the first was a cunning spirit, which hath his dwelling in the secret places of the earth, and hath command over the snow and the hail, and is as a pestilence unto the poor man: for when he is hungry he lifteth up the lid of his meal-garnel, to take out meal, and lo! it is full of strong ice.

22 And the second was a little blind spirit, which hath a number upon his forehead; and he walketh to and fro continually, and is the chief of the heathen which are the worshippers of fire. He also is of the seed of the prophets, and ministered in the temple while he was yet young; but he went out, and became one of the scoffers.

23 But when these spirits heard the words of the man, and perceived his trouble, they gave no ear unto his outcry, neither listened they to the voice of his supplication.

24 And they laughed at the man with a loud laughter, and said unto him, Lo, shall we leave our digging into the bowels of the earth, or our ice, or our fire, with which we deceive the nations, and come down to be as it were servants unto thee and these two beasts, which are lame beasts, and unprofitable? Go to, man; seek thou them which are of thy fellows.

25 And they vanished from his sight: and he heard the voice of their laughter, both he and his two beasts.

26 ¶ But when the spirits were gone he said unto himself, I will arise and go unto a magician which is of my friends: of a surety he will devise some remedy, and free me out of all my distresses.

27 So he arose and came unto that great magician which hath his dwelling in the old fastness hard by the river Jordan, which is by the Border.

28 And the magician opened his mouth and said, Lo, my heart wisheth thy good, and let the thing prosper which is in thy hands to do it:

29 But thou seest that my hands are full of working, and my labour is great. For lo, I have to feed all the people of my land, and none knoweth whence his food cometh; but each man openeth his mouth, and my hand filleth it with pleasant things.

30 Moreover, thine adversary also is of my familiars.

31 The land is before thee: draw thou up thine hosts for the battle on the mount of Proclamation, and defy boldly thine enemy, which hath his camp in the place of Princes; quit ye as men, and let favour be shewn unto him which is most valiant.

32 Yet be thou silent: peradventure will I help thee some little.

33 But the man which is crafty saw that the magician loved him not. For he knew him of old, and they had had many dealings; and he perceived that he would not assist him in the day of his adversity.

34 So he turned about, and went out of his fastness. And he shook the dust from his feet, and said, Behold, I have given this magician much money, yet see now, he hath utterly deserted me. Verily, my fine gold hath perished.

35 But when he had come back unto his house, he found the two beasts which were yet there; and behold the beasts were gabbling together, and making much noise. And when he looked in, behold yet another beast; and they were all gabbling together.

36 Now the other beast was a beast which he loved not. A beast of burden which he had in his courts to hew wood and carry water, and to do all manner of unclean things. His face was like unto the face of an ape, and he chattered continually, and his nether parts were uncomely. Nevertheless his thighs were hairy, and the hair was as the shining of a sattin raiment, and he skipped with the branch of a tree in his hand, and he chewed a snail between his teeth.

37 Then said the man, Verily this beast is altogether unprofitable, and whatsoever I have given him to do, that hath he spoiled: he is a sinful thing, and speaketh abominably, his doings are impure, and all people are astonied that he abideth so long within my gates.

38 But if thou lookest upon him and observest his ways, behold he was born of his mother before yet the months were fulfilled, and the substance of a living thing is not in him, and his bones are like the potsherd which is broken against any stone.

39 Therefore my heart pitieth him, and I wish not that he be utterly famished; and I give unto him a little bread and wine that his soul may not faint; and I send him messages unto the towns and villages which are round about; and I give him such work as is meet for him.

40 But if we go forth to the battle, let him not go with us.

41 For behold the griffin hath heretofore wounded him, and the scorpion hath stung him sorely in the hips and the thighs, and also in the face.

42 Moreover the eagle of heaven also is his dread, and he is terrified for the flapping of his huge wings, and for his cry, which is like the voice of an unknown tongue, also his talons, which are sharper than any two edged sword.

43 And if it cometh to pass that he see them in the battle, he will not stand, but surely turn back and flee.

44 Therefore let us not take him with us, lest he be for an ensample unto the simple ones.

45 And while he was yet speaking, Behold, he heard a knocking upon the stair as if yet another beast had been coming:

46 And lo it was even so.

47 And another beast came in, whose disease was the murrain, who had eyes yet saw not, and whose laughter was like the laughter of them whose life is hidden, and which know not what they do.

48 And I heard a voice cry, Alas! alas! even as if it were Heu! heu!

49 Now the man was sick at heart when he perceived that he was there with the four beasts, and he said, Wretched man that I am, who shall deliver me from the weight of beasts which presseth sore upon me?

50 Then the four beasts waxed very wroth, and they all began for to cry out against the man which is crafty.

51 And he said, O race of beasts, be ye still, and keep silence until I consider what shall be done in this thing.

52 And while he spake, it seemed as if he trembled and were afraid of the four beasts and of the staves wherewith they skipped.


CHAPTER IV

1 But while he was yet trembling, lo, there came in one which was his familiar friend from his youth upwards, who keepeth the Books of the scribes, and is hired to expound things which he knoweth not, and collecteth together the remnants of the wise men.

2 And he opened his mouth and said, Lo, I have come even this hour from the camp of thine enemy, and I have spoken with the man whose name is as ebony.

3 And while I was speaking with him kindly, lo, some of the creatures which are within his gates took notice of me, and they warned him. So he put no faith nor trust in me.

4 But take thou good heed to thyself, for they that are against thee are mighty, and I have seen their numbers.

5 Now when the man heard this, he waxed yet more fearful.

6 Then came there unto his chamber another of his friends, one whose nose is like the beak of a bird of prey, whose mouth is foul, and his teeth reach from the right ear even unto the left, and he said, For why art thou so cast down? be of good cheer, behold I have an old breast plate which I will put on and go forth with thee unto the battle.

7 And further, he began to speak of the north, and the great men of

the north, even the giants, and the painted folk, but they stopped him, for of his speaking there is no end.

8 Then came there into his chamber a lean man, which hath his dwelling by the great pool to the north of the New City;

9 Which had been of the familiars of the man in plain apparel while they were yet youths, before he had been tempted of the man which is crafty.

10 Whose name had gone abroad among the nations on many books, even as his father's name had gone abroad.

11 One which delighteth in trees, and fruits, and flowers; the palm-tree and the olive, the pomegranate and the vine, the fig and the date, the tulip and the lily.

12 Which had sojourned in far lands, gathering herbs for the chief physician.

13 And he had a rotten melon on his head, after the fashion of an helmet.

14 And the man which is crafty began to take courage when his friends were gathered unto him, and he took his trumpet with bold-ness, and began to blow for them over which he had power.

15 But of them which listened to him, their limbs were weak, and their swords blunt, and the strings of their bows were moist.

16 Nevertheless, he made an assembly of them over against the mount of Proclamation: and these are the names of his host, and the number of his banners, whom he marshalled by the mount of Proc-lamation the day that he went forth to make war upon the man whose name is as ebony.

17 Now behold the four beasts were in the first band, yet they trembled and desired not to be in the front of the host.

18 And in the second band was one which teacheth in the schools of the young men, and he was clad in a gray garment whereof one half his wife had weaved.

19 Also, Samuel, a vain young man, and a simple, which sitteth in the King's Courts, and is a tool without edge in the hands of the oppressor.

20 Also, John, the brother of James, which is a man of low stature, and giveth out merry things, and is a lover of fables from his youth up.

21 Also, James, the young man which cometh out of the west coun-try,—which feareth God, and hateth all manner of usury; who babbleth of many things, and nibbleth the shoe-latchets of the mighty; one which darkeneth counsel with the multiplying of vain words:

22 To whose sayings no man taketh heed.

23 And in the third band was a grave man, even George, the chief of the synagogue, a principal man, yea, the leader of the doctors, whose beard reacheth down unto his girdle;

24 And one David, which dwelleth at the corner as thou goest up to the place of the old prison-house, which talketh touching all manner of pictures and graven images; and he came with a feather on his head.

25 And Andrew the chief physician, and Andrew his son, who is a smooth man, and one which handleth all wind instruments, and boweth himself down continually before the horn which is in the forehead of the man which is crafty, and worshippeth it.

26 With James the baker of sweet breads, which weareth a green mantle, which inhabiteth the dwelling of the nobles, and delighteth in the tongue of the strange man.

27 And Peter who raileth at his master.

28 And in the fourth band I saw the face of Samuel, which is a mason, who is clothed in gorgeous apparel, and his face was as the face of the moon shining in the north-west.

29 The number of his bands was four; and in the first band there were the four beasts,

30 And in the second band there were nine men of war, and in the third six, and in the fourth ten.

31 The number of the bands was four: and the number of them which were in the bands was twenty and nine: and the man which was crafty commanded them.

32 And the screaming bird sat upon his shoulder.

33 And there followed him many women which know not their right hand from the left, also some cattle.

34 And John the brother of Francis, and the man which offered Consolation to the man which is crafty.

35 Also seven young men, whereof no man could tell by what name they were called.

36 But when I saw them all gathered together, I said unto myself, Of a truth the man which is crafty hath many in his host, yet think I that scarcely will these be found sufficient against them which are in the gates of the man who is clothed in plain apparel.

37 And I thought of the vision of the man which was clothed in dark garments, and of the leopard, and the lynx, and the scorpion, and the eagle, and the great boar of Lebanon, and the griffin;

38 The stork, and the hyæna, and the beagle, and all the mighty creatures which are within the gates of the man in plain apparel.

39 Verily, the man which is crafty shall be defeated, and there

shall not escape one to tell of his overthrow.

40 And while I was yet speaking, the hosts drew near, and the city was moved; and my spirit failed within me, and I was sore afraid, and I turned to escape away.

41 And he that was like unto the messenger of a king, said unto me, Cry. And I said, What shall I cry? for the day of vengeance is come upon all those that ruled the nations with a rod of iron.

42 And I fled into an inner chamber to hide myself, and I heard a great tumult, but I wist not what it was.

# The Boar

And when all the people beheld the boar of Lebanon and how he fought, lo! their spirits were moved within them with laughter.

For he went forth into the host of the enemy in fury and in great wrath and he contended with them and cursed them and he smote certain of them and plucked off their hair, and they remained not but went and tarried at Jericho until their beards were grown.

And the wounds that he gave were unseemly for he cared not though he took forth their bowels in disorder trampling on them; and many there were who engaged him that were compelled to go over unto those of the circumcision.

But behold while the battle yet raged he came unto a place where dung had been laid upon the face of the ground but the men of the city had carried it forth in waggons to the field.

And he began with the snout of his nose to dig and to grovel in the soil where the abomination had lain in former days and his length of tail was twisted as a serpent twisteth herself before she spring upon the adversary.

And the man in the veil was grieviously offended and the leopard was moved with indignation for his heart is decietful more than the hearts of other beasts and he hath a sting in his tail wherewith he woundeth whom he listeth even though they put their trust in him.

And he came unto the man whose name is as ebony and he said unto him. Wherefore is it that thou sufferest that monster to remain with us behold now and see that he careth not what becometh of thee nor of us for instead of fighting with us he is digging in the ground for small roots and insects and things that are of no profit therefore expel him forth of our array for it is not meet that he go thus forth in the front of our host for seest thou not that the creature is in the gall of bitterness and the bond of iniquity?

And the man answered and said unto him Let him alone, for he is an hungered; and if they throw unto him an acorn he will go over to the other side; they that are not for me be against me.

Therefore let thou the creature alone; when he hath filled his belly peradventure he will go forth again into the host of mine enemies, and the wounds that he inflicteth are not to be borne.

And while he yet spoke, lo! there was a great cry, and all the host of the man that was crafty was scattered abroad into the four winds of the heaven; and there was not left unto him one that pisseth against the wall.

And the great city was moved as with the commotion of an earthquake for the voice of their cry was very great even as of a woman in travail.

For they ran to and fro over the streets of the city and without the gates for the space of three score and ten furlongs as the dust of the desert is moved by the whirlwind, or the leaves that fall from the trees when the storm of the mountains descendeth.

And the beasts themselves were astonied; and they looked one upon another and they said among themselves what meaneth this?

And I heard one beast speaking, and another beast said unto that certain beast which spoke What will be the end of these things and how is that mighty and comely host scattered in a moment in the twinkling of an eye?

And he said unto him it is the mole that walketh in darkness; for he hath looked up from under the earth and breathed upon the host with the breath of his nostrils, and there is in his breath that which decayeth.

For it is like the pestilence that rageth at noon-day, and none dare abide nigh to the place of his habitation for they wot not from what flower of the field it may next arise.

And the man whose name is as ebony was sore dismayed, and he waxed pale; and his face became like the face of a dead man.

For the voice of the outcry of those that were wounded and maimed was exceeding great such as never was heard since the foundation of the city—no nor ever shall be while the Tower of its strength remaineth.

For the host of the man that was crafty was annihilated and there was none who remained with him but his two beasts and certain of the Amalekites and those of Ishmael that had been sold as slaves among the children of the land.

And also much women.

And the two beasts were sorely wounded and the voice of their complaint was heard in every corner of the land and when no one would listen more to the noise of their crying they went and applied to the great physician that draineth the rich till they become empty and until they have no strength remaining.

For they knew that he had saved their master from the gates of death and from going down to the steps of the grave but he had left a mark upon his forehead as thou goest from the left eye-brow around the mighty temple towards the foundation of the great horn that can never be removed.

And when the man whose name is as ebony heard of this he waxed yet more afraid for he dreaded the great physician and he felt as if his substance were passing away like the morning dew that falleth on the tender herb and his whole soul becoming light as the smoke that ascendeth up on high.

And he called together his friends and the creatures of his household and he said what shall be done to the mole that walketh in darkness for lo the people of our city that wont to be our friends and to go with us unto the temple, are wounded and very wroth; and why should they become our enemies? The man also who is crafty is gnashing on us with his teeth; he cannot fight and to curse he is not ashamed.

And they answered with one voice and said unto him let us disown the mole and turn him from our array and cast a stain upon him for it is not meet that we fall out with our brethren and they did so.

And I turned to the man who talked with me and said O my lord dost thou see the unrighteousness of these men? The poor mole hath ventured his life for them and hath wrought a great overthrow in the host of their enemies and yet have they expelled him from the house that he hath defended and blotted out his name from among the captains of the host surely my lord this doing is not good.

And he said unto me mark thou that man whose name is as ebony; darkness is in his name and folly is with him. But his house is of *Wood* and if that mole but once breathe upon it he will shake it to its foundations as a tree is shaken by the winds of heaven.

And I heard a great noise as if many thunders had uttered their voices but when I listened again I percieved by the hearing of the ear that it was only like the voice of the northern wind sounding in a vessel in which there is no water.

And I wondered greatly for mine ears were stunned with the noise it was so great.

And the man that talked with me said be not thou afraid for it is only one of the beasts of him that is crafty; for when he can no more fight on fair and equitable terms of retaliation, he hath hired them and sent them forth to howl in every corner of the city until their voice hath reached unto the ends thereof: and they deemed that it should have win its way to heaven but the clouds that envelope the home of beauty and blessedness hath repelled it–it hath returned to the sewer from whence it arose and scarcely hath it ruffled the scum that stagnates around its native dunghill.

And I said canst thou tell me o my lord what creature is this that howleth so abominably.

And he said the voice is like the voice of Jacob the son of Levi who came from the city that bordereth on the river of the west as thou goest down to the great ocean.

From the land of Tyre and Sidon where the merchants traffic with the men of a far country, where the ships sail and the dolphins of the deep sport themselves the young man whose voice no one regardeth.

Woe is me for the youth for he hath attacted the old and the feeble the low and the vulgar that were afar off and knew not of his sufferings. He hath made war upon a louse and lifted his hand against a flea.

# A Letter to Charles Kirkpatrick Sharpe, Esq.
## On his Original Mode of
# Editing Church History

DEAR SIR,

FROM the time that your edition of Kirkton's Narrative was announced, until last month, I felt all the anxiety to see it natural to one interested in the history of Scotland; and after perusing it throughout, I am convinced that the public is indebted to you for your labour. You have presented it with–rather an interesting and certainly a valuable work,–one that traces to their principles, and depicts, during their utmost fervour, those wide disparities of sentiment respecting religion and government, which characterised the most eventful period in the annals of our country; and all this with a simplicity and candour to which I do not remember any parallel among the productions of that violent age.

I was indeed at first greatly puzzled to find out what could be the meaning of the notes and comments which you have added so liberally; but I think I have at last discovered it; if I have not, I shall be happy to stand corrected by you, or any of our friends who is better informed. But leaving that for the present, which I intend to discuss fully before I conclude this letter, I think, in the history of Kirkton, of which the main body of your work consists, we perceive throughout that singleness of heart which seldom fails in carrying assent along with it. We may have made some trifling miscalculations; and I believe that he has done so in a few instances. I take this, however, solely on your own authority, and have not been at pains to search into minute particulars, as I feel that in no point of view can such small matters affect the general authenticity of his statements.

It is apparent that a poor persecuted and intercommuned Whig could not possibly have that accurate intelligence of the court affairs, and the motives which actuated the council, which one in favour and trust with that party might have commanded. We nevertheless see clearly, that he always himself believes in the truth of what he is asserting; that he proceeds uniformly with calm discussion, a conscious integrity, and a fair estimate of his own discernment.

This much at least is certain, that the relation of a contemporary, such as Kirkton, is entitled to a higher degree of credit than any thing that can be raked up in a subsequent age. He knows that he is addressing persons as well informed as himself, who have the same means of ascertaining the facts stated; and he is sensible, if these are found out to be false, the authenticity of his work is overturned, and consequently the end that he had in view frustrated.

For these reasons I have no hesitation in declaring to you, that I regard the work of Kirkton as an authentic document, of great avail in estimating many curious particulars in our national and ecclesiastical annals, that are no where else clearly developed. And there is one thing for which I particularly respect and love him, he never fails to expose the weak side of his party. It is indeed to be considered, that it was then regarded as the strong side. That high sense which they entertained of the guidance and direction of an over-ruling providence, which was their boast and reliance whether asleep or awake, may, indeed, in this moral and philosophical age, be laughed to scorn, but was the staff and shield of the primitive Covenanters—the compass and star to which they looked throughout such a storm of adversity as never visited these northern regions. It cannot be disputed that this enthusiasm sometimes misled them, and that they mistook the visions of an ardent imagination for the voice of God. Kirkton always shews so much of this, as to mark distinctly the absence of cunning, or any attempt to throw a veil over the failings of those with whom he was joined. His history may thus be viewed not only as an authentic record of the general history of the times in which he lived, but as a true and domestic portrait of the way and manner in which the persecuted Covenanters felt and thought with regard to their oppressors; and certainly no one, whose heart is not prejudiced, can take a near view of this portrait without increasing reverence and esteem.

Is it then possible, sir, that you can truly have published this work with the intent of throwing discredit on these intrepid sufferers in the cause of civil and religious liberty? Can any one believe that you are so imbecile, as to undertake a thing so contrary to all common sense? Did you deem that such a picture of cruelty and oppression, wanton depravity, and contempt of all rights, civil and divine, as is there delineated of the one side, could ever command the respect or reverence of mankind? or that the arbitrary cause which you pretend to espouse, could be in any way advanced thereby? Or did you deem that the patience, manly fortitude, and sufferings of the other party, were likely to excite any other feelings in the human breast than those of love and reverence; especially among a generation for whose freedom the martyrs of that day laid down their lives, and who are reaping the benefits of that dearly purchased freedom at this very day, in all its peaceful and benign plenitude? No, sir, I will never believe that such an anomaly of reverse calculation exists in the material world. It would be like a man exhibiting two different colours to prove that there was no difference between them. I will not, however, believe yourself; though you have, by a sly pretence, which is well maintained throughout, endeavoured to mislead me, I know you to be a gentleman, as well as a man of considerable genius and some research; and though I might have believed that you had in your composition as much ill nature and malignity as might have induced you to attack the venerable cause of piety and freedom, I can never be induced to believe you capable of taking such a foolish and boyish method to accomplish a purpose in itself so absurd.

I have therefore concluded, sir, after mature deliberation, that you must be a Cameronian, and I am sure of it, pretend you what you will. You are of the sect of the primitive Covenanters,—a decided supporter of the doctrines of Donald Cargill, and his successor, old Francis Macmillan. I give you joy of your principles, and hope they will do you credit. For, let me tell you, you have done more for them than any man either of this or the preceding age. Others have supported them by dry reasoning and abstract theories, which few can be at the pains to read, and fewer can comprehend; but you have, by a series of ludicrous and obscene extracts, (which, by the bye, some people, notwithstanding all pretensions to the contrary, do not much dislike,) exhibited such a contrast throughout your work, as is of itself quite decisive. There we have all along the upper part of the page, the manly narrative of honest Kirkton, speaking of his suffering friends with compassion, but of his enemies as became a man and a Christian. And below that, such a medley of base ribaldry, profane stuff, and blasphemous inuendos, as at one view exhibits the character of both parties. Never before did the world so distinctly see that the suffering party were men struggling against oppression with their treasure and their blood; that they burned with a desire after freedom, and were possessed of spirits of which their country have good reason to be proud; and that their persecutors were that slavish cringing set—that fawning sycophant race, who could sacrifice the rights and liberties of their fellow-subjects for a little discretionary advancement, or base worldly lucre,—and bear themselves as if they wished to eradicate every innate feeling of the soul, and dissolve every social tie that binds man to man in the brotherhood of confidence.

There are, indeed, I am sorry to say it, a set of men in the present day, who think it a good jest to caricature humble zeal in matters of religion and conscience, and to exalt not only the tyrants who sanctioned the massacres and spoliage of the south and west of Scotland, but even the slavish and beastly tools by whom these disgraceful schemes were executed—those very scavengers in blood! And such men have got but too many to laugh with them at well-meant but homely sanctity. One would think that a sense of propriety, if not of shame, would deter people from such manifest depravity. Brilliancy of imagination may caricature any thing; and there is perhaps nothing that is so easily caricatured as uncouth zeal and enthusiasm, however noble may be their object.—But I should judge that all abettors of arbitrary kingly power, and aristocratical church government, are unfortunate in making a single allusion to that period. If they once induce to a research, no one can mistake for a moment which of the adverse parties was actuated by the more noble *set* of motives.

Modern wit, it is true, has many advantages over the abstruse and argumentative productions of that gloomy period: but truth will ultimately prevail; and though this refined, reasoning, and deistical generation may raise the profane laugh against their own rude forefathers of the hamlet, who laid down their lives for the sake of preserving a good conscience towards God and towards man,—for the sake of maintaining the reformed religion in all its pristine purity, and free from the secular arm,—yet those great and good characters will have justice done to them at last. An age must come that will do honour to their memories and the noble cause of independence for which they suffered, and not one hair of their heads shall fall to the ground.

You have taken one effective measure, nobody can deny it, of establishing the simplicity and probity of their characters; for by that raking together, out of old musty records and profane jest books, all the aspersions that all their enemies have ever uttered against them, and shewing to the world what a miserable contrast all this affords, when placed in opposition to a portrait drawn by a plain and well meaning, but very unskilful hand, a good deal is effected. But yet had you employed the time you have taken in collecting this rubbish in elucidating the history of the period to which your author refers, your work would have been more uniform. You might then have produced a book to which the historian, the patriot, and the divine, would always have turned with delight. At all events, it would have appeared somewhat like the work of a reasonable being; in which light, I fear, it will hardly as it now stands be regarded by the world.

Your plan, it must likewise be acknowledged, displays great ingenuity, and can scarcely miss having the effect desired. The contrast can never be mistaken, for it is managed by a master who understands grouping well, and is up to all the effects of light and shade. But unless to those that are personally acquainted with you, which all the world cannot be supposed to be, the work must appear very comic and unnatural; and were I to tell you what I think the generality of mankind will say of it, you would perhaps take it amiss. As I am only a single individual, however, and my opinion of small avail, I cannot help dwelling a little on this.

A revered and worthy old friend of mine lately addressed me on the subject, asking me what I thought of my friend Sharpe's book, now that I had seen it? I said it contained much curious matter, but that I was afraid the Editor's plan might be viewed as somewhat equivocal. "The Editor!" exclaimed he, with great indignation; "he is such an editor as I have not met with in the course of my reading! The man must surely be out of his judgment! Would any man in his right senses have sat down to edite a large, splendid, and expensive work, and yet bent all his efforts, from beginning to end, only to prove that it is untrue—that it is mere foolishness—written by a vulgar and ignorant man, not once to be relied on? The thing is out of all rule or comprehension." I said, that at all events you had the credit of originality in your mode of editorship; and that the work could not be productive of any ill effect, for that it contained much more in favour of independence, and its ancient supporters, than against them.

"No thanks to him," said he, in the same passionate tone; "he has done what he could to asperse, but the attempt has been a feeble one. The characters of these men can never be injured by any profane collector of blasphemous and obscene calumnies, and paltry pander to the green appetite of sickly deism. It is not for them that I feel; for I know the more their history is searched into the more they will be admired, as well as the cause for which they stood. But why not let them have fair play? Let the authentic histories of both sides be produced, but let them be laid before the public unadulterated. It is hard, that when one genuine work is produced, it should be mixed up and defaced by all the malignant alloy of ages of hostile bigotry! Still it is only for the spirit that pervades the men of our own time that I grieve; for I hold it as out of the power of any one to attach either blame to the good old cause, or contempt to its professors. But nothing can be more unfair than this, because a few homely and ignorant people, and a few violent spirits, chanced to be of that persuasion, over whom, in their scattered state, the rest had no control,—does this at all imply that the whole body of the reformers were fanatically violent or ignorant? Not by any rule of inference I know of. Yet this is what the waggish Tories of the present day would always inculcate, with as little good sense as generosity.

"It has been a maxim with the sages of all nations," continued he, "to regard with deference, whatever was held sacred by a people. This I conceive to be a deference due to the ideas and feelings of our fellow creatures, even though we put the true nature of the objects of their adoration, and the principles of their belief, entirely out of the question. Now it must be evident to every one, that at least the eminent Presbyterians of Scotland *thought that they were in the right.* A man can do no more for a cause than die for it; and surely the hero that suffers every worldly loss and privation—every torture that cruelty can suggest—and yields to an ignominious death without shrinking, deserves the admiration of mankind, let the cause for which he suffers be what it will. Is it not then lamentable to see, that there are spirits among us so depraved as to mock, and endeavour to hold up to ridicule, those intrepid martyrs for a cause which has been approved of by their country, and the benefits of which we have now reaped for more than 130 years? True, they can never throw contempt upon them nor it; and the heartless unfeeling being who would attempt to do either, is below the notice of a man." This, my dear sir, is no fabricated speech, in order to throw discredit on your mode of editing Church History. It is part of a real and genuine conversation, and, as nearly as I can recollect, the very words. I have inserted it here on purpose to give you the opinion of a man, who may be supposed to have spoken the sentiments of the class to which he belongs; and from this I deem it may be concluded, that, among all the serious and religious part of the community, you will be accused of gossiping and waggery, if not of folly and mere idiocy. If then you really did, as I have suggested, intend, by the publication of these tracts, to do honour to the cause of religious liberty, perhaps it would not be amiss, in your next edition, to make Mr John Ballantyne affix a preface, in his best style, explaining the plan on which you have proceeded; it would prevent many ill-grounded reflections, and I would not trust this to yourself, for, if you did it, there would infallibly be something ambiguous in it, that the simple would misapprehend.

In the second place, do you think the ladies will exactly relish such notices as these about Dainty Davie, Ebenezer, John Knox in the kiln-logie, and all the little nice tasteful stories about servant lasses, ladies' petticoats, and such like things, that you have interspersed so liberally throughout? I should think scarcely; but of these matters I am no great judge. This age, I know, is supposed by many to be fastidious in these matters to a fault. It is, perhaps, from a philosophical regret for this, that you have made so bold an innovation into these fields of superficial delicacy and unwarrantable refinement. I cannot, however, see what you could gain, should you even be successful in overthrowing them. Do you think their opposites would be more agreeable? Or, that if our colloquial conversations were reduced to the standard with which you have favoured us, we would have more respect for one another? perhaps we would. As I said before, I am no great judge of these matters; but, at all events, the field is now fenced by the approbation of the fair, and you ought to have recollected that, in these matters, they are extremely jealous; but, to be sure, you are a shrewd man, and may have your private reasons for what you have done.

In the third place, I do not think your own friends and acquaintance, the country gentlemen and proprietors, will approve of the odium with which they will suppose you have loaded our early reformers. They have learned long ago to distinguish between the two forms of church government, and to estimate the advantages of our own. There is not among them a man who is not sensible of the burdens, even in a temporal point of view, from which these have been the means of extricating them. Their own rent-rolls, from which no tithes or quit-rents to the church need to be subtracted, bear agreeable testimony to them of this every six months. They cannot ride five miles across the Border, in any part from one end of the line to the other, but the face of the country bears testimony of it. Let any man, whatever his persuasion or religious principles may be, survey the state of farming in the interior of the two neighbouring counties of Berwickshire and Northumberland, and then declare, whether or not Scotland has been benefited by the struggle made by our ancestors against the introduction of prelacy. Let any man, whatever are his principles, take experimental proof of the character and endowments of the lower classes in the two sister kingdoms. Let him examine which of them are best educated and instructed,–which of them have the highest sense of religion, and of all the social and domestic duties of life; and I will take his word for it without an appeal. Let him farther take a view of the lives, character, and respectability of the *officiating clergy* of both countries, and declare, whether the half-starved curate to whom the instruction of the community is principally assigned, who has all the drudgery of religious duty to take off the hands of his pampered master, and is fed only on the crumbs that fell from his table,–whether is such a man, let him declare, or the free independent presbyterian minister of Scotland, who bows to no master but one in heaven, the most likely to command respect and deference to the doctrines which he teaches, and to do honour to the cause of true religion and piety? I know of nothing in nature, sir, in which there is a stronger contrast exhibited than in this whole view–not even your ingenious work itself.

You know all this as well as any one, and much better than I do. You *are* sensible of the advantages which Scotland has obtained by the reformation, for you cannot open your eyes without seeing it. You also know at what a dear rate it was purchased, and by whom; and would you dare for your soul to hold up the sufferings of such men to ridicule and contempt?–No! as Burns says,

> Our fathers' blood the kettle bought,
>     And who would dare to soil it?
> By heaven, the sacrilegious dog
>     Should fuel be to boil it.

Your friend,　M. M.

# A Hebrew Melody

*By the Ettrick Shepherd*

### 1.

O SAW ye the rose of the East,
   In the valley of Sharon that grows?
Ye daughters of Judah, how blest
   To breathe in the sweets of my rose!
Come, tell me if yet she's at rest     5
   In her couch with the lilies inwove;
Or if wantons the breeze with her breast,
   For my heart it is sick for my love.

### 2.

I charge you, ye virgins unveil'd,
   That stray 'mong the sycamore trees,     10
By the roes and the hinds of the field,
   That ye wake not my love till she please.
"The garden with flowers is in blow,
   And roses unnumber'd are there;
Then tell how thy love we shall know,     15
   For the daughters of Zion are fair?"

### 3.

A bed of frankincense her cheek,
   And wreath of sweet myrrh is her hand;
Her eye the bright gem that they seek
   By the rivers and streams of the land;     20
Her smile from the morning she wins;
   Her teeth are the lambs on the hill;
Her breasts two young roes that are twins,
   And feed on the vallies at will.

### 4.

As the cedar 'mong trees of the wood,     25
   As the lily 'mid shrubs of the heath,
As the tower of Damascus that stood
   Overlooking the hamlets beneath;
As the moon that in glory we see
   'Mid the stars and the planets above,–     30
Even so among women is she,
   And my bosom is ravished with love!

5.

Return with the evening star,
  And our couch on Amana shall be;
From Shinar and Hermon afar               35
  Thou the mountains of leopards shall see.
O, Shulamite, turn to thy rest,
  Where the olive o'ershadows the land;
As the roe of the desert make haste,
  For the singing of birds is at hand!           40

# The Ettrick Shepherd not the Author of the Poetic Mirror

[…] effect *as the production of Lord Byron*, and that it was criticised as such by all the company.

During the remainder of our visit The Poetic Mirror continued to be the subject of conversation; and as specimens of the other poets' manner of writing, he showed us a most exquisite and friendly letter from Southey on the same subject, and likewise two poems in his own hand writing both sent purposely for the work in question. There was also one from Wordsworth, with a subsequent letter from that gentleman reclaiming it, and promising another in its room. We saw one from Wilson, of considerable length and two from other gentlemen whose names Mr Hogg thought proper to conceal, all in their own hand writing, and all avowedly for the same work. These sir are facts of which I can bring proof, and none of which Mr. Hogg himself will offer to controvert. I heard nothing of Mr. Scott, nor saw I ought of his that I remember of; but I think one of the poems, the author of which Mr. Hogg refused to give, is now attributed to him in the Mirror; and as he is well know [*sic*] to be Hogg's earliest and most constant friend, it cannot be supposed that he would be behind in such a generous effort.

From these circumstances I was very curious to see the work; but it was a full year after this before it made its appearance; and when it came to my hand, I certainly did suppose that every one of the poems were furnished by the gentlemen to whom they are ascribed in the contents. How could I deem otherwise? I had seen the poems collected in the gentlemen's own hand writing for the work, and a positive promise by those who had not contributed; and I saw the whole of this very shortly and simply corroborated in the preface which the editor has prefixed; which is indeed so plain that any farther appeal to him would be an insult. How then was I astonished on coming to Edinburgh a few months ago to hear people with such perfect *sang froid* ascribe the whole of the work to Mr Hogg? From what I have stated this must be impossible; and as the work was originally intended to be of some utility to the editor, I think it is doing him a manifest injury to insinuate that the whole is a thing trumped up by himself.

It is my humble opinion then sir, and you must at least acknowledge that I have not taken it up on very slight grounds, that the principal poems *are* furnished by the gentlemen to whom they are ascribed. On going through the work I had no doubt of it, until I read those ascribed to Wordsworth, which by some accident happened to be the last; and then I began to have my doubts—I read them over again, and soon saw it was impossible such a man would ever suffer himself to write such absolute nonsense. They are manifestly imitations; and as I never am in Edin to hear what is said of such matters, it is impossible for me to solve this. He contributed one, poem for the work as I said, which Mr. Hogg commended as very beautiful; reclaimed it, and promised a better in its place. I scarce can imagine he would be so little of a gentleman as to break a promise given in writing to a brother poet, yet I think it probable, that owing to some neglect, or failure of memory, he had suffered the thing to fall aside; and that some wicked wag of exquisite genius, had either imposed these on poor Hogg as Wordsworths own productions, or in sport as imitations. To ascribe the whole of these poems to *Hogg* as well as the two volumes of dramas would be ascribing to him a versatility of poetical genius which I am afraid no man of our day will ever possess. A solution of any part of these riddles, by any of your correspondents will greatly oblige

Yours &c.

J. P. Anderson

Corseknock by Carlisle

# New Poetic Mirror

## *Hamatory* Verses to a Cow

### Leigh Hunt Esq.

Delicious creature, with sweet gladsome *hair*,
And belly polished round like *welwot* fair!
Thy balmy *hudder* (pressed by maiden fingers

Not half so soft) where creamy beauty lingers;
Thy tail of rural white, with full dark curls          5
Fringing its *hairy* coronet of pearls;
And then its bending gentle curve behind,
And swale *hobsequious* waving in the wind;
These, with thy cheeks, and sidelong looks, confess
Thy blushing, sighing, soft woluptuousness!          10
    O hide from me these lowely lips and *heyes*!
Thy bridal crest, and bosom's fragrant sighs,
That smell so fresh of grass, and *'ay*, and *strawr*,
And all the *'ealthsome 'ealing 'erbs* that *hare*!
There *his* not one poetic gallant being,          15
Whom if his heart were whole, and rank agreeing,
It *hwould* not fire to twice of what he is,
To clasp thee in his *harms* and call thee his.
Thy *hardent* keen and quivering glance of tears;
Thy patient moving mouth, where *vell* appears          20
The smile that's *hunderneath*, but breathed vithin
Is ten times stronger than the *hopen* grin.
I cannot help exclaiming in my woe,
"O gentle creature look not at me so!"
    When I walk out on summer afternoon          25
When *hairs* and gurgling brooks are all in tune,
When grasshoppers *hare* loud, and day-work done,
And shades *'ave 'eavy houtlines* in the sun,
If thou art nigh some rising thoughts *happear*,
With something dark at bottom that I fear.          30
When as I stroll *hinto* some lonely place,
*Hunder* the trees, upon the thick short grass,
And hear thy voice from out the shades emerging
Singing thy *hevening hanthem* to the wirgin,
I look *haround* me with a new-born *heye*,          35
As *hif* some tree of knowledge there were nigh,
To taste of nature primitive and free,
And walk at *hease* in my *'eart's* liberty.
    Thy scowling lover—*Ho* what wild sensation!
Rage, wonder, misery, scorn, 'umiliation!          40
How I *henwy* and *'ate* the *'orrid* creature!
And fear beside, if that were any matter.
I cannot bear the loathed theme, to make
My very solace of distress partake!
For I have longed sometimes, I do confess,          45

To start at once from tones of wickedness;
But work begun, an interest in it, shame
At turning coward to the thoughts I frame;
Necessity to keep firm face on sorrow,
Some flattering sweet-lipped question every morrow,    50
And above all, the poet's task divine
Of making beasts themselves took up and shine,
And turning to a charm the shame that's past
Have *'eld* me *hon* and shall do to the last
   Then come thou forth, queen of the meadow, lowing, 55
At evening come, under the sky-light glowing,
And there I'll meet thee as home thou art coming,
When woods are still, and clouds of insects humming.
With one permitted arm shall be embraced
Thy downy neck, or round substantial waist;    60
And both our cheeks like peaches on a tree
Lean with a touch together thrillingly!
Most meet our compact, generous and high,
Queen of the herd art thou—their cockney monarch I

## To the Whore of Babylon
### The Same

   Rich courtly figure, with thy nods and flushes
Breaking around thee into smiles and blushes,
That floating on the silvery waters sittest
As best thy lovely lucious form befittest!
Never was nobler finish of love sight!    5
'Tis like the coming of a shape of light!
And every pampered gazer, with a start,
Feels the quick pleasure smite across his heart,
Pulls out his 'andkerchief, and gives a shout,
And odours fly, and scents come puffing out,    10
Till shaken by the noise the reeling *hair*
Whisks up thy garments thin, and lifts thy flowing *air*
   Thy *hankle* trim, soft shaded by the stream,
Thy scarlet mantle, round thee shedding beam
Like blushing chrystal tinged by the moon,    15
And fits thy limb like a silk pantaloon,
Sweeter than snowy white from the mid thigh
That catches the *hextrinsic* common *heye*,
But on thy shape the gentler sight attends,
Moves as thou passest, as thou bend'st thee bends,    20

Watches thy air, thy gesture, and thy face,
And thinks it never saw such courtly grace!
So fine is thy bare throat, and curls of black,
So lightsomely dropt on thy polished back;
Thy thigh so fitted for the graceful dance,                    25
So heaped with health, and turned with elegance!
But above all, so meaning is thy look,
Full, and as readable as open book!
Yet there is nothing in it one might call
A stamp exclusive, or professional;                            30
The nose is graceful, and lightsomely brought
Down from a forehead of love-lighted thought;
Desire looks sweet and inward from thine eye,
And round thy mouth of sensibility;
It is a face, in short, seemed made to shew                    35
How far the genuine flesh and blood can go.
    Wert thou my sister, wedded to my brother,
Then would I woo thee rather than another,
And I would win thee too—else there should be
Feeling repulsive—more especially                              40
Should we two meet at court-day, or at feast,
Or better still, in my *hideas* at least,
In summer party to the greenwood shade,
With lutes prepared and cloth on 'erbage laid,
Then would our time most exquisitely pass                      45
With stirring themes, and elbows on the grass;
With harmony of thought and look so finely,
That all we did it would be done divinely.
I see the various scenes, or think I see,
The loose goats sporting round the willow tree,                50
And all thy sweet complaisant nymphs themselves
Some by the water side, on bowery shelves
Leaning at will, some in the water sporting
With sides half swelling forth, and looks of courting;
Some tying up their long moist hair, or sleeping               55
Under the trees with beaus and poets peeping,
Or sidelong eyed, pretending not to see
The latter in the brakes come creepingly.
Never before was seen such scene of gladness!
Of future rapture and perspective madness!                     60
    There we should have many long rounds of blisses,
Feasts, comfits, baths, and bower-enshaded kisses!

But chiefly would I love thy glowing face,
Some eve just flushed from thy husband's embrace;
How would that look thro' every fibre slide!     65
Till I would turn, scarce knowing what I did,
And sigh in whisper—"May I be so free?"
Soft thou would'st answer O yes—certainly!
I could not hold, I could no more dissemble,
But kiss thee mouth to mouth all in a tremble;     70
High be our feelings! sweet be that long kiss!
Sacred be love from sight whate'er it is!!!
Thenceforward, when thy husband made so free
As husbands overnight will sometimes be,
Thou could'st not chuse but fly to meet another,     75
Of course, no less a person than his brother.

# Further Anecdotes of
# The Shepherd's Dog

*Eltrieve-Lake, Feb.* 22, 1818.

MR EDITOR,

IN a former Number of your Miscellany there appeared an affecting instance of the sagacity of a Shepherd's Dog, the truth of which I can well attest, for the owner, John Hoy, was my uncle; that is, he was married to my mother's sister. He was all his life remarkable for breeding up his dogs to perform his commands with wonderful promptitude and exactness, especially at a distance from him, and he kept always by the same breed. It may be necessary to remark here, that there is no species of animals so varied in their natures and propensities as the shepherd's dog, and these propensities are preserved inviolate in the same breed from generation to generation. One kind will manage sheep about hand, about a bught, shedding, or fold, almost naturally; and those that excel most in this kind of service, are always the least tractable at a distance; others will gather sheep from the hills, or turn them this way and that way as they are commanded, as far as they can hear their master's voice, or note the signals made by his hand, and yet can never be taught to command sheep close around him. Some excel again in a kind of social intercourse. They understand all that is said to them, or of them, in the family; and often a good deal that is said of sheep, and of other dogs, their comrades. One kind will bite the legs of cattle, and no species of correction or disapprobation will restrain them, or ever make them give it up; another kind bays at the heads of cattle, and neither precept nor example will ever induce them to attack a beast behind, or bite its legs.

My uncle Hoy's kind were held in estimation over the whole country for their docility in what is termed *hirsel rinning;* that is, gathering sheep at a distance, but they were never very good at commanding sheep about hand. Often have I stood with astonishment at seeing him standing on the top of one hill, and *the Tub*, as he called an excellent snow-white bitch that he had, gathering all the sheep from another with great care and caution. I once saw her gathering the head of a hope, or glen, quite out of her master's sight, while all that she heard of him was now and then the echo of his voice or whistle from another hill, yet, from the direction of that echo, she gathered the sheep with perfect acuteness and punctuality.

I have often heard him tell another anecdote of *Nimble*, she of whom your Correspondent writes; that one drifty day in *the seventy-four*, after gathering the ewes of Chapelhope, he found that he wanted about an hundred of them. He again betook him to the heights, and sought for them the whole day without being able to find them, and began to suspect that they were covered over with snow in some ravine. Towards the evening it cleared up a little, and as a last resource, he sent away Nimble. She had found the scent of them on the hill while her master was looking for them; but not having received orders to bring them, she had not the means of communicating the knowledge she possessed. But as soon as John gave her the gathering word, she went away, he said, like an arrow out of a bow, and in less than five minutes he beheld her at about a mile's distance, bringing them round a hill, called *The Middle*, cocking her tail behind them, and apparently very happy at having got the opportunity of terminating her master's disquietude with so much ease.

I once witnessed another very singular feat performed by a dog belonging to John Graham, late tenant in Ashiesteel. A neighbour came to his house after it was dark, and told him that he had lost a sheep on his farm, and that if he (Graham) did not secure her in the morning early, she would be lost, as he had brought her far. John said, he could not possibly get to the hill next morning, but if he would take him to the very spot where he lost the sheep, perhaps his dog Chieftain would find her that night. On that they went away with all expedition, lest the traces of the feet should cool; and I, then a boy, being in the house, went with them. The night was pitch dark, which had been the cause of the man losing his ewe; and at length he pointed out a place to John, by the side of the water, where he had lost her. "Chieftain, fetch that," said John, "bring her back, sir." The dog jumped around and around, and reared himself up on end, but not being able to see any thing, evidently misapprehended his master; on which John fell a cursing and swearing at the dog, calling him a great many blackguard names. He at last told the man, that he must point out the *very track* that the sheep went, otherwise he had no chance of recovering it. The man led him to a gray stone, and said, he was sure she took the brae within a yard of that. "Chieftain, come hither to my foot, you great numb'd whelp," said John. Chieftain came. John pointed with his finger to the ground, "Fetch that, I say, sir, you stupid idiot—bring that back away." The dog scented slowly about on the ground for some seconds, but soon began to mend his pace, and vanished in the darkness. "Bring her back away, you great calf," vociferated John, with a voice of exultation, as the dog broke to the hill; and as all these good dogs perform their work in perfect silence, we neither saw nor heard any more for a long time. I think, if I remember right, we waited there about half an hour; during which time, all the conversation was about the small chance that the dog had to find the ewe, for it was agreed on all hands, that she must long ago have mixed with the rest of the sheep on the farm. How that was, no man will ever be able to decide. John, however, still persisted in waiting until his dog came back, either with the ewe or without her; and at last the trusty animal brought the individual lost sheep to our very feet, which the man took on his back, and went on his way rejoicing. I remember the dog was very warm, and hanging out his tongue—John called him all the ill names he could invent, which the other seemed to take in very good part. Such language seemed to be John's flattery to his dog. For my part, I went home fancying I had seen a miracle, little weeting that it was nothing to what I myself was to experience in the course of my pastoral life, from the sagacity of that faithful animal the shepherd's dog.

My dog was always my companion. I conversed with him the whole day—I shared every meal with him, and my plaid in the time of a shower; the consequence was, that I generally had the best dogs in all the country. The first remarkable one that I had was named Sirrah, he was beyond all comparison the best dog I ever saw. He was of a surly unsocial temper—disdained all flattery, and refused to be caressed; but his attention to his master's commands and interests never will again be equalled by any of the canine race. The first time that I saw him, a drover was leading him in a rope; he was hungry, and lean, and far from being a beautiful cur, for he was all over black, and had a grim face striped with dark brown. The man had bought him of a boy for three shillings, somewhere on the Border, and doubtless had used him very ill on his journey. I thought I discovered a sort of sullen intelligence in his face, notwithstanding his dejected and forlorn situation, so I gave the drover a guinea for him, and appropriated the captive to myself. I believe there never was a guinea so well laid out; at least, I am satisfied that I never laid out one to so good purpose. He was scarcely then a year old, and knew so little of herding, that he had never turned sheep in his life; but as soon as he discovered that it was his duty to do so, and that it obliged me, I can never forget with what anxiety and eagerness he learned his different evolutions. He would try every way deliberately, till he found out what I wanted him to do; and when once I made him to understand a direction, he never forgot or mistook it again. Well as I knew him, he very often astonished me, for when hard pressed in accomplishing the task that he was put to, he had expedients of the moment that bespoke a great share of the reasoning faculty. Were I to relate all his exploits, it would require a volume; I shall only mention one or two, to prove to you what kind of an animal he was.

I was a shepherd for ten years on the same farm, where I had always about 700 lambs put under my charge every year at weaningtime. As they were of the *short*, or *black-faced* breed, the breaking of them was a very ticklish and difficult task. I was obliged to watch them night and day for the first four days, during which time I had always a person to assist me. It happened one year, that just about midnight the lambs broke and came up the moor upon us, making a noise with their running louder than thunder. We got up and waved our plaids, and shouted, in hopes to turn them, but we only made matters worse, for in a moment they were all round us, and by our exertions we cut them into three divisions; one of these ran north, another south, and those that came up between us straight up the moor to the westward. I called out, "Sirrah, my man, they're a' away;" the word, of all others, that set him most upon the alert, but owing to the darkness of the night, and blackness of the moor, I never saw him at all. As the division of the lambs that ran southward were going straight towards the fold, where they had been that day taken from their dams, I was afraid they would go there, and again mix with them; so I threw off part of my clothes, and pursued them, and by great personal exertion, and the help of another old dog that I had beside Sirrah, I turned them, but in a few minutes afterward lost them altogether. I ran here and there, not knowing what to do, but always, at intervals, gave a loud whistle to Sirrah, to let him know that I was depending on him. By that whistling, the lad who was assisting found me out, but he likewise had lost all traces of the lambs whatsoever. I asked if he had never seen Sirrah? He said, he had not; but that after I left him, a wing of the lambs had come round him with a swirl, and that he supposed Sirrah had then given them a turn, though he could not see him for the darkness. We both concluded, that whatever way the lambs ran at first, they would finally land at the fold where they left their mothers, and without delay we bent our course towards that; but when we came there, we found nothing of them, nor was there any kind of bleating to be heard, and discovered with vexation that we had come on a wrong track.

My companion then bent his course towards the farm of Glen on the north, and I ran away westward for several miles, along the wild track where the lambs had grazed while following their dams. We met after it was day, far up in a place called the Black Cleuch, but neither of us had been able to discover our lambs, nor any traces of them. It was the most extraordinary circumstance that had ever occurred in the annals of the pastoral life! We had nothing for it but to return to our master, and inform him that we had lost his whole flock of lambs to him, and knew not what was become of one of them.

On our way home, however, we discovered a body of lambs at the bottom of a deep ravine, called the Flesh Cleuch, and the indefatigable Sirrah standing in front of them, looking all around for some relief, but still standing true to his charge. The sun was then up; and when we first came in view of them, we concluded that it was one of the divisions of the lambs, which Sirrah had been unable to manage until he came to that commanding situation, for it was about a mile and a half distant from the place where they first broke and scattered. But what was our astonishment, when we discovered by degrees that not one lamb of the whole flock was wanting! How he had got all the divisions collected in the dark is beyond my comprehension. The charge was left entirely to himself from midnight until the rising of the sun; and if all the shepherds in the Forest had been there to have assisted him, they could not have effected it with greater propriety. All that I can say farther is, that I never felt so grateful to any creature below the sun as I did to my honest Sirrah that morning.

I remember another achievement of his which I admired still more, but which I cannot make an Edinburgh man so thoroughly to understand. I was sent to a place in Tweeddale, called Stanhope, to bring home a wild ewe that had strayed from home. The place lay at the distance of about fifteen miles, and my way to it was over steep hills, and athwart deep glens;–there was no path, and neither Sirrah nor I had ever travelled the road before. The ewe was brought in and put into a barn over night; and, after being frightened in this way, was set out to me in the morning to drive home by herself. She was as wild as a roe, and bounded away to the side of the mountain like one. I sent Sirrah on a circular rout wide before her, and let him know that he had the charge of her. When I left the people at the house, Mr Tweedie, the farmer, said to me, "Do you really suppose that you will drive that sheep over these hills, and out through the midst of all the sheep in the country?" I said I would try to do it. "Then, let me tell you," said he, "that you may as well try to travel to yon sun." The man did not know that I was destined to do both the one and the other. Our way, as I said, lay all over wild hills, and through the middle of flocks of sheep. I seldom got a sight of the ewe, for she was sometimes a mile before me, sometimes two; but Sirrah kept her in command the whole way—never suffered her to mix with other sheep—nor, as far as I could judge, ever to deviate twenty yards from the track by which he and I went the day before. When we came over the great height towards Manor Water, Sirrah and his charge happened to cross it a little before me, and our way lying down hill for several miles, I lost all traces of them, but still held on my track. I came to two shepherds' houses, and asked if they had seen any thing of a black dog, with a branded face and a long tail, driving a sheep? No; they had seen no such thing; and, besides, all their sheep, both above and below the houses, seemed to be unmoved. I had nothing for it but to hold on my way homeward; and at length, on the corner of a hill at the side of the water, I discovered my trusty coal-black friend sitting with his eye fixed intently on the burn below him, and sometimes giving a casual glance behind to see if I was coming:–he had the ewe standing there safe and unhurt.

When I got her home, and set her at liberty among our own sheep, he took it highly amiss. I could scarcely prevail with him to let her go; and so dreadfully was he affronted that she should have been let go free after all his toil and trouble, that he would not come near me all the way to the house, nor yet taste any supper when we got there. I believe he wanted me to take her home and kill her.

He had one very laughable peculiarity, which often created disturbance about the house,–it was an outrageous ear for music. He never heard music, but he drew towards it; and he never drew towards it, but he joined in it with all his vigour. Many a good psalm, song, and tune, was he the cause of being spoiled; for when he set fairly to, at which he was not slack, the voices of all his coadjutors had no chance with his. It was customary with the worthy old farmer with whom I resided, to perform family worship evening and morning; and before he began, it was always necessary to drive Sirrah to the fields, and close the door. If this was at any time forgot or neglected, the moment that the psalm was raised, he joined with all his zeal, and at such a rate, that he drowned the voices of the family before three lines could be sung. Nothing farther could be done till Sirrah was expelled. But then! when he got to the peat-stack knowe before the door, especially if he got a blow in going out, he *did* give his powers of voice full scope without mitigation, and even at that distance he was often a hard match for us all.

Some imagined that it was from a painful sensation that he did this. No such thing. Music was his delight: it always drew him towards it like a charm. I slept in the byre-loft–Sirrah in the hay-nook in a corner below. When sore fatigued, I sometimes retired to my bed before the hour of family worship. In such cases, whenever the psalm was raised in the kitchen, which was but a short distance, Sirrah left his lair; and laying his ear close to the bottom of the door to hear more distinctly, he growled a low note in accompaniment, till the sound expired; and then rose, shook his lugs, and returned to his hay-nook. Sacred music affected him most; but in either that or any slow tune, when the tones dwelt upon the key-note, they put him quite beside himself; his eyes had the gleam of madness in them; and he sometimes quitted singing, and literally fell to barking. All his race have the same qualities of voice and ear in a less or greater degree.

The most painful part of Sirrah's history yet remains; but, in memory of himself, it must be set down. He grew old, and unable to do my work by himself. I had a son of his coming up that promised well, and was a greater favourite with me than ever the other was. The times were hard, and the keeping of them both was a tax upon my master which I did not like to impose, although he made no remonstrances. I was obliged to part with one of them; so I sold old Sirrah to a neighbouring shepherd for three guineas. He was accustomed, while I was smearing, or doing any work about the farm, to go with any of the family when I ordered him, and run at their bidding the same as at my own; but then, when he came home at night, a word of approbation from me was recompense sufficient, and he was ready next day to go with whomsoever I commanded him. Of course, when I sold him to this lad, he went away when I ordered him, without any reluctance, and wrought for him all that day and the next as well as ever he did in his life. But when he found that he was abandoned by me, and doomed to be the slave of a stranger for whom he did not care, he would never again do another feasible turn for him in his life. The lad said that he run in among the sheep like a whelp, and seemed intent on doing him all the mischief he could. The consequence was, that he was obliged to part with him in a short time; but he had more honour than I had, for he took him to his father, and desired him to foster Sirrah, and be kind to him as long as he lived, *for the sake of what he had been;* and this injunction the old man faithfully performed.

He came back to see me now and then for months after he went away, but afraid of the mortification of being driven from the farm-house, he never came there; but knowing well the road that I took to the hill in the morning, he lay down near to that. When he saw me coming, he did not venture to come to me, but walked round the hill, keeping always about 200 yards' distance, and then returned to his new master again, satisfied for the time that there was no more shel-ter with his beloved old one for him. When I thought how easily one kind word would have attached him to me for life, and how grateful it would have been to my faithful old servant and friend, I could not help regretting my fortune that obliged us to separate. That unfeel-ing tax on the shepherd's dog, his only bread-winner, has been the cause of much pain in this respect. The parting with old Sirrah, after all that he had done for me, had such an effect on my heart, that I have never been able to forget it to this day; the more I have consid-ered his attachment and character, the more I have admired them; and the resolution that he took up, and persisted in, of never doing a good turn for any other of my race, after the ingratitude that he had experienced from me, appears to me to have a kind of heroism and sublimity in it. I am, however, writing nothing but the plain simple truth, to which there are plenty of living witnesses. I then made a vow to myself, which I have religiously kept, and ever shall, never to sell another dog; but that I may stand acquitted to you, sir, of all pecuniary motives, which indeed those who know me will scarcely suspect me of,—I must add, that when I saw how matters went, I never took a farthing of the stipulated price of old Sirrah.

I have Sirrah's race to this day; and though none of them have ever equalled him as a sheep dog, yet they have far excelled him in all the estimable qualities of sociality and humour. The history of his son, the renowned Hector, shall form the subject of another letter when I have leisure.

JAMES HOGG.

## *April 1818–March 1819 (Volumes 3–4)*

# Sonnet to John Carnegie, Esq.

SWEET Bard of Largo's Vale! yet once again
Strike that wild harp of thine, and to the gale,
Casting the volume of its melody,
The Zephyrs on their wings shall waft the strain,
And the whole world shall ring with Largo's Vale.     5
Carnegie! Yes, the Muse, on bended knee,
Shall wreathe a garland of the brightest dies,
Ivy and laurel deftly mixed for thee,
Thou Bard of tender tears and gentle sighs,
Poet of Largs! in whose most classic line,     10
That loveliest land of Scotia's wild domain
Sees all its long unchanted beauties shine.
Muse of the West, go wipe thine eyes, yet red
For Burns; rejoice, rejoice. All is not fled.

J. H.

# On Carmel's Brow

### *A Hebrew Melody, by the Ettrick Shepherd*

#### 1.

ON Carmel's brow the wreathy vine
    Had all its honours shed,
And o'er the vales of Palestine
    A sickly paleness spread;
When the old Seer, by vision led,     5
    And energy sublime,
Into that shadowy region sped,
    To muse on distant time.

#### 2.

He saw the valleys far and wide,
    But sight of joy was none;     10
He looked o'er many a mountain's side,
    But silence reigned alone;

Save that a boding voice sung on
  By wave and waterfall,
As still, in harsh and heavy tone,          15
  Deep unto deep did call.

3.

On Kison's strand and Ephratah
  The hamlets thick did lie;
No wayfarer between he saw,
  No Asherite passed by;          20
No maiden at her task did ply,
  Nor sportive child was seen;
The lonely dog barked wearily
  Where dwellers once had been.

4.

Oh! beauteous were the palaces         25
  On Jordan wont to be,
And still they glimmered to the breeze,
  Like stars beneath the sea!
But vultures held their jubilee
  Where harp and cymbal rung;     30
And there, as if in mockery,
  The baleful satyr sung.

5.

But who had seen that Prophet's eye,
  On Carmel that reclined!
It looked not on the times gone by,     35
  But those that were behind:
His gray hair streamed upon the wind,
  His hands were raised on high,
As, mirror'd, on his mystic mind
  Arose futurity.          40

6.

He saw the feast in Bozrah spread,
  Prepared in ancient day;
Eastward, away the eagle sped,
  And all the birds of prey.
"Who's this," he cried, "comes by the way   45
  Of Edom, all divine,
Travelling in splendour, whose array
  Is red, but not with wine?

7.

"Blest be the Herald of our King,
  That comes to set us free!                    50
The dwellers of the rock shall sing,
  And utter praise to thee!
Tabor and Hermon yet shall see
  Their glories glow again,
And blossoms spring on field and tree,          55
  That ever shall remain.

8.

"The happy child in dragon's way
  Shall frolic with delight;
The lamb shall round the leopard play,
  And all in love unite;                         60
The dove on Zion's hill shall light,
  That all the world must see.
Hail to the Journeyer, in his might,
  That comes to set us free!"

Letter from James Hogg
# To Timothy Tickler Esq.

Honoured Sir

This blunt way of yours of attacting every body slap-dash name
and surname in the public prints (as my father calls them) will never
do. Upon my word, you have given up all conformity with what is
proper and decorous in life; and if you go on at this rate, you will
only expose your own malignity and spleen, without ruffling a feather
of the game at which your [*sic*] are levelling your old-fashioned
rediculous matchlock. When you first begun, in public, to let fly
your crackers at me, your whole manner and process had so much
originality in it, that I was obliged to laugh with the rest, although I
could scarcely prevent my face from growing red with anger at times.
But now, since I retired again to this my sequestered shieling, and
have had leisure to consider of matters that are past, and weigh the
motives of the actors in these; and have often nothing else to do but
sit "nursing my wrath to keep it warm" I have learned to see things
in a very different light, and must therefore ask you in plain broad

terms Mr. Tickler. What the devil was your business with me?

There is no doubt that as an adventurer in the world of literature I have exposed myself to the rod of every one who thinks it worth his while to apply it. Every smart puppy, and old malevolent, starched, erudite gentleman, (begging your pardon sir) who with all hi[TEAR] greek and latin sentences; and all his inflated trope[TEAR] and figures injudiciously culled from the stupid pros[TEAR] poets of antiquity; and with all his rediculous attem[TEAR] too (begging your pardon again Mr. Tickler, you canno[TEAR] say that I mean you) could never earn a smile of approbation from the muses nor one of their true worshippers may belabour and bedaub me as long as they like I have nothing to say, as far as that I have given to the public is concerned. But pray sir allow me to ask what that had to do with my top boots or gloveless hands? Or how in the world was it connected with the tails of my coat, although these chanced perhaps to hang a little lower than the fashionable cut? Could you think it was to be expected that I should pay any attention to the fashoin [*sic*] of my clothes, or that I could at all be a judge what was the fashion? or that I should enter a drawing room as mim and upright as one who has walked the parliament house at least for thirty years? I can see no connection for my part; and if there is none, the joke is forced and out of place, and manifests a great lack of wit.

But what is much worse than any of these sir, you have fairly insinuated that when I was a shepherd I drank whisky like a fish. I have none of the printed letters by me; but I remember you paint me as sitting in the bield of a craig, wet to the skin, and chumping up my dinner of dry cheese and bread, peeping now and then by the corner of my gourd, and wishing for the love of God that the weather would clear up somewhat—This is a true picture—many a time and oft have I been in that very situation. But what put it into your head that in *such a situation* I could possibly cheer up my heart with the pure and genuine essence of malt? or where was the likelihood that I was to procure it? Besides you knew it was not true; for I have told you often that as far as I could remember when I was twenty years of age, I could not have consumed above *one gill* of spirits; and even from [TEAR]hat time forward, as long as I remained at my pastoral employment, I could not calculate on more than a bottle in the year at an average; and though I may have made up my lee-way considerably since that period, your insinuation was not the less a vile one. Because I have sometimes indulged in a hearty tumbler with you, at your own table o' Saturday nights, was that enough for you to publish to the world that I was a habitual drinker from my youth upward and even enjoyed the grateful beverage when sitting under the shelter of a grey stone or rash bush in the days of my innocence and primitive simplicity, when the highest ambition that I had in life was to be looked on with a favourable eye by some blooming ewe-milker, or to win the foot race at a country wedding or our annual football? After this what must the gentlemen farmers think of that enlightened and meritorious work HOGG ON SHEEP?—And what will the enthusiastical admirers of poetic imagination think of *The Pilgrims of the Sun* the most beautiful and sublime poem that perhaps ever was written, as well as my inimitable witch and fairy ballads?—I blush to think in what a light they will now be viewed! as the ravings of a distempered fancy uncommonly elevated by the fumes of smuggled whisky forsooth. For shame Mr. Tickler! "Nunquam sunt grati qui nocuêre salis."

After all I do not blame you for writing the letters. I was delighted with them in manuscript; but for publishing them without my leave; and though I have never compared the originals with the printed copies, I shrewdly suspect there are some very pointed additions intermingled in the latter. The truth is Mr. Tickler that envy is the leading trait of your character—the prevalent passion that acts as a mainspring to every movement of your mind. I could prove it to you by every thing that you have either said, done, or written, since ever we two fell acquainted; and I will do it should you please to put me to the task. Granting it therefore as a position for the present, you had two very powerful motives for the publication of these two letters. In the first place you saw that it was an attempt to place me in a light that you could not endure; for tho' always in a jocular manner, you have uniformly set yourself against every thing that had a tendency to raise my poetical character. In the second place you saw that the critical letters themselves were the best, and most original things in Constable's Magazine; and however unworthy the subject, that they were in fact superior to any piece of criticism in that Magazine with which so many of our friends are engaged—Therefore it was a galling business to you in every respect, so you determined to knock it on the head; and you certainly have been but too successful in turning the laugh both against my biographer and myself. It was extremely rediculous, when your character and my own are both fairly taken into the account. Well may I exclaim with your old friend Mr Horace "O major tandem parcas insane minore." Think you no body can quote latin but you?

It was moreover excessively ungenerous Mr. Tickler; you know there never was a man struggled harder than I have done for a little literary distinction, without a single advantage, stay, or support—You knew that I would have been the better of a lift, which neither you nor any of my literary friends had the generosity to offer—or granting that you did once promise such a thing, you know well the manner in which you fulfilled it—In a left handed way with a vengeance! Stinging your weetless friend in the dark with a poignancy scarcely to be surmounted.

When I spoke to you some time ago about the publishing of your letters to me, your answer was (for you are never at a loss for a ready one) that Constables magazine was not a fit vehicle to give a fair criticism to the world in—I granted it, and do so still; yet you might surely have suffered one generous heart to give a scope to the enthusiasm and benevolence of its feelings without interposition or insult.

But dear Mr. Tickler have you the vanity to believe that it was your gomral letters that put a stop to the publication of that criticism in Constables Magazine? I wish for the sake of human nature that I could have joined with you in the supposition; but my intelligence was too direct to be doubted; it was Mr. Constable himself that peremptorily ordered its discontinuation, because forsooth my name sometimes appeared as a supporter of his opponnent's Magazine. Now I am extremely sorry for this apparent meanness in my old friend Archy, a man whom I always considered as rather generous and gentlemanly in his demeanour—one who indeed required a little flattery to make him do things liberally, an ingredient which I was so unfortunate as never to be able to bestow because I did not know what to flatter him for. However he and I agreed extremely well for a number of years, and never differed about any thing save once about a certain epitaph, and I believe we would have been the greatest of friends to this day if it had not been for the invincible stupidity of Bob Miller. Therefore you may believe me, when I assure you, that I would rather have given him the copy-right of all the works of which he stopped the review, and a manuscript poem into the bargain, ere I had discovered him to be capable of so much littleness (I wish that be not an Irishism) I never spoke an ill word, nor thought an ill thought of Mr Constable, farther than I have expressed myself to you at present, and that I am now in reason bound to support another publisher is entirely his own blame, for he needed not to have let the incomprehensibility of Bob Miller be a bar of seperation between us unless he had chosen. Men are not all what they seem Mr Tickler more than you are, but a tree will always be known by its fruit. It is needless however for the like of me to make remarks on such doings, for "Quantum quisque sua nummorum condit in arca. Tantum habet et fidei." I may add what some other old latin author says I forgot how they call him "Quem semper acerbum. Semper honoratum (sic dii voluistis) habebo."

With regard to your letter to Mr. Jefferey sir, I thought it was very impertinent, and in bad taste. I have it not by me, for I left all my magazines in Mr. Grieve's liberary, and ever since Whitsunday his books are lying in utter confusion, so that I cannot get a single volume from among them; but the impression left on my mind is, that it falls immeasurably short of all your other letters in producing the desired effect. Your assumed familiarity with such a man as Jefferey diverges at once towards the precincts of ribaldry, and that which applied to one like me, appears laughable, applied to him becomes disgusting. But the whole of this as well as the others may with ease be traced to your ruling passion Envy. You know that Mr Jefferey *is* a great man and that he will be regarded as such so long as the literature of this age continues to be held in estimation, which was sufficient to awaken your spleen, and so you tried to depreciate him in the eyes of the public as well as to hurt his own feelings by a few rude asseverations that are not true, and some ill chosen sarcasms on a mere trifle.

I do not mean by what I have said above to represent the Edin. Review as free from alloy. On the contrary, I think with you that it has been very heavy and stupid of late; but I do not see how blame can be attached to the editor on that account. What can he help it if his associates send him dull drawling papers at times? Engaged in business as he is, he cannot be supposed to write all the Review; and one must put up with the fallings-off of his coadjutors at times, or otherwise affront them and thereby lose them altogether; and in science at least from whence was Jefferey's to be replaced? I was amused beyond measure by a letter that I had the week before last from Mr. Jamieson (not Robert as you may be apt to suppose, as every body knows Robert) wherein he says with the greatest seriousness and concern "I have been anxiously expecting the Edin. Review for a quarter of a year past, according to promise, but have still been dissapointed. The proprietors and editor of that work should really give it up; and all who wish them well I am sure will advise it. It is evident to the whole world, that the work is now dragged on with the utmost difficulty, and when it does appear it is no great things. It reminds me of a loch-leech that I once saw hanging by a cottage window in a vial of water, that was all dead and corrupted but the head, which still kept active and wagging. It would surely be much better to give it up at once with honour and eclat, for the men's wit is fairly run aground, and their subjects exhausted."

Now pray my humoursome old friend do not send this letter to that outrageous Magazine in Prince-street, which I know you will never stop to do for the jest's sake; but a poor devil like me does not want to give any body offence, and besides I have given up writing for that work, farther than a screed of poetry now and then. They refused to admit my articles and returned them all on my hand sometimes, what I could stand worst of all w. a hint that I had better send them to the New Series of the Scots magazine the Dominies magazine, or the new magazine set afoot at Lanark. And now when you presume again to speak of such men as Mr Jefferey and me just keep up your bridle hand a little, and take the way with circumspection. Otherwise I will likewise speak to my friend Mr. Miller, and tip you an eighteen-penny pamphlet on my own bottom. [TEAR] do not think he will again refuse to publish any thing of mine, at least if he bargain fairly for it, as he and I are much better acquainted than we were once. But if he should, I am in good understanding with another firm, whose names no body can read and no body can spell, but who, I am told, in the continuation of the Chaldee Manuscript are denominated "the three brethren, Shadrach, Meshech, and Abednego." If I am driven to this shift I have some anecdotes that will *amuse* the good town at least, and I shall not then have the disadvantage of writing as I do at present among cleverer people than myself.

Yours in the interim as ever<br>James Hogg

ALTRIVE LAKE
*August* 3ᵈ 1818

## April 1819–March 1820 (Volumes 5–6)

# Letter from the Ettrick Shepherd

*Eltrive, March 3, 1820.*

DEAR CHRISTOPHER,

I ENCLOSE you a very curious letter from a cousin-german of my own to his son, who still remains in this country. It has given me so much amusement that I thought it might be acceptable to you for publication in the Magazine. If you think proper to give it a corner, do not alter the orthography, or the writer's singular mode of grammar, in any other way than by pointing it. What he says with regard to the riches and freedom of America must be taken with reserve, it being well known here that he is dissatisfied, but that he wants the son, to whom he is writing, and others of his family, to join him. This indeed is apparent from the tenor of the letter.

The writer was a highly respected shepherd of this country, and as successful as most men in the same degree of life; but for a number of years bygone he talked and read about America till he grew perfectly unhappy; and, at last, when approaching his sixtieth year, actually set off to seek a temporary home and a grave in the new world; but some of his sons had formed attachments at home, and refused to accompany him.

He was always a singular and highly amusing character, cherishing every antiquated and exploded idea in science, religion, and politics. He never was at any school, and what scraps of education he had attained had all been picked up by himself. Nothing excited his indignation more than the theory of the earth wheeling round on its axis, and journeying round the sun; he had many strong logical arguments against it, and nailed them all with Scripture. When he first began to hear tell of North America, about twenty years ago, he would not believe me that Fife was not it; and that he saw it from the Castle Hill of Edinburgh. I remember, and always will, a night that I had with him about seventeen years ago. He and one Walter Bryden, better known by the appellation of Cow Wat, Thomas Hogg, the celebrated flying Ettrick tailor, and myself, were all drinking in a little changehouse one evening. After the whisky had fairly begun to operate, Laidlaw and Cow Wat went to loggerheads about Hell, about which their tenets of belief totally differed. The dispute was carried on with such acrimony on both sides, that Wat had several times heaved his great cudgel, and threatened to knock his opponent down.

Laidlaw, perceiving that the tailor and I were convulsed with laughter, joined us for some time with all his heart; but all at once he began to look grave, and the tear stood in his eye. "Aye, ye may laugh!" said he, "great gomerals! It's weel kend that ye're just twae that laugh at every thing that's good. Ye hae mair need to pray for the poor auld heretick than laugh at him, when ye see that he's on the braid way that leads to destruction. I'm really sorry for the poor auld scoundrel after a', and troth I think we sude join an' pray for him. For my part I sal lend my mite." With that he laid off his old slouched hat, and kneeled down on the floor, leaning forward on a chair, where he prayed a long prayer for Cow Wat, as he familiarly called him, when representing his forlorn case to his Maker. I do not know what I would give now to have a copy of that prayer, for I never heard any thing like it. It was so cutting, that before the end Wat rose up foaming with rage, heaved his stick, and cried, "I tell ye, gie ower, Jamie Laidlaw, I winna be prayed for in that gate."

If there were different places and degrees of punishment, he said, as the auld hoary reprobate maintained—that was to say, three or four hells, then he prayed that poor Cow Wat might be preferred to the easiest ane. "We coudna expect nae better a place," he said, "for sic a man, and indeed we would be ashamed to ask it. But, on the ither hand," continued he, "if it be true, that the object of our petition cheated James Cunningham an' Sandy o' Bowerhope, out o' from two to three hunder pounds o' lamb-siller, why, we can hardly ask sic a situation for him; an' if it be farther true, that he left his ain wife, Nanny Stothart, and took up wi' another, (whom he named name and surname), really we have hardly the face to ask any mitigation for him at a'."

The tailor and I, and another one, I have forgot who it was, but I think it was probably Adie o' Aberlosk, were obliged to hold Wat by main force upon his chair till the prayer was finished. Such are some of the traits of character peculiar to the writer of the enclosed curious epistle.—Your's ever,

JAMES HOGG.

DEAR ROBERT,

*York, September* 9, 1819.

I WRITE you this, to let you know, that we are still alive, which is a great mercy. We Came hear on the 25th of Aprile; but, as there was no Land ready misered, we were obledged to take a House for this Summer, and an acare of a Garden; we had to Stay in it untill we get the Crop of the Garden. When we are for going to our Land, we have got Each of us one 100 acers; and Andrews is a little of from us; Walter and me has 200 acers in one Lott, as we had to Draw it all by Ballot in Two Hundred acers; Andrew and George Bell, from Eskdale, is in one Lott. We are Mostly all Scotts men, and has got a Township to be all togethor, or what is Called, a parish in Scotland. They give 60,000 Acers for one Township. There is a Great meny people Settling hear. Goverment bought a Large Tract of Cuntry from the Indians Last year. This End of it was only about 12 Mills of york, and very good Land, So that people was all for on it, it Being So near the Capital of the provence; but we were Two Long of getting our Grant, that the Land was all taken up Near the Town, So that we will be 30 Mills from york; but the Land is good, for Walter and Andrew has been on it. Andrew has a fine streem of water runs through the middle of his Lott; but I am afraid that Wat and me will be Scarce of Water, unless we dig a well. We have Eighteen Mounths to do our settling deuties in, where we have to Clear five acers Each, and put up a House, and then we get our Deed for Ever to our Selvs and hirs. Robert, I will not advise you to Come hear, as I am afraid that you will not Like this place; So you may take your oun will when you did not Come along with us. I do not Expect Ever to See you hear; I am very glad to hear that you have got a place for you and your wife. May the good will of him that Dwelt in the Bush rest on you and hir; and may you be a blissing to one another. If I had thought that you ould have deserted us, I should not have comed hear; it was my ame to get you all near me made me Come to America; but mans thoughts are vanity, for I have Scattered you far wider, but I Cannot help it now. Them that I have hear is far more Contented than I am; indeed I can do very Little for the Suport of a family, for the work hear is very heavy; it is not a place for old men Lik me, altho it is a fine Cuntry, and produces plenty Robert, if this Comes to you, as I Expect it will, you may take it over to Wolfhope, and Let William See it, as I have Sent one to him with the man that brings them to Scotland. We have had our health midling well Since we Came hear, untill Six weeks ago, that Wat was taken with the ague; he had it only about Two weeks, when he got better; then Andrew took it, and he has had it this mounth, but is now getting Better—but very weak; they have wrought all this Summer with people in the Town for Six Shillings a-day, but did not get ther victules, they have made a good dale of money; but we have to pay dear for the House; but we have a good Garden that we Can Live upon, and has Sold a great dale out of it a 100 Duson of Cowcombres, and therty Bushels of potatoes. We had peas 10 foot High, and Beans 12 foot Some Hundreds after one. It has been a very warm Summer hear, and there is a fine Crop of Every kind of grain, and Hundreds of people Coming from the old Cuntry to eat of it; we get the finest of the wheat hear; Twelve Stone of it is 27 Shillings, and we are Expecting it will be at 20 in a month; we took fifteen acers of meadow Hay to mow and win from one Mr Macgill; we had three Dollars the acre, and we made it in three weeks; and he has given us as much Lea Hay for nothing as will winter our Cow, only we had it to mow and win. He is a very ricth man, and has befriended me more than all the farmers in Esther Ettrick or yearrow ould have Dun. The money here with Merchants and people of tread, is as plenty as Ever I Saw it any Town in Scotland. There is a market hear Every day for beef and mutton, and people Comes in from the Cuntry with Butter and Chease, and Eggs, and potatoes, onions, and Carrots, melons, and Skuashins, and pumpkins,—with many things unknown in Scotland. The people hear Speaks very good English; there is many of our Scots words that they Cannot understand what we are saying; and they Live far more independant than King George; for if they have been any time hear, and got a few acers of there farm Cleared, they have all plenty to Live upon; and what they have to Sell, they get always money for it, for bringing it to york. There is a road goes Straight North from york into the Cuntry for fifty mills; and the farm Houses almost all Two Story High; Some of them will have as good as 12 Cows, and four or five Horces; they are Growing very ricth, for they pay no taxes, but Just a perfict trifell, and rids in ther gig, or Chire, Like Lords. We Like this place far better than the States; we have got Sermon three times Every Saboth; they are the Baptists that we hear; there is no Presbetaren minister in this Town as yet, but there is a Large English Chapel, and a Methidest Chapel; but I do not think that the Methidests is very Sound in their Doctrine; they Save all infants, and Saposes a man may be Justified to day, and fall from it to-morrow; and the English Minister reads all that he Says, unless it be his Clark Craying always at the End of Every peorid, good Lord Dliver us. If Tom Hogg ould Come Over and hear the Methidests one day, it ould Serve him Craking about it for one Year; for the minister prays as Loud as Ever he Can, and the people is all doun on there knees, all Craying, Amen; So that you Can Scarce hear what the prest is Saying; and I have Seen Some of them Jumping up as if they ould have gone to Heaven, Soul and Body—but there Body was a filthy Clog to them, for they always fell down again, altho crying, O Jesus, O Jesus, Just as he had been to pull them up through the Loft. They have there field meetings, where they preach night and day for a week, where Some thousands atends; Some will be asleep, and Some faling down under Convictions, and others Eating and Drinking! Now, Robert, if this Comes to you, write to us how you are all, and all the News that you Can think of; and if you think that William will Come hear or not, we have got as much Land as will Serve us all; but neither you nor him will Like America at the first, as Every thing is New hear, and people has Every thing to Learn. There is not many Carts hear, they all waggons with four wheels. I have Seen three yoke of oxen in one waggon, and they plow with oxen; many of there plewghs has but one Stilt, and no Colter: The wages is not So good hear as formerly on So many people Coming from Briton and Irland. Tell John Riddel that I have as much Hickery on my farm as will be fishing wands to thousands, and many of them a Hundred foot High, and they are for no Ewse to us but to Burn; but it is the best fire wood in the world. I shall Say no more, but wish, that the god of Jacob may be your god, and may he be your gide, for Ever, and Ever, is the Sincer prayer of your Loving Father, till Death,

JAMES LAIDLAW.

Pay your Letters to the Sea, or they will not Come to us.

Account of
# A Coronation-Dinner at Edinburgh,
*In a Letter from* JOHN M'INDOE, *Esq. to*
WILLIAM M'ILHOSE, *Esq. Manufacturer, Glasgow*

MY DEAR FRIEND,

I PROMISED to write you from this boasted city, and my destined route having landed me in it at a most important juncture, I haste to fulfil my engagement. But this letter shall neither be about business, which you detest; nor the appearance of this small eastern metropolis, which you despise. No, sir: this letter, I am resolved, shall be about *the men of genius here*, the only thing worth notice in this their city, and the only article in which we *cannot* excel those who are destined to live in it. You are well aware that my attachment to literature, or rather to literary men, is such, that with unwearied perseverance I have procured introductions to all such of them as verged on the circle of my uttermost acquaintance. But perhaps you do not know, that when I could in noways attain such introductions, I made a piece of business with the gentlemen, put on a brazen face, and favoured them with a call. It is a fact, that I waited on Mr J—y with a political French novel in MS. written by a lady. He received me rather haughtily, with his back stretched up at the chimney, and his coat turned to one side; but I held him excused, for I perceived that he was thinking on something else. I made him a present of the work, however, and have been proud to see what use he has made of it. I also waited on Sir W– S– with a few Saxon coins, and two Caledonian brass javelins; on Mr C– N– with a song from Dr Scott; on Mr – with a specimen of Glasgow ice, and the Gorbals weaver's theory on the mean temperature of the globe; on P– W– with some verses to the moon, said to be written by Finlay; on G– with a German dialogue of Paisley manufacture; and on the E– S– on pretence of buying his wool. But of all the introductions I ever had in my life, the most singular took place here last night, which, as you will see by the post-mark, (should I forget to date this,) was the celebrated 19th of July.

I came from Stirling to this place in the morning, in order to attend at the great public dinner; but being informed by chance, that a club of literary and social friends were to dine together at a celebrated tavern, at which they have been accustomed to meet for many years, I was seized with an indescribable longing to make one of the party, and immediately set all my wits to work in order to accomplish this. Accordingly, I went to the commercial correspondent that was deepest in arrears with our house, and besought his interest. He introduced me to another, and that one to another, who promised, if practicable, to procure me admission; and the manner of this admission being not the least singular part of my adventure, I must describe it to you the more particularly.

This last-mentioned gentleman, (who was a jeweller,) after writing a card of considerable length, gave it me, with a direction where to find his friend, who was a mercantile gentleman whose name I had often heard mentioned: therefore, when I threw my eye on the direction, I was greatly delighted. I soon found his shop, and, the door being open, popped in; where, behold, the first face I saw was that of an elderly reverend-looking divine, a man of the most benevolent aspect. Behind him was a tall dark squinting politician, at a hard argument with an artist whose picture I had seen at an exhibition or two, and knew him at first sight. I do not know his name; but he wears spectacles, has a round quizzical face, and a very little mouth, out at which the words come pouring in flights, like well-ground meal out of a mill. But that meal had some poignancy of taste about it; for it made the politician writhe and wince, and almost drove him beyond all patience. Beyond the counter, at the fire-place, stood two celebrated lawyers, with their fore-fingers laid across, arguing a lost process over again with great volubility. I could see no mercantile-looking person whatever to whom to deliver my letter, save a young well-favoured lad with a Roman nose, busily engaged at one of the windows with his day-book, and to him I shewed the back of my card; but he only nodded his head, and pointed to an inclosed desk on the opposite side. To that I went; and, shoving aside eight or nine spacious subscription-boards for painters, poets, artificers, and all manner of rare and curious things, I set my nose through the spokes, and perceived the bald head of a man moving with a quick regular motion, from the one side to the other alternately, and soon saw, on gaining a little more room for my face among the subscription cards, that he was writing, and tracing the lines with no common celerity. I named him, and at the same time handed him my letter; on which he cocked up his eyes with a curiosity so intense, that I could scarcely retain my gravity, and thought to myself, as he perused the lines, "This must be an extraordinary fellow!"

When he had finished reading the note, he beckoned me to meet him at an opening in the counter, near the farthest corner of the shop. I obeyed the signal; but as he passed the two lawyers, he could not help pricking up his ears to the attestations of one of them, who was urging the case with more fervency than the matter appeared to require. When he came to a pause, the Merchant of Venice, for so I always felt inclined to denominate him, only said to him, "Well, it may be all very true that you are saying, my dear sir; but, for God's sake, don't get into a passion about it. There can be no occasion at all for that." And having given him this sage advice, he passed on, shook me by the hand, and conducted me down stairs.

"So you are for this private dinner, in place of the great public one, with my Lord Provost, and all the nabbs in the country to preside?" said he.–"I would prefer it a great deal," said I, "and would take it as a particular favour, if you could procure me admission into a company made up of gentlemen, whose characters I hold in the highest admiration."–"Ay! God bless the mark!" said he, taking a hearty pinch of snuff with one nostril, and quite neglecting the other; "so you admire them, do you? I should like, an it be your will, to know what it is for. I hope it is not for their detestable political principles? If so, I have done with *you*, friend; let me tell you that."–"I suppose our principles are all much the same in the main," said I; "and I hope you intend to be of the party, for one."–"Me? not I–I love the fellows personally, and should certainly have been there; but then one hears such blarney; so much sycophantic stuff, it makes one sick, and affects one like an emetic after a good hot dinner. By the bye, I have no great objections to their mode of dining;" (at this part, he took another hearty snuff, still with the same nostril, and gave two or three dry smacks with his lips;) "but the truth is, I do not know if I can be admitted myself."–"I thought you and they had been all one," said I.–"Why, so we are, in some respects," replied he; "as I said, I love the blades personally, but as to their political creed, I say, God mend it. But so it is, that I am so often with them, that my own party have almost cut me; and the others, who know my sentiments well, view me with a jealous eye, and would as soon, I fear, want me as have me; so that, at present, I am an alien from both parties. But, I must say this for these luminaries whom you profess to *admire*, that badness of heart is none of their faults. There will be some more of the artists here immediately. I will speak to them–you shall be sure of a ticket of admission."–"Shall I likewise have the pleasure of meeting with the Edinburgh artists too?" said I.–"All of them who pretend to be literary men and tories," said he. "But, heaven be praised, we have not many of them!"

Well, to make a long tale short, to the meeting we both went, where nine-and-twenty of us sat down together to dinner; and as I was merely introduced by name to two of the stewards as the friend of this Merchant of Venice, little farther notice was taken of me, so that I had time to note down a few things that passed, which I subjoin for your amusement, and that of Tod and Finlayson, should they meet you at Dugald's to-morrow evening. In the meantime, I shall describe two or three of the leading members of this literary club, that you may have a guess who they are; for I forgot to tell you, that the obliging Merchant bound me by a promise, before undertaking to introduce me, that whatever I said, wrote, or published, I was to give no names, that having become of late a most dangerous experiment. I gave him my word, which I will not break, though it will cramp me very much in my letters; but the ample field of description is left free and open to me, and to that will I resort, as a general that feels himself cramped in the plain makes his retreat to the mountains.

We shall begin with the president, who was an old man with long grey locks, prominent features, and a great deal of vivacity in his eye; a little lame of both feet, and tottered as he walked, so that I instantly recognized him as one who, of late years, has been, like the cuckoo, often heard of but seldom seen. You will understand well enough who I mean. The gentleman next to the president, on the right hand, was young, sprightly, and whimsical; with hawk's eyes, and dark curled hair. He spoke so quick, and with so short a clipped tongue, that I, who sat at a distance from him, scarcely ever could distinguish a word that he said. He on the president's left hand was a country-looking man, well advanced in life, with red whiskers, strong light-coloured hair that stood upon his crown like quills upon the fretful porcupine, and a black-silk handkerchief about his neck tied over a white one. These two appeared to be intimate acquaintances, and were constantly conversing across the table. The countryman appeared to be often jealous of the other, and at a great loss to understand the ground of his jokes, but he would not let him have a minute's peace. I shall give you one single instance of the sort of conversation that was passing between them, so much to the amusement of the president, and the friends next to them. The young gentleman had been telling the other some literary anecdote about the author of a book called *Marriage*, (which I once saw advertised) but I could not hear distinctly what he said. The other raised his eyes as if in great astonishment, and I heard perfectly what he said, which was as follows:–"Weel, man, that's extraordinar! I never heard ought like it a' my days afore. Hech, but it wad be a queer job, if ane but kend that it was true!"–"What!" said the president, "sure you don't accuse your friend of telling you falsehood, or indeed *suppose* that he would tell you aught that is not strictly true?"–"Whisht, callant. It as a' that ye ken about the matter," said the countryman. "I am only speaking for mysel'. Let every man ride the ford as he finds it. He may have always told the truth to you, and every body else. I'll never dispute that. But let me think; as far as I min', he never in a' his life tauld me the truth but ance, and that was by mere chance, and no in the least intentional." I was petrified, but those who knew the two only laughed, and the accused party laughed the most heartily of any.

The croupier was likewise a young gentleman, tall, fair, and athletic; and had a particular mode of always turning up his face like a cock drinking out of a well when he began to speak. Though rather fluent after he began talking, he seemed always to commence either with pain or difficulty, and often in the middle of a dispute between others, when he disapproved of a sentiment on either side, then he held up his face, and made his mouth like a round hole, without engaging any farther in the debate. I could not help observing, however, that one very ingenious gentleman, with whom I was peculiarly happy to meet, but who is now so publicly known, that I dare not even describe him, kept his eye ever and anon upon the croupier's motions; and though he sometimes laughed at them, if ever the said croupier turned up his face, he held it as good as if he had sworn that the speaker was wrong. And this celebrated character restrained himself, or rose into double energy exactly in proportion to the attitude of the croupier's nose, which he failed not to consult as minutely as a farmer does the state of his barometer.

There were also two, who, by way of precedency, sat opposite to each other in armed chairs at the middle of the table; the one a facetious little gentleman, with an Irish accent; the drollest being, without effort or premeditation, that I ever heard open a mouth. Indeed one would have thought that he often opened his, and let it say what it liked. I was a grieved man when he got so drunk at an early hour that he fell under the table. His fellow was nothing behind him in either good humour or fun, but I thought they were sometimes trying who could speak the greatest nonsense. This last I do not know, for some called him by one name, and some another. He is a stout boardly gentleman, with a large round whitish face,–a great deal of white round the pupil of the eye, and thin curled hair. A most choice spirit; and you must either have known or heard of him when you were in Campbell's house here. I took him at first for a well educated substantial merchant; afterwards for a sea-captain; but I now suspect that he may move in a higher circle than either of these would do.

The next most remarkable man of the party in my eyes was a little fat Gibbon-faced scholar, with a treble voice, and little grey eyes. He is indeed a fellow of infinite wit and humour, but of what profession I could not devise. He may be a doctor of physic, a dominie, a divine, a comedian, or something more extraordinary than any of these; but I am sure his is an artless and a good heart, and that he is not aware of the powers of his own mind in the delineation of human characters, perhaps (and it is a pity) too careless of what he says, and too much addicted to the ludicrous.

There was also a tall elegant old gentleman, from whom I expected something highly original. There were two or three attitudes of body, and expressions of countenance, that he assumed in confuting a young impertinent advocate, that were quite inimitable; but he was placed by some individuals that he seemed not to like, and in a short time drew himself up. I hope I shall have an opportunity of describing some more of them by and by; in the mean time I must proceed with regularity, which leads me at present to something by no means unsubstantial, namely the dinner, a thing which I have always accounted an excellent contrivance wherewith to begin the commemoration of any great event.

The dishes were exclusively Scottish. There was the balmy Scots kail, and the hodge-podge, at the two ends of the table to begin with; and both of these backed by a luxurious healthy-looking haggies, somewhat like a rolled up hedgehog. Then there were two pairs of singed sheep heads, smiling on one another at the sides, all of them surrounded by well scraped trotters, laid at right angles, in the same way that a carpenter lays up his wood to dry; and each of these dishes was backed by jolly black and white puddings, lying in the folds of each other, beautiful, fresh, and smooth; and resembling tiers of Circassian and Ethiopian young maidens in loving embraces. After these came immense rows of wild ducks, teals, and geese of various descriptions; with many other mountain birds that must be exceedingly rare, for though I have been bred in Scotland all my life, I never heard any of their names before. Among them were some called whaups, or tilliwhillies, withertyweeps, and bristlecocks.

As soon as the dinner was over, our worthy president rose and made a most splendid speech, but as you know I do not write the short-hand, I cannot do justice to it by any report. He concluded thus:–"Gentlemen, let us dedicate this bumper to our beloved sovereign, GEORGE THE FOURTH–May he long be spared to wear the crown this day set upon his head, and sway the sceptre put into his hand over a free, a loyal, and a happy people. With all the honours, ten times redoubled."

Here the applause, clapping of hands, waving of handkerchiefs, and shouting, was prodigious, so that I was afraid the people, in the extremity of their loyalty, had been going mad. But after they had sung the King's Anthem in full chorus, they again took their seats quietly, all save the countryman before mentioned, who was placed at the president's left hand, and who had all the time been sitting with open mouth staring in the speaker's face. When the rest sat down, he heaved his fist firm clenched above his head, and vociferated, in a loud and broad dialect, "Faith, callants, ye may say what ye like; but I can tell you, that this auld chap at the end o' the board speaks weel, and hauds a confoundit grip o' good sense too." And with that he came down on the table with such a rap, that he made all the glasses jingle. This set the circle in a roar of laughter, but he held up his hand again as a sign for them to be silent, and seemed disposed to harangue them. Some called to order; others, *Hear, hear*; and, finally, all voices united in the cry of, *Chair, chair*. The orator finding himself thus interrupted in what he intended to have said, looked good-naturedly about, and said, "I fancy I'm maybe like the tail that grew out o' the tup's nose, a sma' bit out o' my place here, and a wee blink farther forret than I should hae been. I was gaun to mak a speech, an' tack a toast to the tail o't; but a' in gude time. Auld cronie, gi'e me your hand in the meanwhile; I hae aye kend you for a leel man and a true, and I think mair o' ye the night than ever!" With that he shook the old president unmercifully by the hand, and added, "Ay, my hearty auld cock, we are a' ane, and there's muckle gude blood i' the land that's a' ane wi' us; and as lang as that is the case, we'll sing the Whigs Leyden's bit auld sang–

> 'My name it is doughty Jock Elliot,
> And wha dare meddle wi' me?'"

After this, a number of loyal and national toasts followed from the chair, the same that are given at every social meeting. When these were exhausted, the croupier being called on for a toast, he rose, and after turning his face three times straight upward, he delivered a very striking speech, and concluded by giving as a toast, "*A pleasant journey, and a hearty welcome to our King to Scotland.*"

This toast was drank with all the honours; and, before the president took his seat, he begged that some gentleman would favour the company with a song corresponding with the toast. "That I'll do wi' a' my heart," said the countryman, "an ye'll excuse me my speech. I'm never at a loss for a sang; and gin I ha'e nae new ane that suits, I can brag a' the country at patching up an auld ane." He then sung the following song with great glee, and every time he pronounced the term *Carle*, he came with a slap on the president's shoulder.

### Carle, an the King come

1.

"Carle, an the King come!
Carle, an the King come!
Thou shalt dance, and I shall sing,
    Carle, an the King come!"
A royal face when have we seen?
When has a King in Scotland been?
Faith, we shall bob it on the green,
    Carle, an the King come.

2.

Raise the loyal strain now!
Carle, thou's be fain now!
We's gar a' our bagpipes bumm,
    Carle, an the King come.
Auld carle, I have heard thee bless
His good auld Sire with earnestness;
Nor shall thy heart rejoice the less,
    Carle, an the King come.

3.

I have heard thee tell, too,
Stuart's race excelled too;
Then, for their sakes, we'll hail their Son,
    Carle, an the King come.
For them our fathers rued fu' sair,
And stood till they could stand nae mair;
Then let us hail their only Heir
    Carle, an the King come.

4.

Who has raised our name high?
And our warrior fame high?
Tell—that snarlers may sing dumb,
    Carle, an the King come.

O loyalty's a noble thing!
A flower in heaven that first did spring;
And every grumbler down we'll fling,
   Carle, an the King come.

5.

Who our band can sever?
Carping croakers, never!
But now their crimes we'll scorn to sum,
   Carle, an the King come.
Then bend the bicker ane an' a',
We'll drink till we be like to fa',
And dance it, cripple stilts an' a',
   Carle, an the King come.

6.

"Carle, an the King come!
Carle, an the King come!
Thou shalt dance, and I shall sing,
   Carle, an the King come!"
When yellow corn grows on the riggs,
And gibbets rise to hang the Whigs,
O then we will dance Scottish jigs,
   Carle, an the King come.

The singer received his due quota of applause; and being reminded that he had a right to call a song, it was hinted, that he should call on the Merchant of Venice, alias the Royal Merchant; but he shook his head, and replied, "Na, na, it is nae his time o' night yet by ten bumpers. I ken him ower weel to ca' on him now;–but he'll gie me, *Wad ye ken what a Whig is?* or twall o'clock yet, for a' his canting about rights an' liberties in the forenoon. He speaks muckle nonsense about thae things. I'm while's just wae for him." Another whispered him to call on the president; but he added, "Na; I'm something like the weaver wi' his grace–I never like to ask ought that I think I ha'e nae some chance o' getting."

The next gentleman who spoke, at least to any purpose, was one before mentioned, whose personal appearance I chuse not to describe. He being clothed in black, I had taken him all the afternoon for a clergyman; and after he spoke, I had no doubt but that he was a celebrated whig minister, who was taken from Perthshire to London some years ago; and yet I could not conceive what he was seeking there. Word followed word, and sentence followed sentence, till he actually winded out his speech to the length of three quarters of an hour's duration. But before he was half done I got fatigued, which, creating some confusion in my ideas, I lost all traces of connection in my notes; and on looking them over to-day, I find so many contractions of superlative terms, most of them meaning the same thing, that I can make nothing of them; and it is a loss for you I cannot, for though the speech was delivered in a preaching style, it was nevertheless a piece of grand and impressive eloquence; insomuch, that I said to myself again and again, "On my word but the seceder minister does well!" The subject was indeed scarcely to be equalled. It was a character of our late venerable and beloved Sovereign–"The father of his people, and the firm defender of their rights, whose image was embalmed for ever in their profound and grateful remembrances, and whose descent to the grave was long overshadowed by the darkest of human calamities." Such were some of the speaker's impressive words; and you can scarcely conceive how much he affected his audience. It was upon the whole a singular mixture of prolixity, pathos, and sublimity. He concluded by giving "The memory of our late beloved and revered Sovereign, George the Third." The toast was drunk with the silent honours, in a way which I never saw done in Glasgow, and which in this instance appeared to me highly impressive. All the company taking example by the president stood up in silence, and waving their emptied glasses slowly around their heads, crossed their hands on their brows and made a reverend bow, after which a long restrained *ruff* of approbation ensued like the sound made by muffled drums.

After this an elderly gentleman with spectacles rose, and said, "He had been favoured with a few verses of a song that day–that they were written by a gentleman in the company, who, he believed, had written more loyal and national songs than any bard now living, more perhaps than all of them put together; and as the verses appeared to suit the foregoing toast in a particular manner, he volunteered to sing them, provided he were allowed to consult the manuscript. This being granted, he sung the following stanzas in a soft under voice, to a most beautiful old air, to be found only in Albyn's Anthology.

### Our good Auld Man

1.

Our good auld man is gane!
Our good auld man is gane!
But I will greet for the auld grey head,
Now cauld aneath the stane.

2.

There's some brag o' their weir,
And some o' their lordly kin;
But a' my boast was his virtuous breast,
And the kindly heart within.

3.

'Tis neither for blight nor blame
That the tear-drap blinds my e'e,
But I greet when I think o' the auld grey head,
And a' that it bore for me.

4.

Though darkness veil'd his eye,
And light o' the soul was nane;
They shall shine bright in a purer light,
When the moon and the stars are gane.

I only took notes of one more speech and two songs; for, indeed, the glass went round so freely, that wine and loyalty got the upper-hand of my judgment, and I lost all recollection of what was afterwards done, said or sung, as completely, as if I had been at a whig dinner, with Kelly in the chair, at the Black Bull.—Yours, &c.

JOHN M'INDOE.

*January–December 1822 (Volumes 11–12)*

# BLACKWOOD'S
# EDINBURGH MAGAZINE.

No. LXXI.      DECEMBER, 1822.      Vol. XII.

## Noctes Ambrosianæ.

### No. VI.

ΧΡΗ Δ᾽ΕΝ ΣΥΜΠΟΣΙΩ ΚΥΛΙΚΩΝ ΠΕΡΙΝΙΣΣΟΜΕΝΑΩΝ
ΗΔΕΑ ΚΩΤΙΛΛΟΝΤΑ ΚΑΘΗΜΕΝΟΝ ΟΙΝΟΠΟΤΑΖΕΙΝ.

ΡΗΟΟ. *ap. Ath.*

[*This is a distich by wise old Phocylides,*
*An ancient who wrote crabbed Greek in no silly days;*
*Meaning,* " 'TIS RIGHT FOR GOOD WINEBIBBING PEOPLE,
" NOT TO LET THE JUG PACE ROUND THE BOARD LIKE A CRIPPLE;
" BUT GAILY TO CHAT WHILE DISCUSSING THEIR TIPPLE."
*An excellent rule of the hearty old cock 'tis—*
*And a very fit motto to put to our Noctes.*]

C. N. *ap. Ambr.*

DIE VENERIS, *Nocte 15ta Mensis Decemb.*
PRESENT—THE EDITOR'S MOST EXCELLENT MAGAZINITY, IN COUNCIL.

NORTH, (*proloquitur.*)

Mr Odoherty, it is to be hoped you have not come to such an affair as this, to eat the flesh of the wild boar of the forest, and the red-deer of the hills, at the expense of our noble friend, without preparing a small canticle in honour of his gifts—something in the occasional way, as it were?

ODOHERTY.

If the Hogg will take the Boar, I will venture on the Deer.

HOGG.

Done for a saxpence—here's my thumb : Sing ye awa, Captain, and I'll be casting for an *cedèa* in the meantime.

ODOHERTY.

Look sharp, if you get a nibble, Shepherd—*I nunc et versus,*—here goes then.

ODOHERTY *sings.*

#### I.

There's a Spanish grandee on the banks of the Dee,
  A fine fellow is he—a finer is none;
For though he's so great, and high in estate,
  He is also first-rate in the peerage of fun.
Then fill to Lord Fife, in condiments rife
  To the end of this life his career may he run;
And his tree that hath stood, at the least since the Flood,
  Oh, may't flourish and bud till our Planet's undone!

# The Women Folk

O SAIRLY may I rue the day
  I fancied first the women-kind,
For aye sinsyne I ne'er can ha'e
  A quiet thought, or peace o' mind.
They ha'e plagued my heart, and pleased my e'e,     5
  And teased and flatter'd me at will;
But aye, for a' their witcherye,
  The pawky things, I lo'e them still.
    O the women folk, O the women folk,
    But they ha'e been the wreck o' me!    10
    O weary fa' the women folk,
    For they winna let a body be.

I've thought, an' thought, but darna tell;
  I've studied them wi' a' my skill;
I've lo'ed them better than mysel';    15
  I've tried again to like them ill.
Wha sairest strives, will sairest rue,
  To comprehend what nae man can:
When he has done what man can do,
  He'll end at last where he began.    20
    O, the women folk, &c.

That they hae gentle forms, and meet,
  A man wi' half a look may see,
An' gracefu' airs, an' faces sweet,
  An' wavin' curls aboon the bree–    25
An' smiles as saft as the young rose-bud,
  An' een sae pawky bright and rare,
Wad lure the lavrock frae the clud;
  But, laddie, seek to ken nae mair.
    O, the women folk, &c.    30

Even but this night, nae farther gane,
  The date is nouther lost nor lang,
I tak' ye witness ilka ane,
  How fell they fought, an' fairly dang;
Their point they've carried right or wrang,    35
  Without a reason, rhyme, or law–
An' forced a man to sing a sang,
  That ne'er could sing a verse ava.
    O, the women folk, &c.

*January–December 1823 (Volumes 13–14)*

# The Hon^ble Captain Napier
# and Ettrick Forest

[*Manuscript Version*]

SIR

There is a work on pastoral economy which has lately made its appearance and as it merits the attention of the public in no ordinary degree at this critical period, I send you a few remarks on it and anecdotes connected with it for publication, knowing that no one is qualified for doing so who is not intimately acquainted with the local circumstances of the country to which the book relates.

This is no work of a capricious and self approving theorist set down to vend the feelings of a party, or set the interests of one part of the Common wealth against another: no dictatorial harangue of learned pedagogue, reasoning about matters of which he knows not the first principles. The author is no Mr Weir, proving the inefficiency of our present mode of pasturage from the eclogues of Virgil, and the works of Aristotle; but the eldest son and heir, of a nobleman, telling a plain unvarnished tale about things in which he is deeply concerned and recommending improvements, and those only by the adoption of which he must ultimately either be a gainer or a loser. There can therefore be no doubt whatsoever with regard to the sincerity and good intentions of its author, and it is impossible to read the work without percieving throughout, the bold, fearless, independent and generous spirit that indited it.

It is not my purpose to enter into a general detail of this genuine pastoral production. Such disquisitions lye exactly four and thirty miles out of your way (the distance betwixt Ambrose's and Ettrick Forest). I know you do not wish to knock a respectable and long established work on the head at once, by monopolizing every dingy art and science but rather take a particular interest in the success of some of your contemporary journals, and have shown that, most forcibly, by shunning every object that lay in their path. You have even avoided the path itself, and the very department which it traverses, for fear of stumbling upon some of these objects; for there is no denying that you have a wonderful facility in striking your foot against certain objects with a deevilish sharp kick; and more than that, the additional volitation acquired by such a stumble is rather apt to make you run your head plump against the next person, or beast, that comes in our way.

I could not however relinquish this opportunity of saying a few words in approbation of the motives of my countryman, motives that do honour to human nature, and add lustre even to the noble class to which he belongs, and with which he is widely connected. Indeed it is impossible to speak of the Honourable Capt. Napier in terms adequate to the sentiments that I entertain of his public and enterprising spirit. He is the eldest son of Lord Napier, and heir apparent to his lands and titles. The lineal descendant and representative, not only of the famous Napiers of Merchiston, but also of a family of Scotts of high Border lineage and fame, the ancient knights of Thirlstane and Howpasley. With an hereditary spirit of enterprise, he went into the Royal Navy when very young, and before he was 19 years of age, served on board THE DEFENCE at the glorious battle of Trafalgar, assisting in the capture of the St. Ildephonsa which the gallant crew carried a prize into Gibraltar. He afterwards served in the same ship with Lord Cochrane; and for many years, whenever there was fame to be won in the teeth of danger, or honour by deeds of generosity and disinterestedness, there was to be found the hon^ble William Napier, more properly William Scott of Thirlstane for the latter was his paternal name. He was twice wounded in battle, and at one time lay three months in an enemy's prison. His deeds of chivalry occassioned his name being mentioned with high approbation in sundry of his admiral's dispatches, and raised him by rapid steps from the rank of a midshipman to that of post captain in the royal navy.

At length, when his country had no more need of his arm, he laid aside the sword and took up the shepherd's crook. From keeping long and indefatigable guard on the sublime elemental bulwark of his country, he retired to her most sequestered wilderness, to one of her inland glens to which cultivation had approached with slow and indignant motion; where antiquated forms, customs, and adages lingered with an obstinacy only to be accounted for in the patriarchal feelings of an intelligent and thinking people. But these rules and adages had been transmitted to them by their fathers—handed down from generation to generation by those whom they were taught to consider as wiser and better men than themselves, and they could not yield them up without reluctance. Against such prejudices Captain Napier soon found that he would be obliged to contend in his new exertions to serve his country. But he was nothing daunted. He set a stout heart to a steep brae and determined to gain the summit, seeing he could no longer benefit the land of his fathers by wreaking vengeance on her enemies, or in defending her naval rights, he resolved to do so by his example, and to cultivate the rural arts of peace to the utmost extent of his interest and ability.

His first exertions were directed towards that sort of improvement which ought ever to be the first in a country, and which necessarily *paves the way* for all others, namely the improvement of the roads. In this he persevered with an obstinacy that was almost ludicrous, for in it as in several other things he was not supported by his coadjutors to the extent that his patriotic intentions merited. But neither fatigue nor opposition either deterred or dispirited him for one moment, he wrote letters, called meetings, and made speeches; threatened some with the law, and others with acts of parliament, to make them acquiesce in that which was their own interests. He surveyed roads over mountains and through glens and cataracts, carrying the end of the chain himself for many a weary day, and stopping at every turn to mark down the altitudes, rocks, bridges, and declivities. In these laborious peregrinations he surveyed many lines of road where roads have never been made, nor ever will be made while the world stands. Among them may be mentioned an excellent one over Minchmoor, and another over Bodsbeck-Law, both rising with an abrupt ascent to the respectable elevation of 2000 feet above the level of the sea, of course excellently adapted for *winter roads* as they would have been always blown quite free of snows during that boisterous season and suppose a few scores of passengers might have perished annually on them that was their own concern, so it behoved them to look to it [MS BREAK] of Annandale to meet him with one at Birkhill Path. He absolutely compelled the men of Tweedale to contribute their quota to a certain line that went through a part of their county, but they have hitherto withstood all his efforts in meeting him with an effective line on the Edinburgh road, which still remains in a disgraceful state considering the excellence of the line, and the expenses that have been laid out on it all to the southward. Every one of these new lines of road is of the utmost importance to the county. They open up a communication with each of the adjoining districts, and through these with every part of the united kingdom; and it cannot be denied that for all these the country is mainly indebted to the unwearied exertions of Capt. Napier.

On reading over the Captain's very curious work the first thing that strikes one is, how it could be possible that the occupiers of land in this celebrated pastoral district of Ettrick Forest should have been so backward in their improvements relating to the rearing and management of sheep, the sole staple commodity of their country. There is no doubt however of the fact it actually was so, and every material change towards improvement was withstood as an innovation till it could be withstood no longer. Till the advanced rents compelled the farmers to adopt the measures that had apparently proved the most lucrative to others. Even after they had been sullenly adopted by the farmers, the old shepherds withstood them to the utmost of their power, and that with a virulence quite unexampled. These being a people that have great influence with [MS BREAK] "swelsh of a gersy heuch. There is nae muckle to be pickit up at the back of a dirty stane dike."

But the greatest innovation of all on the old fashioned bodies, both farmers and shepherds, was the introduction of the Cheviot breed of sheep, in the room of the old rough, hardy, black faced natives of the soil. This was an aera in the annals of sheep-farming never to be forgotten, and far less ever to be blotted out of the *shepherd's callander*. All the upper parts of Tweedale, Ettrick Forest, Annandale, and Clydesdale, were stocked with the latter breed, and these alone; and for many ages the farmers and shepherds in these extensive districts held the white faced, or Cheviot breed, in utter contempt. They called them "poor, beggarly, despicable animals, that needed to be fed with the hand of man, and put into a house in an ill day!" Even the want of horns in the Cheviot breed was made a matter of reflection on them personally. They called them *the Doddies*, and mocked the shepherds and farmers who stood by them in the sheep markets. It was true that when the black faced sheep broke in a market they always run through the Cheviot droves without regarding them as sheep at all. While the white faced lambs would have been lying in St. Boswell's fair peaceably and innocently chewing the cud, down would have come a precipitate and headlong drove of short wedders and run right over them, tumbling numbers of them quite over and over. This naturally incensed the lowland shepherd, who kept crying "Keep thae mad deils o' yours on their stance. D'ye think the green's to be laid waste wi' them? They'll pit away a' my lambs." "Ay gude troth neighbour I think your lambs winna rin very far. Take gude care that they dinna stick ye wi' their horns." Such jibes as that were to be heard in every fair.

But when they began to encroach piecemeal on the original stock the country was put into a ferment. The neighbouring shepherds were so inveterate against them that if they could they would have worried them all with their dogs, and it was often supposed that they did not get over fair play with their own shepherds themselves. Certain it is that they abhorred them, and would rather that their masters had lost a little than they should have been encouraged to persevere in their injudicious improvements. There was no bad epithet however with which the poor creatures were not branded. They called them "vile, bleached, wan looking devils; the very portraits of death. The ghosts of sheep; and whey faced b—hes." The very children, in conformity with the humours and prejudices of their parents, pretended to be frighted for them as *wraiths*: and boys told long winded stories of having met with straglers of the new come stock in the gloaming, and of having run off the hill in great terror, thinking they were "spirits of sheep; or old ewes rowed up in winding sheets!"

One of these old shepherds would have made a good subject for David Wilkie when a drove of small border lambs was first turned in before him at 14/ and 16/ a head. The rueful despair that was painted on his countenance could not miss being noted by every one who saw him. And ever and anon as he spoke of them he turned his face up towards the hill, and took another look of his old, stout, black faced ewes, as if taking a last glimpse of all that belonged to the good and faithful *days of langsyne*. It was even reported that numbers of these old men, both shepherds and masters, when at family worship, prayed against the doddies every night. I have been at some pains to collect a few of these notes from the prayers of some of the most noted votaries of the old system, and must confess, if they were levelled against the Cheviot breed of sheep, they appear to have been managed very obliquely. Auld Watie Bryden was wont to pray every night for two years running, to be "protected and defended from a' new comers, however *whitewashed* their faces might be; for they were but like whited walls, and painted sepulchres full of rottenness within." Another worthy man named James Bryden prayed some once or twice in these words "Repel these invaders of our country that are threatening to come upon us like the locusts in numbers and in power, eating up every green thing. May the nations of our land be enabled to push them down as with the horn of the unicorn, and tread them under their feet, that they may rise no more to spread upon our mountains and encumber our vallies." I think it very probable that this honest man meant the French; but perhaps he alluded to the horns of the black faced sheep, and had the above mentioned scenes of St. Boswell's fair in his eye, and liked to see the old breed treading the others under their feet.

Old John Rieve (perhaps our correspondent means Grieve) was more pointed in his anathemas. When his next neighbour (whom by the by he did not much like) laid first on a stock of the *Doddies*,

John prayed to the following purport. "And what wilt thou do with the fool who hast trode upon the ashes of his fathers, hath scattered his flocks, and brought home those of a far country with great boasting and noise? It would be but justice wert thou to smite both his shepherds and his sheep, that they might fall down dead together, that their stink may come up into his nostrils and their skins remain unto him for a prey." It was reported that Johny's prayer was but too well heard. "Direct us in the right way" said one "in all things temporal, as well as spiritual; and in these newfangled times if it is thy will that *black* should become *white* we have nothing earthly to say."

These are only a few out of a great number that I collected, many of them too familiar with divinity to be inserted. But when the lambing season of the Cheviot flocks came on, the despair of the Forest and the other moorland shepherds reached its acme. They had been accustomed, with the old breed, to pay very little attention to them at such times. The wildest and most savage creatures have all the most powerful parental affections. The short ewe (as she is commonly denominated) would not leave her lamb for the severest of weather. Or if obliged to leave it for a little in search of necessary food, the yeanling would keep to its hole among the snow, or spot where its dam left it, certain of her return; and even, in these deplorable circumstances, the heroic little wretch would tramp with its fore foot, and whistle through its nose, with intent to defend its den against both the shepherd and his dog. It was generally noted too that on the heights and most exposed parts of a farm, there the dams were always kindliest to their young. Instances have been known that when one of their lambs have perished in these inhospitable heights in times of severity the dam came and stood for some hours every day over the carcass till it was altogether consumed. And any of these creatures, when the shepherd stripped of the skin of her own lamb, and put it on another that had been one of twins, or otherwise deserted, would bleat over it at once out of pure affection, offer it the dug, and ever after acknowledge it as her own, showing it even more kindness than ordinary, which seems to have originated in some indefinable feelings of the loss the creature deemed she had suffered and experienced the joys of a parent once more. If the shepherd had no lamb on the hill to supply the place of her own, (it being common to take all such odd lambs into the house to be supplied with cow milk), it was a common practice with him to tie his garter to the dead lamb's foot and trail it after him; the ewe followed him, with her nose close over the body of her dead offspring, bleating all the way in a most melancholly tone, and every now and then chasing the shepherd's dog, which she would scarcely suffer to come within sight. In this manner he could have led her in beyond the fire, or into any corner of any house he chose, in order to get another lamb set to her.

This strong natural affection the Cheviot ewe possessed in a very inferior degree. When straitened with cold or hunger she left her lamb without ever thinking of returning to the spot where she left it. The lamb, if it was able, would trail away after any sheep that came by the by. Then they were all of them so bare and delicate [MS BREAK] attendance ready at the call of whoever wants them. These seem to have acted powerfully as a check to all misdemeanors, for from the day that the prison was erected it has never yet been tenanted although before that, it was so much wanted, that the constables were obliged to lay their prisoners up in an old barn, with two doors neither of which had a lock, and got their heads broken, in the course of their attendance. So long has the round house now stood without one inhabitant, that it is said the Hon. Mrs. Napier has promised to the first delinquent that may chance to be laid in it a guinea to drink with his associates.

These markets have proved, and are like to prove of the greatest utility to Ettrick forest and the districts adjacent. In particular the lamb fair in July, and the ewe fair in September. At both these markets, though, great numbers of the very best stock in Scotland have been exposed, it is asserted that the show has hardly ever been equal to the demand. If the rest should chance not to succeed in the same degree, it will be the fault of the farmers, for it is impossible that any markets can ever suit them so well. They are placed in the very middle of the finest pastoral district of our country, and the sheep appear at them in the freshest state imaginable.

His next great effort was the establishment of the Pastoral Club, a society founded on the most liberal and enlightened views, for the encouragement of pastoral farming in all its branches, and all their ramifications. Every farmer, for the best breeds of stock, of all ages and denominations; and even the servant that has proved himself the most expert and attentive to the charge committed to him, all find liberal premiums paid to them in ready gold. The emulation that these have excited, both among masters and servants, promise to be of the highest utility, acting as a spur in every species of industry.

Captain Napier has moreover proved himself the father of the poor in the fullest sense of the word. The smallest of their deprivations has proved matter of attention to him. Not only in his own parish, but in those adjacent has he been attentive to every case of distress. He has sometimes been blamed for patronising the good and the bad, the worthy and the unworthy, with the same degree of sympathy and perseverance. Concerning this I can say nothing, but suppose that human suffering was always plea sufficient for his interference. He disapproves radically of the principle of the poor's rates and once went so far as to order their discontinuation in his own parish, of which he is patron and one of the elders. The astonished dominie gave over collecting, and the poor ceased their applications, all waiting in gaping suspense the issue of this extraordinary mandate. In any other parish so circumstanced, the thing would have raised an open rebellion, but in Ettrick there was not a murmur, so fully were all convinced of capt. Napier's good intentions. He found in a few months that the poor were all likely to be turned on himself, so he suffered the assessment and distribution of the poor's money to proceed as usual, subjected to some restrictions.

There is another anecdote of our noble author, which is worthy of being related, as it excited a good deal of risibility at the time it occurred, and it shall be the last. He is a strong advocate for all the observances of our holy religion; and as the parishes of Ettrick and Yarrow is the land of shepherds, the consequence is, that one third of these congregations has always been wont to consist of decent, respectable-looking colley dogs. However, there were often some of them but middling well bred, and did not account much of kicking up a stoure in the area, by beginning a battle-general; they were, moreover, often guilty of some other venial improprieties, scarcely becoming the sanctity of the place. So acute are the observations of these creatures, that although, during the course of the service, the people arose twice in time of prayers, that made no difference in the deportment of the minor and subordinate part of the community. But so horribly tired were the rascals of listening to precept and prayer, that the moment the blessing began to be pronounced, they broke all out at once, with one tremendous volley of joy, so that no man or woman in these parishes ever heard a word of the blessing, the response proved so transcendantly vociferous. It had therefore been the custom, time out of mind, in these two parishes, for the people to sit still on their seats, without moving a finger, till the blessing was pronounced. This took the greater part of the dogs at unawares; and the parson got the blessing breathed softly over without much interruption. There were, nevertheless, some old accustomed rascals that generally began a whining and whimpering the moment the minister lifted his hand; and if a single arm was stretched out for a hat, the fray began. But over and above all this, there are numbers of these animals, of a certain extravagant poetical breed, endowed with most unequivocal organs of music, and took it on them to join the clamorous harmony of the mountain church music, bearing a part in every psalm that was sung; and so overpowering were their notes on some occassions, that there was not a voice to be heard in church, save the precentor's and their own. On the whole, there was something in the economy of this mingled congregation that the Captain did not like, so he set his face against the canine part of the community altogether, threatening them with the lesser excommunication, namely an utter expulsion from divine ordinances.

Accordingly, on the next Sunday after this resolution was finally taken, our determined author [MS BREAK] "but the Captain [TEAR] wantit to gie him the jouk as the fo'k were thrangin in, he seized them by the necks at the jeopardy of his hands, and ordered their masters either to go home again with them, or tie their companions up in some out house, till divine service was over."

Perhaps this may have been a joke; I do not precisely know; but the substance of the matter is truth; and in two weeks, that was effected, which had hitherto been held as impracticable; and the church of Ettrick was thereafter as clear of dogs as any church in the kingdom. Every person now rises up reverendly in his pew, during the time the blessing is a pronouncing; and there are as graceful bows and courtesies to be seen there as any where else. Nay, it is said the congregation rather appear to excel in that, the late acknowledged subordination of rank appearing to have given *a new spring* to their devotions. Of all these graceful and becoming attitudes, the people of Yarrow are deprived; they are still obliged to adhere to the old custom, keeping close to their seats in time of the blessing, *in order to cheat the dogs.*

Such is the man, and such the persevering spirit of him whose work I have so lately been perusing. After having done every thing in his power by way of showing an example to his father's tenants, and his countrymen in general, he has now laid the issue of all his experiments openly and fairly before the public, that every man may judge for himself, and profit by that which has cost him nothing. I am now thoroughly perswaded, and am certain that I will be borne out by every gentleman of the Border districts, when I say, that I know of no man who deserves better of his country than Capt. Napier, nor one who has effected so much for its improvement, from the resources of a private fortune. What a pattern is such a man to the young noblemen and gentlemen of our land! Were each of them but to pay one half the attention to their native soil, and the various districts of it with which they are connected, what a difference would soon be made in the appearance of the country; and how much a thousand casual distresses and local inconveniences might thereby be obviated.

With regard to the work itself, I shall only remark in general, that all of it that is the captain's own appears to be the least objectionable. The reasoning is candid and obvious, and the calculations never extravagant. But there are many [MS BREAK] "Gude faith, Clavers lad, ye may gae your ways to your grave!" I cannot [TEAR] really believed in the correctness of this statement.

It will likewise be observed, farther, that whenever he mentions the Shepherds name, he does it with uncommon kindness and deference, which I think is more than your friend deserves; for it cannot fail being remembered, that in his popular poem, "The Queen's Wake," he introduces the Hon[ble] author in a very mysterious equivocal light, as RED WILL OF THIRLSTANE. And after a long unintelligible palaver about his feudal lake, and his fighting in it to the knees, and being killed in it, and the fishes swimming with indignation over his breast, he concludes the character by saying that

> He ne'er in all his restless life
> Did unbecoming thing BUT ONE!

What *one thing* can this have been that he has been so avowedly charged with? It has certainly rather a startling appearance, and I wish the bard had condescended to give some explanation of it in a note, or otherwise. For however well these matters may be understood by him and his agust neighbour, I can assure him that they are not so by the mutual friends of both, and therefore it is but fair that their countrymen should know the meaning of a charge so whimsical. I have indeed heard that it was something about the WATER COW of St. Mary's Loch, against which the Hon[ble] captain had lifted up his hand to the Shepherd's great grief and indignation; but such a supposition is altogether untenable.

There is another shepherd, named Alexander Laidlaw, on whose diary the Captain places a great deal of reliance, as a basis whereon to found his theories. It is a curious document—a very curious one indeed—but I have great reason for doubting its accuracy regarding the losses on such and such farms during the severe winters of the last century, and wish he had consulted the memories of some old shepherds a little more sedulously—the best chronicles of such events. But when a man cannot give correct statements of matters that passed under his own eye, how shall we credit him in those 150 years ago? I could mention several of these inaccuracies in his letter, which, though very trivial in themselves, render his curious diary doubtful. As an instance, in stating the losses in his neighbourhood in the storm of 1794, he says, "Eldinhope lost the greatest number, amounting, it was said, to 100". Now the fact is that Eldinhope lost upwards of Eleven-scores. There were nine scores, and fourteen, all smoored in one place—(the Wolf-Cleuch) they lost all their tups beside, and several other stragglers. Such a misstatement is the more singular, as this was a neighbouring farm, on the hills of which he turned his eyes every day, and must have known what loss was suffered there, as well as as he did on the farm on which he herded.

In 1799, he says, the farm of Sundhope lost in old sheep, 33 per cent; and in lambs, 66 per cent; which comes in all to 99 per cent. What a miserable remnant the poor farmer of Sundhope must have had of a good stock that year!* (The additional sentence here)

In a quotation from an essay by the Rev$^d$. Dr Singers, (p. 67) it is said, that "the stock contained on a farm is generally worth from four to seven year's rents." Well done Doctor! That must have been a valuable stock indeed! Had he said it was worth about two year's rents, he would have been nearer the truth, as things exist at present, than any of the given proportions.

The Hon. Captain likewise gives the authority of his herd, Wattie Scott, to a position, that the last winter, 1821–2, was the worst of the last five years. What will the gardeners on the Clyde and about Edin. say to this? What will every curling club in Scotland say to it, that got not one game on the ice during the whole season? Or the poacher (of which there are several about Ettrick) that never could trace a hare from his own kail yard. What will every other farmer and shepherd on the highest lands throughout the kingdom say to Wattie Scott's extraordinary peice of information, it being a well enough, and well ascertained fact, that the sheep never were better, nor less loss among them, in the memory of man? The Captain had better trust to his bills of mortality than to Wattie Scott's word, as we greatly suspect he will tell him the same story every winter, and produce more vouchers for it into the bargain.

There is another remarkable fact, that I am sorry it behoves me to mention in this place, for I do not dissaprove of one of the Captain's plans of improvement, nor do I think he has stated the benefits likely to result from them in any extravagant point of view; But in any case, the truth should not be concealed; and, singular as it may appear, I assert it as a fact, and shall be glad to hear an explanation of it, *That before any of these expensive improvements were executed on the farm of Thirlstane, the stock of sheep was manifestly better than they are now, with all the drains, rounds, parks, march dikes, and stacks of hay that has been provided for them.* I have not at present the means of ascertaining the exact numbers kept by the foregoing tenant; but I can assert further, and whoever denies or doubts it, I shall prove it to their satisfaction, *that the costs of sale sheep which he exposed every year during his lease, exceeded those exposed by the Captain as much in number as they excelled them in quality.* What will Wattie Scott, with his bad winters, and his 2000 stores of hay, say to this?

The Captain proceeds throughout his work on the apparent and liberal principle that the proprietor and tenant ought to go hand in all improvements and all losses. That what is the interest of the one cannot fail to be the interest of the other, and that it behoves them always to pull together, and never in contrary directions. In all that relates to the transactions between man and man it is impossible to think too highly of his generosity and candor. But on these matters we must allow him to speak for himself. On the subject of *led farms* his sentiments are as follows

There is scarce one of the 'led farms' just mentioned, that would not support a respectable tenant, with the present resident shepherd, now acting as manager and shepherd; who, for a little additional profit, is willing to do more than a resident tenant, without a grown-up son, would be satisfied or inclined to accomplish. Therefore, according to the present system, there is nearly *one-half* of the 'farming population' driven from the country, to gratify the avarice or ambition of individuals, under the false plea of paying more rent to the proprietor than the land could afford under the management of a resident farmer. From our own experience by this time, and from the numberless applicants for farms evinced on a late occasion in the counties of Peebles and Dumfries, we are not afraid to assert, that resident tenants are to be found in abundance, willing to pay as much for their farms as others give who live off them; and as for the expense of farm-house and offices, particularly as required upon 'hill-farms,' the erection of these may be made a profitable investment of capital on the part of the proprietor. A man must pay house-rent somewhere, and he may do it on a farm, as well as in villages or towns. We have already given it as our opinion, that a landlord, in common justice, is not authorized to let his lands at "rack-rent," however willing people may be to take them at such price,—driving on a miserable existence in poverty and filth; but a fair remunerating price to the one, and fair rent to the other, will cement that reciprocal interest and attachment, which is the strength, wealth, and safeguard, of every well regulated community. Look at Ireland—miserable, rack-rented, and 'deserted'

Ireland—how the degraded peasant seeks to wrest from the miserable farmer, not only the occupation of the land, but from the 'absent proprietor' the very possession of it! How should we look in the Forest under the effect of similar commotions? And if these commotions can be identified, *even in part*, with rack-rents and mismanagement of proprietors, why may not similar reasons produce similar effects at more distant times, even in the country which now affords secure and quiet habitations to those that yet remain?

Upon the principle of 'led farms,' we have no doubt whatever; but with the assistance of such faithful shepherds as are intrusted with the charge of those farms already, we could manage a farm-stock, covering an extent of country on both sides of Etterick,—all the way from Etterick Pen to Abbot's Ford, or perhaps below it; and what would then become of all our gallant yeomen, the heart and soul of the country, the terror of her invaders, and—with the magistrate—the constitutional preservers of our liberties and independence? The sooner, therefore, we see the whole of our farms, as opportunities occur, containing once more the legitimate occupiers—in happy independence and faithful adherence to the proprietors of the soil—not bachelors, but sires of an industrious, respectable, and virtuous population,—so much the sooner will every improvement arrive at perfection, and every article of produce, according to increased consumption, afford that rational return which arises from a just connection between produce and proper proportional demand.

To see the honour and independence of landlord, farmer, and peasant, each in his several situation, with the progress of every internal improvement, is what we most ardently do desire; and with such feeling, and for such purpose, we respectfully solicit an unbiassed attention to the plans we have now had the honour to propose.

With regard to the paying of rent according to the value of produce, he has the following observations in which every man of sense and feeling must concur

Arable farms are always subdivided into fields whose measurement is accurately ascertained, and paid for accordingly; whereas our hills, 'in a state of mere open waste,' are generally let according to the number of sheep they are *said* to contain, which must frequently be erroneous in the extreme; especially after the accomplishment of some little improvement effected at the commencement of a lease, perhaps by the liberality of the landlord. A rent, therefore, paid according to the value of produce, and that produce accurately understood, would reconcile many difficulties, preclude many heart-burnings, and confirm that mutual interest between landlord and tenant, which is often more spoken of in moments of general hilarity, than attended to in point of fact.

There may be, and there actually are, differences of opinion upon the subject of *paying of rent according to produce;* and, what is more extraordinary, there are some, whose speculative habits or inclinations would prevent them entering upon the measure at *one* time, while, under other circumstances, they would rejoice at the very proposal. So unsettled and so uncontrollable are the views of men in various stations of life, that even farmers themselves have often been led away and deceived through the vain hope of realizing sudden wealth, by grasping at numerous farms or very extended operations, under the prospect of improving times. Thus it is, that, when a farmer enters upon a lease at what he may conceive a moderate price, nothing short of ruin would induce him to alter the plan, and pay according to produce, because he would then *know at once the amount of his annual profits;* but on a sudden change in the times, attended with the deteriorating effects which we have witnessed of late years, there are many who would willingly renounce their leases, and compound almost at any price to save them from that destruction which must happen to those who, without a great capital, continue to pay a rent above the produce of the soil.

Rent according to produce *insures* to the tenant a return for his capital and industry; and to the landlord, the enjoyment of the fruits of the earth, according to the various degrees of fecundity or abundance which it hath pleased the Almighty to bestow. But farmers are often too speculative to make up their minds to a *certain* profit; they say, 'we are only farming for the landlord, not for ourselves; we are his managers, not his tenants; we risk our capital upon his ground at a *certain* price; we can never make more of it; we are tied down and confined within a certain sphere, and there we must remain without the chance of ever bettering ourselves.' Such are their arguments when they look back to the occasional prosperity which has been exemplified by individuals during these last thirty years, in the progress of reclaiming fertile but uncultivated lands held at low rents, and returning an unnatural profit through the disorganized state of Europe: They forget that there never was before such an anomalous state of things as that which succeeded to the sanguinary revolution of France; one of the principal effects of which was, to derange all classes and orders of society,–to divert the regular course of commerce from the ancient channels, and to give an impulse to the affairs of men in *this* country, which must naturally subside as order and regularity are resumed. One of the effects of these convulsions has been, to occasion a great interchange of landed property, so that in many instances the fortunate farmers have been enabled to purchase the lands they formerly held, from proprietors already incumbered with old standing mortgages or debts, and thus become the *lairds* themselves. No wonder, therefore, that the views of others rising in life, should receive a bias or impression from the peculiar circumstances which have been in operation during the younger part of their lives; but they must now remember, that the 'bubble has burst,' and with the cause must cease the effect, leaving them, as their forefathers were, in the very creditable and distinguished situation of BRITISH FARMERS,—the very heart and soul of this glorious and still-flourishing empire. Farmers, therefore, *must* be farmers; and the sooner they can unite themselves in a common interest with their landlords, which shall secure the just rights and consequent prosperity of either party, so much the sooner will there be an end to that outcry, which, in the middle of peace and plenty, is anomalously termed 'agricultural distress.'

To effect all this, landlords must be satisfied with *their proportion* of the produce; and a tenant need not aspire, in that particular, to be more free than the proprietor from whom he holds his farm; and let the leases run as a security to quiet possession or assedation to the tenant, which secures to him also a return for the value expended on the temporary improvement of the soil.

We believe that in no country in Europe have landed proprietors expended such sums within the last 50 years, for internal improvement, as has been exemplified by the public spirit of heritors and farmers in Scotland; and it is much to be lamented that their generous exertions have been so ill repaid by the sudden and unexpected depreciation in the value of national produce; and as many of them have entailed heavy burdens upon their estates by such operations, it is clear that nothing but a long train of prudent and economical measures can in any wise tend to redeem the original outlay, and so restore to the proprietors of the soil that degree of splendour which is due to their dignity and rank. But we protest vehemently against the too general system of seeking splendour and economy united, by an expatriation from the 'land of our forefathers,' to the 'lilied fields of France,' or the still more fascinating enjoyments of her gay but licentious metropolis. Every man, woman, and child, has a right to *travel*; it is a duty even incumbent on the higher ranks of society, to make themselves acquainted with the manners and customs of other countries, but not slavishly or conceited to adopt them. It strengthens the mind, matures the judgment, and dissipates prejudice and error by a *rational* intercourse with men of other countries; but, above all, to a 'Briton,' it teaches him, when surrounded by the bayonets, prisons, and inquisitions of Continental Europe, to admire, with holy reverence, the deeds of his forefathers—to value that liberty of conscience and that *personal* independence which has been transmitted and held unimpaired to the present time; and it ought, under such enjoyments, to stamp a pledge at his very 'heart's core,' never to desert the land of his nativity, at her utmost need, for the tinsel splendour, acquired at a cheap and shabby rate, the pleasure or profligacy, vice and effeminacy, inherent in the very character of those continental states most approved and resorted to by our national absentees. Let it not be thought that the peasant, the widow, and the orphan, are insensible to the effects of this *continental manianism*; the curses of thousands are borne on the unavailing breeze in the course of rich deserters; while the more patriotic, having it equally in their power to riot in extravagance and luxury, prefer to maintain that conscientious and dignified situation at home which commands the respect and blessings of the poor; with the rigid performance of that Christian duty which is implied in the scriptural text–'Unto whom much is given, *from him much shall be required.*'

There has been nothing said more forcible than this of all that has been said regarding the present distresses of the farming interest; and when we couple it with what follows we concieve that no more need to be [TEAR] to show the sentiments of the Hon<sup>ble</sup> author

It is very probable that sheep-lands paying at *this time* the prices of ten years back, afford a rent perhaps beyond their actual value, as things are; and when a tenant has accumulated a large profit, at the former expense of his landlord, we do not grudge him the pain of a certain disbursement; but, in most instances, farmers have *not* saved that probable superabundant profit. It has either been wasted by improvident expense, or frittered away by persevering in unprofitable speculation. Under these circumstances, it is impossible that the landlord can reclaim any part of the past profits, without imposing utter destruction upon his ill-fated tenant; and, indeed, whatever may be the amount of his free capital, as long as it has not been amassed from the profits of the land, we conceive, in all justice and humanity, let him be ever so much bound by the legal ties of a lease, when a sudden and continued depreciation of produce shall exist, that the landlord, under such circumstances, cannot be authorized to exact that which his land hath not positively produced. It may be argued, indeed, that a tenant takes his farm upon a lease with his eyes open; that a lease is a formal contract–an obligation binding both parties to abide for better or for worse by the specified terms; and although such is the case actually in fact, yet, when the general condition of the country is so much deteriorated as to preclude, on the part of the tenant, the possibility of his realizing that return which was looked for at the commencement of the lease, and upon the faith of which rested all his calculations,–it is then full time, on the part of the landlord, to condescend to such terms as can alone insure a just and permanent rent to himself, and continued security to his tenant. A lease should never be looked upon as the *medium of speculation* between the contracting parties; but as a safeguard to assedation, and the means of encouragement to the tenant–the laws of hypothec affording sufficient security to the landlord. If farmers, therefore, would condescend to pay according to produce, and if the landlords would regulate their expenditure according to a certain medium of income, as the ministers of the kirk are obliged to do, they would then participate in that regular and easy change in the value of the produce of their lands, and be spared that inconvenience which results from a sudden and serious diminution of their incomes.

*Postscript.*–Since the foregoing pages were sent to the press, the different banks have commenced discounting bills at four per cent. which, with the still further depreciation of mountain produce, operates in some measure to derange the profits arising out of our former calculations. We may remark, however, that the value of labour as well as of material, has also declined; and the very highest prices having been set against the improvements, we have no doubt, but, in most situations, they might be acquired, especially when the inclosures are laid together, at little more than *one half* of the sums proposed. Upon the whole, therefore, the diminished return will be balanced by the saving of expenditure, and we have still before us the HOPE of better prices, although the prospect undoubtedly is bad. Nothing at present is more worthy of our serious consideration than the sudden and unexpected fall in the price of wool. It is allowed on all hands, that, during these last two years, the manufacturers have been constantly employed at comfortable wages; and, although the profits of management have not been very great, or even granting them to have been very small, it must be allowed, with fully more justice, that the profits of the farmer, comparatively speaking, have been reduced to a mere cipher; and how the woolstaplers have been enabled to command so great a reduction of price in the value of that commodity, when distress bears harder upon the farmer than the manufacturer, is a subject worthy of the fullest investigation, not only upon the principle of self defence, but with the view to future justice and preservation. If this should prove to be the effect of combination, as many are of opinion, farmers must be more upon their guard for the future; but if it merely results from further depreciation throughout every ramification of the trade, from the raw material to every article of manufactured produce, farmers as well as landlords must just patiently submit to their own and *just proportion* of the common distress, and endeavour, in the mean time, to submit to the legislature such plans as will tend rather to protect the growth of the home material, upon which the prosperity of nine-tenths of the nation depends, than to encourage the importation of similar commodity from foreign states, to the ruin of the proprietors of the soil, and all those depending upon the value of its produce for the daily support of their families and themselves.

We fearlessly assert, in spite of the manufacturers–and we wish them every reasonable success–that as long as the duty upon the raw imported material is so low *as not to give a very decided preference* to the growth of our own country, that the best interests of proprietor, farmer, and peasant, are sacrificed to the weavers, whose numbers or whose importance are of small interest compared with that of the proprietor who upholds the dignity of national character and of the crown;–of the farmer, who directs the toil of the husbandman;–and of the peasant, whose strength and honest industry provides for us the bread of life; and from which three classes united, arise our statesmen, our soldiers, our sailors, and, above all, our COUNTRY GENTLEMEN–a denomination of resolute and patriotic men, unknown among the baser herds of Continental Europe; and that these, or any one of these, should suffer for the sake of eating foreign grain at a low rate, or of working up foreign wool, both of which are a drug in their respective countries, and thereby maintaining an unnatural proportion of manufacturers–we fearlessly assert, again, that for such purpose the best interests of the nation are SACRIFICED. Where is the benefit of collecting the whole fleeces of the world, and returning them in the shape of cloth, to the destruction of our own proprietors? It is a well known fact, that the prosperity of the kingdom depends upon the amount of its *own home consumption*, and that this consumption, again, depends upon the quantity of money circulating through every rank or gradation in society; and that this quantity, again, depends upon the *amount, in pounds, shillings, and pence*, of the value of the produce of the soil. If the country is inundated with corn or wool from other shores, then does the produce of our own country become a *drug;*–the farmer gets nothing for his crop, the proprietor gets nothing for his land, and the peasant may sit counting his fingers, and his children at his door, with little hope of work, and less chance of reward. Under such circumstances, the inevitable consequence of *free trade*, or even an approximation to free trade, before we recover from the tempest of the late mighty conflict in which we were engaged,– there must be a suspension, when the landed interest suffers, of that home consumption which forms the very basis of our national prosperity.–Hence desertion by the 'lords of the land,' with the little they have left, to foreign climes–and hence a natural demoralization and prostration of that national character, and that home-bred feeling, which have hitherto exalted the character of a Briton above the conception and beyond the understanding of other states around.

W. J. N.

*Thirlestane, 6th Sept.* 1822.

Thus it appears, that during the short period that the work has been in the press, farm stocking has undergone a farther depreciation in price, and that to such an extent as to have deranged all the captain's nicely balanced calculations. What is to be the end of this ruinous rise in the value of money to leaseholders in general, it is beyond our power to calculate; but at present it appears to us that all farming, and sheep farming in particular is grown to a mere humbug, and not worth wasting words about, far less good writing, together with

Messrs Balfour & Clark's best stile of printing. Every farmer is either a bankrupt in effect, or hanging on in a state of timid dependence, as completely in his laird's power either to ruin or save him, as ever the vassals of the Black Douglas were, or those of the ancient knights of Thirlstane under the most arbitrary ages of the feudal system. For the last 12 years there has been no money made by farming. Put the good and the bad seasons as to prices and losses over against each other, and it will soon appear that the balance is all on the wrong side; and now things are fairly come to that rate of derogation that a state of villenage must either return, or the present race of farmers cease to exist as the occupiers of the land. Were the proprietors and their factors all to pay the same attention to the actual existing state of the country that the Hon. W. J. Napier has done; or were they even to be at pains to profit by his unsophisticated statements, observations and example there might be some hope that the credit of the most valuable class of the community would still be preserved. But while these gentlemen are wasting their time, and the fruits of the farmer's skill and industry in a routine of elegant and fashionable amusements afar from their native hills and vallies, the ruin of their tenantry will only make an impression on their hearts when it begins to make a palpable deficiency in their yearly incomes, and when the decay in the vitals of their inheritance is too far gone to be retrieved.

# The Honourable Captain Napier and Ettrick Forest

*To Christopher North, Esq.*

SIR,—There is a work on pastoral economy which has lately made its appearance,* and as it merits the attention of the public in no ordinary degree at this critical period, I send you a few remarks on it, and anecdotes connected with it, for publication; knowing that no one is qualified for doing so, who is not intimately acquainted with the local circumstances of the country to which the book relates.

This is no work of a capricious and self-approving theorist, set

---

* A Treatise on Practical Store-Farming, as applicable to the Mountainous Region of Etterick Forest, and the Pastoral District of Scotland in general. By the Hon. William John Napier, F.R.S. Edinburgh, Post-Captain in the Royal Navy; a Vice-President of the Pastoral Society of Selkirkshire, &c. &c. With Engravings. Edinburgh: Waugh and Innes. 1822.

down to vend the feelings of a party, or set the interests of one part of the commonwealth against another—no dictatorial harangue of learned pedagogue, reasoning about matters of which he knows not the first principles. The author is no Mr Weir, proving the inefficiency of our present mode of pasturage from the Eclogues of Virgil, and the works of Aristotle; but the eldest son and heir of a nobleman, telling a plain unvarnished tale, about things in which he is deeply concerned, and recommending improvements, and those only by the adoption of which he must ultimately either be a gainer or a loser. There can, therefore, be no doubt whatsoever with regard to the sincerity and good intentions of its author; and it is impossible to read the work without perceiving throughout, the bold, fearless, independent, and generous spirit that indited it.

It is not my purpose to enter into a general detail of this genuine pastoral production; such disquisitions lie exactly four-and-thirty miles out of your way. (The distance betwixt Ambrose's and Ettrick Forest.) I know you do not wish to knock a respectable and long-established work on the head at once, by monopolizing every dingy art and science, but rather take a particular interest in the success of some of your contemporary journals, and have shewn that most forcibly, by shunning every object that lay in their path. You have even avoided the path itself, and the very department which it traverses, for fear of stumbling upon some of these objects; for there is no denying that you have a wonderful facility in striking your foot against certain objects with a devilish sharp kick; and more than that, the additional volitation acquired by such a stumble, is rather apt to make you run your head plump against the next person, or beast, that comes in your way.

I could not, however, relinquish this opportunity of saying a few words in approbation of the motives of my countryman—motives that do honour to human nature, and add lustre even to the noble class to which he belongs, and with which he is widely connected. He is the eldest son of Lord Napier, and heir-apparent to his lands and titles—the lineal descendant and representative not only of the famous Napiers of Merchiston, but also of a family of Scotts, of high Border lineage and fame, the ancient knights of Thirlstane and Howpasley. With an hereditary spirit of enterprize, he went into the Royal Navy when very young, and before he was nineteen years of age, served on board THE DEFENCE at the glorious battle of Trafalgar. After that, he was in many subsequent engagements—was twice wounded in battle; and at one time lay three months in an enemy's prison;—and these acts of chivalry, together with his family interest, raised him, by rapid steps, from the rank of midshipman, to that of post-captain in the Royal Navy.

At length, when his country had no more need of his arms, he laid aside the sword, and took up the shepherd's crook. From keeping long and indefatigable guard on the sublime elemental bulwark of his country, he retired to her most sequestered wildernesses—to one of her inland glens—to which cultivation had approached with slow and indignant motion—where antiquated forms, customs, and adages, lingered with an obstinacy only to be accounted for in the patriarchal feelings of an intelligent and thinking people. But these rules and adages had been transmitted to them by their fathers—handed down from generation to generation, by those whom they were taught to consider as wiser and better men than themselves; and they could not yield them up without reluctance. Against such prejudices, Captain Napier soon found that he would be obliged to contend in his new exertions to serve his country. But he was nothing daunted. He set a stout heart to a steep brae, and determined to gain the summit; seeing he could no longer benefit the land of his fathers, by wreaking vengeance on her enemies, or in defending her naval rights, he resolved to do so by his example, and to cultivate the rural arts of peace, to the utmost extent of his interest and ability.

His first exertions were directed towards that sort of improvement which ought ever to be the first in a country, and which necessarily *paves the way* for all others, namely, the improvement of the roads. In this he persevered with an obstinacy that was almost ludicrous. But neither fatigue nor opposition deterred or dispirited him for one moment—he wrote letters, called meetings, and made speeches, threatened some with the law, and others with acts of parliament, to make them acquiesce in that which was their own interests. He surveyed roads over mountains, and through glens and cataracts, carrying the end of the chain himself for many a weary day, and stopping at every turn to mark down the altitudes, rocks, bridges, and declivities. In these laborious peregrinations he surveyed many lines of road, where roads have never been made, nor ever will be made while the world stands. Among these may be mentioned an excellent one over Minchmoor, and another over Bodsbeck-Law, both rising with an abrupt ascent to the respectable elevation of 1900 feet above the level of the sea; of course excellently adapted for *winter roads*, as they would have been always blown quite free of snows during that boisterous season; and suppose a few scores of passengers might have perished annually on them, that was their own concern, so it behoved them to look to it.

It is true, a few impassable *wreaths* of snow might occasionally have intervened on these mountain ways; but as these could not have been supposed to have remained above five months at a time, or six at the most, we think it a pity that these lines of road had not been made, as we are sure the adjoining districts will miss them. People would have seen finely about them on a good day, and would have got such of their horses amazingly well tried, as were doubtful with regard to wind. But if the honourable Captain failed in effecting some of his lines of road, he sometimes had the good fortune to procure the making of two roads in the same line, or rather additional ones to those lately made, which might be a sort of indifferent compensation to the country for the loss of the others. A stranger need not be surprised on entering Ettrick Forest, at seeing two excellent roads sweeping along the bottom of a hill, within a few yards of each other, or at the farthest, not separated above a musket-shot–an improvement which, without doubt, tends mightily to the *facilitating of communication*, though not to the increase of the farmer's funds.

After those laborious surveys alluded to above, the Captain's work was but half begun: he had to descend into all the adjoining districts, and harass them without end for new lines to meet with his. He succeeded, by fair or foul means, in causing the upper district of Roxburgh-shire meet him with one in the middle of the inhospitable Moors of Ale–the Eskdale district of Dumfries-shire to meet him at a place called Tamleuchar-Cross, on the border of the two counties– the upper district of Annandale to meet him with one at Birkhill-Path. He was obliged to force one through a part of the county of Tweedale, by subscription, which was, however, readily supported by several gentlemen of that district; but they have hitherto withstood all his efforts, in meeting him with an effective line on the Edinburgh road, which still remains in a disgraceful state, considering the excellence of the line, and the expences that have been laid out on it, all to the southward. Every one of these new lines of road is of the utmost importance to the county. They open up a communication with each of the adjoining districts, and, through these, with every part of the united kingdom; and it cannot be denied, that for all these the country is mainly indebted to the unwearied exertions of Captain Napier.

The readiness that the other gentlemen trustees showed in backing his measures, made it apparent that the country only wanted such a spirit to put it into motion. Still, without such a moving spring, our cross roads might have continued in a state of nature for ages to come.

On reading over the Captain's very curious work, the first thing that strikes one is, how it could be possible that the occupiers of land in this celebrated pastoral district of Ettrick Forest should have been so backward in their improvements relating to the rearing and management of sheep, the sole staple commodity of their county. There is no doubt, however, of the fact—it actually was so; and every material change towards improvement was withstood as an innovation, till it could be withstood no longer—till the advanced rents compelled the farmers to adopt the measures that had apparently proved the most lucrative to others. Even after they had been sullenly adopted by the farmers, the old shepherds withstood them to the utmost of their power, and that with a virulence quite unexampled. These being a people that have great influence with their masters, contributed not a little to the retarding of these necessary improvements. When the draining of the land on which his hirsel grazed began first to be mentioned to the old shepherd, he is said to have replied with teeth clenched in despite, so that the words squeezed through them,—

"Ay, ay, rit and raise, cut and turn up; we'll see wha will be the profiter in the end. Mak seuchs to drown a' the new-drappit lambs, graves for the grit ewes, and canny uppittings for the wauf hoggs. Braw profits there, gudeman! Braw profits there! A wheen fine skins, a' daubit wi' drumble and ha' clay. They will gar somebody's pouches jingle!"

It was in vain that his master represented to him how they would improve the grass, and make dry lairs for his sheep. No reasoning could allay the indignation of old Bonnety, who replied, "Sic an improvement of the gerse as they will make! Raise us a loke soft toth, in place o' our good helsome prie, that used to keep the hearts o' a' the ewes hale in the lang lentrin days. And what will they make dry lairs to? To the blind moudiworts, to help them to turn the wrang side o' the grund outmost."

Now experience has fairly shewn the short-sightedness of these old shepherds; for, laying every other advantage aside, the draining of the country has banished the rot from among the flocks, or rendered its influences so trivial, as scarcely to be worth mentioning; whereas before, on wet and severe seasons, it either destroyed or injured the constitutions of the sheep of whole districts. The stells were not so bitterly opposed by the shepherds, but they were likewise in many instances made very light of. It was a common remark of theirs, when the plans of the new round stells were mentioned, "Na, na, commend me to the lown side of a green hill, after a', or the beildy swelsh of a gersy heuch. There is nae muckle to be pickit up at the back of a dirty stane dike."

But the greatest innovation of all on the old-fashioned bodies, both farmers and shepherds, was the introduction of the Cheviot breed of sheep, in the room of the old rough, hardy, black-faced natives of the soil. This was an æra in the annals of sheep-farming never to be forgotten, and far less ever to be blotted out of the shepherd's calendar. All the upper parts of Tweedale, Ettrick Forest, Annandale, and Clydesdale, were stocked with the latter breed, and these alone; and for many ages, the farmers and shepherds in these extensive districts held the white-faced, or Cheviot breed, in utter contempt. They called them "poor, beggarly, despicable animals, that needed to be fed with the hand of man, and put into a house in an ill day." Even the want of horns in the Cheviot breed was made a matter of reflection on them personally. They called them *the doddies*, and mocked the shepherds and farmers that stood by them in the sheep-markets. It was true, that when the black-faced sheep broke in a market, they always ran through the Cheviot droves without regarding them as sheep at all. While the white-faced lambs would have been lying in St Boswell's fair, peaceably and innocently chewing the cud, down would have come a precipitate and headlong drove of stout wedders, and run right over them, tumbling numbers of them right over and over. This naturally incensed the lowland shepherds, who kept crying, "Keep thae mad deils o' yours on their stance; d'ye think the green's to be laid waste wi' them? they'll pit away a' my lambs."– "Ay, gude troth, neighbour, I think your lambs winna rin very far; tak gude care that they dinna stick ye wi' their horns." Such jibes as these were to be heard in every fair.

But when they began to encroach piecemeal on the original stock, the country was put into a ferment. The neighbouring shepherds were so inveterate against them, that, if they could, they would have worried them all with their dogs, and it was often supposed that they did not get over fair play with their own shepherds themselves. Certain it is that they abhorred them, and would rather that their masters had lost a little, than they should have been encouraged to persevere in their injudicious improvements. There was no bad epithet, however, with which the poor creatures were not branded. They called them "vile, bleached, wan-looking devils–the very portraits of death– the ghosts of sheep; and whey-faced b–hes." The very children, in conformity with the humours and prejudices of their parents, pretended to be frightened for them as *wraiths*; and boys told long-winded stories of having met with stragglers of the new-come stock in the gloaming, and of having run off the hill in great terror, thinking they were "spirits of sheep, or old ewes rowed up in winding-sheets."

One of these old shepherds would have made a good subject for David Wilkie, when a drove of small Border lambs was first turned in before him at 14s. and 16s. a-head. The rueful despair that was painted on his countenance could not miss being noted by every one who saw him; and ever and anon as he spoke of them, he turned his face up towards the hill, and took another look of his old, stout, black-faced ewes, as if taking a last glimpse of all that belonged to the good and faithful *days of langsyne*. It was even reported that numbers of these old men, both shepherds and masters, when at family worship, prayed against *the doddies* every night. I have been at some pains to collect a few of these notes from the prayers of some of the most noted votaries of the old system, and must confess, if they were levelled against the Cheviot breed of sheep, they appear to have been managed very obliquely. *Auld Watie Brydon* was wont to pray every night, for two years running, to be "protected and defended from a' new comers, however *whitewashed* their faces might be; for they were but like whited walls, and painted sepulchres, full of rottenness within." Another worthy man, named James Bryden, prayed some once or twice in these words, "Keep back these invaders of our country, that are threatening to come upon us like the locusts in numbers and in power, eating up every green thing. May the nations of our land be enabled to push them down as with the horn of the unicorn, and tread them under their feet, that they may rise no more to spread upon our mountains, and encumber our valleys!" I think it very probable that this honest man meant the French; but perhaps he alluded to the horns of the black-faced sheep, and had the above-mentioned scenes of St Boswell's Fair in his eye, and liked to see the old breed treading the others under their feet. Old John Rieve (perhaps our correspondent means Grieve) was more pointed in his anathemas. When his next neighbour (whom, by the bye, he did not much like) laid first on a stock of *the doddies,* John prayed to the following purport: "And what wilt thou do with the fool who hast trod upon the ashes of his fathers—hath scattered his flocks, and brought home those of a far country, with great boasting and noise? It would be but justice wert thou to smite both his shepherds and his sheep, that they might fall down dead together, that their stink may come up into his nostrils, and their skins remain unto him for a prey." It was reported that Johny's prayer was but too well heard. "Direct us in the right way," said one, "in all things temporal as well as spiritual; and in these new-fangled times, if it is thy will that *black* should become *white*, we have nothing earthly to say." "O be nae just sae hard upon the auld stock," said auld Will o' Phaup, "but spare a wee bit remnant, to show the generations that are to come what has been afore them, or the very remembrance of the blue bonnets and the cloutit shoon will soon be nae mair, in the land for which they shed their blood."

These are only a few out of a great number that I collected, many of them too familiar with divinity to be inserted. But when the lambing season of the Cheviot flocks came on, the despair of the Forest and the other moorland shepherds reached its acme. They had been accustomed, with the old breed, to pay very little attention to them at such times. The wildest and most savage creatures have all the most powerful parental affections. The short ewe (as she is commonly denominated) would not leave her lamb for the severest of weather; or, if obliged to leave it for a little in search of necessary food, the yeanling would keep to its hole among the snow, or spot where its dam left it, certain of her return; and, even in these deplorable circumstances, the heroic little wretch would tramp with its fore foot, and whistle through its nose, with intent to defend its den against both the shepherd and his dog. It was generally noted, too, that on the heights and most exposed parts of a farm, there the dams were always kindliest to their young. Instances have been known that, when one of their lambs have perished in these inhospitable heights, in times of severity, the dam came and stood for some hours every day, over the carcase, till it was altogether consumed. And any of these creatures, when the shepherd stripped off the skin of her own lamb, and put it on another that had been one of twins, or otherwise deserted, would bleat over it at once out of pure affection, offer it the dug, and ever after acknowledge it as her own, shewing it even more kindness than ordinary, which seems to have originated in some indefinable feelings of the loss the creature deemed she had sustained, on experiencing the joys of a parent once more. If the shepherd had no lamb on the hill to supply the place of her own (it being common to take all such odd lambs into the house to be supplied with cow milk), it was a common practice with him to tie his garter to the dead lamb's foot and trail it after him; the ewe followed him, with her nose close over the body of her dead offspring, bleating all the way in a most melancholy tone, and every now and then chasing the shepherd's dog, which she would scarcely suffer to come within sight. In this manner he could have led her in beyond the fire, or into any corner of any house he chose, in order to get another lamb set to her.

This strong natural affection the Cheviot ewe possessed in a very inferior degree. When straitened with cold or hunger, she left her lamb without ever thinking of returning to the spot where she left it. The lamb, if it was able, would trail away after any sheep that came by the bye; then they were all of them so bare and delicate, that they fell down and died beneath every blast. In short, the latter were creatures that required ten times the attention of the others, consequently the Halcyon days of the shepherds were gone; and it was observed that the old shepherds that had been all their lives used with the Scottish breed of sheep, never could be broke to pay that attention to the newly introduced stock that was requisite, while the young ones that were bred and innured to it, grew as attentive as it was possible to be.

It was not, therefore, for nothing that the shepherds withstood the introduction of the Cheviot stock, nor was it without reason that the farmers disapproved of it. It had been better for them all, not excluding the proprietor, that they had never been introduced into the high lying districts to this day. Every ground kept one-sixth of more stock then than it does at the present time; and if the ground had been drained and sheltered in the same way that it is now, each farm would have kept one-fifth more of the black than white-faced breed. The lambs fed fat in one-half of the time. At least, they were as fat by the middle of July, as the Cheviot lambs are at the end of August, on the same land. What an advantage that would have been in such times as these! There has been a good deal of money made by the change in low-lying farms that were fairly stocked before the rage for Cheviot stock came to its height; but in all high-lying districts, we appeal to the farmers themselves, taking in the loss that was suffered by the change, if the fine stock have not been a losing concern on the whole.

The truth is, that they would never have been introduced but for this reason:—The prices of their wool ran so high, that the rents kept pace with that; and at the commencement of every new lease, the farmer saw no shift, whereby he could make any profit, save by the introduction of the Cheviot breed of sheep. For the one-half of the lease, the time, namely, that he took in stocking up, he was a loser. During the remainder of the lease, perhaps he was a gainer to a certain amount; but then the rent was sure to be raised for the next lease in proportion; and forthwith he found himself engaged with an animal ill adapted to the climate, making ostensible profits at one time, but these all counterbalanced now and then by severe losses, which, for all Captain Napier's ingenious reasoning, *can not* be prevented in some seasons by the power of man.

These assertions might be considered futile, were they not supported by the most obvious of all reasoning. Some of the most extensive and enlightened farmers in the whole country, and some of these the honourable author's next neighbours, after having had a Cheviot stock for upwards of thirty years, and success equal to their neighbours, are again beginning, by degrees, to introduce the old Forest breed. It has never yet been tried how fine the wool of that breed could be made, the coarsest and most shaggy woolled ones always having been preferred as the truest and hardiest kind. I could give you a number of specious reasons, shewing, that by adopting a certain form of that animal, the wool could be brought to much the same quality as that shorn from a cross breed between the Cheviot and short sheep; but, as I said at first, I have no desire to enter into the minutiæ of these matters, but merely to select a number of curious and interesting particulars relating to that pastoral department of our country; but I have no doubt whatever that the aboriginal breed was the best suited both to the soil and climate of the district.

However, as the honourable author, without all dispute, thinks otherwise, and as all, or the greater part of farmers and gentlemen in these bounds, have given evidence that they *once* thought otherwise, by the choice they made, I shall, for the present, proceed with some more anecdotes of our noble sailor's exertions to promote the interests of his country in general, and in particular the spot where his father's estates lie—the parishes of Ettrick and Yarrow.

Knowing that example always goes before precept, he took one of his father's farms into his own hand, the same on which the castle of his forefathers stood in former generations, and immediately set about shewing the farmers and proprietors *what might be done* with a pastoral farm. These experiments are all so fully and so fearlessly detailed in his work now before the public, that to it I must refer the reader; for though the farm is there represented as an ideal one, it is quite manifest to what farm all the calculations allude. In the mean time, he was not negligent, along with the roads and bridges, to push on every improvement in his power. A superb castle arose immediately beside the ruins of that which his ancestors inherited; plantations were laid out suiting the extent of the property and face of the country, for that is exclusively pastoral, and large plantations of wood would only deface it;—neat and elegant cottages were placed along the whole line of his father's property, like gems in the baldrick of a savage: and, above all, public markets for the whole product of the country were established on the Captain's own farm, free of all custom or expences whatever. The exposers find a good stone wall around the market place, plenty of bounds, and excellent ground for the show. Those who have smaller lots, or fat sheep for sale, find plenty of pens erected ready to their hands; and those who delight in eating and drinking, find houses erected for their accommodation, for which even the tavern-keeper pays no rent, but vends the good things of this life to his customers with a liberal hand, and at the cheapest rate, as he well may. The shoemaker vends his sandals, the wife of Lochmaben her crockery ware; the petty ale-house-keeper comes and erects his tent as freely and independently as the Wahabee Indian erects his in his native wood;—the itinerant pedlar, the fruit-erer, and every vender of petty wares, down to the ragged Black-Jock-man, with his three sticks, come there to traffic, without expence, and without reproof. But then there is a substantial round-house erected by the way side, in the full view of every one in the fair, and plenty of constables in attendance, ready at the call of whoever wants them. These seem to have acted powerfully as a check to all misde-meanours; for from the day that the prison was erected, it has never yet been tenanted, although, before that, it was so much wanted, that the constables were obliged to lay their prisoners up in an old barn, with two doors, neither of which had a lock, and get their heads broken in the course of their attendance.

These markets have proved, and are like to prove, of the greatest utility to Ettrick Forest, and the districts adjacent—in particular, the lamb fair in July, and the ewe fair in September. At both these mar-kets, though great numbers of the very best stock in Scotland have been exposed, it is asserted that the show has hardly ever been equal to the demand. If the rest should chance not to succeed in the same degree, it will be the fault of the farmers, for it is impossible that any markets can ever suit them so well. They are placed in the very middle of the finest pastoral district of our country, and the sheep appear at them in the freshest state imaginable.

His next great effort was the establishment of the Pastoral Club, a society founded on the most liberal and enlightened views, for the encouragement of pastoral farming in all its branches, and all their ramifications. In this plan he was joined at once by great numbers of gentlemen, and almost by every respectable farmer in the bounds, manifesting still farther the great utility of such a stirring character to a country. Every farmer, for the best breeds of stock, of all ages and denominations, and even the servant that has proved himself the most expert and attentive to the charge committed to him, all find liberal premiums paid to them in ready gold. The emulation that these have excited, both among masters and servants, promise to be of the highest utility, acting as a spur to every species of industry.

Captain Napier has moreover proved himself the father of the poor, in the fullest sense of the word. The smallest of their deprivations has proved matter of attention to him. Not only in his own parish, but in those adjacent, has he been attentive to every case of distress. He has sometimes been blamed for patronizing the good and the bad, the worthy and the unworthy, with the same degree of sympathy and perseverance. Concerning this I can say nothing, but suppose that human suffering was always plea sufficient for his interference. He disapproves radically of the principle of the poors' rates, in as far as they approximate to those of England, and has been at great pains in modifying them so in the two parishes with which he is connected, that they cannot be increased, but, without some singular dispensation of Providence, must gradually diminish.

He is a strong advocate for all the observances of our holy religion; and as the parishes of Ettrick and Yarrow is the land of shepherds, the consequence is, that one-third of these congregations has always been wont to consist of decent, respectable-looking colley dogs. However, there were often some of them but middling well bred, and did not account much of kicking up a stour in the area, by beginning a battle-general; they were, moreover, often guilty of some other venial improprieties, scarcely becoming the sanctity of the place. So acute are the observations of these creatures, that although, during the course of the service, the people arose twice in time of prayers, that made no difference in the deportment of the minor and subordinate part of the community. But so horribly tired were the rascals of listening to precept and prayer, that the moment the blessing began to be pronounced, they broke all out at once, with one tremendous volley of joy, so that no man or woman in these parishes ever heard a word of the blessing, the response proved so transcendantly vociferous. It had therefore been the custom, time out of mind, in these two parishes, for the people to sit still on their seats, without moving a finger, till the blessing was pronounced. This took the greater part of the dogs at unawares; and the parson got the blessing breathed softly over without much interruption. There were, nevertheless, some old experienced tikes that generally began a whining and whimpering the moment the minister lifted his hand; and if a single arm was stretched out for a hat, the fray began. But over and above all this, there are numbers of these animals, of a certain extravagant poetical breed, endowed with most unequivocal organs of music, and took it on them to join the clamorous harmony of the mountain church-music, bearing a part in every psalm that was sung; and so overpowering were their notes on some occasions, that there was not a voice to be heard in the church, save the precentor's and their own. On the whole, there was something in the economy of this mingled congregation that the Captain did not like, so he set his face against the canine part of the community altogether, threatening them with the lesser excommunication, namely, an utter expulsion from divine ordinances; so in two weeks that was effected, which had hitherto been held as impracticable; and the church of Ettrick was thereafter as clear of dogs as any church in the kingdom. Every person now rises up reverendly in his pew, during the time the blessing is a pronouncing; and there are as graceful bows and courtesies to be seen there as any where else. Nay, it is said the congregation rather appear to excel in that, the late acknowledged subordination of rank, in the expulsion of this minor and riotous class, appearing to have given *a new spring* to their devotions. Of all these graceful and becoming attitudes, the people of Yarrow are deprived; they are still obliged to adhere to the old system, keeping close to their seats in time of the blessing, *in order to cheat the dogs.*

But all the opposition that has been made to the religious principles of these independent animals, seems still to have been of small avail. Like other persecuted sects, their zeal appears to have increased in proportion to the power by which they were opposed. For thirty years and upwards, I have been an occasional attendant on divine service in the church of Ettrick, many of these a constant one; and all that time, no one ever thought of rising during the time of the blessing. But the other day I chanced to be there again, and found my old friends much the same as ever, running races and fighting battles in the area; barking at the blessing, and indulging in all their proscribed ritual, with a considerable shew of ostentation. It might perhaps be no bad hint to the people of Ettrick, (or rather *Etterick*, as Mr Boston and the Captain spell it,) that they had better not boast much of the victory gained over the dogs, and keep to their seats in the time of the blessing as formerly, else every person present must laugh at that most solemn part of the service.

Such is the man, and such the persevering spirit of him whose work I have so lately been perusing. After having done every thing in his power by way of shewing an example to his father's tenants, and his countrymen in general, he has now laid the issue of all his experiments openly and fairly before the public, that every man may judge for himself, and profit by that which has cost him nothing. I am now thoroughly persuaded, and am certain that I will be borne out by every gentleman of the Border districts, when I say, that I know of no man who deserves better of his country than Captain Napier, nor one who has effected so much for its improvement, from the resources of a private fortune. What a pattern is such a man to the young noblemen and gentlemen of our land! Were each of them but to pay one-half the attention to their native soil, and the various districts of it with which they are connected, what a difference would soon be made in the appearance of the country! and how much a thousand casual distresses and local inconveniences might be obviated!

With regard to the work itself, I shall only remark in general, that all of it that is the Captain's own appears to be the least objectionable. The reasoning is candid and obvious, and the calculations never extravagant. But there are many parts extracted from the writings of others, the accuracy of which there is great reason to doubt. In the first place, he introduces a number of Mr Hogg's stories as if they were gospel. They may be truth for ought I know to the contrary, but they do not read very like it. What an enormous scene these *Beds of Esk* must have exhibited after the great thaw in February 1794! "Eighteen hundred and sixty sheep, nine black cattle, three horses, two men, one woman, forty-five dogs, and one hundred and eighty hares!!!" Would not you, sir, have liked to have seen your friend the shepherd running among all this carnage, picking up the hares, and ever and anon exclaiming, "Gude faith, Clavers lad, ye may gae your ways to your grave!" I cannot but wonder if the author really believed in the correctness of this statement himself.

There is another shepherd, named Alexander Laidlaw, on whose Diary the Captain places a great deal of reliance, as a basis whereon to found his theories. It is a curious document,–a very curious one indeed–but I have great reason for doubting its accuracy regarding the losses on such and such farms during the severe winters of the last century, and wish he had consulted the memories of some old shepherds a little more sedulously–the best chronicles of such events. But when a man cannot give correct statements of matters that passed under his own eye, how shall we credit him in those 150 years ago? I could mention several of these inaccuracies in his letter, which, though very trivial in themselves, render his curious Diary doubtful. As an instance, in stating the losses in his neighbourhood in the storm of 1794, he says, "Eldinhope lost the greatest number, amounting, it was said, to 100." Now the fact is, that Eldinhope lost upwards of eleven score. There were nine score and fourteen all smoored in one place–(the Wolf-Cleuch.) They lost all their tups beside, and several other stragglers. Such a mistake is the more singular, as this was a neighbouring farm, on the hills of which he turned his eyes every day, and must have known what loss was suffered there, as well as he did on the farm on which he herded.

In 1799, he says, the farm of Sundhope lost in old sheep, 33 per cent., and in lambs, 66 per cent., which comes in all to 99 per cent. What a miserable remnant the poor farmer of Sundhope must have had of a good stock that year!

In stating the losses in 1799, he says, that Benger Burn had an entire Cheviot stock, but that Crosslee had only hoggs and gimmers. So far from this being the truth, the Crosslee had a complete stock of Cheviots, and Benger Burn had not. In order to refresh Laidlaw's memory a little in this, I beg leave to remind him, that both these farms began the change in the same year, 1793. The farmers bought their lambs conjointly that year, at the Langholm fair; and on the next year following, Mr Bryden of Crosslee bought the Hope's Rigg and Woolee ewes. These brought him nearly into a regular system at once, whereas Mr Scott of Benger Burn only stocked up by buying lambs every year; and in 1799, when his old shepherd died, the half nearly of his pack was of the old breed, and a part of them a cross breed. Though these are things of small consequence, they shew how much Laidlaw writes at random, even of the things of his own day; and therefore people need not be surprised, if in writing of incidents that occurred two hundred years ago, he should place a remarkable æra a few years out of its place, and assert likewise that it happened in March, in place of the latter end of January and begin-ning of February. After all, it must be confessed, that the Captain gives all these with caution, and provisionally, so that they never affect his arguments.

In a quotation from an Essay by the Rev. Dr Singers, (p. 67,) it is said, that "the stock contained on a farm is generally worth from four to seven years' rents." Well done, Doctor! That must have been a valuable stock indeed! Had he said it was worth about two years' rents, he would have been nearer the truth, as things exist at present, than any of the given proportions.

The honourable Captain likewise gives the authority of his herd, Wattie Scott, to a position, that the last winter, 1821–2, was the worst of the last five years. What will the gardeners on the Clyde and about Edinburgh say to this? What will every curling club in Scot-land say to it, that got not one game on the ice during the whole season? Or the poacher (of which there are several about Ettrick) that never could trace a hare from his own kail-yard? What will every other farmer and shepherd on the highest lands throughout the kingdom say to Wattie Scott's extraordinary piece of information, it being a well ascertained fact, that the sheep never were better, nor less loss among them, in the memory of man? The Captain had better trust to his bills of mortality than to Wattie Scott's word, as we greatly suspect he will tell him the same story every winter, and produce more vouchers for it into the bargain.

There is another thing to be taken into consideration. Captain Napier could scarcely have got such another field whereon to carry his operations into effect, as the farm of Thirlestane, there being very few indeed in the south of Scotland, on which a farmer can cope with him on equal terms. The stock was an excellent stock in his predecessor's time, before these improvements were begun–I scarcely ever saw a better; and I know that many of the neighbouring farmers think they were better then than they are now. So do I; but I find the shepherds who have served both masters think otherwise; and it is but reasonable that it should be otherwise. The truth is, that such judges as I am, have no other way of deciding on these matters, but by the sheep brought to market; and from these specimens, taking in both the numbers and quality, I would not hesitate in giving the preference to the stock of the former tenant. But there are so many ways of farming, and of drawing a stock; and the Captain and his predecessor differing so materially in both these points, I must still leave it to a further issue, and the experience of more seasons, before calculating positively on the utility of all these expensive improvements.

The Captain's plan of making the farmer's rent always bear a proportion with his profits, is too minute for a common shepherd like me fully to comprehend; but this is evident, that it has been held up to ridicule by some journalists, (who shall be nameless,) but who have apparently never looked it over, as their remarks bear upon any thing but the conclusion at which he arrives. I would refer to that part of the summary, as an instance of the author's extraordinary acuteness and circumstantiality in making out his inferences; as also to that on the lambing of gimmers, beginning at page 251. That is a subject which I have studied all my life, and yet I cannot tell which is the best way; namely, whether the gimmers should be suffered to have lambs or not. The history of the experiment is simply as follows:–You have all the gimmer lambs additional for sale the first year, but rather less wool. The next year you have still more lambs, for there is no kind of sheep so ticklish in bringing a lamb as an eild gimmer; and at the Martinmas following, they are the worst sheep on the farm–quite inferior in condition to those that have brought two lambs. But how it comes I know not, they uniformly turn out the best sheep in the end, and add greatly to the value of a cast of draft ewes. On the whole, I would rather recommend the lambing of the gimmers, save on very high-lying pastures, or where the farmer values himself much on the character of his draft ewes in the Yorkshire markets.

The Captain proceeds throughout his work on the apparent and liberal principle, that the proprietor and tenant ought to go hand in hand in all improvements and all losses. That what is the interest of the one, cannot fail to be the interest of the other, and that it behoves them always to pull together, and never in contrary directions. In all that relates to the transactions between man and man, it is impossible to think too highly of his generosity and candour. But on these matters, we must allow him to speak for himself. On the subject of *led farms* his sentiments are as follows:–

> "There is scarce one of the 'led farms' just mentioned, that would not support a respectable tenant, with the present resident shepherd, now acting as manager and shepherd; who, for a little additional profit, is willing to do more than a resident tenant, without a grown-up son, would be satisfied or inclined to accomplish. Therefore, according to the present system, there is nearly *one-half* of the 'farming population' driven from the country, to gratify the avarice or ambition of individuals, under the false plea of paying more rent to the proprietor than the land could afford under the management of a resident farmer. From our own experience by this time, and from the numberless applicants for farms evinced on a late occasion in the counties of Peebles and Dumfries, we are not afraid to assert, that resident tenants are to be found in abundance, willing to pay as much for their farms as others give who live off them; and as for the expense of farm-house and offices, particularly as required upon 'hill-farms,' the erection of these may be made a profitable investment of capital on the part of the proprietor. A man must pay house-rent somewhere, and he may do it on a farm, as well as in villages or towns. We have already given it as our opinion, that a landlord, in common justice, is not authorized to let his lands at "rack-rent," however willing people may be to take them at such a price,–driving on a miserable existence in poverty and filth; but a fair remunerating price to the one, and fair rent to the other, will cement that reciprocal interest and attachment, which is the strength, wealth, and safeguard, of every well-regulated community. Look at Ireland–miserable, rack-rented, and 'deserted' Ireland–how the degraded peasant seeks to wrest from the miserable farmer, not only the occupation of the land, but from the 'absent proprietor' the very possession of it! How should we look in the Forest under the effect of similar commotions? And if these

commotions can be identified, *even in part*, with rack-rents and mismanagement of proprietors, why may not similar reasons produce similar effects at more distant times, even in the country which now affords secure and quiet habitations to those that yet remain?

"Upon the principle of 'led farms,' we have no doubt whatever; but with the assistance of such faithful shepherds as are intrusted with the charge of those farms already, we could manage a farm stock, covering an extent of country on both sides of Etterick,—all the way from Etterick Pen to Abbot's Ford, or perhaps below it; and what would then become of all our gallant yeomen, the heart and soul of the country, the terror of her invaders, and—with the magistrate—the constitutional preservers of our liberties and independence? The sooner, therefore, we see the whole of our farms, as opportunities occur, containing once more the legitimate occupiers—in happy independence and faithful adherence to the proprietors of the soil—not bachelors, but sires of an industrious, respectable, and virtuous population,—so much the sooner will every improvement arrive at perfection, and every article of produce, according to increased consumption, afford that rational return which arises from a just connection between produce and proper proportional demand.

"To see the honour and independence of landlord, farmer, and peasant, each in his several situation, with the progress of every internal improvement, is what we most ardently do desire; and with such feeling, and for such purpose, we respectfully solicit an unbiassed attention to the plans we have now had the honour to propose."

With regard to the paying of rent according to the value of produce, he has the following observations, in which every man of sense and feeling must concur:—

"Arable farms are always subdivided into fields whose measurement is accurately ascertained, and paid for accordingly; whereas our hills, 'in a state of mere open waste,' are generally let according to the number of sheep they are *said* to contain, which must frequently be erroneous in the extreme; especially after the accomplishment of some little improvement effected at the commencement of a lease, perhaps by the liberality of the landlord. A rent, therefore, paid according to the value of produce, and that produce accurately understood, would reconcile many difficulties, preclude many heart-burnings, and confirm that mutual interest between landlord and tenant, which is often more spoken of in moments of general hilarity, than attended to in point of fact.

"There may be, and there actually are, differences of opinion upon the subject of *paying of rent according to produce;* and, what is more extraordinary, there are some, whose speculative habits or inclinations would prevent them entering upon the measure at *one* time, while, under other circumstances, they would rejoice at the very proposal. So unsettled and so uncontrollable are the views of men in various stations of life, that even farmers themselves have often been led away and deceived through the vain hope of realizing sudden wealth, by grasping at numerous farms or very extended operations, under the prospect of improving times. Thus it is, that, when a farmer enters upon a lease at what he may conceive a moderate price, nothing short of ruin would induce him to alter the plan, and pay according to produce, because he would then *know at once the amount of his annual profits;* but on a sudden change in the times, attended with the deteriorating effects which we have witnessed of late years, there are many who would willingly renounce their leases, and compound almost at any price to save them from that destruction which must happen to those who, without a great capital, continue to pay a rent above the produce of the soil.

"Rent according to produce *insures* to the tenant a return for his capital and industry; and to the landlord, the enjoyment of the fruits of the earth, according to the various degrees of fecundity or abundance which it hath pleased the Almighty to bestow. But farmers are often too speculative to make up their minds to a *certain* profit; they say, 'we are only farming for the landlord, not for ourselves; we are his managers, not his tenants; we risk our capital upon his ground at a *certain* price; we can never make more of it; we are tied down and confined within a certain sphere, and there we must remain without the chance of ever bettering ourselves.' Such are their arguments when they look back to the occasional prosperity which has been exemplified by individuals during these last thirty years, in the progress of reclaiming fertile but uncultivated lands held at low rents, and returning an unnatural profit through the disorganized state of Europe: They forget that there never was before such an anomalous state of things as that which succeeded to the sanguinary revolution of France; one of the principal effects of which was, to derange all classes and orders of society,—to divert the regular course of commerce from the ancient channels, and to give an impulse to the affairs of men in *this* country, which must naturally subside as order and regularity are resumed. One of the effects of these convulsions has been, to occasion a great interchange of landed property, so that in many instances the fortunate farmers have been enabled to purchase the lands they formerly held, from proprietors already encumbered with old standing mortgages or debts, and thus become the *lairds* themselves. No wonder, therefore, that the views of others rising in life, should receive a bias or impression from the peculiar circumstances which have been in operation during the younger part of their lives; but they must now remember, that the 'bubble has burst,' and with the cause must cease the effect, leaving them, as their forefathers were, in the very creditable and distinguished situation of BRITISH FARMERS,—the very heart and soul of this glorious and still flourishing empire. Farmers, therefore, *must* be farmers; and the sooner they can unite themselves in a common interest with their landlords, which shall secure the just rights and consequent prosperity of either party, so much the sooner will there be an end to that outcry, which, in the middle of peace and plenty, is anomalously termed 'agricultural distress.'

"To effect all this, landlords must be satisfied with *their proportion* of the produce; and a tenant need not aspire, in that particular, to be more free than the proprietor from whom he holds his farm; and let the leases run as a security to quiet possession or assedation to the tenant, which secures to him also a return for the value expended on the temporary improvement of the soil.

"We believe that in no country in Europe have landed proprietors expended such sums within the last fifty years, for internal improvement, as has been exemplified by the public spirit of heritors and farmers in Scotland; and it is much to be lamented that their generous exertions have been so ill repaid by the sudden and unexpected depreciation in the value of national produce; and as many of them have entailed heavy burdens upon their estates by such operations, it is clear that nothing but a long train of prudent and economical measures can in any wise tend to redeem the original outlay, and so restore to the proprietors of the soil that degree of splendour which is due to their dignity and rank. But we protest vehemently against the too general system of seeking splendour and economy united, by an expatriation from the 'land of our forefathers,' to the 'lilied fields of France,' or the still more fascinating enjoyments of her gay but licentious metropolis. Every man, woman, and child, has a right to *travel*; it is a duty even incumbent on the higher ranks of society, to make themselves acquainted with the manners and customs of other countries, but not slavishly or conceitedly to adopt them. It strengthens the mind, matures the judgment, and dissipates prejudice and error by a *rational* intercourse with men of other countries; but, above all, to a 'Briton,' it teaches him, when surrounded by the bayonets, prisons, and inquisitions of Continental Europe, to admire, with holy reverence, the deeds of his forefathers−to value that liberty of conscience and that *personal* independence which has been transmitted and held unimpaired to the present time; and it ought, under such enjoyments, to stamp a pledge at his very 'heart's core,' never to desert the land of his nativity, at her utmost need, for the tinsel splendour, acquired at a cheap and shabby rate, the pleasure or profligacy, vice and effeminacy, inherent in the very character of those continental states most approved and resorted to by our national absentees."

There has been nothing said more forcible than this, of all that has been said regarding the present distresses of the farming interest; and when I couple it with what follows, I conceive that no more need be said by me to shew the sentiments of the honourable author.

"It is very probable that sheep-lands paying at *this time* the prices of ten years back, afford a rent perhaps beyond their actual value, as things are; and when a tenant has accumulated a large profit, at the former expense of his landlord, we do not grudge him the pain of a certain disbursement; but, in most instances, farmers have *not* saved that probable superabundant profit. It has either been wasted by improvident expense, or frittered away by persevering in unprofitable speculation. Under these circumstances, it is impossible that the landlord can reclaim any part of the past profits, without imposing utter destruction upon his ill-fated tenant; and, indeed, whatever may be the amount of his free capital, as long as it has not been amassed from the profits of the land, we conceive, in all justice and humanity, let him be ever so much bound by the legal ties of a lease, when a sudden and continued depreciation of produce shall exist, that the landlord, under such circumstances, cannot be authorized to exact that which his land hath not positively produced. It may be argued, indeed, that a tenant takes his farm upon a lease with his eyes open; that a lease is a formal contract—an obligation binding both parties to abide for better or for worse by the specified terms; and although such is the case actually in fact, yet, when the general condition of the country is so much deteriorated as to preclude, on the part of the tenant, the possibility of his realizing that return which was looked for at the commencement of the lease, and upon the faith of which rested all his calculations,—it is then full time, on the part of the landlord, to condescend to such terms as can alone insure a just and permanent rent to himself, and continued security to his tenant. A lease should never be looked upon as the *medium of speculation* between the contracting parties; but as a safeguard to assedation, and the means of encouragement to the tenant—the laws of hypothec affording sufficient security to the landlord. If farmers, therefore, would condescend to pay according to produce, and if the landlords would regulate their expenditure according to a certain medium of income, as the ministers of the kirk are obliged to do, they would then participate in that regular and easy change in the value of the produce of their lands, and be spared that inconvenience which results from a sudden and serious diminution of their incomes.

"*Postscript.*—Since the foregoing pages were sent to the press, the different banks have commenced discounting bills at four per cent., which, with the still further depreciation of mountain produce, operates in some measure to derange the profits arising out of our former calculations. We may remark, however, that the value of labour as well as of material, has also declined; and the very highest prices having been set against the improvements, we have no doubt but, in most situations, they might be acquired, especially when the inclosures are laid together, at little more than *one-half* of the sums proposed. Upon the whole, therefore, the diminished return will be balanced by the saving of expenditure, and we have still before us the HOPE of better prices, although the prospect undoubtedly is bad. Nothing at present is more worthy of our serious consideration, than the sudden and unexpected fall in the price of wool. It is allowed on all hands, that, during these last two years, the manufacturers have been constantly employed at comfortable wages; and, although the profits of management have not been very great, or even granting them to have been very small, it must be allowed, with fully more justice, that the profits of the farmer, comparatively speaking, have been reduced to a mere cypher; and how the woolstaplers have been enabled to command so great a reduction of price in the value of that commodity, when distress bears harder upon the farmer than the manufacturer, is a subject worthy of the fullest investigation, not only upon the principle of self-defence, but with the view to future justice and preservation. If this should prove to be the effect of combination, as many are of opinion, farmers must be more upon their guard for the future; but if it merely results from further depreciation throughout every ramification of the trade, from the raw material to every article of manufactured produce, farmers as well as landlords must just patiently submit to their own and *just proportion* of the common distress, and endeavour, in the mean time, to submit to the legislature such plans as will tend rather to protect the growth of the home material, upon which the prosperity of nine-tenths of the nation depends, than to encourage the importation of similar commodity from foreign states, to the ruin of the proprietors of the soil, and all those depending upon the value of its produce for the daily support of their families and themselves.

"We fearlessly assert, in spite of the manufacturers–and we wish them every reasonable success–that as long as the duty upon the raw imported material is so low *as not to give a very decided preference* to the growth of our own country, that the best interests of proprietor, farmer, and peasant, are sacrificed to the weavers, whose numbers or whose importance are of small interest compared with that of the proprietor, who upholds the dignity of national character and of the crown;– of the farmer, who directs the toil of the husbandman;–and of the peasant, whose strength and honest industry provides for us the bread of life; and from which three classes united, arise our statesmen, our soldiers, our sailors, and, above all, our COUNTRY GENTLEMEN–a denomination of resolute and patriotic men, unknown among the baser herds of Continental Europe; and that these, or any one of these, should suffer for the sake of eating foreign grain at a low rate, or of working up foreign wool, both of which are a drug in their respective countries, and thereby maintaining an unnatural proportion of manufacturers—we fearlessly assert, again, that for such purpose the best interests of the nation are SACRIFICED. Where is the benefit of collecting the whole fleeces of the world, and returning them in the shape of cloth, to the destruction of our own proprietors? It is a well-known fact, that the prosperity of the kingdom depends upon the amount of its *own home consumption*, and that this consumption, again, depends upon the quantity of money circulating through every rank or gradation in society; and that this quantity, again, depends upon the *amount, in pounds, shillings, and pence*, of the value of the produce of the soil. If the country is inundated with corn or wool from other shores, then does the produce of our own country become a *drug;*—the farmer gets nothing for his crop, the proprietor gets nothing for his land, and the peasant may sit counting his fingers, and his children at his door, with little hope of work, and less chance of reward. Under such circumstances, the inevitable consequence of *free trade*, or even an approximation to free trade, before we recover from the tempest of the late mighty conflict in which we were engaged,—there must be a suspension, when the landed interest suffers, of that home consumption which forms the very basis of our national prosperity.—Hence desertion by the 'lords of the land,' with the little they have left, to foreign climes—and hence a natural demoralization and prostration of that national character, and that home-bred feeling, which have hitherto exalted the character of a Briton above the conception and beyond the understanding of other states around.

"W. J. N.

*"Thirlstane, 6th Sept. 1822."*

Thus, it appears, that during the short period that the work has been in the press, farm stocking has undergone a farther depreciation in price, and that to such an extent as to have deranged all the Captain's nicely balanced calculations, the principle excepted. What is to be the end of this ruinous rise in the value of money to leaseholders in general, it is beyond our power to calculate; but at present it appears that all farming, and sheep-farming in particular, is grown to a mere humbug, and not worth wasting words about, far less good writing, together with Messrs Balfour and Clark's best style of printing. Every farmer is either a bankrupt in effect, or hanging on in a state of timid dependence, as completely in his laird's power either to ruin or save him, as ever the vassals of the Black Douglas were, or those of the ancient Knights of Thirlstane, under the most arbitrary ages of the feudal system. For the last twelve years, there has been no money made by farming. Put the good and the bad seasons, as to prices and losses, over against each other, and it will soon appear that the balance is all on the wrong side; and now things are fairly come to that rate of derogation, that a state of villenage must either return, or the present race of farmers cease to exist as the occupiers of the land. Were the proprietors and their factors all to pay the same attention to the actual existing state of the country that the Hon. W. J. Napier has done, or were they even to be at pains to profit by his unsophisticated observations and example, there might be some hope that the credit of this most valuable class of the community would still be preserved. But while these gentlemen are wasting their time, and the fruits of the farmer's skill and industry, in a routine of elegant and fashionable arrangements afar from their native hills and valleys, perhaps arranging a whole train of winter's amusement in Paris or in Rome, the ruin of their tenantry will only make an impression on their hearts, when it begins to make a palpable deficiency in their yearly incomes, and when the decay in the vitals of their inheritance is too far gone to be retrieved.

Now, Mr North, I need not inform you, for you will at once see, that I am a rude illiterate person, with a slight share of uncommon sense. You will therefore take the trouble to mark my *article* with the proper points, such as commas and periods; about the intermediate ones I don't care so much. But there is one fellow, shaped like Charlie's wain, that asks questions, I forget his name, but he puzzles me worst of all; I request you will put him always at the beginning of a question in my essays, in place of setting him up at the end. Because, in reading, nobody knows where my question begins, and never suspects that the author is asking a query till he comes to the end of it. This is exceedingly awkward, and it is apparent to me that there is something manifestly wrong or defective in the mode. For instance, you would write a sentence thus: "If the charms of variety are universal—if truth is most impressive told as fiction, and fiction most winning related as truth, then is not Blackwood's Magazine the best book in the world?" How absurd!? Where does the question begin? Print all my articles in this latter way, let grammarians say what they will; and if these rural disquisitions can be of any avail to you, you need not want plenty of them from your obedient,

AN ETTRICK SHEPHERD.

BUCCLEUCH
*Jan. 8th,* 1823.

# When the Kye Comes Hame

COME all ye jolly shepherds that whistle thro' the glen,
   I'll tell ye of a secret that courtiers dinna ken.
What is the greatest bliss that the tongue of man can name?
   'Tis to woo a bonny lassie when the kye come hame.
      When the kye come hame, when the kye come hame,     5
      'Tween the gloaming an' the mirk, when the kye come hame.

'Tis not beneath the burgonet, nor yet beneath the crown,
   'Tis not on couch of velvet, nor yet in bed of down—
'Tis beneath the spreading birch, in the dell without the name,
   Wi' a bonny, bonny lassie, when the kye come hame.     10
      When the kye come hame, when the kye come hame,
      'Tween the gloaming an' the mirk, when the kye come hame.

There the blackbird bigs his nest for the mate he lo'es to see,
   And up upon the topmost bough, oh, a happy bird is he!
There he pours his melting ditty, and love 'tis a' the theme,     15
   And he'll woo his bonny lassie when the kye come hame.
      When the kye come hame, &c.

When the bluart bears a pearl, and the daisy turns a pea,
   And the bonny lucken gowan has fauldit up his ee,
Then the lavrock frae the blue lift drops down, and thinks nae shame   20
   To woo his bonny lassie when the kye come hame.
      When the kye come hame, &c.

Then the eye shines sae bright, the hale soul to beguile,
   There's love in every whisper, and joy in every smile:
O wha wad choose a crown, wi' its perils and its fame,     25
   And miss a bonny lassie when the kye come hame?
      When the kye come hame, &c.

See yonder pawky shepherd, that lingers on the hill,
   His ewes are in the fauld, and his lambs are lying still;
Yet he downa gang to bed, for his heart is in a flame,     30
   To meet his bonny lassie when the kye come hame.
      When the kye come hame, &c.

Away wi' fame and fortune, what comfort can they gie?
   And a' the arts that prey on man's life and liberty:
Gie me the highest joy that the heart of man can frame,     35
   My bonny, bonny lassie, when the kye come hame.
      When the kye come hame, &c.

# A Scots Mummy

*To Sir Christopher North*

DEAR SIR CHRISTY,

YOU will remember, that, when you and I parted last at Ambrose's, the following dialogue passed between us. Perhaps you may have forgot; but it was just at the head of the narrow entry, immediately under the door of that celebrated tavern, that it took place; and, at the time when it began, we were standing with our backs toward each other, in what I would have called, had I been writing poetry, a moveless attitude.

"Mr Hogg, what *is* the reason that you write to me so seldom?"

"Faith, man, it's because I hae naething to write about."

"Nothing to write about? For shame! how can you say so? Have you not the boundless phenomena of nature constantly before your eyes?"

"O, to be sure, I hae; but then—"

In the meantime I was thinking to myself, what the devil can this phenomena of nature be, when you interrupted me with, "None of your *but then's*, shepherd. A man who has such an eye as you have, for discerning the goings on of the mighty elements, can never want the choice of a thousand subjects whereon to exercise his pen. You have the night, with her unnumbered stars, that seem to rowl through spaces incomprehensible; the day dawn, and the sunshine; the dazzling splendours of noon, and the sombre hues that pervade the mountains, under the congregated masses of impending vapours."

"Gude sauf us, Christy's mair nor half seas ower!" thinks I; "but I maunna pretend no to understand him, for fear he get intil a rage.—Ay, ye're no far wrang, man," I says; "there are some gayen good things to be seen atween the heaven an' yirth sometimes. Weel, gude night, or rather gude morning, honest Sir Christy. I'll try to pick you up something o' yon sort."

"By all means, Hogg. I insist on it. Something of the phenomena of nature, I beseech you. You should look less at lambs and rams, and he-goats, Hogg, and more at the grand phenomena of nature. You should drink less out of the toddy-jug, shepherd, and more at the perennial spring. However, we'll say no more about that, as matters stand, to-night; only hand me something of the phenomena of nature."

I came home here, and looked about me soon and late with a watchful eye, and certainly saw many bright and beautiful appearances on the face of the sky, and in the ever-varying hues of the mountains; still I had witnessed all these before; so had every old shepherd in these glens; and I could not persuade myself that any of these was the particular thing, a description of which you wanted; because they were, in fact, no phenomenons, if I understand that French word properly, nor ever were viewed as such by any of our country people. But at length the curiosity of two young shepherds, neighbours of my own, furnished me with a subject that hit my fancy to a hair; and the moment that I first heard the relation, I said to myself, "This is the very thing for old Christy." But thereby hangs a tale, which is simply and literally as follows:–

On the top of a wild height, called Cowanscroft, where the lands of three proprietors meet all at one point, there has been, for long and many years, the grave of a suicide, marked out by a stone standing at the head, and another at the feet. Often have I stood musing over it myself, when a shepherd on one of the farms of which it formed the extreme boundary, and thinking what could induce a young man, who had scarcely reached the prime of life, to brave his Maker, and rush into his presence by an act of his own erring hand, and one so unnatural and preposterous; but it never once occurred to me as an object of curiosity, to dig up the mouldering bones of the culprit, which I considered as the most revolting of all objects. The thing was, however, done last month, and a discovery made of one of the greatest natural phenomenons that I ever heard of in this country.

The little traditionary history that remains of this unfortunate youth, is altogether a singular one. He was not a native of the place, nor would he ever tell from what place he came, but he was remarkable for a deep, thoughtful, and sullen disposition. There was nothing against his character that anybody knew of, and he had been a considerable time in the place. The last service he was in was with a Mr Anderson of Eltrieve, who died about 100 years ago, and who had hired him during the summer to herd a stock of young cattle in Eltrieve Hope. It happened one day in the month of September, that James Anderson, his master's son, a boy then about ten years of age, went with this young man to the Hope one day, to divert himself. The herd had his dinner along with him; and, about one o'clock, when the boy proposed going home, the former pressed him very hard to stay and take a share of his dinner; but the boy refused, for fear his parents might be alarmed about him, and said he *would* go home; on which the herd said to him, "Then if ye winna stay wi' me, James, ye may depend on't I'll cut my throat afore ye come back again."

I have heard it likewise reported, but only by one person, that there had been some things stolen out of his master's house a good while before, and that the boy had discovered a silver knife and fork, that was a part of the stolen property, in the herd's possession that day, and that it was this discovery that drove him to despair. The boy did not return to the Hope that afternoon; and, before evening, a man coming in at the pass called *the Hart Loup*, with a drove of lambs, on the way for Edinburgh, perceived something like a man standing in a strange frightful position at the side of one of Eldinhope hay-ricks. The driver's attention was riveted on this strange, uncouth figure; and as the drove-road passed at no great distance from the spot, he first called, but receiving no answer, he went up to the spot, and behold it was the above-mentioned young man, who had hung himself in the hay rope that was tying down the rick. This was accounted a great wonder, and every one said, if the devil had not assisted him, it was impossible the thing could have been done, for in general these ropes are so brittle, being made of green hay, that they will scarcely bear to be bound over the rick. And the more to horrify the good people of the neighbourhood, the driver said, that when he first came in view, he could *almost give his oath* that he saw two people engaged busily about the hay-rick, going round it and round it, and he thought they were dressing it. If this asseveration approximated at all to truth, it makes this evident at least, that the unfortunate young man had hanged himself after the man with the lambs came in view. He was, however, quite dead when he cut him down. He had fastened two of the old hay ropes at the bottom of the rick on one side, (indeed they are all fastened so when first laid on,) so that he had nothing to do but to loosen two of the ends on the other side; and these he tied in a knot round his neck, and then, slackening his knees, and letting himself lean down gradually till the hay rope bore all his weight, he contrived to put an end to his existence in that way. Now the fact is, that if you try all the ropes that are thrown over all the outfield hay ricks in Scotland, there is not one among a thousand of them will hang a colley dog—so that the manner of this wretch's death was rather a singular circumstance.

Early next morning Mr Anderson's servants went reluctantly away, and, taking an old blanket with them for a winding-sheet, they rolled up the body of the deceased, first in his own plaid, letting the hay-rope still remain about his neck, and then rolling the old blanket over all, they bore the loathed remains away the distance of three miles or so on spokes, to the top of Cowan's Croft, at the very point where the Duke of Buccleuch's land, the laird of Drumelzier's, and

Lord Napier's meet; and there they buried him, with all that he had on him and about him, silver knife and fork and all together. Thus far went tradition, and no one ever disputed one jot of the disgusting oral tale.

A nephew of that Mr Anderson's, who was with the hapless youth that day he died, says, that, as far as he can gather from the relations of friends that he remembers, and of that same uncle in particular, it is *one hundred and five years* next month, (that is, September 1823,) since that event happened; and I think it is likely that this gentleman's information is correct. But sundry other people, much older than he whom I have consulted, pretend that it is six or seven years more. They say they have heard that Mr James Anderson was then a boy ten years of age; that he lived to an old age, upwards of four score, and it is two-and-forty years since he died. Whichever way it may be, it was about that period some way, of that there is no doubt. Well, you will be saying, that, excepting the small ornamental part of the devil and the hay-rope, there is nothing at all of what you wanted in this ugly traditional tale. Stop a wee bit, my dear Sir Christy. Dinna just cut afore the point. Ye ken auld fools an' young bairns shouldna see things that are half done. Stop just a wee bit, ye auld crusty, crippled, crabbit, editor body, an' I'll let ye see that the grand *phenomena of Nature's* a' to come to yet.

It so happened, sir, that two young men, William Sheil and W. Sword, were out on an adjoining height, this summer, casting peats, and it came into their heads to open that grave in the wilderness, and see if there were any of the bones of the suicide of former ages and centuries remaining. They did so, but opened only about one half of the grave, beginning at the head and about the middle at the same time. It was not long till they came upon the old blanket,—I think they said, not much more than a foot from the surface. They tore that open, and there was the hay-rope lying stretched down alongst his breast so fresh, that they saw at first sight it was made of *risp*, a sort of long sword-grass that grows about marshes and the sides of lakes. One of the young men seized the rope, and pulled by it, but the old enchantment of the devil remained. It would not break, and so he pulled and pulled at it till behold the body came up into a sitting posture, with a broad blue bonnet on its head, and its plaid around it, as fresh as that day it was laid in. I never heard of a preservation so wonderful, if it be true as was related to me, for still I have not had the curiosity to go and view the body myself. The features were all so plain, that an acquaintance might easily have known him. One of the lads gripped the face of the corpse with his finger and thumb, and the cheeks felt quite soft and fleshy, but the dimples remained, and did not spring out again. He had fine yellow hair about nine inches long, but not a hair of it could they pull out, till they cut part of it off with a knife. They also cut off some portions of his clothes, which were all quite fresh, and distributed them among their acquaintances, sending a portion to me among the rest, to keep as natural curiosities. Several gentlemen have in a manner forced me to give them fragments of these enchanted garments; I have, however, retained a small portion for you, which I send along with this, being a piece of his plaid, and another of his waistcoat breast, which you will see are still as fresh as that day they were laid in the grave. His broad blue bonnet was sent to Edinburgh several weeks ago, to the great regret of some gentlemen connected with the land, who wished to have it for a keepsake. For my part, fond as I am of blue bonnets, and broad ones in particular, I declare I durst not have worn that one. There was nothing of the silver knife and fork discovered, that I heard of, nor was it very likely it should; but it would appear he had been very near run of cash, which, I dare say, had been the cause of his utter despair, for, on searching his pockets, nothing was found but three old Scots halfpennies. These young men meeting with another shepherd afterwards, his curiosity was so much excited, that they went and digged up the curious remains a second time, which was a pity, as it is likely that by these exposures to the air, and from the impossibility of burying it up again so closely as it was before, the flesh will now fall to dust.

These are all the particulars that I remember relating to this curious discovery; and I am sure you will confess that a very valuable receipt may be drawn from it for the preservation of dead bodies. If you should think of trying the experiment on yourself, you have nothing more to do than hang yourself in a hay rope, which, by the by, is to be made of risp, and leave orders that you are to be buried in a wild height, and I will venture to predict, that though you repose there for ages an inmate of your mossy cell, of the cloud, and the storm, you shall set up your head at the last day as fresh as a moorcock. I remain, my worthy friend, yours very truly,

JAMES HOGG.

ALTRIEVE LAKE
*Aug.* 1, 1823.

*January–December 1824 (Volumes 15–16)*

# The Left-Handed Fiddler

### *By the Ettrick Shepherd*

Of all the things in this offensive world,
So full of flaws, inversions, and caprice,
There's nought so truly awkward and ridiculous
As a left-handed fiddler.–There he sits,
The very antitype of base conceit,     5
And the most strange perversity–Scrape, scrape!
With everything reversed,–bow, pegs, and fingers;
The very capers of his head absurd;
With the left ear turn'd upmost:–O ye Gods,
This thing's not to be suffer'd; I declare     10
'Tis worse than my good Lord * * * * * * * * * * * *,
Who danced so very queer before a Queen!

I know of no anomaly in nature
With which I can compare the integer;
It stands alone without the Muse's range,     15
No metaphor or simile to be had,
The *ne-plus-ultra* of ludification.
Were great Ned Irving of old Hatton Garden
To turn the wrong end of the Bible up,
   And read the text backward,     20
   It would not look so awkward
   As a left-handed fiddler!

Were princely Jeffrey, at a Jury trial
Of life and death, in the middle of his speech
To break off with a minuet, and swim     25
Around with sailing motion, his pert eye
Ray'd with conceit and self-magnificence,
Bent like a crescent, and the wee black gown
Blown like a bladder or full-bosom'd sail,
   All would not be so bad,     30
   For we'd think the man gone mad,
   But not so with the fiddler.

We see a wretched sycophant, the tool
Of rustic merriment, set up,

Straining and toiling to produce sweet sounds,    35
In huddled rank confusion; every note
The first, last, and the middle, crowding on,
Uncertain of precedence; sounds there are
Forthcoming, without doubt, in bold success;
But here's the screw of th' rack—mark how they spring,    40
Each from a wrong part of the instrument,
Of the hoarse, hackney'd, and o'erlabour'd jade!
    This is the nerve-teazing,
    The blood and soul-squeezing
    Vice of the heteroclite.    45

I knew a man—a good well-meaning hind,
With something odd in his mind's composition;
He was devout, and in his evening prayer—
A prayer of right uncommon energy—
This man would pause, break off, and all at once,    50
In a most reverend melancholy strain,
Whistle sublimely forth a part, and then
Go on with earnest and unalter'd phrase:
This, I confess, look'd something odd at first,
A mode without a parallel—and then    55
It came so unexpectedly. Yet still
I not disliked it, and I loved the man
The better for such whim, his inward frame
And spirit's communings to me unknown.
But here, Lord help me! ('tis pity 'twere a sin    60
To hate a fellow-creature,) I perceive
A thing set up in manifold burlesque
Of all the lines of beauty.—Scrape, scrape, scrape!
Bass, treble, tenor, all turn'd topsy-turvy!

What would old Patriarch Jubal say to this—    65
The father of the sweetest moving art
E'er compassed by man?—O be his name
Revered for aye! Methinks I see the father,
With filaments of bark, or plaited thongs,
Stretch'd on a hurdle, in supreme delight,    70
Bumming and strumming at his infant science,
Whilst the seraphic gleaming of his eye
Gave omen of that world of harmony,
Then in its embryo stage, form'd to combine
The holy avocations of mankind,    75

And his delights, with those of angels.–Think
   Of this and of the fiddler!

What's the most lovely object here on earth?–
'Tis hard to say. But for a moment think
Of a fair being, cast in beauty's mould,          80
Placed at her harp, and to its tuneful chords
Pouring mellifluous concord; her blue eyes
Upraised as 'twere to heaven; her ruby lips
Half open, and her light and floating locks
Soft trembling to the wild vibration          85
Of her own harp–Is there not something holy,
Sweet, and seraphic, in that virgin's mien?–
Think of it well; then of this rascal here,
With his red fiddle cocking up intense
Upon perverted shoulder, and you must          90
Give him the great MacTurk's emphatic curse–
"The de'il paaticularly d–n the dog!"–Amen.
   I've settled with the fiddler.

# Examination of the School
# of Southside
## *By Mr W. W.*

*Minister.* Now, Mr Strap, I well approve the mode
In which your pupils have been taught the first
Fair rudiments of science. 'Tis a task
Of weighty import, thus to train the minds
Of all the youth o' the parish, Mr Strap:          5
Of weighty import, sir, not unfulfill'd.
Still, there is one small item yet omitted,
Which I, as ghostly pastor, long to prove.
What progress have they made in sacred lore?
Know they aught of the leading principles          10
Of our religion?–Not one word of that
Hath been this day put to them, Mr Strap!
   *Strap.* Sire, I'm a diffident and modest man,
And wish not to encroach on the department

Of such respected neighbour—well aware 15
How much adapted to the grateful task
Is his capacious mind. That part belongs
Unto yourself—not me. Besides, I lay
It down as maxim not to be controll'd,
As plain as that the A, B, C, must come 20
Before that great and fundamental rule
Call'd "The Cat's Lesson," or the glorious square
Of file and column—that eternal base
On which so many fabrics have been rear'd,
Reaching to heaven, struggling with the stars 25
And planets in their courses—nay, have dared,
As with a line and plummet, to mete out
Seas, orbs, and the most wondrous works of God—
Multiplication table!—that I mean.
Simple it is—nay, almost laughable— 30
Two twos make four! two fours make eight, and so forth;
But what a force springs there! O science! science!
How small is thy beginning! But how vast
Are thy attainments!—Pray now, note but this:
Two ones make two—two threes make half a dozen. 35
Ye gods, how beautifully simple 'tis!
Think of it, sire—and of the heights sublime
A Newton gain'd. Yet he began with this—
Two ones make two!—Then of a Napier think,
A David Brewster! 40
   *Minister*. Prithee, Mr Strap,
Where art thou going? Whereto tends this speech?
I ask of thee to hear a specimen
Of the religion taught within thy school;
And lo! thou fliest off at a tangent, like 45
A schoolboy's rocket—whizz away to heaven—
Crack! pluff!—then down to earth thou comest again
In trivial flitters. Prithee, Mr Strap,
Where is this speech to end?
   *Strap*. Where it began, 50
If so you please, most reverend worthy sir.
I say, I lay it down as maxim clear,
Nor subject to perversion, that, as in
The science of numbers, man must first begin
With trivial things, and move up by degrees, 55
And only reach to the sublimest last;

So is it with religion—'Tis the highest,
The most sublime of all celestial things
Which God hath yet reveal'd to mortal man;
Therefore, it ought to be the last instill'd                    60
Into his mind, when that hath reach'd the goal
Of its capacity.
    *Minister.* Ah, Mr Strap!
Wrong, wrong—Sir, thou art grievously wrong.
Hast thou ne'er heard me preach? or has thy mind               65
Been hunting tropes and figures at the time?
Religion ought to be administer'd
To youthful minds as an emollient;
A seasoning to every mess with which
Their spirits are dilated, that it may                         70
Grow with their growth, and strengthen with their strength.
In a young scion grafted, then its roots
Spread in the earth, its tendrils in the heavens;
But in an old and crabbed stock it dies,
And withers ere it bloom. Strap, thou hast laid               75
A false foundation on a dangerous base,
And all in poor excuse; because, forsooth,
Thou teachest no religion in thy school.
Go send thy pupils to me, one by one,
That there be no collusion. I have long                        80
Suspected thee a sceptic, Mr Strap;
If I can prove it on thee, I shall rend
The Southside school from out thy dangerous grasp.

    *Enter a Scholar.*
Come hither, little fellow. Thou'rt acute
In all the branching elements of lore.                         85
Now, dost thou know who made thee?
    *Boy.* Yes.
    *Minister.* Who was it then?
    *Boy.* My parents.
    *Minister.* O heavens! I knew it. These brave boys are lost  90
Lost! lost! for lack of learning the great truths
Of primitive religion!—My brave boy,
Thou err'st exceedingly. Dost thou not know
'Twas God who made thee, and all things beside?
    *Boy.* That I deny most promptly. True, he made             95
Adam and Eve, and the first parent pairs

Of every living thing. But since that time
He's left all creatures to make one another,
As best they may. Heaven mend thy wits, good sir,
Think'st thou that God makes all the little brats,                    100
Bastards, and blackamoors; foals, calves, and kids;
The lion's growling whelps; the fox's litter;
The infant whales; the little grovelling moles;
And all the unlick'd cubs throughout the world?
I hold such thoughts as blasphemy.                                    105
    *Minister*. Alack the day!–alack the day!–Strap, Strap!
Thou art a heathen–a rank renegado
From gospel light!–Still as the old cock crows,
So learns the young!–I have him on the hip!
He leaves the Southside school!–Thou chattering rogue,   110
So like thy master, hast thou ever read
A plain old-fashion'd book yclept the Bible?
    *Boy*. Yes; often.
    *Minister*. So? And how dost thou esteem it?
    *Boy*. A good old book–a very worthy book.                 115
    *Minister*. Ay! say'st thou so? which may your wisdom deem
The best book in the world?
    *Boy*. Blackwood's Magazine.
    *Minister*. O hideous, hideous! Most deplorable!
This is the very summit of misrule,                                   120
And horrid miscreance. Incongruous elf,
Wherefore this answer? Who taught thee to give
That mass of vile scurrility the preference
To works of sacred worth? Base sciolist,
Your reasons?–Come, most sage philosopher?                            125
    *Boy*. Because I deem that little lightsome work
The greatest bulwark in our native land,
Around its holy faith, its sacred rights,
Its principles of loyalty and truth,
And all that cherishes content and peace                              130
Among a bold, a free, and happy people.
    *Minister*. Ay, ay, brave sir–'Tis very well with thee!
Thou'rt in the high way to preferment, master.
Thou'st seen a certain stage of great regard,
Right opposite our good friend David's corner?                       135
Thither thy steps are tending. Fare thee well.
God speed thee to thy venerable goal.
Shake hands, and part we friends. Whom dost thou deem

The worthiest man of the parish?
   *Boy.* O! Mr Tickler, beyond all compare!   140
The sage, the gay, the proud, the loyal Tickler!
   *Minister.* Ay, ay! All of a piece! All of a piece!
Like Mr Pringle's butler of the Yair.
Beshrew me, but I smell a vicinal rat!
What is thy name, brave boy?   145
   *Boy.* My name, sir, forms no portion of my creed;
On that alone am I examined here.
   *Minister.* Thou art a dapper fellow—somewhat tall
Too for thy years. Wast thou brought up at home,
Or in a certain cottage at the end   150
Of a large town, call'd Duddingston? Eh? What?
Have I discovered thee?
   *Boy.* Bid thee, good sir;
Most reverend sir, good day; and thank you, sir.
   *Min. (solus.)* Ah me! What will this wicked world become!   155
I've heard a foolish burden of a song
That runs to the following purport:—

"An' eh what a parish! an' O what a parish!
And eh sic a parish as Little Dunkeld!
They stickit the minister, hang'd the precentor,   160
Dang down the kirk steeple, an' drank the bell!"

I cannot get that foolish rhyme cancelled
From out my heart, for O what a parish
Is Little Southside!

       *Enter a young Lady.*
Come hither, pretty maiden, full sore I dread   165
To ask at so much innocence and beauty,
Of that which most concerns her welfare here,
And happiness hereafter, knowing well
The base pestiferous stuff early instill'd
Into thy plastic mind.   170
   *Girl.* You may or may not, sir,
As fits your inclination. 'Tis the same.
But I can answer all the pretty questions
Of sound morality, and truth, and love.
   *Minister.* Eh? Love? What love? I shall go mad!   175
   *Girl.* I hope not now, sir? Not on my account?
First try me ere you turn outrageous,

I'll warrant you shall note me for a tickler.
   *Minister.* A what! a what! there are some words and terms
That make me nervish! But let us proceed. 180
Which do you deem the best book of the world?
   *Girl.* The Bible, sir. The holy blessed Bible.
What book on earth can e'er compare with that?
   *Minister.* Bless thee, thou lovely one! for thou hast caught
A spark divine amid a hive of sin. 185
Dost thou believe in all the truth supreme
Within that blessed book?
   *Girl.* O yes, I bow
To them with reverence, and never let
My heart doubt one of them. And I believe 190
In that compendium made by holy men,
My little Catechism. Next unto
The Holy Scriptures, I approve of that.
Pray am I right, good sir?
   *Minister.* Right? Yes. Thou art a gem of the first water 195
In God's own sanctuary. Whom dost thou deem
The worthiest and best man of the parish?
   *Girl.* Whom should I deem the best, but him commission'd
By one who cannot err, to teach his word,
And keep a watch for my immortal soul? 200
   *Minister.* Heaven bless thee, pretty maid, and o'er thee watch
For everlasting good! Forgive these tears,
The tears of an old man. Here is a purse
To buy thee a new Bible. Let it be
A gilded one, gilded with gold all over, 205
And I'll put down thy name above the donor's.
Pry'thee, what is thy name?
   *Girl.* I've said it, sir.
   *Minister.* Not that I did remark.
   *Girl.* Maids do not always choose to tell their names. 210
   *Minister.* Where wast thou bred? sure thou may'st tell me that.
   *Girl.* I've heard it said that I was bred with care
And caution, at a place call'd Duddingston.
   *Minister.* God grant me grace! Art thou a Tickler too?
Now I remind thou said'st thou wert a Tickler. 215
   *Girl.* Ay, so are all the scholars of Southside,
But half of them will not tell thee their names.
Good morrow, reverend sir, and pray accept
A little maiden's thanks.

*Minister, (solus.)*

"An' eh what a parish! an' O what a parish!                220
"An eh sic a parish as little Dunkeld!"

Strap shall not flit. That is decisive now,
And all for sake of that sweet maiden's wit;
That very lovely and ingenious thing.
Strap *shall not* flit; for if he train the maids          225
In any path whatever, right or wrong,
They most assuredly shall train the men
Right onward after them. Strap shall not flit.
        *(Calling in at the window as passing.)*
Good morrow, Mr Strap. Farewell, good sir,
To thee and to thy *Ticklers*. Take good care            230
Of them and their religious principles.
Take care of their religion, Mr Strap.                *[Exit.*


ALTRIVE
*December* 1*st*, 1824.

# January–December 1825 (Volumes 17–18)
# Correspondence Between
# Mr James Hogg and Lord Byron
### To C. N. Esq.

DEAR SIR,

I ENCLOSE you a parcel of Lord Byron's letters to me, a part of which I have at length discovered; the rest, I suppose, are lost for ever, if some of my fair friends of the Blue Stocking Club have not the kindness to return them, for I am sure they are safe in somebody's possession. I therefore take this opportunity of requesting copies of them, in whosesoever hands they are, and the originals they are welcome to preserve. If you think there is any impropriety in publishing the enclosed, I beg that you will let it alone, and by all means take care of the originals, and return them to me. His first letter to me, inclosing one from Mr Murray, I have entirely forgot. If it had not been for the mention of it here, I would not have known that it existed. I think it must have been merely a few lines written inside of an envelope of a complimentary nature, and that I have given them to some friend to keep as a curiosity. I am not sure but that Mr Gillies has the note. Pray ask him. Do not publish my own letters, unless you think them necessary to the understanding of Lord B.'s.

Yours, &c.

J. H.

LETTER I.–TO THE RIGHT HONOURABLE THE LORD BYRON

*Dean-Haugh, near Edinburgh, March 7th, 1812.*

MY GOOD LORD,

It is impossible for me to express the supreme glow of delight that your approval has afforded me. The slight intimation of that, in your letter to myself, was well enough, and more than either my merit deserved or my vanity anticipated. But yesterday, when Mr Scott read me the page in your letter to him, wherein your sentiments regarding me are more fully displayed, really I felt all my hair creep on my head, and stand upright like a bottle brush; and all with sensations which you yourself, in all your glory, might have envied. I daresay I looked very queer, as I said to Mr Scott, "Weel, that's aye some encouragement. What d'ye think of that?" He answered me with enthusiasm, in something to the following purport:

That he was exceedingly glad to find your lordship's sentiments coincide so entirely with his own—that here they were given freely and disinterestedly, from a full conviction, and the feeling of the moment, by one whose capacity to judge of such a poem no one would dispute; and he added, that he would have given his sentiments of the work full publicity before this time, had it not been that all the general remarks which it behoved him to have made, would have applied as fully to his own poetry as to mine; for that they were both so much of a traditionary and local nature, that, had he reviewed mine, it would have been regarded by the world as a review of his own.

You charge me to cultivate the acquaintance of this my illustrious friend, and to be ruled by his advice. You need not bid me, my lord; I am truly anxious to maintain that hold on his friendship which I have now enjoyed without interruption for these many years. But no man can cultivate *his* friendship farther than he chooses himself. It is impossible. He is always ready to oblige others; but he will accept of no obligation from either inferiors or equals, (if any of the latter are to be found, begging your Lordship's pardon,) or if he does, it is only on purpose to have some pretence for tripling it, or rather returning it an hundred fold. In short, no man, woman, or child, can cultivate his acquaintance one jot farther than he chooses. It is precisely with him, "hitherto shalt thou come, but no farther."

As to walking by his advice, that is quite easily done. I generally ask his advice in everything. He is, however, very shy of giving it, till once he discovers what way my inclinations tend, and then he advises me that way without fail. He never sends one away displeased with his advice, and there is no man's more easily followed.

It was he who first recommended Childe Harold to me, and gave me a copy of the quarto edition. I had a prejudice against it ere ever I opened it, and after I had read it through, I was perfectly mad at it. I wrote a review of it for a work that is going on here just now, but the article was so severe, and of so taunting a nature, that the chaps would not take it in, and I was obliged to write it over again. Resolved, however, to have at you, I sent the original article to a London Review, but they also returned it, and I have it lying by me to this day—a humbling memorial how hardly a novice in the poetical art can brook the appearance of one who is manifestly his superior.

The great fault that I found with you as a poet, was your want of an ear for harmony. I had all my life been led to consider harmony of numbers as the principal genuine gold stamp of poetry; as the quality farthest removed from prose, and the one most necessary to constitute true poetry. I am not going to defend this feeling through thick and thin, but only inform you, that I possess it in no ordinary degree, and am satisfied of its validity. I hold Campbell's numbers as the true standard of melody. Moore's are far too liquid; and as for Scott's, they are scarcely a hair better than your own. He has a rough rugged sort of ear, that would seem to relish the war-pipe even above the Harmonicon. With these impressions, and this properly modulated poetical ear, I confess that they were absolutely torn to flinders by the harshness of The Childe's numbers. The more strong and original that the expressions were, they sounded to me still the harder. Had they been more light and flimsy, they would then have sounded on like the wheels of an empty waggon over a rough pavement, but as they were, they paused, bumped, and grated on like one overloaded with gold. In fact, I could find no parallel to such broken and dislocated numbers among our genuine and approved poets, and therefore I noted the peculiarity down as illegitimate to all intents and purposes.

I'll tell you what I think of you plump. There is no poet of the age can touch you in sublimity. I am almost afraid to say it; but I think I could find in your poetry full sentences of the truest sublime that ever was written in English rhyme.—I say *rhyme*, for I never compare mortal man to Shakspeare, though, with all my heart, I shall give you the preference to Mr Milton, which I believe none will do but myself; but, in fact, the old democrat was never a great favourite of mine. Wordsworth comes next to you of all men living; but then his are only touches, and generally coupled with something imperfect. Yours are never so, for your best metaphors are as clearly made out as they are powerful. Campbell is next. Southey often tries it, with what effect this is not the place to decide. I love the man; you hate him, which is enough for the present. But is it not curious, that there is not an instance of the sublime in all Scott's poetry, nor one that approaches to it, as far as I can judge.

But this is all nonsense, therefore, to cut it short, I give you the gree of all your contemporaries in the true and genuine sublime. Yet, I know not how it is, I do not think you have a very brilliant imagination neither. If I had a tail to balance myself properly, I could outfly you a hundred thousand miles in this respect; but then your muse has more nerve, bone, and sinew, than other people's, and consequently bears you through where most others stick. You never once aim at what you cannot accomplish, and the reason is, because you draw principally from yourself, and take the measure of the human heart and human feelings rather too much by your own. But,

O dear, my lord, your want of melody is dreadful. It is out of my power to read or recite one of your verses aloud, without being compelled to do it as blank verse. You certainly are an anomaly in body and mind, soul and spirit, and all that relates either to this world or the next. I have heard it said, and have no doubt of the fact, that you are a little cracked, or, as we express it much better in Scots, "a kind o' half-daft chield." Admitting this to a certain extent, my greatest fear is, that the reviewers laud you, and the ladies flatter you till they put you clean horn daft altogether, and then, God knows what may be the upshot. If you die a young man, you will die a spoiled one, and then posterity will account you much what I have expressed above. If you live to be an old man, you have a great chance, when the heyday of passion and vanity has subsided, to become a pattern of virtue, benevolence, and even of sanctity and devotion. You will laugh at present at such an insinuation, but I am fully persuaded that you have the germs of all these in your composition, though a thousand conflicting energies have jumbled them into such a chaos that it is impossible, as things exist, to separate either the good or the bad from the store.

When I took up the pen to-day to answer your lordship's kind letter, inclosing Murray's, I determined that mine should not be above twice as long as yours. You see how much I have been deceived, and still I have never yet mentioned the main subject. The truth is, I am half crazed to-day, by reason of your decided approval of my humble efforts—for what can be so delightful to a poor peasant attempting the steeps of Parnassus, as to be beckoned on by the lord of the region; but my intentions, when I began, was to ask a favour of your lordship, not to send you a lecture on poetical composition.

I purpose, at the beginning of next year, to publish a volume about the size of a monthly review, and to continue it annually for some time. It is to be called The Poetic Mirror; or, The Living Bards of Britain; and I want contributions for it from young and old, high and low, all who ever strung a rhyme, or measured iambics by counting their fingers, from the very highest to the worst, and the worse the latter sort are, the better. Now, I am not going to commence my canvass for contributions till I know whether you will furnish me with a poem for the work or not. The greater part of the poets of the North are my friends, at least so far my friends, that they will cheerfully lend a hand to aught that is likely to amend or ameliorate my circumstances. I can calculate with perfect certainty on Mr Scott, Mr Wilson, Mr Southey, and I think Wordsworth also, besides many others whose names may not be known to you, but whose genius I hold in high estimation. I am also a little acquainted with Campbell personally, but really his muse is so costive, I do not think I can in conscience ask him for an original poem, and I can take nothing else. I would like exceedingly to have a piece of yours in my first number, the larger the better, but as long or short as you list. Do not think I am begging or entreating for the poem as a thing I cannot do without; for if I did not think you had more pleasure in giving than withholding such a thing, I would neither ask nor accept of it; but such a trifle would be an easy matter to you, and might prove of great value to me. At all events, this request is likely to procure the pleasure of another letter from your lordship, and in that case will not have been made in vain.

I am, with all respect, your Lordship's most obedient servant,

JAMES HOGG.

P. S.–Address to the care of John Grieve, Esq. North Bridge, Edinburgh.

[WE shall continue this series regularly. Mr Hogg ndy sre[asaaen us no less than seven of his own letters and five of Lord Byron's, and we earnestly hope that Mrs Gray of Belfast, or whoever has the others, which the Shepherd alludes to, will forthwith attend to the hint given in his introductory note, and transmit accurate copies of them at least either to Mr Hogg or to us.]

LETTER II.
TO MR JAMES HOGG,
*Care of John Grieve, Esq. North Bridge, Edinburgh.*
*Albany, March* 24.

DEAR SIR,

I HAVE been out of town, otherwise your letter should have been answered sooner. When a letter contains a request, the said request generally figures towards the *finale*, and so does yours, my good friend. In answering perhaps the other way is the better: so not to make many words about a trifle, (which any thing of mine must be,) you shall have a touch of my quality for your first Number–and if you print that, you shall have more of the same stuff for the successors. Send me a few of your proofs, and I will set forthwith about something, that I at least hope may suit your purposes. So much for the Poetic Mirror, which may easily be, God knows, entitled to hang higher than the prose one.

You seem to be a plain spoken man, Mr Hogg, and I really do not like you the worse for it. I can't write verses, and yet you want a bit of my poetry for your book. It is for you to reconcile yourself with yourself.—You shall have the *verses*.

You are mistaken, my good fellow, in thinking that I (or, indeed, that any living verse-writer—for we shall sink *poets*) can write as well as Milton. Milton's Paradise Lost is, as a whole, a heavy concern; but the two first books of it are the very finest poetry that has ever been produced in this world—at least since the flood—for I make little doubt Abel was a fine pastoral poet, and Cain a fine bloody poet, and so forth; but we, now-a-days, even we, (you and I, *i.e.*) know no more of their poetry than the *brutum vulgus*—I beg pardon, the swinish multitude, do of Wordsworth and Pye. Poetry must always exist, like drink, where there is a demand for it. And Cain's may have been the brandy of the Antideluvians, and Able's the small still.

Shakespeare's name, you may depend on it, stands absurdly too high, and will go down. He had no invention as to stories, none whatever. He took all his plots from old novels, and threw their stories into a dramatic shape, at as little expense of thought as you or I could turn his plays back again into prose tales. That he threw over whatever he did write some flashes of genius, nobody can deny: but this was all. Suppose any one to have the *dramatic* handling for the first time of such ready-made stories as Lear, Macbeth, &c. and he would be a sad fellow, indeed, if he did not make something very grand of them. As for his historical plays, properly historical, I mean, they were mere re-dressings of former plays on the same subjects, and in twenty cases out of twenty-one, the finest, the very finest things, are taken all but *verbatim* out of the old affairs. You think, no doubt, that *A horse, a horse, my kingdom for a horse!* is Shakspeare's. Not a syllable of it. You will find it all in the old nameless dramatist. Could not one take up Tom Jones and improve it, without being a greater genius than Fielding? I, for my part, think Shakspeare's plays might be improved, and the public seem, and have seemed for to think so too, for not one of his is or ever has been acted as he wrote it; and what the pit applauded three hundred years past, is five times out of ten not Shakspeare's, but Cibber's.

Stick you to Walter Scott, my good friend, and do not talk any more stuff about his not being willing to give you real advice, if you really will ask for real advice. You love Southey, forsooth—I am sure Southey loves nobody but himself, however. I hate these talkers one and all, body and soul. They are a set of the most despicable impostors—that is my opinion of them. They know nothing of the world; and what is poetry, but the reflection of the world? What sympathy have this people with the spirit of this stirring age? They are no more able to understand the least of it, than your *lass*–nay, I beg her pardon, *she* may very probably have intense sympathy with both its spirit, (I mean the whisky,) and its body (I mean the bard.) They are mere old wives. Look at their beastly vulgarity, when they wish to be homely; and their exquisite stuff, when they clap on sail, and aim at fancy. Coleridge is the best of the trio–but bad is the best. Southey should have been a parish-clerk, and Wordsworth a man-midwife– both in darkness. I doubt if either of them ever get drunk, and I am of the old creed of Homer the wine-bibber. Indeed I think you and Burns have derived a great advantage from this, that being poets, and drinkers of wine, you have had a new potation to rely upon. Your whisky has made you original. I have always thought it a fine liquor. I back you against beer at all events, gill to gallon.

By the bye, you are a fine hand to cut up the minor matters of verse-writing; you indeed think harmony the all-in-all. My dear sir, you may depend upon it, you never had *name* yet, without making it rhyme to *theme*. I overlook all that sort of thing, however, and so must you, in your turn, pass over my real or supposed ruggedness. The fact is, that I have a theory on the subject, but that I have not time at present for explaining it. The first time all the poets of the age meet–it must be in London, glorious London is the place, after all–we shall, if you please, have a small trial of skill. You shall write seventeen odes for me, anything from Miltonian blank down to Phillupean namby, and I a similar number for you, and let a jury of good men and true be the judges between us. I name Scott for fore- man–Tom Campbell may be admitted, and Mrs Baillie, (though it be not exactly a matron case.) You may name the other nine wor- thies yourself. We shall, at all events, have a dinner upon the occa- sion, and I stipulate for a small importation of the peat reek.

Dear sir, believe me sincerely yours,

BYRON.

# Hymn to the Devil

Speed thee, speed thee!
Liberty lead thee!
Many this night shall hearken and heed thee.
    Far abroad,
    Demigod!                                    5
    What shall appal thee?
Javel, or Devil, or how shall we call thee?

Thine the night voices of joy and of weeping,
The whisper awake, and the vision when sleeping:
The bloated kings of the earth shall brood     10
On princedoms and provinces bought with blood,
Shall slubber, and snore, and to-morrow's breath
Shall order the muster and march of death:
The trumpets shall sound, and the gonfalons flee,
And thousands of souls step home to thee.     15
     Speed thee, speed thee, &c.

The warrior shall dream of battle begun,
Of field-day and foray, and foeman undone;
Of provinces sacked, and warrior store,
Of hurry and havoc, and hampers of ore;     20
Of captive maidens for joys abundant,
And ransom vast when these grow redundant.
Hurray! for the foray. Fiends ride forth a-souling,
For the dogs of havock are yelping and yowling.
     Speed thee, speed thee, &c.     25

     Make the bedesman's dream
     With pleasure to teem;
     To-day and to-morrow
     He has but one aim.
     And 'tis still the same, and 'tis still the same.     30
But well thou know'st the sot's demerit,
His richness of flesh, and his poorness of spirit;
And well thy images thou canst frame,
On canvass of pride, with pencil of flame:
A broad demesne is a view of glory,     35
For praying a soul from purgatory:
And, O, let the dame be fervent and fair,
Amorous, and righteous, and husband beware!
For there's a confession so often repeated,
The eyes are enlightened, the life-blood is heated.     40
Hish!–Hush!–soft foot and silence,
The sons of the abbot are lords of the Highlands.
Thou canst make lubbard and lighthead agree,
Wallow a while, and come home to thee.
     Speed thee, speed thee, &c.     45

Where goest thou next, by hamlet or shore,
When kings, when warriors, and priests are o'er?
These for thee have the most to do,

And these are the men must be looked unto.
On courtier deign not to look down, 50
Who swells at a smile, and faints at a frown.
With noble maid stay not to parle,
But give her one glance of the golden arle.
Then, oh, there's a creature thou needs must see,
Upright, and saintly, and stern is she! 55
'Tis the old maid, with visage demure,
With cat on her lap, and dogs on the floor.
Master, she'll prove a match for thee,
With her psalter, and crosier, and Ave Mari.
Move her with things above and below, 60
Tickle her and teaze her from lip to toe;
Should all prove vain, and nothing can move;
If dead to ambition, and cold to love,
One passion still success will crown,
A glorious energy all thine own! 65
'Tis envy; a die that never can fail
With children, matron, or maiden stale.
Shew them in dreams from night to day
A happy mother, and offspring gay;
Shew them the maiden in youthful prime, 70
Followed and wooed, improving her time;
And their hearts will sicken with envy and spleen,
A leperous jaundice of yellow and green:
And though frightened for hell to a boundless degree,
They'll singe their dry periwigs yet with thee. 75
  Speed thee, speed thee, &c.

Where goest thou next? Where wilt thou hie thee?
Still there is rubbish enough to try thee.
Whisper the matron of lordly fame,
There's a greater than she in splendour and name; 80
And her bosom shall swell with the grievous load,
And torrents of slander shall volley abroad,
Imbued with venom and bitter despair:
O sweet are the sounds to the Prince of the Air!
Reach the proud yeoman a bang with a spear, 85
And the tippling burgess a yerk on the ear;
Put fees in the eye of the poisoning leech,
And give the dull peasant a kick on the breech:
As for the flush maiden, the rosy elf,
You may pass her by, she will dream of herself. 90

But that all may be gain and nothing loss,
Keep eye on the men with the cowl and the cross;
Then shall the world go swimming before thee,
In a full tide of liberty, licence, and glory.
        Speed thee, speed thee, &c.                                    95

Hail, patriot spirit! thy labours be blest!
For of all great reformers, thyself wert the first;
Thou wert the first, with discernment strong,
To perceive that all rights divine were wrong;
And long hast thou spent thy sovereign breath,                         100
In heaven above and in earth beneath,
And roared it from thy burning throne,
The glory of independence alone;
Proclaiming to all, with fervour and irony,
That kingly dominion's all humbug and tyranny;                         105
And whoso listeth may be free,
For freedom, full freedom's the word with thee!
That life has its pleasures—the rest is a sham,
And all that comes after a flim and a flam!
        Speed thee, speed thee!                                        110
        Liberty lead thee!
Many this night shall harken and heed thee.
            Hie abroad,
            Demigod!
        Who shall defame thee?                                         115
King of the Elements! how shall we name thee?

# If E'er You Would Be a
# Brave Fellow, Young Man

AIR,—*Whistle, and I'll come to ye, my Lad.*

1.

If e'er you would be a brave fellow, young man,
Beware of the Blue and the Yellow, young man;
        If ye wud be strang,
        And wish to write lang,
Come join wi' the lads that get mellow, young man.                      5
Like the crack o' a squib that has fa'en on, young man,
Compared wi' the roar o' a cannon, young man,

So is the Whig's blow
To the pith that's below
The beard o' auld Geordie Buchanan, young man.     10

### 2.

I heard a bit bird in the braken, young man,
It sang till the Whigs were a' quaking, young man,
    And ay the sad lay
    Was, Alack for the day!
For the Blue and the Yellow's forsaken, young man.     15
The day is arriv'd that's nae joking, young man;
'Tis vain to be murmuring and mocking, young man:
    A Whig may be leal,
    But he'll never fight weel,
As lang as he dadds wi' a docken, young man.     20

### 3.

O wha wadna laugh at their capers, young man?
Like auld maidens, fash'd wi' the vapours, young man,
    We have turned them adrift
    To their very last shift,
That's–*puffing the Radical Papers, young man.*     25
If ye wad hear tell o' their pingle,* young man,
Gae list the wee bird in the dingle, young man;
    Its note o' despair,
    Is sae loud in the air,
That the windows of heaven play jingle, young man.     30

### 4.

I'll give you a toast of the auldest, young man;
The loyal head ne'er was the cauldest, young man;
    "Our King and his Throne,
    Be his glory our own,"
And the last of his days aye the bauldest, young man.–     35
But as for the loun that wad hector, young man,
And pit us at odds wi' a lecture, young man,
    May he dance cutty-mun,
    Wi' his neb to the sun,
And his doup to the General Director,† young man.     40

---

* *Pingle*–difficulty.
† This is a mysterious allusion to that part of the town where Executions take place.

# The Laird o' Lamington

CAN I bear to part wi' thee,
Never mair your face to see?
Can I bear to part wi' thee,
  Drunken Laird o' Lamington?
Canty war ye o'er your kale,                        5
Toddy jugs, an' caups o' ale,
Heart aye kind, an' leel, an' hale,
  Honest Laird o' Lamington.

He that swears is but so so,
He that lies to hell must go,                       10
He that falls in bagnio,
  Falls in the devil's frying-pan.
Wha was't ne'er pat aith to word?
Never lied for duke nor lord?
Never sat at sinfu' board?                          15
  The Honest Laird o' Lamington.

He that cheats can ne'er be just;
He that prays is ne'er to trust;
He that drinks to drauck his dust,
  Wha can say that wrang is done?                   20
Wha was't ne'er to fraud inclin'd,
Never pray'd sin' he can mind?
Ane wha's drouth there's few can find,
  The Honest Laird o' Lamington.

I like a man to tak' his glass,                     25
Toast a friend or bonny lass;
He that winna is an ass—
  Deil send him ane to gallop on!
I like a man that's frank an kind,
Meets me when I have a mind,                        30
Sings his sang, an' drinks me blind,
  Like the Laird o' Lamington.

620  *Noctes Ambrosianæ. No. XX.*  [May,

OMNES.

Mr Brougham! (*all the honours.*)

HOGG (*sings.*)

THE LAIRD O' LAMINGTON.

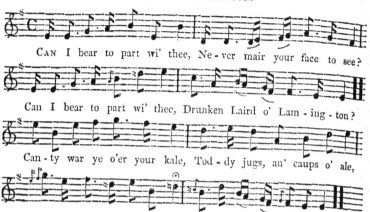

Can I bear to part wi' thee, Ne-ver mair your face to see?

Can I bear to part wi' thee, Drunken Laird o' Lam-ing-ton?

Can-ty war ye o'er your kale, Tod-dy jugs, an' caups o' ale,

Heart aye kind, an' leel, an' hale, Honest Laird o' Lam-ing-ton.

He that swears is but so so,
He that lies to hell must go,
He that falls in bagnio,
        Falls in the devil's frying-pan.
Wha was't ne'er pat aith to word?
Never lied for duke nor lord?
Never sat at sinfu' board?
        The Honest Laird o' Lamington

He that cheats can ne'er be just;
He that prays is ne'er to trust;
He that drinks to drauck his dust,
        Wha can say that wrang is done?
Wha was't ne'er to fraud inclin'd,
Never pray'd sin' he can mind?
Ane wha's drouth there's few can find,
        The Honest Laird o' Lamington.

I like a man to tak' his glass,
Toast a friend or bonny lass;
He that winna is an ass—
        Deil send him ane to gallop on!
I like a man that's frank an kind,
Meets me when I have a mind,
Sings his sang, an' drinks me blind.
        Like the Laird o' Lamington.

NORTH.

Thank you, James. Never heard you in better voice. By the way, Mullion, you said there was a poem in praise of the Chancellor of the Exchequer in your bag—I wish to hear it—now's your time.

MULLION.

In the anonymous bag, sir?—O yes, I recollect it—(*reads.*)

# Some Passages in the Life of
# Colonel Cloud

*In a Letter by the Ettrick Shepherd, to the Hon. Mrs A—r—y.*
*Dated Edinburgh, August* 11, 1816

HONOURED MADAM,

FOR a circumstance of which you are not aware, I owe you an ample apology; but as, some day or other, the extent of my error may reach your ear, or be unfurled to your discovering eye, I deem it incumbent on me to offer you some explanation in writing. I have, therefore, set myself down with the intent of inditing a long letter, giving you some account of the most singular character I have ever met with; and though the circumstances I have to relate are trivial in themselves, and things of no value, I am certain they will strike you, as they did me, with a novelty altogether peculiar.

When I visited you in May last, on my way to Glen-Lyon, what did you think of my companion? You certainly showed him every attention and kindness; and, on the whole, appeared a good deal captivated by his manner and conversation. But I have some impression which did not strike me till very lately, that on the day we took the ride up the river, you either said something, or looked something, or hinted something, in one way or other, that you had suspicion of something equivocal in his character. I assure you, my dear madam, that I had none; and whether I had any reason or not, the following detail will fully evince.

In December last, I chanced one evening to stray into a billiard-room with a Mr Robertson, a friend of mine; but being only a looker-on at that engaging game, I had to saunter about, waiting for Mr Robertson, with whom I was going to sup at a tavern. I had not well entered, till my eye caught a gentleman with whose face I felt conscious of being intimately acquainted. He was an on-looker like myself, and was watching the game very attentively through a quizzing-glass. I was assured I knew him perfectly well, and, as I thought, for something very remarkable; but for all that I could toil in a confusion of reminiscences, I could not recollect his name, (indeed, I rarely ever recollect anybody's name at first,) so, for the present, I was obliged to defer addressing this intimate and interesting acquaintance. The party at the table where we both stood, were playing a pool, and some of the on-lookers were making casual remarks, when this mysterious gentleman made a chance reference to me, naming me at the same time in that easy familiar way, as if we had not only been daily, but hourly companions.

I was now more puzzled than ever, and before I left the room, I asked Mr Robertson, I asked Captain Harper, the master of the billiard-room, and several others, who was the gentleman in black, with the gold chain and quizzing-glass? All of them declared an acquaintance with his face–none with his name; and for several days and nights I could not forget the circumstance, but neither could I tell why I was so much interested in it.

Some weeks subsequent to that, as I was sitting in the Turf Coffee-room, an officer, dressed partly in a Highland uniform, came in, and began reading the papers straight opposite to me. I knew the face quite well, and he likewise tipped me a nod of recognition. I do not know what I would have given to have been able to recollect that officer's name, for it struck me that I had been particularly obligated to him at some former period; but his name I *could not* recollect, so I was obliged to go away highly dissatisfied with myself for my stupidity, and suspecting that I had lost my small portion of memory altogether.

On the same day I again perceived this gallant and respectable-looking officer, coming up the street after me, still walking by himself; and so much did I feel interested in knowing him, that I determined to wait his coming up, and address him at all hazards. I thought him one of the Highland chiefs that had entertained me in the north, but where, Heaven knew!–I did not. I moved my bonnet to him, and bade him good day. He instantly held out his hand, gave mine a hearty shake–named me, and expressed much satisfaction that I recognized my old friend, having of late suspected I had forgot him.

"I am in a worse predicament now than ever," thought I; and I am sure I looked very sheepish; for, indeed, no situation could be more awkward than the one in which I stood, having forced an introduction of myself on a gentleman of whom I still knew not the least circumstance. I am sure, my dear Mrs A——, you will think that was a dilemma that must soon have come to an end? I thought so too; but, on the contrary, it still increased–never came to an end–and never will come to an end while I live. There was one thing, however, that I now discovered, which stunned me still the more. I perceived that he was the very individual whom I had met in the billiard-room, but so transformed, that a witch could not have known him.

It was necessary for me to say something; and so I did. "I beg pardon, sir," says I. "But I was so sure we were old acquaintances when we met at billiards the other evening, that I have been both grieved and angry with myself ever since for forgetting your name."

"And what was the great matter for that?" said he. "You might have called me *Captain*, which never comes wrong to one of my countrymen; or *Colonel*, which would have *sounded* a little better; or Duncan, or Donald, or M'Devil, or any patronymic you listed. What was the matter how you denominated an old acquaintance? It is a long time, Mr H——, since you and I first met. Do you remember that morning, at a fishing-party, in Major Campbell's boat?"

"Perfectly well, sir," says I, (which was not true.) "Was it at Ensay, in the sound of Harries, that you mean?"

"Yes, to be sure!" said he.

"I was at so many fishing parties at Ensay, that I can hardly at this distance of time recollect one from another," said I. "Was it that morning that Dr M'Leod, and Luskinder, and Scalpa, were with us, when we caught the enormous skate, that weighed 300 weight?"

"Yes, to be sure, the very same," said he, "that was such a morning, and such a day, ay, and such a night!"

"We had sad doings at Ensay, certainly," said I, "but shame fa' me, if I remember of meeting you there, Cornel. I hope I am right in calling you Cornel?"

To this last question he shortly nodded assent, and then went on. "It is very likely you may not, for I was then only sort of a—a—a—boy, or a something between a boy or a lad—a stripling, in short. My father, the Colonel, had set me out on a ramble that summer, and happy I was to come several times in contact with you. We met again at Tarbet and at Greenock, you know."

I was utterly confounded. "Tarbet? Tarbet?" says I. "Sure, Colonel, I never *did* meet you at Tarbet? You were not of that ridiculous party, when we sailed away with the man's two daughters to Cowal, and then took them with us to Bute for two or three days."

"Was I not? But I was, though," said he; "For though I could not get my father's brigandine, the Empress, left, as he had allowed me to take her out on a pleasure jaunt that summer, I treated your party at the inn, and saw you fairly away. We met again at Greenock, and had a brilliant party at the Tontine.—But this is my domicile for the present," added he, stepping up to the door of a hotel in Prince's Street. "Dine with me here to-day at half past five, or six—say six, punctually, and we will have a chat about old matters, and some literary things. We shall have a quite sober dinner, and I promise you that we shall not have above a bottle and a half a-piece—or *two* bottles—well, say *two* bottles each. Will you come, now? Give me your hand on it."

"With the utmost pleasure, sir," says I. "At six o'clock precisely? And whose party shall I ask for?"

"Oh, no party. We dine by ourselves in my own room," said he. "Ask for me—just for me."

I went away over to Charles' Street, scratching my ears and beating my brains to no purpose, trying to find out who the devil this grand Colonel was. I had been engaged in all these scenes that he had mentioned, but I could have made oath that he was not present at one of them, unless it had been as a servant. As to his father the Colonel's splendid pleasure-vessel, the EMPRESS, I could remember nothing, either at Ensay, Rothsay, or Tarbet. I recollected something of a Mr M'Neill coming into Loch-Fine in a little stout square-rigged vessel of his own from some of the western isles, and of his being bound to the Clyde, but nothing at all of ever coming in contact with the gentleman. I was fairly bamboozled, and began to suspect that the man was a warlock or an enchanter.

At the hour appointed, to a very second, I went to the hotel, rung the porch bell, and taking the waiter aside, asked him very ingeniously for the proper designation of the Highland gentleman who lodged there, for that I was engaged to dine with him privately, and it looked so exceedingly awkward to have lost his address.

The lad said, there was no Highland gentleman lodging there at present but Major Cameron, who was dining out; but there was a gentleman in No. 6, who had ordered dinner for two, and whose address he supposed was Colonel Cloud.

"M'Leod, you mean," says I.

"No, no," said he; "not *Mac*Leod; that is my own name, which it is not likely I would forget. The gentleman, I think, gave his address as Colonel Cloud of Coalpepper. But he does not lodge here. I never saw him before to-day."

"You astonish me, callant, more ways than one," says I. "Such a designation as Cloud of Coalpepper I never in my life either heard or read, and this gentleman and I are old and intimate acquaintances. That cannot be the gentleman I want."

"Come up stairs and look at him," said the lad; "and if he is not your man, you have nothing ado but to beg pardon, and come down again."

I did so, and found my friend in the full insignia of his honourable office. He was, as I judged, extremely polite, only that he took the greater part of the conversation on himself, which proved a great

ease for your awkward friend in his awkward predicament. To have
heard him talk, you would have thought that I had been in his company for the greater part of a number of years. He never instanced a
party in which I had not been; but then he never represented one of
them as they were; the greatest part of the particulars he mentioned,
I was certain, were purely imaginary, but yet I did not like to tell the
gentleman to his face that he was lying. He mentioned the Right and
Wrong Club with great *sang froid*–said he was only one night there,
and had no inclination ever to go back again. I asked who was in the
chair that night?

"Confound me, if I recollect," said he. "But whoever it was, he
was as often on the floor as in the chair. However, there was a great
battle that night, so that you cannot have forgot it, unless you had
one every night."

"Cornel, I declare, I never saw any fighting at that famous club,"
said I. "I think there was a sort of row one night between some
M'Leods and M'Donalds, which gave the designation to the club,
but there was nothing serious; merely a drunken rally."

"What! have you forgot your rising to knock Norman M'Leod
down? and how he tripped the feet from under you, so that you fell
against a green screen, and down went you and screen together with
a tremendous rattle? And don't you remember what you said when
you arose, which set us all into such a roar of laughter, that, saving
two at the farther end of the room, we all took to our seats again, and
no one could ever tell that night again, what we quarrelled about?"

"I remember nothing about it at all?" said I.

"But I do," said the Colonel; "you got up, and held your elbow,
which seemed to have got some damage,–'D–n the Hieland blude
o' him,' says you, 'an it warna for his father's sake, I wad pit the life
out o' him.' I may well remember the circumstances of that night's
fray, for, being a stranger, I had meddled too rashly in the dispute,
and had like to have paid very dearly for my temerity. This won't do,
thinks I; I must show the lads some play before I am overpowered in
this way. I had, at one time, five of them floored at once, all lying as
flat as flounders. And don't you remember of two that fought it out?–
That was the best sport of all! After the general row, we had all
taken our seats again, and sat I know not how long, when the president, whose name I think was Mr Gildas, or Gillies, or something of
that sound, says in a queer quizzical voice, 'Gentlemen, I wish you
would look in below the table, for I think always that there are some
of the party missing.' The room being very large, there was a screen
set round behind us, and, on a search commencing, it was discov-

ered that there were two still fighting at the farther end of the room. 'I wonder when they began?' says you; 'for if they hae feughten *very* lang, it wad maybe be as gude to pairt them.'–'I think,' says the president, ringing the bell, 'that we had as well ascertain that fact.– Pray, waiter, do you know when these two gentlemen began fighting?'–'About two hours ago, sir.'–'That is very illustrious,' says the president. 'And have they fought all this while?'–'O no, sir; I don't think it. They were both sleeping when I was last up.'–'O, very well!' says the president. 'Bring two stoups more of bourdeaux.'

"They were both on the floor at that time fighting like men in a dream, and neither of them could get above the other. We never regarded them in the smallest degree, but set to work again. We never noted when they joined the party; and when supper was set at one in the morning, not one amongst us knew who the two were that had fought all the night, and I suppose none ever knew to this day."

This was certainly an amusing picture, and I believed it; not because it was so like truth, but because it was so unlike truth, that I thought I was sure no man could ever have contrived it. I was sure, meantime, that my distinguished entertainer was never at the club when I was present, else he had been there either as a waiter or an invisible being. He had the wit, however, of never suffering me to make any remarks on his narrations, for he always began a new subject with the same breath in which he ended the preceding one; and here he began with the query, "When I had seen our worthy friend, Mr M'Millan?"

"M'Millan, of Millburgh?" said I. "Is he an acquaintance of yours?"

"Yes; an intimate one, and a near neighbour," was the reply. "Do you not remember of his sending for me to a shooting-party in the Wood of Culloch-More, one day?"

"I remember of being there a roe-shooting two days," said I, "but knew not who the laird had sent for besides."

"My father, the Colonel, had a party of fourteen that day, all engaged in the same sport," said he. "I would gladly have been of your party, but our own could do nothing without the assistance of my dogs. Without them, the sport would have been entirely blown up. I shot seven roe-bucks that day for my own part, and never once fired at a doe. But my dogs are so completely trained to the driving, that it would be an easy matter to root out the whole breed of roes in the kingdom with their assistance."

He then entered into a long detail of the marvellous feats he had performed on the moors, describing them with a great deal of animation, and I fairly set him down as a most wonderful and highly-gifted gentleman. He next described his various breeds of dogs, which were without end. He had three Russian pointers, and two Russian terriers, most valuable and interesting animals of their kind; but he had a handsome bitch, of a Transylvanian breed, that surpassed everything. He never took less than 100 guineas for every one of her blind pups. I never had heard of such a beast in the world as that! He had far too high a value for her, that was the truth! for she had been the cause of much mischief to him. Owing to some disputes about her, he had been compelled to cowe one young nobleman on the moors, and challenge another, so that she had very nigh cost him his life; but he did not value her a bit the less of that, he rather valued her the more. Besides these, the breeds he enumerated were prodigious, so that I rather got confused among them, never knowing which he talked of; till at last he was so good as give me all their names, every one of which was either German or classical.

All this time I had never been able to recollect where I had seen this distinguished officer and sportsman; and, in order if possible to effect this, I asked bluntly, what regiments they were which he and his father commanded? He did not answer the question directly, but began a long explanatory story, the substance of which was as follows:–

That though he allowed his companions to call him Colonel, he was not one in fact, having the title and emolument only in reversion. His father, the Colonel, held the lucrative office of Deputy-Adjutant-General, under the Emperor of Austria, which office he had secured for this his only son, long ago, the Colonel's hope and delight. That his father had reared him solely with the view of filling that important station; and though he had restricted him in none of his pleasures, he had kept him at hard work as a student, both in arts and arms. He said a great deal more to the same purpose, for he was very long and very minute on this interesting topic.

At a late hour we parted, with mutual professions of esteem, and I had, before that, accepted of an invitation to the mansion-house of Coalpepper, close beside the celebrated village of that name. The Colonel and I were to leave Edinburgh together in the spring, make a tour of the middle Highlands, and arrive at his father's house by a certain day–have fishing-parties, and pleasure-parties in the Empress, and I cannot tell you what all.

From that day forth, I saw not the Colonel for three months, nor did I ever, during that period, meet with a single individual who knew him either by name, title, or appointment. I applied to the Almanack, but found it vain to consult it for the staff-officers of the

Emperor of Austria. Matters remained *in statu quo.*

It approached toward the end of March, at length; and as I had engaged to be at Alloa on the 23d of April, and in Athol and Glen-Lyon early in May, I began to be impatient at not meeting again with my friend, the Colonel, for I intended introducing him to all my friends and correspondents in that tract, and show him that I had honourable, noble, and respectable friends, as well as he. One day, about that period, I had been walking with my friend Mr Forbes, the wine-merchant, and as I knew he had a great number of the nobility and gentry on his books, I stopped him on the street, just as we were going to part, and asked him if he could give me the Edinburgh address of young Cloud of Coalpepper. Forbes fell a-laughing, until he had almost fallen down on the street, and, without giving me any explanation, left me standing there quite dumfoundered. As I was turning round to go away, what should pop out of Mr Laing's shop but the very image and likeness of the gentleman I was in quest of, but in such a dishabile habit, that I knew not what to think. He looked me full in the face, but did not see me, and away he went, carrying three books below his arm. "I'll see where this singular apparition goes," thought I; and accordingly I dogged him until he entered a lodging down two pair of stairs, in an elegant eastern street in Edinburgh. I followed close at his heels, and said to the girl that opened the door, that I wanted to speak with the gentleman who entered just now. Accordingly, I was shown into a darkish shabby apartment, and there was my friend, the Colonel, who had just set himself down amongst an immense number of papers and a few books. I could not help addressing him by his title, though still dubious as to the identity of my man. He received me with perfect ease and great kindness, and at once assumed his high ground and exalted character. He said his father the Colonel (and Deputy-Adjutant-General to the Emperor of Austria) had compelled him, as a test of his improvement, to write out essays in thirteen different languages, and that in order to finish these in time for our northern and western jaunt, he had been obliged to conceal himself in that most quiet of all retreats, and study almost night and day, but that he would now be ready to set out with me in the course of a fortnight.

We had settled everything, before we parted, regarding our tour, but in place of sending for the Colonel's carriage, as had been previously intended, we resolved to proceed to Alloa in the steam-boat, take a chaise the length of your mansion, angle from that to Crief, and so on to Athol, Glen-Lyon, and Glen-Orchay, and then turn to the southward on our way to Coalpepper Castle, where pleasures without number awaited us, and where we were to remain for a whole month.

Accordingly we set out together on the 20th, attended the annual festival held at Alloa in commemoration of the anniversary of Shakspeare; spent eight or nine days with the kind and intelligent gentlemen of that place, and for several of these days the Colonel and I went a-fishing in the Devon, on the forenoons.

It was here that I experienced the first disappointment in my illustrious friend; and, trivial as it may appear in your eyes, it made me feel very queer. He had boasted fully as much of his angling as his shooting, and as I had determined not to be beat at that sport, on any consideration, I went from Edinburgh, fully provided with fishing apparatus; and lest the trouts of the Devon should despise the Edinburgh flies, I went to M'Isaac of Alloa, and picked all his. The Colonel had nothing—he had not so much as a fishing-rod, which I thought very shabby, but Mr Bald supplied him with everything, and away we set.

When we went to begin, he could not so much as put on his flies, for his father the Colonel's servant, who always went with him, was so completely master of these things, that neither he, nor his father the Colonel, ever paid the least attention to them. This was very well. So accordingly he put on magnifying glasses, which he kept for the purpose of angling, that he might trepan the trouts the moment they were so imprudent as to snap at his fly, or even to toy with it. I never saw a gentleman go forth to the water side with such an important look; it was so knowing, and at the same time so confident and so profound, that I did not know whether to quake or laugh. "I shall be beat at the fishing for once, though I had a thousand guineas on it," thought I, with a sigh, as I followed this champion down the bank.

But an experienced angler knows another the moment he first sees him throw the line. The mason word is a humbug; but the very first wave of a rod is sufficient between anglers. Colonel Cloud, younger of Coalpepper, and, in reversion, deputy adjutant-general to the Emperor of Austria, began that finest and healthiest of rural sports. Good and gracious! Madam! if you had seen how he began it! With what an air! What a look of might and majesty through the magnifying glasses! I never was so petrified in all the days of my life. I cannot describe to you the utter absurdity of his address in the art, as I am afraid you have never regarded it; but, in the first place, he fixed upon a smooth, shallow part of the river, where no fish in his right judgment would ever take a fly; and then he held the rod with both his hands; set out his lips, as also an immense protuberance behind, and thrashed on the smooth stream with such violence, as if he intended to strike the trouts on the head, in the majesty of his power. I was like to burst with laughter, and wist not what to do, yet still I contained myself. But at length a par rose at his fly, a small, insignificant fish, not thicker than a lady's little finger–the Colonel perceived this through the magnifying glasses, (magnifiers they were with a vengeance,) and he pulled the line with such force, that his rod sounded through the atmosphere like a whirlwind. Yea, with such violence did he pull it, that his feet slid in a reverse direction, and he fell. "By the L–, I had on one a stone weight," cried he. "Nay, he was more. I'm sure he was more."

This was altogether beyond my capacity of bearing any longer. I crept in beyond an alder bush, laid me down on my face, and laughed till I was weak. The tears ran from my eyes till the very grass was steeped; but it was in vain that I held my sides, and tried to refrain laughing. I had some fears I should never do more good. I waded across the river, and no more durst I come near the Colonel that day, but I despised him in my heart. He lost in my good opinion that day more than he has ever since regained. He caught not one fish, either great or small. I filled my basket. I overtook him at the village of Cambus, about two o'clock. Mr Alexander Bald had come up to meet us; the two were sitting on a rock conversing, when I came immediately opposite, and I heard him informing Mr Bald that he had not caught any, but that he had hooked one which was fully a stone weight. The whole scene again presented itself to my imagination in vivid and more vivid colours, my knees lost their power, and I had no shift but to turn about, lie down on the bank, and fall again into a convulsion of laughter. Mr Bald called again and again, what ailed me, but I was unable to make him any answer, and never knew till he had waded the river, and was lifting up my head. "What ails you?" said he, "I think you have been crying?"

"Yes," said I, "I suppose I *was* crying."

The Colonel was a great favourite with the good folks of Alloa, for he was eminently intelligent, and well versed in both ancient and modern literature; argumentative, civil, and courteous. But at length we left them with regret, as I had often done before, and that night we arrived at your hospitable mansion.

This was precisely the bearing of our acquaintance before we visited at your house; and you yourself acknowledged to me that you thought me lucky in my travelling companion. There is no dispute with regard to his capabilities and general intelligence, yet I know

now that there had been something about him, of which, or *with* which you were not perfectly satisfied; and as I have learned a good deal more of him since that period, I shall, as in duty bound, proceed to communicate that knowledge very shortly to you.

If you at all regarded the thing, you might remember, that before we took leave of you, everything was amicably arranged between my honoured friend and me regarding our tour; we were to fish up to Crief that day, and so on by Glen-Almond and Amberlee to Kinnaird. But before we had proceeded two miles, he informed me, with apparent regret, that he was compelled to abandon his northern tour, as he had received an express from his father the Colonel, ordering him home. I was greatly astounded at this, being perfectly convinced in my own mind that he had never received a letter since he left Edinburgh. He had no possible chance, save at Alloa, and on sounding him a little, I found he did not so much as know where the post-office of that town was situated. It was vain, however, for me to expostulate, after he informed me that there were some foreign dispatches arrived at the castle of Coalpepper, which required both dispatch and decision; that his father required his immediate assistance; and the carriage was to meet him at Dunira that day. I was compelled to submit to the emergency, and we parted; but before doing so, he again exacted my solemn promise, that I was to spend a month with him at his father's mansion. I repeated such promise for the thirtieth time, and with a bow so profound that my bonnet, which I held in my left hand, touched the ground, I parted from my illustrious friend.

I spent the month of May in Strath-Tay and Glen-Lyon, the month of June in Appin and Lorn, and though the weather was eminently ungenial, I never enjoyed any excursion with greater zest. Often in my heart did I pity Colonel Cloud, younger of Coalpepper, and ASSISTANT DEPUTY ADJUTANT-GENERAL to the EMPEROR OF AUSTRIA!

With a heavy heart I was at last obliged to turn my back on the romantic lands of Ossian and of Fingal; and, descending on the populous valleys of the west, on the 9th of July I arrived at the environs of the far-famed village of Coalpepper; but instead of going straight to the house of the Austrian staff-officer, I went to Millburgh, Mr M'Millan being my oldest acquaintance. I had not been many hours in the house ere I began to ask for my friend the Colonel. No one of the family understood who I meant, and I found it impossible to explain myself.

"It cannot be Mr Jacob Cloud whom Mr H. means?" said one of the young ladies.

"The very same man," said M'Millan, "and that will be some title given him in banter among his associates at Edinburgh. Do you stile Jacob the Colonel now?"

"Yes, I understand he gets that title for the most part," said I. But hearing them call him *Mr* Cloud, or simply *Jacob*, I recollected the honour and integrity of my friend, who had previously informed me that he was only a colonel, and adjutant-general in reversion; and, admiring his modesty about his own native place, I mentioned his name no more. But the next day Mr M'Millan says to me, "Were you not saying that Jacob Cloud was an acquaintance of yours?" I answered in the affirmative, when he added, "Very well, I will invite him to dinner to-day. I have always been wishing to have him here since he came home."

The dinner party was very numerous, and among the last who came into the drawing-room was my friend the Colonel, with the very identical magnifying glasses across his nose that had exaggerated the par of the Devon to such an enormous bulk. I felt some very tickling sensations, but behaved myself middling well. He came up to me, shook hands with great frankness, and far more affability than I had any right to expect, welcoming me to that district, in which he hoped I should never be so great a stranger again, &c. &c.

It so happened, that the Colonel and I were placed at different ends of the table, and during the whole evening I never had an opportunity of exchanging another word with him save one. I called on him at dinner to drink a glass of wine, and asked him if he had reached home in time to get the dispatches written out?

"O, yes, thank you; quite in good time," was the answer.

I then heard Mr M'Millan inquiring what papers they were to which I alluded, and he said they were "some of those ridiculous formal affairs. A great botheration, certainly, and quite FOREIGN to all useful purposes."

I noted that he pronounced the term *foreign* very loud and sonorously, while the magnifying glasses gleamed in the light of our candles. As I am never among the first risers from a social board, I saw no more of my friend that night, nor did I hear aught of the invitation to a month's diversion; and, in spite of many appearances rather equivocal, I that evening believed everything to exist precisely as he had so often described them to me at the Castle of Coalpepper. It was not till next day that my eyes were opened to the truth, the whole truth, and nothing but the truth; and never in my life shall I again be as much astonished at anything I shall hear or see.

We were to have a fox-chase the following day in Glen-Sheagy, and there were sportsmen laws laid out for us, which we were not to transgress. We were to be allowed to shoot a roe-buck or a brocket, but neither a doe nor a fawn on any account. The description of that day's sport would take a long paper by itself: I must stick by my text for the present. I never doubted that my friend the Colonel would be the leading man in the sport. How could I, after the descriptions he had given me of his unequalled prowess in that line? I thought it would be a day amongst a thousand with him, and a party in which I should see him then appear in all his glory. I thought of the Transylvanian bitch Penelope—of the Russian pointers, and the terriers from the sources of the Wolga, that would tear either a fox or an otter to pieces—of the Hungarian dog Eugene, that had once belonged to the Archduke John—and Hector and Cressida—and, though last not least, of Sobieski, the great blood-hound from the forests of Poland; and I thought what a day there would be in the woods of Sheagy More!

When we were making ready, I says to Mr M'Millan carelessly, "Mr Cloud will be of the party, of course?"

"O, no! he cannot enjoy such a thing," said he; and "he is of no use either,—that's worse."

I was petrified and speechless. "Do I hear with my ears, and understand with my heart?" thought I; "what was it the malicious, ill-willie man was saying? 'He cannot enjoy such a thing! and is for no use at it neither! that's worse!' Worse with a vengeance! The gentleman is raving, or speaking through his sleep. Mr *Mac-Millan!*" exclaimed I aloud, (for I had been exclaiming internally before for the space of a minute or two,) "Mr *Mac-Millan!* ye dinna mean, or pretend to say, that Cloud is not a good shot?"

"It is impossible for me, or any man living, to determine that point," said he, "for one very good reason, he never fired a shot in his life." My ears tingled, and I was struck dumb.

Not being able to bring my mind to think about anything else, however, in the course of our preparations, I was obliged once more to propose that *the Colonel* should still be of our party, for the sake of his *dogs*.

"Dogs! What do you mean?"

"Why, hath not Jacob a variety of very superior dogs, bred from foreign countries?"

"He a breed of dogs? pooh! He never had a single dog in his life. His father had once a half-blind terrier that lay in below the loom, but it is dead, and has been for these three years and a half."

I grew dizzy, my head birled round like a mill-wheel, and I could not help repeating into myself an hundred times these words, *"Lord, what is man?"*

We hunted a whole day–got no foxes; but I caught a beautiful young roe-buck alive, and Mr M'Millan shot a fine old one. We drank some whisky at the Strone of Sheavy, and on our walk home I took Mr M'Millan apart; and the *blind terrier* and the *loom* having been uppermost in my mind from the morning, the following dialogue passed between Mr M'Millan and me. I give it verbatim, without colouring or addition.

"What rank does old Mr Cloud hold in society?"

"He is a manufacturer; a very honest, worthy man."

"Has he not some foreign commission?"

"No, no; he just works for the people of the village."

"He does not attend to the manufactory in person, surely?"

"That he does. He has no other to attend to it. In plain terms, he is a common weaver, and has just two looms in the house, one for himself, and one for an apprentice, or an occasional journeyman in a strait."

"Did he never serve in any army, either abroad or at home?"

"Never. He has lived in the village all his life, and his father before him."

"What sort of character does my friend sustain in general?"

"He has some strange peculiarities about him; there are, however, good points in his character. He is sober, industrious, and a most kind and affectionate son. His father has pinched himself to bring him out as a dominie, and he has requited his parent by a course of the hardest studies, as well as the utmost gratitude and attention."

"That is enough for me," said I in my heart; "Jacob and the shepherd shall be friends still. I hold these qualities in higher estimation than a reversion of a lucrative post at the court of Austria." I said not a word to Mr M'Millan how I had been hoaxed. He continued:–

"The truth is, that if the young man had not too fertile an imagination–a fancy that has a scope beyond that of any other man's that ever existed–he would have been a first-rate character."

Well might I assent mentally to that remark, when I thought of the Castle of Coalpepper–the great staff officer–the square-rigged brigandine–the Empress–the Colonel's carriage with three outriders–the dogs–the rural sports–and a thousand things beside, all vanished in a breath. All the creation of a fancy, over which truth, reason, and ultimate disgrace, had no control. Mr M'Millan perceiving me thoughtful, went on. "He was once in our family teaching the children, and gave us much satisfaction by his attention."

Never was there a day so fertile of disclosures to me. I was sure, from the beginning, that I had been intimately acquainted with this singular person. It was true, I had. But never, till that moment, did it strike me how, where, or when. "We had him teaching our children," said Mr M'Millan. I then recollected that I had, indeed, known him previously, but in circumstances so extremely degrading, that they cannot be mentioned to you along with the name of the Hon. Colonel Cloud of the staff of Austria.

Were some people to read this long epistle, they would regard it as an extravagant romance, so far does truth sometimes overreach fancy. You know that it is true, and to you it needs no confirmation, as I introduced him to you in all his borrowed plumage, for which, madam, I humbly ask your pardon: Not for introducing to you the son of a poor operative weaver; as such, he had as good a right to be there as the son of a poor shepherd, but it is for introducing to your kindness and hospitality an impostor. There's the rub! But I entreat that you will only laugh at it, and regard it as a harmless and unaccountable lunacy. I am, with the utmost respect, my honoured and esteemed friend, yours most faithfully,

JAMES HOGG.

# There's Nought Sae Sweet

Air—*Auld Langsyne*

There's nought sae sweet in this poor life
    As knittin' soul to soul;
And what maist close may bind that knot?
    The glass and bowl!
The glass and bowl, my boys,                     5
    The glass and bowl;
So let us call, for this is out,
      Anither bowl.
        *Chorus.* The glass and bowl, &c.

We never dabbled in the burn,               10
    Nor pull'd the gowan droll,
But often has the sun's return
    Surprised our bowl.

*Chorus.*–Our glass and bowl, my boys,
   Our glass and bowl;     15
  So let us call, as this is out–
   Another bowl.

And aft did we the merry catch
 And cheering ditty troll,
And hooted mony a whiggish wretch   20
 About the bowl.
   *Chorus.*–Our glass and bowl, &c.

And, therefore, hills betwixt may rise,
 And though ocean water roll,
Yet we'll ne'er forget the lads who met  25
 About the bowl.
   *Chorus.*–Our glass and bowl, &c.

And whan yer poet's dead and gane,
 And laid beneath the moul',
Let those who sung his memory, drink  30
 About the bowl.
   *Chorus.*–The glass and bowl, my boys,
    The glass and bowl;
   So let us call, for this is out–
    Another bowl.     35

# The Brakens Wi' Me

AIR–*Driving the Steers*

1.

I'LL sing of yon glen o' red heather,
 An' a dear thing that ca's it her hame,
Wha's a' made o' love-life together,
 Frae the tie o' the shoe to the kembe.
Love beckons in ev'ry sweet motion,   5
 Commanding due homage to gi'e;
But the shrine of my dearest devotion
 Is the bend o' her bonny e'e bree.

2.

I fleeched and I prayed the dear lassie
 To gang to the brakens wi' me,   10

But though neither lordly nor saucy,
　　Her answer was, "Laith will I be.
Ah, is it nae cruel to press me
　　To that which wad breed my heart wae,
An' try to entice a poor lassie                    15
　　The gate she's o'er ready to gae.

### 3.

"I neither hae father nor mither,
　　Good counsel or caution to gie,
And prudence has whisper'd me never
　　To gang to the brakens wi' thee.                 20
I neither hae tocher nor mailing,
　　I hae but ae boast—I am free;
But a' wad be tint without failing
　　Amang the green brakens wi' thee."

### 4.

"Dear lassie, how can ye upbraid me,                25
　　And try your ain love to beguile,
For ye are the richest young lady,
　　That ever gaed o'er the kirk-stile.
Your smile that is blither than ony,
　　The bend o' your sunny e'e-bree,               30
And the love-blinks aneath it sae bonny,
　　Are five hunder thousand to me."

### 5.

There's joy in the blithe blooming feature,
　　When love lurks in every young line;
There's joy in the beauties of nature,              35
　　There's joy in the dance and the wine;
But there's a delight will ne'er perish
　　'Mong pleasures so fleeting and vain,
And that is to love and to cherish
　　The fond little heart that's our ain.          40

# *January–December 1826 (Volumes 19–20)*

## Songs for the
# Duke of Buccleuch's Birth Day

TICKLER What sort of festival had you last November James in Ettrick on the young duke of Buccleuch's birth day?

SHEPHERD O man a real grand ane! Mitchell set us down a dinner as we had a' been deuks the'gither. It is true we thought the wine rather plishy-plashy stuff; but our chayerman wadna suffer us to gie up wi't an' brik on the toddy till we had drunken the healths of a' the Buckleuchs, Montagues, and Douglasses man woman an' bairn o' them in healths five fathom deep. And then there was sickan shouting and scraughing at the honours that I thought weel the auld borough wad topple down about our lugs and rowe stane aboon stane into the Ettrick.

TICKLER Was the party so very numerous?

SHEPHERD Aye to be sure. Every man o' the Forest was there frae the chief Magistrate down to the Tailor o' Yarrowford. The cheild that reads twa o' our Magazines ye ken.

TICKLER That does not answer my question James. I want to know how many sat down to dinner in order to form some estimate of the strength and copiousness of mountain voices.

SHEPHERD That's mair than I can tell you Tim; for though I can count fifty scores o' sheep on Mount-Benger Law without erring in ane yet I never could count the company that night though I tried it three times ower. And when Mitchell and the president came to settle about the reckoning how mony think you were atween them in numbers?

TICKLER I cannot possibly guess. Perhaps half a score?

SHEPHERD Just three score and thirteen lad. I'll assure ye when I heard that I thought there wad be nae bill sittled that night.

TICKLER Why? Could they not count the guests over again?

SHEPHERD Aha! That *was* impossible! for lang afore that time they were a' run abreed athwart the town, some looking after their horses, some after the lasses, some after auld Wattie Henderson for crock-siller, and some after Geordie Scott for the price o' swine. Ye might as weel have tried to have countit how many hielandmen there were at Falkirk tryste.

TICKLER How then was the matter settled?

SHEPHERD O our president was nae coward, sae him and Mitchell just raid the mare for four and twenty punds. But the farmers and burgesses lost it!

TICKLER Aye! That brings a deep sigh from your breast to this day James. Why does it so?

SHEPHERD It was a gay trying night that, mae ways than ane.

TICKLER Little doubt of it. Had you much speechifying?

SHEPHERD O capital speeches for a coontry place ye ken. Some pith and nerve with but little elegance. Our president Tam Anderson spoke like a prince far better than Joseph Hume—

TICKLER James! James!

SHEPHERD I heard them baith, and on my honour I thought sae. As for the Tailor o' Yarrowford he was quite superb! I'll never forget the close o' his speech as lang as I leeve, it was sae capital and sae muckle in character. These were the words (*shepherd rises*) And noo freens brethren, and coontrymen; I winna presoome to draw out the *thread* o' my discoorse till it *nick* the *knuckles* o' your patience, but I maun just observe that we're a *tackit* an' *sewed* to the auld honourable house o' Buccleuch by a *seam* that the power o' mortal man never can *slite*!!!

OMNES Ha—ha—ha! Hurra for the Tailor o' Yarrowford Here's to the Tailor.

TICKLER No laughing if you please Mr Ambrose.

SHEPHERD Aye Tim look to the honour and respectability of our Noctes I trust always to your high old aristocratic feelings for that. But faith and troth let Ambrose take a hearty nicker honest man. Better twa laugh than ane greet. Another reaming jug Maister Ambrose. Od bless your honest chubby face for Care an' it never stared on mine at the same time.

TICKLER More of the Forest festival dear James if you please. A little more of the Forest. Our town festivals are grown quite naseous. Fudge! flummery! headaches! glysters and cammomile tea! ! I want something fresh from the country, rough rabid and raging like the season. The very sight of your own weatherbeaten face and burly head is an anodyne to my spirit. Some of the original songs sung at the meeting my good fellow.

NORTH Were there really such things there?

SHEPHERD Gude faith man ye need hardly speer that and me there. Davie Tamson the poet o' Galashiels an' I screeded them off poetry by the yard. But the best thing that could have happened to me was, that they were a' sae drunk afore my original sang was asked that the deevil tak them if ane o' them kend what it was about or wha it was about. A gay while after that they thought it behoved them to encore this new sang, merely out o' respect to me lest I should have been affronted; for a' that they recollected about the sang was just that I had sung ane, and some warna quite sure even of that. I suspected how the land lay and gae them a different ane, sae they were highly pleased wi't thinking it was the same. They war baith extempories the songs but I'll gye a' that I can mind o' them.

## Songs for the Duke of Buccleuch's Birth day Held at Selkirk the 25 of Nov[r] 1825

Air– *Killiecrankie*

### 1

Rejoice ye wan and wildered glens
  Ye dowie dells o' Yarrow
This is the day that heaven ordains
  To banish a' your sorrow
Ilk forest shaw an' lofty law
  Frae grief an' gloom arouse ye
What gars ye snood your brows wi' snaw
  An' look sae grim an' grousy

### 2

What though the winter storm an' flood
  Set a' your cliffs a quaking
An' frost an' snaw leave nought ava
  On your green Glens o' braken
Yet soon the spring wi' bud an' flower
  An' birds an' maidens singing
The bonny rainbow an' the shower
  Shall set your braes a ringing

### 3

We saw our sun set in the cloud
  For gloaming far too early*
An' darkness fa' wi' eiry shroud
  While hearts beat sad an' sairly
But after lang an' lanesome night
  Our morn has risen mair clearly
An' O to wan an' waefu' wight
  Sic blithesome morn is cheery

* We suppose our shepherd here alludes to the deaths of the late duke and duchess of Buccleuch both cut off in the middle of life's day "For gloaming far too early"

4

This is the day that wakes our spring
   Our rainbow's arch returning
This is the dawning sent by heaven
   To banish care an' mourning
O young Buccleuch our kinsman true
   Our shield and firm defender
To thee this day our love we pay
   Our blessings kindly render

5

O young Buccleuch O kind Buccleuch
   What thousand hearts yearn o'er thee
What thousand hopes await thy smile
   And prostrate lie before thee
Be thou thy Border's pride and boast
   Like sires renowned in story
And thou shalt never want an host
   For country king and glory

Song Second
## Wat o' Buccleuch.
Air–*Thurot's defeat.*

1

Some sing with devotion
   Of feats on the ocean
And nature's broad beauties in earth and in skies
   Some rant of their glasses
   And some of the lasses
And these are twa things we maun never despise
   But down with the praises
   Of lillies and daiseys
Of posies and roses the like never grew
   That flimsy inditing
   That poets delight in
They're kend for a havering halfwitted crew

CHORUS
   But join in my chorus
   Ye blades o' the Forest
We'll lilt of our muirs and our mountains of blue

And hallow for ever
Till a' the town shiver
The name of our master Young Wat o' Buccleuch

2

Of Douglas and Stuart
We'd many a true heart
Wha stood for auld Scotland in dangers enew
    And Scotts wha kept order
    So lang on the Border
Then wha heardnae tell o' the Wats o' Buccleuch
    Now all these old heros
    Of helms and monteros
O wha wad believe that the thing could be true
    In lineage unblighted
    And blood are united
In our noble master young Wat o' Buccleuch
        Then join in my chorus &c.

3

In old days of wassail
Of chief and of vassal
O these were the ages of chivalry true
    Of reif and of rattle
    Of broil and of battle
When first our auld forefathers followed Buccleuch
    They got for their merit
    What we still inherit
Those green towring hills and low vallies of dew
    Nor feared on their mailings
    For hornings or failings
The broad sword and shield paid the rents of Buccleuch
        Then join in my chorus &c.

4

From that day to this ane
We've lived but to bless them
To love and to trust them as guardians true
    May heaven protect then
    And guide and direct then
This stem of the generous old house of Buccleuch
    The Wats were the callans
    That steadied the balance

When strife between kinsmen and Borderers grew
  Then here's to our scion
  The son of the lion
The lord of the Forest the chief of Buccleuch

  CHORUS
  Then join in my chorus
  Ye lads of the Forest
We'll lilt of our muirs and our mountains of blue
  And hallow for ever
  Till a' the town shiver
The name of our Master Young Wat o' Buccleuch

# The Great Muckle Village
# of Balmaquhapple

AIR—"*Soger Laddie.*"

I.

D'YE ken the big village of Balmaquhapple,
The great muckle village of Balmaquhapple?
'Tis steep'd in iniquity up to the thrapple,
And what's to become of poor Balmaquhapple?
Fling a' off your bonnets, and kneel for your life, folks,      5
And pray to Saint Andrew, the god o' the Fife folks;
Gar a' the hills yout wi' sheer vociferation,
And thus you may cry on sic needfu' occasion:

II.

"O blessed Saint Andrew, if e'er ye could pity folk,
Men folk or women folk, country or city folk,      10
Come for this aince wi' the auld thief to grapple,
And save the poor village of Balmaquhapple!
Frae drinking, and leeing, and flyting, and swearing,
And sins that ye wad be affrontit at hearing,
And cheating, and stealing, O grant them redemption,      15
And save and except the few after to mention.

III.

"There's Johnny the elder, wha hopes ne'er to need ye,
Sae pawkie, sae holy, sae gruff, and sae greedy,
Wha prays every hour, as the wayfarer passes,
But aye at a hole where he watches the lasses:        20
He's cheated a thousand, and e'en to this day yet
Can cheat a young lass, or they're leears that say it;
Then gie him his way, he's sae sly and sae civil,
Perhaps in the end he may cheat Mr Devil.

IV.

"There Cappie the cobler, and Tammie the tinman,      25
And Dickie the brewer, and Peter the skinman;
And Geordie, our deacon, for want of a better;
And Bess, that delights in the sins that beset her.
O, worthy Saint Andrew, we canna compel ye,
But ye ken as weel as a body can tell ye,        30
If these gang to heaven, we'll a' be sae shockit,
Your garrat o' blue will but thinly be stockit.

V.

"But for a' the rest, for the women's sake, save them!
Their bodies at least, and their souls, if they have them;
But it puzzles Jock Linton, and small it avails,      35
If they dwell in their stomachs, their heads, or their tails.
And save, without frown or confession auricular,
The clerk's bonny daughters, and Bell in particular;
For ye ken that their beauty's the pride and the stapple
Of the great wicked village of Balmaquhapple."      40

# Meg o' Marley

1.

O KEN ye Meg o' Marley glen,
   The bonny blue-ee'd deary?
She's play'd the deil amang the men,
   An' a' the land's grown eiry;
She's stown the Bangor frae the clerk,      5
   An' snool'd him wi' the shame o't;
The minister's fa'en through the text,
   An' Meg gets a' the blame o't.

2.

The plowman plows without the sock,
  The goadman whistles sparely,          10
The shepherd pines amang his flock,
  An' turns his ee to Marley;
The tailor's fa'en out-ower the bed,
  The cobler ca's a parley,
The weaver's fa'en out-through the web;    15
  An' a' for Meg o' Marley.


3.

What's to be done? for our goodman
  Is flyting late an' early;
He rises but to curse an' ban,
  An' sits down but to ferly.          20
But ne'er had love a brighter lowe,
  O light his torches warly,
At the bright ee an' blithesome brow
  Of bonny Meg o' Marley.


# My Bonny Mary

WHERE Yarrow rowes amang the rocks,
  An' wheels an' boils in mony a linn,
A blithe young Shepherd fed his flocks,
  Unused to branglement or din.
But Love its silken net had thrown     5
  Around his breast so brisk an' airy,
And his blue eyes wi' moisture shone,
  As thus he sung of bonny Mary.


"O Mary, thou'rt sae mild an' sweet,
  My very being clings about thee,    10
This heart wad rather cease to beat,
  Than beat a lonely thing without thee.
I see thee in the evening beam,
  A radiant glorious apparition;
I see thee in the midnight dream,    15
  By the dim light of heavenly vision.

"When over Benger's haughty head
   The morning breaks in streaks sae bonny,
I climb the mountain's velvet side,
   For quiet rest I get nae ony.          20
How sweet the brow on Brownhill cheek,
   Where many a weary hour I tarry!
For there I see the twisted reek
   Rise frae the cot where dwells my Mary.

"When Phœbus mounts outower the muir,     25
   His gowden locks a' streaming gaily,
When morn has breathed its fragrance pure,
   An' life, an' joy, ring through the valley,
I drive my flocks to yonder brook,
   The feeble in my arms I carry,        30
Then every lammie's harmless look
   Brings to my mind my bonny Mary.

"Oft has the lark sung o'er my head,
   And shook the dew-draps frae her wing,
Oft hae my flocks forgot to feed,        35
   And round their shepherd form'd a ring.
Their looks condole the lee-lang day,
   While mine are fix'd an' canna vary,
Aye turning down the westlan brae,
   Where dwells my loved, my bonny Mary.    40

"When gloaming o'er the welkin steals,
   And haps the hills in solemn grey,
And bitterns, in their airy wheels,
   Amuse the wanderer on his way;
Regardless of the wind or rain,        45
   With cautious step and prospect wary,
I often trace the lonely glen,
   To steal a sight o' bonny Mary.

"When midnight draws her curtain deep,
   And lays the breeze amang the bushes,    50
And Yarrow, in her sounding sweep,
   By rocks and ruins raves and rushes;
Then, sunk in short and restless sleep,
   My fancy wings her flight so airy,
To where sweet guardian spirits keep    55
   Their watch around the couch of Mary.

"The exile may forget his home,
　Where blooming youth to manhood grew,
The bee forget the honey-comb,
　Nor with the spring his toil renew;　　　　60
The sun may lose his light and heat,
　The planets in their rounds miscarry,
But my fond heart shall cease to beat
　When I forget my bonny Mary."


# O Weel Befa' the Maiden Gay

O WEEL befa' the maiden gay,
　In cottage, bught, or penn;
And weel befa' the bonny May
　That wons in yonder glen,
Wha lo'es the modest truth sae weel–　　　5
Wha's aye say kind, an' aye sae leal,
An' pure as blooming asphodel,
　Amang sae mony men.
O weel befa' the bonny thing,
　That wons in yonder glen.　　　　10

'Tis sweet to hear the music float
　Alang the gloaming lea;
'Tis sweet to hear the blackbird's note
　Come pealing frae the tree;
To see the lambkin's lightsome race–　　　15
The dappled kid in wanton chase–
The young deer cower in lonely place,
　Deep in his flowery den;
But sweeter far the bonny face
　That smiles in yonder glen.　　　　20

O, had it no been for the blush
　Of maiden's virgin-flame,
Dear Beauty never had been known,
　And never had a name.
But aye sin' that dear thing of blame　　　25
Was modell'd by an angel's frame,
The power of Beauty reigns supreme
　O'er a' the sons of men;

But deadliest far the sacred flame
    Burns in a lonely glen.                                    30

There's beauty in the violet's vest—
    There's hinny in the haw—
There's dew within the rose's breast,
    The sweetest o' them a'.
The sun will rise an' set again,                               35
And lace with burning gowd the main—
And rainbow bend outower the plain,
    Sae lovely to the ken;
But lovelier far my bonny thing,
    That smiles in yonder glen.                                40

# A Pastoral Love Scene

## *By the Ettrick Shepherd*

### SCENE FIRST

What are ye ay greeting for that gate the day Keatie?

I'm greeting nane. I wonder to hear ye.

Why dear woman you're greeting till your very heart is like to burst.
    If ye sob that gate ye'll gar me greet too and that's the thing I
    wadna wish to do.

O fie no fie no! I wad like ill to see *you* crying like a bairn or a poor
    young lass like me gaun away frae amang a' that she likes or that
    hae any regard for her.

Do ye no like to gang to this grand place?

Oo ay; I like weel enough.

Then keep up your heart and behave yoursel like a woman. The
    place will soon grow a hame to you, and your neighbours a' like
    sisters and brothers.

Yes, I hope so. It will grow a hame to me for I maun suit mysel to my
    circumstances and make it a hame but it will never be like my
    auld hame nor the foks like them I am leaving to me. What gars
    that bit lamb bleat that gate Duncan?

It is bleating for its mither. It has lost its mither poor thing.

Do the lambies never like ony creatures better than their mithers?

No; nor ony ither half sae weel either.

Aih! but they be happy creatures! Come away. What are ye dighting
    your een for?

O there's a mote gaen into ane o' them, that's a'. Walk on a wee bit
I'll follow you—it will be better immediately.

Let me look at it. I'll take it out with the corner of a silk napkin or
with the tip of my tongue.

The tip of your!—Oh no—no—no that will never do. The tip of your
tongue at *my* eye! and your blue een looking into it?—it wad be
blinded. It wad never see mair. Oh no that will never do. Never
mind it, it will soon be better.

You had better let me take it out. It is may be a grain of sand which
is very ill to bide.

Oo no; some wee bit item of a thing; walk on I'll be wi' you just
now.

I think you hae gotten ane in the ither ee too Duncan.

I think sae but they will soon come out again. Walk on I'll soon
overtake you.

May the shame fa' me gin that little simple soul hasna gart me make
a fool o' mysel. I winna tell her how weel I like her though. Yes I
think I will—I may just as weel out wi' it and be done. Poor dear
dear lassie!—heaven bless her! "Do the lambs like nae creatures
better than their mithers Duncan?" "Ah! they are happy creatures!"
Od I thought my heart wad rive into twa pieces!—There was never
ought said like it for taking ane by the heart—I'll tell her—Yes I
will—Faith I'll tell I'm in love though I had made a resolution not
to do it—I'll rin till I come at her and I'll pit my arm round her neck
and I'll say "Keatie, my dear Keatie what will you gie me gin I tell
you a secret?"—No—that winna do either. "What will you gie me?"
That will *not* do—Then she will say "What kind o' secret Duncan?"
I think it *will* do gay an weel. O it will be sae sweet to tell her. But
stop, an' let me consider, if this sweetness may not lead to something that's sour. I canna marry at this time—that's clear—then will
it be prudent in me to come under engagements that I may never
live to fulfil—it would be better un-done but—poor Keatie! I canna
take leave o' her without letting her ken that my heart is a' her ain.

You are not very ill to overtake the day Kate.

I did not like to gar you heat yoursel rinning after me. How's the
een?

Een, whatten een? Plague on't I had forgotten the motes. But Keatie—
hem—I say Keatie what will ye gie me if I tell you a secret?

What will you hae Duncan?

Aye that's the question. What I'll hae. There I'm fixed at aince! What
wad ye think an I war to ask the secret itsel—that is—I mean the
thing of the secret—I'm no quite sure what I mean—but tell me

Kate What is the greatest secret about a woman?

The heart.

Thank you—that is a good answer and a sensible answer and a proprate answer, an' it is the very thing I wad hae been at—That's my secret.

You are speaking beside your good sense Duncan, I dinna understand ae word you are saying.

I'll tell you then Keatie—you'll understand this—If any body were to offer you his heart and ask your's in return what wad ye say?

I wad say I couldna do it, for I had parted wi' mine already.

That wad be a nabber for him! But I hope that wadna be true Keatie, for if that were to prove true I'm little better nor a dead man.

We are queer creatures Duncan and ye are amang the queerest of us. There are feelings of love that we should cultivate wi' a' our hearts an' wi' a' our minds, and there are others that the less we think of the better. I hae done wrang, and sair wrang, but my dynasty is settled. I hae given away my poor bit heart and the bargain I hope is signed and sealed never to be altered or shaken.

Then fareweel to a' hope of happiness in this world for me. I came this day to offer you my heart and beg your's in return but the dike is shot the gimmer's to the brae an' a' the hinds in the town can never bring her hame again. I may lay my head i' the mools when I like.

It is needless for me to lie to you Duncan your heart is a dear present to me but indeed and in troth I canna give you mine in exchange for it.

It is a hard case and mair than my life is worth. Is it fair to spier what is the reason you cannot give me your heart?

Because I gave you it lang syne. Ay an' made a resolution an' a vow to mysel never to gie it to another.

Ah what's this what's this? The warld is rinning round about wi' me. Thae extremities in life are unco hard to thole. Now gie me your hand, and here I pledge me to be your's only and your's for ever.

I do the same, but we maunna set a time as yet; we maun baith be richer an' better providit afore we venture to change our state. O I am so happy at this right understanding afore we part.

I never kend what real happiness was afore a' my life. I am baith daft an' dizzy wi happiness. I am like a creature transported into another sphere. And now dear Keatie take care o' yoursel in this grand house; be upright, and faithfu', and just; an' read muckle on your bible. But of a' things in this world take care o' the flunkies.

Aye an' take ye care o' the ewe-milkers Duncan. There will be

happing wi' plaids and setting on o' leglins and muckle toying
gaun on at the bught when poor Keatie's out o' sight. But whenever ye find your heart gaun astray after a pair o' ripe lips an'
pawkie een then think on me, an' on this solemn engagement—
Eh? What ails ye?—That was an unco sair sigh frae a hale heart.
There was a serious thought came o'er my mind that I coudna help—
But I'll just gang in sight o' your new habitation wi' you an' then I
maun take fareweel o' you till the Lammas fair.

---

## Scene Second

*Duncan solus.* Oh wae's me wae's me! I hae jumpit ower a linn wi'
baith my een open. I am maimed. I am dumfoundered ever sin I
engaged mysel to Keatie M,Cheyne. Had I been married—down-
rightly married it had been brookable; but here I am like a dog
tied to a kirn that maunna taste the cream for days an' months an'
years. An' waur than a' that, though a' the dainteths o' the land
stand round about him he maunna taste them. When I gang to
kirk or merkat I'm like a tike gaun to the hunting wi' a clog about
his neck—It's no that I'm rued o' the lass for I like nae single individual half sae weel, but it's my bondage I rue. That man is doited,
daft and bedeviled who makes any engagements to a woman till
he comes afore the minister! But ho! hush and be quiet! for here
comes no less a person than the mother that bore me.
Ha son Duncan! So you are speaking to yourself this morning and
that is a sign you are in love. No young man ever talks to himself
unless he be in love.
An' what though I be dear mother. There would be nought unnatural in that scene.
No—if that love were fixed on a proper object—If not it would be
highly un-natural—You are come of a good house and though only
a poor lad have high blood in your veins. You should keep that in
remembrance. You ought never to say ane kindly word to a maid
without keeping that in remembrance.
It is what I never in a' my life spent a thought on. I hae often heard
you brag that ye war bred a lady an' what the better were we o'
that? Were ye a better wife to a poor but honest man o' that? Or
did ye no rather help to bring the house about his lugs?
Lugs! To hear a son o' mine say *lugs* instead of ears! pah! A son of the
ancient house of Cowhally who has royal blood in his veins to be
so degraded. You have no spirit, no ambition son Duncan. What
is poverty? Nothing—But let a man still keep up his dignity his
respectability his deportment his—

Blow lowne a wee bit mother. It isna sae easy to keep up dignity wi' no a sixpense in ane's pocket.

But will ever low manners low connections and low pursuits put money in your pockets? I have fears of you Duncan but I have made a great exertion to establish you in life and I have succeeded provided your humble ideas throw no obstacles in the way. Whom do you think the hansomest and most accomplished girl of your acquaintance?

It is hard to say there are sae mony nice anes. But I could name ane.

What do you think of your cousin Matty of Glenbuoy?

Hout, gude guide us she's a lady! The like o' me maunna think about her. She has ower lang a tocher, and carries her head ower high for Duncan.

Nevertheless she is your own if you have but the spirit to accept, for you have not even to ask, that is all settled to your hand.

I dinna gie credit to that dear mother. That is a height of fortune to which I never looked.

Your uncle wishes it−is anxious for it−He has no son of his own and has need, great need of you. He has likewise made up his daughter's mind to perfect acquiescence−for hark ye−It strikes me you are the heir of entail−You never thought of that poor coof.

How could I, and both the families of Petherdale nearer of kin?

Aye but they are elder branches, and the entail must descend.

That's news indeed. Then may I not get the estate without the lady?

Yes if she have no son before her father's death.

Then there is some chance, for that is the only one. Ah such a lady and such a residence as I might have had−But it is over−past!−lak-a-day!

What is the matter son Duncan?−I am frightened−agitated−all in a tremor.

It is all over−past−settled−I am engaged−bound up−shakeled hand and foot.

Oh!−oooh!−I shall faint−go into hystericks−die−What you low grov-elling thing are you married? Married to some trull? Some coun-try wench? Some dowdy with beef cheeks and bulby eyes, red arms and feet like a toadstool. The son and heir of the house of Cowhally shekeled−collared to the female cub of a red headed Danish serf.

Married! Aye war than that−muckle war than that.

Oh me! The misery that mothers are made to endure. Come out with it all, for it cannot be worse than I deem it.

I am engaged, solemnly pledged and engaged to Kate M,Cheyne

and I have never had an hour's peace o' mind sinsyne. I feel like
ane out o' the warld, an' see the lasses and the very weans whispering and pointing at me with their fingers.

Go break with the minikin—Break with her at once—Lovers' pledges
and vows go for nothing. Think of a lady and the braes of Glen-
buoy, and go instantly and cut your little westland flower. She is
the offspring of an Irish gilly, a boor, a serf of the lowest description unmeet to clean the shoes of the heir of Cowhally.

I would give all I have in the world to be free but I cannot ask it, for
the engagement was of my own seeking—She is a sweet girl—I can
never ask it.

Bating her extract the girl is very well; wonderful well all things
considered—But what is she compared with the stately Matilda of
Cowhally—These fond parting engagements are a sort of matters
of course—they signify nothing—This is one that *must* be broken—If
you cannot do it I will do it for you.

But then you must not be severe or harsh with her, for a woman has
no pity on one of her own sex—She is blameless and a sweet and
amiable creature—But free I must be, else bound altogether, for in
this state I cannot live.

### Scene Third

Well dearest mother how have you sped in your request to poor
Keatie?

She will do nothing but whimper and whine refusing to believe me
but she says if you ask it yourself she will free you so far you are
safe. Tell me then your success at Cowhally.

Why it was but so so—I canna brag muckle o't. Did Kate say she
would free me at once if I asked it?

She did.

That is a sort of dead weight off one's shoulders however.

Were your uncle and cousin not kind to you?

O yes—kind enough—Very kind I daresay in their own way.

What did you say? Did you broach the subject to the lady?

I wat weel I gae her some gayan braid hints, but I couldna see that
they were ought weel taen. There was a good deal o' blushing
and snirting and laughing, an' some bits o' made coughs as if to
keep down a complete gaffaw. I hae nae grit notion o' courting
ladies.

It is all owing to those vulgar low notions you have imbibed my
heart is in a fever for fear of your bad behaviour there tell me your
whole procedure, demeanour and reception.

That will take a lang time–I rapped at the front door as ye bade me–
"Is the laird at hame"–"No he is not" quo the lass a gay dink
sonsy quean she was–"Is Miss Matilda at hame then" says I–
"She is" quo the lass a nice huzzy as could be. Keatie declared she
would free me?

I told you so; the thing is not worth a thought–Go on.

"Yes she is at home" says the lass a funny looking pawky slut as ever
ye saw. Do ye ken wha she is mother or ought of her pedigree?

What is her pedigree to you? You have no concern about that.

True true very true. She is a queer ane though–It is a mercy that
Kate is willing to let me off however.

It is most incongrous son Duncan that your mind should be thus
running on three different objects all at the same time. The thing I
want–

True true I ran through my story. What is it they ca' that lass? Bell?
I think it is Bell–Bell M,Ava or something like that. Yes that's the
very name I remember now. Well, this Bell M,Ava says to me
"Yes sir she is at home. Will it please you sir to walk into the
kitchen a little and I will inform her?" The kitchen! thinks I to
myself. That's hardly consistent with my mother's dignity and a
wooer's prerogative. However I couldna refuse to follow the quean,
so into the kitchen I goes shoulder to shoulder wi' Bell M,Ava.

O son son dinna rend my heart–It is all over! You will be a clown
and a coof and a booby as long as you have breath.

No sae bad as ye trow mother I didna bide aboon an hour wi' this
bonny lass M,Ava.

An hour! Rather a fair proportion of time with a low vulgar house-
maid.

I couldna help it, for she had a girdlefu bread to bake and put on
before she could wash her hands and clean hersel; and she says
to me this Bell M,Ava. "If you are not in a great hurry sir" says
Bell says she "will you favour me with your company till I put out
one girdlefu scones" (she *allways* sir'd me). "If you are not in a
hurry sir" says Bell M,Ava.

"But I am in a great hurry" says I.

"No doubt of it"; says she, "they that have least ado are always in
the greatest hurry" says this saucy Bell M,Ava. If I were quite
sure that Keatie would not insist–

Son! Good gracious son what are you raving about? Not another
word about these low persons in my ears. What passed between
you and your lady cousin? Say what or hold your peace.

O but I canna gang on unless you suffer me to take in both courtships; because you see the one has a reference to the other.

Both courtships? You would not sure insinuate that you began a courting the maid as well as the mistress?

Ah mother! Be reasonable now mother, and yield to the dictates o' nature an' humanity. If ye saw a bonny creature lonely by hersel', an' using a' her art, an' a' her bits o' wiles to gar ye stay a while beside her, could ye for the life o' your body help complying, or avoid saying some kind things while there?

How can you talk in that strain to me?

True true—Ye're a woman—she's another; an' of a' things in the warld a bonny young woman is that which an auld ane hates the maist—But reverse the incidency mother—reverse the question and then I have ye—If a bonny young lad were meeting you, an' the tid o' love sair sair on him.

Ah! ah! I have seen the day!

There I have you now!—And if he were to beg, and pray, and look melancholly; and then look in your een with the tear in his.

Oh—Oh! No more of that dear Duncan. It brings me amind of other days—No more of that if you love me!

I kend nature wad speak, an' will speak wi' the tongues o' the hale creation. Was I to blame then for having a syllabub made of a' the sweets o' the soul with lovely Bell M,Ava?

M,Ava M,Ava! Nothing but Bell M,Ava. Pray what comparison is there between a handsome young man and such a huzzy as she? A pig! a porker! A very weed, a mushroom to be rooted out of the walks of gentility. What has she to do with one of the lords of the creation!

A great deal. I can tell you—I'll venture a comparison if you dare. Eye for eye, foot for foot, heart for heart and head for head I stand for lovely woman; kind, ingenious, and affectionate woman!

None of your flights with me son. If you had any conversation with your cousin say it. If you had nothing but gossip with her maid go not to stun my ears and mortify me farther.

I never designedly mortified you mother, but a callan canna help his nature, and mine's wonderfully turned to the love o' women. I am sure I dinna inherit that quality frae you—so when Bell said to me—(This was at the hinder-end of a)—Bell M,Ava says to me "Now" says she "if ye dinna get a good reception up stairs you will haply gie a poor body a flying bode when ye come down again." "There's my hand on't bonny lass" quoth I "and take that for your arles." I said sae, and walked up stairs wi' her hand in hand, and when I left her I fand she had burnt a hole in my heart.

Poor man! poor man! So you made an engagement with the maid before you asked the mistress.

Aha! But I made an engagement wi' her too, an' if other six ilka ane bonnier than another had come in my way that night I believe I wad hae made some kind o' engagement wi' them a'. You shall hear–so pretty M,Ava she flings open the drawingroom door and cries out "Mr Duncan Stewart me'm from Inverglashan." Wi' that up rises lady Mat wi' the grace of a very angel of light or rather ane of seduction and she comes sailing through the floor wi' her head sweed a wee to the tae side and her bit mou primmed like the tying of a purse her chin bridled in and a dimple in ilka cheek. This will never do for me thinks I–Weel I bows as weel as I could for three or four times and I had my plaid round me and my blue bonnet in my right hand.

Good gracious son! Did you go into the drawing-room in that stile?

That I did; till the hempy M,Ava took hold of the plaid with one hand and my bonnet with the other, saying "I will hang these up for you sir"–"The deil be there then!" says I. "Take the bonnet and hang it up where you like but I canna part wi' my plaid."

"Pray dear sir what are t'going to do with your plaid in the drawing room?" says lady Mat.

"Never you say a word my lady cousin I'll maybe find an use for it" says I. So away goes Bell M,Ava laughing with the bonnet in her hand and I saw brawly her ee and her mistress's meet as muckle as if they said to ane another "He's a gay comical billy this. There's mair in him than what has come out o' the brose bicker." I saw they were thinking as much and fand mysel quite in the key for a frolic. "Pray be seated sir" says she pointing to a grand twa-armed chair. "Thank ye I wad rather stand a wee bit" says I. "Why?" says she. "Because I have not made choice o' my seat yet" says I "I am very particular that gate" and there I stands leaning on the chimlaw brace wi' my plaid hanging loose about me. Lady Mat didna ken what to make o' me sae down she sits on one end of a sopha wi' the finest slyest air you ever saw. "I find I'm rather tired with my walk" says I "it will be as good to take your kind offer of a seat" and down I claps close beside her and in the twinkling of an ee I had my plaid wrappit round her and a firm grip o' the sopha with both hands. She giggled and made a feckless struggle. "Na na but ye're no gaun to flit sae easily" says I "for I hae a great deal o' fine things to say to you." "Well well say away and be done then. What are you going to say?" says she. "I'm not quite certain yet" says I "but I ken finely what I'm gaun to do" and wi' that I gi'es her twa or three hearty smacks up against the neuk o' the sopha.

Ha–ha–ha I say son that was behaving like a man. It was rather a downright way of going to work with a young lady of quality. But *never the less* I approve of your bold measures. For whatever innocent freedoms a man may use with a young lady he knows and she knows too that he may always go the same length again— there was one great point gained. Well say on say on I am all impatience. How did she take it?

Faith only middling–she said I was rude–and impertinent and I daresay would have looked very much offended had I not kept her so closely rowed in the plaid that she could not get looked at all until she was forced to come into better humour. "They are bad things these plaids" says she. "What way?" says I. "Because they make people do things that they could never have the face to do without them."

"O blessings on the plaid!" exclaimed I in grand theatrical stile. "Blessings on the shepherd's plaid whether highland or lowland tartan or marled. The defender from the storm the bond of union between kinsmen and the triple triple bond between kind hearted lovers. Blessings on it an' a' the sweet thrilling kisses and vows that have been exchanged under its darkling and kindly influence. The keen ee o' malice canna see through the plaid the sterns o' heaven canna pierce it the lady Moon may glimmer hersel' blind afore she see what's doing underneath it and even the blessed sun can only slightly marble the deep deep rose on the cheek of love

> O weels me on my cozy plaid
>   O weel's on my plaidie
> If I had her my plaid has hap'd
>   I'd be a joyful laddie
>
> Sweet cakes an' wine for gentlemen
>   All other fare surpasses
> Good sack and shugar for auld wives
>   But bonny lads for lasses
>
> But for a bonny lad an' lass
>   In glen or green wood *gladie*
> There's nought in a' the world's wide round
>   Like thee my cozie plaidie
>     O weels me on my cozy plaid &c."

"Pray go on sir" say's she "favour us with the chorus again."

"This is the chorus my bonny lady cousin" says I an' gae her twa or three hearty smacks on the cheek next me. "Now isna the auld sang a true ane?"

"No it is not" said she "I detest both that and the plaid."

"Ye're no that blate" says I "but if I get time and opportunity If I dinna gar you change your sentiments ca' me nae mair Duncan Stewart o' Inverglashan."

"Either sit in peace and quietness and behave like a gentleman" says she "else I will ring for Bell to show you to your own room till father comes home."

"Do so. Do so." says I. "I have no particular objections to the measure provided you let Bell bear me company in my own room. I like the girl very much and as I don't chuse to come here to sit by myself "–With that I put by my hand to pull the bell thinking there would be some good fun in the change, but behold and observe! my lady Mat laid hold of my hand and would not let me pull the bell. "Stop for an instant" says she. "I was just going to remark that Bell M,Ava is a very clever and very superior girl"–"I thought so" says I "pray allow me to ring for her. I hope it will be long before father comes home?" "What an impertinent wretch!" says she laughing. "That is not what I was going to propose. I was going to remark that Bell would make an excellent wife for you." "O thank you kindly cousin" says I "that's a different story. That I am sorry to say cannot be." "Why?" says she. "Wherefore may it not be"–"O that cannot be" said I. "You know well enough that cannot be"–"Not I" says she "I know of no impediment why you two may not be joined in the lawful bonds of wedlock." "Ay but that you do" says I. "You know well enough that I am engaged don't you?"

That was well said son. That was rather well given in.

"No I do not" says she. "Pray who is to be the happy fair?"

"Ah! That's a secret" says I. "Do you know one Miss Katherine M,Cheyne?"

Sure son Duncan you did not say so? You could not insult the lady by telling her of your engagements with that low girl. And *such* a lady too the like of whom is not to be found in a country side though I say it who am of her nearest kin.

"No" says she. "I don't know her I even never heard of her."

"But she has heard of you though" says I "and that no to her profit. Pray did you never hear a whisper that I was engaged to be married to a fair saucy cousin of mine a great heiress and as great a jilt?"–"Well you are such an impertinent puppy!" says she. "That is some of my crazy aunt's palavers which you know as well as I are never to be regarded."

Her what? Her crazy aunt? She dared not put such an epithet to my name. And a tatler too whose word is not to be regarded! On my credit a very pretty allusion!

"O it is quite true this story however" says I. "I shall be immensely rich very soon–positively engaged to be married to an old cousin of my own with a great fortune who is very much disposed for a husband–Like her no the worse–Pity she had not been more pretty though."

"She is old and ugly I suppose?" says lady Mat with a caper.

"Why–y-y-yes–rather" says I.

"Well you are such an intolerable wretch" says she "that you are actually unbrookable. And yet I cannot help laughing at you–He-he-he. You are such a scape-grace! Old and ugly! and very much disposed for a husband! Well you may tell your old doited, crazy, meddling officious mother from me–"

She *durst* not say so sirrah. Or if she did I'll never speak to her again nor suffer one of mine to speak to her.

She's a very nice lady mother for all that.

On my credit and mine honour I am used with a great deal of freedom by her ladyship and that I shall tell her.

Pray do so. She deserves it mother. "You may tell my aunt" say's she "that this is a masterpiece of impertinence in her to send her wild uncultivated puppy of a son here on such ridiculous pretences."

How could you submit to such an insult son? If you had no regard for yourself you ought to have resented it on your mother's account.

Never let on I heard her. What signifies it what a woman says? "Ah but she has a much worse fault than any of these the friend that I am engaged to" continued I quite seriously. "She is a d–d shrew– a most intolerable shrew–Yet I think there might be a way of taming her–Must take her–No alternative–The worst thing of all I'm no sure about her character–I have heard that there's some claymazee about an auld laird o' What's-this they ca' the place–an' a journey to Edinbrough–Eh? what ails you cousin?" (For by this time she was manoovering accross and across the floor wringing her hands shaking her apron and crying bitterly.) "What ails you dear cousin" says I. "Are you vexed at our kinswoman's behaviour? So am I, I assure you. But for all that I'll take her."

"But for all that I am her warrandice that she shall never take you"

says she. "Never–never shall she be buckled to a low-bred uncultivated clown–connected with all his vulgar relations and be cum-
bered with his crazy deranged mother sitting next *me* at the head
of my table."

"O no; begging your pardon mem" says I "not *your* table the table
will be my own and my mother shall always sit next me–always
at my right hand as long as she lives though the first nobility of the
kingdom were present–Who was talking of your table?"

My dear son you have behaved yourself like a man. Your behaviour
was far superior to her's. May the Almighty bless you and reward
your kind heart. Were I sure you would succeed to the property
without her she should never–

Say nae mair mother, say nae mair. Leave me to manage the lasses
mysel'. "Who was talking of your table?" says I–She had not a
word to say–She was clean dumfoundered at having taken a' to
hersel' so I took pity on her then. "But what need you pit yoursel'
out o' humour?" says I. "We canna help the fauts o' our relations.
To be sure it is our duty to be grieved for them but no to get into
a rage. Come sit down beside me, and let us have a chat. I have
not seen you for a lang lang time."

"So you think there is no probability that this notorious cousin of
your's will refuse you?" continued she sitting down.

"None in the least" says I. "Do you think she could refuse youth,
beauty, and manhood when proffered to her seriously?" She then
eyed me with a half malicious half pleased look and said "As far as
form and features go you are well enough certainly but there is a
great deal wanting"–"What more is wanting to a young woman
who has plenty of her own?" said I–"Ah yes" said she "something
must be allowed for quality"– "But then her quality and mine are
the same," says I; "our family, name, and connections; so these
can never be an upcast between us."

She then fell a boring me to tell her more of the qualities and defects
of my betrothed cousin, but I was tired of the joke and waived it
on pretence of putting her out of humour. Her father came–welcomed me formally–not very heartily–we drank some weak tea,
and then I took my leave for a more social treat–so ended my first
genteel courtship.

You have behaved on the whole tolerably well son. But by all means
keep aloof from low bred women.

You did not make choice of a very high bred husband.

I made choice of him for his good taste–He never followed
after low bred women. He made choice of me.

True true—An excellent palliative for low marriages. Goodnight—
must write express to Keatie—cannot live longer in a state of Egyptian bondage to one woman.

### SCENE FOURTH A CHURCHYARD

*Duncan aside from the congregation poring over a letter*

Ay ay! So I have gotten my release with a vengeance! My mother
would have it so—Yes, and *I* would have it so. Therefore I deserve
it all—But yonder's the doctor looking and the elder's looking too
they suspect something—I maun put up the letter till I get hame to
my mother—But if I dinna gie it to her for her interference I's be
nae mair Duncan Stewart of Inverglashen (*reads*) "for there is a
young gentleman here who has offered me marriage, but hitherto
I have refused to listen to him. His name is David Hutchison"—
Devil hutch him! if he reave me o' my Keatie he had better hae
never been born—David Hutchison truly! Heard ever ony body
sic a name? sic a Liker like cadger like name and to think that my
bonny Keatie M,Cheyne is to be a Mrs David Hutchison! (*reads*)
"He is grieve and steward here and is nephew to my master the
Colonel and my lady is"—what—"my lady is a-n-g-i-n-st against the
match." That's some comfort. It will hardly take place with my
lady against it—But I fear that's not the true reading (*reads*) "my
lady is a-n-g" no that's not g it has not a long enough tail (*reads*)
"my lady is anxiousest for it of all." Oho! Then fare-ye-weel
Whitefoot—An what am I? That needs some consideration. What
am I but a forsworn decietfu' blackguard that has decoyed and
taken in as kind a hearted amiable and ingenious girl as ever
breathed the breath o' life—But there's Geordie Scott has up that
poor drivelling snivelling tune of St Pauls. I'll be obliged for
decency's sake to gang in and join the hum-drum congregation.

### SCENE FIFTH A COTTAGE

Come away ben the house son Duncan. What are you sitting there
for like one bereaved both of sense and appetite when dinner
waits you in the other end?

I'm sitting very well here. Gae away to your dinner you that has a
heart for it. I shall give you my share for a penny.

That is a good foretoken son. You have dined on the sermon to
day? much good may it do you! It must have sunk deep into your
inner man to have expelled the cravings of nature, with you none
of the gentlest. Or, are you sick? or fatigued? Pray let me feel your

pulse.

You may read that and then feel whose pulse beats highest.

What is this son Duncan? A love letter—K. M,Cheyne. So this is from the huzzy (*reads*) "Mr Stewart—sir. I had a visit of your mother who came ordering me to relinkish you and give you up, but she used me so harshly that I would not condescend to any thing for her—I was very sorry, for I took her for a civil and well bred lady and fain would have obliged her; I thought I could even have kneeled down on the ground at her feet and embraced and kissed her knees for your sake, but I got nothing but pride and harshness, so I was forced to fall a crying and refused her orders. I then got your letter yesterday at the market and it is a letter that I do not understand for it is both kind and unkind and seems to have a double meaning as all men's letters to women have. As to our engagement it was none of my seeking. I entered into it to oblige you, and to oblige you I as cheerfully resign it; the more so that it leaves me at liberty to oblige others whom I respect; for there is a young gentleman here who has offered me marriage but hitherto I have refused to listen to him. His name is David Hutchison he is grieve and steward here and is nephew to my master the Colonel, and my lady is anxiousest for it of all, and has mentioned all her plans of providing for us in the most genteelest way and I assure you every thing is to be very grand. I did not like to do nothing without your approbation, and am glad I have gotten you told, for I like you yet, though I have no respect for you. I see you tried to impose on me and decieve me and you did it; and now you are trying to break my heart but you cannot; for the man shall never have my hand who has the smallest hankering thought that he can do better. My kindest love to your lady mother tell her that I esteem and respect her still. I thought then she was decieving me, but now see my error for the fault lay with you whom I could never have suspected. I was going to subscribe myself 'Your's' but that's what I am not, and never now can be, but alas must soon be somebody's

     K. M,Cheyne."

A fair riddance son I congratulate you—And yet after all the girl has some good parts.

She must soon be somebody's Keatie M,Cheyne!—that is to say she must soon be David Hutchison's—David Hutchison!—blast the monster!—Did you ever in your life mother hear such a name?

Who could have thought she had as much spirit and discernment?

David Hutchison!

This now leaves you at liberty to push your fortune to its proper and primary altitude.

David Hutchison! Confound the dolt, the dumpling, the gnarled crab! He must be hunchbacked, with his head turned to one side and his mouth to the other. I see him. I percieve him bodily. David Hutchison! Goodbye mother—thank you for your interference—your *kind* interference.

Where are you going to son Duncan?

David Hutchison.

Your senses are astray and you will run yourself on.

David Hutchison! Goodbye.

SCENE A GRAVE—HAYMAKERS IN THE DISTANCE

*Enter Duncan meeting Mr Hutchison*

Pray sir wha do a' yon hayworkers belang to?

They work for Colonel Clapperton.

Is the auld grieve wi' them?

Whom do you mean?

You'll may no ken an auld humple backit womanish lickerish tike wha's a kind o' whipper-in hare a grieve or slave-driver as it were? His name's David Hutchison.

Sir?

O ye dinna ken the auld villain it is like—'Tis as well for ye.

My name sir is Hutchison.

Eh?—Your name Hutchison? No David though? Oh no no—You can never be David Hutchison.

My name sir is Mr Hutchison Mr David Hutchison. I act in the quality of Steward and overseer here. Have you any business with such a man?

Bee my faith an' that I hae. You the identical David Hutchison? Well that beats glaumory—I'm glad of it that I hae sic a good looking tagonist for d'ye see Maister David Hutchison afore ye be five minutes aulder ye maun fight a battle wi' me (*strips off his clothes*).

I can only fight as a gentleman sir not as a common ruffian.

O you're a gentleman are you? An' ye think I'm nane? I'm come o' good blood and a good extract too—As sure as death I am. Cast off your coat if ye be a true man and a leel—My name is Duncan Stewart of Inverglashan I think nae shame o't mair than you do Maister David Hutchison.

Oho! I have heard the name—It is that of an arrant blackguard if it is proper to judge from one act of his. You were affianced to a maid of our family?

Fianced? What's that? Weel say that I was. What's your quarrel there?

And you first sent an old impertinent termagant to insult her and then insulted her yourself under your own hand and seal.

That old impertinent termagant was my mother sir. What I have done myself I'll answer for but not to you.—*Ye* think to trapan my sweetheart—thraw off your coat lad—or take this as part payment.

Keep your distance young bully or here is what will silence you.

Ah! pistols!—That's not fair. I'll meddle none with them things.

Either this way or no way—You may gape and stare—Come not you near the Colonel my master's house to tirle at doors or scratch at windows like a cat by night or make any of your flagrant announciations else a salutation from this shall be your guerdon. Betake you to your moors again—the sooner the better my duffle hero (*Exit*).

He's no the David Hutchison I took him for this chap—He's but a coward though—I count a man a coward that darena fight without puing out a pistol—there's nae chance ata' against that. Duffle hero troth! He's no blate! He's but a coward and that I'll tell him to his face. Hilloa you chap there. Come back and speak a word—I say— I count you a great coward man—a downright coward that darena gang without a bendit pistol aneath your doublet ready to pu' out and fire in the first man's face that gies you a clout on the haffat. Od sir my blood rises at you and here's for you again pistol an' a' the gether (*knocks him down—he sits up. Shoots Duncan and exeunt*).

# Dramas of Simple Life

## No. II

### *By the Ettrick Shepherd*

SCENE A FARMER'S KITCHEN. *Enter the Goodwife among a number of ewemilkers.*

*Goodwife*—What are ye a' gaffawing an' gabbling on there for? Now when the sun's at the south kip, the herds hungry on the hill an' the kie rowting on the lone? Idley inclined limmers! Glaikit giglets! Do ye think to get through the warld that gate tee-hee-heeing about men an kintry havers an' kissing strings, an' your master's wark lying at the wa'? An' *ye'll* set up your faces and ask the biggest wages an' the best o' fare, an' a' for doing what? The deil-be-lickit as I should say sick a word! but curling your hair, trigging out your bits o' mortal clay bodies, primming wi' your smiles an' your dimples, an' rinning reed-wood gyte about the cheilds.

*Mary*–I wat weel goodwife ye needna say sae about me, ye ken weel
   I never mind the men. (*sighs deeply*) An' as few cares about me!

*Ann*–Nor me goodwife. I think on them nae mair than on a seed in
   my teeth.

*Girzy*–Nor me–I never think about ane on them sin I left Minnyive.

*Henny*–I would scorn to think about the best of them.

*Goodwife*–There now! There we go! Ilk ane o' us ready wi' a lee in
   our mouth a' to cloak the frailty o' nature–the besetting weakness–
   the clog, the stain, the fruit maele o' the original transgression!
   Poor things poor things! Some auld fo'ks like me wad envy you!
   Some flee intil a raige at you; but I pity you. Bloom, blouse; flirt
   and flash for a day, a short simmer day; and then a' down to poverty, pains, dudds and debility. Poor things poor things! It is a
   primary curse on us, an' we canna get aboon it! We were the first
   to sin an' we're ay the first to suffer! But bless my heart! Will you
   stand clatter clattering and haver havering there this hale blessed
   day an' no ane o' ye setting about business?

*Ann*–Dear Goodwife I think ye're getting a' to say yoursel'.

*Goodwife*–Now heard ever ony body sic impertinence! I'll refer to
   auld Henny there–she's a douce decent body–I'll refer to auld
   Henny if I hae ever said a word.

*Henny*–Auld Henny! Douce Henny! Be my certy but ye auld an'
   douce weel the day goodwife.

*Goodwife*–There we go! There we go! (*courtseying*) Crave your pardon beautiful young maiden o' fifty four. Wae light on the auld
   wizzened carcage o' ye, has the original sin no lost the owrance o't
   yet? I'm sure the cheek has lost the hue o' the apple lang syne!
   Wae's me that the wicked sap o't is still rangkling about the heart
   O minny Eve minny Eve! I wish ye had lain still in your goodman's
   bosom that morning when ye slippit away to steal apples, for O ye
   hae left us an ill hive to claw.

*Girzy*–What's she saying about Minnyhive?

*Ann*–Whisht ye tawpy an' let us hear the goodwife's good sensibility. Dear Goodwife I'm sure that original sin that ye wite for a'
   things i' this world hasna gi'en us an inklin to steal either apples
   or ought else.

*Girzy*–(*aside*) I wadna like to hear ony body speaking ill o' Minnyhive.

*Goodwife*–No gien you an inklin to steal miss smirker? No left you
   an inclin to steal? What for then do ye like better to take a piece in
   the pantry out o' my sight than at the kitchen table afore a' our
   een? Ye dinna ken I fancy, that I'm obliged to hide the meat in the

pantry that I want first eaten, and then it soon gangs–soon van-
ishes–the cats take it–But were I presenting it for a meal ne'er a
snap o't wad be tastit. Ye dinna ken your ain natures poor things;
it is a good thing that some kens them for ye. An' tell me this.
What gars you like to kiss an' clap an' toy wi' a bonny lad out o'
sight, an' yet, for as weel as ye like him, what wad ye say if he were
to use sic freedoms wi' you afore our een?

*Ann*–I wad tak him in the teeth.

*Goodwife*–There for't now! There we go! A' frae the same source
Anny! A' frae the same fountain head that the first sin puddled an'
stained sae it will never clear. If a spring be suddled and fouled in
its way down the brae it will soon brighten up again, for the clear
water behind will wash away a' impurities, but when the fountain
head has a foul die the stream will keep it till the end o' time.

*Girzy*–A' that aw say is this that there's as decent fouks about the
town o' Minnyhive an' as little sleeperyheadit as ony that belongs
to her.

*Goodwife*–What's the corky saying?

*Ann*–She's speaking through her sleep goodwife. At least through a
kind o' sleep o' stupidity; that's our Girzy's original sin I mean it's
her heirskep frae her auld forbeirs.

*Goodwife*–Weel weel, away to your work. Hurry hurry! for ye wad
stand an' clatter a hale day an I wad but let ye, or listen to you. Get
the kie milkit an' the hay raikit, and ane o' you gang to the hill wi'
the poor lad's whey wha has been waking a' night wi' his new
spained lambs. There's never ane o' ye minding him. Mary it's
your day to gang to the hill, an' ane o' ye maun gang an' bide wi'
him a' night else he'll fa' asleep an' let the lambs scatter.

*Mary*–I wat weel goodwife ye hae read us sic a lesson an' gien us sic
a picture that I am determined no to gang near a man again nor
yet trust mysel in the pantry. Aih-wow I wadna like to hae sae
muckle good sense an' deep learning as you.

*Henny*–It's my day Goodwife. I'll gang wi' Sandy's whey the day.

*Mary*–The woman's dreaming. Ye were there the last day but ane.

*Henny*–I can gang the day too. I dinna count travel muckle.

*(Exit Henny)*

*Goodwife*–There we go! There we go! A' the same an' the same!
There's that auld gaw'd glide wad fainer hae a husband this day
than the youngest amang ye. I wadna wonder that she takes in the
young simple lad. She's very set on't.

*Mary*–Take in him! I's warrant him!–He has mair sense; he hates
the very sight o' her. He'll neither gie her a piece o' his plaid nor

set on the same heather bush wi' her.

*Goodwife*–Hout ay Mary, if it comes on a shower he will surely gie her a piece o' *his* plaid.

*Mary*–Na–na. If it come on a shower he'll gie her the plaid thegether. I wonder what ye loot her gang for.

*Goodwife*–Dinna fa' to the crying about it Mary, an' as I ken you to be a decent lassie, and ane that has some little fear o' your Maker ye shall gang out an' wake wi' him a' night.

*Mary*–Na na, I'm no seeking to gang goodwife, nor am I wanting to gang; but ye ken if ye bid me I maun gang an' will gang too, for ye never bade me do aught that was unreasonable yet. I milkit a' your three bonny bred ewes wi' my ain hand Goodwife; an' your hawkit cow kens me as weel on the lone as my ain mother does. She rowts an mums when she sees me coming an' winna let ane o' them cross her wi' their ten fingers but me. An' I mendit poor little Jock's trousers yestreen. I kend ye didna like to see him gawn tattering half naked, sae I mendit them weel when I should hae been sleeping in my bed.

*Goodwife*–Ay ay Mary, you did very weel. You're a good lassie as times gae, but ye hae a wee tint o' the primeval curse hanging about you as weel as ither fo'k. It is blooming on that cheek Mary an' it is flightering in that bosom. It is glintin in your blue ee and dimpling in your chin, an' if it dinna land you in the mire it will breed your simple heart wae. Nevertheless you shall wake wi Sandie this night. *The lasses sing*

> Air Maid that Tends the Goats
> By a bush on yonder brae
>    Where the airy Benger rises
> Sandy tuned his artless lay
> Thus he sang the lee-lang day
> Thou shalt ever be my theme
>    Yarrow winding down the hollow
> With thy bonny sister stream
>    Sweeping through the broom so yellow
> But your bonniest flower to me
> Milks her ewes on yonder lea
>
> A' the days o' foray gane
>    Health and pleasure bless our border
> Age is free and youtheid fain
> Dule shall beg a hauld invain

Bloodless now in thousand hues
  Flowrets bloom our hills adorning
There my Mary milks her ewes
  Fresh and ruddy as the morning
Yarrow's Flower could ne'er outvie
Mary's hue and glancing eye

Wind my Yarrow down the howe
  Round thy bows o' dazzling siller
Meet thy titty yont the knowe
Wi' my love I'll join like you
Flow sweet Ettrick–oer thy glade
  Sweetly fa' the morn and even
There my Mary–bonniest maid!
  Breathed at first the breeze of heaven
And there I'll hope that happen may
A dear and blithesome bridal day

SCENE 2d *Sandy solus looking at the sun and then down a wild glen*
*Sandy*–I think this morning be the length o' three days–I have either
  tint the airts or the Sun's wearing hard on the south. It is surely
  mair than time a poor body had broken his fast wha has stooden
  ower his staff sin' the fa' o' the gloaming–But I ken how it will be;
  a' will be in confusion at hame wi' cheese-making an' butter kirning
  and whey-brikking; an' the lasses they will be giggling about an'
  hindering wark mair than furthering it; an' the goodwife honest
  woman she will be fliting and raging about amang them an' laying
  the wite of the hale on original depravity. Sae that it is just a change
  if a poor hungry herd be minded amang them ata'. Hech wow
  Cutty man but ye are grown howe at the flank like me. Mony a
  lang look ye hae cast down that cleuch the day. But my poor dog
  shall hae his share though I take the less mysel'. Ha Cutty if I had
  naething to took for but my meal as you hae, the morning wadna
  hae been sae lang to me. Were ye ever in love Cutty? Ay! Ye look
  as if ye kend something about it–Yon is naething but a white sheep
  lad looking ower the knowe; ye maunna bow-wow and rin away
  to meet yon–Keep up your courage Cutty. I wadna wonder that
  ye get the hale o' my brikfast the day; for there's ane coming wi't
  that will rather take the heart for eating an' supping away frae me.
  Ay Cutty lad there's ane coming out wi' your whey that ye like
  worst about a' the town; ane that ye'll no gie a kind look to, nor a
  wag o' your tail, nor wad ye lick her hand for a bickerfu' curds an'

cream. She wonders what ye ail at her, but I ken brawly what's the matter. Ye're jealous o' her, ye sly thief, because ye think I like her better than you. O man ye hae little sense about these things Cutty! To think that my love for her can interfere wi' my affection for you. It is really very absurd in you man, an' very bairnly like, to return a' sic a bonny lassie's carresses wi' a gurr and a gloom. Ah grace and beauty yonder she comes now—lie still poor fond heart lie still—dinna flutter away out o' your bit frail tenement a' thegither, burning hot as it is. What will I do! for this is a glow o' pleasure I can hardly stand. What an air an' what a grace in every movement!—How swiftly and sweetly she trips it!—If ever a human thing was endowed with the maike of an angel!—Hobgoblins of despair! May I never stir off this bit if it be nae auld Henny an' the beard—Oh when will I get my breath again—It is a kind o' relief too—I'll take my breakfast heartily now—It will be a bitter ane, but had it been her the never a drop wad hae gaen down my wizen.

(*Enter Henny*)

*Henny*—I fear you would be looking lang for me the day Sandy?

*Sandy*—Aye. I was looking for somebody.

*Henny*—Another than me of course. But the Gudwife has made Mary sic a day about you she wadna come, and I was obliged to take her place.

*Sandy*—It was very kind in you. She's obliged to you. An' sae are we a'. We're a' obliged to you there's no doubt of it.

*Henny*—I think ye hae but a cauldrife way o' expressing your obligation Sandy—just say plainly ye wad rather no have seen my face the day.

*Sandy*—I couldna want my whey ye ken. Ye might have had it here an hour ago.

*Henny*—Ye little ken how fast I hae gaen, an' how sair I hae warmed mysel. Winna ye gie me a piece o' your plaid for fear I get cauld?

*Sandy*—I's gie you it a' thegither. Hae, there it is. Rowe yoursel up in it.

*Henny*—Hech-wow! This is cauldrife wark! What o'clock is it?

*Sandy*—I hae nae rule but the sun. It's near eleven.

*Henny*—(*Pulling a fine watch from her bosom*) It is half past nine only. How do you contrive to live in this wilderness without a watch?

*Sandy*—I ken when daylight rises, and when it grows dark, and as for a' the rest I maun just be guidit by circumstances. Ilk ane's no sae routh o' auld siller as you.

*Henny*—But wad ye like to hae a watch Sandy?

*Sandy*—I canna say but I wad if it war convenient.

*Henny*–What will you gie me if I'll gie you this ane?

*Sandy*–O I hae naething to gie you–I dinna want her.

*Henny*–Will ye no gie me a pair o' gloves on your wedding day?

*Sandy*–That's no muckle–Yes I will.

*Henny*–An' promise to rowe her up every night?

*Sandy*–Yes I will.

*Henny*–Then it is a bargain. The watch is yours.

*Sandy*–Hout Henny it is a joke. I winna hae your watch.

*Henny*–It is a fair bargain. You give me all I ask, a pair o' gloves when you are married, and to wind her up ilka night or pay the forfeit.

*Sandy*–Na na. There was nae forfeit mentioned. She's a grand watch tho'.

*Henny*–Put her up, put her up. Now ye ken Sandy there was a forfeit.

*Sandy*–What was it? I never heard tell of it.

*Henny*–A kiss on the bridal eve–

*Sandy*–Na na. My kisses winna then be my own to bestow.

*Henny*–It is but a sma matter I ask. I want to make you a present but merely to ask some little favour by way o' remuneration.

*Sandy*–You are a real good body. I never thought you had been sic a kind body as you are. The watch wad be good company to me, and ye shoudna want half a dozen kisses provided they were my ain to gie.

*Henny*. Then what is to hinder you parting wi' them as lang as they *are* your ain to gie?

*Sandy*. That is rather a hame stroke! But what signify kisses when they're no to pass as love tokens?

*Henny*–If I be pleased to take them as I get them what is that to you?

*Sandy*–Very weel then. Take a stick and nick on the number, and I's yerk ye aff plenty o' them, and then the grand watch is mine. That's ane mind–twa–three–four–five–half a dozen–ten–seventeen. Now. Henny the watch is mine and what the better are you?

*Henny*–Ye may weel say't–Ye're a nice lad Sandy–Ye're a dear lad to some that like ye an' canna get ye. Have ye a full stock o' sheep for your fee?

*Sandy*–I hae a full stock, but they're no just free as yet.

*Henny*–How muckle will make them free?

*Sandy*–Mair than I'll win this year.

*Henny*–Will this do ony thing for you. Take this ten pound note and make your sheep free, if ye never pay it again I shall not lay you in prison for it.

*Sandy*–Dear Henny that is quite ridiculous. I winna hae your money.

*Henny*–Take it–I brought it for you, for I heard somebody complain-

ing that you coudna pay them out your stock. Take a lang loan of
it at ony rate an' make yoursel clear wi' the warld.

*Sandy*–Henny ye are the best body ae way an' a' ways I hae ever met
wi'. I will take the loan o' your ten pounds since my neighbour
wants it, which I didna ken of afore.

*Henny*–Take it an' welcome–Now I maun away hame. Ah but ye
will hae a blithe night wi' Mary! She is to wake the night wi' you,
for I heard the goodwife say it–Goodbye Sandy–blessings on you.

SCENE THE KITCHEN. *Ewemilkers standing at table laughing. &*
*then enter the Goodwife*

*Goodwife*–Weel you're a' there again, steghing in you an' giggling as
fast as ever! A braw dayswark I hae gotten out o' ye! No as muckle
as will haud a' your grinders gaun! Daft haillucket ne'erdoweels!

*Ann*–Gooodwife gin ye kend what I ken ye wad giggle as fast as ony
o' us.

*Goodwife*–Me giggle? Heard ever ony body sic impudence? What's
this come out amang ye the day. Nae good I's warrant.

*Ann*–Look at Henny how she is dizzened out the day.

*Goodwife*–Peace be wi' us sirs the body's crazed! I declare she's like
a countess in a morning dress–false curls an' a' thegither! Hech-
wow sirs the corruption o' our nature!

*Ann*–But goodwife ye dinna ken what she has tauld me in a great
secret. Ye will hardly believe it.–Our Sandy kissed her seventeen
times in the glen the day; borrowed ten pounds frae her, an' has
taken her grand watch to carry till they be married.

*Goodwife*–Hout, fie fie! This is really too bad! It is a shame to be
heard! Goodness to the day my face burns to the bane at hearing
it; an' yet I maun laugh. Ha–ha–ha! Hee-hee-hee!(*The Goodwife*
*sinks on the longsettle in a fit of laughter and all the rest join her*)

*Ann*–Now didna I tell you goodwife that ye wad laugh as weel as the
worst of us.

*Goodwife*–Wha can help it? Fie fie for shame Henny! A woman come
to your years wi' grey hairs and wrinkles should be thinking about
ither things than young men. Did he just gie you seventeen kisses
neither mae nor fewer? If I had been him I would hae made out
the clad score Hee–hee–hee. For shame ye auld roudess! ye
weatherbeaten witch! ye sybow! ye bik that you are! Sic an example as you are to the young an' the simple. Ye shall never gang
your lane to a young man belonging to my family again. What for
do ye look sae pale my good Mary? Ye look as ye wad faint.

*Mary*–I jaloused ay she was a witch, now I am sure of it, else our

Sandy has lost a' the feelings of a man.

*Girzy*–A witch! The woman's daft, that's what ails her.

*Ann*–But are ye sure that's no your ain original sin too Girzy?

*Girzy*–Od I wonder fo'k disna think shame to speak sae muckle about thae originals.

*Ann*–It is weel kend that there's mair originality about Minnyhive than any ither place in a' this country Girzy.

*Girzy*–It's a great untruth. They are as douce fo'k about it as ony ither place, an' no ae speck of originality amang them. The last year when the meal was sae dear there wasna ane sat on the stool o' repentance for seven months. Was that ony sign of originality?

*Ann*–Hout aye Girzy ye ken Jenny Girdwood sat on't.

*Girzy*–It's no to heed her. She's never off't.

*Omnes*–Ha–ha–ha!

*Girzy*–What are ye a' gaffawing at? The poor auld woman sits on it for a seat to hear the word. Ye're a' as daft as Henny.

*Henny*–I can bide a' your taunts an' a' your jeers the day. It's a' spite. There's no ane of ye but what wad hae gien the claes aff her back to have been where I was and to have got what I got the day. Taunt away! I'll be upsides wi' the best of you yet. (*Sings*)

> O weels me on my shepherd lad
> My blythesome shepherd laddie
> Wha gae to me a pledge of love
> An' rowed me in his plaidie
> Wha gae to me a pledge of love
> That gars me look sae gaudy
> An' makes my very heart to sing
> Of my dear shepherd laddie

*Mary*–Have some pity on our lugs woman wi' that voice of yours. I declare it is waur than the ring of a cracked pot or the jing of a rusty door-hinge. It has gart the sweat break on my brow.

*Goodwife*–Dinna be jealous of sic a runt my good Mary. Ye shall gang to Sandy the night to keep him waking, or herd an' let him sleep, and he will tell you it is either all a lee, or all a frolic this ridiculous story o' auld Henny's.

*Henny*–Say ye're no sure Goodwife–Dinna count afore your host. (*sings*)  O weels me on my shepherd lad.

*Goodwife*– Out on you old crack-voiced crack-brained dikelouper. If I hear another word of your shameless impudence I'll turn you out of my door–Off off to the bught. Away away. Ye hae keepit me up wi' your jaunders frae wark that has muckle need to be done.

Kissed *you* seventeen times! Ha–ha–ha. I have a great mind to kick her.

SCENE THE GLOAMING. A WILD GLEN. *Sandy solus*

*Sandy*—Weel I think there has been a great battle in the East the day, and that the sun has aince mair stood still ower the valley of Jehoshaphat; for sic a day of length never was in my remembrance. It has been like a season; an' sair sair have I played the fool sin' it began. My dear, my beloved Mary is coming to wake with me a' this night, and rather than she should ken that I kissed the auld brock I wold rather never be seen in this country. My lovely, my pure angelic Mary, a creature too modest, sweet and comely for the hand of man to touch! I declare I have not the heart nor the conscience to take her to my bosom or vow to be her ain. Cutty man, I wish ye had torn the harrigalds of the auld hunk, but instead of that ye thought it grand sport and cockit your tail an' barkit ye great rascall. (*Sings*)

> The day-beam's unco laith to gang
>   It lingers sair ayont the willow
> An' O it blushes deep an' lang
>   As if ashamed to kiss the billow
> The gloaming starn keeks o'er the Yoke
>   An' strews wi' gowd the stream sae glassie
> The raven sleeps aboon the rock
>   An' I wait for my bonny lassie
>
> Weel may I tent the siller dew
>   That comes at eve sae softly stealing
> The silken hue the bonny blue
>   Of nature's rich an' radiant ceiling
> The lily lea, the vernal tree,
>   The night-breeze o'er the broomwood creeping;
> The fading day, the milky way,
>   The star-beam on the water sleeping.
>
> For gin my Mary were but here,
>   My flower sae lovely an' sae loving,
> I'll see nought but her een sae clear,
>   I'll hear nought but her accents moving;
> Although the bat wi' velvet wing
>   Wheels round our bed sae damp and grassy,
> O I'll be happier than a king
>   Lock'd in thy arms my bonny lassie!

Nae art hast thou, nae pawkie wile,
   The rapid flow of love impelling;
But O the love that lights thy smile
   Wad lure an angel frae his dwelling.
Can I–can ane o' human race
   E'er wound thy peace or evil treat thee?
For sure thy bonny guileless face
   Wad melt the lion's heart to pity.

Alas that love's relucent lowe
   A bleer'd regret should ever slaken,
That heavenly gleed, that living glow,
   Of endless happiness the token.
I'll fling my fears upon the wind,
   Ye worldly cares I'll lightly pass ye,
Nae thought shall waver through my mind
   But raptures wi' my bonny lassie.

This blooming heath shall be our bed,
   Our canopy the waving willow,
This little brake shall guard our head,
   The wild rose nodding o'er our pillow;
Her lips her bosom pressed to mine,
   Ah, paradise, it must surpass ye
I'll ask nae purer joys divine
   Than sic a bower an' sic a lassie.

Now yonder she comes like a streamer o' light. O blessed be the grey gloaming for it sheaths a lover in armour–My fears are a' gane–Here will I lie close till she is passing bye me and then will I seize her in my arms and kiss her a thousand times giving full vent to the bounding raptures that vibrate about my heart. (*he springs up and seizes her*) Ah my love! my joy! my dearest girl! are you come at last? and do I hold you in my arms and feel the pressure of those dear arms which till this delicious moment I never felt before? (*She speaks half smothered*) "Dear Sandy dinna worry me wi' kindness" Ha! charnel banes and dead men's breath! what do I hear, and what do I feel? Is this Henny? (*he pukes*) Oh I'm choaked! I'm bewitched! I'm bedeviled! Out upon thee thou owl, thou goatsucker, what seek'st thou here with that croaking voice enough to gather all the male frogs of the Flesh-Cleuch Howe about our ears. Thou harpie, thou green lizard, thou she adder, go trail in the dark for a mate like thyself. Devil that thou wert in the howe of thy own greasy bed covered with clouts and vermin with thy cat in thy bosom. What in the name of sin and Satan art thou seeking here?

*Henny*–Is that a' the thanks I get for dreeing the scorn o' the hale family young an' auld, and losing my night's rest to assist you, and bring you a good warm supper?

*Sandy*–I wish it had been the will o' heaven that ye had been somewhere else howsoever.

*Henny*–Now you are dissapointed for want o' that bit slip-slop wench Mary; but an ye kend her as weel as I do ye wadna think sae muckle o' her. She may do weel enough to court an' toy with, but will ever she provide for the wants of a family as some ane can do? I can tell ye, gin a' be true that's said about her she's very little worth, and will never mense either a young man's bed or board. Ye dinna ken that she's the goodman's mistress. Aye you may stare his kept mistress.

*Sandy*–Hae. There's your watch an' your ten pound note again, gin that be the gate ye speak; an' let me never see either their face or yours as lang as the dun hide wi' the beard's on it. (*flings them at her*)

*Henny*–Dear Sandy ye hae lost your reason for want o' sleep. Lye down and take a nap and you will be better when you waken. I'll watch the lambs sickerly enough, as I was bidden.

*Sandy*–Then gang clean away outbye off me, for if ye come within a stane-cast o' me I'll murder ye for a nightmare through my sleep. (*She retires and he falls sound asleep*)

*Henny*–(*returning and speaking aside*) There he lies as sound as midnight. What a grand noble creature a young man is, wi' the bushy locks, the curling lip, and the dark beard just keeking out as if it thought shame o' itsel.–I like a beard like that–Poor fellow! he's lying quite exposed to the night air. I'll e'en hap him wi' his ain plaid, an' if he winna take me in his bosom I'll take him in mine. (*she covers him with the plaid and lies down beside him. Scene closes*)

SCENE A FARM HOUSE AT BREAK OF DAY. *Enter Robert the ewe-herd who looks up to the left and calls out*

*Rob*–Lasses are ye waking there? Hilloa kimmers I say are ye waking?

*Voice above*–No.

*Rob*–(*mimicking*) No–But I say waken ye up then this moment an' come away; and if ye canna waken rise in your sleep, you'll maybe waken afore ye won the bught. Get up, get up, for gudesake for a' is gane to utter profusion thegither. Annie are ye waking?

*Ann*–Ay Rob I'm waking.

*Rob*–Because if ye say sae I can trust you. Get up my bonny agitaceous woman, and rouse the rest, and make haste and come away, for Sandy has fawn asleep, and letten away a' the lambs and there will be nothing but mischief and manifest insensuality (*goes to a side door*) Goodman are ye waking?

*Goodwife*–I *am* waking Robbie, What's the matter? The Goodman's no here.

*Rob*–The matter Goodwife! What think ye? Hasna Sandy fawn asleep in the glen wi' some o' his myrmidons, an' a' the lambs are come off and landit amang their mithers again. Every thing is in rank deplority.

*Goodwife*–There we go! There we go! Oh sirs the natural infirmity and profligacy o' mankind! That's a' come o' that luckless lassie Mary for I ordered her to the glen thinking the twosome wad be ower fand o' ane another to sleep ony. Fy Robbie gae raise the goodman, he's sitting drinking wi' his twa cronies o' the knowe and the Mill, and gar him gallop to the glen and waken Sandy and his deary, for without him and Cutty we winna get the lambs back to the glen this day.

(*Enter the Goodman drunk.*)

*Goodman*–What's astir what's astir billy? Eh? Wha are ye? Eh? Rob I say Mr Philosopher, you billy? What were ye saying about the lambs?

*Rob*–Why in troth goodman they have all got away, and joined their dams or mithers. Indeed are they goodman; they're a' comed away, and I little wat what will be done.

*Goodman*–What will be done man? Does that puzzle ye? Why I think the first thing to do is to take them back again? mh? Will nae that do think ye? mh?

*Rob*–O but then Sandy's sleeping in the glen wi' ane o' the lasses and I canna leave my ewes and take them back mysel'.

*Goodman*–Sandy sleeping in the glen wi' ane o' the lasses! No but Rob the like of that I heard never. Sandy sleeping in the glen wi' ane o' the lasses? An' the lambs a' away? I'll tell you what you do Robbie lay the saddle on Chess. Fetch me my nibbit staff an' tell a' the lasses for till get their leglins and follow me.

*Rob*–Dear Goodman what are ye gaun to do wi' the lasses and their leglins in the glen? There's neither cow nor ewe to milk there. Naething but just Sandy an' ane o' the lasses.

*Goodman*–I'll tell you Robbie. The best thing for you is just ay for till do as you're bidden. Eh? Mh? Will nae that do think ye? Mh?

*Scene changes to the glen as before. Sandy and Henny sleeping. Enter the goodman heaving his cudgel—he strikes and the lasses gather round with their leglins full of water. Henny squeaks and Sandy springs up and bounds away. All the lasses continue to fling water on Henny and the Goodman lays on her with his staff. (Scene closes)*

# Act Second

### SCENE A HAY FIELD *Mary and Ann*

*Ann*–Wow Mary but ye are douf an' dowie now a days!

*Mary*–Me douf an' dowie? I never had a lighter nor a merrier heart sin I was born. Ye just take it on ye to say sae ay sin Sandy ran away.

*Ann*–Aye but how often do I catch ye greeting by yoursel? An how often do I hear ye sobbing a' the night. That's no a' for naething Mary ye needna try to gar me trow't.

*Mary*–What an it be for my sins? We a' sigh an' sob o'er little I doubt Annie.

*Ann*–*Your* sins! Lak-a-daisy poor lassie whaten sins hae ye to sigh an' sob for. Whilk o' the commands hae ye been breaking?

*Mary*–The hale o' them I fear.

*Ann*–Na that's impossible Mary. There is but twa o' them ye are capable o' breaking an' these are the fourth an' the seventh. Pray my dear Mary hae ye been committing adultery? Eh? Has the Goodman been meddling w'ye when he was drunk sometimes?

*Mary*–Fy for shame Annie how can ye speak that gate? The man's no born shall ever lay a foul finger on me.

*Ann*–Dinna say o'er far. I hae kend as good resolves made an' broken, an' made again an' broken fifty times.

*Mary*–I downa bide to hear the like o' that laid in lasses' names. I wadna rin as loose amang the men as ye do Annie for the hale warld.

*Ann*–I like to hae some fun wi' the callans. It is but a wee while in our young days that we can hae it. My tocher is but a sma' ane; but it is my ain. My Goodman shall hae full possession o't when he gets me an' gin I keep my health I's no make it ony less till him. There for't! What are ye sobbing at now? Was that for a sin come i' your head? Or was't only the original sin that our goodwife's sae troubled about?

*Mary*–Ye're a great gowk Annie! I wonder to see a woman o' as muckle sense as great a gowk.

*Ann*–There's twa of us met. Had ye no been the greatest gowk o' the twa ye wad never hae banished your lad for a wee mistake wi' auld Henny–Depend on't it wasna his blame, an' for me I wad forgie a sweetheart ony thing where the heart wasna concerned.

*Mary*–Ye may forgie Rob then as muckle as ye like. If ye haena muckle to forgie in him he will have enough to forgie in you. But the lips that could condescend to kiss Henny's (the auld brock) shall never kiss mine again, an' the arms that were twined round sic a waist as hers shall never clasp mine.

*Ann*–There we go there we go as our goodwife says, Hech wow sirs the natural corruption o' female nature! How often have thae fine lips o' his smackit at a broxy haggies, and how mony thousand times have his arms claspit a tarry ewe? And yet he maun be banished frae your heart, an' a for bestowing a charity kiss on a fellow creature. Had she been a great toast an' great beauty I wad hae been jealous o' my sweetheart had he done sic a thing, but if he had gien auld Henny a hunder kisses an' something mair beside I wad only have held it as a grand frolic, and something to have taunted him about.

*Mary*–Wi' a' your beauty Annie ye hae the coarsest notions about mony things that I ever heard expressed.

*Ann*–Aye but I hae the proper notions nevertheless. We canna make men and things as we wad hae them and what can a sensible maid do but take them as they are. If we stand up shilly-shallying and taking offence at every bit trifle we may sit out our simmer day and be drafted off for eild crock ewes in the back year. I know ane had better put up wi' twa or three affronts than bring hersel to this. Take my advice and send a kind message to Sandy and desire him to back to his place like a wise decent lad and no rin away at a trifling affront like a fool.

*Mary*–He shall rin to the farrest corner o' the warld afore I send ony sic message. But the goodman has sent your philosopher after him to bring him back and we'll soon hear what resolution he has taken.

*Annie sings*

> Dinna look sae high lassie
> Dinna look sae high lassie
> If ilka kiss ye tak amiss
> Ye'll drink ere ye be dry lassie
> Ye'll drink the very dregs o' grief
> The lees o' pride an' a' lassie
> Till past your bloom an' wrinkles come
> An' that's the warst of a' lassie

Weels me on the men lassie
Weels me on the men lassie
An' wae betide the mincing thing
Their worth that disna ken lassie
If my dear laddie tak a smack
At bught or breery shaw lassie
The maist revenge that I shall tak
I'll gie another twa lassie
Dinna look sae high lassie &c

Yonder's our young master coming to us now for some sport.


SCENE A FARMER'S PARLOUR *The Goodman and Rob*

*Good*—Weel Rob did ye find out your neighbour Sandy?

*Rob*—I wat did I goodman I fand him out indeed. But I hae been little the better o' finding him out. The chield's gane daft—clean out of a' reason! What d'ye think goodman?—The like was never kend in this country! He has sold his sheep to the dandy jobber and is gaun hynd-wynd off to America.

*Goodman.* Dear Rob man that is madness in *him* for till gang to America. Ye should have perswaded him for till come back to his service and have told him that I was willing for till let a' byganes be byganes.

*Rob*—O Goodman I preached to him till I was tired but I might as weel hae spoken to the stanes o' that wa' or to the wind that's rearding through the firmament—Off he'll gang to America. He says after he has been cudgelled by his master taken in and affronted by auld Henny, and exposed to a' the lasses an' his ain sweetheart amang them, afore he come back he'll rather gang to the boddom o' the sea.

*Goodman*—The bottom of the sea? Hm? How think ye that will do Rob? Eh? That'll no do! Poor Sandy maunna gang to the bottom o' the sea nor till America neither. We maun prevent him by force. How will that do think ye? Hmh?

*Rob*—I think we should send for the Goodwife and take her advice afore we do any thing; she's a gayan lang headit body and has a great deal of preventative circumlocution in her stratum.

*Goodman*—And a gayan lang tongued ane too. Eh? How dis that do think ye? We wad be daft to send for her, for ye ken she has a' the wit o' the warld and winna suffer ane to gie an advice but hersel. She sees a' body's original sin but her ain. Hm? How dis that do think ye?

*Rob*–Ah but Goodman I hae a great deal to lippen to her animadversions.

*Goodman*–It's mair than I hae honest man. For I can tell you if we were for till send for her–Oho! the devil!

(*Enter the Goodwife*)

*Goodwife*–Wha's the devil Goodman? What reason have ye to take his name invain this morning? Was he in the whisky bottle last night that has made your nose sae red this morning?

*Goodman*–Peggy my bonny woman!–Are ye gaun for till make a fool o' yoursel an' me baith? What are ye saying about whisky?

*Goodwife*–Ha–ha–ha for as fond as ye are of it ye downa bide to hear it spoken about–O sirs the corruption o' our nature! What are ye seeking in here lad? Were ye trying to wheedle a dram or twa frae your master?

*Rob*–I was telling him about Sandy and I was just coming to seek you to gie us your preponderance.

*Goodman*–Have ye no heard the story about poor Sandy woman?

*Goodwife*–What story? Nane o' your lang windit stories an it be your will.

*Goodman*–Dear Peggy woman has not he taken it intil his head for till gang away till America.

*Goodwife*–But are ye sure that somebody hasna gane *for till* take it *intil* his head *for till* speak nonsense? Eh? How will that do think ye? What's this about Sandy Rob? Tell us in few words for I hate mony words an' lang stories.

*Goodman*–Aye when they come frae ony body but yourself?

*Goodwife*–Wha's speaking to you? I daresay the poor man's no weel. Rob rin away ower to Mr Spiers an' tell him to come directly and gie your master some drogs–some little o' the cordial for he's very ill wi' the trouble o' the M,Gregors this morning.

*Goodman*–Rob d'ye hear? There's advice for ye lad! How will that do think ye?

*Goodwife*–O he maun speak! The tongue maun gang on like the clack of a wind mill when the breeze is up. Tell your story to me Rob an' let him just him rave on to himsel, he will be as weel pleased as if a' the parish heard him.

*Rob*–The story's soon tauld goodwife. Sandy has taken his passage out for America and will neither rue nor hear reason.

*Goodman*–And has been sae ill advised as for till sell his sheep to the dandy jobber.

*Goodwife*–Say away goodman. Ye hae surely been ill advised to haud your tongue this morning. What for will ye no speak?

*Goodman*–So I will speak Peggy my woman if ye'll but let a body lye. See I was just saying to Rob that the best way was for till seize him by force and bring him back whether he wad or no.

*Goodwife*–Hhegh man but that is a grand advice! I daresay ye hae dived to the very fountains o' wisdom for that–the very centre o' gravity?–How think ye did your confused head fish up sic a profound sentiment. What right have ye to seize him by force? Has he stown? Has he swindled? Has he embezzled? Isna this the land o' freedom and hasna every honest man has a right to gang where he will? And if ye were to bring him back by force wha wad keep him by force? WAD ye be willing to hire a brace o' constables to take care o' him twa or three years. I fancy ye think he is like ane o' your cronies that ye can bring back by the coat-tails ony night.

*Goodman*–Ay but Peggy my woman ye maun confess that I can keep him too.

*Goodwife*–There it is now! There we go! Corrupt nature still! An' how do ye keep him joe? By setting the thing afore him that he likes best? Tumbler upon tumbler, jug upon jug, here a little and there a little. Aye aye that is your besetting sin goodman! I think if Eve had brought Adam a bottle o' whisky ye wad hae believed in original depravity.

*Goodman*–I'll tell ye what it is goodwife; atween you an' me, she might hae brought him a waur thing. Eh? How will that do think ye?

*Goodwife*–Ha–ha–ha some trees are planted in a dry soil! But as I was saying you see Rob (For there's nae end in talking wi' the Goodman) As I was saying he keeps his drunken neighbours by sitting that afore them that they like best–We maun manage the same way wi' Sandy. We maun lure him back to see Mary–gie her a hint aforehand–and she'll gar him stay–take my word for it and say an auld fool said it.

*Goodman*–I tauld you sae–That is the very plan. Eh? How will that do think ye?

*Goodwife*–You tauld us sae did you?

*Goodman*–I'm sure I tauld you something like it to bring him back by the coat-tail as I did Mr Eckford and then set the thing afore him he likit best.

*Rob*–Now Goodman didna I say that we should ask her advice afore we gaed to ony obstreperous measures. I never saw her far wrang yet an' I'll lay my lug she has the right thread by the end at the very first. He is out o' himsel about that lassie for as saucily as she uses him. Fo'ks say ye ken that I am as ill about some ither body, but that's atween oursels. However, as I was saying to Annie the other night.

*Goodwife*–Whisht Rob–Nearest the heart nearest the mouth. What were ye going to tell us about Sandy an' Mary?

*Rob*–She is the wyte o' the hale–He is affrontit about Henny, and Mary she pretends to be waur affrontit, and has denounced him whilk has put him beside himsel. But he says he canna leave the country without seeing her aince mair. I have taken in hand to speak for him and (*whispering*) I hae brought a lang letter to her.

*Goodwife*–We have it a' before us–Snap your thumbs goodman–Ye are a clever–sapient–deep–profound chiel. Ye hae a brain that could apprehend and comprehend ony thing, only the skull is sae thick that ideas have very hard getting out and in.

(*Exit.*)

*Goodman*–Hear till her Rob–Heard ye ever the like o' that? Hmh? I say Rob–How wad it do for you and me for till throw some grand obstacles in the way of this scheme o' her's? Eh? How will that do think ye?

*Rob*–The truth is goodman that her wit is worth baith your's and mine put thegither.

*Goodman*–She's a gayan clever body though I say it. But she has twa great failings Rob. The first is original sin. I'm gaun to try the preest o' Traquair to make her quat o' that–an the tither is a devil of a canty conceit o' hersel. You and I maun try to cure her o' that. Eh? How will that do think ye?

(*Exeunt*)

Scene A Wood. *Mary crying over a long letter. Enter the Goodwife behind the bush peeping over and listening.*

*Mary*–(*reading*) "I must have acted foolishly, for had I acted wisely I would never have been driven to this but however I have acted my heart was never in the fault. (*cries bitterly*) My heart was never in the fault nor my love of you dearest Mary affected in the smallest degree." I believe it I believe it! and m–m–my h–heart will break in a hunder an' fifty thousand pi–pi–pieces.

*Goodwife*–(*Aside*). Aih goodness preserve us! Heard ever ony body the like o' that.

*Mary*–(*reading on*) "I have loved you Mary and do love you with the most perfect, pure and sincere affection–and–to–think of *leaving* you–of shaking hands and saying 'Mary–Fare–ye–weel for ever.' (*cries convulsively*) Of shaking ha–ha–hands and saying Mary–my own de–ea–earest Mary fare–ye–fare–ye." Oh oh OO! (*Faints: the goodwife springs forward, lifts the love letter, folds it delicately and puts it in her pocket then assists Mary*)

*Goodwife*–Mary, dear heart what for are ye lying hoo–hooing and fainting in the wood this gate for? Sit up an' behave yoursel like a wise woman and dinna gang to fa' into extericks as gin ye war possessed. I say sit up Mary and tell me what's the matter.

*Mary*–(*looking wildly about*) Did ye see ought of a wee bit letter?

*Goodwife*–Was it a *very* wee ane hinney?

*Mary*–Aye. It was a gay bit ordinar letter.

*Goodwife*–I saw Rob have a great letter like a epistle but he wadna let me see it.

*Mary*–Did ye see ony body pass this gate sin I fell a dovering?

*Goodwife*–Na na nae body at a'. Have ye lost ony thing?

*Mary*–I hae tint a bit letter an' wad rather hae tint the heart out o' my breast.

*Goodwife*–O the weakness and subtilty o' our corrupt nature! Are ye sure your bit heart is there to lose hinny?–Nae mair than the letter is. An' the warst thing is that ye'll never see ony o' them again.

*Mary*–O dear Goodwife gin ye hae that bit foolish letter hae pity on me and gie me it again. Mind that ye war aince young and fand and lovebitten yoursel.

*Goodwife*–But I never fell into a swarf for a love letter. Na na hinney the less o' thae things for maidens the better.

*Mary*–Do ye mind goodwife when the bairns had the fever I sat up wi' them when no another servant about the house wad enter the nursery door?

*Goodwife*–I mind it weel Mary and never will forget it.

*Mary*–An' when ye were yon way ye ken.

*Goodwife*–Nae mair about that. I have it a' noted down here.

*Mary*–An' when the goodman wanted to kiss me ye ken I came straight an' tauld you.

*Goodwife*–That was wrang. Ye war ower honest there. That was silly. These bits o things should never be tauld ower again.

*Mary*–An I can tell you mair. He has a plot against you even now to break a joke on you and put your deep wit to ridicule. I was applied to, to bear a part but wadna hear them speak of ought against you.

*Goodwife*–He execute a plot on me! It will be like the plot that he tried on his ain mare; dressed himsel like a bogle to fright her out o' the corn never to come back again. He did fright the mare; but the next time she came by the spot she threw him and brak his head. An' now she is frighted for every thing. That grand plot o' his has cost him fifty fa's. If his scull had been in the least like ither men's it had been crushed ere now like an egg shell. He contrive a plot on me! I wish he were the man! But Mary we'll be aforehand wi' him. Do ye set a tryste to meet him the night.

*Mary–Me* set a tryste to meet a married man? That would be ruin without a chance.

*Goodwife–*O dear bairn ye'll no be sae muckle the waur as ye trow. Set ye a tryste to meet him in the hay nook at midnight, then come to me and I'll put on your claes an' gang in your place.

*Mary–*Will you give me my letter then?

*Goodwife–*Whisht whisht bairn. Nae mair about that.

*Mary–*Ah honest man! I coudna find in my heart to put him sae sair out as that neither.

*Goodwife–*Think how grand sport it will be. I'll let you be by to listen.

*Mary–*He–he–he! I canna help laughin. Will ye gie me my letter then?

*Goodwife–*It was for your ain sake I wanted to keep it from you, but this corrupt nature maun work. There's your letter and muckle good may it do you. An' now we will douss the goodman! He an' Mr Speirs are to hae a bout at Clapperton's the night. I'll send you for him and then do you set a love tryste. O he'll be sae upliftit! Then he'll caress ye a' the gate hame but there's nae help for it, ye maun just bear wi' him. He'll be sure to slip a guinea or twa into your hand, and tell you maybe half a dozen times "Now Mary my bonny lassie I was aye just wanting for till have an opportunity to gie you as muckle as for till buy a silk gown for the wedding. Eh? How will that do think ye? And then I wad maybe be expecting the beverage. How wad that do think ye?"

*Mary–*It is a better joke and hardly fair for there never was a better honester man when the sup o' whisky's out of his head. But indeed Goodwife I have other matters that lie heavier at my heart.

*Goodwife–*O blessings on that bit waefu' heart! Do ye ken bairn I came here solely for the purpose of speaking about the very thing that lies nearest it but ae thing dings out another wi' me. Now you are to do my bidding in this *positively* for it is your interest that I have at heart. Your sweetheart Sandy has sold his sheep and taken his passage for America and he's neither to haud nor to bind but to America he'll gang. Haud your tongue and hear me speak will ye? You're neither to greet nor sob nor speak till I be done. Ye're just like the goodman ye wad ay have a' to say yoursel'. I say your sweetheart for I ken a' an' I ken he's coming back to see you afore he gang away. Am not I right now?

*Mary*–He writes sae. But I wot not whether to see him or no.

*Goodwife*–O lakaday! what for no? Let alone pu'ing the gerse will ye? There's little enough for the kie already an' hear me speak. It's an unco thing that fo'k maun either be saying or doing that a body canna get a word spoken though a body has naething at heart but a body's weel. Sandy's coming to see you–You like him better than your ain heart's blood I ken that–Will ye forgie him?

*Mary*–Never–I'll never forgie him the usage he has gien me.

*Goodwife*–There we go! Aye that's ane o' the original curses engrafted on our nature that we maun ay pretend aversion to the thing we're fondest of having. Now ye ken mair sense than no to believe that a' the ridiculous story about Henny was a mere frolic to devert the auld clacker.

*Mary*–Since he has made sic a fair choice as old Henny he may keep her and take her out to America wi' him. My very heart vexes at him.

*Goodwife*–A woman maun ay cleave to the choice that's sairest against hersel' poor proud foolish thing! Forgie your lover at once on condition that he bide at hame and come back to his service. That will be like a sensible girl and we'll provide for you baith and dinna gang to ruin a' your happiness and his baith wi' foolish pride. Wow woman ye surely think little of yoursel to be jealous of auld Henny. I can tell ye he flang her money and her watch baith in her face when she began to speak ill o' you.

*Mary*–Did he poor fellow? I never heard o' that.

*Goodwife*–He did sae an' ca'd her a' the ill names he could invent. Now say at aince that ye forgie him. (*Mary hides her face in the goodwife's clothes and sobs*) That is as it should be a' is right now. Up an come away and by and by we will snool the Goodman! I trow I hae mair reason to be jealous than you have.                    (*Exeunt*)


Scene continues. *Enter Sandy*

*Sandy*–Ah me this is the place we were wont to meet. Well I'll go and sit me down on the seat on which we have often sat together and croon the bit parting sang I have made. I'll learn to sing it in such a pathetic stile she shall not be able to stand it. (*He sings*)

> Whene'er I try the word to say
>     There comes a pang that strikes me dumb

Though a' the lave are on their way
    The word FAREWEEL it winna come
I've spelled it ower within my breast
    Yet still its sound I darena frame
The word has sic a waesome fa'
    I downa add it to her name

2

Were it but till the term o' May
    An' my dear lassie weel to be
Or were't even for a year and day
    And hope remain'd my love to see
Then I could take a kiss with glee
My arms around her waist sae sma'
    And then the round tear in her ee
Wad be the sweetest sight of a'

3

But a' my heart hauds dear on earth
    Its only valued worldly gain
In all its beauty all its worth
    To leave it ne'er to see again
    O that's a pang an afterpain
The spirit dares not live to feel
    The breath will break my heart in twain
That says the weary word FAREWEEL

I think that should melt her. But it is the queerest thing ever I knew that I never made a good affectionate sang to sing to that dear lassie but I gat a grievious dissapointment. I hope it will not be sae to night but it has happened sae often that I have sair forebodings. What's yon I see? If yon be as it appears to me I wish the corbies had pickit out my een afore I saw it. (*He squats close. Enter the Goodman hugging Mary*)

*Goodman*–Mary. I say. Mary–my bonny lassie. Mh? Dinna ye think it wad be as good for us for till sit down in this dark corner even now, as for till wait till midnight? Mh? How will that do think ye?

*Mary*–O goodman I wadna for the hale warld sit down wi' you there even now. The goodwife bade me haste back, and I wad be missed at the kie milking, and you an' me wad baith get our deaths. In troth wad we.

*Goodman*–I'm saying–Mary–My dear bonny Mary. Ye maybe think that I'm drunk?

*Mary*–O no goodman–no drunk but doitrified a wee.

*Goodman*—Ooo–no. No–no–I say–speak–Ye ken I have ay been wanting an opportunity to make you a bit present to buy the wedding gown. Eh? You are a good lassie; here, take this, and never let on.

*Mary*—Thank you Goodman. But there's far ower muckle here.

*Goodman*—Never mind–I say–never mind–nothing between you and me–I say. I'll maybe be for the first kiss after its on. Eh? How will that do think ye?

*Mary*—In troth Goodman ye deserve the first half dozen. How will that do think ye?

*Goodman*—Ah you're a dear ane! Ah you're a sweet ane! Ah you're a delightful, dear, roguish sweet, sweet, sweet creature!–I say Mary–wad it not be as good for us for till sit down ahint this bush and take a chat, and maybe a buss, just now as for till wait till midnight?

*Mary*—I wat Goodman I wad do it wi' a' my heart but I am feared some body see us or hear us that should do neither. And then think how we would face the goodwife.

*Goodman*—Aye they're cursed things these goodwives. But I say–Mary, my dear sweet Mary are ye no joking about giving me the meeting at midnight?

*Mary*—No indeed I am not. Did I ever decieve you?

*Goodman*—You are to be in the hay nook then at twelve?

*Mary*—Precisely. And for your own sake, not for mine but for your own sake; you are neither to offer nor say one uncivil word to me.

*Goodman*—Ooo–no–no. Of course you know–I say–Ah! you're a dear one!–How long will you stay?

*Mary*—As long as you like.

*Goodman*—Blessings on you! Eh?–How will that do think ye? I say dear Mary–When you are married which you will soon be–I have all that planned–Oo yes–But I say. I must have you to live close beside me then. How will that do I think ye?

*Sandy*—The devil confound you then!

*Mary*—Hush Goodman! haste and come away. I heard somebody. Sure you are drunker than you were? Take care and dinna fa!

(*Goodman singing and capering supported by Mary*)

Hey for Sandy Don
Hey for Cock-o-Lorum
Hey for Bobbing John
And his canty quorum
Hey for twall at night

Hour of dearest blisses
Hey for maiden's smile
And for maiden kisses
Faraladdle–lay &c

I have seen the day
When my love was wally
Sighing sobbing ay
Sickening shilly shally
Now I've lived to see
Maiden beauty blink me
Goodwives here's to your–Eh?
How will that do think ye?
Faraladdle-lay &c            (*Exit singing and dancing*)

*Sandy*–(*rising and coming forward*) I'll gang and cut my throat! That is the *first* thing that I'll do–For really there's nought in this wicked world that's worth the living for–But of a' things that ever it produced this is the most monstrous unaccountable and unnatural. To think that my Mary–the pure the modest retiring Mary that had not even confidence to turn her face to the mid day breeze as if the embrace of the pure wind of heaven could contaminate her gentle and maidenly form–No–She could not–I have seen her turn from it with blushes like those of a new opened rose–And yet to see that same being gallanting with an auld married man mair than half drunk, and trysting to meet him in the hay mow at midnight–The thing is beyond human conception–I'm surely bewitched–Or dreaming–I have dreamed such things–Oh yes God be thanked I hope it is a dream–sic a thing cannot exist but in a dream–And yet let me see–Where am I? There's the changehouse–there's the Mill and there's the bush aboon Traquair. Aye and here is the seat where I have met with my dear Mary I know not how oft–Ah but then I have often dreamed of this and often seen this very scene in my sleep though never so painfully– It is, it must be a dream. The Goodman wadna do sickan a thing– And yet–let me try–I can walk; and jump; and speak; and sing– Ah but I have done all these a hunder times in my sleep and far mair for I have flown away over hill and dale; this way the most delightfully and seen wonderfu' things but never aught to this. I'm either bewitched or in a dream and I think it is the latter–I wish to heaven ony body wad come and waken me–I'll try to call if nae body will waken me I shall waken somebody. Hilloa!
                            (*Shouts  Enter Robert*)

*Rob*–Who's there? What's a' this outrageous disclamation for?

*Sandy*–I was calling through my sleep. Honest neighbour will ye be sae good as waken me. For I canna do it mysel wi' a' the power I hae. Hilloa!

*Rob*–The man has seen a warlock or is possessed with demonology! I declare you have thrown me intil a constirpation.

*Sandy*–My worthy neihbour Robert is this you?

*Rob*–Aye.

*Sandy*–Aye! Why dinna you speak then? Am I awake? Am I in my right senses?

*Rob*–I coudna say–There's rather an inconstituency in your comprehension.

*Sandy*–Speak out Rob and do not put me clean mad man. Is this the Bush aboon Traquair? Am I standing in this place, and have you by the hand?

*Rob*–(*after a pause of consternation*) Aih? What's your will?

*Sandy*–Do you not know what I say? Is that the mill. And that the changehouse?

*Rob*–What's your opinion of these dissiderations?

*Sandy*–On my soul I do not know–tell me.

*Rob*–I'm interlabouring with some sonspulosity of intellectual magic at present.

*Sandy*–Oh dear Robert drop your learned words and resolve me do not you see that I am beside myself?

*Rob*–Yes and sorry I am to interview it. You have come very suddenly this way.

*Sandy*–I came to day to see–you know who–But that's over.

*Rob*–I had a commissionary for you when you came, that Mary was to meet you at this spot at any hour you chose.

*Sandy*–I will tell you what it is Rob. I'll rather meet the devil here.

*Rob*–(*starting*) Mercy on us! Can it be love has made this wreck. But neithbour–My dear neighbour and friend do not be alarmed at meeting with Mary for the Goodwife comes with her to agree you and it will do you a great inordination of good to meet with her and will soon leviate all your wild lucinations. Come name your hour.

*Sandy*–Twelve at night Rob. Twelve at night–Will she come then? Nay nay–pre-engaged and better engaged–something into pocket too! O woman! woman! How I have been decieved of thy lovely sex–And of its loveliest flower! But what in the wide world can now be lovely to me. Weel may I sing "the flowers of the Forest are a' wed away!" There's a scene to act this night Rob at which nature will sicken and the very inanimate creation stand aghast. This night or rather nigh the first hour of morning the horses will quake at the manger and the kie give over ruminating at the stake staring round them in dread and wonder but yet they winna believe what's gaun on—Why then should I?—I wont believe it either—But I'll go and see, and hear, and judge for myself—Yes I shall be there for ane—At twelve. Yes at twelve *precisely*—Say I'll wait on her at twelve—Goodbye. (*Exit*)

*Rob*—The man is as mad as the roaring oceanic sea. I must run to my master and mistress and approximate them of this strange dispension of providence. I am as deeply extricated in love as he and yet I have a' the sober sympathetics of naturality about me. It is an unco thing that a man canna get a naysay frae a bonny lass without falling into a state of incapacious absolution. (*Sings*)

Some love it is like a novelle
   All made up of romantication
But mine is as sound as a bell
   A glorious amalgamation
I joy in the science of truth
   The even down circumlocution
And thanks to the toil of my youth
   I am bless'd with a good restitution
(*Exit singing obstreporously*) Falal-deral-laddie-falay &c

SCENE A FARMER'S PARLOUR
(*Goodman Robert*)

*Goodman*—Is it a fact that ye are telling me Rob?

*Rob*—It is as true as evangelistical gospellity sir—Mad as the wind—and the lassie Mary and the goodwife are to meet him at twelve prescisionally.

*Goodman*—(*rubbing his hands and chuckling*) He–he–he–Rob–I say–O Rob man that is grand—We'll have sic a grand play on the goodwife—We'll get her to keep the tryste—I'll find a plan of preventing Mary—Then the goodwife will be obliged to sit wi' Sandy hersel', and you and I will gang an catch them thegither. He–he–he! I have her in the branx now! How will that do think ye?

*Rob*—Ah you have a great deal of duplicity and fun in your comprehension goodman—But take my word for it the goodwife will degenerate us baith.

*Goodman*—Keep her to the tryste keep her to the tryste. I'll prevent Mary. We will snub her for aince—Oho here she comes.

*Goodwife*–(*Behind speaking loud*) I think I'll be put out o' my seven senses amang them! Sorrow tak the hale population o' them, an I haena to think for them a' and act for them a'. Goodwife this; Goodwife that! Bairns, broods, beggars and tawpies fiend be in my feet if I ken whilt end o' me's uppermost. (*Enter Goodwife*) Hech wow what have we here? What are your twa clear heads a brewing some great event nae doubts o't? The national debt is it? Or the death of a paulie lamb?

*Goodman*–Dear Peggy my woman ye're ay sae captious. I was just gieing Rob some directions about bringing down an auld crock ewe frae the height and garring her settle hersel a wee laigher down. He–he–he wasna I Rob?

*Rob*–O Goodman ye're ay sae conceptious its no easy to answer you but I can tell you the auld crock ewe will mak fools o' us baith.

(*Exit Rob*)

*Goodman*–Now Peggy my woman I hae a wee bit engagement the night an ye're no to gang for till be angry though I should stay out gayan late. I hae promised for till meet a friend ower at the changehouse the night but it is on some serious business and we're no gaun to drink ony feck.

*Goodwife*–If it be a serious business wi' you it is nae good ane I ken you o'er weel no to ken that. But as I hae a bit engagement mysel the night I will be better quit of you sae ye may gang an drink till day if ye like. Hech wow I maun gae prepare mysel for my engagement. Goodbye a pleasant night to you.     (*Exit goodwife*)

*Goodman*–Mh? I never saw her in better humour in my life. I'm a lucky man He–he–he I amaist wonder at my own luck. I'll ower to Clappertons and have another half mutchkin–Eh? How will that do?

SCENE A HAY MOW DARKNESS
(*Enter Sandy cautiously who climbs up to a loft and conceals*)

*Sandy*–Here I am then to be a witness of that which will make me the most miserable of mankind. But it is proper I should be satisfied for who would pine or fret himself for a girl such as I concieve Mary to be just now. By heaven if he offer any violence or rudeness to her I'll commit ane murder to night at least. (*Enter Mary softly dressed in the goodwife's clothes*) Who in the name of confusion is this! The goodwife by all that is comical and outrageous–she has got private wit of the meeting and now for a blow up–She comes straight to my hiding place. What shall I do? (*Mary climbs up and hides close beside Sandy. They hear one another and squat close. Enter the goodman)*

*Goodman (groping about)* Mary? I say–Mary my dear heart are you here? Eh? I say–Where are you? Ah you little sweet cunning rogue where are you? I heard you breathing like to burst with laughing but I'll stop your laughing if I had a hold of you. Eh? Where are you? *(gropes his way off at the side and then comes staggering back)* Oh d–n it that's a cow–He-he-he! I got such a flegh. Weel weel it will be as good to take a snuff and sit down till I see if the baggage comes. It would be a pity to lose a chance of such a girl for want of an hour's sleep. But what if I should fa' sound asleep for that whisky toddy has rather mazelled me. That last half mutchkin was rather a kneveller! It's an awesome thing that toddy! Od it gies a man a face for ony thing–I could face up a lass in the dark fu' weel–or ought else except a horned cow–He-he-he I got a devil of a glofe when I got the brocket cow's muckle nose in my arms–Hee-he-he. Only to think when ane expects to catch a bonny lass in his arms and the very first thing he gets haud of is the face of a horned cow he-he-he. *(Enter the goodwife in Mary's clothes the Goodman catches her in his arms)* Ah you sweet little rogue have I really got you–Blessings blessings on your dear bonny sweet delightful face–I thought you were hoaxing me–I did not think my dear Mary would trust herself with me dearly as she knows I like her–Come let us sit down–sit down here that I may get you all in my arms. *(They sit down)* Now I'm just so happy! I havena been as happy I dinna mind the time. What for are ye sigh sighing that gate–cheer up your heart and chat with me and give me a kiss. Ah that's worth a hunder kisses of an auld wife. Had she a cheek o' velvet like that! Or sic lips sprinkled wi' heather hinny.

*Goodwife–(Whispering)* Whisht! Whisht I'm fear'd some ane hear us. Oh I'm terrified some may hear us.

*Goodman–*Yes faith and I can tell you of ane my sweet lassie that hears us for there's a brocket cow wi' sharp horns within twa yards of us hears us weel enough. I was gaun groping for you thinking I heard you breathing and got her muckle head in my arms, but she gart me flee aff like a wild drake sae that my heart is hardly gien ower beating yet–But I say–Gie me a buss dear Mary and I'll tell you a queer secret–Ah you are a sweet rogue! Plague on auld wives!

*Goodwife–*What's the secret–Speak laigh for O I'm terrified some body hear; if we should be found out thegither it's absolute ruin. And then the goodwife

*Goodman*–The goodwife! Wha cares for her and her puffs o' ill nature? Od an she wad behave hersel better she wad meet wi' mair respect–But I have her otherwise engaged the night, for I have wised her out on a gowk's errand for till meet a young man on some business that she's gaun to try her deep wisdom in. Now there's a third ane necessary and I have contrived for till keep that ane out of the way that my goodwife and the young chield may be obliged to sit waiting together till they're caught; for ye see Rob is to gang wi a bouet and a candle an' discover them afore witnesses– He–he–he–O I have her on the hip! Eh? How will that do think ye?

*Goodwife*–You have so! You have so! He–he–he. (*they both laugh*)

*Goodman*–I say–Mary–ye ken–Eh? How will this do? Eh? I say–I have her for aince–Eh? And some ither body too–Ods mercy!

(*Enter Rob with a lanthorn and light–takes out the candle and looks about*)

*Rob*–I thought I heard some speakulation in here. I wish nae blackguards may be comed to steal my master's beastiality. (*Percieves the goodman lying hid*) By the Gordons here's ae thumping thief at ony rate. (*locks the door and puts up the key*) I shall keep a' in that is in till I get a satisfactionary prostitution–Gude gracious goodman is that your ain sel? Weel that beats a' the concuchology that I ever beholded–Wha's this wi' you that has her face sae weel hidden? Oho! I think I ken the claes–I'm utterly adumbrated!

*Goodman*–Rob. I say Rob. I believe I'm rather catched–But–hmm– ye ken–it's neither here nor there–Hae–there's a snuff–just gae your ways Rob, and leave the door as it was, and I'll take care o' this ane. Eh? How will this do think ye?

*Rob*–Na the deil a bit will I leave you in that state goodman. If ye had had a' your wits about ye ye wadna hae been here in this clandestine way. There's naething in my mind so bad as antinuptial collaterality.

*Goodman*–Come now Rob be reasonable–I say–ye're no to look wha this is–she thinks a great deal o' shame poor thing–It's no Annie sae you needna care.

*Rob*–Na na. I have seen enough–I want to see nae farther. I dinna wish to explicate ony man's doxology. (*The goodwife draws her skirt over her head and exeunt*) Na na goodman I'll see her fairly into the house afore I suffer you to follow her. There's nae saying what a decent man will do when he has ower muckle volability in his pericandeum–Now sir gang your ways and slip cannily in ayont the goodwife and if ye sleep sound the night I hae nae arthmeticial calculation in husbandry. (*he percieves Mary escaping wrapt in the goodwife's gown-skirt.*) By the Gordons here is the goodwife too. Nae doubt she has heard every thing–There will be the confusion of Babylon about our town–I'm sure I wish Annie and me were away frae about it for I hae seen and heard ower muckle of this clandestine sexuality.

*Sandy–(above)* How's a' w'ye now Robin?

*Rob–*Aih?

*Sandy–*How's a' w'ye I say?

*Rob–*Thanks t'ye honest man–I canna complain–Forgie my sins! Are you there too? And in the same snug hole wi' the goodwife! I think you have all sold yourselves to work wickedness with greediness to night. You were half mad at least the last time I met with you if you have the sense of a hyppopatamus you must be ten times madder now.

*Sandy–*No. I am quite settled now. I take leave of you all this day and set off for the new world. There is no woman worth loving or regretting. Robert, could human heart have divined a conjunction so unnatural as this?

*Rob–*It was certainly a most inapplicable juxtaposition.

*Sandy–*Well I'm free–I care not *that* for the whole sex–I'll run them down and rhyme them down and sing them down. Here goes neighbour give us a hand.

*Rob–*What shall it be? THE WOMEN FOCKS?

*Sandy–*No that's hackneyed.

*Rob–*Suppose we have one stave of it?

*Sandy–*Well–Blow up then.

> That they have gentle forms and meet
>    A man wi' half a look may see
> And gracefu' airs and faces sweet
>    And waving curles aboon the bree
> And smiles as saft as the young rose-bud
>    And een sae pawky bright and rare
> Wad lure the laverock frae the cludd
> (*pause*) But laddie seek to ken nae mair
>      O the women focks! the women focks!
>       But they have been the wreck of me!
>      O weary fa' the women focks
>      For they winna let a body be!

*Sandy–*They are just things made of a' contrarieties Robin courtesy and deceit, beauty and wickedness. The Goodwife's right, the Goodwife's right; the Goodwife's right after a'. There must be some inherent principle in them that induces evil else maiden beauty and modesty would never submit to a deed like this. Of a' things on earth women are the most incomprehensible–they hate a little sin terribly–They wadna gie a bawbee for that–But put a tremendous big ane in their way–ane that has RUIN printed on the front of it and–plump!–they fa' into that.

*Rob*–The reason I take to be this–It is because the contumely of their nature indicates them to cognition.

*Sandy*–That's deep–That's clever and *very* profound. It never struck me before that that was the cause of their inconsistencies.

*Rob*–The palpable cause sir–and it is principally owing to this their inveterate conducement to hydrostatics.

*Sandy*–G–d bless my soul! What think ye of another verse on them?

*Rob*–Verse about w'ye as lang as you like Mr Alek.

> *Sandy*
> Whoever has bow'd at Beauty's dear shrine
>   Bonny lad cannie lad tell me who
> Will find his quiet a wreck like mine
>   Whenever he gangs to love and to woo
> O can ye believe that beauty's bloom
>   Bonny lad cannie lad tell me now
> Is nought but the blush of an early doom
>   Wherever we gang to love and to woo

> *Rob*
> And wha wadna trow that woman's dear smile
>   Was inflamability body and bone
> And blessed wi' a blink of the cockatrice bile
>   And fierce inextingishe-a-ti-on
> Camisad*o*!–Camisad*o*
>   Down with femenity body and bone
>       (*hems and pauses*)
> I want a long word, but since it be so
>   We'll try uncertifi-ca-ti-on.

*Sandy*–Well done Robert! What a pity such profound sense should always be introduced on stilts making a monster of a mouse. Come let us go into the kitchen and rouse up the lasses. I should like to see how somebody will look.

*Rob*–But my dear friend tell me this. Were nae you an' the goodwife nestled first?

*Sandy*–We were, but she never knew of me. We met by chance as listeners.

*Rob*–That story disna seem weel; as the man said when he sang a chapter; I wish it be nae a qualification.

*Sandy*–No no true on my word. I heard the tryst set at the corner of The Bush aboon Traquair an' coudna believe my ain senses till I came here to see whither she wad keep the tryste or no. What a senseless abandoned lassie! Had you no popp'd in wi' the lanthorn what wad hae been the consequences!

*Rob*–I pat a stop for aince to their litigation–I wish you had a sweetheart like mine–ane whom ye could trust out o' sight and in o' sight in a' places an' situations. As for this poor lassie she has fairly lost her equinoxial gravity–Come let us to the kitchen I want to have a single embrace of my dear Annie–my piece of bright adamantine chrystaline empyremal purity.        (*Exeunt*)

SCENE A FARMER'S KITCHEN AS BEFORE
(*Enter the Goodman and Annie meeting*)

*Goodman*–(*in a loud whisper*) Wha's this? Mary, dear, is this you?

*Annie*–Na Goodman–it's no your dear Mary. Ha–ha! This is grand?

*Goodman*–Ha Annie–you gypsie–you wild slut–Where have you been till this time o' the morning. Have you been courting a gliff wi' some chield for a change?

*Annie*–In troth have I goodman but say naething about it. My joe maunna ken a' things.

*Goodman*–Nor mine neither. He–he–he–I say Annie–come this way–Ye needna be saying ought–but the truth is I was at the courting too–Did ye get enough o't?

*Annie*–No half enough goodman.

*Goodman*–There's twa o' us–my case exactly–I came very ill on–I say–He–he–he! What wad ye think o' ganging into the coal-house here and trying for till make up a bad meal wi' a sort o' desert. Eh? How will that do think ye?

*Annie*–Are ye nae the waur o' drink the night goodman?

*Goodman*–What has put it in your light head to ask that?

*Annie*–Because if ye be sober I can trust mysel ony gate wi' you but I am no sae sure about that when you're tipsy.

*Goodman*–Vice-versa my woman vice-versa. D'ye ken that? Eh?

*Ann*–Aih Goodman I fear that has some very ill meaning. I darena gang wi' you. It's something like ane o' my Rob's words but no just sae lang tailed.

*Goodman*–Come along Annie come along. Nae trust like trist.
(*Exeunt*)

*(Enter Sandy and Rob, who call above)*

*Both*–Lasses–Hilloa lasses! Are ye waking there? Come down here and see lads a piece for you.

*Girzy*–*(above)* Aye trouth honest man no very mony will see us if ye kend what some kens–I'm coming nane down t'ye.

*Sandy*–Waken the rest Girzy waken the rest.

*Girzy*–Aye but where will I gang *to* waken them? Ye ca' ay Minnyhive an ill place but this is a hell till it. (*Enter Girzy*) An' ye're there snipelting after your deary? An' ye're there snipelting after your's– Gin ye haena seen them the night afore ye hae bonny bargains to look after–Gude guide us to the day! It is naething ava for lasses to gang out wi' lads but it's an awfu' like thing to gang out wi' bachelors!

*Rob*–What do you mean Girzy? You're driving at some bad insignification.

*Girzy*–Bad? There's naething but badness amang ye. When the young focks in Minnyhive gang a wooing they sit decently at their sweet-hearts' fire side. But here it is a' skulduddery thegither. Stay there till I speak a word to a friend an' I'll show you a sight that's good for sair een–I'm no ay sleeping when I'm winking–I hae gayan lang lugs an' I can lay them in my neck an' listen at times too– Hegh! Ye are fine focks hereaway–It will be lang or ony o' our lasses gang a splunting wi' bachelors.

*(Exit Girzy who returns followed by the goodwife undressed)*

*Goodwife*–What's ado here? What has the tawpie raised me for? Nought but men! men! men! I think the original curse has changed sides an' their desires are to us–But if that's to be the case mind we are to rule over you–an' we'll do it wi' a rod of iron too–Sandy I'm glad to see your crazy face again, untimely hour as it is–I hope you have come to your right reason again. If no ye maun be brought to it. We maunna let the corruption of your nature ruin you poor senseless insignificant gowk! I'll give you your corn if I had time– What thought you o' yon scene Rob? Was there ever ought like you seen in a christian land–Aye ye may look asklent at your comrade, but no ae word to him for your life. But you will never let a lady ask a question or speak a single word–What was it that ye raised me for ye dowdy?

*Girzy*–I'm nae howdy, nor never needit ane yet, an' that's mair nor some focks are like to say or the play be done. Come here and I'll show you whether your focks or them o' Minnyhive be warst. (*She opens the coal cellar door, the goodwife drags out the Goodman and Girzy hauls out Annie*) If this be nae skulduddery I never saw it.

*Sandy*–Is this the piece of chrystaline empyrean purity [MS OBSCURE] can be trusted &c?

*Goodwife*–Now ye poor drunken–intemperate–effeminate, womanish carle what have ye to say for yoursel? No ae word? No sae muckle as a bit lie to hide your wickedness? Weel I'm rather sorry for you now–On a pickle hay in the coal cellar at twa in the morning.

*Goodman*–I say–Will ye take a snuff? (*presenting the great snuff box*)

*Goodwife*–No I thank you honest man–Ha–ha–ha. No a shift but that? No a single affcome at a'. O really for the credit o' the house frame some story however unfeasible. Ye gaed in to say your prayers didna you? And found Annie there by chance? Wasna that the gate of it? Say something or really I'll be very wae for you.

*Goodman*–I say–callants I'm rather in a bad scrape. Eh? But this I'll say an' swear till it. The bonny lass is not the worse of me.

*Goodwife*–Hech-wow! is that really true man? Ha–ha–ha! There are some here that need nae oracle to be satisfied in that–I can tell you a' sirs that though appearances are sair against my poor goodman, yet he has ane principle of honour in him that I could trust against the world.

*Goodman*–I say–Peggy my woman–I think–after a'–It will be as good for you for till take a snuff.

*Goodwife*–You're very good sir–thank you–You're pleased with this principle of honour. Now Rob you that is sic a grand gramarian and a philosopher, What do you think the strongest principle that can bind a man from doing evil?

*Rob*–The strongest I take to be an inmate postulation of homogenousness.

*Goodwife*–I dinna ken what that is but I can tell you of a stronger and thats the want of power. That I'll back against all other principles in the world.

*Goodman*–(*Aside*) Oho! Is she landed there!

*Rob*–Ah but goodwife that's no fair mathewmaticks. That's no a principle. If ye be gaun to reason do it metaphysically.

*Goodman*–Doited body! Think you every body is like you, and that a man o' taste hasna sense for till distinguish objects?

*Goodwife*–That you have!–That you have–I say. "Ah that is worth a hunder kisses of an auld wife!–Had she a cheek of velvet like that! Or sic lips sprinkled wi' heather hinney!" (*The Goodman looks amazed and frightened Sandy bursts into laughter*) What ails you my man? What gar's you gape and stare that way as if you saw a ghost? (*fawning*) "Come let us sit down–sit down here that I may get you all in my arms–Now I am so happy–I have not been so happy I dinna ken the time–The Goodwife! Wha care's for her? He–he–he I have *her* on the hip." Is not that a bonny story?

*Goodman*–Things are muckle waur here than I excpectit! How the devil has she come by all this–Oh–oh–oh! There's no trusting of these young jades.

*Goodwife*–Did you ever hear a story goodman of ain honest carle that once wiled away a bonny innocent young bride to debauch her, but instead of her he got the head of an illwillie cow wi' sharp horns in his arms? What did such a man deserve think you?

*Goodman*–After all it was too bad in him–D–d bad! I can stand this nae langer–I say–Goodwife–Think you you could manage the farm for twa or three years yoursel?

*Goodwife*–Why do you ask?

*Goodman*–Because I'm thinking of ganging up to London to live a while till I get Jock intil the parliament house, and then I'll get my wale o' bonny skelping lasses and no ane to say Goodman what for did ye do sic a thing. That's my plan!–And I'll do it too.

(*Exeunt*)


## [MS BREAK]

[...] night after that (*Enter the Goodman hastily behind*)

*Goodwife*–(*aside*) Hech wow the boundless corruption of our nature!

*Rob*–Heavens such boundless cautionry.

*Goodman*–(*in a loud whisper*) Will you in faith Annie? Bless you for a girl of spirit–I say–Here's five notes to buy the wedding things.

*Ann*–(*aloud*) No–I'll not have them–I'll have no hire either to do good or evil, but the pleasure of doing them.

*Rob*–Well well you *shall* do as you chuse. Only don't go to break with me for really and truly my life is bound up with you.

*Ann*–Never make me or any woman alive your equal unless you can trust her as well out of your sight as in it. Ah lak-a-day! Before I am lang your's I will not be a thing to court! We all see what is before us and yet we run headlong into it as foam-bells do into the eddy of the whirlpool.

*Rob*–(*half crying*) It is delightful to hear from the lips of purity and chrystalized semenality such heavenly vestments of prostitution.

*Goodman*–Eh? Of what? Ye're surely wrang man? I'll thank you for till to say that over again.

*Rob*–Oh Goodman you must excuse phraseologicality in one that is in such raptures with his ideosyncrasy.

*Goodman*–Eh? Ideo-what?

*Goodwife*–Peace be wi' us honest man have you found your tongue again? And gaun to overpower us wi' your wit too?

*Goodman*–I say–How lang will it take to gang up to Lonnen in the James Watt?

*Goodwife*–Haud your tongue about that daft project. I'll rather make you a bed in the coal cellar awthegither, and gie you the chance of a' the lasses that gang out an' come into the house.

*Goodman*–That would rather be too much of a good thing. Lunnen for my money! and strapping lasses for that. (*snapping his fingers*)

When I was a young man striking at the studdy
I had a pair o' blue breeks and they were a' duddy
When I streuk they sheuk like a lamb's taillie
But yet I'm turned a gentleman my wife she wears a *raillie*
Yet though I'm turned an auld man and steady at my duty
I like a bonny lassie yet–But only for her beauty
Shame fa' the heart that wadna glow in wildest agitation
At the sweetest thing the bonniest thing in a' the lord's
creation
Fal-de-ral fal-de-ral &c            (*Exeunt goodman*)

*Goodwife*–There's nae fools to an old fool! Shame fa' me gin I dinna like to see him a wee cagy about the bonny lasses. As for you Sandy ye have made the greatest fool of yourself ava; first to suffer yoursel to be taken in and slandered wi' an auld abandoned slut like Henny and then to run away and leave your hirsel and your lass–And *sic* a lass.

*Sandy*–Aye you may weel say it! Sic a lass! Sic a lass as I ever wish to see again. So you're no gaun to tell me aught about the tryste in the hay neuk yestreen?

*Goodwife*–He–he–he! Gude forgie me! Do ye ken about that too? Muckle hallershaker that you are. (*Marches him about the stage with her open hand and laughs immoderately*) What the deil were ye gaun peeping about and spying wicked fock's doings for? I am sure *she* hasna tauld you and gin Rob has tauld you he has begun at the wrang end. Sae ye maunna heed him but just let a' byganes be byganes wi' Mary and you. For ye may take ane's word for it wha has nae very high opinion o' corrupt nature and particularly of that luckless part of it that belongs to her ain sex that Mary's ane of the best o' us.

*Sandy*–Now I never saw a brighter instance of the corruption of female nature than this. Because Mary has taken you in you want her to take me in too. But I heard the tryste set and shamelessly set in the very darkest corner of the bush aboon Traquair. I hope it will never be profaned by sic a tryste again and I could not believe my senses till I went and hid myself and heard the meeting and every thing that passed.

*Goodwife*–Then I can tell you lad there were more listeners there than a brocket cow.

*Rob*–Ah! goodwife goodwife! Who would think that you were so full of conceptionality!

*Goodwife*–What does the pedagogue mean?

*Rob*–There are some people that have things that are rather as one might say somewhat heterogenielogical. (*looking very wise*)

*Goodwife*–Eh?

*Rob*–I discovered your supererogator rather in an awkward incumbancy in the way of collaterality–you witnessed it–What would the incumbent have said if I had informed him that you and the circumstantiator here were procrastinating in the same den both antecedentally and intermediately? Hay–hay–hay! Tell me that hay–hay–hay.

*Goodwife*–I'm quite in the dark Mr Philosopher.

*Rob*–So you were then. Hay–hay! In plain Scottish then What would the goodman have said had I told him that you and Sandy were lying snug courting in the same hole before he came?

*Goodwife*–You would have told him a manifest lee then.

*Sandy*–To say the truth we were very close–I could have touched you with my hand all the while.

*Goodwife*–(*Screaming with laughter*) So so man? Was that the gate o't? What a strange night we have had! Blessings on that bonny bush aboon Traquair for it tells a' secrets. (*calls*) Mary! Hilloa Mary. Come out o' your holes and your bores there, just as you are, and let this honest lad see wha he was lying in the dark loft beside. (*Enter Mary in the Goodwife's clothes*)

*Sandy*–I am bewildered with joy, and see it all. How could I suspect such perfect innocense?

*Goodwife*–It was all a scheme of mine and I got the courting and kissing in the hay mow myself. Come join hands like true lovers and let us have a sang afore we part.

*Sandy*–And was I lying so near my own Peggy in the hay loft and did not know? O had I but seized on her in the bonny Bush that night, misbelieving all the lies ever heard, secure of innocense with such beauty and simplicity as Goodwife a sang we shall have.

*Sandy*

Thou Bonny bush aboon Traquair
    That wav'st our valley over
O never bush so sweet so fair
    Eer shrouded faithful lover
The powers of love have watered thee
    With dews in heaven compounded
And hallowed every shrub and tree
    To heal the heart that's wounded

In days when virtuous love was young
    Thy scions of devotion
Stole from the western star that hung
    Red blushing o'er the ocean
Upon this lea so lovely fair
    Were grafted safe and soundly
Thou bonny bush aboon Traquair
    May earthly joys surround thee

*Goodwife*–Come now let us a' gang and leave the reconciled couple to settle the wedding–Annie suppose you and your joe should try the coalhouse aince mair–Goodbye good luck to you all. (*Exeunt severally all but Sandy and Mary*)

*Sandy*–Now my beloved my dearest Mary is all forgiven between us.

*Mary*–There has been little to forgive but grievous lies told on us both.

*Sandy*–Come then let us join hands and vow to be one for ever. (*Enter Henny*)

*Henny*–I forbid the bans! The process and the conjunction! Here I stand a wronged and ruined woman a bar of separation between you two for ever.

*Sandy*–Wretch what right have you to meddle with ought relating to us?

*Henny*–I'll show my right–I'll make that good here where I stand– Did not your false tongue swear to me on the blessed gospel and engage to be mine? Can you deny that?

*Sandy*–The woman is insane! I declare–

*Henny*–*You* declare? What do *you* declare? Have not you ruined me? taken away my youthful virtue and would now leave to scorn and contumely? And *you* minx! How have *you* the face to lay claim to my betrothed degraded as you are? You would indeed be a fit wife for a betrayer of youthful innocence after being a *miss* a ready miss both to father and son. (*Mary cries and shrinks enter the Goodman running at Henny she flies and he follows*)

*Goodman*–The deil gie me good of you if I dinna gar you for aince. (*He calls behind*) Hilloa come a' here and bring a blank wi' you. (*Enter omnes with a blanket the Goodman tosses a form into it*) Now toss her to the clouds and down again till she squeak like a worried wulcat. She has been the breeder of a' the mischief in the parish. That way! Up wi' her lads and lasses! gie her some good bumps on the cassa. Hurra! There she goes like the witch of Fife! (*They toss the light form outrageously high and at every flight Henny utters a squeak behind. They then throw the form into a pond*) There lucky! Take tat for a cooler! Splash like an otter and swim for your life I say–How will that do think ye?                                                    *Scene closes*

### Enter Mr Pom and Mr Murphy

*Pom*–You shan't go away Murphy I cannot live here in this rustic vile retirement without you and besides what shall I do with all my mother's pretty maids? I shall have them all on my hands together without you?

*Mur*–They are very pretty maids but I understand they are to be married shortly.

*Pom*–They are no the worse of that surely?

*Mur*–Sure Mr Pompey you do not seriously intend to debauch these innocent maids?

*Pom*–Every one of them I do assure you. I have bespoke them all already–I love a little change in that way. I seduce all the pretty girls in the parrish. Always glad to see me come home–There's Mr Pom now! We shall have some sport now!–And even the old dowagers of mothers "Oh how dye do Mr Pom–Have you been well since you went to college Mr Pom–Hope you'll call." Then when they catch me in the dark with their daughters "Oh tis no body but Mr Pom. No body minds him." What sport we shall have if you will but stay.

*Mur*–What an unconscionable dog you are! Well sir these are scenes in which I never will join. I wish you all manner of virtuous pleasure. But take my advice. Never meddle with your mother's servants adieu.                                                    (*Exit*

*Pom*–Virtuous pleasure! What does he mean by that? The fellow has no spirit. I'll seduce all the girls to a certainty. That little rose Mary gave my love a sharp reception. I'll have her nevertheless the other beauty is at my steps. She is even more forward than me. The third is a drab but I shall use her as a sort of foil and to keep her quiet. *Virtuous* pleasure forsooth! I know of no pleasure so fraught with virtue as mine shall be.

> Gin you meet a bonny lassie
>   Be sure ye dinna let her gae [MS BREAK]

> Wheneer I try the word to say
>   There comes a pang that strikes me dumb
> Though a' the lave are on their way
>   The word fareweel it winna come
> I've spelled the word within my breast
>   Yet still its sound I darena frame
> The word has sic a waesome sound
>   I downa add it to thy name

> Were't but till the month o' May
>   An' my dear lassie weel to be
> Or were't but for a year and day
>   And hopes again my love to see
> Then I could take a kiss wi' glee
>   Wi' arms about thy wast sae sma
> And then the round tear in thy ee
>   Wad be the sweetest sight of a'

> But a' my heart hauds dear on earth
>   Its only valued worldly gain
> In all its beauty all its worth
>   To leave and never meet again
> Ah that's a pang an afterpain
>   The spirit dares not live to feel
> The breath will rend my heart in twain
>   That says the weary word fareweel

*Mary*–He's an intolerable puppy that young master of ours.

*Ann*–I like him exceedingly. He is a lad that very much may be made of. I anticipate a great deal of fun with him. He has been making love to me and I assure you I have given him every encouragement.

*Mary*–He was making love to me too and that of the most impertinent sort. But I gave him a settler. I told his mother all before his face.

*Ann*–O that was too bad poor fellow that was a shameful damper. I think you are not saying ought Girzy. I am afraid he has got the upper hand of you.

*Girzy*–Touts!

*Ann*–Ah Girzy what will the natural philosophers about Minnyive say to this?

*Girzy*–There's none about Minnyive will ever ken.

*Ann*–Will ever ken What?

*Girzy*–Touts ye're ay on about naturality yet I wonder ye dinna think shame.

*Ann*–I wadna say but somebody may have to change seats wi' Jenny Girdwood next winter.

*Girzy*–It's naething but ill will and jealousy because I have taken the young law-war from you. Goodness to the day here he comes. Ye may just gang and leave us by oursels twa for I ken he'll want to speak to me in preevat.

*Enter Pompey*

*Pom*–Fine day girls–Fine day for blooming maids–makes them blush like roses–How d'ye do Maria? Any better humoured as yet? Pretty Miss Ann I want one private word with you. It is from your sweetheart you know Maria will you favour us? Hunks get you gone. (*Girzy retires growling with Mary*) Well lovely Ann have you been thinking of my proposal?

*Ann*–Indeed I have sir I have thought about nothing else and am quite delighted but am afraid our marriage–

*Pom*–Our what? Marriage? O my pretty girl nothing like that. That is a horrible concern! quite stale. I want you for my mistress.

*Ann*–O dear sir I cannot hire you into my service, for I have no money to give you for wages, and no work for you; but I am willing to be your servant, not your mistress, or your wife; would not that be better?

*Pom*–No, no, no. I tell you no I don't court you for marriage. I hate it; and don't want it. The thing in short that I desire is seduction.

*Ann*–Seduction? O that must be a grand thing! I should like it extremely. Is that one of the scences you learn at the Colledge?

*Pom*–Say *sciences* my dearest Annie not *scences*. Yes charming girl it is the sweetest of all sciences and we learn it in the school of nature.

*Ann*–O that must be natural philosophy then the thing that our Rob has studied so deeply. Is it done by figures?

*Pom*–Yes love it is natural philosophy. The very fountain head of all science intellect and truth.

*Ann*–Is it? I'll take lessons immediately. (*courtesies*) Thank you kindly sir. When shall we begin?

*Pom*–This very night sweetest maiden. When all the rest go to sleep come to my chamber and we'll begin our lessons.

*Ann*–I will, depend on it. Have you candles ready? I can buy some from Betty Nicol.

*Pom*–O we shan't need them.

*Ann*–Not need candles? Teach me in the dark? I cannot concieve that? Then it is not done by figures?

*Pom*–Figures! Ha-ha–figures! No simpleton. I can teach it you lying in my arms and quite in darkness. How will you like that?

*Ann*–I should like that best of all–But dear me–

*Pom*–No *buts*. I'll have no *buts*, nor *dear me's*. Come to my chamber when the rest go to sleep, and I'll begin you in the first branch of Natural Philosophy.

*Ann*–Yes sir. Thank you sir–I will–How is it you call that introductory branch again I have forgot it? Prod–

*Pom*–Hush here's my mother. (*Enter the Goodwife*)

*Goodwife*–What do you here you graceless impertinent puppy keeping up my girls from their work and demeaning yourself in sic a way as this?–Rather like a blackguard than a gentleman schollar.

*Pom*–You know nothing about life at all mother pray hold thy peace. A mere country drudge, a dungyard goodwife. (*laughs affectedly*) You should not meddle in gentlemen's amusements.

*Goodwife*–Not meddle? Sic a gentleman! Trying to bring himself to a level with the meanest servant about his father's house. I'll let you ken what's what as lang as you are under my tuition I will. Do I not know that you have been endeavouring to ruin every servant girl that we have?

*Pom*–No-no-no I tell you–I have'nt. I never meddle with girls, save in giving them some hints useful in life. It is accounted a most genteel amusement to converse with blooming country maids. I assure you it is among we learned and enlightened gentlemen. You know nothing about a collegian's lawife at all.

*Goodwife*–I doubt your hints very much son. Pray what useful hints have you been giving them. Tell me truly now and if I am satisfied I shall suffer you to converse with them when you please providing you dinna take them off my work. What does your coxcombship teach them–Let us hear. Do you teach them their fallen and corrupt state by nature and their liability to err?

*Pom*–(*Taking off his hat and bowing very low*) Yes–I do. The very fundamental principle that I begin with.

*Goodwife*–I should rejoice if this were true–But I can hardly believe it knowing what a selfish degenerate thing you were from the cradle. I'll ask them all in your presence. (*calls*) Come hither you two. (*Enter Mary and Girzy*)

*Goodwife*–Now I ask at you Mary who art truth itself. Did this my son ever give you any good hints anent your life?

*Mary*–No–Anything but good hints–I think him a very bad lad.

*Ann*–Ah now Mary how can you say so?

*Goodwife*–Let her alone–No tampering with the evidence. Did he ever give you any lessons on that first principle of true morality the corruption of your nature?

*Mary*–If he did they were practical ones for he has tried all his art to corrupt my nature. (*He makes signs to Mary*)

*Goodwife*–Ah thou art a true chip of the old block. Now Girzy tell me what he has ever taught you.

*Girzy*–Awm no obliged to confess here; an' aw wanna confess naething nawther. There's no a nicer spirited chap in aw Minnyive.

*Goodwife*–Ah! You mean spirited selfish wretch, have you overcome this poor halfwitted low insignificant dowdy?

*Girzy*–What's she saying about a howdy?

*Pom*–Pon the honour of a gentleman mother, you are extremely vulgar.

*Ann*–You are indeed grieviously mistaken Goodwife. The young gentleman is ane of the most civil, kind, and obliging gentlemen that ever was born. He is and I know it–and have proofs of it.

*Girzy*–So say I–He's a ceevil obliging young man.

*Goodwife*–Hold your peace fool! I tremble for your recommendation and as for you Annie you are so much of a wag ane never kens how to read you.

*Pom*–She's a very sensible civil well bred girl. She has more common sense than you all put together.

*Goowife*–There we go! There we go! Favours at a' hands I fear.

*Ann*–I never meant to tell but I cannot hear the kind good young gentleman accused falsely and not vindicate him which I *will* do and you may believe me Goodwife that you *do* accuse him *very* falsely indeed. He's the most generous disinterested of human beings and as a proof of it he has kindly offered to teach me gratis the first principle of natural philosophy.

*Goodwife*–I am glad to hear it. Oh Annie you rejoice a mother's heart for let a son be as bad as he will a mother is still a mother. Poor fellow I have wronged him. (*takes his hand and Ann's*)

*Ann*–You *have* wronged him. He is to teach me the rudiments the very first principle of all social happiness, love, joy, and truth.

*Goodwife*–You make me cry for joy at hearing such delightful news. Forgive my bad suspicions Pompey. You are my son still! What is this noble art? How is it called?

*Ann*—Oh it is the sweetest of all arts the most enchanting! Mr Pompey says it. It is called seduction. Is not that the name of it Mr Pompey?
    *The Goodwife stares and lets go both their hands*
*Pom*—No–no–no I tell you. That's not the name at all.
*Ann*—It is—You called it so. When you asked me to become your mistress you know and I refused. It is duction something *se*duction or *pro*duction the ane or the other. And what is more Goodwife the young gentleman is so civil and so generous that he will not even suffer me to lay out any of my wages on candles but is going to teach me in the dark.
*Goodwife*—*Se*duction and *pro*duction and teach you them in the dark?
*Ann*—Yes. Which must be very troublesome you know. And is so very kind in him! I am to go to his chamber when all the rest are asleep and we are to begin our lessons this very night. Are we not Mr Pompey?
*Goodwife*—(*furiously*) Do you know what you are saying huzzy?
*Ann*—Dear me it is quite true. Do you not believe me? He is even to take me in his arms and teach me in his bosom the good kind generous hearted young gentleman! I have engaged to go and so I will.
*Goodwife*—Ah you dog! You base unworthy wretch! How dare you presume to practice under your parents' roof and your parents' eye! I'll turn you out of doors disgraceful puppy but first I'll give you a mark to ken you by. (*wounds him with the poker*) *Exeunt*


# I Lookit East–I Lookit West

I lookit east–I lookit west,
    I saw the darksome coming even;
The wild bird sought its cozy nest,
    The kid was to the hamlet driven;
    But house nor hame aneath the heaven,                    5
Except the skeugh of greenwood tree,
    To seek a shelter in was given,
To my three little bairns and me.

I had a prayer I couldna pray,
    I had a vow I couldna breathe,                           10
For aye they led my words astray,

And aye they were connected baith
  Wi' ane wha now was cauld in death.
I lookit round wi' watery ee—
  Hope wasna there—but I was laith         15
To see my little babies dee.

Just as the breeze the aspin stirr'd,
  And bore aslant the falling dew,
I thought I heard a bonny bird
  Singing amid the air sae blue;         20
  It was a lay that did renew
The hope deep sunk in misery;
  It was of one my woes that knew,
And ae kind heart that cared for me.

O, sweet as breaks the rising day,         25
  Or sun-beam through the wavy rain,
Fell on my soul the charming lay!
  Was it an angel poured the strain?
  Whoe'er has kenn'd a mother's pain,
Bent o'er the child upon her knee,         30
  O they will bless, and bless again,
The generous heart that cares for me!

A cot was rear'd by Mercy's hand
  Amid the dreary wilderness,
It rose as if by magic wand,         35
  A shelter to forlorn distress;
  And weel I ken that Heaven will bless
The heart that issued the decree,
  The widow and the fatherless
Can never pray and slighted be.         40

# Tam Nelson

Tam Nelson was a queer, queer man,
  He had nae ill nor good about him,
He oped his een when day began,
  And dozed ower night, ye needna doubt him.

But many a day and many a night,         5
  I've tried wi' a' the lights o' nature,

To settle what's come o' the wight,
    The soulless, senseless, stupid creature!

Tam lo'd his meltith and his clink
    As weel as any in the nation,                    10
He took his pipe, he drank his drink,
    But that was nought against salvation.

But were a' the sants and slaves o' sin
    Opposed in rank an' raw thegither,
Tam ne'er did aught to cross the ane,               15
    And ne'er did aught to mense the ither.

Tam graned an dee't like ither men;
    O tell me, tell me you wha know it—
Will that poor donsy rise again?
    O sirs, I canna, winna trow it.                  20

Nae doubt, but he wha made us a'
    Can the same form an' feelings gie him,
Without a lack, without a flaw—
    But what the de'il wad he do wi' him?

He'd make nae scram in cavern vile,                 25
    Nor place that ony living kens o',
He's no worth ony devil's while,
    Nor upright thing to take amends o'.

If borne aboon the fields o' day,
    Where rails o' gowd the valleys border,         30
He'd aye be standing i' the way,
    And pitting a' things out of order.

At psalm, or hymn, or anthem loud,
    Tam wadna pass, I sairly doubt it,
He couldna do't—an' if he could                     35
    He wadna care a doit about it.

O thou who o'er the land o' peace
    Lay'st the cold shroud and moveless fetter,
Let Tam lie still in careless ease,
    For d—n him, if he'll e'er be better.            40

# There's Some Souls
# 'ill Yammer and Cheep

There's some souls 'ill yammer and cheep,
    If a win'le strae ly in their way;
And some through this bright world 'ill creep,
    As if fear'd for the light o' God's day.

And some would not lend ye a boddle,        5
    Although they would borrow a crown,
And some folk 'ill ne'er fash their noddle
    Wha's waukin, if they can sleep soun'.

And some wi' big scars on their face,
    Point out a prin scart on a frien',        10
And some black as sweeps wi' disgrace,
    Cry out the whole world's unclean.

Some wha on the best o't can cram,
    Think a' body else maun be fu',
Some would na gi'e misery a dram,        15
    Though they swattle themsels till they spew.

Sure's death! there can be but sma' pleasure
    In livin' 'mang sic a cursed crew,
An't were na the soul's sacred treasure,
    The friendship that's found in a few.        20

That treasure, let's hoord it thegither,
    Enjoy my gude luck or thole ill,
Nor grudge though wine's sent to a brither
    In hoggits, when I've but a gill.

Then here's to the chiel wha's sae bauld        25
    As to trust his ain thought to his tongue,
Wha e'en though his trunk's growin auld,
    Has a soul and a heart that are young.

Before I an auld frien' forget,
    My memory first I maun tine;–        30
Here's a glass for anither health yet,
    Need'st thou guess, angel woman!–it's thine.

# January–December 1827 (Volumes 21–22)

# Ode for Music
# On the Death of Lord Byron

### By the Ettrick Shepherd

PRELUDE

O came ye by Dee's winding waters,
   That rave down the Forests of Marr,
Or over the glens of the Gordons,
   And down by the dark Loch-na-Gaur?
For there, at the fall of the even,       5
   Was heard a wild song of despair,
As if the sweet seraphs of heaven
   Had mix'd with the fiends of the air.

The angels in songs were bewailing
   The fall of a bard in his prime;      10
While demons of discord were yelling
   A coronach loud and sublime.
The cliff, like a bay'd deer, was quaking;
   The hill shook his temples of grey;
The stars drizzled blood on the braken,    15
   As pour'd this dread strain from the brae:

CHORUS OF DEMONS
    Sound! sound
    Your anthem profound,
Spirits of peril, unawed and unbound!
    Clamour away,      20
    To mortals' dismay,
Till the Christian turn on his pillow to pray.
    Sound, sound, &c.
Wake up your pipe and your carol with speed,
The pipe of the storm, and the dance of the dead;   25
Light up your torches, the dark heavens under,
The torch of the lightning, and bass of the thunder!
Roar it and revel it, riot and rumble,
Till earth from her inmost core grovel and grumble;

And then in deep horrors her moody front swaddle,          30
Till all these dark mountains shall rock like a cradle!
     Sound, sound, &c.

For he, the greatest of earthly name,
Whose soul, of our own elemental flame,
Was a shred of so bright and appalling a glow,          35
As ne'er was inclosed in a frame below—
Spirits, that energy, all in prime,
Must join this night in our revels sublime!
     Then sound, sound
     Your anthem profound,          40
Spirits of peril, unawed and unbound!
     Sound overhead
     Your symphony dread,
Till shudders the dust of the sleeping dead.

    CHORUS OF ANGELS
     Hail, hail,          45
    With harp and with vaile,
Yon spirit that comes on the gloaming gale!
     Sing! Sing!
    Till heaven's arch ring,
To hail the favour'd of our King!          50

Grey Shade of Selma, where art thou sailing?
Light from thy dim cloud, and cease thy bewailing;
Though the greatest of all the choral throng
That ever own'd thy harp and song,
Hath fallen at Freedom's holy shrine,          55
Yet the light of his glory for ever shall shine.
Spirit of Ossian, cease thy bewailing,
Our spirits atone not for human failing;
But let us rejoice, that there is above
A Father of pity, a God of love,          60
Who never from erring being will crave
Beyond what his heavenly bounty gave:
And never was given in Heaven's o'erjoy
So bright a portion without an alloy.
     Then hail to his rest,          65
     This unparallel'd guest,
With songs that pertain to the land of the blest!

　　　For stars shall expire,
　　　And earth roll in fire,
Ere perish the strains of his sovereign lyre;                    70

That spirit of flame that had its birth
In heaven, to blaze for a moment on earth,
Mid tempest and tumult, mid fervour and flame,
Then mount to the glories from whence it came.–
And there for his home of bliss shall be given                  75
The highest hills on the verge of heaven,
To thrill with his strains afar and wide,
And laugh at the fiends in the worlds aside.
　　　Then hie thee, for shame,
　　　Ye spirits of blame,                                       80
Away to your revels in thunder and flame;
　　　For our's the avail
　　　To hallow and hail
Yon spirit that comes on the gloaming gale.

　　Then bounding through the fields of air,                    85
A spirit approach'd in chariot fair,
That seem'd from the arch of the rainbow won,
Or beam of the red departing sun,
A hum of melody far was shed,
And a halo of glory around it spread;                           90
For that spirit came the dells to see,
Where first it was join'd with mortality,
Where first it breathed the inspired strain,
And return its harp to heaven again.
Then far above the cliffs so grey,                              95
This closing measure died away:
　　　With joint acclaim
　　　Let's hail the name
Of our great Bard, whose mighty fame
　　　Must spread for aye,                                      100
　　　Ne'er to decay
Till heaven and earth shall pass away.

# Hogg on Women!!!

Aye now I've light upon a theme
Unbounded thrilling and supreme
So let me try my mountain lore
In the delirious theme once more
For what is bard with all his art                    5
Who scorns to take the fair one's part
And never hath in life percieved
What once I sparingly believed
That woman's fair and lovely breast
Was framed the sanctuary blest                       10
The home all other homes above
Of virtuous and of faithful love
   Sweet sex I fear with all my zeal
I ne'er can laud you as I feel
If nature's glowing hand imbue                       15
The early bloom with beauty's dew
Stamp in thine eye the witching wile
And light with love thy opening smile
Ere prudence rises to thine aid
A thousand snares for thee are laid                  20
While still to revel wrong or right
Among these snares is thy delight
'Tis thus that thousands wreck'd and hurled
From virtue's paths traverse the world
Regardless of creation's scorn                       25
Unblest unfavoured and forlorn
   But as well woman may compare
A David Haggart with a Blair
A Hunt with Southey or I wot
A lord of Buchan with a Scott                        30
A Jeffery with a tailor spruce
Strutting with ellwand and with goose
A Peter Rob<sup>t</sup>son with a clown
Or Doctor Brown with Doctor Browne
As man take one degraded mind                        35
For model of dear womankind
   Nay let us rise in our compare
To beauties of the earth and air
With their reverses—range the sea
The wood the waste the galaxy                        40

And rather urge a paralell
'Twixt rays of heaven and shades of hell
Than woman's fair and virtuous fame
Should suffer but in thought or aim
Or from her sacred temples fall                        45
The smallest flower celestial
   Take woman as her God hath made her
And not as mankind may degrade her
Else as well may you take the storm
In all its hideousness to form                         50
An estimate of nature's cheer
And glories of the bounteous year
As well compare the summer flower
With dark December's chilling shower
Or summer morning pearled with dew                     55
With winter's wan and deadly hue
The purple ocean calm and glowing
With ocean when the tempest's blowing
Then say with proud discourtesy
"This is the earth, and that the sea                   60
And this is woman—what you will
Please you to say she's woman still,
And will be woman, more or less
A being prone to perverseness.
Hath it not flowed from sage's tongue                  65
And hath not moral poet sung
That men to war or business take
But woman is at heart a rake?"
   Injurious bard such thing to say
Degraded be thy shameless lay                          70
Such ruinous principle to own
And damning dogma to lay down
'Tis false—Wo to the blighted name
That would attach promiscuous blame
To all the gentle fair and wise                        75
And only view to generalize
   For me I'm woman's slave confest
Without her hopeless and unblest
And so are all gainsay who can
For what would be the life of man                      80
If left in desert or in isle
Unlighted up by beauty's smile

Even though he boasted monarch's name
And o'er his own sex reigned supreme
With thousands bending to his sway                          85
If lovely woman were away
What were his life? What could it be?
A vapour on a shoreless sea!
A troubled cloud in darkness toss'd
Alongst the waste of waters lost!                           90
A ship deserted in the gale
Without a steersman or a sail
A star or beacon light before
Or hope of haven evermore
A thing without a human tie                                 95
Unloved to live unwept to die
    Then let us own through nature's reign
Woman the light of her domain
And if to maiden love not given
The dearest bliss below the heaven                          100
At least due homage let us pay
In reverence of a parent's sway
To that dear sex whose favour still
Our guerdon is in good or ill
A motive that can never cloy                                105
Our glory honour and our joy
And humbly on our bended knee
Acknowledge her supremacy

Mount-Benger
April 6th 1827

# The Marvellous Doctor
## *By the Ettrick Shepherd*

WHEN my parents lived in the old manse of Ettrick, which they did
for a number of years, there was one summer that an old gray-headed
man came and lived with them nearly a whole half year, paying my
mother at the rate of ten shillings a-month for bed, board, and wash-
ing. He was a mysterious being, and no one knew who he was, or
what he was; but all the neighbourhood reckoned him *uncanny*; which

in that part of the country means a warlock, or one some way conversant with beings of another nature.

I remember him well; he was a tall ungainly figure, dressed in a long black coat, the longest and the narrowest coat I ever saw; his vest was something like blue velvet, and his breeches of leather, buckled with silver knee-buckles. He wore always white thread stockings, and as his breeches came exactly to the knap of the knee, his legs appeared so long and thin that it was a marvel to me how they carried him. Take in black spats, and a very narrow-brimmed hat, and you have the figure complete; any painter might take his likeness, provided he did not make him too straight in the back, which would never answer, as his formed a segment of a great circle. He was a *doctor;* but whether of law, medicine, or divinity, I never learned; perhaps of them all, for a doctor he certainly was—we called him so, and never knew him by any other name; some, indeed, called him the *Lying* Doctor, some the *Herb* Doctor, and some the Warlock Doctor, but my mother, behind his back, called him always THE MARVELLOUS DOCTOR, which, for her sake, I have chosen to retain.

His whole occupation was in gathering flowers and herbs, and arranging them; and, as he picked a number of these out of the churchyard, the old wives in the vicinity grew terribly jealous of him. He seemed, by his own account, to have been over the whole world, on what business or occupation he never mentioned; but from his stories of himself, and his wonderful feats, one might have concluded that he had been everything. I remember a number of these stories quite distinctly, for at that time I believed them all for perfect even-down truth, though I have been since led to suspect that it was scarcely consistent with nature or reason they could be so. One or two of these tales I shall here relate, but with this great disadvantage, that I have, in many instances, forgot the names of the places where they happened. I knew nothing about geography then, or where the places were, and the faint recollection I have of them will only, I fear, tend to confuse my narrative the more.

One day, while he was very busy arranging his flowers and herbs, and constantly speaking to himself, my mother says to him, "Doctor, you that kens sae weel about the nature of a' kinds o' plants and yirbs, will ye tell me gin there be sic a yirb existing as that, if ye pit it either on beast or body, it will gar it follow you?"

"No, Margaret, there is not an herb existing which has that power by itself; but there is a decoction from certain rare herbs, of which I have had the honour, or rather the misfortune, to be the sole discoverer, which *has* that effect infallibly."

"Dear doctor, there was sic a kind of charm i' the warld hunders o' years afore ye were born."

"So it has been said, Margaret, so it has been said, but falsely, I assure you. It cost me seven years' hard study and hard labour, both by night and by day, and some thousands of miles' travelling; but at last I effected it, and then I thought my fortune was made. But—would you believe it, Margaret?—my fortune was lost, my time was lost, and I myself was twenty times on the eve of being lost too."

"Dear doctor, tell us some o' your ploys wi' that drog, for they surely must be very curious, especially if you used it as a love-charm to gar the lasses follow you."

"I did; and sometimes got those to follow me that I did not want, as you shall hear by and by. But before I proceed, I may inform you, that I was offered a hundred thousand pounds by the College of Physicians in Spain, and twice the sum by the Queen of that country, if I would impart my discovery to them in full, and I refused it! Yes, for the sake of human nature I refused it. I durst not take the offer for my life and existence."

"What for, doctor?"

"What for, woman? Do you say, what for? Do you say, what for? Don't you see that it would have turned the world upside down, and inverted the whole order of nature? The lowest blackguard in the country might have taken away the first lady—might have taken her from her parents, or her husband, and kept her a slave to him for life; and no opiate in nature to counteract the power of the charm. The secret shall go to the grave with me; for were it once to be made public in any country, that country would be lost; and for the sake of good order among mankind, I have slighted all the grandeur that this world could have bestowed. The first great trial of my skill was a public one;"—and the doctor went on to relate that it occurred as follows:

## THE SPANISH PROFESSOR

HAVING brought my valued charm to full perfection abroad, I returned to Britain to enjoy the fruit of my labours, convinced that I would ensure a patent, and carry all the world before me. But on my arrival in London, I was told that a great Spanish professor had made the discovery five years before, and had arrived at great riches and preferment on that account, under the patronage of the Queen. Convinced that no man alive was thoroughly master of the charm but myself, I went straight to Spain, and called on this eminent professor, whose name was Don Felix de Valdez. This man lived in a style superior to the great nobility and grandees of his country. He had a palace that was not exceeded in grandeur by any in the city, and a suite of lacqueys, young gentlemen, and physicians, attending him, as if he had been the greatest man in the world. It cost me great trouble, and three days' attendance, before I could be admitted to his presence, and even then he received me so cavalierly that my British blood boiled with indignation.

"What is it you want with me, fellow?" says he.

"Sir, I would have you know," says I, "that I am an English doctor, and master of arts, and *your* fellow in any respect. So far good. I was told in my own country, sir, that you are a pretender to the profound art of attachment; or, in other words, that you have made a discovery of that divine elixir, which attaches every living creature touched with it to your person. Do you pretend to such a discovery? Or do you not, sir?"

"And what if I do, most sublime doctor and master of arts? In what way does that concern your great sapience?"

"Only thus far, Professor Don Felix de Valdez," says I, "that the discovery is my own, wholly my own, and solely my own; and after travelling over half the world in my researches for the proper ingredients, and making myself master of the all-powerful nostrum, is it reasonable, do you think, that I should be deprived of my honour and emolument without an effort? I am come from Britain, sir, for the sole purpose of challenging you to a trial of skill before your sovereign and all his people, as well as the learned world in general. I throw down the gauntlet, sir. Dare you enter the lists with me?"

"Desire my lacqueys to take away this mad foreigner," said he to an attendant. "Beat him well with staves, for his impertinence, and give him up to the officers of police, to be put in the House of Correction; and say to Signior Philippo that I ordered it."

"You ordered it!" said I. "And who are you, to order such a thing? I am a free-born British subject, a doctor, and master of arts and sciences, and I have a pass from your government officers to come to Madrid to exercise my calling, and I dare any of you to touch a hair of my head."

"Let him be taken away," said he, nodding disdainfully, "and see that you do to him as I have commanded."

The students then led me gently forth, paying great deference to me; but when I was put into the hands of the vulgar lacqueys, they made sport of me, and having their master's orders, used me with great rudeness, beating me, and pricking me with needle-pointed stilettos, till I was in great fear for my life, and was glad when put into the hands of the police.

Being quickly liberated on making known my country and erudition, I set myself with all my might to bring this haughty and insolent professor to the test. A number of his students having heard the challenge, it soon made a great noise in Madrid; for the young King, Charles the Third, and particularly his Queen, were half mad about the possession of such a nostrum at that period. In order, therefore, to add fuel to the flame now kindled, I published challenges in every one of the Spanish journals, and causing three thousand copies to be printed, I posted them up in every corner of the city, distributing them to all the colleges of the kingdom, and to the college of Toledo in particular, of which Don Felix was the Principal–I sent a sealed copy to every one of its twenty-four professors, and caused some hundreds to be distributed amongst the students.

This challenge made a great noise in the city, and soon reached the ears of the Queen, who became quite impatient to witness a trial of our skill in this her favourite art. The King could get no more peace with her, and therefore was obliged to join her in a request to Professor Don Felix de Valdez, that he would vouchsafe a public trial of skill with this ostentatious foreigner.

The professor pleaded to be spared the indignity of a public exhibition along with a crazy half-witted foreigner, especially as his was a secret art, and ought only to be practised in secret. But the voices of the court and the colleges were loud for the trial, and the professor was compelled to condescend and name a day. We both waited on their Majesties to settle the order and manner of trial, and drew lots who was to exhibit first, and the professor got the preference. The Prado was the place appointed for the exhibition, and Good Friday the day; when I verily thought all Spain was assembled together. The professor engaged to enter the lists precisely at half past twelve o'clock; but he begged that he might be suffered to come in disguise, in order to do away all suspicions of a private understanding with others; and assured their Majesties that he would soon be known to them by his works.

I was placed next to the royal stage, in company with many learned doctors, the Queen being anxious to witness the effect that the display of her wonderful professor's skill produced on me, and to hear my remarks on it; and truly the anxiety that prevailed for almost a whole hour was wonderful, for no one knew in what guise the professor would appear, or how attended, or who were the persons on whom the effect of the unguent was to be tried. Whenever a throng or bustle was perceived in any part of the parade, then the buzz began, "Yonder he is now! Yon must be he, our great professor, Don Felix de Valdez, the wonder of Spain and of the world!"

The Queen was the first to perceive him, perhaps from some private hint given her in what guise he would appear; on which she motioned to me, pointing out a mendicant friar as my opponent, and added, that she thought it but just and right that I should witness all his motions, his feats, and the power of his art. I did so, and thought very meanly of the whole exhibition, as a sort of farce got up among a great number of associates, all of whom were combined to carry on the deception, and share in the profits accruing therefrom. The friar did nothing till he came opposite to the royal stage, when, beckoning slightly to her Majesty, he began to look out for his game, and perceiving an elegant lady sitting on a stage with her back towards him, he took a phial from his bosom, and letting the liquid touch the top of his finger, he reached up that finger and touched the hem of the lady's robe. She uttered a scream, as if pierced to the heart, sprung to her feet, and held her breast as if wounded; then, after looking round and round, as if in great agitation, she descended from the stage, followed the friar, kneeled at his feet, and entreated to be allowed to follow and serve him. He requested her to depart, as he could not be served by woman; but she wept and followed on. He came to a thick-lipped African, who was standing grinning at the scene. The professor touched him with his unguent, and immediately blackie fell a-striving with the lady, who should walk next the wonderful professor, and the two actually went to blows, to the great amusement of the spectators, who applauded these two feats prodigiously, and hailed their professor as the greatest man in the world. He walked twice the length of the promenade, and certainly every one whom he touched with his ointment followed him, so that if he had been a stranger in the community as I was, there could not have been a doubt of the efficacy of his unguent of attraction. When he came last before the royal stage, and ours, he was encumbered by a crowd of persons following and kneeling to him; apparently they were of all ranks, from the highest to the lowest. He then caused proclamation to be made from a stage, that if any doubted the power of his elixir, he might have it proved on himself without danger or disgrace; a dowager lady defied him, but he soon brought her to her knee with the rest, and no one of the whole begged to be released.

The King and Queen, and all the judges, then declaring themselves satisfied, the professor withdrew, with his motley followers, to undo the charm in secret; after that, he returned in most brilliant and gorgeous array, and was received on the royal stage, amid rending shouts of applause. The King then asked me, if I deemed myself still able to compete with his liege kinsman, Professor Don Felix de Valdez? or if I joined the rest in approval, and yielded the palm to his merits in good fellowship?

I addressed his Majesty with all humility, acknowledging the extent of the professor's powers as very wonderful, provided they were all *real;* but of that there was no proof to me. "If he had been a foreigner, and a stranger, as I am, in this place, and if prejudices had been excited against him," added I, "then I would have viewed this exhibition of his art as highly wonderful; but, as it is, I only look on it as a well-got-up farce."

The professor reddened, and bit his lip in the height of scorn and indignation; and indeed their Majesties and all the nobility seemed offended at my freedom; on which I added, "My exhibition, my liege, shall be a very short one; and I shall at least convince your Majesty, that there is no deceit nor collusion in it." And with that I took a small syringe from my bosom, which I had concealed there for the purpose, as the liquor, to have due effect, must be always warm with the heat of the body of him that sprinkles it; and with that small instrument, I squirted a spray of my elixir on Professor Don Felix's fine head of hair, that hung in wavy locks almost to his waist.

At that moment there were thousands all standing a-gape, eager to witness the effect of this bold appeal. The professor stood up, and looked at me, while the tears stood in his eyes. That was the proudest moment of my life! For about the space of three minutes, his pride seemed warring with his feelings; but the energy and impulse of the latter prevailed, and he came and kneeled at my feet.

"Felix, you dog! what is the meaning of this?" says I. "How dare you go and dress yourself like a grandee of the kingdom, and then come forth and mount the stage in the presence of royalty, knowing, as you do, that you were born to be my slave? Go this instant! doff that gorgeous apparel, and put on my livery, and come and wait here at my heel. And, do you hear, bring my horse properly caparisoned, and one to yourself; for I ride into the country to dinner. Take note of what I order, and attend to it, else I'll baste you to a jelly, and have you distilled into the elixir of attraction. Presumption indeed, to come into my presence in a dress like that!" and with that I lent him two or three hearty blows, and kicked him off the stage.

He ran to obey my orders, and then the admiration so lately expressed was turned into contempt. All the people were struck with awe and astonishment. They could not applaud, for they were struck dumb, and eyed me with terror, as if I had been a divinity. "This exceeds all comprehension," said the judges. "If he had told me that he could have upheaved the Pyrenean mountains from their foundations, I could as well have believed it," said the King. But the Queen was the most perverse of all, for she would not believe it, though she witnessed it; and she declared she never would believe it to be a reality, for I had only thrown glamour in their eyes. "Is it possible," said she, "that the most famous man in Spain, or perhaps in the world, who has hundreds to serve him, and run at his bidding, should all at once, by his own choice, submit to become a slave to an opponent whom he despised, and be buffeted like a dog, without resenting it? No; I'll never believe it is anything but an illusion."

"There is no denying of your victory," said King Charles to me; "for you have humbled your mighty opponent in the dust. You shall dine with me to-night, as we give a great entertainment to the learned of our kingdom, over all of whom you shall be preferred to the highest place. But as Don Felix de Valdez is likewise an invited guest, let me entreat you to disenchant him, that he may be again restored to his place in society."

"I shall do myself the distinguished honour of dining with your exalted and most Catholic Majesty," says I. "But will it be no degradation to your high dignity, for the man who has worn my livery in public, to appear the same day at the table of royalty?"

"This is no common occurrence," answered the King. "Although by one great effort of art, nature has been overpowered, it would be hard that a great man's nature should remain degraded for ever."

"Well, then, I shall not only give him his liberty from my service, but I shall order him from it, and beat him from it. I can do no more to oblige your Majesty at present."

"What! can you not then remove the charm?" said he. "You saw the professor could do that at once."

"A mere trick," said I, "and collusion. If the professor, Don Felix, had been in the least conscious of the power of his liquor, he would at once have attacked and degraded me. It is quite evident. I expected a trial at least, as I am sure all the company did; but I stood secure, and held him and his art at defiance. He is a sheer impostor, and his boasted discovery a cheat."

"Nay, but I have tried the power of his unguent again and again, and proved it," said the Queen. "But, indeed, its effect is of very short duration; therefore, all I request is, that you will give the professor his liberty, and take my word for it, it will soon be accepted."

I again promised that I would; but at the same time I shook my head, as much as to let the Queen know she was not aware of the power of my elixir, and I determined to punish the professor for his insolence to me, and the sound beating I got in the court of his hotel. While we were speaking, up came Don Felix dressed in my plain yellow livery, leading my horse, and mounted on a grand one of his own, that cost two hundred gold ducats, while mine was only a hack, and no very fine animal either.

"How dare you have the impudence to mount my horse, sir?" says I, taking his gold-headed whip from him, and lashing him with it. "Get off instantly, you blundering booby, take your own spavined jade, and ride off where I may never see your face again."

"I beg your pardon, honoured master," said he, humbly; "I will take any horse you please, but I thought this had been mine."

"You thought, sirrah! What right have you to think?" said I, lashing him; "get about your business. I desire no more of your attendance. Here before their Majesties, and all their court and people, I discharge you my service, and dare you, on the penalty of your life, ever to come near me, or offer to do even a menial's turn to me again."

"Pardon me this time," said he; "I'll sooner die than leave you."

"But you shall leave me or do worse," says I, "and therefore get about your business instantly;" and I pushed him through the throng away from me, and lashed him with the whip till he screamed and wept like a lubberly boy.

"You must have some one to ride with you and be your guide," said he; "and why will you not suffer me to do so? You know I cannot leave you."

The King, taking pity on him, sent a livery-man to take his place, and attend me on my little jaunt, at the same time entreating him to desist, and remember who he was. It was all in vain. He fought with the king's servant for the privilege, mounted my hack, and followed me to the villa, about six miles from the city, where I had been engaged to dine. The news had not arrived of my victory when I got there. The lord of the manor was at the exhibition, but not having returned, the ladies were all impatience to learn the result.

"It becomes not me, noble ladies," said I, "to bring the news of my own triumph, which you might very reasonably suspect to be untrue, or over-charged; but you shall witness my power yourselves."

Then they set up eldrich screams in frolic, and begged for the sake of the Virgin that I would not put my skill to the test on any of them, for they had no desire to follow to England even a master of the arts and sciences, and every one assured me personally that she would be a horrid plague to me, and that I had better pause before I made the experiment.

"My dear and noble dames," said I, "there is nothing farther from my intention than to make any of you the objects of fascination. But come all hither," and I threw up the sash of the window—"Come all hither, and satisfy yourselves in the first place, and if more proof is required, it shall not be lacking. See; do you all know that gentleman there?"

"What gentleman? Where is he? I see no gentleman," was the general titter.

"That gentleman who is holding my horse. He on the sorry hack there with yellow livery. You all know him assuredly. That is your great professor, Don Felix Valdez, accounted the most wonderful man in Spain, and by many of you the greatest in the world."

They would not believe it until I called him close up to the door of the chateau, and showed him to them like any wild beast or natural curiosity, and called him by his name. Then they grew frightened, or pretended to be so, at being in the presence of a man of so much power, for they all knew the professor personally; and if one could have believed them, they were like to go into hysterics for fear of fascination. Yet, for all that, I perceived that they were dying for a specimen of my art, and that any of them would rather the experiment should be made on herself than not witness it.

Accordingly, there was a very handsome and engaging brunette of the party, named Donna Rashelli, on whom I could not help sometimes casting an eye, being a little fascinated myself. This was soon perceived by the lively group, and they all gathered round me, and teased me to try the power of my philtre on Rashelli. I asked the lady's consent, on which she answered rather disdainfully that "she *would* be fascinated *indeed* if she followed *me*, and therefore she held me at defiance, provided I did not *touch* her, which she would *not* allow."

Without more ado, I took my tube from my bosom, and squirted a little of the philtre on her left foot shoe—at least I meant it so, though I afterwards perceived that some of it had touched her stocking.

"And now, Donna Rashelli," said I, "you are in for your part in this drama, and you little know what you have authorised." She turned from me in disdain; but it was not long till I beheld the tears gathering in her eyes; she retired hastily to a recess in a window, covered her face with her hands, and wept bitterly. The others tried to comfort her, and laugh her out of her frenzy, but that was of no avail; she broke from them, and, drowned in tears, embraced my knees, requesting in the most fervent terms to be allowed the liberty of following me over the world.

The ladies were all thrown by this into the utmost consternation, and besought me to undo the charm, both for the sake of the young lady herself and her honourable kin; but I had taken my measures, and paid no regard to their entreaties. On the contrary, I made my apology for not being able to dine there, owing to the King's commanding my attendance at the palace, took a hasty leave, mounted my horse, and, with Don Felix at my back, rode away.

I knew all their power could not detain Donna Rashelli, and, riding slowly, I heard the screams of madness and despair as they tried to hold her. She tore their head-dresses and robes in pieces, and fought like a fury, till they were glad to suffer her to go; but they all followed in a group, to overtake and entreat me to restore their friend to liberty.

I forded the stream that swept round the grounds, and waited on the other bank, well knowing what would occur, as a Spanish maiden never crosses even a rivulet without taking off her shoes and stockings. Accordingly she came running to the side of the stream, followed by all the ladies of the chateau, calling to me, and adjuring me to have pity on them. I laughed aloud at their tribulation, saying, I had done nothing but at their joint request, and they must now abide by the consequences. Rashelli threw off her shoes and stockings in a moment, and rushed into the stream, for fear of being detained; but before taking two steps, the charm being removed with her left-foot shoe, she stood still abashed; and so fine a model of blushing and repentant beauty I never beheld, with her raven hair hanging dishevelled far over her waist, her feet and half her limbs of alabaster bathing in the stream, and her cheek overspread with the blush of shame.

"What am I about?" cried she. "Am I mad? or bewitched? or possessed of a demon, to run after a mountebank, that I would order the menials to drive from my door!"

"So you are gone, then, dear Donna Rashelli?" cried I. "Farewell, then, and peace be with you. Shall I not see you again before leaving this country?" but she looked not up, nor deigned to reply. Away she tripped, led by one lady on each hand, bare-footed as she was, till they came to the gravel walk, and then she slipped on her morocco shoes. The moment her left-foot shoe was on, she sprung towards me again, and all the dames after her full cry. It was precisely like a hare hunt, and so comic that even the degraded Don Felix laughed amain at the scene. Again she plunged into the stream, and again she returned, weeping for shame, and this self-same scene was acted seven times over. At length I took compassion on the humbled beauty, and called to her aunt to seize her left-foot shoe, and wash it in the river. She did so; and I, thinking all was then over and safe, rode on my way. But I had not gone three furlongs till the chase again commenced as loud and as violently as ever, and in a short time the lady was again in the stream. I was vexed at this, not knowing what was the matter, and terrified that I might have attached her to me for life; but I besought her friends to keep her from putting on her stocking likewise, till it was washed and fomented as well as her shoe. This they went about with great eagerness, an old dame seizing the stocking, and hiding it in her bosom; and when I saw this I rode quickly away, afraid I would be too late for my engagement with the King.

We had turned the corner of a wood, when again the screams and yells of females reached our ears. "What, in the name of St Nicholas, is this now?" says I.–"I suppose the hunt is up again, sir, but surely our best plan is to ride off and leave them," said Don Felix.–"That will never do," returned I; "I cannot have a lady of rank attending me at the palace, and no power on earth, save iron and chains, can detain her, if one-thousandth part of a drop of my elixir remain about her person." We turned back, and behold there was the old dowager coming waddling along with a haste and agitation not to be described, and all her daughters, nieces, and maidens, after her. She had taken the river at the broadest, shoes and all, and had got so far a-head of her pursuers that she reached me first, and seizing me by the leg, embraced and kissed it, begging and praying all the while for my favour, in the most breathless and grotesque manner ever witnessed. I knew not what to do; not in the least aware how she became affected, till Donna Rashelli called out, "O, the stocking, sir, the stocking!" on which I caused them take it from her altogether and give it to me, and then they went home in peace.

I dined that night with their Majesties, not indeed at the same table, but at the head of the table in the anteroom, from whence I had a full view of them. I was a great and proud man that night, and neither threats nor persuasions could drive the great professor from waiting at the back of my chair, and frequently serving me kneeling. After dinner I had an audience of the Queen, who offered me a galleon laden with gold for the receipt of my divine elixir of love. But I withstood it, representing to her Majesty the great danger of imparting such a secret, for that after it had escaped from my lips, I could no more recall it, and knew not what use might be made of it,–that I accounted myself answerable to my Maker for the abuse of talents bestowed on me, and, in one word, was determined that the secret should go to the grave with me. I was, however, reduced to the necessity of promising her Majesty a part of the pure and sublime elixir ready prepared, taking her solemn promise meanwhile not to divulge it; which I did, and a ready use she had found for it, for in a few days she requested more, and more, and more, till I began to think it was high time for me to leave the country.

Having now got as much money as I wanted, and a great deal more than I knew what to do with, I prepared for leaving Spain, for I was affrighted at being made accountable for the effects produced by the charm in the hands of a capricious woman. Had I yielded to the requests of the young nobles for supplies, I might almost have exhausted the riches of Spain; but as it was, I had got more than my own weight in gold, part of which I forwarded to London, and put the remainder out to interest in Spain, and left Madrid not without fear of being seized and sent to the Inquisition as a necromancer. In place of that, however, the highest honours were bestowed on me, and I was accompanied to the port by numbers of the first people of the realm, and by all the friends of the Professor Don Felix de Valdez. These people had laid a plot to assassinate me, which they would have executed but for fear that the charm would never leave their friend; and as Felix himself discovered it to me, I kept him in bondage till the very day I was about to sail; then I caused his head to be shaved, and washed with a preparation of vinegar, alum, and cinnamon; and he returned to his senses and right feelings once more. But he never could show his face again in the land wherein he had been so much caressed and admired, but changed his name and retired to Peru, where he acquired both fame and respectablility.

## THE COUNTESS

WHEN a man gains great wealth too suddenly and with ease, it is not uncommon for him to throw it away with as little concern as he had anxiety in the gathering of it. This I was aware of, and determined to avoid. On the contrary, I began without loss of time to look about me for a respectable settlement in life; and having, after much inquiry, obtained a list of the unmarried ladies possessing the greatest fortunes in England, I fixed on a young Countess, who was a widow, had an immense fortune, and suited me in every respect. Possessing as I did the divine cordial of love, I had no fears of her ready compliance; so, after providing myself with a suitable equipage, I set off to her residence to court and win her without any loss of time.

On arriving at her mansion about noon, I was rather drily received, having no introduction; for I trusted to my own powers alone. She was shy and reserved, and after a good deal of hanging on, she ventured to invite me to an early dinner, letting me know at the same time that no gentlemen remained there overnight when her brother was not present. Thinks I to myself, my pretty Countess, could I get a quiet squirt at your auburn locks, or any part of your dear self, I should make you not so haughty. I waited my opportunity, and ventured a chance shot as she was going out at the door, aiming at her bushy locks, but owing to a sudden cast of her head, as in disdain, the spray of my powerful elixir of love fell on an embroidered scarf that hung gracefully on her shoulder.

I was now sure of my game, provided she did not throw the scarf aside before I got her properly sprinkled anew, but I had hopes the effect would be too instant and potent for that. I judged right; in three minutes she returned into the drawing-room, and proposed that we two should take a walk in her park before dinner, as she had some curiosities to show me. I acquiesced with pleasure, as may well be supposed. "I have you now, my pretty Countess," thought I; "escape me if it be in your power, and I shall account you more than woman."

This park of hers was an immense field inclosed with a high wall, with a rail on the top. She had some roes in it, one couple of fallow deer, and a herd of kine. This last was the curiosity she wanted to show me; they were all milk-white, nay, as white as snow. They were not of the wild bison breed, but as gentle and tame as lambs—came to her when called by their names, and seemed so fond of being caressed, that several were following and teasing her at the same time. One favourite in particular was so fond, that she became troublesome; and as the lady was every minute becoming fonder of me, she wished to be quit of her. But the beast would not go away. She followed on, humming and rubbing on her mistress with her cheek. Then what does the unlucky being, but, taking her scarf, she struck the cow sharply across the face with it! The tassels of the scarf fastened on the far horn of the cow, and the animal being a little hurt by the stroke, as well as blinded, sprung away, and in one moment the lady lost hold of her scarf. This was death and destruction to me; for the lady was thus bereaved of all her attachment to me in an instant, and what the countess had lost the cow had gained. I therefore pursued the animal with my whole speed, calling her many kind and affectionate names to make her stop. These she did not seem to understand, for stop she would not; but perceiving that she was a little blindfolded with the scarf, I slid quietly forward, and making a great spring, seized the embroidered scarf by the corner. The cow galloped, and I ran and held, determined to have the scarf, though I should tear it all to pieces, for I knew too well that my divine elixir had the effect of rousing animals into boundless rage and madness, so it was little wonder that I held with a desperate grasp. I could not obtain it! All that I effected was to fasten the other horn in it likewise, and away went the cow flaunting through the park like a fine madam in her gold embroidery.

I fled to the Countess as fast as my feet could carry me, and begged her, for Heaven's sake, to fly with me, for our lives were at stake. She could not understand this; and moreover, she, that a minute or two before had been clinging to me with such fondness, that I was almost ashamed, would not now suffer me to come nigh or touch her. There was no time to parley, so I left her to shift for herself, and fled with all my might towards the gate at which we entered, knowing of no other point of egress. Time was it; for the creature instantly became furious, and came after me at full speed, bellowing like some agonized fiend escaped from the infernal regions. The herd was roused by the outrageous sounds, and followed in the same direction, every one roaring louder and faster than another, apparently for company's sake; but, far a-head of them all, the cow came with the embroidered scarf flying over her shoulders, hanging out her tongue and bellowing, and gaining every minute on me. Next her in order came a stately milk-white bull, tall as a hunting steed, and shapely as a deer. My heart became chill with horror; for of all things on this earth, I stood in the most mortal terror of a bull. I saw, however, that I would gain the wicket before I was overtaken; and, in the brightness of hope, I looked back to see what was become of the Countess. She had fallen down on a rising ground in a convulsion of laughter! This nettled me exceedingly; however, I gained the gate; but, O misery and despair! it was fast locked, the Countess having the pass-key. To clear the wall was out of my power in such a dilemma as I then was, so I had nothing left for it but swiftness of foot. Often had I valued myself on that qualification, but little expected ever to have so much need of it. So I ran and ran, pursued by twenty milk-white kine and a bull, all bellowing like as many infernal spirits. Never was there such another hunt! I tried to make the Countess for shelter, thinking she might be able, by her voice, to stay them, or, at all events, she would tell me how I could escape from their fury. But the drove having all got between her and me, I could not effect it, and was obliged to run at random, which I continued to do, straining with all my might, but now found that my breath was nigh gone, and the terrible hunt drawing to a crisis.

What was to be done? Life was sweet, but expedients there were none. There were no trees in the park save young ones, dropped down, as it were, here and there, and palings round them, to prevent the cattle destroying them. The only one that I could perceive was a tall fir, I suppose of the larch species, which seemed calculated to afford a little shelter in a desperate case; so towards that I ran with a last effort. There was a triangular paling around it, and setting my foot on that, I flew to the branches, clomb like a cat, and soon vanished among its foliage and tresses.

Then did I call aloud to the Countess for assistance, imploring her to raise the country for my rescue; but all that she did, was to come towards me herself, slowly and with lagging pace, for she was feeble with laughing; and when she did come, they were all so infuriated that they would not once regard her.

"What is the matter with my cattle, sir?" cried she. "They are surely bewitched."

"I think they are bedeviled, and that is worse, madam," returned I. "But, for Heaven's sake, try to regain the scarf. It is the scarf which is the cause of all this uproar."

"What is in the scarf?" said she. "It can have no effect in raising this deadly enmity against you, if all is as it *should be*, which I now begin to suspect, from some strange diversity of feelings I have had."

"It is merely on account of the gold that is on it, madam," said I. "You cannot imagine how mad the sight of gold, that pest of the earth, puts some animals; and it was the effort I made to get it from the animal that has excited in her so much fury against me."

"That is most strange indeed!" exclaimed she. "Then the animal shall keep it for me, for I would not for half my fortune that these favourites should be driven to become my persecutors."

She now called the cattle by their names, and some of them left me, for it was evident that, save the charmed animal, the rest of the herd were only running for company or diversion's sake. Still their looks were exceedingly wild and unstable, and the one that wore the anointed shawl, named fair Margaret, continued foaming mad, and would do nothing but stand and bellow, toss her adorned head, and look up to the tree. I would have given ten thousand pounds to have had a hold of that vile embroidered scarf, but to effect it, and retain my life, at that time was impracticable.

And now a scene ensued, which, for horror to me could not be equalled, although, to any common beholder, it would have appeared nothing. The bull perceiving one of his favourite mates thus distempered, showed a great deal of concern about her; he went round her, and round her, and perceiving the flaunting thing on her head and shoulders, he seemed to entertain some kind of idea that it was the cause of this unwonted and obstreperous noise. He tried to fling it off with his horns, I know not how oft, but so awkwardly and clumsily, that he could not. What think you he then did? He actually seized the scarf with his great mouth, tore it off, and in a few seconds swallowed it every thread!

What was I to do now? Here was a new enemy, and one ten times more formidable, who had swallowed up the elixir, and whom, therefore, it was impossible ever to discharm; who, I knew, would pursue me to the death, even though at the distance of fifty miles. I was in the most dreadful agony of terror imaginable, as well I might, for the cow went away shaking her ears as if happily quit of a tormentor, and the bull instantly began a-tearing up the earth with hoof and horn, and the late bellowings of the cow were, to his, like the howl of a beagle to the roar of a lion. They made the very earth to quake; while distant woods, and walls, and the very skies, returned the astounding echoes. He went round the tree, and round the tree, digging graves on each side of it, and his fury still increasing, he broke through the paling as if it had been a spider's web, and setting his head to the tree, pushed with all his mighty force, doubled by supernatural rage. The tree yielded like a bulrush, until I was merely hanging by the stem; still I durst not quit my hold, having no other resource, but I uttered some piercing cries of desperation as I saw the Countess speeding away. The tree was young and elastic, and always as the infuriated animal withdrew his force for a new attack, it sprung up to its original slender and stately form, and then down it went again; so that there was I swinging between heaven and earth, expecting every moment to be my last, and if he had not, in his mad efforts, wheeled round to the contrary side, I might have been swinging there to this day. When he changed sides, the fibres of the tree weakened, and then down I came to the earth, and he made at me full drive; it was in vain that I called to him to keep off, and bullied him, and pretended to hunt dogs on him; on he came, and plunged his horns into the foliage; the cows did the same for company's sake, and, I'm sure, never was there a poor soul so completely mobbed by a vulgar herd. Still the tree had as much strength left as to heave me gently above their reach, and no more, and I now began to lose all power through terror and despair, and merely held my gripe instinctively, as a drowning man would hold by a rush. The next push the tree got I was again laid flat, and again the bull dashed his horns into the foliage, and through that into the earth. How I escaped I scarce can tell, but I did escape through amongst the feet of the cows.

At first I stole away like a hare from a cover, and could not help admiring the absurdity of the cows, that continued tossing and tearing the tree with their horns, as if determined not to leave a stiver of it; whilst the bull continued grovelling with his horns, down through the branches and into the ground. Heavens! with what velocity I clove the wind! I have fled from battle–I have fled from the face of the lions of Asia, the dragons of Africa, and the snakes of America– I have fled before the Indians with their scalping knives; but never in my life was I enabled to run with such speed as I did from this infuriated monster.

He was now coming full speed after me, as I knew he would; but I had got a good way a-head, and, I assure you, was losing no time, and as I was following a small beaten track, I came to a stile over the wall. I never was so thankful for anything since I was born! It was a crooked stone stair, with angles to hinder animals from passing, and a locked door on the top, about the height of an ordinary man. I easily surmounted this, by getting hold of the iron spikes on the top; and now, being clear of my adversary, I set my head over the door and looked him in the face, mocking and provoking him all that I could, for I had no other means of retaliation. I never beheld a more hideous picture of rage! He was foaming at the mouth, and rather belching than bellowing; his tail was writhing in the air like a serpent, and his eyes burning like small globes of bright flame. He grew so enraged at length, that he rushed up the stone stair, and the frame-work at the angles began to crash before him. Thinks I to myself, "Friend, I do not covet such a close vicinity with you; so, with your leave, I'll keep a due distance;" and then descending to the high road, I again began to speed away, though rather leisurely, knowing that he could not possibly get over the iron-railed wall.

There was now a close hedge on every side of me, about eight or ten feet high, and as a man who has been in great jeopardy naturally looks about him for some safe retreat in case of an emergency, so I continued jogging on and looking for such, but perceived none; when, hearing a great noise far behind me, I looked back and saw the irresistible monster coming tumbling from the wall, bringing gates, bars, and railing, all before him. He fell with a tremendous crash, and I had great hopes his neck was broken, for at first he tried to rise, and could not; but, to my dismay, he was soon again on the chase, and making ground on me faster than ever. He came close on me at last, and finally, I had no other shift but to throw off my fine coat, turn round to await him, and fling it over his horns and eyes.

This not only marred him, but detained him long, wreaking his vengeance on the coat, which he tore all to pieces with his feet and horns, taking it for a part of me. By this time, I had reached a willow-tree in the hedge, the twigs of which hung down within reach. I seized on two or three of those, wrung them together like a rope, and by the assistance of that, swung myself over the hedge. Still I slackened not my pace, convinced that the devil was in the beast, and that nothing but blood would allay his fury. Accordingly, it was not long till I saw him plunging in the hedge, and through it he came.

I now perceived a fine sheet of water on my left, about a mile broad, I knew not whether a lake or river, never having been in those bounds before; towards that I made with all my remaining energy, which was not great. I cleared many common stone-walls in my course, but these proved no obstacles to my pursuer, and before I reached the lake, he came so close upon me, that I was obliged to fling my hat in his face, and as he fortunately took that for my head, it served him a good while to crush it in pieces, so that I made to the lake, and plunged in. At the very first, I dived and swam under water as long as I could keep my breath, assured that my enemy would lose all traces of me then; but when I came to the surface, I found him puffing within two yards of me. I was in such horror, that I knew not what to do, for I found he could swim twice as fast as me, so I dived again, but my breath being gone, I could not remain below, and whenever I came to the surface, there was he.

If I had had the smallest reasoning faculty left, or had once entertained a thought of resistance, I might easily have known that I was now perfectly safe. The beast could not harm me. Whenever he made a push at me, his head went below the water, which confounded him. Seeing this to be the case, I took courage, seized him by the tail, clomb upon his back, and then rode in perfect safety.

I never got a more complete and satisfactory revenge of an enemy, not even over the Spanish professor, and that was complete enough; but here I had nothing to do but to sit exulting on the monster's back, while he kept wallowing and struggling in the waves. I then took my pen-knife, and stabbed him deliberately over the whole body, letting out his heart's blood. He took this very much amiss, but he had now got enough of blood around him, and began to calm himself. I however kept my seat, to make all sure, till his head sunk below the water, while his huge hinder parts turned straight upmost, and I left him floating away like a huge buoy that had lost its anchor.

------

"Now, Doctor, gin a' tales be true, yours is nae lee, that is certain. But I want some explanations. It's a grand story, but I want to take the consequences alang wi' me. What did the Queen o' Spain wi' a' the ointment you left wi' her? I'm thinking there wad be some strange scenes about that Court for a while."

"Why, Margaret, to say the truth, the elixir was not used in such a way as might have been expected. The truth appeared afterwards to have been this: The King had at that time resolved on that ruinous, and then very unpopular war, about what was called the Family Compact; and finding that the clergy, and a part of the principal nobility, were in opposition to it, and that without their concurrence the war could not be prosecuted with any effect, the Queen took this very politic method of purchasing plenty of my divine elixir of attachment, and giving them all a touch of it every one. The effect was, of course, instant, potent, and notorious; and it is a curious and incontestable fact, that the effects of that sprinkling have continued the mania of attachment among that class of Spain unto this day."

"And how came you on wi' your grand Countess? Ye wad be a bonny figure gaun hame again to her place half-naked, and like a droukit craw, wi' the life of her favourite animal to answer for."

"That is rather a painful subject, Margaret—rather a painful subject. I never saw her again! I had lost my coat and hat. I had lost all my money, which was in notes, in swimming and diving. I had lost my carriage and horses, and I had lost my good name, which was worst of all; for from that day forth, I was branded and shunned as a necromancer. The abrupt and extraordinary changes in the lady's sentiments had not escaped her own notice, while the distraction of the animals on the transference of the enchanted scarf to them, confirmed her worst suspicions, that I was a dealer in unlawful arts, and come to gain possession of herself and fortune, by the most infamous measures; and as I did not choose to come to an explanation with her on that subject, I escaped as quietly from the district as possible.

"It surely can be no sin to dive into the hidden mysteries of nature, particularly those of plants and flowers. Why then have I been punished, as never pharmacopolist was since the creation; can you tell me that, Margaret?"

"Indeed, can I—weel enough—Doctor. Other men have studied qualities o' yirbs to assist nature, but ye have done it only to pervert nature, an' I hope you hae read your sin in your punishment."

"The very sentiment that my heart has whispered to me a thousand times! It indeed occurred to me, whilst skulking about on my escape after the adventure with the Countess; but it was not until farther and still more bitter experience of the dangerous effects of my secret, that I could bring myself to destroy the maddening liquid. It had taken years of anxiety and labour to perfect a mixture, from which I anticipated the most beneficial results. The consequences which it drew upon me, although, at first, they promised to be all I could wish, proved in the end every way annoying, and often wellnigh fatal, and I carefully consumed with fire every drop of the potion, and every scrap of writing, in which the progress of the discovery had been noted. I cannot, myself, forget the painful and tedious steps by which it was obtained. And even after all the disasters to which it has subjected me—after the miserable wreck of all my high-pitched ambition, I cannot but feel a pride in the consciousness that I carry with me the knowledge of a secret never before possessed by mortal man, which no one shall learn from me, and which it is all but certain that none after me will have perseverance enough, or genius, to arrive at!"

The learned Doctor usually wound up the history of an adventure with a sonorous conclusion like the above, the high-wrought theatrical tone of which, as it was incomprehensible to his hearers, always produced a wonderful effect. Looking upon the gaunt form of the sage, I was penetrated with immeasurable reverence, and though the fascination of his marvellous stories kept me listening with eager curiosity while they lasted, I always retired shortly after he ceased speaking, not being able to endure the august presence of so wise a personage as he appeared to me to be.

Many of his relations were still more marvellous than those I have preserved; but these are sufficient for a specimen, and it would be idle to pursue the Doctor's hallucinations farther. All I can say about these adventures of his is, that when I heard them first, I received them as strictly true; my mother believed them most implicitly, and the Doctor related them, as if he had believed in the truth of them himself. But there were disputes every day between my mother and him about the invention of the charm, the former always maintaining that it was known to the chiefs of the gipsy tribes for centuries by-gone; and as proofs of her position, cited Johnie Faa's seduction of the Earl of Cassillis's lady, so well known in Lowland song, and Hector Kennedy's seduction of three brides, all of high quality, by merely touching the palms of their hands, after which no power could prevent any of them from following him. She likewise told a very affecting story of an exceedingly beautiful girl, named Sophy Sloan, who left Kirkhope, and followed the gipsies, though she had never exchanged a word with one of them. Her father and uncle followed, and found her with them in an old kiln on the water of Milk. Her head was wounded, bloody, and tied up with a napkin. They had pawned all her good clothes, and covered her with rags, and though weeping with grief and despair, yet she refused to leave them. The man to whom she was attached had never asked her to go with him; he even threatened her with death if she would not return with her father, but she continued obstinate, and was not suffered long to outlive her infatuation and disgrace. This story *was* a fact; yet the Doctor held all these instances in utter contempt, and maintained his prerogative, as the sole and original inventor of THE ELIXIR OF LOVE.

There was not a doubt that the Doctor was skulking, and in terror of being apprehended for some misdemeanour, all the time he was at Ettrick Manse, and never one of us had a doubt that it was on account of some enchantment. But I had reason to conclude, long afterwards, that his seclusion then, and all the latter part of his life, was owing to an unfortunate and fatal experiment in pharmacy, which deprived society of a number of valuable lives. The circumstances are related in volume third of Eustace's *Pharmacopœia*, and it will there be seen that the description of the delinquent suits exactly with that of THE MARVELLOUS DOCTOR.

ALTRIVE LAKE
*August* 11, 1827.

# Ane Pastorale of the Rocke
## *Maide be Maister Hougge*

THERE wals ane Egil satte on a hille,
Quhen alle the voycis of hevin were stille;
The whew of the clyffe, the yowle of the caive,
The soughe of the woode, and the whushe of the waive;
That solemme disembodyit chyme,　　　　　　　5
That ayreal symphonye sublyme,
Whiche semis, to the eire of the shepherde lone,

A thousande voycis alle in one—
It semit to haif sunke in its deipe recesse,
To slumber in awsome sylentnesse.            10
   Now this Egil he satte on his airye byrthe,
Quhare he hardlye semit ane being of yirthe;
For als he lokit from his yermit riven,
His greye heide movit in the vaile of hevin,
In that pale shroude of grizelye hewe               15
That joynis the yirthe with the valis of blewe,
And myndis mee ofte of the curtaine grimme,
That borelesse shade, so deidlye dimme,
Which nefer wals percit be mortal eye,
And shadowis Tyme from Eternitye.             20
   O but that Egil he wals als proude,
Als he loked from the frynge of his amber cloude,
Als euir wals Czar or crownyt Khanne,
Or Turke in the myddis of his dyvanne;
For hee geeyt his cheike with soche disdaine,      25
Als he turnit his one eye to the plaine,
And glancit with the oder, throughe portale dunne,
Unblynked, upon the nonedaye sone;
And then he shoke his fedderis graye,
And bore his croune in soche ane waye,         30
Als if he helde in high disdaine
The valleys, the shore, and the soundyng maine;
He semyt all naiture to deryde,
And lycked his hornye lippis in pryde,
Quhille his yellow eye hald soche ane lychte,       35
That the golde of Ophir wals never so brychte;
It euin crepit backe belowe the skynne,
Or sanke his haughtye brayne wythinne;
Quhille his cruked beke wolde the hefinis mocke,
So very proude wals this kyng of the rocke.       40
   And quharefore all this frowardnesse?
Ane gentil daime alone maye guesse,
Soche as have felit, for pompous thyngis,
Envye, with all its thousande styngis;
Or als ane kyng with pride elaite,              45
Quhen his first mynistere of staite,
Ane drone the comberance of the byke,
Turnis rounde him's taille lyke saucye tyke,
And sayis, "Sir kyng, this is not fitte;

You haif lost your jodgmente and your wytte." 50
Als that graite kyng withoute dispute
Wolde holde his purpose resolute,
With eye majestick, calme, and proude,
So loked this yellper of the cloude.
    And quharefore all? No more than this— 55
Straighte downe belowe him on ane dysse,
Quhare grewe ane crabbed crompilit thorne,
There had there satte since brikke of morne
Ane glossy Raven, brychte of blee,
Als busye als ane burde colde bee, 60
Pookyng his fedderis sleike and blewe,
Semyng theire brychtnesse to renewe,
Als with his bigge unshaiplye bille
He combit them over with gode wille;
And euery flapper on his tre, 65
And glymmer of his pawkye ee,
Showit that he mockit with mumpis and mumis,
Proude Maister Egillis motelye plumis.
    The Egil had sore dispyte that daye,
But yet ane worde he scornit to saye, 70
But satte with indignatione fulle,
Movyng his heide lyke graite Mogulle;
Quhille Corbye, who percevit his takyng,
Out of mere funne and myschefe makyng,
Turnit up his darke and wycked loke, 75
And sayit, with leire no burde colde broke:
"How faris goode maister Egil nowe,
Perchit on Gilborachis barren browe?
And how is the godewyffe on the strawe?
I hope soche daye sho neuir sawe, 80
Of inwarde joyis so swete and ryffe,
And collapis of yong trembilyng lyffe!"
    The Egil laughit ane laughe so loude,
It percit the gorget of the cloude,
Broke all its muffis and grande myneviris, 85
And shoke its storyit pylis to shyviris;
But it did not onlye maike ane rente
Alangis the frynge of the fyrmamente,
But it enterit oft als it wente bye
The littil borelis of the skye; 90
Whiche maide the ladye angelis skreime,

And sterted sanctis oute of theyre dreime;
That splendyd dreime consaivit so welle,
On whiche our docter lofis to dwelle—
It is ane awful dreime of blisse,                                    95
Ane bathe of endlesse happynesse,
Steiped in delychtis up to the eiris,
Withoute all future hopis or feris,
Enoughe to maike ane verye drone
Bever and blenche to thynke upon.                                    100
    But then this Egillis yelloche broke
From caive to caive, from rocke to rocke,
Tille all arounde Gilborachis steipe
From yowlyng woode and yauping deipe,
Ane thousande voycis issuit forth,                                   105
Not lyke the voycis of this earthe,
But nycheris of ane tongueless brode,
Ane gorbelyng brawlyng broderhode
Of spyritis of the rocke and lynne,
That sojournit euirmore therynne.                                    110
    The Corbye wals fulle sore astounded,
And his capacious mynde confounded;
For not ane worde, for all his braye,
Did this cursit Egil deign to saye.
The Corbye satte demore and gruffe,                                  115
And raisit his fedderis lyke ane ruffe,
His yukit stirlis to relieve,
He dychte his nebbe upon his sleive,
While the brychte twynkiling of his eine,
The lychtening chainge from darke to greine,                        120
Stille glemyng, depenyng, and renewyng,
Showit that some myschiefe wals a-brewyng.
    "Goode maister Egil, quhatis the funne?
Tell us the sport, that we may wonne
Our shaire of this confounded cackle,                                125
This tinckell of our tabernacle.
Haif you no feris for youre godewyffe,
That winsome swetener of your lyffe,
That soche ane yelloch o'er hir bedde
Maye haif effectis of dole and dredde,                              130
Maye reife hir of hir tender wyttis,
Or throwe hir into moderis fyttis?
Or, quhat is worse than swairf or swone,

Produce hir sootye sonnis ower sone?
Haif some respeck, if not for myne, 135
For that most charmyng lofe of thyne,
In hir swete bedde so sweitlye bounded
With bainstelis and with bonis surrounded,
With morefulis feite and curlewe trammis,
And hedis and harrigillis of lammis, 140
And broket hofis of high degre,–
Sothe, sho is ane comelye sychte to se!
Her bearded beke and haffetis drye,
Hir towzye tap and yellowe eye,
Hir hairye houghis and dingye breste, 145
The verye hewis of raffe and reiste.
And then her size! ane shaime to telle!
Ane wyffe far bygger nor yourselle,
Moste altogedder be confeste
Graite comforte to ane Egillis breste!" 150
    "Yelle," quoth the Egil, with ane neighe,
That quashit the growlyng of the se,
And maide the cluddis of hefen to frylle,
Als dancyng of ane Frenche quadrylle;
Then als ane wylde and wycked meide, 155
But grand expedyente in ane neide,
To eize his heart with raige that burnit,
Outower the clyffe his taille he turnit,
And pourit adowne its breste sublyme
Ane cataracke of liquide lyme, 160
That dashit the Corbye from his throne,
Blynded his eyne, and sent him prone,
Head-foremoste, croakyng with despyte,
Dyit lyke ane pyatte blacke and whyte.
    Then joynit the Egillis in ane hewe, 165
Whiche maide the echois swell anewe,
Far far abroade incontinente,
On billowis of the fyrmamente,
Als all the spyritis of the glennis
Had wakenit from theyre mouldye dennis, 170
And reyne the stamocke of the yirthe,
With one confoundit skreide of myrthe.
    This mockryffe laugh was worse than badde,–
It almoste pat the Corbye madde;
Downe from the clyffe he heidlong bore, 175

And ay he cursit and he swore,
But sone he washit his soylit wyng,
In greine Gilborachis silver spring;
Then did he shaike his fedderis blacke,
And rousit them on his plookye backe,                          180
Shoke his grate nebbe his ruffe to drye,
And turnit his cheike up to the skye,
And ay, with euerye braithe he drewe,
He cursit the Egil blacke and blewe;
And als he satte upon that stone,                              185
Drying his fedderis in the sone,
Quhare no proude sovraine heard nor sawe,
Thus moralyzit the Corbye Crawe:
"Goode Lorde, how lowe the grait are hurlit!
This is ane baisse and wycked worlde,                          190
Quhare trothe and wysdome are owerrunne,
And plaice be dirtye favour wonne;
By lowe and skavenjar deceite,
Is overpowrit the goode and graite;
Tossit from on highe, he fallis forlorne,                      195
And with the skaithe gettis all the skorne.
How harde it is the wyse and graite
Shoulde thus be tombelit from the staite;
Knockit from the presynkis of the throne,
To be debaisset and bloterit on,                               200
Ane skorne and laughyng stocke indeide,
To baisse-born Kytis risen in his steide!
    "Ill speide the lucke! Quhate'er the coste,
The Raven yet shalle reulle the roste!
Shall it be toulde, shall it be saide,                         205
In fair Gilborachis greine-wode glaide,
That e'er ane Howlet and ane Haake,
Ane Keystrel and ane Kittywaake,
Ane gabbillying Gose and fawnyng Mewe,
Ane Cooternebbe and damit Curlewe,                             210
Sholde chatteryng rounde our monark stande,
And guide the counsilis of the lande?
Forbydde it, faite, and foraigne fee!
Forbydde it, proude nobylitye,
Ye gallant Rokis, and Gleddis, and Gorbyis,                    215
And all the blode of all the Corbyis!
    "I'll skaille the ayre withoutten feiris,

And ryng ane solo in his eiris,
Of mysdemainners and myschance,
Shall gar him loke two gaites at once!                    220
By the blacke cloude that holdis in store
The flickering flaime and thonderis rore,
(The Corbyis terror and dismaye,)
I swear to share the sovraigne swaye,
Ellis shalle myne comelye maite and mee                   225
Synke deide upon the sounding se!"
    With that, quha sholde there come in haiste,
And face the Corbye breste to breste,
But his dark daime of proude degre—
The ladye of the lonelye tre.                             230
And thus she spoke hir counsellis deipe,—
Whiche wyffis are ne'er disposit to keipe,
For theye moste spekyng bee and jeering,
An it were but for the pryde of heiring:
"Thou blousteryng, bloterit barleyfummil,                235
Quhy sittis thou there to groulle and grummil,
Als if thyne othis and bostyngis graite
Colde maike the mynistere of staite,
Or fors the lordlye Egillis pryde
To plaice the by his sovraigne syde?                      240
Swith steike thyne graite and gorbellyng gabbe,
Thou droukit, droyten, dryvellyng swabbe,
And use gode language to thyne kyng;
Beatte up the ayre on dauntlesse wyng,
And place the on thyne regal tre,                         245
And seye some straine of mynstrelsye,
Some song of lofe, or song of leire,
That may affect thyne sovraigne's eire.
Go laude thine mystresse to the skye,
That will command ane meike replye."                      250
    The Corbye lokit asklente the whyle,
Then shoke his heide and smylit ane smyle.
"Myne mystresse! That is ane thaime indeide
Which neuir wolde haif rechit myne heide.
Daime, I shoulde taike youre kindlye proffer,             255
But quhat the deuil colde I saye of hir,
Saif that she is ane wycked hagge,
Of carrione sluttis the very slagge;
Ane brymstone brangler, ferce and felle,

Als doure as dethe, and black as helle? 260
If that will fytte I'll sing ane song,
Shall bee als snappie as it is long."
    "Soche language to thyne better hauffe
Bespeekis thee but ane menselesse cauffe,
Ane cowarde and ane baughlesse bummil, 265
Ane cockilit and ane barleyfummil.
Thou bullit-heedit, burlye beiste,
Speike but soche oder worde in jeste,
And I shall teche the quhom to laugh at;
Ill pycke the eyne out of thyne haffat, 270
And set ane fyer unto thyne taille,
In mydis of thonder and of haille!
    "Swith, since thou'lt nouther saye nor syng,
To reconcyle us with oure kyng,
Go sytte the eggis and breide the yongue, 275
Quhill I assaye, with flatteryng tongue,
Favor to winne by mynstrelsye,
And bryng the Egil to his kne;
'Twill conjure up some senis of myrthe,
And raise our soulis abone the yirthe, 280
Bryng backe theyre youthfulle deidis to mynd,
And mounte them on the mornyng wynde."
    The Corbye, who had hearit with dreidde
Of pycking the eyne out of his heidde,
And forssing him, withouten baille, 285
By byrnyng fyer set to him's taille,
Into the myddis of murmuris loude
And bellowyngis of the thonder cloude,
With boltis of terror byzzing sheine,
And spatteryng brymstone in his eyne, 290
Evin though the yocke his spyrit gallit,
Yet found his very herte appallit;
And demit it better to suckumm,
Lyke odir husbandis, and syng dumm;
Or brykke ane joke als beste might bee, 295
On sadde and sore necessitye.
    "Swith, for the jockis sake, I sobmytte
Ane while upon the eggis to sytte.
But quhat, in name of him that shroudis
The rairyng thunder in the cloudis, 300
And blends the forwarde with the paste,

Will this madde worild come tille at laste?
To heire ane wyffe set up her faice
To praise hir beautie, wytte, and graice,
Whiche well sho knowis, and moste allowe,                                    305
None oder in the worlde wolde doo,
Is soche ane breche of common sense,
Soche bare and brazen impudence,
Als nevir braifit cremationis marke
Synce my old gutchere left the arke.                                          310
    "Och, but ane wyffis ane blousterous craiture,
The very yooldaye blare of nature;
This houre in smylis and dymplis flairying,
The neiste in stormis and tempestis rairyng,
The saime to maiden meike and gaye                                           315
Als ferce Dezember is to Maye.
Well will it sute soche daime austere
To be hir owne grande trumpetere,
Whyche wycked wyffis too oft haif beine,
To heire the praise for whiche theye griene.                                 320
    "I wolde gif all the fedderis blacke
That growe upon myne boordlye backe,
That maister Egil sholde descrye,
With his unbleste and topaz eye,
This maisterpece of femaile trikkis,                                         325
Ane Corbyis wyffe weiryng the brykkis,
Ryngyng hir praises lyke ane belle,
And alle her lofe unto herselle;
Quhat solaisse to his herte 'twill be,
For he is wyffepeckit wofullye!                                              330
But, mystresse myne, for all your granne,
And all your haiste to be goodemanne,
If maister Egil fyndis the chete,
Lorde, quhat ane downcome wee shall gete!"
    But with ane croke of proude disdaine,                                   335
Ane floryshe and ane jybe profaine,
Yearnyng for lawlesse ryvalrye,
Mounted in ayre the darke ladye,
And toke hir sate in puffyng pryde
Neire by the Egillis lordlye syde;                                           340
And thus byganne in tonefulle croke,
This first grand "Pastorale of the Rocke."

## THE RAVENIS SONGE

"Quhat burde, that sailis the waif or skye,
Can boste of soche ane maite als I?—
In all hir virtuis so compleite,             345
So kynde, so comelye, and so sweite,
So swyfte the mornyngis raye to ryng,
So proude of breste and bold of wyng,
So cleire of eye—for eye so brychte
Ne'er percit the darkness nor the lychte,      350
Or threwe the glance, at morne or even,
From heven to yirthe, from yirthe to heven;
Of all the daimis of ayre, gif me
Myne ladye of the lonelye tre.
   "I maide myne choyce at Ravenis waike,     355
On mairgin of the Baykel lake,
Quhare I had flowne with amorous speide,
For daime of Caledonyais breide;
For welle I knowit that then there were
Ane thousande vyrgin Corbyis there,        360
All bredde in stormye clyffis betweine
Ben-hope, Ben-alder, and Loch-skeine,
And banyshit there ane aige to messe,
For feire of over corbyousnesse,
The reine-deiris flankis to howke supine,     365
To dabbe out yongue Syberianis eine,
Kydnappe the omal and the eile,
Feiste on the Baykelis gorgeous seile,
And ower the sorges of the se
Bewaile theyre darke vyrginitye.          370
   "There did I take myne aumorouse flychte,
Outower the cloudis by daye and nychte,
And to ane clyffe of granyte graye
Fulle cunnynglye I toke myne waye;
And there I sat with pantyng breste,        375
Untille the daye rose in the eiste,
That, mirrorit in that glassye waife,
The maidenis formis I mychte persaife,
And watche withynne the wateris blewe
Theyre shaiplye bosomis als they flewe;     380
For hee wolde bee of wysedom slacke
Qhua wailit his mystresse be the backe.

"Foule fall the wychte, devoyde of graice,
Quha fallis in lofe als faice to faice,
Quhare all is mymmis and myrgeons maide,     385
The maydenis false and airtfulle traide,
Maide up of tryckis I shun to telle,
Enoughe to cheite the deuil himselle!
No, no—if you the trothe wolde knowe,
Go watch theyre shadowis them belowe,     390
And farre wythinne the wateris brychte,
You will se the comelye daimis arychte,
Joste als theye are from naturis hande,
With graicefulle eise at theyre commande,
Theyre shaiplye shankis and bosomis faire,     395
Theyre fedderis floatyng in the ayre,
And strengthe of jointis belowe the wyng,
The vyrgin Ravenis master stryng.
    "Och, how myne herte begoude to jompe,
And on myne fedderye breste playe dompe,     400
Quhen my sweite daime wente soryng over,
And ower myne heide begoude to hover
The mofementis of hir comelye breste,
And molde that colde not be expressit,
So roundit for the love-sycke sighe,     405
So sharpe to stryke, so bold to flye!
The eye-beime of virgynitye,
And mysticke sychtis wythinne the se,
More than enoughe I founde, in sadnesse,
To fyer ane Corbyis breste with madnesse."     410

    At this pairte of the Ravenis song,
The Egil shoke with passionis strong;
He stretchit his yellow legge behynde,
Spredde his brode fedderis on the wynde,
And with ane wycked aumorous eye,     415
He lycked his lippis and sighed ane syghe.
The Corbye hoped to wynne the daye,
And thus wente on hir heinous laye:—

    "Och, lofe is ane moste potente thyng
Beyonde the mychte of burde to syng;     420
The Egillis lofis ane stounde of pryde,
Ane tyrantis swaye ower cryngyng bride;

The lofe of manne, if I heire trewe,
Hathe in it tinctis of vyleste hewe,
Ane selfysh, sordyd policye,                                    425
Ane shaime to heire, and wors to se;
But all the glowyng passionis giuen
To burde or beiste belowe the heuin,
For ardente, pure, and ferse esteime,
The Ravenis lofis the paradeigm.                                430
    "Myne very herte wals laide in steipe
With this faire visione of the deipe.
I lofit so moche, I lofit more
Nor euir Corbye did before.
I wooit hir on the rowntre greine,                              435
Als kyng behofit to woo ane queine,
With eye of lambe, and herte of deire,
And kidneye of ane Tartar steire;
And after feiste that scairse wolde cloye,
Sesonit with lofe and fooryous joye,                            440
With eiris that byrnit als in ane flaime,
I hearit this anser from myne daime:
    "'Braif maister Corbye, coulde I roame,
Ower Scotlandis hillis, myne naitif home,
And there the flowre of Ravenis reigne,                         445
Hosbande lyke the I wolde disdaine;
But sothe to saye, I dredde to se
The marche of paile virgynitye;
It is so baisse to sytte and brode
On old and moustenit maydenhoode—                               450
The laste graite dredde of femailis breste,
From Egillis to the Howlettis neste;
And often I can eithlye se,
From clyffe of cloude and top of tre,
That this harde swaye of vyrgin thralle,                        455
The wemyng beare the worste of alle.
So, to elude this blastyng skaithe,
This issue dredded more than dethe,
I hold you at youre proffer graite,
And take you for myne wynsum maite.                             460
    "'Now shalle I kno that staite of wyffe,
Whiche I haif grenit for all myne lyffe,
That staite of paine and blisse unnaimit,
For whiche the female herte is fraimit.

And O I eithlye can divyne                                                    465
Quhat disappoyntmente shall be myne;
Alaike, quhare spryngis the joye unsung
Of sytting eggis and fedyng yongue,
Of gadderyng byrnis from daille and downe,
And beryng tauntis from crabbed lowne?                                         470
For all that I can heire or se,
This ernyng is ane mysterye,
Ane thyng implanted in oure fraime,
At somethyng forwarde still to aime,
Ane pressure urgyng burde and manne                                            475
To bee immortal if they canne.
    "'Of mankyndis faithe 'tis harde to saye;
That theye haif soulis that fende for aye,
Is somethyng derke; but this I kenne,
That there be gostis als welle als menne.                                      480
Yet this disputed bee can never,
The Corbyis chaunce to live for ever
Moste onlie bee in flesche and blode,
By living in theyre comelye brode;
Thus maye wee fende, by rocke and fyrthe,                                       485
Quhille there is flesche upon the yerthe;
And after soche unhallowit daye,
Live theye for mee quha will, quha maye.–
'Tis this that maikis me yielde myne lyffe
Unto the shekilis of ane wyffe.'                                                490
    "Rejoicit to fynde myne comelye deire
Wals soche ane graite philosophere,
I joynit with hir myne harte and hande,
And brochte hir home to fayre Scotland,
Plaicyng hir in Gilborachis glaide,                                            495
To be hir sovraignis waityng maide,
And mystresse, too, if hee sholde deime
Soche lofe ane Egil mochte beseime.
    "This I shalle saye, in language plaine,–
And flattery is myne grande dysdaine,–                                         500
That soche ane daime, for seimlye graice,
For comelynesse of forme and faice,
For all that loferis bosome warmis,
Ne'er lay in loferis pantyng armis.
Her eye is of the daizzelyng hewe                                              505
Of starre wythin the oceane blewe,

Quhen its brychte streimeris gleime and curle
On every waifis redoundant furle;
Her taper lymbe—ane queinly gemme!
So lyke the brakenis staitlye stemme,                    510
And every beautye that you se,
Beire the high markis of majesty."

"Skreime," quod the ladye Egil then,
And aye sho yellit and yellit againe;
For all this while her queinlye herte               515
Had byrnit with ane deedly smarte
Of jealousye and raige extreime,
Which lente soche venom to hir skreime,
That the Egillis golden eye turnit blewe,
Then chaingit into an olive hewe;               520
For hee begoude to dredde the stryffe
And vengeance of ane jealous wyffe—
That storme the mychtye hefenis under
Neiste to the lychtenyng and the thunder.
The ladye Egil gaif ane raire,               525
Then left the eggis and toke the aire,
And als she hoverit ower the rocke,
These wordis the queinlye femaile spoke:
"I'll not upbraide with haughtye worde
Myne husbande and myne honourit lorde:               530
For it dothe beste ane wyffe become
On husbandis follyis to be dumbe,
To shutte hir eyne ower every blotte,
Or se them als sho sawe them notte;
But this I'll saye, and holde it gode,               535
That everilke burde of nobil blode,
Or manne or beiste, quhate'er it bee,
Sholde keipe himselfe to his degre;
And neuer yeilde to mix or melle
With craituris farre below himselle:               540
For he that venturis to repose
In dunghill drabbis and carrion crowis,
Maye chaunce to catche the blychtyng staine,
That will not sone washe out againe.
"My lorde, I haif hearit this shaimlesse thyng               545
In your high eiris ane solo ryng
Enoughe to make ane queinlye bryde

From the fair sone hir faice to hyde.
I will not chyde, but go with mee,
And this moste lofelye mystresse se;                    550
Cowryng hir sootye eggis upone
We will fynde this matchlesse paragone."
　　Goode hefenis! could theye beliefe theyre eyes!
Quhat wals theyre wonder and surpryis,
Quhen theye behelde, in anguish graite,                 555
Theyre laite graite mynistere of staite,
Sytting upon the eggis fulle lowe,
With mootit wyng and herte of woe.
The lordlye Egillis laughit amaine,
With youte of anger and disdaine,                       560
Until theyre very yermit shoke,
And Corbye kennit not quhare to loke;
Thus to be caughte he thoughte soche shaime,
Sytting the eggis lyke eldron daime.
　　Then the Egillis bothe upone him felle,              565
And with theyre bekis layit on pelle-melle;
And they daddit him down from rocke to rocke,
Quhille hee colde nouther stande nor croke;
And pluckit off all his fedderis blacke,
Tille he wals as baire as ane paddockis backe.          570
Then they chasit his menselesse maite awaye,
Farre ower Gilborachis craigy brae—
Turnit back upon her neste forlorne,
And tore it from the aigit thorne,
And brakke the eggis, and spytefullye                   575
Disgracit the Corbyis regal tree—
Ane speche to all benethe the sone,
Nefer to doo als hee had done,
Trying to gaine him's ranke and plaise
By spousis favoris and dysgraice.                       580
　　From that time furthe it so befelle,
Ane curious fack I haif to telle,
The Corbye fumit and lokit bigge,
And from that houre he turnit a Whigge—
Ane crokyng, mockyng, pesterous tyke,                   585
That kepit his soveraigne still in fyke,
And held his growlyng, grumbilyng mode,
Whudder at evil or at gode;
The very bane of gloryis helthe,

The mildewe of the commonwelthe,                    590
And only happy stille to bee
Plaigue of his sovraignis dynastie.
Old Maister Sauthan wals the firste
Sette up the trade of Whigge accursit,
And after him the Corbye drewe,                     595
The same in naiture als in hewe.
With oder Whiggis we shalle haif funne,
Before myne pastoralis bee done.

Mount Benger
*Nov.* 14, 1827.

*January–December 1828 (Volumes 23–24)*

# Trials of Temper

### *By the Ettrick Shepherd*

"I SAY she is neither handsome, nor comely, nor agreeable, in any one respect, Mr Burton; and I cannot help considering myself as rather humbugged in this business. Do you account it nothing to bring a man of my temperament a chase of three hundred miles on a fool's errand?"

"My dear sir, I beg a thousand pardons. But really, if you esteem Miss Eliza Campbell, your own relation as well as mine, as neither handsome, beautiful, nor accomplished, why, I must say you have lost, since you went abroad, every sense of distinction; every little spark that you once possessed of taste and discernment in female accomplishments. Why, now, I suppose, a lady, to suit your taste, Doctor, must be black—as black as a coal, and well tatooed over the whole body?"

"None of your gibes and jeers with me, Mr Burton. I did not, and do not, mean to give any offence; but it is well known to all your friends, and has been known to me these thirty years, what a devil of a temper you have. As to my taste and discernment in female beauty, I have seen too much of life to be directed in these by a petty dealer in Galashiels gray-cloth, corduroy breeches, and worsted stockings,— ay, even though he add Kilmarnock bonnets, pirnie caps, and mittens, to the inventory. And if you had any degree of temper, I would tell you, that your niece, Miss Campbell, is one of the worst-looking, worst-conditioned middle-aged women, that I ever looked on!"

"Temper! I short of temper? Why, I must say, sir, that I would not be possessed of a temper as irritable as yours, to be made owner of all the shops in this street, as well as the goods that are in them. You are a very nettle, sir,—a piece of brown-paper wet with turpentine,— a barrel of gunpowder that can be ignited by one of its own grains, and fly in the face of the man who is trying and exerting himself to preserve it. I am a clothier. I do not deny it; and think no shame of my business. But though I have not poisoned so many Pagans and Mahometans as you have done, nor been paid for so doing, by a thousand lacs of rupees, I can nevertheless keep the crown of the causeway, and look all my creditors in the face. Ay, and moreover, I can kneel before my Maker, sir, and entreat his blessing on myself and others, with *a clear conscience*, and that is more than some of your Nabob sort of people can do! Miss Campbell is too good—much too good—for you, sir; and I must say, that I regret exceedingly having invited you so far to come and insult her—in my presence, too, her nearest relation! I must say, sir, that you had better take care not to say as much again as you *have* said, else you may chance to be surprised at the consequence."

"Why certainly the devil has entered personally into this retailer of gray-cloth and carpets! There, he would persuade me, that I am irritable and passionate, and he the reverse; while, in the meantime, here he has got into a violent rage, and chafing like the vexed ocean, and I as cool as a summer evening in Kashmere!"

"Cool?—you cool, sir? Why you are at this moment in a furnace of a passion! Wherefore else should you knock on my counter in that way? You think to intimidate me, I suppose; but you shall neither fright me out of my reasonableness nor equanimity."

"*Your* equanimity! St Patrick save the mark! How long is it since you were sued at law, and heavily fined, for knocking down your shopman with the ellwand? And how many honest customers have you threatened across that counter with the same infernal weapon, before you could bring your reason to control your wrath? And when we were at school together, how often did the rest of the boys combine to banish you from all their games, calling you 'the crabbed tailor,' and pelting you without mercy? And what was worst of all, how often did I get my head broken in your defence?"

"It is too true,—perfectly true!—I remember several of the circumstances quite well. Give me your hand, my old and trusty friend, and come and dine with me to-morrow; for my heart warms to you when I think of our early friendship, and the days of our youthful enjoyments."

"And well may mine warm to you, for you assisted me out, when no other friend would venture, and, I had reason to fear, put your little credit right hardly to stake on my account. And do you know, Burton, that when I left Scotland, and took leave of all my friends, with much probability that it would be for the last time, not a man or woman amongst them shed tears at parting with me but yourself. That simple circumstance has never been erased from my memory, nor ever will. And before I left India I made a will, which is safe in the Register-Chamber of Fort William, and whereby, in the event of my dying without a family, you will find yourself entitled to the half of my fortune."

"My dear sir, that little pecuniary matter has been doubly repaid long ago; and as for that part of the will which is deposited at Fort William, and that devises to me, I shall do all in my power to render it of none effect. Come and dine with me to-morrow."

"I will, with all my heart."

"That's well. And we will have some conversation about the exploits and joys of our youthful years; for, though much has past over our heads, as well as through our hands and our hearts, since that period, still one single reminiscence of it is like a warm blink of sunshine in a winter day. I have often wondered, Doctor, what it is that makes the recollections of youth so delightful; for, as far as I remember my sensations at that time, they were anything but desirable, my joys being transient, and wofully mingled up with vexations and disappointments."

"There is something in the buoyancy of youthful spirits so akin to happiness, that the existence of the one almost implies the presence of the other. The ardency of hope, the first breathings of youthful affection, all render that a season to be thought on with delight.– Have you not some daughters of your own, Mr Burton?"

"I have two very amiable girls, and one of them marriageable, too; but, after hearing your opinion of the most accomplished young lady of the realm, I dare not submit them to your scrutiny. You shall not meet them at dinner to-morrow."

"I insist on meeting them at dinner–What! shall I not be introduced to the daughters of my best friend?"

"Your taste has become so horribly sophisticated, and then you speak out your sentiments so plainly, that no girl is safe from insult with you. Remember, my girls are not blackamoors any more than Miss Campbell is."

"There the bad temper flies out again! This Miss Campbell is a sore subject. Would that I had never seen her!–The truth is, I must speak my sentiments, and, with regard to her, they are anything but those of approbation."

"Why, sir, you're not only blind, but utterly perverse and obstinate. Miss Campbell is the most approved beauty in Edinburgh at the present time; but she is an orphan, and has no fortune–there your antipathy lies! Money is your object! money, money!–that is manifest. Pray, could you not have got a blackamoor, with a camel's load or two of rupees, for a spouse, and so saved the expense of a journey to Britain?"

"I will tell you what, friend–I have a great mind to break your head, and so save the expense of a rope to hang you in. A piece of presumption, indeed, to think to dictate to my tastes, or analyze the springs of my affection and dislike!"

Here the clothier seized his massy mahogany ellwand, and his friend the Doctor, having heard of the feats of arms performed by that unlucky weapon, thought proper to decamp, which he did with a kind of forced laugh, half in wrath at the ridiculous exhibition the two had made. Nevertheless, he returned, after walking about thirty paces, and, setting his head over the half-door, said, emphatically, "Now, after all, you must be sensible that she is very homely, vulgar, and disagreeable; and confoundedly affected?" Then, perceiving the ellwand once more emerging from its dark corner, he made a hasty retreat, desecrating, all the way, the misfortune of a bad temper.

That evening Mr Burton got a note from Miss Campbell, which puzzled him a great deal; it ran thus:

> "MY DEAR UNCLE,
> "I am quite delighted with your friend Dr Brown. I expected to have met an elderly gentleman, but was agreeably surprised at meeting with so much elegance, conjoined with youth. He is certainly the most engaging and courteous gentleman I have ever seen, and has already made me an offer, which I think it would be imprudent in me to reject. As I have much to say to you on this subject, I will come down and see you in the coach to-morrow.
> "Your ever affectionate niece,
> "ELIZA CAMPBELL."

"So, the Nabob has been hoaxing me all this while," said the clothier to himself, chuckling. He then laughed at Miss Campbell's mistake about his friend's age, and slily remarked, that money was all powerful in modifying ages to suit each other. After considering the matter a little more seriously, he became suspicious that some mistake had occurred, for he knew it to be his friend the Doctor's disposition always to speak his sentiments rather too freely, and, in the present instance, he seemed to be quite chagrined and out of humour whenever Miss Campbell was named. The good clothier had a sincere affection for his niece, and, having a large family of his own to provide for, he was anxious to see her settled in life by a respectable marriage, particularly as she had of late begun to be noted as a great beauty, and was toasted by the beaux. So the clothier remained involved in a puzzle until the next day, when his niece arrived; and still from her he could learn nothing, but that all was as it should be. He asked who introduced Dr Brown to her. It was the very friend to whom the clothier had written to perform that friendly office. He made her describe Dr Brown's person and address, and, as far as the clothier could see, they corresponded to a very tittle.—Very well, thinks the clothier to himself, as I am uncertain whether the crabbed loon will come to dinner to-day or not, I will say nothing about it, and then I will see how the two are affected when they meet.

Four o'clock came, so the clothier went home to his house, and put on his black coat and silk stockings; and then he paced up and down his little snug parlour, which served as a drawing-room, with much impatience, going every five minutes up stairs to look out at the window.

"Who dines with my uncle to-day?" said Miss Campbell to her cousin, Ellen Burton;—"I see you have an extra cover set, and he seems rather in the fidgets because his guest is not come."

"I do not know who it is," returned Miss Burton; "he merely said that he expected a stranger to dine with him to-day—some English bagman, I suppose. We have these people frequently with us; but I never regard them, always leaving them with my father, to consult about markets and bargains, as soon as dinner is over; and we will leave them the same way to-night, and go to Mrs Innes's grand tea party, you know."

"O, by all means."

With that the Doctor entered, and was welcomed by a hearty and kindly shake of the hand; and, leading him forward, Burton said, "This is my daughter Ellen, sir, and her sister Jane." Of Miss Campbell he made no mention, conceiving that she and the Doctor were well acquainted before. But either the Doctor and she had not been acquainted before—or else the room was so dark that the Doctor could not see distinctly, (for he was very much out of breath, which mazes the eye-sight a great deal,)—or the beauty of the young ladies had dazzled him—or some unaccountable circumstance had occurred, for the Doctor did not recognise Miss Campbell, nor did the young lady take any notice of him. On the contrary, Jane Burton being only a little girl, and below the Doctor's notice at that time of night, he took the other two for the clothier's daughters, and addressed them as such all the time of dinner. The two young giglets being amused by the simple mistake, encouraged the stranger in it, answering to their names, and quizzing one another about the bagman and his patterns, of all which the Doctor understood not one word; but the clothier thought it altogether a very odd business; yet he carved his beef and his chuckies, and held his peace, suffering the girls to have out their joke, deeming it all affectation on Miss Campbell's part, and some strange misconception of the Doctor's, which he resolved to humour.

The Doctor was so polite and attentive to the young ladies, and appeared so highly delighted with them, that they were insensibly induced to stay longer at table than they intended, and on their going away, he conducted them to the door, kissed both their hands, and said a number of highly flattering things to them. On again taking his seat, being in high spirits, he said, "Why, in the name of wonder, my dear friend, should you endeavour to put grist by your own mill, as the saying is? These daughters of yours are by far the most accomplished and agreeable young ladies whom I have seen since my return from India. The eldest is really a masterpiece, not only of Nature's workmanship, but of all that grace and good-breeding can bestow."

"I thank you kindly, sir; I was afraid they would be a little too fair of complexion for your taste. Pray have you never met with that eldest one before? for it struck me that you looked as you had been previously acquainted."

"How was it possible I could ever have seen her? But you know a bachelor of my years assumes a privilege with young ladies which would be widely out of place with our juniors, while it not unfrequently has the effect of rendering us the greater favourites of the two.—It is quite well known, Mr Burton, what my errand to Britain is at this time. I have never concealed it from you. It is to obtain a wife; and now to receive one out of your family, and from your own hand, would be my highest desire; settlements are nothing between us. These shall be of your own making. Your eldest daughter, the tallest I mean, is positively the most charming woman I ever saw. Bestow her upon me, and I am the happiest man in his Majesty's dominions."

"You shall have her, Doctor—you shall have her with all my heart; and I think I have a small document on hand to show that you can likewise have her consent for the asking, if indeed you have not obtained it already."

"I will double your stock in trade, sir, before I leave this country, if you realize this promise to me. My jaunt from India beyond the Ganges is likely to be amply compensated. Why, the possession of such a jewel is worth ten voyages round the world, and meeting all the lines at Musselburgh. But I'll warrant I may expect some twitches of temper from her—that I may reckon upon as a family endowment."

"And will there be no equivalent on the other side? No outbreakings of violence, outrage, and abuse? The Ethiopian cannot change his skin, nor the leopard his spots; no more can he of an unruly temper sit beneath the sway of reason. At all events, the reflection on me and my family comes with a bad grace from such a firebrand as yourself."

"Stop, for heaven's sake, my good friend, stop; let us not mar so excellent a prospect, by sounding the jarring strings of our nature together. Why, sir, whenever a man comes within the bounds of your atmosphere, he treads on phosphorous—he breathes it, and is not for a moment certain that he may not be blown up in an electric flash. Why get into such a rage at a good-natured joke?"

"It was a very ill-natured joke; and I have yet to learn that you ever did a genuinely good-natured thing in your life. Even now you are all this while playing at hide-and-seek with me—playing at some back game, that I cannot comprehend, in order to make a fool of me. Do you wish me to tell you what I think of you, sir?"

"And pray what do I care what you think of me? Does it any way affect me what may be the opinion of such a being as you?—*You* think of me!"

"There goes! There goes the old man, with all his infirmities on his head."

"Who is an old man, Mr Burton? Who is an old man full of infirmities? Old!—to your teeth, sir, you are years older than myself."

"Do you know, sir, who you are speaking to, sir? or whose house you are in, sir?"

"Yes, I do, sir. I know very well whose house I am in, and whose house I shall soon be out of, too; and whose house I shall never enter again as long as I live. Do I not know all these, sir? What *you* think of me, forsooth! I have thought more of you than ever it behoved me to have done; and this is the reception I have met with in return!"

"Now pardon me this once, Doctor, and I shall never get angry with you again. I'll bear all your infirmities with the patience of Job; but you must not leave my house in this humour."

"*My* infirmities, sir? What do you mean by my infirmities? And who the devil is to bear with yours, sir? I assure you it shall not be me! That I was once obliged to you, I confess, and that I have long thought on you with the affection of a brother, I likewise confess, but—"

"Hold there. Go no farther at present until the furnace-heat of your temper be somewhat allayed. We are friends, and must be friends as long as we live, notwithstanding of our failings. We have all much to forgive one another in this life. But you took me so short, when it was Miss Campbell only that I wanted to talk about."

"Miss Campbell whom you wanted to talk about! A singular sub-ject truly, so immediately after the cessation of hostilities. I tell you once for all, Mr Burton, that I will have nothing to do with Miss Campbell–nothing to say to her; for she is absolutely my aversion."

"It is false, sir–every word of it is false; for you shall have to say to her and do with her both, and she is *not* your aversion. Nay, do not go to get into one of your boundless fits of rage again, for out of your own mouth will I condemn you; and if you deny your own words and mine, I will show you the lady's writ and signature to the fact."

"I was not even able to say a civil thing to the lady."

"You were. You said the most civil things to her that you could invent. You made an offer of your hand to her, and you made the same offer to me."

"I'll fight the man either with sword or pistols who would palm such an imposition on me."

The clothier made no answer to this save by handing over Miss Campbell's note to the astonished physician, who read as follows:–"'I am quite delighted with your friend Dr Brown.' Hem! Thank you, Miss Eliza Campbell. So is not his friend Dr Brown with you, I assure you. 'I expected to have met with an elderly gentleman, but was agreeably surprised–' Oho! hem, hem! What is all this? The girl has some sense and discernment though; for, do you know, I am never taken for a man above thirty."

"That I think does not show much discernment either in them or in her."

"I beg pardon, sir; I only meant to say that the girl saw with the same eyes as the generality of mankind, which at least manifests some degree of common sense. But it is all very well; I see through the letter–a trap to catch a badger, I suppose. As to the insinuation that I made her an offer, she has made it, or dreamed it, or conceived it, of herself, one way or other, for the deuce an offer I made to her of any sort whatever."

"Why, now, Doctor, the whole of your behaviour on this occasion is to me a complete mystery; for the young lady who sat on your right hand to-day at table, is no other than the same Miss Campbell, my niece, whom you have been all along so undeservedly abusing."

"Are you telling the truth, Mr Burton? Are you not dreaming?–I see you are telling me the truth. Why then did you introduce them to me as your daughters?"

"I introduced my two daughters only, believing that you two were perfectly acquainted before."

"She has then been introduced to me in a mask. There is not a doubt of it. She has spoke to me under a disguise of false form and false features, yet I thought all the while that I recognised the voice. And was yon lovely, adorable creature, with the auburn hair and dark eyes, the seamaw's neck, and the swan's bosom, the same who wrote that pretty card about me?"

"The same, I assure you."

"Give it me again that I may kiss it, and look at every elegant letter it contains. I have had flatterers of the sex, black and white, brown and yellow, but never before received flattery from such a superlative being as she is. Where are the ladies? Let us go to them and have tea, for I have an intense longing to look on the angel again. How right you were in your estimation of the young lady, and how grievously I was in the wrong! I would now shoot any man who dared to use such language of her as I did. I would rather she had been your daughter though, for sake of the days of langsyne, even though she is my own half-cousin by the mother's side."

Never was there a more impassioned lover than the Doctor was with this fair cousin; he raved of her, and fumed with impatience, when he found she had gone to Mrs Innes's party, and that he could not see her again that night. He lost no time, however, in writing out the schedule of a contract, a most liberal one, and to this scroll he put his name, desiring his friend to show Miss Campbell the writing preparatory to his visit the next day. The clothier did this, and found his lovely ward delighted with the match, who acknowledged that the annual sum settled on her was four times what she expected with such an agreeable husband; and although she begged for time and leisure to make some preparations, yet, at her kind uncle's request, she unhesitatingly put her name to the document by way of acquiescence; and thus was the agreement signed and settled, and wanted only the ratification of the parson to render it permanent. He then informed her that the Doctor would wait on her next day to ask her formally, and then they might settle on such time for the marriage as suited both.

Next day the Doctor arrived at an early hour, and found the young lady dressed like an Eastern princess to receive him, and in the highest glee imaginable; but as he did not then know the success of his offer, he kept aloof from the subject till the arrival of his friend the clothier. The latter, perceiving his earnest impatience, took him into another apartment, and showed him the lady's signature and acceptance. Never was there a man so uplifted. The intelligence actually put him beside himself, for he clapped his hands, shouted—hurra!

threw up his wig, and jumped over one of the chairs. His joy and hilarity during dinner were equally extravagant—there was no whim nor frolic which he did not practise. He drank tops and bottoms with the young lady every glass, and at one time got on his legs and made a long speech to her, the tenor of which she did not, or pretended that she did not, comprehend; but all the family group applauded him, so that he was elated, and even drunk with delight.

Not being able to rest, by reason of the fervour of his passion, he arose shortly after dinner, and, taking his friend the clothier into the other room, requested of him to bring matters to a verbal explanation forthwith. He accordingly sent for Eliza, who looked rather amazed when she entered, and saw only these two together.

"Come away, my dear Eliza," said her uncle; "take a seat here, and do not look so agitated, seeing the business is already all but finished. My friend, Dr Brown, has come down to-day for the purpose of having a ratification of your agreement from your own hand, and your own mouth."

"Very well, my dear uncle; though I see no occasion for hurrying the business, I am quite conformable to your will in that respect. Why did not Dr Brown come to dinner? Where is he?"

I wish I had seen the group at this moment; or had Mr David Wilkie seen it, and taken a picture from it, it would have been ten times better. The Doctor's face of full-blown joy was changed into one of meagre consternation, nothing of the ruddy glow remaining, save on the tip of his nose. The internal ligaments that supported his jaws were loosened, and they fell down, as he gazed on the clothier; the latter stared at Eliza, and she at both alternately. It was a scene of utter bewilderment, and no one knew what to think of another. The clothier was the first to break silence.

"What ails you, my dear niece?" said he. "Are you quizzing? or are you dreaming? or have you fallen into a fit of lunacy? I say, *what is* the matter with you, child? Is not this my friend, Dr Brown, whom I have known from his childhood?—the gentleman whom I sent for to be introduced to you, and the gentleman, too, to whom you have given yourself away, and signed the gift by an irrevocable deed?"

"What! To this old gentleman? Dear uncle, you must excuse me, that I am in a grievous error, and a quandary besides. Ha, ha, ha!— Hee, hee, hee! Oh, mercy on us! I shall expire with downright laughing."

"What do you mean by such insulting behaviour, madam? Have I come here to be flouted, to be cheated, to be baited by a pack of terriers, with an old fox-hound at their head? But beware, madam, how you press the old badger too hard. I have your signature here, to a very serious deed, signed before witnesses, and if you *do not* fulfil your engagement to me, I have you at my mercy; and I'll use the power which the deed puts in my hands–use it to the utmost–make yourself certain of that."

"Pray, sir, do not get into such a rage, lest you terrify me out of my wits. I am but a poor timorous maiden, sir, and not used to so much obstreperousness; yet I have so much spirit in me, that I shall never be imposed upon by such effrontery–never."

"Mercy on us!" exclaimed the clothier. "We shall all go in a flame together, and be consumed by collision.–My dear niece, you know not what you are doing or saying. This is no person to be despised, but the celebrated Dr Brown from India, chief of the medical staff of a whole Presidency–your own kinsman–my friend, of whom you approved in your note to me, and in conjunction with whom you have signed a contract of marriage. So none of your bantering and flagaries; for have him you must, and have him you shall. The deed cannot be annulled but by mutual consent."

"Well, then, it shall never be farther ratified by me. This may be *your* Dr Brown, but he is not *mine;* and however worthy he may be, he is not the man of my choice."

"Is not this the gentleman of whom you wrote to me in such high terms of approval?"

"*That* the gentleman! Dear uncle, where would my seven senses have been, had that been he?"

"And is this not the lady, sir, whom you met in Edinburgh?"

"I know nothing at all about it. If this be not she, I like her worse than the other."

"There is some unfortunate mistake here. Pray, Dr Brown, who was it that introduced you to the lady, with whom you met?"

"Your friend, Mrs Wright, to be sure; whom else could it have been?"

"And you did not see Mr Anderson, then?"

"No; but I left your letter at his office, thinking there might be something of business."

"There it goes! Mrs Wright has introduced you to a wrong Miss Campbell, and Mr Anderson has introduced a wrong Dr Brown to her.–Plague on it, for you cannot now throw a stone in Edinburgh, but you are sure to hit either a Brown or a Campbell."

This was simply the case: The clothier wrote to his friend, Mrs Wright, to find means of introducing the bearer, Dr Brown, to their *mutual friend,* Miss Elizabeth Campbell. Mrs Wright, having an elderly maiden sister of that name, mistook, in perfect simplicity of heart, the term mutual friend, and, without more ado, introduced the Doctor to her sister. Now, the Doctor knew perfectly well that the other letter, which he carried to Mr Anderson, related likewise to some meeting with Miss Campbell, but not caring about any such thing, he merely popped the letter into the shop as he passed; and Mr Anderson, knowing nothing about Dr Brown's arrival from India, sent for the only unmarried Dr Brown whom he knew, and introduced him to Mr Burton's niece, as desired, and there the attachment proved spontaneous and reciprocal. Miss Campbell, finding now that she was in a bad predicament, having given her heart to one gentleman, and her written promise to another, threw herself on the old Doctor's mercy, explained the mistake, and the state of her affections, and besought him to have pity on a poor orphan, whose choice might be wrong, but which she was incapable of altering. The worthy Esculapius of the East was deeply affected. He took both the young lady's hands in his, kissed first the one and then the other, and, invoking on her all earthly happiness, he not only returned her the bond, but alongst with it a cheque on his banker for a considerable sum, as a marriage-present.

Miss Campbell was shortly after married to a dashing student of medicine, and they now reside in a distant province, very poor, and not over happy; and Dr Brown married the eldest daughter of his old benefactor, a simple, modest, and unassuming young creature, whom he carried off with him to the paradise of India, and placed her at the head of a magnificent Eastern establishment. I have seen several of her letters, in all of which she writes in the highest terms of her happiness and comforts. The two old friends quarrelled every day while together, but at parting, they both shed the warm tears of affection, and words of regret passed between them such as to be remembered for ever.

## Moralitas

She that giveth heart away
For the homage of a day,
To a downy dimpling chin,
Smile that tells the void within,—
Swaggering gait, and stays of steel,—
Saucy head, and sounding heel,—
Gives the gift of woe and weeping—
Gives a thing not worth the keeping—
Gives a trifle—gives a toy.
Sweetest viands soonest cloy.

Gains?–Good Lord! what doth she gain?–
Years of sorrow and of pain;
Cold neglect, and words unkind;
Qualms of body and of mind;
Gains the curse that leaves her never;
Gains the pang that lasts for ever.

And why? Ah hath not reason shown it?
Though the heart dares hardly own it,
Well it traces love to be
The fruit of the forbidden tree;
Of woman's woe the origin;
The apple of the primal sin;
The test of that angelic creature;
The touchstone of her human nature:
Which proved her, though of heavenly birth,
An erring meteor of the earth.

And what, by Heaven's sovereign will,
Was trial once is trial still;
It is the fruit that virgin's eye
Can ne'er approach too cautiously;
It is the fruit that virgin's hand
Must never touch but on command
Of parent, guardian, friends in common–
Approved both by man and woman;
Else woe to her as maid or wife,
For all her days of mortal life;
The curse falls heavy on her crime,
And heavier wears by length of time;
And, as of future joys to reft her,
Upon her race that follows after.

But oh, if prudence and discretion
Baulk the forward inclination,–
Cool the bosom, check the eye,
And guide the hand that binds the tie,–
Then, then alone is love a treasure,
A blessing of unbounded measure,
Which every pledge of love endears;
It buds with age, and grows with years,–
As from the earth it points on high,
Till its fair tendrils in the sky

Blossom in joy, and ever will,
And woman is an angel still.

MOUNT BENGER
*Dec.* 10, 1827.


# I'll No Wake Wi' Annie

O MOTHER, tell the laird o't,
   Or sairly it will grieve me, O,
That I'm to wake the ewes the night,
   An' Annie's to gang wi' me, O.
I'll wake the ewes my night about,         5
   But ne'er wi' ane sae saucy, O;
Nor sit my lane the lee-lang night
   Wi' sic a scornfu' lassie, O.
      I'll no wake, I'll no wake,
      I'll no wake wi' Annie, O,         10
      Nor sit my lane o'er night wi' ane
      Sae thraward an' uncannie, O.

Dear son be wise an' warie,
   But never be unmanly, O,
I've heard you tell another tale         15
   O' young an' charming Annie, O,
The ewes ye wake are fair enough,
   Upon the brae sae bonny, O;
But the laird himsell wad gie them a',
   To wake the night wi' Annie, O.        20
      He'll no wake, &c.

I tauld ye ear', I tauld ye late,
   That lassie wad trepan ye, O,
In ilka word ye boud to say,
   When left your lane wi' Annie, O.        25
Tak' my advice this night for ance,
   Or beauty's tongue will ban ye, O,
An' sey your leel auld mother's skeel,
   Ayont the moor wi' Annie, O.
      He'll no wake, &c.        30

The night it was a simmer night,
   An' O the glen was lanely, O,

For just ae sternie's gowden ee
  Peep'd o'er the hill serenely, O.
The twa are in the flow'ry heath,        35
  Ayont the moor sae flowy, O,
An' but ae plaid atween them baith,
  An' wasna that right dowy, O?
      He maun wake, &c.

Neist morning at his mother's knee,     40
  He bless'd her love unfeign'dly, O;
An' aye the tear fell frae his ee,
  An' aye he clasp'd her kindly, O.
Of a' my griefs I've got amends,
  Up in yon glen sae grassy, O.       45
A woman only woman kens;
  Your skill has won my lassie, O.
      I'll aye wake, I'll aye wake,
      I'll aye wake wi' Annie, O,
      I'll ne'er again keep wake wi' ane     50
      Sae sweet, sae kind, an' cannie, O!

# In Embro Town

TUNE,–*O'er the muir amang the heather.*

In Embro town they made a law,
  In Embro at the Court o' Session,
That Kit and his lads were fautors a'!
  An' guilty o' a high transgression.
    Decreet o' the Court o' Session,     5
    Act sederunt o' the Session;
  Kit North and his crew were fautors a',
    And guilty o' a high transgression.

In the Parliament House the Whigs were croose,
  In the Parliament House at the Court o' Session;    10
There was Cobrun to blaw, and Jamffrey to craw–
  Crooseness and gabs their best possession.
    Decreet o' the Court o' Session,
    Act sederunt o' their Session;
  Whiggery's light, and Whigs are bright,    15
    An' a Tory creed is a fool's transgression.

In Embro' town there dwalls a man
  That never gangs near their Court o' Session,
A vif auld man, wi' a drap in his cann,
    Has gien a' the Whigs in the land a threshin'.          20
      Decreet o' his Court of Session,
      Act sederunt o' his Session;
    The Whigs they are neerdoweels, great and sma',
      And cheap, cheap o' a hearty threshin'.

Frae Embro town his word gangs out,                         25
  Frae Ambrose' spence, his Court o' Session,
And the deevil a prig that stinks o' Whig,
    But dumfounder'd he sinks in consternation.
      Decreet o' this Court o' Session,
      Act sederunt o' the Session;                          30
    The Whigs are found out, and in siccan a rout,
      That their hurdies are scantily worth a threshin'.


# Chalk! Chalk!

Chalk! chalk! why the devil dinna ye chalk?
  Stand to your ladders, and blaze in good order;
Up wi' your capitals, catch, catch the Cockneys all,
  Frae the Hampstead hills and the Battersea border.
      Chalk! chalk! puffing-men,                            5
      Fyke nae mair wi' the pen,
Here's better service, and cheaper for Colburn;
      Try the new-farrant hum,
      Gar gable, yett, and lum,
Stare like a strumpet, frae Hounslow to Holborn.            10

Chalk! chalk! baith "GRANBY" and "NORMANBY,"
  Chalk them ahint ye and chalk them afore ye;
Chalk ilka crossing, and canny bit corner by,
    "HARRIETTE WILSON," and "CLUB-LAND, A STORY."
      Chalk every mither's son,                             15
      Till we read as we run
WRIGHT'S IN THE COLONNADE!—SOHO HOLDS EADY!
      BUY, IF YOU BEN'T A BEAR,
      BUY BOBBY WARD'S DE VERE!
Glower, gaupus, and shool out the ready!                    20

# Good Night and Joy
# Be Wi' You A'

THE night is wearing to the wane,
    And daylight glimmering east awa';
The little sternies dance amain,
    And the moon bobs aboon the shaw.
    But though the tempest tout an' blaw        5
Upon his loudest midnight horn,
    Good night an' joy be wi' you a',
We'll maybe meet again the morn.

O, we hae wander'd far and wide,
    O'er Scotia's land of firth and fell:        10
And mony a bonny flower we've pu'd,
    And twined them wi' the heather bell
    We've ranged the dingle and the dell,
The hamlet and the Baron's ha',
    Now let us take a kind farewell,–        15
Good night and joy be wi' you a'.

Ye hae been kind as I was keen,
    And follow'd where I led the way,
Till ilka poet's love we've seen
    Of this and mony a former day.        20
    If e'er I led your steps astray,
Forgie your Minstrel aince for a';
    A tear fa's wi' his parting lay,–
Good night an' joy be wi' you a'.

# A Strange Secret
### Related in a Letter from the Ettrick Shepherd

DEAR SIR,

YESTERDAY there was a poor man named Thomas Henderson came to our door, and presented me with a letter from a valued friend. I was kind to the man; and as an acknowledgment, he gave me his history in that plain, simple, and drawling style, which removed all doubts of its authenticity. It is not deserving of a recital; but as I am constantly on the look-out for fundamental documents of any sort relating to Scotland, there was one little story of his that I deemed worthy of preservation; and consequently here have I sat down to write it out in the man's own words, while yet they are fresh in my memory.

I was nine years a servant to the Earl of —, and when I left him, he made me a very handsome present; but it was on condition that I should never again come within a hundred miles of his house. The truth is, that I would have been there to this day, had I not chanced to come at the knowledge of something relating to the family that I ought not to have known, and which I never would have known, had I gotten my own will.

"Pray, what was that, Thomas? Above all things, I should like to hear some of the secrets of a noble family."

Weel, ye shall hear a' that I ken, sir; which, to say the truth, is but very little after a'. But it was this. When the auld Earl died there was an unca rumpus an' confusion, and at length the young lord came hame frae abroad, an' tuke the command. An' I think he hadna been master aboon twa years when he rings the bell ae morning, an' sends for me. I was merely a groom, and no used to gang up stairs to my lord; but he often spoke to me in the stables, for I had the charge o' his favourites Cleopatra and Venus, and I thought he wanted to gie me some directions about them. Weel, up the stair I rins, wanting the jacket and bonnet, and I opens the door and I says, "What is't, my lord?" "Shut the door and come in," says he. "Hech! what in the world is in the wind now!" thinks I. "Am I gaun to be made some grand secreter?"

"Tom, has the Lady Julia ordered the coach to-day?" says he.

"I believe she has, my lord. I think Hector was saying so."

"And is it still to the old spot again in the forest?"

"That winna be kend till Hector is on the seat. But there is little doubt that it is to the same place. She never drives to any other."

"Tom, I was long absent from home, but you have been in the family all the while, and must know all its secrets. What is it supposed my sister Julia has always ado with the forester's wife at the shieling of Aberduchra?"

"That has never been kend to ane o' us, my lord. But it is supposed there is some secret business connected wi' her visits there."

"That is a great stretch of supposition, indeed, Tom! Of that there can be no doubt. But what do the servants suppose the secret relates to? Or what do *you* suppose it does? Come, tell me honestly and freely."

"O, naebody kens that, my lord; for Lady Julia just lights at a certain point o' the road, and orders the coach to be there again at a certain hour at night; an' that's a' that has ever been kend about it. But we a' notice that Lady Julia is sair altered. An' the folks say,—but as to that I'm ignorant—The folks say, ye ken, that auld Eppie Cowan's a witch."

"And that it is on some business of enchantment or divination that my sister goes to her?"

"Na, na, I dinna say that, my lord; for a' that I say is just this, that I believe naebody in this world, excepting Lady Julia an' auld Eppie themsells twa, kens what their business is thegither, or how they came to be connected."

"Well, well, Tom, that is what I want particularly to know. Do you set out just now; go over the shoulder of Beinny-Veol, and through Glen-Ellich, by the straight route. Get to Aberduchra before my sister. Conceal yourself somewhere, in the house or out of the house, in a thicket or in a tree. Note all that you see Lady Julia engaged in— who meets her there—what they do, and what they say, and bring me a true report of everything, and your reward shall be according to your success."

Weel, aff I rins, and ower the hills at the nearest, and sair wark had I afore I got mysell concealed, for auld Eppie was running out and in, and in and out again, in an unco fike, weel kenning wha was to be her visitor that day; for every time she came to the door she gae a lang look down the glen, and then a' round about her, as if feared for being catched in a fault.

I had by this time got up to the top of a great elm-tree that almost overlooked the door o' the shieling, but when I saw the auld roudess looking about her sae sternly, I grew frighted, for I thought, if she be a witch, I shall soon be discovered; and then, should she cast any cantrips that may dumfounder me, or should I see ought to put me beside myself, what a devil of a fa' I will get! I wad now hae gien a' the claes on my back to have been safe down again, and had begun to study a quick descent, when I perceived Lady Julia coming rapidly up the glen, with manifestly a kind o' trepidation o' manner. My heart began now to quake like an aspin leaf, for I suspected that some awesome scene was gaun to be transacted, that could bring the accomplished Lady Julia to that wild retired spot. And yet when she drew near, her modest mien and fading beauty were sae unlike onything wicked or hellish, that in short I didna ken what to think or what to fear, but I had a considerable allowance o' baith.

With many kind and obsequious courtesies did old Eppie receive the lady on the green, and after exchanging a few words, they both vanished into the cottage, and shut the door. Now, thinks I, the infernal wark will begin; but goodness be thankit, I'll see nane o't frae here. I changed my place on the tree, however, and came as near to the top of the lum as the branches would carry me. From thence I heard the voices of the two, but knew not what they were saying. The Lady Julia's voice was seldom heard, but when it was, it had the sounds of mental agony; and I certainly thought she was imploring the old hag to desist from something which the other persisted in. The voice of the latter never ceased; it went on with one continued mumble, like the sound of a distant waterfall. The sounds still increased, and I sometimes made myself believe that I heard the voice of a third person. I cannot tell what I would then have given to have heard what was going on, but though I strained my hearing to the uttermost, I could not attain it.

At length, all at once, I heard a piercing shriek, which was followed by low stifled moanings. "L–d J—s, they are murdering a bairn, an' what *will* I do!" said I to myself, sobbing till my heart was like to burst. And finding that I was just going to lose my senses, as well as my hold, and fall from the tree, I descended with all expedition, and straightway ran and hid myself in below the bank of the burn behind the house, that thereby I might drown the cries of the suffering innocent, and secure myself from a fall.

"Now, here shall be my watch," thinks I; "for here I can see every ane that passes out or into the house; and as for what is gaun on in the inside, that's mair than I'll meddle wi'."

I had got a nice situation now, and a safe ane, for there was a thick natural hedge of briers, broom, and brambles, down the back o' the kail-yard. These overhung the burn-brae, so that I could hide mysell frae every human ee in case of great danger, and there was an opening in the hedge, a kind of thin bit, through which I could see all that passed, and there I coured down on my knees, and lay wi' my een stelled on that shieling o' sin and iniquity.

I hadna lain lang in this position till out comes the twasome, cheek for chowe, and the auld ane had a coffin under her arm; and straight on they comes for the very opening o' the hedge where I was lying. Now, thinks I, I'm a gone man; for in below this very bank where I am sitting, are they coming to hide the corpse o' the poor bairn, and here ten might lie till they consumed, unkend to the haill warld. Ay, here they are coming, indeed, for there is not another bit in the whole thicket where they can win through; and in half a minute, I will have the witch and the murderess baith hinging at my throat like twa wulcats. I was aince just setting a' my joints to make a clean splash down the middle of the burn like an otter; but the power was denied me, an' a' that I could do, was to draw mysell close into my cove, like a hare into her form; an' there I sat and heard the following dialogue, and I think I remember it every word.

"Now, my *good Eppie*, are you certain that no person will come upon us, or within view of us, before we have done?" (*Good* Eppie! thinks I, Heaven preserve us a' frae sic goodness!)

"Ay, ay, weel am I sure o' that, Lady Julia, for my ain goodman is on the watch, an' he has a signal that I can ken, which will warn us in good time if anybody leave the high-way."

"Then open the lid and let me look into it once more; for the poor inanimate remains that are in that chest have a hold of this disconsolate and broken heart, which nothing else in this world can ever have again. O my dear boy! My comely, my beautiful, my murdered boy!"

Here Lady Julia burst into the most violent and passionate grief, shrieking and weeping like one in distraction. I was terrified out of a' bounds, but I coudna help thinking to mysell what a strange unconsistent creature a woman was, first to take away a dear little boy's life, and then rair and scraugh over what she had done, like a madwoman. Her passion was sae violent and sae loud that I coudna take up what the auld crone was saying, although her tongue never lay for a moment; but I thought a' the time that she was trying to pacify and comfort Lady Julia; and I thought I heard her saying that the boy wasna murdered. Now, thinks I, that dings a' that ever I heard! If a man aince understands a woman, he needna be feared to try ought in nature.

"Now here they are, my Lady July, just as your own fair hands laid them. There's no ane o' them out o' its place yet. There they a' lie, little an' muckle, frae the crown o' the head to the soles o' the feet."

"Gude forgi'e the woman!" says I into mysell–"Can these be the banes o' bairns that she is speaking about? It is a question how many has been put into that black kisty afore this time, and there their banes will be lying, tier aboon tier, like the contents of a candlemaker's box!"

"Look, here is the first, my leddy. This is the first year's anes. Then, below that sheet o' silver paper, is the second year's, and on sae to the third and the fourth."

"I didna think there had been as muckle wickedness in human nature," thought I; "but if thae twa escape out o' this world without some visible judgment, I'm unco sair mista'en."

"Come now, Leddy July, and let us gae through them a' regularly, an' gie ower greeting. See, as I said, this contains the first year's suits of a' kinds, and here, amang others, is the frock he was baptized in, far, far frae here. Ay, weel I mind that day, an' sae may ye, Leddy July; when the bishop flung the water on your boy's face, how the little chub looked at him! Ech—ech—ech—I'll never forget it! He didna whimper and whine like ither bairns, but his little arms gae a quiver wi' anger, an' sic a look as he gae the priest! Ay, it was as plain as he had said it in gude Scots, 'Billy, I'll be about wi' you for this yet.' Hee—hee—hee—my brave boy! Ay, there needed nae confessions, nor parish registers, to declare wha was his father! 'Faith, billy, I'll be about wi' you for this insult!' Hee—hee—hee. That was what he thought plainly enough, and he looket *very* angry at the Bishop the hale night. O fie, Leddy July, dinna stain the bonny frock wi' your tears. Troth, they are sae warm and sae saut, that they will never wash out again. There now, there now. We will hing them a' out to the sun ane by ane."

Shame fa' my stupidity, says I into mysell. Is the haill terrible affair endit in a bichel o' baby-clouts? As I then heard that they were moving farther away from me, I ventured to peep through the boughs, and saw the coffin standing open, about three feet from my nose. It was a small low trunk, covered with green velvet, lined with white satin, and filled with clothes that had belonged to a princely boy, who, it appeared, from what I overheard, had either been privately murdered, or stolen away, or had somehow unaccountably disappeared. This I gathered from the parts of the dialogue that reached me, for always when they came to the trunk, they were close beside me, and I heard every word; but as they went farther away, hanging out the bairn's claes to air, I lost the parts between. Auld Eppie spake without intromission, but Lady July did little else save cry, and weet the different parts of the dress with tears. It was excessively affecting to see the bonny young lady, wha was the flower o' the haill country, bending ower a wheen claes, pressing them to her bosom, and greeting till the very heart within her was like to melt, and aye crying, between every fit o' sobbing, "O my boy, my dear boy! my noble, my beautiful boy! How my soul yearns after thee! Oh, Eppie, may you never know what the misery is to have but one only son, and to be bereaved of him in such a way as I have been!"

At one time I heard the old wife say, "See, here is the silk corslet that he wore next his breast that very day;" on which Lady July seized the little tucker, and kissed it an hundred times, and then said, "Since it once was warmed in his dear little bosom, it shall never cool again as long as his mother's is warm." So saying, she opened her gown, and laid the remnant on her breast, weeping bitterly.

Eppie's anecdotes of the boy were without end; the bereaved and beautiful mother often rebuking her, but all the while manifestly indulging in a painful pleasure. She showed her a pair of trews that were discoloured, and added, "Ah, I ken brawly what made them sae din. His foster-brother, Ranald, and he were after a fine painted butterfly one day. The creature took across a mire, a perfect stank. Ranald stopped short, but Lewie made a bauld spring to clear it. He hardly wan by the mids, where he stuck up to the waist in mire. Afore my goodman reached him, there was naething aboon but the blue bonnet and the feather. 'You little imp o' darkness, how gat you in there?' said my husband. 'That's not your concern, sir, but how I shall get out again,' says the little pestilence. Ah, he was the bairn that had the kind heart when kindness was shown to him; but no ae thing in this versal world wad he do by compulsion. We could never make him comprehend the power of death; he always bit his lip and scowled wi' his eebrows, as if determined to resist it. At first he held him at defiance, threatening to shoot or run him through the body; but when checked so that he durst not openly defy him, his resolution was evidently unchanged. Ha! he was the gallant boy; and if he lives to be a man, he winna have his match in the three kingdoms."

"Alack, alack! my dear boy," exclaimed Lady Julia; "his beauty is long ago defaced, his princely form decayed, and his little unripe bones lying mouldering in some pit or concealed grave. Perhaps he was flung from these rocks, and his fair and mangled form become the prey of the raven and the eagle."

The lady's vehemence some way affected my heart, an' raised sickan a disposition in me to join her in crying, that in spite o' my heart I fell a fuffing like a goose as I was, in below the burn brae. I was overheard; and then all was silence and consternation for about the space of a minute, till I hears Eppie say, "Did you hear that, Lady July? What say ye? What in the world was that? I wish there may be nae concealed spies. I hope nae unhallowed ee has seen our wark the day, or unblest ear heard our words. Eh?

> "Neck butt, neck ben,
> I find the smell o' quick men;
> But be he living or be he dead,
> I'll grind his bones to mix my bread."

So saying, the old hag in one moment rushed through the thin part of the brake, in a retrograde position, and drapping down from the hanging bank in the same way, she chanced to light precisely with a foot on each side of my neck. I tried to withdraw my head quietly and peaceably, but she held me as if my head had been in a vice, and, with the most unearthly yells, called out for *a knife! a knife!* I had now no other resource left but to make a tremendous bolt forward, by which I easily overturned the old dame, and off I ran plash for plash down the burn, till I came to an opening, by which I reached the only path down the glen. I had lost my bonnet between the old wife's feet, but got off with my head, which was more than the roudess intended.

Such screaming and howling as the two carried on behind me, I never heard. Their grand secret was now out; and I suppose they looked upon the discovery as utter ruin, for both of them knew me perfectly well, and guessed by whom I had been sent. I made the best of my way home, where I arrived before dark, and gave my master the Earl a full and faithful account of all that I had seen and all that I had heard. He said not a word until I had ended, but his face grew dark, and his eyes as red as a coal, and I easily perceived that he repented having sent me. When I had concluded my narrative, he bit his lip for some time, and then said in a low smothered voice,—"I see how it has been—I see how it has been; I understand it all perfectly well. Good G—! what a fate has been mine! But I believe, Tom, it will be unsafe for you to stay longer here; for, if you do, you will not be alive before to-morrow at midnight. Therefore haste to the south, and never for your life come north of the Tweed again, or you are a dead man, depend on that. If you promise me this, I will make you a present of L.10, over and above your wages; but if you refuse, I will take my chance of having your motions watched, and you may take yours."

As I had often heard that some certain officious people had vanished from my Lord's mansion before this time, I was glad to make my escape; and taking him at his offer, I was conveyed on shipboard that same night, and have never again looked towards the north.

"It is a great loss, Thomas," said I, "that you can give me no account of the boy, whose son he was, or what became of him. Was Lady Julia ever married?"

I coudna say, sir. I never heard it said either that she was married or unmarried. I never had the slightest suspicion that she was married till that day; but I certainly believe sinsyne, that she aince *had* been married at ony rate. Last year I met with one John Ferguson from that country, who told me the Earl was dead, and that there was some dispute about the heirship, and that some strange secrets had come out; and he added, "For you know very weel, Thomas, that that family never could do anything like other people."

"Think you there is no person in that country to whom I could apply," said I, "for a developement of these mysterious circumstances?"

"There is only one person," said Henderson, "and I am sure he knows everything about it, and that is the Bishop; for he was almost constantly in the family, was sent for on every emergency, and was often away on long jaunts with Lady Julia alone. I am sure he can inform you of every circumstance; but the danger is, that he may not dare to disclose them."

Having twice met with the Bishop, and been exceedingly happy with him, I wrote to him on the instant, requesting some explanation of the curious story related by Henderson. I am almost certain he will not withhold it; and if it be of such a nature as to suit publicity, I shall send it you as soon as it arrives.

MOUNT BENGER
*May* 10*th.*

This story of Henderson's made so strong an impression upon me that I could not refrain from addressing a letter to the Bishop, requesting, in as polite terms as I could, an explanation of the events to which it referred. I was not aware that the reverend prelate had been in any way personally connected with the events referred to, nor did his answer expressly admit that he was; but I could gather from it, that he had a very intimate share in them, and was highly offended at the liberty I had taken, upon an acquaintance that was certainly slight, of addressing him on the subject. I was sorry that I should have inadvertently disturbed his reverence's equanimity, for his reply betrayed a good deal of angry feeling; and as in it he took the trouble of entering at some length into a defence of the Roman Catholic religion, against which I had made no insinuation, nor even once referred to it, I suspected that there had been something wrong, and, more and more resolved to get to the bottom of the affair, I next wrote to the Protestant clergyman of the place. His reply informed me that it was altogether out of his power to furnish the information desired, inasmuch as he had come to the pastoral charge of his parish many years subsequently to the period alluded to; and the Earl of —'s family being Catholic, he had no intercourse with them. It was considered unsafe to meddle with them, he said; they had the reputation of being a dangerous race, and, interfering with no man's affairs, allowed no interference with theirs. In conclusion, however, my reverend correspondent referred me to a Mr MacTavish, tenant of Innismore, as one who possessed more knowledge concerning the Earl's family than any one out of it. This person, he farther stated, was seventy years of age, and had lived in the district all his life, though the late Earl tried every means to remove him.

Availing myself of this clew, I made it my business to address Mr MacTavish in such a way as was most likely to ensure compliance with my wishes. I was at some pains to procure introductions, and establish a sort of acquaintance with him, and at last succeeded in gaining a detail of the circumstances, in so far as he knew them, connected with the adventure of Henderson at the shieling of Aberduchra. This detail was given me in a series of letters of different dates, and many of them at long intervals from each other, which I shall take the liberty of throwing into a continuous narrative, retaining, however, the old gentleman's own way of telling the story.

---

About the time when the French were all to be killed in Lochaber (Mr MacTavish's narrative commences), I was employed in raising the militia soldiers, and so had often to make excursions through the country, both by night and day. One morning, before dawn, as I was riding up the Clunie side of the river, I was alarmed by perceiving a huge black body moving along the road before me. I knew very well that it was the Bogle of Glastulochan, and kept at a respectful distance behind it. After I had ridden a considerable way in great terror, but yet not daring to turn and fly, the light became more and more clear, and the size of the apparition decreased, and, from a huge undefined mass, assumed sundry shapes, which made it evident that it meditated an attack on me, or, as I had some faint hopes, to evanish altogether. To attempt to fly from a spirit I knew to be needless, so I held on my way, in great perturbation. At last, as the apparition mounted an eminence over which the road winded, and so came more distinctly between me and the light, I discovered that it was two persons on horseback, travelling the same way as myself. On coming up, I recognised the Popish Bishop accompanied by the most beautiful young lady I had ever seen.

"Good morrow to you, pretty lady, and to you, reverend sir," said I; but not one of them answered a word. The lady, however, gazed intently at me, as if she expected I had been some other, while the Bishop seemed greatly incensed, and never once turned round his head. I cannot tell how it was, but I became all at once greatly in love with the lady, and resolved not to part till I discovered who she was. So when we came to the house of Robert MacNab, I said, "Madam, do you cross the corrie to-day?"

"No," said she.

"Then I shall stay on this side too," said I.

"Young soldier, we desire to be alone," said the Bishop, (and this was the first time he had spoken,) "therefore be pleased to take your own way, and to free us of your company."

"By no means," said I; "neither the lady nor your Reverence can be the worse of my protection."

When I said "your Reverence," the Bishop started, and stared me in the face; and after a long pause, once more desired me to leave them. I would not do so, however, although I must acknowledge my behaviour was exceedingly improper; but I was under the influence of a strange fascination at the time, which I am the more convinced of now that I know the events that have followed upon that rencounter.

"We travel by the Spean," said he.

"It is the nearest way," I replied, "and I shall go that way too." The Bishop then became very angry, and I, I must confess, more and more impertinent. "I know better," said I, "than to trust a Popish priest with such a lovely and beautiful, and amiable dear lady in such a wild and lonely place. I bear his Majesty's commission, and it is my duty to protect all the ladies that are his true subjects." This was taking a good deal upon me, but I thought I perceived that the Bishop had an abashed look, as if detected in an affair he was ashamed of; and so I determined to see the end of it. We travelled together till we arrived at Fort William, where we were met by a gallant gentleman, who took the lady from her horse, and kissed her, and made many fine speeches; and she wept, and suffered herself to be led away towards the beach. I went with them, and there being a great stir at the shore, and fearing that they were going to take the lady on board by force, I drew my sword, and advancing to the gentleman, commanded him not to take the lady on board against her will, adding, that she was under my protection.

"Is she indeed, sir?" said he. "And pray may I ask to whom she is indebted for this kind and gratuitous protection?"

"That is to myself, sir," said I.

He pushed me aside in high disdain, and as I continued to show a disposition to oppose by force his purpose of taking the lady on board, I was surrounded by nine or ten fellows who were in readiness to act upon his orders; they disarmed me, and persuading the spectators that I was insane or intoxicated, bound me, as the only means of preventing me from annoying their master. The whole party then went on board, and sailed down the frith; and I saw no more of them, nor discovered any more concerning the lady at that time.

Soon after this adventure, the Bishop returned home, but whenever he saw my face, he looked as if he had seen a serpent ready to spring on him. Many a sore and heavy heart I had about the lady that I saw fallen among the Papists, and carried away by them; but for a long while I remained in ignorance who she was, being only able to conjecture that she was some young woman about to be made a nun, contrary to her own inclination.

At length a fearful report began to spread through the country of the loss of Lady Julia, and of her having been last seen in the company of her confessor; but the Bishop frequented the Castle the same as before, and therefore people shook their heads whenever the subject was mentioned, as if much were suspected, though little durst be said. I wondered greatly if that lady with whom I fell so much in love in our passage through the Highlands, could have been this Lady Julia. My father died that year, so I left the regiment in which I had been an officer, and being in Glasgow about the end of September, I went from thence in a vessel to Fort-William. As we passed the island of Illismore, a lady came on board rather in a secret manner. She had a maid-servant with her, who carried a child. The moment the lady stepped up the ship's side, I perceived it to be the identical beautiful creature with whom I had fallen in the year before, when the Bishop was carrying her away. But what a change had taken place in her appearance! her countenance was pale and emaciated, her looks dejected, and she seemed to be heart-broken. At our first rencounter, she looked me full in the face, and I saw that she recognised me, for she hurried past me into the cabin, followed by her maid.

When we came to the fortress, and were paying our fares, I observed some dispute between the lady and the mate or master of the boat and a West-Islander, the one charging her for boat-fare, and the other for board and lodging. "I give you my word of honour," she said, "that you shall be paid double your demands in two weeks; but at present I have no means of satisfying you."

"Words of honour won't pass current here, mistress," said the sailor; "money or value I must have, for I am but a servant."

The West-Islander was less uncivil, and expressing his reluctance to press a gentlewoman in a strait, said, if she would tell him who she was, he would ask no more security.

"You are very good," said she, as she wiped away the tears that were streaming down her cheeks; but she would not tell her name. Her confusion and despair became extreme, so much so, that I could no longer endure to see one who appeared so ingenuous, yet compelled to shroud herself in mystery, suffer so much from so paltry a cause; and, interfering, I satisfied the demands of the two men. The look of gratitude which she cast upon me was most expressive; but she said nothing. We travelled in company to Inverness, I supplying her with what money was necessary to meet the expenses of the road, which she took without offering a word of explanation. Before we parted, she called me into an apartment, and assuring me that I should soon hear from her, she thanked me briefly for the assistance I had afforded her. "And this little fellow," continued she, "if he live to be a man, shall thank you too for your kindness to his mother." She then asked if I could know the child again, and I answered that I could not, all infants were so much alike. She said there was a good reason why she wished that I should be able to recognise the child at any future period, and she would show me a private mark by which I should know him as long as I lived. Baring his little bosom accordingly, she displayed the mark of a gold ring, with a ruby, immediately below his left breast. I said it was a very curious mark indeed, and one that I could not mistake. She next asked me if I was a Roman Catholic? but I shook my head, and said, God forbid! and so we parted.

I had learned from the West-Islander that his name was Malcolm M'Leod, a poor and honest Roman Catholic, and that the child was born at his house, one of the most remote places in the world, being on a sequestered and inaccessible peninsula in one of the Western Isles. The infant had been baptized privately by the Bishop of Illismore, by the name of Lewis William. But farther the man either could not or would not give me any information.

Before I left Inverness I learned that the lady was no other than the noble and fair Lady Julia, and shortly after I got home to Innismore, I received a blank letter, enclosing the sum I had expended on her behalf. Not long after, a message came, desiring me to come express to the Bishop's house. This was the whole amount of the message, and although no definite object was held out to me, I undertook the journey. Indeed, throughout the whole transactions connected with this affair, I cannot understand what motives they were that I acted on. It seems rather that I was influenced by a sort of fatality throughout, as well as the other persons with whom I had to deal. What human probability was there, for instance, that I would obey a summons of this nature? and yet I was summoned. There was no inducement held out to procure my compliance with the request; and yet I did comply with it. Upon what pretext was I to gain admittance to the Bishop's house? I could think of none. And if I am called upon to tell how I did gain admittance, if it were not that subsequent events demonstrate that my proceedings were in accordance with the decrees of a superior destiny, I should say that it was by the mere force of impudence. As I approached the house, I heard there was such a weeping, and screaming, and lamentation, that I almost thought murder was going on within it. There were many voices, all speaking at once; but the cries were heard above all, and grew more woful and bitter. When I entered the house, which I did without much ceremony, and flung open the door of the apartment from which the noise proceeded, there was Lady Julia screaming in an agony of despair, and holding her child to her bosom, who was crying as bitterly as herself. She was surrounded by the Bishop and three other gentlemen, one of them on his knees, as if imploring her to consent to something, and the other three using gentle force to take the child from her. My entrance seemed to strike them with equal terror and astonishment; they commanded me loudly to retire; but I forced myself forward, while Lady Julia called out and named me, saying I was her friend and protector. She was quite in a state of derangement through agony and despair, and I was much moved when I saw how she pressed her babe to her bosom, bathed him with tears, and kissed him and blessed him a thousand times.

"O Mr MacTavish," cried she, "they are going to take my child from me,—my dear, dear boy! and I would rather part with my life. But they cannot take my child from me if you will protect me. They cannot—they cannot!" And in that way did she rave on, regardless of all their entreaties.

"My dear Lady Julia, what madness has seized you?" said a reverend-looking gentleman. "Are you going to bring ruin on yourself and your whole family, and to disgrace the holy religion which you profess? Did you not promise that you would give up the child? did you not come here for that special purpose? and do not we all engage, in the most solemn manner, to see him bred and educated as becomes his birth?"

"No, no, no, no!" cried she; "I cannot, I cannot! I will not part with him! I will go with him to the farthest ends of the world, where our names were never heard of,—but, oh! do not separate me from my dear boy!"

The men stared at one another, and held their peace.

"Madam," said I, "I will willingly protect your baby and you, if there is occasion for it, as long as there is a drop of blood in my body; but it strikes me that these gentlemen are in the right, and that you are in the wrong. It is true, I speak in ignorance of circumstances; but from all that I can guess, you cannot doubt of your baby's safety, when all these honourable men stand security to you for him. But if it is necessary that you should part with him, and if you will not intrust him to them, give him to me. I will have him nursed and educated in my own house, and under mine own eye."

"You are very good—you are very good!" said she, rather calmly. "Well, let this worthy gentleman take the charge of him, and I yield to give him up."

"No, no!" exclaimed they all at once, "no heretic can have the charge of the boy; he must be brought up under our own auspices; therefore, dearest Lady Julia, bethink you what you are doing, before you work your own ruin, and his ruin, and the ruin of us all."

Lady Julia then burst into a long fit of weeping, and I saw she was going to yield; she, however, requested permission to speak a few words with me in private. This was readily granted, and all of them retired. When we were alone, she said to me softly, "They are going to take my child from me, and I cannot and dare not resist them any longer, for fear a worse fate befall him. But I sent for you to be a witness of our separation. You will know my poor hapless child as long as he lives, from the mark that I showed you; and when they force him from me, O watch where they take him, and to whatever quarter that may be, follow, and bring me word, and high shall be your reward. Now, farewell; remember I trust in you,—and God be with you! I do not wish any one to see my last extremity, save those who cause it, for I know my heart must break. Desire them to come in, and say that you have persuaded me to yield to their will."

I did so; but I could see that they only regarded me with looks of suspicion.

I lingered in the narrow lobby, and it was not two minutes, till two persons, one of whom I had previously ascertained by his accent to be an Irish gentleman, hurried by me with the child. I should have followed, but, as, in their haste, they left open the door of the apartment where Julia was, my attention was riveted on the lady; she was paralysed with affliction, and clasped the air, as if trying to embrace something,—but finding her child was no longer in her bosom, she sprung up to an amazing height, uttered a terrible shriek, and fell down strongly convulsed. Shortly after, she uttered a tremulous moan, and died quite away. I had no doubt that her heart was broken, and

that she had expired; and indeed the Bishop, and the other gentleman, who remained with her, seemed to be of the same opinion, and
were benumbed with astonishment. I called aloud for assistance,
when two women came bustling in with water; but the Bishop ordered one of them, in an angry tone, to retire. He gave the command
in Gaelic, and the poor creature cowered like a spaniel under the
lash, and made all haste out of his sight. This circumstance caused
me to take a look at the woman, and I perceived at once that I knew
her,—but the hurry and confusion of the moment prevented me from
thinking of the incident, less or more, until long afterwards.

Lady Julia at length gave symptoms of returning animation, and
then I recollected the neglect of the charge she had committed to me.
I hurried out; but all trace of the child was lost. The two gentlemen
who took him from his mother, were walking and conversing deliberately in the garden, as if nothing had happened, and all my inquir-
ies of them and of others were unavailing.

After the loss of Lady Julia's child, I searched the whole country,
but no child could I either see or hear of; and at length my only hope
rested on being able to remember who the old woman was whom
the Bishop ordered so abruptly out of his presence that day the child
was disposed of. I was sure, from the manner in which she skulked
away, as if afraid of being discovered, that she had taken him away,
either dead or alive. Of all the sensations I ever experienced I was
now subjected to the most teasing: I was sensible that I knew the
woman perfectly well,—so well, that at first I believed I could call her
to my recollection whenever I chose; but, though I put my memory
to the rack a thousand and a thousand times, the name, residence,
and connexions of the woman went farther and farther from my
grasp, till at last they vanished like clouds that mock us with forms of
the long-departed.

And now I am going to tell a very marvellous story: One day,
when I was hunting in Correi-beg of Glen-Anam, I shot so well that
I wondered at myself. Before my unerring aim, whole coveys of
moor game fluttered to the earth; and as for the ptarmigans, they fell
like showers of hailstones. At length I began to observe that the
wounded birds eyed me with strange, unearthly looks, and recol-
lecting the traditions of the glen, and its name, I suspected there was
some enchantment in the case. What, thought I, if I am shooting
good fairies, or little harmless hill spirits, or mayhap whole flocks of
Papists trying feats of witchcraft!—and to think that I am carrying all
these on my back! While standing in this perplexity, I heard a voice
behind me, which said, "O Sandy MacTavish, Sandy MacTavish,

how will you answer for this day's work? What will become of me! what will become of me!"

I turned round in great consternation, my hairs all standing on end—but nothing could I see, save a wounded ptarmigan, hopping among the greystones. It looked at its feathery legs and its snow-white breast all covered with blood,—and at length the creature said, in Gaelic, as before, for it could not be expected that a ptarmigan should have spoken English, "How would you like to find all your family and friends shot and mangled in this way when you gang hame? Ay, if you do not catch me, you will rue this morning's work as long as you live,—and long, long afterwards. But if you catch me, your fortune is made, and you will gain both great riches and respect."

"Then have with you, creature!" exclaimed I, "for it strikes me that I can never make a fortune so easily;" and I ran at it, with my bonnet in both hands, to catch it.

"Hee–hee–hee!" laughed the creature; and away it bounded among the grey stones, jumping like a jackdaw with a clipped wing. I ran and ran, and every time that I tried to clap my bonnet above it, down I came with a rattle among the stones—"Hee–hee–hee!" shouted the bird at every tumble. So provoking was this, and so eager did I become in the pursuit, that I flung away my gun and my load of game, and ran after the bird like a madman, floundering over rugged stones, laying on with my bonnet, and sometimes throwing myself above the little creature, which always eluded me.

I knew all this while that the creature was a witch, or a fairy, or something worse,—but natheless I could not resist chasing it, being resolved to catch it, cost what it would; and on I ran, by cliff and corrie, till I came to a cottage which I remembered having seen once before. The creature, having involved me in the linns of the glen, had got considerably ahead of me, and took shelter in the cottage. I was all covered with blood as well as the bird, and in that state I ran into the bothy after my prey.

On entering, I heard a great bustle, as if all the inmates were employed in effecting the concealment of something. I took it for a concern of smuggling, and went boldly forward, with a "Hilloa! who bides here?"

At the question there appeared one I had good reason to recollect, at sight of whom my heart thrilled. This was no other than the old woman I had seen at the Bishop's house. I knew her perfectly well, for I had been in the same bothy once before, when out hunting, to get some refreshment. I now wondered much that I should never have been able to recollect who the beldam was, till that moment, when I saw her again in her own house. Her looks betrayed the utmost confusion and dismay, as she addressed me in these words, "Hee–hee, good Mr MacTavish, what will you be seeking so far from home to-day?"

"I am only seeking a wounded ptarmigan, mistress," said I; "and if it be not a witch and yourself that I have wounded, I must have it,– for a great deal depends upon my getting hold of the creature."

"Ha, ha! you are coming pursuing after your fortune the day, Mr MacTavish," said she, "and mayhap you may seize her; but we have a small piece of an operation to go through before that can take place."

"And pray, what is that, Mrs Elspeth?" said I; "for if it be any of your witchcraft doings, I will have no hand in it. Give me my bird; that is all I ask of you."

"And so you really and positively believe it was a bird you chased in here to-day, Mr MacTavish?"

"Why, what could I think, mistress? It had the appearance of a bird."

"Margati Cousland! come hither," said the old witch; "what is ordained must be done;–lay hold of him, Margati."

The two women then laid hold of me, and being under some spell, I had no power to resist; so they bound my hands and feet, and laid me on a table, laughing immoderately at my terrors. They then begged I would excuse them, for they were under the necessity of going on with the operation, though it might not be quite agreeable to me in the first instance.

"And pray, Mrs Elspeth, what is this same operation?" said I.

"Why," said she, "you have come here chasing after a great fortune, and there is no other way of attaining it save by one,–and that is, YOUR HEART'S BLOOD MUST BE LET OUT."

"That is a very uncommon way of attaining a fortune, Mrs Elspeth," said I, as good-humouredly as I could, although my heart was quaking within me.

"It is nevertheless a very excellent plan," said the witch, "and it is very rarely that a fortune can be made without it." So saying, the beldam plunged a skein-ochil into my breast, with a loud and a fiendish laugh. "There goes the heart's blood of black Sandy MacTavish!" cried she; and that instant I heard the sound of it rushing to the floor. It was not like the sound of a cataract of blood, however, but rather like the tinkling of a stream of gold guineas. I forced up my head, and behold, there was a stream of pure and shining gold pieces issuing from my bosom; while a number of demons, some in black gowns, and others in white petticoats, were running off with them, and flinging them about in every direction! I could stand this no longer; to have parted with a little blood I found would have been nothing, but to see my vitals drained of a precious treasure, which I knew not had been there, was more than human nature could bear; so I roared out, in a voice that made all the house and all the hills to yell, "Murder! thieves! thieves! robbers!–Murder! Ho! ho! ho!" Thus did I continue loudly to shout, till one of the witches, or infernals, as I thought, dashed a pail of water on my face, a portion of which going into my mouth and windpipe, choked my utterance; but natheless the remorseless wretch continued to dash water upon me with an unsparing hand, till at last the spell was broke, and the whole illusion vanished.

In order to establish the credibility of the above relation, I must tell another story, which shall be a very short one.

"Our mhaster slheeps fery lhang this tay, Mrs Roy MacCallum," said my man, Donald, to my old housekeeper.

"Huh aye, and that she does, Tonald; and Cot pe plessing her slheep to her, honest shentlemans! Donald MacIntosh."

"Huh aye, Mrs Roy MacCallum. But hersell looked just pen te house to see if mhaster was waking and quite coot in health; and, would you pelieve it, Mrs MacCallum? her is lying staring and struggling as if her were quite mhad."

"Cot forpit, Tonald MacIntosh!"

"Huh aye, to be sure, Mrs MacCallum, Cot forpit, to be sure; but her pe mhad for all tat; and tere pe one creat trial, Mrs Roy MacCallum, and we mhust mhake it, and tat is py water."

"It pe te creat and lhast trial; let us ply te water," rejoined the sage housekeeper.

With that, Mrs Roy MacCallum and Donald MacIntosh came into my sleeping-room with pails of water, and began to fling it upon me in such copious showers that I was wellnigh choked; and to prevent myself from being drowned, I sprung up; but still they continued to dash water upon me. At length I knew my own man Donald's voice as I heard him calling out, "Clash on, Mrs MacCallum! it pe for life or teath."

"Huh aye, ply on te water, Tonald!" cried the other.

"Hold, hold, my good friends," cried I, skipping round the room all dripping wet–"Hold, hold, I am wide awake now, and better."

"Huh! plessit pe Cot, and plessit pe te creat MacTavish!" cried they both at once.

"But where is the witch of the glen?" cried I. "And where is the wounded ptarmigan?—and where is all the gold that came out with my heart's blood?"

"Clash on te water, Mrs MacCallum!" exclaimed Donald; and the indefatigable pails of Donald and the housekeeper were again put in requisition to some purpose. Having skipped about for some time, I at last escaped into a closet, and locked the door. I had then leisure to remonstrate with them through the key-hole; but still there were many things about which we could not come to a right understanding, and I began to dread a tremendous shower-bath from above, as I heard them carrying water up stairs; and that dread brought me first to my proper and right senses.

It will now be perceived that the whole of my adventure in the glen, with the ptarmigan and the witches, was nothing more than a dream. But yet in my opinion it was more than a dream, for it was the same as reality to me. I had all the feelings and sensations of a rational being, and every circumstance was impressed on my mind the same as if I had transacted it awake. Besides, there was a most singular and important revelation imparted to me by the vision: I had discovered who the old woman was whose identity had before perplexed me so much, and who I was sure either had Lady Julia's boy, or knew where he was. About five years previous to this I had come into the same woman's house, weary and hungry, and laden with game, and was very kindly treated. Of course, her face was quite familiar to me; but till I had this singular dream, all the efforts of my memory could not recall the woman's name and habitation, nor in what country or circumstances I had before seen her. From that morning forth I thought of nothing else save another visit to the forester's cottage in the glen; and, though my heart foreboded some evil, I rested not till I had accomplished it.

It was not long till I made a journey to Aberduchra, in search of the old witch whom I had seen in my dream. I found her; and apparently she had recently suffered much from distress of mind; her eyes were red with weeping, her hairs were hanging in elf-switches, and her dress in much disorder. She knew me, and said, "God bless you, Mr MacTavish, where are you travelling this way?"

"In truth, Mrs Cowan," I replied, "I am just come to see after Lady Julia's little boy, poor Lewis William, you know, who was put under your care by the Bishop, on the first of November last year."

She held up her hands and stared, and then fell a-crying most bitterly, striking her breast, and wringing her hands, like one distracted, but still without answering me one word.

"Ochon, ochon!" said I; "then it is all as I suspected, and the dear child is indeed murdered!"

On this she sprung to her feet, and uttered an appalling scream, and then yelled out, "Murdered! murdered! Is the dear boy murdered? Is he–is he murdered?"

This vehemence of feeling on her part at the idea of the boy's being cut off, convinced me that she had not murdered the child herself; and being greatly relieved in my heart, I sat still as in astonishment, until she again put the question if her dear foster-child was murdered.

"Why, Mrs Cowan, not to my knowledge," I replied. "I did not see him murdered; but if he has not been foully dealt with, what has become of him?–for well I know he was put under your charge; and before the world, and before the judges of the land, I shall make you render an account of him."

"Was the boy yours, Mr MacTavish," said she, "that you are so deeply interested in him? For the love of Heaven, tell me who was his father, and then I shall confess to you every thing that I know concerning him."

I then told the old woman the whole story as I have here related it, and requested her to inform me what had become of the boy.

"He was delivered to me after the most solemn injunctions of concealment," said she; "and these were accompanied with threatenings, in case of disobedience, of no ordinary nature. He was to be brought up in this inaccessible wild with us as our grandson; and farther than that, no being was to know. Our reward was to be very high–too high, I am afraid, which may have caused his abstraction. But O he was a dear delightful boy! and I loved him better than my own grandson. He was so playful, so bold, and, at the same time, so forgiving and generous!

"Well, he lived on with us, and grew, and no one acknowledged or noticed him until a little while ago, that one Bill Nicol came into the forest as fox-hunter, and came here to board, to be near the foxes, having, as he pretended, the factor's orders for doing so; and every day he would sport with the two boys, who were both alike fond of him,–and every day would he be giving them rides on his pony, which put them half crazy about the man. And then one day, when he was giving them a ride time about, the knave mounted behind poor little Lewie, and rode off with him altogether into the forest, and there was an end of him. Ranald ran crying after them till he could run no farther, and then, losing sight of them, he sat down and wept. I was busy at work, and thought always that my two little fellows were playing not far off, until I began to wonder where they could be, and ran out to the top of the little birky knowe-head there, and called, and louder called them; but nothing answered me, save the echoes of my own voice from the rocks and trees; so I grew very greatly distracted, and ran up Glen-Caolas, shouting as I went, and always praying between whiles to the Holy Virgin and to the good saints to restore me my boys. But they did not do it—Oh no, they never did! I then began to suspect that this pretended fox-hunter might have been the Wicked One come in disguise to take away my children; and the more so, as I knew not if Lewie had been blessed in holy church. But what could I do but run on, calling, and crying, and raving all the way, until I came to the pass of Bally-keurach, and then I saw that no pony's foot had passed on that path, and turned and ran home; but it was growing dark, and there was nobody there, so I took to the woods again. How I spent that night I do not know, but I think I had fallen into a trance through sorrow and fatigue.

"Next morning, when I came to my senses, the first thing I saw was a man who came by me, chasing a wounded bird, like a white moorfowl, and he was always trying to catch it with his bonnet, and many a hard fall he got among the stones. I called after him, for I was glad to see a human being in that place, and I made all the speed I could to follow; but he regarded me not, but ran after the wounded bird. He went down the linns, which retarded him a good deal, and I got quite near him. Then from that he went into a small hollow straight before me, to which I ran, for I wanted to tell him my tale, and beg his assistance in raising the country in the strath below. When I came into the little hollow, he had vanished, although a hare could not have left it without my seeing it. I was greatly astonished, assured that I had seen a vision. But how much more was I astonished to find, on the very spot where he had disappeared, my grandson, Ranald, lying sound asleep, and quite motionless, through hunger and fatigue! At first I thought he was dead, and lost all recollection of the wonderful way in which I had been led to him; but when I found he was alive and breathing, I took him up in my arms, and carried him home, and there found the same man, or rather the same apparition, busily employed hunting the wounded bird within this same cottage, and he declared that have it he must. I was terrified almost out of my wits, but tried to thank the mysterious being for leading me to my perishing child. His answer—which I shall never forget—was, 'Yes, I have found one, and I will find the other too, if the Almighty spare me in life.' And when the apparition said so, it gave me such a look in the face—Oh! ah! What is this! what is this!"

Here the old woman began to shriek like one distracted, and appeared in an agony of terror; and, to tell the truth, I was not much better myself, when I heard the story of the wounded ptarmigan. But I tried to support the old woman, and asked what ailed her.

"Well you may ask what ails me!" said she. "Oh Mr MacTavish, what did I see just now but the very same look that the apparition gave that morning! The same look, and from the very same features; for indeed it was the apparition of yourself, in every lineament, and in every article of dress:—your very self. And it is the most strange vision that ever happened to me in all my visionary life!"

"I will tell you what it is, Mrs Elspeth Cowan," said I, "you do not know one half of its strangeness yet; but tell me the day of the week and the day of the month when you beheld this same vision of myself."

"Ay, that day I never shall forget," answered Elspeth; "for of all the days of the year it was the one after I lost my dear foster-son, and that was the seventh of Averile. I have always thought my boy was stolen to be murdered, or put out of the way most unfairly, till this very day; but now, when I see the same man in flesh and blood, whom I saw that day chasing the wounded bird, I am sure poor Lewie will be found; for with that very look which you gave me but a minute ago, and in that very place where you stand, your apparition or yourself said to me, 'Yes, I have found the one, and I will find the other if the Almighty spare me in life.'"

"I do not recollect of saying these words, Mrs Cowan," said I.

"Recollect?" said she; "what is it you mean? Sure you were not here your own self that morning?"

"Why, to tell you the solemn truth," replied I, "I was in the glen that very morning chasing a wounded ptarmigan, and I now have some faint recollection of seeing a red-haired boy lying asleep in a little green hollow beside a grey stone,—and I think I did say these words to some one too. But was not there something more? Was not there something about letting out somebody's heart's blood?"

"Yes; but then that was only a dream I had," said she, "while the other was no dream, but a sad reality. But how, in the name of the blessed saints, do you happen to know of that dream?"

"It is not easy, now-a-days," answered I, "to say what is a dream and what is a reality. For my part, from this moment I renounce all certainty of the distinction. It is a fact, that on that very morning, and at that hour, I was in this glen and in this cottage,—and yet I was neither in this glen nor in this cottage. So, if you can unriddle that, you are welcome."

"I knew you were not here in flesh and blood. I knew it was your wraith, or *anam,* as we call it; for, first, you vanished in the hollow before my eyes; then you appeared here again, and when you went away in haste, I followed you to beg your assistance; and all that I could hear was your spirit howling under a waterfall of the linn."

This confounded me more than ever, and it was some time before I recovered my self-possession so far as to inquire if what she had related to me was all she knew about the boy.

"Nothing more," she said, "save that you are destined to discover him again, either dead or alive–for I can assure you, from the words that I heard out of your own spirit's mouth, that if you do not find him, and restore him to his birthright, he never will be discovered by mortal man. I went, poor, sachless, and helpless being as I was, to the Bishop, and told him my woful story; for I durst do nothing till I asked counsel of him. He was, or rather pretended to be, very angry, and said I deserved to be burnt for my negligence, for there was no doubt the boy had fallen over some precipice. It was in vain that I told him how my own grandson had seen him carried off on the pony by the pretended fox-hunter; he persisted in his own belief, and would not suffer me to mention the circumstances to a single individual. So, knowing that the counsel of the Lord was with his servant, I could do nothing but weep in secret, and hold my peace."

Thus ended my interview with Elspeth of the glen.

After my visit to the old sibyl, my mind ran much on the extraordinary vision I had had, and on the old witch's having actually seen a being in my shape at the very instant of time that I myself weened and felt that I was there.

I have forgot whether I went to Lady Julia that very night or some time after, but I did carry her the tidings, which threw her into an agony of the deepest distress. She continued for a long space to repeat that her child was murdered,–her dear, her innocent child. But before I left her, she said her situation was a very peculiar one, and therefore she entreated me to be secret, and to tell no one of the circumstance, yet by all means to lose no time in endeavouring to trace the fox-hunter, and to find out, if possible, whether the boy was dead or alive. She concluded by saying, "Exert yourself like a man and a true friend, as you have always been to me. Spare no expense in attaining your object, and my whole fortune is at your disposal." I was so completely involved in the business, that I saw no alternative but that of proceeding,–and not to proceed with vigour was contrary to my nature.

Lady Julia had all this time been kept in profound ignorance where the child had been concealed, and the very next day after our interview, she paid a visit to old Elspeth Cowan at the remote cottage of Aberduchra, and there I again met with her as I set out on the pursuit. Long and serious was our consultation, and I wrote down all the marks of the man and the horse from Elspeth's mouth; and the child Ranald also gave me some very nice marks of the pony.

The only new thing that had come out, was that the boy Ranald had persisted in saying, that the fox-hunter took his brother Lewie *down* the glen, in place of up, which every other circumstance seemed to indicate. Elspeth had seen them go all three up the glen, the two boys riding on the pony, and the fox-hunter leading it, and Ranald himself was found far up the glen; but yet when we took him to the spot, and pointed up the glen, he said, No, they did not go that way, but the other. Elspeth said it was not possible, but I thought otherwise; for when I asked at Ranald where he thought Nicol the fox-hunter was going with his brother, he said he thought he was taking him home, and that he would come back for him. Elspeth wanted me to take the route through the hills towards the south; but as soon as I heard the boy's tale, I suspected the Bishop had had some share in the abstraction of the missing child, and set out on my search in the direction of his mansion. I asked at every house and at every person, for such a man and such a pony as I described, making no mention of a boy; but no such man had been seen. At length I chanced to be asking at a shieling, within a mile of the Bishop's house, if, on such a day, they had seen such a man ride by on a black pony. They had not seen him; but there was a poor vagrant boy chanced to be present, and heard my inquiry, and he said he saw a man like that ride by on a black pony one day, but it could not be the man I wanted, for he had a bonny boy on the horse before him.

"Indeed?" said I. "O, then, it could not be the man I want. Had the pony any mark by which you could remember it?"

"*Cheas gear,*" said the boy. This was the very mark that little Ranald had given me of the pony. Oho! I have my man now! thought I; so I said no more, but shook my head and went away. Every thing was kept so close about the Bishop's house, I could get no intelligence there, nor even entrance—and in truth, I durst hardly be seen about the premises.

In this dilemma, I recollected the words of the sibyl of the glen, as I had heard them in my strange vision, namely, that my only sure way of making a fortune was by letting out my heart's blood; and also, that when my heart's blood was let out, it proved to be a flood of guineas. Now, thought I to myself, what does making a fortune mean but carrying out successfully any enterprise one may have in hand? and though to part with money is a very hard matter, especially in an affair in which I have no concern, yet I will try the efficacy of it here, and so learn whether the experiment is worth making in other cases where I am more closely interested.–The truth is, I found that I *was* deeply interested in the affair, although, not being able to satisfy my own mind with reasons why I should be so, I affected to consider myself mightily indifferent about it. In pursuance, therefore, of the plan suggested in my dream, and on a proper opportunity, by means of a present administered to one of the Bishop's servants, I learnt, that about the time when the boy had been carried off by the fox-hunter, a priest of the name of O'Callaghan had made his appearance at the Bishop's house; that he was dressed in a dark grey jacket and trowsers, and rode a black pony with cropped ears; that he was believed to have some secret business with the Bishop, and had frequent consultations with him; and my informant, becoming more and more free in his communications, as the facts, one after another, were drawn from him, confessed to me that he had one night overheard quarrelling between O'Callaghan and his master, and having stolen to the door of the apartment, listened for some time, but was unable to make out more of the angry whisperings within than a threat from O'Callaghan, that if the Bishop would not give him more, "he (O'Callaghan) would throw him overboard into the first salt dub he came to." On interrogating my informant if he knew whom O'Callaghan meant, when he said he would "throw him overboard," he replied that he could not guess. I had, however, no doubt, that it was the boy I was in search of, and I had as little doubt that the fellow knew to whom the threat referred; but I have often known people have no scruple in telling all about a secret, so as to give any one a key to the complete knowledge of it, who would yet, upon no consideration, give utterance to the secret itself; and judging this to be the case in the present instance, I contented myself with learning farther, that when the priest left the Bishop's, he went directly to Ireland, of which country he was a native, and would, in all probability, ere long revisit Scotland.

Possessed of this clew, I was nevertheless much at a loss to determine what was the most advisable way of following it out. My inclination led me to wait the fellow's return, and to have him seized and examined. But then I bethought me, if I could be instrumental in saving the boy's life, or of discovering where he was placed, or how circumstanced, it would avail me more, and give Lady Julia more satisfaction than any punishment that might be inflicted on the perpetrators of this deed afterwards. So after a troubled night and day, which I spent in preparation, I armed myself with a pair of pistols and a pair of Highland dirks, a long and a short one, and set out in my arduous undertaking, either to recover the boy or perish in the attempt. And it is needless for me to deny to you, sir, that the vision, and the weird wife of the glen's prophecy, had no small part in urging me to this adventure.

I got no trace of the priest till I went to Abertarf, where I found out that he had lodged in the house of a Catholic, and that he had shown a good deal of kindness and attention to the boy, while the boy seemed also attached to him, but still more to the pony. I went to the house of this man, whose name was Angus Roy MacDonald; but he was close as death, suspicious, and sullen, and would tell me nothing of O'Callaghan's motions. I succeeded, however, in tracing him till he went on board of a Liverpool sloop at Arisaig. I was much at a loss how to proceed, when, in the evening, perceiving a vessel in the offing, bearing against the tide, and hoping that the persons I sought might be aboard of her, I hired a boat to take me out; but we lost sight of her in the dusk of the evening, and I was obliged to bribe the boatmen to take me all the way to Tobermory, having been assured that the Liverpool vessel would be obliged to put in there, in order to clear at the custom-house. We did not reach Tobermory till the next day at noon; and as we entered the narrow passage that leads into the harbour, a sloop came full sail by us right before the wind, and I saw a pretty boy standing on the poop. I called out "Lewis" to him, but he only looked over his shoulder as for some one else, and did not answer me. The ship going on, as she turned her stern right towards us, I saw "The Blake of Boston" in golden letters, and thought no more of the encounter till I went on shore, and there I learned on the quay that she was the identical Liverpool vessel of which I was in pursuit, and the boy I had seen, the very one I was in search of. I learnt that he was crying much when ashore, and refused to go on shipboard again till taken by force; and that he told the people boldly, that that man, Nicol the fox-hunter, had taken him from his mother and father, and his brother Ranald, having enticed him out to give him a ride, and never taken him home again. But the fellow telling them a plausible story, they durst not meddle in the matter. It was known, however, that the vessel had to go round by the Shannon, as she had some valuable loading on board for Limerick.

This was heavy news, as how to get a passage thither I wist not. But the thoughts of the poor boy crying for his home hung about my heart, and so, going to Greenock I took a passage for Belfast, and travelled on foot or on horseback as I could, all the way to Limerick. When I got there, matters looked still worse. The Blake had not come up to Limerick, but discharged her bales at the mouth of the river, and again sailed; and here was I in a strange country with no one perhaps to believe my tale. The Irish, however, showed no signs of apathy or indifference to my case, as my own countrymen did. They manifested the utmost sympathy for me, and the utmost indignation against O'Callaghan; and the man being known in the country, he was soon found out by the natives. Yet, strange to say! though found out by twenty men all eagerly bent on the discovery, as soon as he gave them a hint respecting the person by whom he was employed, off they went, and never so much as came back to tell either the Mayor or myself that their search had been successful or not.

But two or three officers, who were Protestants, being dispatched in search of him, they soon brought him to Limerick, where he and I were both examined, and he was committed to jail till the next court day. He denied all knowledge of the boy, and all concern whatever in the crime he was charged with; and the ship being gone I could procure no evidence against him. There was nothing but the allegations of parties, upon which no judgment could be given: I had to pay the expenses of process, and he gave securities for his appearance at the court of Inverness, if he should be cited. I spent nine days more in searching for the boy on the Clare side of the river; but all my efforts were fruitless. I found that my accusation of their vagrant priest rendered me very unpopular among the natives, and was obliged to relinquish the investigation.

O'Callaghan was in Scotland before me, and on my arrival I caused him to be instantly seized, secure now of enough of witnesses to prove the fact of his having taken off the boy. Old Elspeth of the glen and her husband were summoned, as were Lady Julia and Angus Roy MacDonald. When the day of trial came, O'Callaghan's indictment was read in court, charging him with having abstracted a boy from the shieling of Aberduchra. The Bishop being present, and a great number of his adherents, the panel boldly denied every circumstance; and what was my astonishment to find, on the witnesses' names being called, that not one of them was there! The officers were called and examined, who declared that they could not find one of the witnesses in the whole country. The forester and his wife, they said, had left Aberduchra, and gone nobody knew whither; Lady Julia had gone to France, and Angus MacDonald to the Lowlands, it was supposed, with cows. The court remarked it was a singular and rather suspicious circumstance, that the witnesses should all be absent. O'Callaghan said something in his own defence, and having made a reference to the Bishop for his character, his reverence made a long speech in his praise. The consequence was, that as not one witness was produced in support of the accusation, O'Callaghan was once more liberated.

I would never have learned what became of the boy, had not a young soldier, a cousin's son of mine, come to Innismore the other year. He was a fine lad, and I soon became a good deal attached to him; and he being one of a company stationed in the neighbourhood to guard the passes for the prevention of smuggling, he lived a good deal at my house, while his officer remained nightly at the old mansion-house, the guest of Lady Julia and the young Lord.

It is perhaps proper here to mention that Lady Julia was now the only remaining member of the late Earl's family, and the heir of entail, being the son of a distant relation, had been sent from Ireland to be brought up by Lady Julia. He was a perverse and wicked boy, and grieved her heart every day.

The young man, my relation, was one day called out to follow his captain on a private expedition against some smugglers. The next day one of his comrades came and told me that they had had a set battle with a great band of smugglers, in which several were killed and wounded. "Among the rest," said he, "our gallant commander, Captain MacKenzie, is killed, and your nephew is lying mortally wounded at the still-house."

I lost no time in getting ready, and mounting one horse, and causing the soldier to take another, I bade him lead the way, and I followed. It may well be supposed that I was much astonished on finding that the lad was leading me straight to the cottage of Aberduchra! Ever since the old forester and his wife had been removed, the cottage had stood uninhabited; and it seems that, from its inaccessible situation, it had been pitched upon as a still-house, and occupied as such, for several years, by a strong band of smugglers from the Deveron. They were all bold, resolute fellows, and when surprised by MacKenzie and his party, and commanded to yield, they soon showed that there was nothing farther from their intention. In one moment every one had a weapon in his hand; they rushed upon the military with such fury that in a few minutes they beat them back, after having run their captain and another man through the body, and wounded several besides. Captain MacKenzie had slain one of the smugglers at the first onset; but the next instant he fell, and his party retired. The smugglers then staved their casks, and fled, leaving the military in possession of the field of battle, and of the shieling,

in which nothing was found save a great rubbish of smashed utensils and the killed and wounded of both sides.

In this state I found the cottage of Aberduchra. There were one
smuggler and a soldier quite dead, and a number badly wounded;
and among the latter was the young man, my relative, who was sore
wounded in the left shoulder. My whole attention was instantly turned
towards him. He was very faint, but the bleeding was stanched, and
I had hopes of his recovery. I gave him some brandy and water,
which revived him a great deal; and as soon as he could speak, he
said, in a low voice, "For God's sake, attend to our gallant captain's
wound. Mine is nothing, but, if he is still living, his, I fear, is dangerous; and a nobler youth never breathed."

I found him lying on a bed of rushes, one soldier supporting his
head, and another sitting beside him with a dish of cold water. I
asked the captain how he did; but he only shook his head, and pointed
to the wound in his side. I mixed a good strong cup of brandy and
water, and gave it him. He swallowed it greedily, and I had then no
doubt that the young man was near his last. "I am a great deal the
better of that," said he. I requested him not to speak, and then asked
the soldiers if the wound had bled freely, but they said no, it had
scarcely bled any. I was quite ignorant of surgery, but it struck me
that, if possible, the wound should be made to bleed, to prevent it
from bleeding inwardly. Accordingly, the men having kindled a good
fire in the cottage, I got some warm water, and began to foment the
wound. As the stripes of crusted blood began to disappear, judge of
my astonishment, when I perceived the mark of a ruby ring below
his left breast! There was no mistaking the token. I knew that moment that I was administering to Lady Julia's son, for whom I had
travelled so far in vain, and over whom my soul had yearned as over
a lost child of my own. The basin fell from my hands, my hair stood
on end, and my whole frame grew rigid, so that the soldiers stared at
me, thinking I was bewitched, or seized with some strange malady.
The captain, however, made signs for them to proceed with the fo-
mentation, which they did, until the wound bled considerably; and I
began to have some hopes that there might be a possibility of saving
his life. I then sent off a soldier on one of my horses for the nearest
surgeon, and I myself rode straight to the Castle to Lady Julia, and
informed her of the captain's wound, and the miserable state in which
he was lying at the shieling of Aberduchra. She held up her hands,
and had nearly fainted, and made a lamentation so grievous, that I
was convinced she already knew who the young man was. She instantly ordered the carriage to be got ready, and a bed put into it, in

order to have the captain conveyed straight to the Castle. I expected she would have gone in the carriage herself, but when she only gave charges to the servants and me, I then knew that the quality and propinquity of her guest were not known to her.

My reflections on the scenes that had happened at that cottage, made a deep impression on me that night, as well they might, considering how singular they were. At that cottage I had once been in spirit, though certainly not in the body, yet there my bodily form was seen speaking and acting as I would have done, and as at the same moment I believed I was doing. By that vision I discovered where the lost boy was to be found, and there I found him; and when he was lost again, on that very same spot was I told that I should find him, else he never would be discovered by man. And now, after a lapse of fifteen years, and a thousand wanderings on his part overgone, on that very same spot did I again discover him.

Captain MacKenzie was removed to the Castle, and his recovery watched by Lady Julia and myself with the utmost solicitude—a solicitude on her part which seemed to arise from some mysterious impulse of the tie that connected her with the sufferer; for had she known that she was his mother, her care and anxiety about him could scarcely have been greater. When his wound was so far recovered, that no danger was to be apprehended from the agitating discovery, the secret of his birth was communicated to himself and Lady Julia. It is needless for me to trace farther the details of their eventful history. That history, the evidence adduced before the courts of law for the rights of heritage, and before the Peers for the titles, have now been divulged and laid quite open, so that the deeds done in darkness have been brought to light, and that which was meant to have been concealed from the knowledge of all mankind, has been published to the whole world, even in its most minute and intricate windings. It is therefore needless for me to recapitulate all the events that preceded the time when this narrative begins. Let it suffice, that Lady Julia's son has been fully proved legitimate, and we have now a Protestant Earl, in spite of all that the Bishop did to prevent it. And it having been, in a great measure, owing to my evidence that the identity of the heir was established, I have now the prospect of being, if not the richest, at least, the most independent man of either Buchan or Mar.

# Songs for the Baloon!!!

## Song First

Hurra Hurray the spirit's away
    A rocket of air with her bandelet
We're up in the air on our bonny grey mare
    But I see her yet and I see her yet
We'll ring the skirts of the gowden wain         5
    If this steed of the heavens will rein or bit
Or catch the Bear by the frozen mane
    But I see her yet and I see her yet

### 2

O how I rejoice aloft to rise
    Above the thunder-cloud so high         10
For sore I should dread to break my head
    Against the artillery of the sky
Away thou bonny Witch o' Fife
    On the foam of the air to heave and flit
Nor think thou once of a poet's life         15
    For he sees thee yet and he sees thee yet

---

## Song Second

Fareweel fareweel thou lady moon
    With thy dark look of majestye
For though thou hast a queenly face
    Tis yet a fearsome sight to see
Thy lip is like Ben-Lommond's base         5
    Thy mouth like vast unmeasured dell
Thine eye-brow like the grampian range
    Fringed with the brier and heather bell

### 2

Still on that cast of human face
    There is a ghostly dignitye         10
As if some emblem man might trace
    Of him that made both man and thee
Thou pale vicegerent of the sun
    Fareweel a while—I must away

But when my mortal course is run                    15
  With thee I'll try a while to stay

---

## Song Third

Speed on thou bird without a wing
  Why lean'st thou on the cloudlet gray
While vallies, trees mountains and seas
  Are rushing in one tide away
Breast up the feckless waves of space            5
  And let this potent charm avail
The grey-haired pilgrim of the Sun
  Here hangs exulting at thy tail

### 2

O for Sir Robert's pencil true
  With canvas of the ocean's span                  10
For such a panoramic view
  Ne'er met the eye of mortal man
There goes Loch-Awe! like baldrick bright
  She's speeding to the south away
And there's Cruachan's clefted height             15
  Less than Mount-Benger coils of hay

### 3

Now god thee speed my wonderous steed
  Though now thou'rt skiffing on the sky
In kind George Laidlaw's snuggest shed
  We'll find a shelter by and by                   20
There goes Ben-Nevis' sovereign head
  Soon o'er the Border will he be
Ha speed thee, speed my wonderous steed
  The world's on wing from under thee!

---

## Song Fourth

The tempest may tout and its winds may blaw
  With their whoo, rhoo! morning and even
For now the auld Shepherd's aboon them a'
  Winging his way through the stories of heaven
He has had dreams of night and of day             5
  Journies sublime o'er streamer and rainbow

Over the cloughs of the Milky-way
    Led by the light of the seraphim's window

2

Now in his flesh his blood and his bone
    Far o'er his cliffs and mountains of heather          10
Here he carreers through the starry zone
    Bounding away on the billows of aether
Whoo rhoo! Gillan-an-dhu!
    This is a scene from the future we borrow
This is the way each spirit must stray              15
    Mazed in delight in fear and in sorrow

Hech-hey! God be with us, and all good people. AMEN

———————————

Please edge in somewhere two of the verses to the Comet in 1811

Where hast thou roamed these thousand years?
    Why sought out polar paths again?
From wilderness of glowing spheres
    To fling thy vesture o'er the Wain.

And when thou climb'st the milky way               5
    And vanishest from human view
A thousand worlds should hail thy ray
    Through wilds of yon empyreal blue

Oh on thy rapid prow to glide!
    To sail the boundless skies with thee,           10
And plow the twinkling stars aside
    Like foam-bells on a tranquil sea!

To brush the embers from the Sun
    The icicles from off the pole
Then far to other circles run                       15
    Where other moons and planets roll

# The Stuarts o' Appin

I SING of a land that was famous of yore,
    The land of Green Appin, the ward of the flood,
Where every grey cairn that broods over the shore,
    Marks grave of the royal, the valiant, or good.

The land where the strains of grey Ossian were framed,–    5
  The land of fair Selma, and reign of Fingal,–
And late of a race, that with tears must be named,
  The noble CLAN STUART, the bravest of all.
    Oh-hon, an Rei! and the STUARTS of Appin!
    The gallant, devoted, old STUARTS of Appin!    10
        Their glory is o'er,
        For the clan is no more,
    And the Sassenach sings on the hills of green Appin.

In spite of the Campbells, their might and renown,
  And all the proud files of Glenorchy and Lorn,    15
While one of the STUARTS held claim on the crown,
  His banner full boldly by Appin was borne.
And ne'er fell the Campbells in check or trepan,
  In all their Whig efforts their power to renew,
But still on the STUARTS of Appin they ran,    20
  To wreak their proud wrath on the brave and the few.
    Oh-hon, an Rei! and the STUARTS of Appin, &c.

In the year of the Graham, while in oceans of blood
  The fields of the Campbells were gallantly flowing,–
It was then that the STUARTS the foremost still stood,    25
  And paid back a share of the debt they were owing.
O proud Inverlochy! O day of renown!
  Since first the sun rose o'er the peaks of Cruachin,
Was ne'er such an host by such valour o'erthrown,
  Was ne'er such a day for the STUARTS of Appin!    30
    Oh-hon, an Rei, and the STUARTS of Appin, &c.

And ne'er for the crown of the STUARTS was fought
  One battle on vale, or on mountain deer-trodden,
But dearly to Appin the glory was bought,
  And dearest of all on the field of Culloden!    35
Lament, O Glen-creran, Glen-duror, Ardshiel,
  High offspring of heroes, who conquer'd were never,
For the deeds of your fathers no bard shall reveal,
  And the bold clan of STUART must perish for ever.
    Oh-hon, an Rei! and the STUARTS of Appin, &c.    40

Clan-Chattan is broken, the Seaforth bends low,
  The sun of Clan-Ranald is sinking in labour;
Glenco, and Clan-Donnachie, where are they now?
  And where is bold Keppoch, the loved of Lochaber;

All gone with the house they supported!–laid low,          45
  While dogs of the south their bold life-blood were lapping,
Trod down by a proud and a merciless foe.
  The brave are all gone with the STUARTS of Appin!
    Oh-hon, an Rei! and the STUARTS of Appin, &c.

They are gone! They are gone! The redoubted, the brave!          50
  The sea-breezes lone o'er their relics are sighing,
Dark weeds of oblivion shroud many a grave,
  Where the unconquered foes of the Campbell are lying.–
But, long as the grey hairs wave over this brow,
  And earthly emotions my spirit are wrapping,          55
My old heart with tides of regret shall o'erflow,
  And bleed for the fall of the STUARTS of Appin,
    Oh-hon, an Rei! and the STUARTS of Appin!
    The gallant, devoted, old STUARTS of Appin!
      Their glory is o'er,          60
      For their star is no more,
And the green grass waves over the heroes of Appin!

# John Nicholson's Daughter

THE daisy is fair, the day lily rare,
  The bud o' the rose as sweet as it's bonnie–
But there ne'er was a flower, in garden or bower,
  Like auld Joe Nicholson's bonnie Nannie.
    O my Nannie,          5
    My dear little Nannie,
  My sweet little niddlety-noddlety Nannie,
    There ne'er was a flower,
    In garden or bower,
  Like auld Joe Nicholson's Nannie.          10

Ae day she came out wi' a rosy blush,
  To milk her twa kye, sae couthie an' cannie–
I cower'd me down at the back o' the bush,
  To watch the air o' my bonnie Nannie.
    O my Nannie, &c. &c.          15

Her looks so gay, o'er Nature away,
  Frae bonnie blue een sae mild and mellow—
Saw naething sae sweet, in Nature's array,
  Though clad in the morning's gouden yellow.
      O my Nannie, &c. &c.           20

My heart lay beating the flowery green,
  In quaking, quavering agitation—
And the tears came trickling down frae my een,
  Wi' perfect love, an' wi' admiration.
      O my Nannie, &c. &c.           25

There's mony a joy in this world below,
  And sweet the hopes that to sing were uncannie—
But of all the pleasures I ever can know,
  There's none like the love o' my dearest Nannie.
      O my Nannie,              30
      My dear little Nannie,
    My sweet little niddlety-noddlety Nannie—
      There ne'er was a flower,
      In garden or bower,
    Like auld Joe Nicholson's Nannie.      35

# Appendix A
# Chaldee Manuscript 'Continuation'

And the first that I beheld was smoothe and beautiful in his appearance and his face was like the sun shining in his strength, and there was brightness there.

And I said to my lord seest thou this man whose face shineth, and whose form is as that of the porpoise of the great deep; certainly there is great folly and emptiness in this man else why should he be a footstool to one not better than himself.

And he said grieviously hast thou erred in judgement for the man is prudent among the children of his people and when he yeildeth to become a footstool to his neighbour it is not for nought.

And moreoever he hath great wisdom for if any man say unto him come thou and eat of my bread and drink of my drink, thither he goeth and eateth and drinketh abundantly.

And when these things are fulfilled he lifteth up his face that shineth unto heaven, and he openeth his mouth which is comely, and out of it there proceedeth a sound that is sweeter than that of a ten stringed instrument. If this is not wisdom where is it to be found. Nevertheless the nat. have scof and said that the substance of a man is not in him whosoever hath an ear to hear let her hear.

And John that liveth in the place of the great Sanhedrim was there also a man of low stature comely in his apparrel and knoweth not what the workings in the spirit of man meaneth.

Likewise his fellow whose countenance is darkened by reason of great tribulation and the clouds that hang over the minds of the foolish ones.

And I saw one whose name was like unto the great beast of the desert but his nature attained not thereunto and his brother also an upright man and one that walketh in the paths of holiness and is stately even unto great laughter.

For he lifteth up his head on high and repeateth many wise and godly sayings which those that do him know in nowise regardeth but take them as the ass taketh the words of his rider to whom he trusteth not.

Also one whose voice was as the voice of a child and whose name was as if it had been the colour of amber or certain strong drink which cherisheth the heart of man but he straineth at a gnat and flyeth at his own shadow.

And then I beheld him whose name is like the chariot of the Isle of the west who is rude in speech and whose voice is heard afar off for he calleth aloud in the assemblies of the beasts and striketh with mighty power as a smith striketh on the anvil.

[...] lo I will kill thee for thou hast take[n] [TEAR] me my silver and my gold and hast consumed my [TEAR] very vanity and things of no value and behold I am compelled to unlearn all that thou didst teach me.

And he answered and said unto him so be it unto thee and worse also thou perverse and foolish one for thou lookest not upon the works of na[tu]re as they are but on the works of men and thou takest one thing from one man and another from another putting them together to dishonour.

And thy skies are like the ceiling of a house in which men drink strong drink thy moons are like the holes that are in thy own green curtain and thy mountains like the mountains of the wrath of God.

And when the man whose name was as if it had been a kitten that is a male heard this he waxed wroth and went away saying unto himself why should I contend with one who has been a fool from his youth upward I have gained nothing thereby.

And he came to another who was a stranger to him and he heaved up his broken pillar and smote him on the palms of his hands.

And he said unto him [i]t is nought that thou dost; what miserable thing is that? Go to now, give it up and cast it into the fire.

And the man said so do thou to me and more also if I do not make thy head to smite against the wall.

And ere ever I was aware the clamour combat was begun and the chamber resounded with the noise thereof for the stranger flew at the man and gave him many wounds and bruises and bit off one of his members with the teeth of his mouth.

And the battle was very fierce for the stranger threw him down and struck him on the face about the mouth and below the left ear.

At which the man waxed very wroth and he beat the stranger and overcame him and kicked him out into the street of the city.

And moreover he followed him up to the hill of the fortress of the land for the stranger had been a man of war from his youth and finding him there he kicked him before the eyes of his brethren at which he was sorely offended and ashamed.

And the man became proud of his victory but he rejoiced not therein for his mouth became very small by reason of the striking wherewith the stranger struck him on the mouth.

And by the time that he returned behold there was another man came in even he which liveth at the corner and weareth on his head a feather of red and of green for he is a mischievous person and stirreth up strife and debate or maketh peace at hi[s] pleasure and wherever two or three of the smiths are met together there is he in the midst of them to plague them.

And he came to this wicked artificier and he said unto him thou hast done glorious and [ex]cellent things but what manner of sky is this? Take thou in thy horizon one half that the thing may appear like a thing of this world.

Here also is a fountain that is running with the foam of the ocean and this falling of the stream is wool in place of water lo now I will take unto me a hammer and a chissel and deface every part of thy images.

And his wrath was again rekindled and he lifted up his broken pillar of the temple and thought to smite down the man with the [TEAR]ther behind his back but his bl[TEAR] availed not.

And he defended his graven images with great valour but there was none who came to his aid and he was overcome at the last.

And he came and bowed himself down before the man with the feather and said unto him hold now thine hand I pray thee: what right hast thou to come and destroy my images the work of mine hands?

Behold I will give unto thee the choisest of them all take it away and place it in the house of thy gods; only let me work my work, and possess that which is mine own in peace; for thou art a snare unto me.

And the man laughed aloud and he took the image and went his way.

And the next that I saw was a young man who came from the New fortress by the great river as thou goest down towards Urr of the Chaldeans and he was descended from one of the fathers.

His images were made of silver and overlaid with pure gold very beautiful the work of a cunning artificier for his likenesses of the daughters of men were comely as the angels that are in heaven.

And he delighted in the beasts that went forth to battle and he made all their images and bowed down before them and engraved them on copper and brass and wood and stone that they might remain for ever and ever.

And I said surely this also is folly why should a man waste the days of his youth for nought on a race that are crooked in their ways and for whom no man careth farther than they administer to his own vanity of heart.

And the next that I saw was named after the king of the isles of the north and he dwelt in the street of the river as thou goest down towards the haven of ships.

He made also likenesses of men and of women and they were formed partly of gold and partly of silver mixed with tin and the man was a good man and a just.

And he delighted in the scalp of the aged man when the hairs of his head have fallen off and decayed and the light of a candle shineth thereon also in the daughters of his own houshold.

[...] made also the forms of singing men [TEAR] women and of the nobles of the land and their children and likewise one of the daughters of Babylon after whom the hearts of all the men of the nation were turned until their folly became unspeakable.

For they bowed themselves down before it and paid homage and d[ILLEGIBLE] therunto until their idolatry became an abomination in the sight of all men.

And this man's graven images and likenesses of men and of women were good but they came not forth at all from the wall by which they were placed.

And the next that I saw was a mighty man of great stature and when I saw him I said unto him that talked with me lo there be giants in the earth in those days and his name was as it had been the summer when it becomes abominable by reason of the rain [...]

And he said be not thou alarmed, neither be thou terrified, for it is only one of the beasts of the man that is crafty, which he hath sent forth to howl in every corner of the city; for his battle is turned into cursing and the bray of his wounded beasts is [...]

And I said wilt thou lead me to a place where we can see this beast the voice of whose howling is so great?

And he took me and set me down before him; and lo it was the pitiful creature that I had seen fighting in [...] whose flesh [...]

And moreoever that miserable creature which thou seest hath laid his hand upon the mane of the leopard and sported around the den of the scorpion but the forcing of the wrath of the mighty bringeth forth strife and the wringing of the nose bringeth forth blood [...] toward the [...]

NOTES

The 'Chaldee Manuscript "Continuation"' is published from the manuscript preserved in the University of Otago Library as 'Remains of the Original Chaldee Mss. by James Hogg', DeBeer Mss, Special Collections, MS 16. The manuscript is described by Gillian Hughes as 'a single leaf, a 4-page booklet, and 2 conjugate scraps. The booklet is a subscription paper for the fifth edition of "The Queen's Wake", the printed material being upside-down on the last page. The scraps seem to represent the top portion of another 4-page booklet, as they are conjugate, one leaf being numbered 13–14, and the other 15 on the recto. The first leaf is roughly 23.4 x 18.6 cm, without a watermark. The booklet has a page size of roughly 24.8 x 20.2 cm and a watermark of C WILMOTT | 1815, and the scraps are each roughly 6 x 19.8 cm'.

The Otago manuscript appears to be the remains of what Hogg described in his 'Memoir of the Author's Life' as his 'long continuation' of the original 'Chaldee Manuscript':

> So little had I intended giving offence by what appeared in the Maga-
> zine, that I had written out a long continuation of the manuscript,
> which I have by me to this day, in which I go over the painters, poets,
> lawyers, booksellers, magistrates, and ministers of Edinburgh, all in
> the same style; and with reference to the first part that was pub-
> lished, I might say of the latter as king Rehoboam said to the elders of
> Israel, "My little finger was thicker than my father's loins." It took all
> the energy of Mr. Wilson and his friends, and some sharp remon-
> strances from Sir Walter Scott, as well as a great deal of controversy
> and battling with Mr. Grieve, to prevent me from publishing the
> whole work as a large pamphlet, and putting my name to it. (*Altrive
> Tales*, ed. by Gillian Hughes (S/SC, 2003), p. 45)

As in the original 'Chaldee', Hogg imitates the language of the Authorised Version of the Bible, although for the most part Hogg's biblical references are less specific in the 'Continuation' than in the original. It is not certain that Hogg completed the 'Continuation' or that the first page of the extant manuscript is in fact the first page of the 'Continuation': the manuscript is not titled, the opening paragraph of the manuscript suggests that introductory remarks are wanted, and only the scraps of pages 13–15 have visible page numbers. The contexts of the descriptions of Hogg's subjects in the Otago manuscript are not clear, so most of the characters' identities are obscure. Hogg perhaps was deliberately obscure because of the controversy surrounding the original 'Chaldee'; Hogg comments on his purposeful vagueness in regard to another satire, 'John Paterson's Mare', in a letter to William Blackwood, 15 July 1818: 'I am writing for another Magazine with all my birr and intend having most excellent sport with it as the editors will not understand what one sentence of my celebrated allegories mean, till they bring the whole terror of Edin aristocracy on them. For the soul that is in your body mention this to no living'—see *The Collected Letters of James Hogg: Volume 1 1800–1819*, ed. by Gillian Hughes, assoc. eds Douglas S. Mack, Robin MacLachlan, and Elaine Petrie (S/SC, 2004), p. 363. The notes that follow specu-late on the identities of the subjects where feasible, although the identifications cannot be considered authoritative. Acknowledgement is made to Professors Duncan Macmillan and Ian Campbell for their suggestions for the notes. Information about the artists generally is from the *Oxford Dictionary of National Biography* (*Oxford DNB*) and Peter J. M. McEwan, *The Dictionary of Scottish Art and Architecture*, 2nd edn (Ballater: Glengarden Press, 2004).

The Otago manuscript is included in an appendix instead of the main body of *Contributions to Blackwood's* because the work is too fragmented to provide a consistent narrative and Hogg's intention for the manuscript is not clear. The text follows the Otago manuscript, including Hogg's occasional idiosyncratic spelling, except that end punctuation is silently added where Hogg would have expected the printer to add it. In a few places where small tears have resulted in the loss of a letter or two, the letters have been supplied in brackets if the missing letters are obvious. The text also includes the following emendations for clarity:

353(a) afar off] afar of MS
353(c) bit off] bit of MS
354(a) smiths] smith's MS

**352(a–c) And the first that I beheld [...] substance of a man is not in him** possibly John Graham Dalyell, whose description in the published version of the original 'Chaldee' manuscript includes a reference to his lameness: 'the substance of a living thing is not in him'—see p. 40, III, 36–44 in the present edition and note. Dalyell was not one of the characters described in Hogg's original version of the 'Chaldee'; perhaps Hogg in his 'Continuation' was trying to distance himself from the libellous description of Dalyell in the *Blackwood's* version. In the first line of the manuscript 'I beheld likewise a man who' is marked through and replaced by 'the first that I beheld'.

**352(a) face was like the sun shining in his strength** echoes Revelation 1. 16: 'and his countenance was as the sun shineth in his strength'.

**352(a) and there was brightness there** from Ezekiel 1. 27: 'I saw as it were the appearance of fire, and it had brightness round about'.

**352(a) form is as that of the porpoise of the great deep** Dalyell was lame as a result of a fall as an infant.

**352(a) footstool** a common biblical image. See Psalm 110. 1, for example.

**352(b) erred in judgement** echoes Isaiah 28. 7: 'they err in vision, they stumble in judgment'.

**352(b) eat of my bread and drink of my drink** echoes Paul's instructions regarding the Lord's supper in I Corinthians 11. 26.

**352(b) ten stringed instrument** see Psalm 92. 3 or Psalm 144. 9, for example.

**352(b) If this is not wisdom where is it to be found** echoes Job 28. 12: 'But where shall wisdom be found?'

**352(c) nat. have scof** Hogg probably intended 'nations have scoffed'. The abbreviations here are part of a manuscript revision in Hogg's hand. In the manuscript it is evident that the verse in which these words appear originally ended with 'instrument' and that Hogg added the last two sentences of this verse after he had written the verse that follows. The last two sentences are inserted between the lines of the original text and written in a much smaller hand. Hogg probably uses the word 'nations' as it frequently appeared in the Authorised Version of the Bible in the more general sense of 'people'. In this case, the 'nations' who 'scoffed' at Dalyell were John Wilson, John Lockhart, and William Blackwood.

**352(c) whosoever hath an ear to hear** a common exhortation from Jesus to his listeners at the conclusion of his parables. See Matthew 13. 43, for example.

**352(c) John [...] Likewise his fellow** unidentified.

**352(c) place of the great Sanhedrim** Sanhedrin, in biblical literature the Jewish high court or council of judges. Hogg is probably referring to Parliament Square on the south side of High Street, home to the justice courts. Also bordering one side of Parliament Square is St Giles Cathedral, the meeting place of the General Assembly of the Church of Scotland, the governing body of the Church.

**352(c) name was like unto the great beast of the desart** unidentified.

**352(d) ass taketh the words of his rider** perhaps a reference to the story of Balaam in Numbers 22. Balaam and the ass on which he was riding engaged in a dispute after the ass repeatedly stopped in the road to avoid God's angel, whom Balaam was not able to see.

**352(d) whose name was as if it had been the colour of amber or certain strong drink** Duncan Macmillan suggests that William Yellowlees (1796–1856) is intended. Yellowlees, a portrait printer, was from Berwickshire but worked in Edinburgh from about 1815 to 1830 before moving to London. He was known as 'the Little Raeburn' because of his stylistic resemblance to Raeburn and small size of his portraits. The 'colour of amber' echoes Ezekiel 1. 27.

**352(d)–353(a) as if it had been [...] his own shadow** in the manuscript this replaces 'like unto a horse on which princes do ride and to which the chariots of the great are yoked and he had a mark on his forehead between his eyes'.

**352(d) straineth at a gnat** from Matthew 23. 24: 'Ye blind guides, which strain at a gnat, and swallow a camel'.

**353(a) whose name is like the chariot of the Isle of the west** Gillian Hughes suggests that Alexander Carse (*bap.* 1770, *d.* 1843) may be intended. Carse, originally from Haddingtonshire, was a genre painter who studied in Edinburgh and exhibited with the Associated Artists in Edinburgh. Carse spent time in London in the 1810s, where he came under the influence of David Wilkie. For additional information, see the *Oxford DNB* article on Carse by Lucy Dixon.

**353(a) beasts** the two primary 'beasts' in the original 'Chaldee' are Thomas Pringle and James Cleghorn, Blackwood's original editors who became editors for Constable. However, the 'Chaldee' assigns animal characters to many of the writers for both Constable and Blackwood. See especially p. 27(a) in the present edition and notes.

**353(b) name was as if it had been a kitten that is a male** possibly John Thomson (1778–1840), a landscape painter originally from Dailly in Ayrshire. Thomson attended Edinburgh University in preparation for the ministry and also studied art under Alexander Nasmyth. In 1805 Thomson became minister of the Duddingston kirk near Edinburgh. Thomson was involved in the cultural life of Edinburgh and enjoyed a friendship with Sir Walter Scott, who had a strong influence on Thomson's paintings. For additional information about Thomson, see the *Oxford DNB* article on Thomson by J. L. Caw, rev. Mungo Campbell.

**353(c) Go to now** see the note for 29(b).

**353(c) clamour combat** Hogg probably intended to delete 'clamour' and replace it with 'combat'. 'The man' and 'the stranger' who are the combatants have not been identified.

**353(d) the fortress of the land** Edinburgh Castle, which overlooks the city at the head of the Royal Mile.

**354(a) another man came in even he which liveth at the corner** probably David Bridges, who had a clothing shop with his father at the corner of High Street and Bank Street in Edinburgh. See p. 43, IV, 24 in the present edition and note.

**354(a) wherever two or three of the smiths [...] in the midst of them** echoes the words of Jesus in Matthew 18. 20: 'For where two or three are gathered together in my name, there am I in the midst of them'.

**354(a) wicked artificier** unidentified.

**354(b) [TEAR]ther** probably 'feather'.

**354(b) bl[TEAR]** probably 'blows'.

**354(b) graven images** echoes Exodus 20. 4.

**354(c) the house of thy gods** Bridges kept a large collection of art in a room below the clothing shop. Lockhart in *Peter's Letters to His Kinsfolk*, '3rd edn', 3 vols (Edinburgh: Blackwood, 1819) referred to Bridges's art room as the '*Sanctum Sanctorum* of the Fine Arts' (II, 232).

**354(c) a young man who came from the New fortress [...] Urr of the Chaldeans [...] one of the fathers** William Nicholson (1781–1844), portrait painter and etcher. Although Nicholson was born in Ovingham, Northumberland, he grew up in Newcastle (on the River Tyne), after his father became schoolmaster of the grammar school there. Nicholson moved to Edinburgh in 1814 and became a successful portrait painter. Portraits of Hogg were among works exhibited by Nicholson in 1815 and 1816. Other subjects of Nicholson's portraits and etchings include Walter Scott (and his daughters, Sophia and Anne), Francis Jeffrey, John Wilson, and William Allan. See the *Oxford DNB* article by J. M. Gray, rev. Marshall Hall. The biblical Ur of the Chaldees was a city in southern Mesopotamia on the Euphrates River and the home of Abram (later Abraham). See Genesis 11. 28, 31, for example. Acknowledgement is made to Duncan Macmillan for identifying Nicholson as the subject of Hogg's description.

**354(d) cunning artificier** from Isaiah 3. 3.

**355(a) named after the king of the isles of the north [...] street of the river as thou goest down towards the haven of ships** possibly William Douglas (1780–1832), prominent miniature and portrait painter. Douglas lived on Hart Street in Edinburgh, just off Forth Road. Newhaven was a fishing village on the Firth of Forth near Leith. Douglas painted portraits of families and staff of several members of the Scottish aristocracy, including those of the fourth Duke of Buccleuch. In 1817 he became miniature painter to Prince Leopold of Saxe-Coburg-Saalfeld and painted a miniature of Princess Charlotte of Wales, daughter of George IV and wife of Prince Leopold. James Grant writes of Douglas that 'his social worth and private virtues were acknowledged by all who had the pleasure of knowing him'—see *Cassell's Old and New Edinburgh*, 3 vols (London: Cassell, [1880–83]), III, 190. For additional information, see the *Oxford DNB* article on Douglas by V. Remington.

**355(b) d[ILLEGIBLE]** the word that is obscured by a repair to the manuscript appears to be 'devotion'.

**355(b–c) mighty man of great stature [...] name was as it had been the summer when it becomes abominable by reason of the rain** unidentified.

**355(c) there be giants in the earth in those days** quoted from Genesis 6. 4.

**355(c) be not thou alarmed, neither be thou terrified** echoes John 14. 27: 'Let not your heart be troubled, neither let it be afraid'.

**355(c) beasts of the man that is crafty, which he hath sent forth to howl in every corner of the city** Archibald Constable was known as 'Crafty' among the Blackwoodians and referred to as such in the original 'Chaldee'—see p. 28(a) in the present edition and note. This verse is similar to a verse that appears in 'The Boar': 'And the man that talked with me said be not thou afraid for it is only one of the beasts of him that is crafty; for when he can no more fight on fair and equitable terms of retaliation, he hath hired them and sent them forth to howl in every corner of the city until their voice hath reached unto the ends thereof'—see pp. 46(d)–47(a) in the present edition. This similarity suggests a connection between 'The Boar' and Hogg's 'Continuation' of the 'Chaldee'. It is possible that when Blackwood would not publish the lengthy 'Continuation', Hogg extracted bits from the 'Continuation' and wrote the shorter and more-focused 'Boar'—which Blackwood also did not publish.

**355(d) the leopard** John Wilson (1785–1854). See p. 29(d) in the present edition and note.

**355(d) scorpion** John Lockhart (1794–1854). See p. 36, II, 12 in the present edition and note.

# Appendix B

Appendix B provides musical notation for the songs in *Blackwood's Edinburgh Magazine* for which Hogg published music in *Blackwood's* or for which Hogg identified the name of a traditional tune to which the song should be sung. Hogg composed original music for at least four of the songs in *Blackwood's*. For each of eight other songs, Hogg identified an appropriate traditional tune that fit his lyrics. *Blackwood's* published the musical notation for the melody line for five songs, all of which appeared in the *Noctes Ambrosianæ*. Musical notation in Appendix B for the songs published in *Blackwood's* follows the notation in the magazine. For the songs for which a tune is only named, for consistency the present edition follows the *Blackwood's* practice of publishing only the melody line. The primary source for the tunes named but not published by Hogg is James Johnson, *The Scots Musical Museum Consisting of Six Hundred Scots Songs with proper Bases for the Piano Forte &c.*, 6 vols (Edinburgh, 1787–1803). Robert Burns was the main contributor of songs to *The Scots Musical Museum*. A facsimile reprint of the 1853 edition of *The Scots Musical Museum* has been edited with an introduction by Donald A. Low (Aldershot: Scolar Press, 1991). The 1853 edition retains the numbering and pagination of the original six-volume publication.

In the annotations that follow, the page numbers following the title of the song refer to the printed work in the present edition. The reader is directed to the Notes to each work in the present edition for additional information. For a full bibliography of musical sources relevant to Hogg, see the Bibliography in James Hogg, *The Forest Minstrel*, ed. by P. D. Garside and Richard D. Jackson, with musical notation prepared by Peter Horsfall (S/SC, 2006), pp. 377–94. Acknowledgement is made to Thomas B. Richardson for his assistance and advice in preparing the musical notation.

## 1. 'The Women Folk' (p. 95)
'The Women Folk' was first published in *No. of the Border Garland* (Edinburgh: Nathaniel Gow and Son, [1819]), pp. 6–7, with an original 'Air' by Hogg. The melody line, based on the *Border Garland* publication, was published in *Blackwood's* with the song.

## 2. 'When the Kye Comes Hame' (p. 138)
Hogg published 'When the Kye Comes Hame' with music in *Blackwood's*, although in the magazine he does not indicate the name of the tune or a source. In a letter to George Thomson, 14 December 1821, Hogg claims to like to hear the song 'sung exceedingly to the tune of "The Bladrie of't" to which I have subjoined a second part to suit my chorus'– see *The Collected Letters of James Hogg: Volume 2 1820–1831*, ed. by Gillian Hughes, assoc. eds Douglas S. Mack, Robin MacLachlan, and Elaine Petrie (S/SC, 2006), p. 132. Hogg's tune in *Blackwood's* contains a few

variations on the version of 'The Blathrie o't' in *The Scots Musical Museum*, I (1787), no. 33, p. 34, and in *Blackwood's* Hogg has added a 'second part' for his chorus as he indicated in his letter to Thomson.

### 3. 'If E'er You Would Be a Brave Fellow' (pp. 162–63)
Hogg identifies the 'Air' in *Blackwood's* as 'Whistle, and I'll come to ye, my Lad'. However, in his introduction to the song in *Songs By the Ettrick Shepherd* (Edinburgh: William Blackwood, 1831), Hogg claims that the 'air is my own, and a very capital one. I believe it is preserved in the Noctes, and nowhere else' (p. 28). The tune was not published in *Blackwood's* as Hogg later seems to have thought, so it is not clear how Hogg's version of 'Whistle, and I'll come to ye, my Lad' might be unique, or if Hogg in fact later composed a tune for this song that was popular among the *Blackwood's* writers. The tune published in the present edition is based on the version in *The Scots Musical Museum*, II (1788), no. 106, p. 109.

### 4. 'The Laird o' Lamington' (p. 164)
The music for 'The Laird o' Lamington' is Hogg's composition. The song was first published in *No. of the Border Garland* (Edinburgh: Nathaniel Gow and Son, [1819]), pp. 18–19, with an 'Air' by Hogg. The song is published in *Blackwood's* with music for the melody line; the *Blackwood's* 'Air' is based on the *Border Garland* version.

### 5. 'There's Naught Sae Sweet in this Poor Life' (pp. 180–81)
This song is based on Robert Burns's song, 'Auld Lang Syne', and the *Blackwood's* text indicates that it is sung to that tune. There are two versions of 'Auld Lang Syne' in *The Scots Musical Museum*. The tune printed in the present edition is based on the second version, by Burns, in *The Scots Musical Museum*, V (1796), no. 413, p. 426; the lyrics of this version correspond to the lyrics of the version discussed in the *Noctes* dialogue. The first version is from Allan Ramsay—see *The Scots Musical Museum*, I (1787), no. 25, p. 26.

### 6. 'The Brakens wi' Me' (pp. 181–82)
This song is published with music in *Blackwood's*; Hogg indicates that the 'Air' is 'Driving the Steers'. In a letter to William Baynes and Sons in 1825, Hogg refers Baynes to Captain Simon Fraser's *Airs and Melodies Peculiar to the Highlands of Scotland and the Isles* (1816) for a version of 'Driving the Steers' ('Ioman nan gamhna') to be used with Hogg's 'Scottish Ode (for Music) | On the death of Lord Byron'—see *Collected Letters, Volume 2* (S/SC, 2006), pp. 229–32. Hogg's version of 'Driving the Steers' is adapted to the lyrics of 'The Brakens wi' Me', and Hogg uses the key of 'D major' rather than Fraser's 'F major'.

### 7. 'Rejoice ye wan and wilder'd glens' (pp. 185–86)
This is the first of two 'Songs for the Duke of Buccleuch's Birth day'. Hogg does not provide music for this song, but he indicates that the 'Air' is 'Killiecrankie'. The musical notation for 'Killiecrankie' in the present edition is based on the version in *The Scots Musical Museum*, III (1790), no.

292, p. 302. For other versions of 'Killiecrankie', see *The Forest Minstrel* (S/SC, 2006), pp. 163–64, and notes, pp. 337–40, and *The Jacobite Relics of Scotland [First Series]*, ed. by Murray G. H. Pittock (S/SC, 2002), pp. 28–33, and notes, pp. 434–37.

## 8. 'Wat o' Buccleuch' (pp. 186–88)

This is the second of two 'Songs for the Duke of Buccleuch's Birth day'. Hogg does not publish music for this song, but he indicates that the 'Air' is 'Thurot's Defeat'. A tune entitled 'Thurot's Defeat' has not been discovered, however, so it is unclear which tune Hogg intended for this song. The siege of Carrickfergus by the French forces under François Thurot, and the subsequent, important defeat of Thurot and the French by the British navy under John Elliot in 1760, were popular subjects for songs and ballads for about four decades after the events. There are several extant versions of poems and songs on the subject of 'Thurot's Defeat' that were published as broadsides and chapbooks in the late eighteenth century, and there are also various metrical forms for these works. Most versions do not indicate a specific tune for singing, and none have been discovered that name a tune that corresponds with the metrical form of 'Wat o' Buccleuch'. There are two manuscript songs about 'Thurot's Defeat' among the Minto Papers in the National Library of Scotland (NLS) that name tunes for singing, although there is no music with the songs: 'Thurot's Defeat', by Peter Nettle, to be sung to the tune of 'To all ye Ladies now at Land' (NLS, MS 12,820, fols 1–2), and 'A Song to the Tune of Moll Roe', author not named (NLS, MS 12,820, fol. 3). Neither song's metre is comparable to that of 'Wat o' Buccleuch'. Although 'To all ye Ladies now at Land' and 'Moll Roe' (and comparable tunes—see the Early Irish Tune Title Index, http://www.csufresno.edu/folklore/Olson/IRTITLE3.HTM) do not work for 'Wat o' Buccleuch', Richard Jackson noted that in his 'vain' search 'for a tune specifically headed "Moll Roe"' the versions that he discovered 'are headed "Moll in the Wad(d)"' (personal correspondence). 'Moll in the Wad' generally suits the meter of 'Wat o' Buccleuch'. The musical notation for the present edition is adapted from 'Moll in the Wad', in James Aird, *A Selection of Scotch, English, Irish, and Foreign Airs Adapted to the Fife, Violin, or German-Flute*, 6 vols (Glasgow, *c.* 1782–1801), V, no. 115, p. 44. Acknowledgement is made to Richard D. Jackson for his extensive research into 'Thurot's Defeat' and for providing the source for the tune used in the present edition. Acknowledgement is also made to Julia Gardner, Reference and Instruction Librarian at the Special Collections Research Center, the University of Chicago Library, for providing a copy of a broadside of 'Thurot's Defeat' from the Library's Song Sheet and Broadside Poems collection.

## 9. 'The Great Muckle Village of Balmaquhapple' (pp. 188–89)

The music is not printed in *Blackwood's*, although Hogg indicates that the song is to be sung to the 'Air' of 'Soger Laddie'. The musical notation published in the present edition is based on the version of 'The Soger Laddie' in *The Scots Musical Museum*, IV (1792), no. 323, p. 334.

### 10. 'By a bush on yonder Brae' (pp. 212–13)

Hogg indicates in the manuscript of 'Dramas of Simple Life No. II' that the 'Air' for this song is 'Maid that Tends the Goats'. Of the dozen songs in the manuscript of 'Dramas of Simple Life No. II', 'By a Bush' is the only song for which Hogg provides the name of a tune. In the posthumously-published dramatic work, 'A Bush Aboon Traquair', which is an expanded and 'finished' version of 'Dramas II', the tune titles are provided, perhaps intended as guidance for performance of the drama. The version of 'Maid that Tends the Goats' printed here is from *The Scots Musical Museum*, I (1787), no. 40, p. 40. For another version of the tune, see *The Forest Minstrel*, (S/SC, 2006), pp. 179–80, and notes, pp. 352–55.

### 11. 'I'll No Wake wi' Annie' (pp. 312–13)

This song was first published with an 'Air' by Hogg in *No. of the Border Garland* (Edinburgh: Nathaniel Gow and Son, [1819]), pp. 2–3. The song is published with music in *Blackwood's* based on the melody line from the *Border Garland* version.

### 12. 'In Embro Town They Made a Law' (pp. 313–14)

Hogg identifies the tune for this song as 'O'er the muir amang the heather', but there is no music published in *Blackwood's*. Musical notation for the present edition is based on 'O'er the moor amang the heather' from *The Scots Musical Museum*, IV (1792), no 328, p. 338. For other versions, see *The Forest Minstrel* (S/SC, 2006), pp. 95–96, and notes, pp. 287–90, and *The Jacobite Relics of Scotland, Second Series*, ed. by Murray G. H. Pittock (S/SC, 2003), pp. 409–10, and notes, p. 526.

# The Women Folk

O— sair-ly may I— rue the day I fan-cied first the

wo-men - kind, For aye sin-syne I ne'er can ha'e A qui-et thought, or

peace o' mind. They ha'e plagued my heart, and pleased my e'e, And

teased and flat - ter'd— me at—will; But aye, for a' their

witch - er - ye, The paw - ky things, I lo'e them still. O the

wo-men folk, O the wo-men folk, But they ha'e been the

wreck o' me! O— wear - y fa' the wo-men folk, For they

win - na let a bo - dy be.

# When the Kye Comes Hame

Come ___ all ye jol - ly shep - herds that

whis - tle thro' the glen, I'll ___ tell ye of a se - cret that

court - iers din - na ken. What ___ is the great - est bliss that the

tongue of man can name? 'Tis to woo a bon - ny las - sie when the

Chorus

kye ___ come ___ hame. When the kye come hame, when the

kye come hame, 'Tween the gloam - ing an' the mirk, when the

kye come hame.

# If e'er you would be a brave fellow, young man

*Air--Whistle, and I'll Come to Ye, My Lad*

If __ e'er you would be a brave fel·low, young man, Be -

ware of the Blue and the Yellow, young man; If __ ye wud be strang, And wish

to write lang, Come join wi' __ the lads that get __ mel·low, young man. Like __

the crack o' a squib that has fa'en on, young man, Com -

pared wi' the roar o' a can - non, young man, So __

is the Whig's blow To the pith that's be - low The

beard o' auld Geor - die Bu - chan - an, young man. To the

beard o' auld Geor - die Bu - chan - an, young man.

# The Laird o' Lamington

Can I bear to part wi' thee, Ne-ver mair __ your __ face to see?

Can I bear to part wi' thee, Drunk - en Laird __ o' __ Lam - ing-ton?

Can - ty war ye o'er your kale, Tod - dy jugs, an' caups o' ale,

Heart aye kind, an' leel, an' hale, Hon-est Laird __ o' __ Lam-ing-ton.

# There's Nought Sae Sweet

## Air--*Auld Langsyne*

There's nought sae sweet in this poor life As

kint - tin' soul to soul And___ what maist close may bind that knot? The

**Chorus**

glass and___ bowl! The glass and___ bowl, my boys, The

glass___ and___ bowl; So___ let us call, for this is out, An -

ith - - - er___ bowl.

# The Brakens wi' Me

**Air--*Driving the Steers***

I'll _____ sing of yon glen o' red_____ heath - er An' a
dear thing that ca's it her_____ hame, Wha's _____
a' made o' love - life to - ge - ther, Frae the
tie o' the shoe to the kembe. Love_____
beck - ons in ev' - ry sweet mo - tion, Com -
mand - ing due hom - age to gi'e; But the
shrine of my dear - est de - vo - tion Is the
bend o' her bon - ny e'e_____ bree.

# Rejoice, ye wan and wildered glens

**Tune--*Killiecrankie***

Re - joice ye wan and — wild - ered glens Ye —

dow - ie dells — of — Yar - row This — is the day — that —

heaven or - dains To — ba - nish — all your sor - row Ilk —

for-est shaw an - loft-y — law Frae grief an' gloom a - rouse — ye What —

gars ye snood your — brows — wi' — snaw An' look — sae — grim an

grous — y

# Wat o' Buccleuch

### Air--*Thurot's Defeat*

Some sing with de - vo - tion Of feats on the o - cean And
But down with the prais - es Of lil - lies and dai - seys Of

na-ture's broad beau-ties in earth and in skies Some rant of their glass-es And
po-sies and ro - ses the like nev-er grew That flim-sy in - dit- ing That

some of the lass-es And these are twa things we maun ne - ver de - spise
po - ets de-light in They're kend for a hav - er - ing half-wit-ted crew

But join in my chor-us Ye blades o' the For - est We'll

lilt of our muirs and our moun-tains of blue And hal-low for ev-er Till

a' the town shiv-er The name of our mas-ter Young Wat o' Buc-cleuch

# The Great Muckle Village
## of Balmaquhapple
### Tune--*Soger Laddie*

D' - ye ken the big vil - lage of Bal-ma - quhap-ple, The

great ___ muck-le vil-lage of Bal - ma-quhap-ple? 'Tis steep'd in in - iq - ui-ty

up to the thrap-ple, And what's ___ to be - come of poor

Bal - ma - quhap - ple Fling ___ a' off your bon-nets, and

kneel for your life, folks, And pray to Saint An - drew, the

god o' the Fife folks; Gar a' the hills ___ yout wi' sheer vo - cif-er-a-tion, And

thus ___ you may cry on sic need - fu' oc - ca-sion:

# By a Bush

**Air--*Maid that Tends the Goats***

By a bush on yon - der brae    Where the air - y Ben - ger ris-es

Sand-y tuned his art - less lay    Thus he sang the lee - lang day

Thou shalt e - ver be my theme    Yar-row wind-ing down the hol - low

With thy bon - ny sis - ter stream    Sweep-ing through the broom so yel - low

But your bonni - est flower to me    Milks her ewes on yon - der lea

# I'll No Wake wi' Annie

O moth-er tell the laird o't, Or

sair-ly it will grieve me, O, That I'm to wake the

ewes the night, An' An-nie's to gang wi'____ me,____ O. I'll____

wake the ewes my night a-bout, But ne'er wi' ane sae____

sau-cy, O; Nor____ sit my lane the____ lee-lang night Wi'____

sic a____ scorn-fu'____ las-sie, O. I'll____ no wake, I'll

no wake, I'll no_____ wake wi' An-nie, O, Nor

sit my lane o'er night wi ane Sae thra-ward an' un -

can - - - nie, O.

# In Embro Town

**Tune--*O'er the muir amang the heather***

In Embro town they made a law, In Em-bro at the Court o' Ses-sion,

That Kit and his lads were fau-tors a'! An' guilt-y o'a high trans-gres-sion.

De - creet o' the Court o' Ses-sion, Act sed-er-unt o' the Ses- sion;

Kit North and his crew were fau-tors a', And guilt-y o' a high trans-gres-sion.

# Appendix C

Appendix C is intended to provide a convenient reference for Hogg's publishing relationship with *Blackwood's Edinburgh Magazine*. Part I is a complete chronological listing of James Hogg's publications in *Blackwood's Edinburgh Magazine*, including works published in other volumes of the S/SC edition of Hogg's *Collected Works*. Part II is a list of works attributed to Hogg within *Blackwood's* from 1817 to 1828, but for which reasonable evidence exists to suggest that these were not written by Hogg. Part III is a list of Hogg's works apparently intended by Hogg for publication in *Blackwood's* from 1817 to 1828 but which never appeared there. Works frequently referenced in Appendix C are abbreviated as follows:

**BEM** *Blackwood's Edinburgh Magazine*
**Letters 1** *The Collected Letters of James Hogg: Volume 1 1800–1819*, ed. by Gillian Hughes, assoc. eds Douglas S. Mack, Robin MacLachlan, and Elaine Petrie (S/SC, 2004)
**Letters 2** *The Collected Letters of James Hogg: Volume 2 1820–1831*, ed. by Gillian Hughes, assoc. eds Douglas S. Mack, Robin MacLachlan, and Elaine Petrie (S/SC, 2006)
**Strout** Alan Lang Strout, *A Bibliography of Articles in Blackwood's Magazine 1817–1825* (Lubbock, Texas: Texas Tech Press, 1959)

## I. Complete List of Hogg's Publications
### in *Blackwood's Edinburgh Magazine*, 1817–1835

The following list is a complete chronological listing of James Hogg's publications in *Blackwood's Edinburgh Magazine*, including works published in other volumes of the S/SC edition of Hogg's *Collected Works*. The title of the work is followed by the volume and page references for the *BEM* publication. For those works not appearing in the present edition, the list also includes the title of the S/SC volume in which they have appeared or will appear.

'Tales and Anecdotes of the Pastoral Life. No. I', *BEM*, 1 (April 1817), 22–25

'Verses, Recited by the Author, in a Party of his Countrymen, On the Day that the News Arrived of Our Final Victory Over the French', *BEM*, 1 (April 1817), 72

'Tales and Anecdotes of the Pastoral Life. No. II', *BEM*, 1 (May 1817), 143–47

'Shakspeare Club of Alloa', *BEM*, 1 (May 1817), 152–54

'A Last Adieu', *BEM*, 1 (May 1817), 169

'Tales and Anecdotes of the Pastoral Life. No. III', *BEM*, 1 (June 1817), 247–50

'Elegy', *BEM*, 2 (October 1817), 47

'Translation From an Ancient Chaldee Manuscript', *BEM*, 2 (October 1817), 89–96

'A Letter to Charles Kirkpatrick Sharpe, Esq. On his Original Mode of Editing Church History', *BEM*, 2 (December 1817), 305–09

'A Hebrew Melody', *BEM*, 2 (January 1818), 400

'Further Anecdotes of the Shepherd's Dog', *BEM*, 2 (March 1818), 621–26

'Sonnet to John Carnegie, Esq.', *BEM*, 3 (April 1818), 58

'On Carmel's Brow', *BEM*, 3 (April 1818), 90

'Verses Addressed to the Right Hon. Lady Anne Scott of Buccleuch', *BEM*, 4 (October 1818), 74–76 [*The Brownie of Bodsbeck; And Other Tales*]

'The Shepherd's Calendar. Storms', *BEM*, 5 (April 1819), 75–81 [*The Shepherd's Calendar*]

'The Shepherd's Calendar. Storms', *BEM*, 5 (May 1819), 210–16 [*The Shepherd's Calendar*]

'Letter from the Ettrick Shepherd, Enclosing a Letter from James Laidlaw', *BEM*, 6 (March 1820), 630–32

'Account of a Coronation-Dinner at Edinburgh, In a Letter from John M'Indoe, Esq. to William M'Ilhose, Esq. Manufacturer, Glasgow', *BEM*, 10 (August 1821), 26–33

'The Women Folk', *BEM*, 12 (December 1822), 705–06

'The Honourable Captain Napier and Ettrick Forest', *BEM*, 13 (February 1823), 175–88

'The Shepherd's Calendar. Class Second. Deaths, Judgments, and Providences', *BEM*, 13 (March 1823), 311–20 [*The Shepherd's Calendar*]

'When the Kye Comes Hame', *BEM*, 13 (May 1823), 598

'The Shepherd's Calendar. Class Second. Deaths, Judgments, and Providences', *BEM*, 13 (June 1823), 629–40 [*The Shepherd's Calendar*]

'A Scots Mummy', *BEM*, 14 (August 1823), 188–90

'The Shepherd's Calendar. Class IV. Dogs', *BEM*, 15 (February 1824), 177–83 [*The Shepherd's Calendar*]

'The Shepherd's Calendar. Class V. The Lasses', *BEM*, 15 (March 1824), 296–304 [*The Shepherd's Calendar*]

'The Left-Handed Fiddler', *BEM*, 16 (November 1824), 528–29

'Examination of the School of Southside', *BEM*, 16 (December 1824), 653–57

'The Grousome Caryl. Ane Most Treuthful Ballant', *BEM*, 17 (January 1825), 78–85 [*A Queer Book*]

'The Shepherd's Calendar. Class V. The Lasses', *BEM*, 17 (February 1825), 180–86 [*The Shepherd's Calendar*]

'Hymn to the Devil', *BEM*, 17 (March 1825), 367–69

'If E'er You Would Be a Brave Fellow, Young Man', *BEM*, 17 (March 1825), 382–83

'The Laird o' Lamington', *BEM*, 17 (May 1825), 620

'Ringan and May. Ane Richte Mournfulle Dittye', *BEM*, 17 (June 1825), 712–14 [*A Queer Book*]

'The Witch of the Gray Thorn', *BEM*, 17 (June 1825), 714–16 [*A Queer Book*]

'Some Passages in the Life of Colonel Cloud. In a Letter by the Ettrick Shepherd, To the Hon. Mrs A–r–y. Dated Edinburgh, August 11, 1816', *BEM*, 18 (July 1825), 32–40

'There's Naught Sae Sweet in This Poor Life', *BEM*, 18 (September 1825), 391–92

'The Brakens Wi' Me', *BEM*, 18 (December 1825), 753–54

'Songs for the Duke of Buccleuch's Birth Day ['Rejoice, Ye Wan and Wilder'd Glens' and 'Wat o' Buccleuch']', *BEM*, 19 (February 1826), 217–19

'The Great Muckle Village of Balmaquhapple', *BEM*, 19 (June 1826), 739–40

'Meg o' Marley', *BEM*, 19 (June 1826), 756

'My Bonny Mary', *BEM*, 20 (July 1826), 93–94

'O Weel Befa' the Maiden Gay', *BEM*, 20 (July 1826), 108

'I Lookit East–I Lookit West', *BEM*, 20 (October 1826), 622–23

'Tam Nelson', *BEM*, 20 (October 1826), 623

'There's Some Souls 'ill Yammer and Cheep', *BEM*, 20 (October 1826), 630–31

'The Shepherd's Calendar. General Anecdotes', *BEM*, 21 (April 1827), 434–48 [*The Shepherd's Calendar*]

'Ode for Music. On the Death of Lord Byron', *BEM*, 21 (May 1827), 520–21

'The Shepherd's Calendar. Dreams and Apparitions', *BEM*, 21 (May 1827), 549–62 [*The Shepherd's Calendar*]

'The Shepherd's Calendar. Dreams and Apparitions. Part II', *BEM*, 21 (June 1827), 664–76 [*The Shepherd's Calendar*]

'The Shepherd's Calendar. Dreams and Apparitions, Containing Smithy Cracks, &c. Part III', *BEM*, 22 (July 1827), 64–73 [*The Shepherd's Calendar*]

'The Shepherd's Calendar. Dreams and Apparitions.–Part IV', *BEM*, 22 (August 1827), 173–85 [*The Shepherd's Calendar*]

The Perilis of Wemyng. Ane Most Woeful Tragedye', *BEM*, 22 (August 1827), 214–21 [*A Queer Book*]

'The Marvellous Doctor', *BEM*, 22 (September 1827), 349–61

'Ane Pastorale of the Rocke', *BEM*, 22 (December 1827), 675–84

'Trials of Temper', *BEM*, 23 (January 1828), 40–47

'I'll No Wake Wi' Annie', *BEM*, 23 (January 1828), 113–14

'The Shepherd's Calendar. Class IX. Fairies, Brownies, and Witches', *BEM*, 23 (February 1828), 214–27 [*The Shepherd's Calendar*]

'The Shepherd's Calendar. Class IX. Fairies, Deils, and Witches', 23 (April 1828), 509–19 [*The Shepherd's Calendar*]

'In Embro Town They Made a Law', *BEM*, 23 (May 1828), 782

'Chalk! Chalk!', *BEM*, 23 (May 1828), 794

'Good Night and Joy', *BEM*, 23 (May 1828), 802

'A Strange Secret. Related in a Letter From the Ettrick Shepherd', *BEM*, 23 (June 1828), 822–26

'Ane Rychte Gude and Preytious Ballande', *BEM*, 24 (August 1828), 177–83 [*A Queer Book*]

'The Brownie of the Black Haggs', *BEM*, 24 (October 1828), 489–96 [*The Shepherd's Calendar*]

'The Stuarts of Appin', *BEM*, 24 (October 1828), 535–36

'The Goode Manne of Allowa. Ane Most Strainge and Treuthfulle Ballande', *BEM*, 24 (November 1828), 561–69 [*A Queer Book*]

'John Nicholson's Daughter', *BEM*, 24 (December 1828), 688

'Jock Johnstone the Tinkler', *BEM*, 25 (February 1829), 173–78 [*A Queer Book*]

'Mary Melrose', *BEM*, 25 (April 1829), 411–20

'Sound Morality', 25 (June 1829), 741–47

'Will and Sandy. A Scots Pastoral', *BEM*, 25 (June 1829), 748–51 [*A Queer Book*]

'A Tale of the Martyrs', *BEM*, 26 (July 1829), 48–51

'O Love's a Bitter Thing to Bide', *BEM*, 26 (July 1829), 135

'A Letter About Men and Women', *BEM*, 26 (August 1829), 245–50

'Elen of Reigh', *BEM*, 26 (September 1829), 271–77 [*A Queer Book*]

'Let Them Cant About Adam and Eve', *BEM*, 26 (September 1829), 403–04

'The p and the q; or, The Adventures of Jock M'Pherson', *BEM*, 26 (October 1829), 693–95

'A Singular Letter from Southern Africa', *BEM*, 26 (November 1829), 809–16

'The Last Stork', *BEM*, 27 (February 1830), 217–22 [*A Queer Book*]

'The Lairde of Lonne. Ane Rychte Breiffe and Wyttie Ballande', *BEM*, 27 (April 1830), 571–77 [*A Queer Book*]

'A Greek Pastoral', *BEM*, 27 (May 1830), 766–71 [*A Queer Book*]

'The First Sermon', *BEM*, 27 (June 1830), 879–80

'Some Remarkable Passages in the Remarkable Life of the Baron St Gio', *BEM*, 27 (June 1830), 891–905

'Story of Adam Scott', *BEM*, 28 (July 1830), 41–46

'A Real Vision', *BEM*, 28 (July 1830), 63–65

'The Origin of the Fairies', *BEM*, 28 (August 1830), 209–17 [*A Queer Book*]

'When Bawdrons, Wi' Her Mousin' Paw', *BEM*, 28 (August 1830), 385

'The Cuttin' of My Hair', *BEM*, 28 (August 1830), 406

'Maga at No. 45', *BEM*, 28 (August 1830), 422–23

'Jocke Taittis Expeditioune till Hell', *BEM*, 28 (September 1830), 512–17 [*A Queer Book*]

'A Horrible Instance of the Effects of Clanship', *BEM*, 28 (October 1830), 680–87

'A Sunday Pastoral', *BEM*, 28 (November 1830), 737–41 [*A Queer Book*]

'The Raid of the Kers', *BEM*, 28 (December 1830), 895–99

'The Mysterious Bride', *BEM*, 28 (December 1830), 943–50

'King Willie', *BEM*, 29 (January 1831), 17–18

'O Weel Befa' the Maiden Gay', *BEM*, 29 (March 1831), 546–47

'A Story of Good Queen Bess', *BEM*, 29 (April 1831), 579–93

'Johnne Graimis Eckspeditioun Till Heuin', *BEM*, 29 (April 1831), 641–44 [*A Queer Book*]

'The Miser's Grave', *BEM*, 29 (June 1831), 915–18

'Would You Know What a Whig Is', *BEM*, 30 (August 1831), 415

'An Awfu' Leein'-like Story', *BEM*, 30 (September 1831), 448–56

'The Magic Mirror', *BEM*, 30 (October 1831), 650–54

'Lyttil Pynkie', *BEM*, 30 (November 1831), 782–89

'The Monitors', *BEM*, 30 (November 1831), 843–44

'Mora Campbell', *BEM*, 35 (June 1834), 947–54

'A Screed on Politics', *BEM*, 37 (April 1835), 634–42

## II. Works Attributed to Hogg but for which Hogg's Authorship Is Unlikely, *Blackwood's Edinburgh Magazine*, 1817–1828

The following works are attributed to Hogg within *Blackwood's Edinburgh Magazine* or elsewhere, but as there is external evidence to suggest that Hogg was not the author these works are not included in the present edition.

'Remarkable Preservation from Death at Sea', *BEM*, 2 (February 1818), 490–94. This story is signed 'H. M.' in *BEM* and is attributed to John

Wilson by Strout (p. 35). Wilson claims authorship of the story in a note to 'The Mariner's Return', a poem by Wilson that was published in *BEM*, 27 (June 1830), 906–16. The story was reprinted in the United States of America, slightly revised but under the same title, in Ebenezer Porter, *The Rhetorical Reader*, 5th edn (Andover: Flagg, Gould, & Newman, 1833), pp. 210–14; there the story is attributed to 'Professor Wilson'. However, a greatly revised version of the story, retitled 'Escape from Death–At Sea' was published in an American periodical, the *Miscellaneous Magazine*, 1 (March and April 1824), 58–60, 81–83. In the *Miscellaneous Magazine* the story is signed 'James Hogg'. The authority for the attribution of this story has not been discovered. Because the evidence for the authorship of the *BEM* version weighs heavily in favour of John Wilson, the story has not been included in the present edition. For a full discussion of the authorship question and the two versions of this story, see Janette Currie, 'The Authorship of "Escape from Death–At Sea": A Literary Puzzle', http://jameshogg.stir.ac.uk/showrecord.php?id=75&fulltext=1.

'To the Publisher', *BEM*, 2 (March 1818), [612]. Strout (p. 37) assigns this work to Thomas Hamilton.

Hogg wrote to Margaret Phillips on 14 February 1820 that the 'Blackwood's Magazine-mongers' had 'attached my name to several of their grovelling productions, but not a line in that work has been wrote by me for the last nine months' (*Letters 2*, p. 7). The period of 'the last nine months' would rule out the next five items as Hogg's works:

'Song to a Salmon', *BEM*, 5 (August 1819), 610–11

'L'Envoy; An Excellent New Song in Honour of Dr Scott', *BEM*, 5 (September 1819), *640

'I pity you, ye stars so bright', *BEM*, 5 (September 1819), 731

'Letter from the Ettrick Shepherd, Enclosing a Fragment of the Mad Banker', *BEM*, 6 (January 1820), 390–93. Lockhart was the author of the long poem, 'The Mad Banker of Amsterdam', that was published over several issues of *BEM*. A proof of part of 'Letter from the Ettrick Shepherd' is preserved in the National Library of Scotland as MS 4822, fol. 1. The date of the proof is November 1819, so apparently the work was originally intended for publication in that issue of *BEM*. The work was significantly revised before its publication in January 1820.

'Sonnet, By the Ettrick Shepherd; Addressed to Christopher North, Esq. On Receiving the Last Number of This Magazine, By the Hands of John Dow, Esq. W. S.', *BEM*, 6 (January 1820), 464. Strout (p. 63) tentatively attributes the 'Sonnet' to John Lockhart.

'Letter from James Hogg to his Reviewer', *BEM*, 8 (October 1820), 67–76. Strout (p. 72) quotes a letter from Thomas Gillespie acknowledging Lockhart's authorship. Hogg, too, indicates that he was not the author in a letter to Blackwood: 'My letter seems to be exceedingly strong but too much of the braggadocia in it. The reviewer is however fairly set on his hams It will create a great deal of merriment' (*Letters 2*, p. 52).

'On the Head of George Buchanan', *BEM*, 13 (March 1823), 384. Strout (p. 106) credits William Maginn with this work.

'New Christmas Carol', *BEM*, 16 (December 1824), 680. In a manuscript listing of his publications in *BEM*, D. M. Moir takes credit for this poem—see National Library of Scotland Acc. 9856, no. 25. See also David Groves, 'James Hogg and the "New Christmas Carol": A Misattribution', *Notes and Queries*, 46 (December 1999), 474.

'To O'Doherty, In Answer to "Farewell"', *BEM*, 17 (January 1825), 120. The evidence regarding 'Answer to Farewell' is complex. Strout (p. 127) acknowledges Edith Batho's unsubstantiated attribution of the song to Hogg but offers no evidence of his own. Although the 'Hogg' character sings this song in the *Noctes Ambrosianæ*, Hogg's authorship seems unlikely. The song is reprinted in *BEM* from the *Dumfries Journal* for 28 December 1824, and in the *Journal* the song was signed from 'Kirkmahoe, 22d Dec. 1824'. The poem is printed in the *Journal* immediately below 'Odoherty's Farewell to Scotland', which itself was reprinted from the November 1824 number of *BEM*. However, the 'Farewell to Scotland' was not original to *BEM*; the song was one of three to appear in the story 'Captain Colville', by 'Nalla' (Allan Cunningham), which had been published in the *London Magazine*, 7 (February 1823), 132–40. There the song was represented as a 'Yorkshire ditty' and has no connection to 'Odoherty'. Much of the *Noctes* in which the 'Answer to Farewell' appears was committed to a humorous send-up of Hogg's recently-published book-length poem, *Queen Hynde*, which had also been reviewed in the *Dumfries Journal* for 28 December 1824. The correspondence between Hogg and Blackwood regarding this *Noctes* suggests that Hogg had no involvement in it (*Letters 2*, pp. 220–23). Furthermore, Hogg does not mention the song when he sends Blackwood 'The Grousome Caryl' for the January 1825 number of *BEM* (*Letters 2*, p. 220).

### III. Hogg's Works Written for but not Published in *Blackwood's Edinburgh Magazine*, 1817–1828

The importance of *Blackwood's Edinburgh Magazine* to Hogg is further underscored in the large number of works that Hogg wrote for or submitted to Blackwood but which were not published in the magazine. The following list represents works that either were rejected by William Blackwood for publication in *BEM* or for some other reason did not appear in the magazine. Most of the rejected works are published in the present edition; for information about these works, the reader is referred to the text and notes of the present edition. Publication information is provided for those works which are not included in the present edition. The works are listed in chronological order as far as it is possible to determine the date of composition or submission to *BEM*.

### Extempore Song

'Extempore Song' was not published in Hogg's lifetime. It is published in the present edition from the manuscript preserved in the National Library of Scotland (see pp. 24–25 and notes).

### On the Smearing of Sheep

Hogg wrote to Blackwood on 19 October 1817:' I have not however been unmindful of you I have written a long essay "on the Smearing of Sheep as it affects the qualities of the wool and the flock"' (*Letters 1*, p. 305). On 28 October 1817 Hogg wrote to Blackwood again, enclosing the article on sheep that he wanted published in the next issue 'for the sake of the season as it contains practical truths of which I wish my countrymen to avail themselves' (*Letters 1*, p. 307). The essay was not published in *BEM*. Gillian Hughes notes that Hogg published a letter to the editor of the *Dumfries and Galloway Courier*, 21 September 1824, on the subject of sheep-smearing (*Letters 1*, p. 308).

### Chaldee Continuation

In his *Memoir* Hogg indicated that he had written a 'long continuation' of the 'Chaldee Manuscript' in which he parodies 'the painters, poets, lawyers, booksellers, magistrates, and ministers of Edinburgh, all in the same style'—see *Altrive Tales*, ed. by Gillian Hughes (S/SC, 2003), p. 45. A fragment of a manuscript that possibly is Hogg's 'Chaldee' continuation is preserved in the University of Otago library; the manuscript fragment is included in Appendix A in the present edition.

### The Boar

'The Boar' was not published in Hogg's lifetime and is published in the present edition from the manuscript preserved in the National Library of Scotland (see pp. 44–47 and notes). Apparently there is no extant correspondence to establish the context for 'The Boar', but given that the manuscript was preserved by Blackwood it is reasonable to assume that Hogg intended the work for publication there. It is also possible that 'The Boar' was extracted from the 'Chaldee continuation'. See Appendix A.

### The Ettrick Shepherd not the Author of the Poetic Mirror

This article was announced in the *BEM* 'Notices' for January 1818, but it was never published. It is published in the present edition from the incomplete manuscript preserved in the National Library of Scotland (see pp. 56–57 and notes).

### New Poetic Mirror

'New Poetic Mirror' was never published in Hogg's lifetime. It is published in the present edition from the manuscript preserved in the National Library of Scotland (see pp. 57–61 and notes).

### An Old Soldier's Tale

'An Old Soldier's Tale' was probably submitted to Blackwood on 13 January 1818 (see *Letters 1*, pp. 325–26). Hogg wrote to Blackwood on 31 January 1818: 'What became of my Old Soldiers' Tale–Not even acknowledged?' (*Letters 1*, p. 329). The story was published later that year in the *Clydesdale Magazine*, 1 (July 1818), 106–12, and reprinted in *Winter Evening Tales* (1820)—see *Winter Evening Tales*, ed. by Ian Duncan (S/SC, 2002), pp. 98–106 and notes.

### John Paterson's Mare

Hogg corresponded with Blackwood about 'John Paterson's Mare' as early as July 1818 (*Letters 1*, p. 365). He sent a revised version of the story to Blackwood in June 1822 (*Letters 2*, pp. 163–64), but Blackwood was not interested in publishing any more of Hogg's literary sports that satirised the Edinburgh literary scene. This sketch eventually was published as 'Annals of Sporting. No. I.–John Paterson's Mare' in the *Newcastle Magazine*, 4 (January 1825), 3–12.

### Letter to Timothy Tickler

'Letter to Timothy Tickler' was not published in Hogg's lifetime. It is published in the present edition from the manuscript preserved in the Alexander Turnbull Library (see pp. 72–77 and notes).

### A Ballaunte

Hogg wrote to Blackwood on 28 July 1820: 'I send you *a ballaunte* which I wrote 18 months ago before I dreamed of such blackguardism in the hero or any man' (*Letters 2*, p. 36). Although Blackwood wrote back that he liked the 'Ballate', the work apparently was never published in *BEM* and has not been identified.

### No I of Hints to Reviewers

Hogg's 'Hints to Reviewers' was originally intended for publication in the *Edinburgh Magazine*. Hogg sent the work to Robert Cadell, who rejected it. The work was then offered to Blackwood, who also rejected the work. A partial manuscript of the work survives in private ownership (*Letters 2*, pp. 145, 159). It is not included in the present edition since it was originally intended for the *Edinburgh Magazine* rather than *BEM*.

### The Highlanders

Hogg mentions this poem in the same letter with which Hogg sent Blackwood 'Hints to Reviewers', although apparently he had sent this poem to Blackwood at some earlier time and Blackwood had not published it or returned it. The poem has not been identified—see *Letters 2*, p. 159.

### 'I send you the paper I was talking of'

Hogg wrote this to Blackwood on 4 August 1823 (*Letters 2*, p. 192). The 'paper' has not been identified.

### The Noctes

In Hogg's letter to Blackwood of 4 August 1823 mentioned above, Hogg also noted that he had not finished the 'Noctes', but that it would 'be forthcoming in good time' (*Letters 2*, p. 192). It is not certain when Hogg finished and submitted the 'Noctes', but in a letter to Blackwood of 19 March 1826 Hogg reminded Blackwood that he had 'sent a complete Noctes once which of course I never saw again' (*Letters 2*, p. 243). Hogg's 'Noctes' has not been identified.

### Correspondence with Byron

Hogg's 'Correspondence with Byron' was not published in Hogg's lifetime. It is published in the present edition from the proof pages preserved among the Blackwood papers in the National Library of Scotland (see pp. 153–59 and notes).

### Fife Gypsies

In a letter to William Blackwood, 6 June 1825, Hogg wrote: 'I inclose you the last chapter of the Fife Gypsies, if it is too long you may let it lie over till I come in to Holy Fair which will be some time next month' (*Letters 2*, p. 234). This work apparently was never published and has not been identified.

### There Cam a Fiddler Out of Fife

In the letter of 6 June 1825 quoted above, Hogg also included a four-stanza song, beginning with instructions that if it would 'suit the noctes you may clap it in old Ticklers mouth' (*Letters 2*, p. 234). The song was not published in *BEM*; however, the song had originally been published in Hogg's *Jacobite Relics* (1819). See *The Jacobite Relics of Scotland. [First Series]*, ed. by Murray G. H. Pittock (S/SC, 2002), pp. 21–22.

### Some Remarkable Passages in the Life of an Edinburgh Baillie and The Adventures of Colonel Peter Aston

Hogg had completed these stories in late 1825 or early 1826 (*Letters 2*, p. 240). Hogg wanted Blackwood to publish these two stories as part of a series of 'Lives of Eminent Men' that would also include 'Some Passages in the Life of Colonel Cloud', which was published in the July 1825 number of *BEM* (see pp. 166–80 and notes in the present edition). Upon the recommendation of D. M. Moir Blackwood rejected their publication in *BEM* and as a collection. The stories later were published in revised forms in *Tales of the Wars of Montrose* (1835). For additional information about these stories, see Gillian Hughes's Introduction and notes to the S/SC edition of *Tales of the Wars of Montrose* (1996).

### Forest Dialogue

Hogg wrote a *Noctes* dialogue to introduce his two 'Songs for the Duke of Buccleuch's Birth Day'. The two songs were published in *BEM* in the *Noctes Ambrosianæ* for February 1826, but Blackwood, or rather John Wilson, rejected the dialogue, as Blackwood wrote to Hogg: 'Christopher did not take the Forest dialogue, but he liked the songs' (NLS, MS 30,309, pp. 163–65). The dialogue is published for the first time in the present edition along with the songs from the manuscript preserved in the National Library of Scotland (see pp. 183–88 and notes).

### The Cameronian in Love

Hogg wrote to Blackwood on 19 March 1826: 'I never saw again [...] the Cameronian in love' (*Letters 2*, p. 243). Blackwood responded on 25 March that 'As to The Cameronian in Love it went out of my hands, and I never saw it again' (NLS, MS 30,309, pp. 163–65). This work has not been positively identified; Gillian Hughes suggests that this might be 'The Elder in Love', which was published in *Fraser's Magazine*, 5 (March 1832), 234–37 (*Letters 2*, p. 245).

### *A Pastoral Love Scene, or Dramas of Simple Life | Drama First*

'A Pastoral Love Scene' is the first of three pastoral dramas proposed by Hogg for publication in *BEM*. After Blackwood rejected 'A Pastoral Love Scene', Hogg rewrote it and published it as 'Katie Cheyne' in *Sharpe's London Magazine*, 1 (August 1829), 56–63. Hogg's original version is published in the present edition from the manuscript preserved in the Mitchell Library, Glasgow (see pp. 193–209 and notes).

### *Dramas of Simple Life No. II*

Although Blackwood agreed to publish this second of Hogg's three pastoral dramas, Hogg would not permit it to be published without the first. The work is published in the present edition from the incomplete manuscript preserved in the Alexander Turnbull Library (see pp. 209–53 and notes). The drama was revised substantially for publication as *A Bush Aboon Traquair*, which first appeared in the posthumously-published *Tales and Sketches*, 6 vols (Glasgow: Blackie, 1836–37), II, 275–338.

### *Dramas of Simple Life No. III*

This third of Hogg's three pastoral dramas has not been identified and apparently was never published, if in fact it was ever completed.

### *Hogg on Women!!!*

Hogg apparently sent Blackwood 'Hogg on Women!!!' in early April 1827, but Blackwood declined publication and returned the manuscript of 'the Verses on Women' to Hogg on 25 May 1827 (NLS, MS 30,310, pp. 128A–30). The poem is published in the present edition from the manuscript preserved in the National Library of Scotland (see pp. 260–62 and notes).

### *Songs for the Baloon*

These songs were intended for a special *Noctes Ambrosianæ* that was to include an aerial voyage in a hot-air balloon. Hogg wrote to Blackwood expressing his enthusiasm for the proposal and promising to send songs for the *Noctes* (*Letters 2*, p. 276). John Wilson had planned to write this *Noctes*, but the work was never completed and Hogg's songs were not published in *BEM*. The songs are published in the present edition from the manuscript preserved in the National Library of Scotland (see pp. 346–48 and notes). Hogg eventually wrote his own balloon story to provide a context for his ballooning songs; this work was published as 'Dr David Dale's Account of a Grand Aerial Voyage' in the issue of the *Edinburgh Literary Journal* for 23 January 1830, pp. 50–54.

### *Some old records*

Hogg wrote to Blackwood on 21 December 1827: 'I send you some old records that will puzzle and astonish the people' (*Letters 2*, p. 280). These 'records' have not been identified and apparently were not published in *BEM*.

### Polar Curiosities

Hogg sent Blackwood a work he referred to as 'Polar curiosities' on 5 January 1828 (*Letters* 2, p. 282). Hogg claimed the work was true and extracted from John Harris's *Navigantium Atque Itinerantium Bibliotheca* (1705). Blackwood rejected the work because he thought that people would not understand it (NLS, MS 30,310, p. 280). The 'Polar curiosities' probably served as the basis for Hogg's story 'The Surpassing Adventures of Allan Gordon', which was published posthumously in *Tales and Sketches*, 6 vols (Glasgow: Blackie, 1836–37), I, 241–316. Apparently Hogg's manuscript for the 'Polar curiosities' has not survived.

### An Egyptian Story

Hogg sent Blackwood 'an Egyptian story' on 12 February 1828 (*Letters* 2, p. 287). Blackwood rejected the story, and subsequently it was published as 'A Remarkable Egyptian Story' in *Fraser's Magazine*, 7 (February 1833), 147–58.

### Love's Legacy

Although Hogg may have written 'Love's Legacy' with the intention of publishing it in *BEM*, it is likely that he never showed the long poem to Blackwood. Hogg commented on this poem in the letter to Blackwood of 12 February 1828 quoted above: 'I have likewise apoem [*sic*] about the length of The Pleasures of Memory. Entitled LOVE'S LEGACY or A FAREWELL GIFT but after my grievious dissapointment with Queen Hynde neither dare I offer it to the public' (*Letters* 2, p. 287). A portion of the poem was published as 'Mora Campbell' in the June 1834 number of *BEM* and will be included in the second volume of the S/SC edition of Hogg's *Contributions to Blackwood's Edinburgh Magazine*. The remainder of the poem was published in *Fraser's Magazine* in three instalments, 10 (October, November, December 1834), pp. 403–08, 556–60, 639–44. For discussion of the publication history of *Love's Legacy*, see David Groves's edition of the original poem in *Altrive Chapbooks*, 5 (September 1988), 1–53, as well as his article '"This Thrilling Tempest of the Soul": An Introduction to *Love's Legacy*', *Newsletter of the James Hogg Society*, 7 (1988), 10–17.

### M, Corkindale Letters

Hogg wrote to Blackwood on 1 August 1828 that he had 'a series of M,Corkindales letters' ready for Blackwood (*Letters* 2, p. 299), and on 6 August 1828 Hogg sent Blackwood the completed work (*Letters* 2, p. 300). In a letter to Allan Cunningham of 17 October 1828, Hogg also indicated that he intended this work to be part of the 'Lives of Eminent Men' series (*Letters* 2, p. 312). The 'M,Corkindales letters' have not been identified with certainty, but it is possible that they were edited by Hogg's nephew, Robert Hogg, and published in *The Shepherd's Calendar* (1829) as the second part of Hogg's story 'A Strange Secret'—see pp. 315–45 and notes in the present edition.

# Hyphenation List

Various words are hyphenated at the ends of lines in this edition of *Contributions to Blackwood's Edinburgh Magazine*. The list below indicates those cases in the present volume in which hyphens should be retained in making quotations. Each item is referred to by page number and line number; in determining line numbers, titles and headings have been ignored.

p. 1, l. 16  a-swoomin
p. 1, l. 32  hearth-rug
p. 2, l. 25  Pool-Midnight
p. 9, l. 28  hop-step-and-leap
p. 10, l. 31  Ramseycleuch-burn
p. 11, l. 41  Ramseycleuch-burn
p. 12, l. 6  anti-prelatic
p. 21, l. 36  "sun-ways-about"
p. 29, l. 1  blow-fly
p. 42, l. 10  palm-tree
p. 54, l. 14  half-starved
p. 64, l. 25  weaning-time
p. 68, l. 16  farm-house
p. 80, l. 37  a-day
p. 84, l. 20  well-ground
p. 93, l. 17  upper-hand
p. 117, l. 25  Birkhill-Path
p. 120, l. 8  black-faced
p. 124, l. 12  Black-Jock-man
p. 125, l. 42  church-music
p. 136, l. 31  lease-holders
p. 141, l. 9  hay-ricks
p. 141, l. 38  hay-rope
p. 143, l. 34  moor-cock

p. 166, l. 21  billiard-room
p. 166, l. 22  looker-on
p. 167, l. 11  Coffee-room
p. 167, l. 21  respectable-looking
p. 171, l. 42  highly-gifted
p. 172, l. 24  Deputy-Adjutant-General
p. 173, l. 3  Glen-Lyon
p. 173, l. 8  wine-merchant
p. 178, l. 22  ill-willie
p. 197, l. 27  lak-a-day
p. 198, l. 5  Glen-buoy
p. 199, l. 27  house-maid
p. 202, l. 10  dare-say
p. 204, l. 15  He-he-he
p. 216, l. 20  Hech-wow
p. 226, l. 13  coat-tails
p. 235, l. 34  He-he-he
p. 263, l. 20  church-yard
p. 263, l. 26  even-down
p. 280, l. 5  willow-tree
p. 318, l. 41  wul-cats
p. 331, l. 5  snow-white
p. 339, l. 15  fox-hunter

# Notes

In the Notes that follow, page references to prose works include a letter enclosed in parentheses: (a) indicates that the passage concerned is to be found in the first quarter of the page, while (b) refers to the second quarter, (c) to the third quarter, and (d) to the final quarter. Page references to the poetry are followed by line numbers. Where it seems useful to discuss the meaning of particular phrases, this is done in the Notes; single words generally are explained in the glossary. Where appropriate, the Notes also include pertinent textual discussions. Quotations from the Bible are from the Authorised King James Version, the translation familiar to Hogg and his contemporaries. References to Shakespeare's plays are to *The Complete Works*, ed. by Stanley Wells and others, 2nd edn (Oxford: Clarendon Press, 2005). For references to other volumes of the Stirling/South Carolina Research edition, the editor's name is given after the title, followed by the abbreviation 'S/SC' and date of first publication. The geographical references in the notes rely heavily on Francis H. Groome, *Ordnance Gazetteer of Scotland: A Survey of Scottish Topography*, 6 vols (Edinburgh: Jack, 1882–85), and David Munro and Bruce Gittings, *Scotland: An Encyclopedia of Places & Landscape*, Royal Scottish Geographical Society (Glasgow: Collins, 2006). The Notes are also greatly indebted to the following standard reference works: *Oxford Dictionary of National Biography, Oxford English Dictionary, Scottish National Dictionary,* and *Concise Scots Dictionary.*

Works frequently referenced in the Notes are abbreviated as follows:

**Anecdotes of Scott** James Hogg, *Anecdotes of Scott*, ed. by Jill Rubenstein (S/SC, 1999)

*BEM Blackwood's Edinburgh Magazine*

**BL** British Library

**Child** *The English and Scottish Popular Ballads*, ed. by Francis H. Child, 5 vols (Boston: Houghton Mifflin, 1882–98)

**Confessions** James Hogg, *The Private Memoirs and Confessions of a Justified Sinner*, ed. by P. D. Garside, afterword by Ian Campbell (S/SC, 2001)

*ELJ Edinburgh Literary Journal*

**GED** Colin Mark, *The Gaelic-English Dictionary* (London: Routledge, 2004)

**Kinsley** Robert Burns, *The Poems and Songs of Robert Burns*, ed. by James Kinsley, 3 vols (Oxford: Clarendon Press, 1968)

**Letters 1** James Hogg, *The Collected Letters of James Hogg: Volume 1 1800–1819*, ed. by Gillian Hughes, assoc. eds Douglas S. Mack, Robin MacLachlan, and Elaine Petrie (S/SC, 2004)

**Letters 2** James Hogg, *The Collected Letters of James Hogg: Volume 2 1820–1831*, ed. by Gillian Hughes, assoc. eds Douglas S. Mack, Robin MacLachlan, and Elaine Petrie (S/SC, 2006)

*Life of Scott* J. G. Lockhart, *Memoirs of Sir Walter Scott*, 5 vols (London: Macmillan, 1900)

*Memoir* James Hogg, 'Memoir of the Author's Life' and 'Reminiscences of Former Days', *Altrive Tales*, ed. by Gillian Hughes (S/SC, 2003)

**NLS** National Library of Scotland

*New Statistical Account The New Statistical Account of Scotland*, 15 vols (Edinburgh: William Blackwood, 1845)

*ODEP The Oxford Dictionary of English Proverbs*, ed. by William George Smith and F. P. Wilson, 3rd edn (Oxford: Clarendon Press, 1970)

*OED Oxford English Dictionary*

*Oxford DNB Oxford Dictionary of National Biography*

*Peter's Letters* J. G. Lockhart, *Peter's Letters to His Kinsfolk*, '3rd' edn, 3 vols (Edinburgh: Blackwood, 1819)

*Poetical Works* James Hogg, *The Poetical Works of James Hogg*, 4 vols (Edinburgh: Constable, 1822)

*Shepherd's Calendar* James Hogg, *The Shepherd's Calendar*, ed. by Douglas S. Mack (S/SC, 1995)

*SND Scottish National Dictionary*, ed. by William Grant and David Murison, 10 vols (Edinburgh: The Scottish National Dictionary Association, 1941–76)

*Songs* James Hogg, *Songs, by the Ettrick Shepherd* (Edinburgh: Blackwood, 1831)

**Strout** Alan Lang Strout, *A Bibliography of Articles in Blackwood's Magazine 1817–1825* (Lubbock, Texas: Texas Tech Press, 1959)

*WET* James Hogg, *Winter Evening Tales*, ed. by Ian Duncan (S/SC, 2002)

# April 1817–March 1818 (Volumes 1–2)

### Tales and Anecdotes of the Pastoral Life. No. I

'Tales and Anecdotes of the Pastoral Life. No. I' was first published in the first issue of *Blackwood's Edinburgh Magazine* (then entitled *Edinburgh Monthly Magazine*), 1 (April 1817), 22–25. The story is signed 'H' in *BEM*, although Hogg's authorship is not otherwise indicated. 'Tales and Anecdotes' is the first of three stories of the same title that appeared in the first three consecutive issues of William Blackwood's new monthly magazine. The 'Tales and Anecdotes' stories were reprinted with minor revisions as chapters III, IV, and V of 'The Shepherd's Calendar' in *Winter Evening Tales*, 2 vols (Edinburgh and London: Oliver & Boyd, 1820), II, 142–59; see also *Winter Evening Tales*, ed. by Ian Duncan (S/SC, 2002), pp. 392–409.

The date of composition of the 'Tales and Anecdotes' series is not known. As early as May 1813 Hogg had written to Archibald Constable with a proposal for a collection of Scottish stories: 'I have for many years been collecting the rural and traditional tales of Scotland and I have of late been writing them over again and new-modelling them, and have the vanity to suppose they will form a most interesting work They will fill two large vols 8vo price £1 or 4 vols 12mo price the same'. Hogg proposed to Constable that the collection be called '*The Rural and Traditionary Tales of Scotland* by J. H. Craig of Douglas Esq' (*Letters 1*, p. 145). Constable did not publish the collection, and Hogg later sought William Blackwood's assistance. Hogg wrote to Blackwood on 4 January 1817 that a collection of stories he proposed calling 'Cottage Winter Nights' was ready for publication, and he hoped Blackwood would publish it: 'The work consists of "The Rural and Traditionary Tales of Scotland" They are simple carelessly and badly written but said to be very interesting The Bridal of Polmood which you read is the longest tale, not the best, but a fair specimen' (*Letters 1*, p. 289). Blackwood did not publish Hogg's collection under Hogg's title, but in 1818 Blackwood published a two-volume collection of 'rural' tales, *The Brownie of Bodsbeck; And Other Tales.* The two-volume collection that became *Winter Evening Tales*–and that included the 'Tales and Anecdotes' stories– eventually went to Oliver and Boyd. (For a thorough discussion of the publication history of Hogg's 'rural and traditionary tales' and related works, see Ian Duncan's introductory essay to the S/SC edition of *Winter Evening Tales*, pp. xi–xxii.)

The third sketch in the 'Tales and Anecdotes' series concludes with the note that the stories are to be continued. Hogg does not continue the series under the 'Tales and Anecdotes' title, though. In the April 1819 number of *BEM* Hogg begins a new series of pastoral anecdotes under the title 'The Shepherd's Calendar'. The first two instalments of this series, entitled 'Storms', were collected with the three 'Tales and Anecdotes of the Pastoral Life' to form 'The Shepherd's Calendar' in *Winter Evening Tales*. The *BEM* series of 'The Shepherd's Calendar' ran intermittently through the April 1828 number; the stories were then collected with a few additional works and published by Blackwood in two volumes in 1829 under the title *The Shepherd's Calendar*–see *The Shepherd's Calendar*, ed. by Douglas S. Mack (S/SC, 1995).

The present publication of 'Tales and Anecdotes' follows the *BEM* text. The text silently corrects inconsistencies in the printing of quotation marks in the *BEM* text, but otherwise the sketch is printed without emendation.

1(a) **Mr Grumple** [...] **of** *Woolenhorn* apparently fictitious. The characters in the first number of 'Tales and Anecdotes' all appear to be fictitious, although in the second and third numbers of the series Hogg introduces some of his pastoral acquaintances.

1(a) **rights of teind, and the claims** [...] **has for a grass glebe** Callum G. Brown writes in *Religion and Society in Scotland since 1707* (Edinburgh: Edinburgh University Press, 1997): 'In principle the burden of maintaining church finances rested with the landowners who formed the board of heritors in each parish. The board was responsible for the construction and maintenance of a church capable of accommodating two-thirds of the population over the age of twelve, for the provision of a manse and a glebe of four acres arable or pasture for sixteen cattle, and for the payment of the minister's stipend from the teinds–an annual tax exacted by "teind-holders", usually landowners, equal to one fifth of the agricultural rental value of the parish' (p. 68). The obligation to make adequate provisions for ministers was established early in the Reformation in Scotland in *The Book of Discipline* (1561), written by a committee of church leaders, including John Knox. The 'rights of teind' were controversial even into the twentieth century as the heritors and the church frequently disagreed over appropriate support. Brown writes: 'In practice heritors ensured that costs were minimised and passed on to the lower social groups in the parish. Heritors challenged claims for expenditure, kept salaries low (especially schoolmasters'), and made tenants responsible for the payment of their proportion of the teinds' (p. 69).

1(b) *come ben* an expression meaning 'come inside', an invitation to the inner part or 'best room' of the house.

1(c) **clouted shoes** shoes that have been patched or reinforced with a thin metal plate (*SND*).

2(b) **sport they had in killing the salmon** in *Anecdotes of Scott* Hogg relates a story of midnight 'leistering kippers in Tweed' with Scott and James Skene of Rubislaw (pp. 41–42).

2(d) **shaugle shauglin a' his pith** that is, 'shuffling' along with all his energy.

3(a) **the grains o' the leister** a leister is a three-pronged spear used in catching salmon; the grains are the prongs.

3(d) **gae owre** gave up, stopped.

4(a) **they wad turn unco milk-an'-water things** [...] **wantin a broolzie** that is, they would become weak or feeble without an opportunity for a scuffle.

4(a) **close-time** the time when catching or killing certain kinds of wildlife is illegal. The salmon fishing industry was an important facet of the Scottish economy, and as a prerogative of the government, salmon fishing was closely regulated. Close time for salmon fishing in Hogg's time would have been approximately September until February. Apparently, as Peter Plash suggests, close-time was frequently ignored. See James Ballantyne, 'Hogg's Role in *The Scotch Gentleman*', *Studies in Hogg and his World*, 16 (2005), 131–33.

5(a) **the mense of a miller's horse** echoes the proverbial expression of disparagement 'like a miller's mare' (*ODEP*, p. 532).

5(c) **I have** [...] **future communications** Hogg continues his story of the country wedding in parts II and III of 'Tales and Anecdotes of the Pastoral Life', which are published in the May 1817 and June 1817 numbers of *BEM* respectively (see pp. 6, 19 of the present edition).

### Verses, *Recited [...] On the Day that the News Arrived of Our Final Victory Over the French*

'Verses, Recited [...] On the Day that the News Arrived of Our Final Victory Over the French' was first published untitled in the *Edinburgh Evening Courant* in the issue for Monday, 11 April 1814. The newspaper introduces the poem with a note about the occasion at which the song was performed: 'A party of social friends having met on Friday evening last, in honour of the glorious news which arrived that day of the taking of Paris, Mr Hogg (the Ettrick Shepherd) was called on for a song, when he recited the following verses'. In his introduction to the poem in *Songs* (1831), Hogg noted that the poem was 'written for, and sung at, a large social meeting of friends, who met by appointment at Young's tavern, to celebrate the entry of the Allies into Paris in 1814' (p. 258). The Allied forces entered Paris and defeated the French forces on 31 March 1814, which led to the abdication of Napoleon in early April and his exile to Elba. This was not the 'final victory over the French', however, as Napoleon returned from Elba in March 1815 and reestablished an army. Napoleon was defeated at Waterloo and abdicated again in June 1815. (For a full discussion of the newspaper context of this and related works, see Gillian Hughes's article, 'James Hogg and Edinburgh's Triumph over Napoleon', *Scottish Studies Review*, 4 (Spring 2003), 98–111. Acknowledgment is made to Dr Hughes, who discovered the newspaper publication of the song, for her suggestions for these annotations.)

The poem was substantially revised for publication in the first issue of *Blackwood's Edinburgh Magazine* (*Edinburgh Monthly Magazine*), 1 (April 1817), 72. In addition to frequent revisions in wording throughout the poem, the *BEM* version adds a stanza after the sixth stanza of the newspaper version:

> Come, jaw your glasses to the brim!
> Gar in the air your bonnets flee!
> "Our gude auld king!" I'll drink to him,
> As lang as I hae drink to pree. (ll. 25–28)

Although the poem was identified as Hogg's in the newspaper printing of the work, in *BEM* the poem was signed 'H' and Hogg's authorship was not otherwise acknowledged.

The poem was further revised and reprinted in the 1822 *Poetical Works* (IV, 276–77); the extended title of 'Verses' was changed in *Poetical Works* to address specifically the allied victory in Paris: 'Stanzas *Recited in a party of Social Friends, met in honour of the entry into Paris by the Allies.–1814'*. In addition to changes in wording throughout the poem, the fifth, sixth, and seventh stanzas of the *BEM* version were omitted from *Poetical Works*. In the opening line of the last stanza in *Poetical Works*, the poem returns to the wording of the newspaper version and celebrates 'Britain' rather than just 'Scotland' as in *BEM*: 'Lang may auld Britain's banner pale' (IV, 277). The poem was reprinted again with further revisions in *Songs* (pp. 258–59) under the title 'A National Song of Triumph'. The *Songs* version follows the revisions for *Poetical Works* except that the fifth and sixth stanzas of *BEM* were restored in a slightly revised form for *Songs*. The *Songs* version also has four eight-line stanzas instead of the nine four-line stanzas of *BEM*.

The present edition reprints the *BEM* version without emendation.

**5, l. 1 cliffs o' snaw** perhaps a reference to the chalky white cliffs of southeast England, near Dover, which look across the English Channel towards the French coast.

**5, l. 3 bastard Eagle** Napoleon selected the eagle as an emblem of his empire, and it adorned palaces, weapons, and flag staffs. Hogg here expresses his sense of the illegitimacy of Napoleon's rule.

**5, l. 7 lions** representations of both England and Scotland. The lion rampant has been a symbol of Scottish kings since William I, 'the Lion' (1143–1214). The lion as a royal symbol of England may date as early as Henry I (1068–1135).

**6, l. 13 Gae hang the coofs wha boded wae** an attack on those who publicly suggested that Britain's involvement in the Peninsular War was doomed to failure. Francis Jeffrey and the *Edinburgh Review* undoubtedly were particular targets of Hogg's criticism. In the October 1808 number of the *Edinburgh Review* (vol. 13, pp. 215–234), Jeffrey published an article, 'Don Pedro Cevallos on the French Usurpation in Spain', that was critical of the British military campaign in Spain and lauded the strength of the French army under Napoleon. This led many prominent subscribers to the *Review*, including Sir Walter Scott, to cancel their subscriptions, and it also spurred Scott to support John Murray in the establishment of the *Quarterly Review*.

**6, l. 27 "Our gude auld king"** a toast to King George III (1738–1820). George III was king of Great Britain from 1760 to 1820, although his eldest son became Prince Regent in 1811 when the king's mental disease rendered him incapable of ruling.

**6, l. 30 The Rose and Shamrock**  representations of England and Ireland, respectively. The rose as the national flower of England dates from the fifteenth century and the War of the Roses. The shamrock became a popular, if unofficial, symbol of Ireland in the seventeenth century for its association with legends of St Patrick.

**6, l. 32 "*The Thristle o' the Norlan' hill*"**  the thistle of the Northern hill. The thistle is an emblem of Scotland. The *SND* gives 'thristle' as a Scots word for 'thistle'; however, the spelling was changed to 'thistle' in all versions after *BEM*. Hogg apparently uses italics here for emphasis, and as Gillian Hughes suggests, the quotation marks probably also represent a toast drunk at Young's Tavern on the original occasion of the performance of the poem. See also l. 27. Later versions of the poem do not use either italics or quotation marks.

**6, ll. 35–36 lions paw the gale [...] dewlaps to the sun**  an image of the Royal Standard of Scotland, a red lion rampant on a yellow background. The lion stands erect on its hind legs with its 'dewlap' exposed and the fore legs appearing to 'paw' the air.

### Tales and Anecdotes of the Pastoral Life. No. II

'Tales and Anecdotes of the Pastoral Life. No. II' was first published in *Blackwood's Edinburgh Magazine* (*Edinburgh Monthly Magazine*) in the second issue, 1 (May 1817), 143–47. The story is signed 'H', but Hogg's authorship is not otherwise noted. The story is a continuation of 'Tales and Anecdotes of the Pastoral Life. No. I' from the April 1817 issue of *BEM* (see p. 1 of the present edition). The story was reprinted as Chapter IV of 'The Shepherd's Calendar' in *Winter Evening Tales* (1820), II, 147–54; see also *WET*, pp. 397–404. See the notes for 'Tales and Anecdotes of the Pastoral Life. No. I' in the present edition for more information about the publication of this series.

The present edition reprints the *BEM* version without emendation.

**7(a) Stridekirtin**  apparently fictitious.

**7(b) teinds**  see note for 1(a).

**7(b) Arcadia of Britain** Arcadia, a mountainous region of Peloponnesus, Greece; in literature, from Virgil's *Eclogues* forward, Arcadia has come to represent pastoral simplicity and peacefulness. Hogg describes the Ettrick and Yarrow valleys as the 'Arcadia of Britain' in his 1802 'Journey through the Highlands of Scotland', first published in *The Scots Magazine*, October 1802: 'The two rivers, Etterick and Yarrow, form properly what is called Etterick Forest— which was the Sylva Caledonia of the ancients and is now the Arcadia of Britain, the whole scene, life and manners of the inhabitants being truly pastoral' (vol. 64, p. 815).

**7(c) in some late ages, noted for its zeal in the duties of religion**  during the Covenanting wars of the seventeenth century, fugitive Covenanters scattered throughout the region of Hogg's native Ettrick. Hogg's novel, *The Brownie of Bodsbeck*, incorporates traditional tales of the Covenanters, and in his *Anecdotes of Scott* Hogg emphasises the truth of his story: 'It is the picture that I hae been bred up in the belief o' sin ever I was born an' mair than that there is not *one* incident not one in the whole tale which I cannot prove to be literally true from history' (p. 22). Also, Thomas Boston (1676–1732), who was minister of Hogg's native parish church in Ettrick from 1707 until his death in 1732, was at the centre of the major religious controversies of his time, including, most famously, the antinomian controversy that arose out of the re-publication of Edward Fisher's *The Marrow of Modern Divinity*, which Boston had encouraged. The General Assembly of the Church of Scotland ordered the ministers to warn the congregation against the antinomian theology of the *Marrow*. Boston was a leader of the opposition to the General Assembly's action and was formally rebuked by the Assembly. Boston later published an annotated edition of the *Marrow* under the pseudonym Philalethes Irenaeus (see also 'Thomas Boston' by P. G. Rykem, *Oxford DNB*).

**7(c) that practical religion should be losing ground [...] and scepticism [...] gaining ground in proportion** in the character of Mr Grumple, the narrator's relative, Hogg satirises what he perceives as the secular interests of the Moderates in the Church of Scotland—interests that are in part a consequence of patronage. Mr Grumple is much more conscious of the monetary affairs of the parish than the spiritual needs of the parishioners. The Moderates were largely represented by the landowning gentry, who had gained the right to appoint ministers of their parishes (patronage) rather than allowing the local congregation to exercise its traditional right to elect and call its own minister. The Moderates were in conflict with the Evangelicals, who regarded the 'rational religion' of the Moderates as '"cold morality" or "legalism" without a touch of gospel to stir or comfort souls'—see J. H. S. Burleigh, *A Church History of Scotland* (London: Oxford University Press, 1960), p. 304. Hogg addresses the conflict between the Moderates and Evangelicals again in a story in *BEM*, 'Sound Morality', which was published in the June 1829 issue (vol. 25, pp. 741–47).

**7(d) ministers of religion [...] sanctity of character** John Lockhart in *Peter's Letters* underscores the importance of the 'sanctity of character' of the minister in the Presbyterian Church of Scotland: 'To the devout Presbyterian—the image of his minister, and the idea of his superior sanctity, come instead not only of the whole calendar of the Catholic Christian, but of all the splendid liturgies, and chauntings, and pealing organs of our English cathedrals [...] the Ministers were often not the chief only, but the sole symbols of the faith of those who followed their system' (III, 71).

**8(c) "green coats kilted to the knee"** Hogg quotes the fourth line of the opening stanza of his long poem *The Pilgrims of the Sun* (London: John Murray; Edinburgh: William Blackwood, 1815):

> Of all the lasses in fair Scotland,
> That lightly bound o'er muir and lee,
> There's nane like the maids of Yarrowdale,
> Wi' their green coats kilted to the knee.

This line also echoes a line repeated throughout the well-known ballad 'Tam Lin': 'Janet has kilted her green kirtle | A little aboon her knee' (James Johnson, *The Scots Musical Museum*, 6 vols (Edinburgh: James Johnson, 1787–1803), v, 423.

**8(c) "pat on their hose [...] trig an' witching"** the source of this quotation has not been discovered. The quotation marks perhaps represent the point of view of the characters in the story rather than indicating a quotation from a published source.

**8(d) contest at leaping** the athletic competitions described by Hogg were common occurrences among the shepherds. In *The Shepherd's Calendar*, Hogg describes the unsurpassed athleticism of his maternal grandfather, Will o' Phaup: 'For feats of frolic, strength, and agility, he had no equal in his day' (S/SC, 1995), p. 103. Hogg himself was an accomplished shepherd-athlete, and later (1827) Hogg founded the St Ronan's Games. For more on Hogg's athleticism see David Groves, *James Hogg and the St Ronan's Border Club*. (Dollar: Douglas S. Mack, 1987).

9(d) **whenever two or three young shepherds are gathered together** echoes the words of Jesus in Matthew 18. 20: 'For where two or three are gathered together in my name, there am I in the midst of them'.

9(d) **the broose!** 'a race at country weddings from the church or the bride's home to the bridegroom's' (*SND*). In 'Tales and Anecdotes of the Pastoral Life. No. III', Hogg describes a second 'broose', where the race is run on foot from the starting line to a point five hundred yards distant, and then the runners finish at the starting point. See p. 20(a) of the present edition.

10(c) **Jock o' the Meer–Cleuch** unidentified. In Nos II and III of the 'Tales and Anecdotes' series, Hogg apparently blends fictitious characters with real characters from among his shepherding acquaintances. Those characters that are known to be real are identified in the notes.

10(c) **Aedie o' Aberlosk** Adam Bryden (1766–1850) of Aberlosk farm in Eskdalemuir, about ten miles south of Ettrick. Bryden was a partner with Hogg in Locherben farm, which Hogg tenanted 1807 to 1810. Hogg wrote to Blackwood on 7 March [1821?]:

> Gang away down to Ambrose's and see Aedie o' Aberlosk. He is much fallen off: indeed quite doited by worldly misfortune now, but he *was* the greatest original I ever saw. Be sure to give him half a mutchkin for my sake and the laughing you have got at him. It was he you know who wrote the letter to the king. When ever you weary of him desire him to take his glass with his friend till you come back, and leave him, telling Ambrose to give them so much. I thought you would be angry if I did not introduce you to him. He is come to Edin. on a very disagreeable business to seek redress against a brother in law for withholding his rights (*Letters 2*, p. 67).

Aedie's 'letter to the king' is printed in the third part of 'Tales and Anecdotes' (p. 26 of the present edition). For more on Adam Bryden, see the 'Notes on Correspondents' in *Letters 1*, pp. 450–51.

10(c) **Ramseycleuch-burn** this stream flows into Ettrick Water near Ramseycleuch. See also note for 14(b).

11(a) **Kirkhope** a hamlet on Ettrick Water about one mile southwest of Ettrickbridge.

12(a) **Cameronian naig** the Cameronians were followers of Richard Cameron (1648–80), Scottish Covenanting minister. Even after the covenanting wars ended, the Cameronians continued to oppose government interference in their religion and movements towards moderation in the Presbyterian church. Aedie comically characterises his horse as something of a stalwart rebel.

12(a) **auld Clavers mounted on Hornie** John Graham of Claverhouse (1648?–89), later Viscount Dundee, had a reputation for cruelty as he led government troops in pursuit of the Covenanters in the early 1680s. Hogg notes here Claverhouse's reputation also for superior riding skills. In *Anecdotes of Scott*

Hogg comments on leading Scott, William Laidlaw, and Sir Adam Ferguson through a 'wild region by a path, which, if not rode by Clavers, as reported, was never rode by another gentleman' (p. 42). In *The Brownie of Bodsbeck* Hogg also associates Claverhouse's riding skills with the devil: 'Clavers exerted himself that day in such a manner, galloping over precipices, and cheering on his dragoons, that all the country who beheld him believed him to be a devil, or at least mounted on one. The marks of that infernal courser's feet are shewn to this day on a steep, nearly perpendicular, below the Bubbly Craig, along which he is said to have ridden at full speed, in order to keep sight of a party of the flying Covenanters' (ed. by Douglas S. Mack (Edinburgh: Scottish Academic Press, 1976), p. 75). 'Hornie' is the devil.

12(b) *the five kirks o' Eskdale* the parishes of Eskdalemuir, Ewes, Staplegorton, Wauchope, and Westerkirk. According to the Rev. William Brown in *The New Statistical Account of Scotland*, the 'kirks' constituted a gift of land from King James V to Robert Maxwell, the fifth Lord Maxwell, for his service to the King. Along with receiving the gift of land in 1537, Maxwell was appointed one of the kingdom's six vice-regents. Brown notes that 'the Five Kirks, then, were not the same as those comprehended under that name, now; but were Upper and Nether Ewis, Wauchope, Staplegordon, and Westerkirk, which last included Eskdalemuir, before it was erected into a separate parish' (IV, 400).

12(c) a *Tam-Park* of a glass 'a small drinking-glass. The origin of the name is not traced' (*SND*). The *SND* cites only this example from Hogg. Ian Duncan suggests that the expression might refer to a local who was 'notorious for serving his guests (or customers) short measure' (*WET*, p. 581, note for 402(c)). 'Park' was a well-known name in Selkirkshire; most notable among the Parks was the African explorer, Mungo Park (1771–1806).

12(c) *Bailey's Dictionary An Universal Etymological English Dictionary* (1721), compiled by Nathan Bailey (*bap*. 1691, *d*. 1742). Bailey's *Dictionary* was a popular and influential work throughout the eighteenth and nineteenth centuries and went through many editions. The dictionary was distinctive for its thoroughness and for its focus on etymology and pronunciation, as well as word meanings. Samuel Johnson was heavily influenced by Bailey in developing his dictionary, and Bailey's dictionary has occasionally appeared in literature, from *Tom Jones* to *Middlemarch* (see also 'Nathan Bailey' by Michael Hancher, *Oxford DNB*). Hogg in his *Memoir* cites a Bailey's anecdote referring to his own difficulty in first reading 'The Life and Adventures of Sir William Wallace' and 'The Gentle Shepherd': 'Thus, after I had got through both works, I found myself much in the same predicament with the man of Eskdalemuir, who had borrowed Bailey's Dictionary from his neighbour. On returning it, the lender asked him what he thought of it. "I dinna ken, man," replied he; "I have read it all through, but canna say that I understand it; it is the most confused book that ever I saw in my life!"' (*Memoir*, p. 16).

12(d) welcome hame till us 'welcome-hame' is also used as a noun, 'a reception or party given for a bride on entering her new home' (*SND*).

14(b) Wattie Bryden Hogg may have had in mind Walter Bryden who, with his brother George, had the farm of Ramsey-cleuch. Hogg met Sir Walter Scott at the Brydens' farm in the summer of 1801 when Scott was collecting ballads for his *Minstrelsy of the Scottish Border*; Hogg describes this meeting in *Anecdotes of Scott*, pp. 37–39. A different Walter Bryden, or Cow Wat, also figures in 'Letter from the Ettrick Shepherd', *BEM*, 6 (March 1820), 630–32, in a comic dispute with Hogg's cousin, James Laidlaw, over their beliefs about hell. See pp. 78–79 of the present edition and note to 78(d).

**14(c) decently and in order** from I Corinthians 14. 40: 'Let all things be done decently and in order'.

**14(c) future opportunity** the story is concluded in the June number of *BEM* (pp. 247–50). See p. 19 of the present edition.

## Shakspeare Club of Alloa

'Shakspeare Club of Alloa' was first published in *Blackwood's Edinburgh Magazine* (*Edinburgh Monthly Magazine*), 1 (May 1817), 152–54, and has not been reprinted. The work was identified as Hogg's by David Groves in his article 'James Hogg: A Parody of Robert Southey', *Notes and Queries*, 46 (December 1999), 474–77, and confirmed by Gillian Hughes in her preparation of Hogg's *Collected Letters* (S/SC, 2005), I, 293–94. The verses included within 'Shakespeare Club of Alloa' apparently were written by Hogg for Alexander Bald to read at the annual meeting of the Shakespeare Club of Alloa in Bald's role as club president. Hogg wrote to Bald on 21 April 1817, enclosing the verses:

As it is likely I will not see you before Wednesday afternoon I inclose you a few pages I have written in a great hurry this day thinking it would be necessary for you to read them over at your leisure in order to give them the full effect when read in public.

You will observe that they are not designed to follow the toast 'To the Memory of Shakespeare' but after your health is given as President of the club which will not likely be for some time afterward. (*Letters 1*, p. 293)

Alexander Bald (1783–1859) was a prominent business person in Alloa as a timber merchant and brick manufacturer. Bald and Hogg may have met as early as 1803 when Bald was visiting John Grieve, a mutual friend of Hogg's and Bald's. Bald himself was a poet and frequent contributor to the *Scots Magazine*. (For more information on Bald, see 'Notes on Correspondents' in *Letters 1*, p. 443, and the article in the *Oxford DNB* by Sidney Lee, rev. Sarah Couper.) The Shakespeare Club of Alloa was established by Bald in 1804, and the Club met annually on or about 23 April, the birthday of the poet. The entry for Alloa in *The New Statistical Account of Scotland* indicates that the Shakespeare Club 'was formed by a native of this parish, who is distinguished for literary taste, in the year 1804, and prior to that even in the poet's birthplace; and at the different anniversaries, it has occasionally been visited by several distinguished poets, and other literary characters, honorary members of the club. The late Mr Hogg's beautiful Ode to the Genius of Shakespeare was written for the anniversary of 1815' (VIII, 'Clackmannanshire', p. 63). Hogg apparently attended the celebrations of the Club for several years, where he enjoyed the pleasant company not only of his friend Bald, but also of the Club members, whom Hogg came to admire. Hogg had written to Bald on 14 November 1813:

But among all the incidents, and all the traits that I saw or met with among my own species, there was nothing pleased me so much as the notice taken of me by the young gentlemen of your town, for which I

was indebted to your introduction. [...] I could not help feeling a little hurt when I found that no means were left me of making any return *in kind* to my shakesperian brethren for all their hospitality, I may perhaps have my turn by and by; at all events I desire that, whoever of the number come to Edin. that they will call on me as an acquaintance at N°. 10 St. Ann street which I will take extremely kind. (*Letters 1*, p. 166)
The present edition reprints the *BEM* version without emendation.

**14(title) Alloa** a port town on the River Forth in Clackmannanshire.

**14(d) newspapers, for some years bygone** as Gillian Hughes has noted, an account of the 1815 celebration of the Shakespeare Club appeared in the *Edinburgh Evening Courant*, 4 May 1815 (*Letters 1*, p. 248). The article printed Hogg's poem, 'To the Genius of Shakespeare', which was written for the occasion. The poem was reprinted in Hogg's 1822 *Poetical Works* (IV, 252–54).

**14(d) famous STEAM BOAT, on a new plan** this allusion is probably multi-faceted. The Forth and Clyde rivers were important navigable rivers and the centre of steamboat development at the beginning of the nineteenth century. William Symington (1764–1831), inventor and designer of engines, developed an engine for use in steamboats based on an engine he had built for an Alloa colliery, and he also designed one of the best-known prototypes of steam travel, the *Charlotte Dundas*. (See also 'William Symington' by T. H. Beare, rev. Michael S. Moss, *Oxford DNB*.) Regular steamboat traffic between Alloa and Leith began in 1815.

Perhaps more to the point, though, is Hogg's allusion to the 'steamboat' association with John Wilson. In a letter from Hogg to Alexander Bald, 23 April 1815, Hogg wrote:

Let the bust of Shakspeare be crowned with laurel on Thursday, for I expect it will be a memorable day for the club, as well as in the annals of literature,–for I yesterday got the promise of being accompanied by both *Wilson*, and *Campbell*, the bard of Hope. I must, however, remind you that it was very late, and over a bottle, when I extracted this promise–they both appeared, however, to swallow the proposal with great avidity, save that the latter, in conversing about our means of conveyance, took a mortal disgust at the word *steam*, as being a very improper agent in the wanderings of poets. I have not seen either of them to-day, and it is likely that they will be in very different spirits, yet I think it not improbable that one or both of them may be induced to come. (*Letters 1*, p. 248)

Hogg's *Poetic Mirror* (1816) includes a parody of John Wilson's poetry, 'The Morning Star, or the Steam-Boat of Alloa'. *Morning Star* is the actual name of a steamboat that navigated the Forth.

**15(b) Mr Stevenson** unidentified.

**15(c) style of the Poet Laureate** Robert Southey (1774–1843) became Poet Laureate in 1813. Hogg corresponded with Southey and met the poet on a visit to the Lake District in 1814. Southey contributed a poem in 1811 to Hogg's periodical *The Spy*, and in June 1814 Hogg solicited a poem from Southey for his proposed 'Poetical Repository'. Hogg describes his relationship with Southey in his *Memoir*, pp. 65–66. David Groves suggests that the poem for the Shakespeare Club is a parody of Southey's poetry–see *Notes and Queries*, 46 (December 1999), 474–77.

**16, ll. 33–34 threat | Of stern invasion** presumably a threat from France under Napoleon. Hogg notes that the need for military preparedness against foreign enemies has diminished, and he hopes that domestic disturbances will not require the use of military force. See also ll. 51–66.

**16, l. 35 Ochils** the Ochil Hills, a range of hills extending from near Stirling to near Perth.

**16, l. 36 Grampian glens** the Grampians, a range of mountains that extends through central Scotland from near Stonehaven in the east to Dumbarton in the southwest. The Grampians include the highest mountains in Britain and mark the division between the Highlands and Lowlands.

**16, l. 38 Bancho's old unalienable line** in Shakespeare's *Macbeth* the third witch says to Banquo: 'Thou shalt get kings, though thou be none' (I. 3. 73). Traditionally, the Stuart kings are descended from Banquo.

**16, ll. 39–40 'mid a land and race | By man ne'er conquered** Douglas Mack has suggested that Hogg is referring to Scotland's proud claim that the Highlands were never conquered by the Romans. This is a recurring image in Hogg's work: see *Mador of the Moor*, ed. by James E. Barcus (S/SC, 2005), p. 9, l. 27, and note, p. 109; *Queen Hynde*, ed. by Suzanne Gilbert and Douglas S. Mack (S/SC, 1998), p. 5, ll. 20–21, and note, p. 248; and 'The Stuarts of Appin', p. 349, ll. 36–37, and note, in the present edition.

**17, l. 62 Pale discontent sits on the Labourer's brow** a reference to the agitation of the radical reformers in the early nineteenth century. Compare 'Pale discontent appear'd on each dark brow', from Mary Abel Clinckett's poem, 'Contest between Beauty & Wealth, For the Sovereignty of the Island of Barbados', *Early Attempts at Poetry, Written at Different Periods, From 1811 to 1816* (Bristol: Wm. Major, 1817), p. 142.

**17, ll. 65–66 Prince of Israel, who despised | The old men's counsel** a reference to King Rehoboam in 1 Kings 12. 13: 'And the king answered the people roughly, and forsook the old men's counsel that they gave him'. See also 1 Kings 12. 8.

**17, l. 71 The mob's enormities** in 1817 the French Revolution and the threats of Napoleon still would have been fresh in people's minds.

**18, l. 104 No 5, Devon Sreet** Hogg uses an Alloa address. The River Devon joins the River Forth near Alloa.

### A Last Adieu

'A Last Adieu' was first published in the second number of *Blackwood's Edinburgh Magazine* (*Edinburgh Monthly Magazine*), 1 (May 1817), 169; it was signed 'H' but was not otherwise identified as Hogg's. The poem was reprinted in the 1822 *Poetical Works* (IV, 300–302) with only minor printing differences attributable to the publisher's preferences. 'A Last Adieu' was written by Hogg as a tribute to his mother, Margaret Laidlaw Hogg, who died in 1813 (the exact date is not known). The date of composition of 'A Last Adieu' is also uncertain, although it seems to have been written within a few weeks after Mrs Hogg's death. Hogg mentions the poem in a letter of 14 November 1813 to his friend Alexander Bald of Alloa: 'I have not forgot the promise I made to send her [Mrs Anne Bald] some verses of mine in my own manuscript to add to her little store of original scraps and I think I mentioned the elegy which I had written on the death of my mother and which I have copied but which I hesitate about sending, something more appropriate to friendship may haply be found' (*Letters 1*, p. 166).

Margaret Laidlaw Hogg (1730–1813) was the daughter of William Laidlaw, shepherd on the farm of Phaup, or Phawhope, at the head of the Ettrick Valley. Margaret married Robert Hogg in May 1765; James was the second of Margaret and Robert's four sons. 'A Last Adieu' expresses Hogg's deep affection for his mother, as well as her strong influence on Hogg's literary interests and knowledge of the traditional songs and stories of the Borders. Hogg acknowledges his relationship with his mother in a letter to Bernard Barton, dated 5 July 1813, soon after Mrs Hogg's death:

> I received your three last [letters] all on the same day owing to my having been absent for some weeks in Ettrick forest where I was called on rather a melancholly occassion. I have lost the warmest the sincerest and in a word the best friend that ever I had in this world or am ever likely to have My old mother to whom my attachment was such as cannot be described is no more and I am just returned from paying the last sad duties to her to whom I owed every thing that a son could pay and from comforting an aged father who is now left right solitary. I have however this solace that her existence was lengthened while it could be comfortable to herself valuable to her friends it always was. (*Letters 1*, p. 150)

Although the exact date of Margaret Hogg's death is not known, apparently she died sometime in June 1813. In Hogg's letter to Bernard Barton, dated 5 July 1813 (quoted above), Hogg writes that he had not answered Barton's recent letters because he had been away from home 'some weeks' in consequence of his mother's death. In an earlier letter to Barton, dated 7 June 1813, Hogg made no mention of his mother, so it would be reasonable to assume that she died after 7 June 1813. Also, a letter from William Hogg to James Gray, dated 20 November 1813, noted that Mrs Hogg died '5 months ago' (James Hogg Collection. General Collection, Beinecke Rare Book and Manuscript Library. GEN MSS 61, Box 1, folder 19).

The present edition reprints the *BEM* text of 'A Last Adieu' with the following emendation:

18, l. 20 fairies] faries *BEM*

**18, l. 6 But riches, unknown, were unvalued by thee** Hogg's father had enjoyed modest success as a shepherd, which led to his leasing the farms of Ettrick House and Ettrick Hall after his marriage to Margaret. However, a series of misfortunes led to Robert Hogg's bankruptcy, which James describes in his *Memoir*: 'but, at length, owing to a great fall in the price of sheep, and the absconding of his principal debtor, he was ruined, became bankrupt, every thing was sold by auction, and my parents were turned out of doors without a farthing in the world. I was then in the sixth year of my age, and remember well the distressed and destitute condition that we were in'. Robert Hogg was returned as a shepherd to Ettrick House through the 'compassion' of Walter Bryden of Crosslee (*Memoir*, p. 12).

**18, l. 7 In the wild wast thou born, in the wild didst thou dwell** Margaret Laidlaw grew up on the farm of Phaup, which Hogg described in *The Shepherd's Calendar* as 'one of the most lonely and dismal situations that ever was the dwelling of human creatures. [...] It is on the very outskirts of Ettrick Forest, quite out of the range of social intercourse' (p. 107). William Hogg echoes his brother's assessment, describing Phaup as 'the highest and most sequestered corner of the Parish of Etterick [...]. Nothing was to be seen but long tracts of Heath & on the tops of the Hills frequently sat a dark and thick mist. Nothing was to be heard but the howl of the winds and dash of waters' (James Hogg Collection. General Collection, Beinecke Rare Book and Manuscript Library. GEN MSS 61, Box 1, folder 19). As the wife of Robert Hogg, a shepherd in Ettrick, Margaret continued to live 'in the wild'.

18, ll. 15–16 O how I would long [...] attend to thy song William Hogg describes how Mrs Hogg entertained her sons with traditional stories and songs: 'her memory was stored with tales and songs of spectres, ghosts, Faries, Brownies, voices, &c. These had been often both seen and heard in her time among the Glens of Phaupe. And many a winter night to keep us boys sober has she told us how the Faries would have tripped with much mirth and speed along the bottom of some lonely Dell. [...] These songs and tales, which were sung & told in a melancholy, plaintive air, had an influence on James's mind altogether unperceived at the time, and perhaps undescribable even now' (James Hogg Collection. General Collection, Beinecke Rare Book and Manuscript Library. GEN MSS 61, Box 1, folder 19).

18, ll. 22–23 shield thy grey head; | But fortune denied it on 7 March 1813 Hogg wrote to the Duchess of Buccleuch to request the lease of a small farm of Eltrive Moss, in part to support his aging parents: 'Now there is a certain poor bard who has two old parents each of them upwards of 84 years of age; and that bard has no house nor home to shelter those poor parents in, or cherish the evening of their lives' (*Letters 1*, p. 132). Hogg was not granted the farm until after his mother's death—and after the death of the Duchess, when the Duke of Bucclecuch acceded to Hogg's wishes.

19, l. 29 no tombstone is seen Margaret Hogg is buried in the Ettrick churchyard. A tombstone was erected some years later that records the death of Margaret and her husband, Robert, as well as 'three of their sons'; Gillian Hughes suggests that the three unidentified sons are 'children who died in early infancy' (see note for 12(b) in *Altrive Tales*, ed. by Gillian Hughes, (S/SC, 2003), p. 216).

19, l. 32 Where the minstreless lies of the Border the last Mrs Hogg's title as 'minstreless' of the Border was affirmed by Sir Walter Scott's visit to her in the process of collecting Border ballads. Hogg writes of this meeting in his *Anecdotes of Scott*:

> I had seen the first volumes of the 'Minstrelsy of the Scottish Border,' and had copied a number of ballads from my mother's recital, or chaunt rather, and sent them to the editor preparatory to the publication of a third volume. [...] My mother chaunted the ballad of Old Maitlan' to him, with which he was highly delighted, and asked her if she thought it ever had been in print? And her answer was, 'O na, na, sir, it never was printed i' the world, for my brothers an' me learned it an' many mae frae auld Andrew Moor, and he learned it frae auld Baby Mettlin, wha was housekeeper to the first laird of Tushilaw. She was said to hae been another nor a gude ane, an' there are many queer stories about hersel', but O, she had been a grand singer o' auld songs an' ballads'. (pp. 37–38)

Sir Walter Scott collected 'Auld Maitland' from Mrs Hogg for his *Minstrelsy of the Scottish Border*. In his introduction to 'Auld Maitland' Scott writes that the ballad is 'the most authentic instance of a long and very old poem, exclusively thus preserved. It is only known to a few old people, upon the sequestered banks of the Ettrick; and is published, as written down from the recitation of the mother of Mr James Hogg, who sings, or rather chaunts it, with great animation' (*Minstrelsy of the Scottish Border*, 3rd edn, 3 vols (London: Longman; Edinburgh: Constable, 1806), I, 15). Hogg also recalls the occasion—and his mother's honorary title—in his poem 'Lines to Sir Walter Scott, Bart.,' published in the 1822 *Poetical Works* (IV, 131–40):

> Scarce grew thy lurking dread the less
> Till she, the ancient Minstreless,
> With fervid voice, and kindling eye,
> And withered arms waving on high,
> Sung forth these words in eldritch shriek,
> While tears stood on thy nut-brown cheek— (ll. 66–71).

## Tales and Anecdotes of the Pastoral Life. No. III

'Tales and Anecdotes of the Pastoral Life. No. III' is the final instalment in the 'Tales and Anecdotes' series and was first published in *Blackwood's Edinburgh Magazine* (*Edinburgh Monthly Magazine*) in the third number, 1 (June 1817), 247–50. Like the first two stories, the work is signed 'H' in *BEM*, but Hogg's authorship is not otherwise acknowledged. The story was reprinted as Chapter V of 'The Shepherd's Calendar' in *Winter Evening Tales* (Edinburgh, 1820), II, 197–204; see also *WET*, pp. 404–09. For further information about the publication of this series, see the notes to 'Tales and Anecdotes of the Pastoral Life. No. I' in the present edition.

The present edition follows the *BEM* printing with the following emendation: 22(b) *dead!*"] *dead!* *BEM*

**19(d) "thumpin luck and fat weans"** a large portion of luck and fat (healthy) children.

**19(d) "a bien rannle-bauks, and tight thack and rape o'er their heads"** a 'rannle-bauks' is 'a bar of wood or iron fixed across the chimney from which the chain and hook for holding cooking utensils is suspended' (*SND*). The blessing on the bride and groom is for prosperity: a rannle-baucks in good condition so that it will hold a full pot, and a good roof over their heads.

**19(d) "a routh aumrie and a close nieve"** a plentiful pantry and a clenched fist. Again, the wish for the couple is for prosperity.

**20(a) the broose!** see note for 9(d).

**20(c) Liddesdale** the valley of Liddel Water, which runs southwest from Saughtree in Roxburghshire to just north of Carlisle, a distance of about twenty miles.

**20(d) Hobby** Border diminutive for Robert.

**21(a) Tam the tailor** in his note to 'Tam the tailor' in *WET* (p. 581), Ian Duncan acknowledges Gillian Hughes's suggestion that Tam is Thomas Hogg, James Hogg's cousin, who also appears as 'the celebrated flying Ettrick tailor' in Hogg's 'Letter from the Ettrick Shepherd' in the March 1820 number of *BEM*, vol. 6, pp. 630–32. See p. 78(d) of the present edition. As Gillian Hughes notes, Thomas Hogg, 'tailor in Thirlestane', was the source for 'Lady Linley' in Alexander Campbell's *Albyn's Anthology*, 2 vols (Edinburgh, 1816–

18), II, 8; the *Anthology* also included several songs by James Hogg—see *Letters 1*, p. 8.

21(a) **my Cameronian** see note for 12(a).

21(a) **Aberlosk** Aedie o' Aberlosk. See note for 10(c).

21(a) **"him that beats a Cameronian has but another to beat."** perhaps Aedie means the devil.

21(d) **"sun-ways-about"** from left to right, the direction of the apparent movement of the sun. Sun-ways-about is a traditional sign of good luck, as opposed to 'withershins', which is the opposite direction of the sun and a sign of disaster or ill luck.

22(a) **benty-necks** weaklings.

22(b) **Willie Beattie [...] Bellendine** Hogg had a fondness for this name, although it is not known if he had a specific person in mind. A shepherd named 'Willie Beattie' appears in Hogg's story 'The Renowned Adventures of Basil Lee' (*WET*, p. 9). Also, in the second 'Editor's Narrative' of Hogg's *Confessions of a Justified Sinner*, the Editor mentions a 'fine old shepherd, W—m B—e, a great original' (p. 170). For further discussion of this name, see note for 170(c) in *Confessions*, p. 251. Bellendine, Bellendean, or Bellendaine is a hill in Roxburghshire that supposedly was the gathering place for the Scott Clan in preparation for war. 'A Bellendaine' was the war cry of the Scotts. See also note for 202(b) in *WET*, p. 567.

22(b) **By Jehu** an oath, possibly a milder form of 'by Jesus'. The oath is appropriate for the context of the race, though, as 'Jehu' was also an expression associated with speed and recklessness, usually in reference to driving fast. The expression is derived from II Kings 9. 20: 'And the watchman told, saying, He came even unto them, and cometh not again: and the driving is like the driving of Jehu the son of Nimshi; for he driveth furiously'.

22(b) **like the rushing of many waters** from Isaiah 17. 13: 'The nations shall rush like the rushing of many waters'.

23(b) **Jamie Sword** unidentified, but Sword was a common Border name. Hogg uses the name W. Sword in 'A Scots Mummy' (p. 142 in the present edition) and again in his novel *The Private Memoirs and Confessions of a Justified Sinner* (1824) from the portion of 'A Scots Mummy' that was incorporated into the novel. See note for 142(c) in the present edition.

23(c) ***George the Third*** (1738–1820) became king of Great Britain in 1760. Because of the king's mental illness, the Prince of Wales was appointed regent in 1811.

24(b) **(*To be continued.*)** Hogg wrote to Blackwood on 24 September 1817 that the 'continuation of my pastoral anecdotes would scarcely do now as they are not in the published contents but they shall be continued by and by' (*Letters 1*, p. 301). The series was not continued under the title of 'Tales and Anecdotes of the Pastoral Life'. However, beginning with the April 1819 issue of *BEM* and continuing intermittently through 1828, Hogg published in *BEM* a series of similar pastoral anecdotes under the title *The Shepherd's Calendar*. See *The Shepherd's Calendar*, ed. by Douglas S. Mack (S/SC, 1995).

### Extempore Song

'Extempore Song' is published for the first time in the present edition. Hogg sent 'Extempore Song' to William Blackwood along with 'Elegy', which was published in the October 1817 issue of *BEM* (pp. 25–26 of the present edition).

A note by Hogg on the manuscript of 'Elegy' indicates that both poems were written on the same occasion, although the specific individual who is the subject of the poems has not been identified. The date of composition of 'Extempore Song' is not known, but it is likely that the poem was written much earlier than 1817. A version of 'Elegy' had been published in 1811 in Hogg's periodical *The Spy*, so it is possible that 'Extempore Song' was also written in 1811 or earlier. Hogg apparently intended to acknowledge authorship in *BEM* since the manuscript is signed 'J. Hogg' at the end of the poem.

Hogg borrows language from 'Extempore Song' for two later elegiac poems: 'In Memory of Mr Robert Anderson' (Anderson died 20 November 1823), which is preserved in a manuscript letter of 28 April 1828 to the subject's father and published in *Songs* as 'A Father's Lament' (see *Letters 2*, pp. 290–91); and 'I downa laugh, I downa sing', which was published in *Select and Rare Scottish Melodies* (1829). Hogg's repetitions are illustrated in the opening stanzas of each of the later works. 'In Memory of Robert Anderson' begins:

> How can you bid this heart be blithe
> When blithe this heart can never be
> Ive lost the jewel from my crown
> cast round your eyes and here you'll see
> That there is own [*sic*] out of the ring
> who never can forgotten be
> Aye there's a blank at my right hand
> that never can be made up to me

The first stanza of 'I downa laugh, I downa sing' reads:

> I downa laugh, I downa sing,
> Though sweet beseeching looks I see,
> Though smiles abound, wine goes round,
> And ev'ry eye is turn'd on me;
> For there is ane out o' the ring,
> Wha never can forgotten be!
> Aye, there's a blank at my right hand
> That ne'er can be made up to me!

The texts of 'In Memory of Robert Anderson' and 'I downa laugh, I downa sing' diverge substantially from 'Extempore Song' in the second and third stanzas, reflecting the differences in the subjects. Hogg explains the occasion of 'In Memory of Robert Anderson' in the introductory note to 'A Father's Lament' in *Songs*: 'A young friend of mine, whom I greatly admired for every manly and amiable virtue, was cut off suddenly in the flower of his age, (Mr R— A—n.) The next time that I visited the family, his parent's distress and expressions of fond remembrance affected me so deeply, that I composed the following verses in his character' (p. 79). In his introductory note to 'Elegy' in *Songs*, however, Hogg claims the subject of 'Elegy' (and thus 'Extempore Song') was the 'death of a natural child, of the most consummate beauty and elegance' (p. 202).

A fair-copy manuscript of 'Extempore Song' is preserved among the Blackwood papers in the National Library of Scotland as MS 4805, fol. 99. The manuscript consists of a single sheet *c.* 23 cm x 37 cm folded to *c.* 23 cm x 18.5 cm. The paper is watermarked IVY MILL | 1813. 'Extempore Song' is written on the recto of fol. 99; 'Elegy' is written on the verso of fol. 99 and the recto of fol. 100. (Robert Southey's poem 'To Mary' is written on the verso of fol. 100). 'Extempore Song' is included in the present edition because Hogg clearly intended the song for publication in *BEM*, and he did not publish the song elsewhere in its original form. The poem is published herein from the manuscript without emendation.

## Elegy

'Elegy' was first published in *The Spy*, No. 39, 25 May 1811. The poem was revised for publication in *Blackwood's Edinburgh Magazine*, 2 (October 1817), 47, and the *BEM* version was published from a fair-copy manuscript. 'Elegy' was reprinted in the 1822 *Poetical Works* (IV, 246–48), based on the *BEM* version. It was reprinted again in *Songs* (pp. 202–03), although the title in *Songs* was 'Fair was thy blossom' from the first line of the poem. In his introduction to the *Songs* version of 'Elegy', Hogg notes that the poem is an 'elegiac song on the death of a natural child' (p. 202); in the *Songs* version Hogg omits the second, fourth, and fifth stanzas from *BEM* because he considered them 'too particular' (p. 202). The child has not been identified, however.

Hogg intended 'Elegy' to be published in *BEM* along with 'Extempore Song' (see p. 27 of the present edition), although the latter work was not published in *BEM*. Hogg's note on the manuscript of 'Elegy' indicates that 'Elegy' and 'Extempore Song' were 'written on the same occassion' [*sic*]. The fair-copy manuscript from which the *BEM* version of 'Elegy' was published is preserved in the National Library of Scotland as MS 4805, fols 99–100. The manuscript consists of a single sheet *c.* 23 cm x 37 cm folded to *c.* 23 cm x 18.5 cm. The paper is watermarked IVY MILL | 1813. 'Extempore Song' is written on the recto of fol. 99; 'Elegy' is written on the verso of fol. 99 and the recto of fol. 100. (Robert Southey's poem 'To Mary' is written on the verso of fol. 100).

'Elegy' is the first of two works that Hogg published in the October 1817 issue of *BEM* (the second is the 'Chaldee Manuscript'—see pp. 26–44 and notes in the present edition). The October issue is significant both for Blackwood and Hogg. The October issue is the first under Blackwood's new title, *Blackwood's Edinburgh Magazine*, and the first under Blackwood's new editorship. 'Elegy' is the first of Hogg's works in *BEM* to be signed by Hogg. 'By the Ettrick Shepherd' appears as part of the title in *BEM*, and the poem is signed 'J. Hogg' at the end of the work. Hogg's authorship is also addressed in an editorial introduction, which was probably written by John Wilson (the verses are signed 'Wilson', although the verses apparently have not been published elsewhere):

> [WE return our best thanks to the ETTRICK SHEPHERD for the following very beautiful lines, and will, at all times, be happy to receive his communications. He would be conferring upon us a signal favour, were he occasionally to enrich our Work with a few of his exquisite Songs; for, in our opinion, he is, in that department, little, if at all inferior to Burns himself. Why does not the Author of "Kilmeny" show what might be made of a regular Pastoral Poem? There a delightful field lies open to his genius, peopled not with human life alone, but also with the aërial creatures whom he loves, and has described better than any other modern poet. We may quote the words of another Scottish bard.
> > "Sweet voices! circling all the cloudy tops
> > Of the green mountains, and from mossy caves
> > Piping at midnight! like the little wren
> > At times heard singing from some ruin'd wall,

> Now like a burst of choral instruments
> Filling with bliss the blue arch of the heavens,
> Music fit for the stars! There is he seen,
> The green-robed Harper, sitting on the cairn
> Where sleeps some Chief of Old—or on the turf
> Of the lone sheep-fold, where the lambs are lying
> All round as calm as snow,—or the grey stone
> Which the hawk, waking from his slumber, leaves
> To that sudden Fairy! And there the Fairy plays,
> And sings his wild low tunes unto the soul
> Of some night-wandering man—oftenest to Him
> Who found in youth a Harp among the hills,
> Dropt by the Elfin-people, and while the moon
> Entranced hangs o'er still St Mary's Loch,
> Harps by that charmed water, so that the Swan
> Comes floating onwards through the water-lilies,
> A dreamlike creature listening to a dream;
> And the Queen of the Fairies, rising silently
> Through the pure mist, stands at the Shepherd's feet,
> And half forgets her own green paradise,
> Far in the bosom of the Hill,—so wild!
> So sweet! so sad! flows forth that Shepherd's Lay!" WILSON.
> Such a recommendation as this from the pen of a kindred writer, ought,
> we feel, to weigh more with Mr Hogg than any thing we could say to
> him, and we hope that he will tune his harp to the themes thus wildly
> alluded to, in which, both by his habits and his native genius, he cannot
> fail to excel. EDITOR.]

Wilson's introduction initiates the magazine's frequent, and sometimes caustic, public commentaries on Hogg's works and personal character. Wilson invokes a comparison of Hogg with Burns; comparisons of Hogg with Burns, Byron, and Wordsworth become common methods of satirising Hogg in *BEM*, especially after the *Noctes Ambrosianæ* series begins in March 1822. Wilson also echoes images of Hogg's most famous poem at this time, *The Queen's Wake*, particularly the various harp images that are central to *The Queen's Wake* (see the Introduction to the S/SC edition of *The Queen's Wake* for a detailed discussion of the role of harps in the poem). Wilson's introduction to 'Elegy', then, offers a clear invitation to Hogg to accept a strictly-delineated role in *BEM* as a peasant, pastoral poet, writing of the traditional Border lore but remaining outside the mainstream of literature. Furthermore, Wilson's verses perhaps were intended as a parody of Hogg's poetry and his reputation as a poet, reminiscent of the parodies Hogg wrote of his contemporaries, including Wilson, in *The Poetic Mirror* (1816). Wilson's image of the 'entranced' moon hanging 'o'er still St Mary's Loch' becomes a satiric response to Hogg's image of a 'watery Moon' reflecting the 'Moon aërial' in 'Hymn to the Moon', one of Hogg's parodies of Wilson in *The Poetic Mirror*. Douglas Mack argues that later, in *The Three Perils of Woman* (1823), Hogg exposes Wilson's 'false and unreal' portrayal of Scottish life and continues his attacks on Wilson's 'sentimental narratives' as 'merely the windy and insubstantial effusions of a "brain-stricken" votary of the moon'—see Douglas S. Mack, *Scottish Fiction and the British Empire* (Edinburgh: Edinburgh University Press, 2006), pp. 22–23; see also the note for 25(b) in *The Three Perils of Woman*, ed. by David Groves, Antony Hasler, and Douglas S. Mack (S/SC, 1995), p. 441.

'Elegy' is published in the present edition from the *BEM* version with the following emendation:

26, l. 35 Stand] Start *BEM*

**26, l. 43 daisy, emblem meet** the daisy is a traditional symbol of childhood innocence.

### Translation of an Ancient Chaldee Manuscript
*Supposed to have been Written by Daniel* [Manuscript Version]

'Translation of an Ancient Chaldee Manuscript' was first published in *Blackwood's Edinburgh Magazine*, 2 (October 1817), 89–96, the first issue of William Blackwood's reorganised and renamed periodical. The work was not reprinted in Hogg's lifetime; furthermore, the work was so controversial that it was omitted from the second edition of the October 1817 issue, although the clamour about the 'Chaldee' contributed to the demand for a second edition. (For further discussion of the history and reception of the 'Chaldee Manuscript', see the Introduction to the present edition.)

The 'Chaldee Manuscript', written in the style of the Authorised Version of the Bible, is a satirical sketch of the history of William Blackwood's attempts to establish a monthly literary magazine. The sketch lampoons the rivalry between the publishing firms of Blackwood and Archibald Constable, as well as various authors who wrote for both publishers. Blackwood began publication of the *Edinburgh Monthly Magazine* (the original title of *BEM*) with the April 1817 issue, but by June Blackwood's frustration with the ineptitude of his editors, James Cleghorn and Thomas Pringle, led him to decide to cease publication with the September 1817 issue and dissolve the relationship with his editors under the original arrangement. Before leaving Blackwood's employment, however, Cleghorn and Pringle negotiated an agreement with Constable to edit his *Scots Magazine*, which Constable then renamed the *Edinburgh Magazine and Literary Miscellany*.

Hogg, who also had professional ties to Constable, believed that the marketplace would support the periodicals of both publishers, although Hogg promised to support Blackwood; however, the competition between the two rivals appealed to Hogg's sense of literary sport. On 24 September 1817 Hogg wrote to Blackwood: 'I am highly amused at this terrible trial of strength that is commencing between you and Constable and have a great mind to write something original on the occassion' (*Letters 1*, p. 300). Hogg apparently wrote the 'Chaldee' before the day was over. On 25 September Hogg wrote to Blackwood again, enclosing the 'Chaldee Manuscript': 'Please read over this beautiful allegory of mine with the editor of the Magazine and cause him to add a short history of its preservation in the archives of Rome or somewhere and by whom it came to be noticed and translated into our language' (*Letters 1*, p. 303). The 'editor' added the explanatory introduction as Hogg requested, but the editor also added much more. John Lockhart, in a letter to his friend Jonathan Christie, explains how the final version developed: 'The history of it is this: Hogg, the Ettrick Shepherd, sent up an attack on Constable the bookseller, respecting some private dealings of his with Blackwood. Wilson and I liked the idea of introducing the whole panorama of the town in that sort of dialect. We drank punch one night from eight till eight in the morning, Blackwood being by with anecdotes, and the result is before you'—see Andrew Lang, *The Life and Letters of John Gibson Lockhart*, 2 vols (London: Nimmo, 1897), I, 157.

The additions to Hogg's original were extensive, but Hogg was generally pleased with the new 'Chaldee', as he writes to Blackwood on 19 October: 'I have laughed at least as heartily at the continuation of *Daniel* as you did at the original the conciet is excellent indeed I see that mine was quite an imperfect thing without some description of the forces on the other side—the third chapter however is very faulty—the characters are made too plain and the language of scripture compleatly departed from. I have remedied that in proof in a great measure but alas it is out of time!' (*Letters 1*, p. 304). Hogg's revisions were not included in the printed version since *BEM* was published the next day, 20 October. The published version that resulted from the long night of drinking punch differs so significantly from Hogg's original version of the 'Chaldee Manuscript' that they represent distinct works; the present edition, therefore, includes both versions. The *BEM* version appears on pp. 30–44 of the present edition.

Hogg's manuscript of the 'Chaldee' is preserved among the Blackwood papers in the National Library of Scotland as MS 4807, fols 2–4. The manuscript consists of two sheets: one sheet, *c.* 23 cm x 37 cm, folded to make two folios, and a second sheet, *c.* 23 cm x 18.5 cm, torn from a larger sheet. The full sheet is watermarked VALLEYFIELD | 1815; there is no watermark on the half sheet. Hogg numbered the pages 1 through 6. The title of the work in the manuscript is 'Translation of an ancient Chaldee Manuscript *Supposed to have been written by Daniel*'. Hogg's original version reflects the purported authorship of Daniel by drawing heavily on the apocalyptic imagery of the second half of the biblical book of Daniel. In the printed version, however, the attribution of the work to Daniel has been omitted and replaced with an introduction that establishes a fictitious context for the work, although the introduction connects the 'Chaldee' to the well-known contemporary orientalist, Antoine Isaac, Baron Silvestre de Sacy. The revisions to Hogg's original work are begun on the second sheet (fol. 4) of Hogg's manuscript; the manuscript revisions appear to be in Lockhart's hand. The complete manuscript of Lockhart's and Wilson's additions apparently has not survived.

Hogg's manuscript version of the 'Chaldee' consists of forty-six unnumbered verses. The final published version, however, consists of 181 verses divided into four chapters. The *BEM* version includes Hogg's first thirty-eight verses with only minor revisions, except that verses 32 and 33 are combined and two-thirds of verse 16 is deleted. Twenty-eight verses are added by Lockhart and Wilson to complete what becomes Chapter I. Hogg's next five verses, describing the calling together of Ebony's 'beasts', are significantly revised and incorporated into verses 10 through 18 of Chapter II, which totals twenty-two verses. There is nothing of Hogg's in Chapter III. Although Hogg made stylistic revisions to Chapter III in proof, his revisions were not included in the published version. Finally, Hogg's last three verses, slightly revised, are printed as the last three verses of the forty-two-verse Chapter IV.

The authors' familiarity with the language and style of the Authorised Version of the Bible is evident throughout the 'Chaldee'. Hogg, especially, was steeped in the biblical language, having regularly heard the Bible read by both of his parents and having memorised portions of it even before he was able to read. The explanatory notes that follow identify significant references to biblical texts, although there is no attempt to identify the sources of each common biblical expression used by the authors, such as 'sore afraid', 'gave ear unto', 'fruits of our labours', and 'wist not'. The notes identify as far as possible the people represented in the satire; the information about the people is indebted to the *Oxford DNB* and Gillian Hughes's 'Notes on Correspondents' to her editions of *The Collected Letters of James Hogg*. For those people whose biographies are included in the *Oxford DNB*, the notes refer the reader to the appropriate articles. The National Library of Scotland 'Chaldee' materials include several 'keys' to the people described in the 'Chaldee', although none of the keys is complete, there are discrepancies in the identifications, and most of the keys are not contemporary with the 'Chaldee'. One manuscript key, however, appears to be in Lockhart's hand and seems to be the most reliable, though it, too, is incomplete; this manuscript key is preserved in the NLS as MS 4807, fols 42–43, and is referenced occasionally in the notes.

The text of the manuscript version follows Hogg's manuscript without emendation except to add silently punctuation where Hogg would have expected it to be added.

**26(c) (title) Chaldee Manuscript | *Supposed to have been written by Daniel*** Chaldea was a region of southern Babylonia at the head of the Persian Gulf. The Chaldeans appear throughout the Old Testament but figure prominently in the book of Daniel and are associated with the magicians and astrologers with whom Daniel competed to interpret king Nebuchadnezzar's dreams. Hogg's 'Chaldee' is dominated by imagery from the biblical book of Daniel, especially the apocalyptic images of the second half of Daniel.

**26(d) I saw in my dream** the dream vision of the 'Chaldee' is derived from Daniel's dream vision in the second half of the book of Daniel, chapters 7 through 12.

**26(d) great city** Edinburgh.

**26(d) moving of a straw [...] whirlwind** echoes Hosea 13. 3: 'as the chaff that is driven with the whirlwind out of the floor'.

**26(d) shaking of a reed** echoes I Kings 14. 15: 'For the Lord shall smite Israel, as a reed is shaken in the water'.

**26(d) man clothed in plain apparrel [...] colour of ebony** William Blackwood, often referred to among the Blackwood's writers simply as 'Ebony'. The image of 'plain apparel' echoes Daniel 10. 5 and Acts 1. 10.

**26(d) the number of his name** see Numbers 1.

**27(a) his number was the number of a maiden** Blackwood's publishing firm was located at '17' Princes Street, Edinburgh.

**27(a) two beasts [...] borders of the south** James Cleghorn (1778–1838) and Thomas Pringle (1789–1834), Blackwood's editors of the first six issues of the *Edinburgh Monthly Magazine* (later *BEM*). Both men were from the 'borders of the South': Cleghorn was a native of Duns in Berwickshire, and Pringle was a native of Teviotdale in Roxburghshire. Cleghorn was a farmer before moving to Edinburgh in 1811 to edit the *Farmer's Magazine*. He was the author of a prize-winning work, *The Depressed State of Agriculture* (1822), and wrote on agriculture for the *Encyclopaedia Britannica*. After leaving Constable's employment in 1826, Cleghorn worked as an actuary and established the

Scottish Provident Assurance Company. Thomas Pringle took a position at the Edinburgh Register House in 1808 after finishing at Edinburgh University and remained there until becoming an editor for Blackwood's *Edinburgh Monthly Magazine*. Pringle developed friendships with both Hogg and Walter Scott. Pringle contributed 'Epistle to Mr R– S * * * *' to Hogg's *The Poetic Mirror* (1816), and he published a collection of poetry, *The Autumnal Excursion, and Other Poems*, in 1819. He collaborated with Scott on a series of articles, 'Notices Concerning the Scottish Gipsies', for early numbers of the *Edinburgh Monthly Magazine*. In 1820 Pringle settled in South Africa, where he worked as a librarian and established an academy, a newspaper, and a literary journal. He returned to Great Britain in 1826 and became active in the anti-slavery movement and continued his work as a writer, including serving as editor of the annual, *Friendship's Offering* (see David Finkelstein's article on Pringle in the *Oxford DNB*). The image of the beasts is from Daniel 7.

27 (a) **one beast was like a lamb, and the other like a bear** Pringle's personality was mild and pleasant, whereas Cleghorn was more aggressive and gruff. Hogg wrote in his *Memoir* that 'from the time I heard that Pringle had taken in Cleghorn as a partner I declined all connexion with it, farther than as an occasional contributor' (p. 43). Blackwood unsuccessfully attempted to keep Pringle with *BEM* after he dissolved the *Edinburgh Monthly Magazine*.

27 (a) **the joints of their legs like the polished cedars of Lebanon [...] touched not the ground as they went** both Cleghorn and Pringle were lame and walked with crutches. Cleghorn was born with a disability, and Pringle was injured in an accident when he was an infant. Lebanon was widely known for its cedar trees, and there are numerous biblical references to the 'cedars of Lebanon'; see, for example, Psalm 92. 12 and Isaiah 2. 13.

27 (b) **for a time, times or half a time** from Daniel 12. 7: 'And I heard the man clothed in linen, which was upon the waters of the river, when he held up his right hand and his left hand unto heaven, and sware by him that liveth for ever that it shall be for a time, times, and an half'.

27 (b) **I will teach the people of thy land to till and to sow** Cleghorn was a farmer in Berwickshire before moving to Edinburgh in 1811 to become editor of the *Farmer's Magazine*.

27 (c) **I will teach the children [...] learning, and knowledge, and understanding** Pringle worked at the Register Office in Edinburgh before becoming an editor of the *Edinburgh Monthly Magazine*.

27 (c) **proffered unto him a book** the *Edinburgh Monthly Magazine*.

27 (c) **light to thy feet and a lamp unto thy path** an echo of Psalm 119. 105: 'Thy word is a lamp unto my feet, and a light unto my path'.

27 (c) **bread to thy houshold and a portion to thy maidens** from Proverbs 31. 15: 'She riseth also while it is yet night, and giveth meat to her household, and a portion to her maidens'.

27 (d) **went away rejoicing in heart** echoes Acts 8. 39: 'he went on his way rejoicing', but Hogg also adds the common biblical expression of 'rejoicing in heart'.

27 (d) **noise of many chariots, and of horsemen horsing on their horse** a reference to the noise made by the crutches of Cleghorn and Pringle. The imagery echoes Ezekiel 26. 10 and 23. 6, 12.

27 (d) **\*singular as this formation [...] language** this note is not included in *BEM*.

**28(a) all those on whose wisdom he could rely and he pressed them** was revised in *BEM* to read 'all those whose heart was as his heart, and he entreated them'.

**28(a–b) a man who was *Crafty* in counsel [...] comely and well-favoured** Archibald Constable (1774–1827), Edinburgh publisher. In 1801 Constable purchased the long-standing *Scots Magazine*, and in 1802 he established the highly-successful *Edinburgh Review*; Constable's magazine successes in part inspired Blackwood to venture into the magazine market. When Pringle and Cleghorn left Blackwood's service, they had already negotiated positions with Constable as editors of the *Scots Magazine*, which Constable renamed the *Edinburgh Magazine and Literary Miscellany*. Hogg had published in the *Scots Magazine*, and Constable published several of Hogg's works prior to Hogg's publishing association with Blackwood, including *The Mountain Bard* (1807) and *The Forest Minstrel* (1810). Even after the 'Chaldee', Hogg published occasionally in the *Edinburgh Magazine*, and Constable published Hogg's *Poetical Works* in 1822. In his *Life of Scott* John Lockhart notes that it was in the 'Chaldee' 'that Constable first saw himself designated in print by the *sobriquet* of "The Crafty," long before bestowed on him by one of his own most eminent Whig supporters' (III, 165n). The 'Crafty' designation appears in letters of both Blackwood and Hogg before the publication of the 'Chaldee'. Constable's appearance, too, is described by Lockhart in *Peter's Letters to His Kinsfolk*: 'a good-looking man [...] very fat in his person, but with a face with good lines, and a fine healthy complexion' (II, 175–76). The printed text omits 'and the man was an upright [...] among the children of men'. The clause 'one that feared God and eschewed evil' is from Job 1. 1. For additional information about Constable, see David Hewitt's article in the *Oxford DNB*.

**28(a) and the man was an upright [...] children of men** this portion of text was omitted from *BEM*.

**28(b) a notable horn in his forehead [...] had eyes, and a mouth speaking great things** *The Edinburgh Review*. The image is from Daniel 7. 8: 'I considered the horns, and, behold, there came up among them another little horn, before whom they were three of the first horns plucked up by the roots: and, behold, in this horn were eyes like the eyes of man, and a mouth speaking great things'. See also Daniel 7. 20.

**28(b) prince of the host** from Daniel 8. 11: 'Yea, he magnified himself even to the prince of the host'.

**28(b) cast down the truth [...] practised and prospered** from Daniel 8. 12: 'it cast down the truth to the ground; and it practised, and prospered'.

**28(b) devouring sword in the hand of mine adversary** from Jeremiah 46. 10: 'a day of vengeance, that he may avenge him of his adversaries: and the sword shall devour'.

**28(c) put your trust under the shadow of my wings** from Psalm 36. 7: 'therefore the children of men put their trust under the shadow of thy wings'. Constable hired Cleghorn and Pringle to edit the *Scots Magazine*, which he renamed the *Edinburgh Monthly and Literary Miscellany*, after Blackwood announced the discontinuation of the *Edinburgh Monthly Magazine.*

**28(d) I will overturn, overturn, overturn, it** from Ezekiel 21. 27: 'I will overturn, overturn, overturn it: and it shall be no more, until he come whose right it is; and I will give it him'. The devil preaching at Auchtermuchty uses this text for his sermon in Hogg's novel *The Private Memoirs and Confessions of a*

*Justified Sinner*, ed. by P. D. Garside (S/SC, 2001), p. 138, and note, p. 243. This verse is omitted from the *BEM* version of the 'Chaldee'.

**28(d) cast it out like dung** echoes Zephaniah 1. 17: 'and their blood shall be poured out as dust, and their flesh as the dung'.

**28(d) And we will tread him down [...] grind him to powder [...] brook Kidron** the river Kidron runs from near Jerusalem to the Dead Sea. There are several references to Kidron in the Bible, but the most appropriate for Hogg's purposes here is II Kings 23. 6: 'And he brought out the grove from the house of the Lord, without Jerusalem, unto the brook Kidron, and burned it at the brook Kidron, and stamped it small to powder, and cast the powder thereof upon the graves of the children of the people'. The images here also echo II Samuel 22. 43: 'Then did I beat them as small as the dust of the earth; I did stamp them as the mire of the street, and did spread them abroad'.

**28(d) horn of the unicorn** Psalm 22. 21: 'Save me from the lion's mouth: for thou hast heard me from the horns of the unicorns'.

**28(d) bulls of Bashan** Bashan was a fertile region in southern Syria, and the expression 'bulls of Bashan' was used metaphorically even in biblical times to refer to oppressive strength and prosperity. See, for example, Amos 4. 1: 'Hear this word, ye kine of Bashan, that are in the mountain of Samaria, which oppress the poor, which crush the needy, which say to their masters, Bring, and let us drink'.

**28(d)–29(a) from the emmet, and the spider, [...] and the maggot after his kind** The use and repetition of the phrase 'after his kind' echoes God's command to Noah to gather specimens 'of every living thing [...] after their kind'. See Genesis 6. 19–20. It is not clear if Hogg had in mind specific individuals in his list of creatures at this point in the satire or if he were simply reflecting Constable's point of view about the general character of Blackwood's associates. However, in the manuscript of 'The Boar' (pp. 48-51 in the present edition), 'the mole that walketh in darkness' has a prominent place in the satirical imagery. In the published version, 'canker-worm' is added to this list of creatures (see 33, l. 27)

**29(a) things that are low shall be exalted** from Ezekiel 21. 26: 'Thus saith the Lord God; Remove the diadem, and take off the crown: this shall not be the same: exalt him that is low, and abase him that is high'. This concept is also an important one in the gospels. See Matthew 23. 12, Luke 14. 11, and Luke 18. 14.

**29(a) bowed down before him with their faces to the earth** echoes I Chronicles 21. 21: 'Ornan looked and saw David [...] and bowed himself to David, with his face to the ground'. The second part of Hogg's verse, 'and his heart was lifted up, and I saw them marshalling their hosts for the battle', was omitted from the printed version.

**29(a) and his heart [...] the battle** this portion of text was omitted from *BEM*.

**29(b) it repented him that he had taken the book [...] call unto thee thy friends** 'Blackwood at first discouraged, but then rallies and collects his friends' (NLS, MS 4807, fols 42–43). In a letter to John Murray, 28 April 1818, Blackwood comments on the effect of the 'Chaldee' for his business: 'I gained much more than I lost by it, as my friends rallied round me, and many came forward who were formerly unknown to me' (NLS, MS 30,001, fols 107–110).

**29(b) burn it with fire, and give its ashes to the winds of heaven** echoes Exodus 9. 10: 'And they took ashes of the furnace, and stood before Pharaoh; and Moses sprinkled it up toward heaven'.

**29(b) certain sons of Belial** the expression, which means 'worthless persons', is from Judges 19. 22, although a variation on the expression is used frequently in the Bible. Hogg probably intended this expression to refer to John Wilson and John Lockhart, whose antics would both entertain and anger Hogg for the rest of his life. This phrase 'sons of Belial' does not appear in the printed version. The printed version also combines this verse and the following verse, beginning 'Go to now', into a single verse.

**29(b) why is thy countenance fallen** from Genesis 4. 6: 'And the Lord said unto Cain, Why art thou wroth? and why is thy countenance fallen?'

**29(b) Go to now** see Ecclesiastes 2. 1 and James 4. 13.

**29(b) behold and see** from Lamentations 1. 12.

**29(b) they that are for thee […] those that be against thee** echoes Matthew 12. 30: 'He that is not with me is against me; and he that gathereth not with me scattereth abroad'. See also Luke 11. 23.

**29(c) gem of curious workmanship […] snuffed it up** a reference to William Blackwood's silver snuff box and his fondness for snuff.

**29(d) to destroy, and to pass over** Exodus 12 records the story of God's destroying the firstborn of all the Egyptian families and 'passing over' all the families of the Israelites, whose houses had been marked with blood. See especially Exodus 12. 13: 'and when I see the blood, I will pass over you, and the plague shall not be upon you to destroy you, when I smite the land of Egypt'.

**29(d) to pass over […] And he called unto him the beautiful leopard** at this point in the *BEM* version, Lockhart and Wilson have added thirty-seven verses, corresponding to 33, I. 38 through 36, II. 9.

**29(d) beautiful leopard from the valley of the palm trees […] eyes like the lightening of flame** John Wilson (1785–1854), who began sharing editorial duties for *BEM* with the publication of the October 1817 issue and who quickly became the person on whom Blackwood most relied for the magazine's publication. Wilson became associated with 'Christopher North', the fictional editor of *BEM*. Wilson's first collection of poems was entitled *The Isle of Palms and other Poems* (1812). His other works include *The City of Plague* (1816), *Lights and Shadows of Scottish Life* (1822), *The Trials of Margaret Lyndsay* (1823), and *The Foresters* (1825). Wilson is described in Lockhart's *Peter's Letters* as 'a very robust athletic man, broad across the back—firm set upon his limbs— and having altogether very much of that sort of air which is inseparable from the consciousness of great bodily energies. […] His hair is of the true Cicambrian yellow; his eyes are of the lightest, and at the same time of the clearest blue' (I, 130). For additional information about Wilson and his role in *BEM* see the Introduction to the present edition. The image of the leopard is from Daniel 7. 6.

**29(d) curlew and the falcon from among the birds that fly in the firmament of heaven** unidentified.

**29(d)–30(a) fiery lynx also that lurked behind the white cottage** Arthur Mower, author of the novel *The White Cottage*, which was published by William Blackwood in 1817. There is no evidence, however, that Mower published in *BEM* prior to the 'Chaldee'.

**30(a) the dark wolf that delighted in the times of ancient days** John Gibson Lockhart (1794–1854), who was often described as having the look of a Spaniard because of his dark features. Hogg describes Lockhart in 'Account of a Coronation-Dinner' as 'young, sprightly, and whimsical; with hawk's eyes, and dark curled hair' (p. 86(c) in the present edition). Lockhart was an exceptional classics scholar and studied Greek and Latin at Glasgow University and Balliol College, Oxford. Lockhart himself changed his character to a scorpion in the printed version of the 'Chaldee Manuscript', and the revisions to Hogg's original manuscript are begun on the manuscript in Lockhart's hand. See also the note for 36, II. 12.

**30(a) great wild boar from the forest of Lebanon [...] whetting his dreadful tusks for the battle** James Hogg, who was from Ettrick Forest. Hogg uses this image of the boar to refer to himself at least as early as 1811, when he wrote in *The Spy*: 'Sir! the *boar* that from the *forest* comes, doth waste it at his pleasure–I beg your pardon, Sir; I was not meaning you' (S/SC, 2000), p. 476. The image is taken from Psalm 80. 13, which Hogg quotes in *The Spy* from the Church of Scotland's metrical version of the Psalms. John Lockhart describes Hogg's teeth in *Peter's Letters*: 'His mouth, which, when he smiles, nearly cuts the totality of his face in twain, is an object that would make the Chevalier Ruspini die with indignation; for his teeth have been allowed to grow where they listed, and as they listed, presenting more resemblance, in arrangement, (and colour too,) to a body of crouching sharp-shooters, than to any more regular species of array' (I, 143).

**30(a) the griffon** Thomas McCrie (1772–1835), minister and church historian, author of an important biography of John Knox (1811); 'the body of one that had been buried long in the grave' refers to Knox. McCrie was a Secessionist, Anti-Burgher minister and staunch defender of the traditions of the Presbyterian Church and the Reformation in Scotland. His sympathetic treatment of Knox proved to be very popular in the early nineteenth century. Like Hogg, McCrie objected to Scott's unsympathetic portrayal of the Covenanters in his novel *Old Mortality*. McCrie wrote one article for *BEM*, 'Account of Mackenzie's MS. History of Scotland', which appeared in the June 1817 number. For additional information about McCrie, see James Kirk's article in the *Oxford DNB*.

**30(a) the slow-hound and the beagle after their kind** unidentified, but see the note for 32–33, I. 26–27. This verse is divided into two verses in *BEM*–see 37, II. 17, 18.

**30(a) the hyena [...] gnaweth the bones of the dead** John Riddell (1785–1862), genealogist and specialist in peerage law. He was known for both his vast knowledge of records and his vigorous pursuit of genealogical accuracy. Riddell published several articles in the early numbers of *BEM*. The *BEM* version adds 'and is as a riddle unto the vain man' to Hogg's description, perhaps as a means of more-readily identifying the subject–see 37, II. 17. For additional information on Riddell, see Lionel Alexander Ritchie's article in the *Oxford DNB*.

**30(b) beasts of the field** see Genesis 2. 20: 'And Adam gave names to all cattle, and to the fowl of the air, and to every beast of the field'.

**30(b) cry. And I said what shall I cry** from Isaiah 40. 6: 'The voice said, Cry. And he said, What shall I cry?'

**30(b) ruled the nations with a rod of iron** echoes Revelation 12. 5; 'And she brought forth a man child, who was to rule all nations with a rod of iron'. See also Revelation 19. 15.

**30(b) I fled into an inner chamber to hide myself [...] I knew not what it was** from I Kings 22. 25: 'Behold, thou shalt see in that day, when thou shalt go into an inner chamber to hide thyself'.

### Translation from an Ancient Chaldee Manuscript [*BEM* Version]

'Translation from an Ancient Chaldee Manuscript' was first published in *Blackwood's Edinburgh Magazine*, 2 (October 1817), 89–96. The text published in *BEM* is a greatly-enlarged version of Hogg's original satire at the hands of John Lockhart and John Wilson. The published version differs so significantly from Hogg's original version of the 'Chaldee Manuscript' that they represent distinct works; the present edition, therefore, includes both versions. The text of Hogg's manuscript appears on pp. 26–30 of the present edition. For discussion of the history of the composition of the 'Chaldee', see the annotations for the manuscript version of the 'Chaldee' in the present edition. In the annotations that follow, the page number is followed by the chapter and verse number of the printed version. The annotations address in full those points that are unique to the *BEM* version; for notes that are common to both *BEM* and the manuscript, the reader is directed to the appropriate reference in the notes to the manuscript version. A proof of the published version with Hogg's manuscript corrections is preserved in the British Library among the printed texts as C.60.k.4; the most significant revisions made by Hogg to the proof are identified in the notes.

The *BEM* version printed in the present edition follows the *BEM* text with the following emendations:

31, I. 8 you do unto] you unto *BEM.*
33, I. 29 earth.] earth *BEM.*

**30, (title) Chaldee** see the note for 26(c) (title).
**30(c) The Eruditi of Milan** unidentified.
**30(c) B.A.M.M.** perhaps the authors are offering the reader a hint that the story is a 'bam', or hoax.
**30(d) Silvester De Sacy** Antoine Isaac, Baron Silvestre de Sacy (1758–1838) was widely regarded as the leading orientalist of his time and a pioneer in Arabic studies in France. He held a variety of academic and government positions, including professor of Persian at the Collège de France and rector of the University of Paris.
**30, I. 1 I saw in my dream** see the note for 26(d).
**30, I. 1 great city** Edinburgh.
**31, I. 2 moving of a straw** see the note for 26(d).
**31, I. 2 shaking of a reed** see the note for 26(d).
**31, I. 3 man clothed in plain apparel [...] colour of ebony** see the note for 26(d).
**31, I. 3 the number of his name** see the note for 26(d).
**31, I. 3 his number was the number of a maiden** see the note for 27(a)
**31, I. 4 two beasts [...] borders of the South** see the note for 27(a).
**31, I. 5 one beast was like unto a lamb, and the other like unto a bear** see the note for 27(a).
**31, I. 5 the joints of their legs like the polished cedars of Lebanon [...]**

touched not the ground as they went see the note for 27(a).

**31, I. 7 for a time, times, or half a time** see the note for 27(b).

**31, I. 9 I will teach the people of thy land to till and to sow** see the note for 27(b).

**31, I. 10 I will teach the children [...] learning, and knowledge, and understanding** see the note for 27(c).

**31, I. 11 proffered unto him a Book** the *Edinburgh Monthly Magazine*.

**31, I. 12 light unto thy feet, and a lamp unto thy path** see the note for 27(c).

**31, I. 12 bread to thy household, and a portion to thy maidens** see the note for 27(c).

**31, I. 13 noise of many chariots, and of horsemen horsing upon their horses** see the note for 27(d).

**32, I. 15** In the proof Hogg has revised the opening sentence of verse 15 to read: 'And the man knew that evil was determined; and he called together'.

**32, I. 16 ¶** the pilcrow, or paragraph sign, was used in the Authorised Version of the Bible to indicate the equivalent of a new paragraph, or section, within a chapter.

**32, I. 16–17 a man who was crafty in counsel [...] comely and well-favoured** see the note for 28(a–b).

**32, I. 17–18 a notable horn in his forehead [...] had eyes, and a mouth speaking great things** see the note for 28(b).

**32, I. 18 Prince of the Host** see the note for 28(b).

**32, I. 18 cast down the truth [...] grew and prospered** see the note for 28(b). In the manuscript Hogg follows the quotation from Daniel 8. 12, writing 'practised' in place of 'grew' in the *BEM* version.

**32, I. 20 devouring sword in the hand of mine adversary** see the note for 28(b).

**32, I. 22 trust under the shadow of my wings** see the note for 28(c).

**32, I. 23 cast it out like dung** see the note for 28(d).

**32, I. 24 And we will tread him down [...] grind him to powder [...] brook Kedron** see the note for 28(d). The most common spelling, *Kidron*, is in Hogg's manuscript, and Hogg changed the spelling back to *Kidron* in his proof, although his proof corrections and revisions were not used in the printed version.

**32, I. 25 horn of the unicorn** see the note for 28(d).

**32, I. 25 Bulls of Bashan** see the note for 28(d).

**33 I. 26–27 from the emmet and the spider, [...] and the maggot after his kind** see the note for 28(d)–29(a).

**33, I. 28 things that are low shall be exalted** see the note for 29(a).

**33, I. 29 bowed down before him with their faces to the earth** see the note for 29(a).

**33, I. 31–32 it repented him that he had taken the Book [...] call unto thee thy friends** see the note for 29(b).

**33, I. 31 burn it with fire, and give its ashes to the winds of heaven** see the note for 29(b).

**33, I. 32 certain that were there present** the manuscript has 'certain sons of Belial'. See the note for 29(b).

**33, I. 32 why is thy countenance fallen** see the note for 29(b).

**33, I. 32 Go to now** see the note for 29(b).

**33, I. 32 behold and see** see the note for 29(b).

**33, I. 32 they that are for thee [...] those that be against thee** see the note for 29(b).

**33, I. 34 gem of curious workmanship [...] snuffed it up** see the note for 29(c).

**33, I. 37 to destroy, and to pass over** see the note for 29(d).

**33, I. 38 Old City [...] New City** the Old Town and New Town, Edinburgh. The Old Town was originally the area from the Castle eastward. The New Town, designed by James Craig in 1766, begins at Princes Street, north of what had been the North Loch. Constable's publishing firm, on the High Street, was in the Old Town; Blackwood's, on Princes Street, was in the New Town.

**33, I. 39 aged man [...] a mirror** verses 39–43 refer to Henry Mackenzie (1745–1831), who was 72 years old in 1817. Mackenzie was a well-respected man of letters in his time and is perhaps best known as the author of the popular novel, *The Man of Feeling* (1771). He also edited and wrote most of the articles for two weekly publications, *The Mirror* (1779–80) and *The Lounger* (1785–87). Mackenzie was an ardent supporter of Burns, Scott, and Byron.

**34, I. 44 great magician [...] Border** verses 44–48 refer to Sir Walter Scott (1771–1832). Scott's grand home, Abbotsford, was on the river Tweed, near Selkirk. Scott had collaborated with Thomas Pringle to write a series of articles, 'Notices Concerning the Scottish Gipsies', for early numbers of *BEM*, and he continued to write occasionally for *BEM* for several years. Blackwood and Scott had a short-lived publishing relationship in 1816, when Scott left Archibald Constable's publishing firm for the publication of *Tales of My Landlord* (*Old Mortality* and *The Black Dwarf*), but Blackwood and Scott clashed over editorial issues and Scott did not continue to publish his books with Blackwood.

**34, I. 47 place of Princes** Princes Street, Edinburgh, where Blackwood had his business.

**34, I. 47 mount of the Proclamation** a reference to the cross on High Street, Edinburgh, the site of the reading of proclamations. Constable's publishing business was located at 255 High Street.

**34, I. 48** In the BL proof Hogg revised verse 48 to read: 'paradventure I will help thee in the time that is to come'.

**34, I. 49–51 wise man which had come out of Joppa [...] speaketh of trees and of beasts [...] all manner of precious stones** verses 49–53 refer to Robert Jameson (1774–1854), who was from Joppa, a suburb of Edinburgh on the Firth of Forth near Portobello. Jameson was professor of natural history at the University of Edinburgh and keeper of the University's museum of natural history. His published studies of the geology of Scotland include *Mineralogy of the Scottish Isles* (1800), *System of Mineralogy* (1804–08), and *A Mineralogical Description of Dumfriesshire* (1805). He wrote several articles for *BEM*, including 'Account of the Wernerian Natural History Society of Edinburgh' (June 1817); Jameson founded the Society in 1808 and remained its president until his death. For more information about Jameson, see the *Oxford DNB* article by Dennis R. Dean. The biblical Joppa was a seaport northwest of Jerusalem.

**35, I. 54 wise man which had a light in his hand [...] crown of pearls** David Brewster (1781–1868), minister, scientist, and author, published important studies on the properties of light, especially related to polarisation. He published several articles in the early issues of *BEM*, including 'On the Optical Properties of Mother-of-Pearl' in the October 1817 issue. Brewster became editor of the *Edinburgh Encyclopædia* in 1808, and in 1819 became co-editor with Robert Jameson of the *Edinburgh Philosophical Journal*. Over his lifetime he published numerous articles in a variety of journals beyond *BEM*, including the *Edinburgh Review* and the *Quarterly Review*, as well as the *Encyclopædia Britannica*. Brewster's books include *A Treatise on New Philosophical Instruments* (1813), *Life of Sir Isaac Newton* (1831), and *Martyrs of Science: Lives of Galileo, Tycho Brahe, and Kepler* (1841). Brewster also is known for inventing the stereoscope and the kaleidoscope. For additional information, see the *Oxford DNB* article by A. D. Morrison-Low.

**35, l. 55 a wise young man, which is learned in the law, even as his father was learned [...] with his fellow** Patrick Fraser Tytler (1791–1849) was the son of Alexander Fraser Tytler, Lord Woodhouselee (1747–1813), who had a distinguished career as an advocate, judge, and professor of history. Patrick attended Edinburgh University and joined the Scottish bar in 1813. In 1816 he was awarded the position of king's counsel in exchequer. Patrick's major interest, however, was history, and his best-known work is his *History of Scotland* (1828–43), which was written at Sir Walter Scott's encouragement. Tytler published several articles in the early issues of *BEM*. The 'fellow' is probably Archibald Alison, later Sir Archibald (1791–1867), who was also a lawyer and a historian. Tytler and Alison were friends and had travelled in Europe, especially France and Belgium, in 1814–15; in 1815 Alison published a book based on these and other of Alison's travels. Alison also published numerous articles in *BEM*, although apparently none prior to the 'Chaldee'. For additional information on Tytler, see the *Oxford DNB* article by Michael Fry.

**35, l. 56 a learned man who sendeth all the King's messengers** 'Mr Henderson, Surveyor, General Post Office' (NLS, MS 4807, fols 42–43). R. Shelton Mackenzie adds this note: 'The coachmen, guards, and letter-carriers, then wore a uniform of which a scarlet coat was the most remarkable portion'– see *Noctes Ambrosianæ*, ed. by R. Shelton Mackenzie, 5 vols (New York: Worthington, 1868), I, xxv note; hereafter referred to as 'Mackenzie'.

**35, l. 57 a sweet singer** perhaps Robert Pearse Gillies (1789–1858), as suggested by the 'Chaldee' key preserved as NLS, MS 4807, fols 42-43. Gillies was a regular contributor to *BEM* in its early years, although apparently not before December 1818; his special interest was German literature. Gillies later was the model for 'Kempferhausen' in the *Noctes* dialogues. He became a founding editor of the *Foreign Quarterly Review* in 1827, and in 1851 published his reminiscences of his literary acquaintances, *Memoirs of a Literary Veteran*. Early in his writing career Gillies had been a poet, whose works elicited the comment from Byron: 'No one should be a rhymer who could be anything else' (quoted in *Oxford DNB* article on Gillies by Francis Watt, rev. David Finkelstein). However, Mackenzie (I, xxv note), suggests that Peter Hill is intended here. Hill was an Edinburgh bookseller, who is described by Lockhart in *Peter's Letters*: 'while his forenoons are past in the most sedulous attention to the business of a flourishing concern, his genteel and agreeable manners have made him a universal favourite with everybody, so that one frequently meets with him at evening parties, when "it is good to be merry and wise;" and I declare to you, that you never heard a sweeter pipe. Our friend Tom Moore himself is no whit his superior' (II, 180–81).

**35, I. 58–59 a physician in his youth [...] dealer in wine and oil** 'Charles Mackenzie Esq' (NLS, MS 4807, fols 42–43).

**35, I. 61 one cunning in sharp instruments** 'A person who sent an article on the sharpening of Rasors' (NLS, MS 4807, fols 42–43), but otherwise unidentified.

**35, I. 62 a voice of one screeching at the gate** verses 62–63 refer to Charles Kirkpatrick Sharpe (1781–1851). Sharpe is described by Sir Walter Scott in his *Journal*: 'He was bred a clergyman but did not take orders owing I believe to a peculiar effeminacy of voice which must have been unpleasant in reading prayers'–see *The Journal of Sir Walter Scott*, ed. by W. E. K. Anderson (Oxford: Oxford University Press, 1972), p. 2; Sharpe's voice earned him the nickname 'cheeping Charlie'. Sharpe's edition of James Kirkton's *Secret and True History of the Church of Scotland* is reviewed by Hogg in the December 1817 number of *BEM* (see pp. 47–54 in the present edition and notes). Sharpe had approached Blackwood about publishing Kirkton's *History*, but Sharpe would not agree to Blackwood's editorial conditions and, furthermore, Sharpe insulted Blackwood's social standing. Sharpe wrote to Robert Surtees, though, in a letter postmarked 1 October 1817 (before the 'Chaldee'): 'Blackwood and I have in some sort made up matters–but this will not long continue, I guess; Wilson, the Palm and Plague man, is now the editor of his Magazine, which of course must soon fall, or fall into other hands–the worthy in question being as shifting as the northern lights, and stark mad to boot–Constable drives on in triumph, with new Editors and a new title page–for my part, as both of these Magazines are staft with vulgar antedeluvian Whiggery, I cannot endure them–but I give Constable some trifles, because he gives me many better things' (NLS, MS 9309, fols 22–23).

**35, I. 65 wist not** in the BL proof this concluding verse is number 60 rather than 65. Hogg revised the verse to read: 'So the man was sore perplexed, and his cogitation troubled him'.

**36, II. 1 Oman, and the road of Gabriel [...] land of Ambrose** 'Blackwood's Back Window looks towards Oman's Tavern, as likewise to Gabriel's Road in which is Ambrose's Tavern' (NLS, MS 4807, fols 42–43). At the time of the 'Chaldee' Charles Oman operated a hotel at 22 St Andrew Street. Previously he owned a tavern in West Register Street and in 1810 established a hotel at 14 Princes Street–see Marie W. Stuart, *Old Edinburgh Taverns* (London: Robert Hales, 1952), pp. 82–83, 86–89. Ambrose's Tavern, located at 1 Gabriel's Road, became a regular feature of *BEM* in 1822 with the advent of the long-running and popular series, *Noctes Ambrosianæ*.

**36, II. 2 a veil upon his head** a reference to the 'veiled editor' of *BEM*. William Blackwood did not hire an editor for *BEM* after his disappointment with Pringle and Cleghorn, and he maintained a deliberate secrecy about his editorial practices with his new magazine. In a letter dated 12 August 1817 Hogg complained to Blackwood about not knowing Blackwood's plans for his new magazine: 'I regret much that you have told me so little of your plan; if the name is to change who is to be Editor &c.' (*Letters 1*, p. 295). John Wilson, especially, and John Lockhart–in conjunction with Blackwood himself–took on the lion's share of editorial responsibilities in the early years, with D. M. Moir frequently acting as an advisory reader for Blackwood.

However, whenever Blackwood was confronted with the question of Wilson's or Lockhart's editorship, he denied that he had an editor. Yet, when faced with responding to controversial articles in *BEM*, such as the 'Chaldee', he claimed that 'I myself have no controul over the measures of my Editor' (NLS, MS 30,001, fols 66–67).

**36, ll. 3 let not thine heart be discouraged [...] afraid** from John 14. 27: 'Let not your heart be troubled, neither let it be afraid'.

**36, ll. 9 knew not who they were which came** most of the works in the early numbers of *BEM* were published anonymously or with pseudonymous names or initials. As *BEM* developed, a series of fictional authorial personae developed with it. Works also frequently were written jointly, and at times the person whose name was signed to the work was not the author of the work. In many cases, the authorship of articles in *BEM* remained purposely enigmatic.

**36, ll. 10 beautiful leopard, from the valley of the palm trees** John Wilson. See the note for 29(d)–30(a).

**36, ll. 11 lynx that lurketh behind the white cottage** Arthur Mower. See the note for 29(d).

**36, ll. 12 the scorpion** John Gibson Lockhart (1794–1854), who was from the 'far country' of Glasgow. The sting of Lockhart's pen is evident in other works in the October 1817 issue, specifically 'On the Cockney School of Poetry' (pp. 38–41), which attacked Leigh Hunt and his poem, *The Story of Rimini*, and the 'Letter to the Lord High Constable, from Mr Dinmont' (pp. 35–36), which, like the 'Chaldee', attacked Archibald Constable and his literary associates. Like Wilson, Lockhart took some share in the editorial responsibilities for *BEM*, and he was an important contributor throughout most of his life, even after he moved to London in December 1825 to become editor of John Murray's *Quarterly Review*. Lockhart published a volume of poetry translations with Blackwood in 1823, *Ancient Spanish Ballads*, and he published four novels with Blackwood over a four-year period: *Valerius* (1821), *Adam Blair* (1822), *Reginald Dalton* (1823), and *Matthew Wald* (1824). Lockhart is perhaps best known for the biography of his father-in-law, Sir Walter Scott, which was first published in 1837–38. Lockhart seems to have been a 'dark wolf' in Hogg's manuscript; see the note for 30(a). The change of Lockhart's character to a scorpion is made on Hogg's original manuscript in Lockhart's hand. For additional information about Lockhart and his role in *BEM* see the Introduction to the present edition.

**36, ll. 13 great wild boar from the forest of Lebanon [...] whetting his dreadful tusks for the battle** see the note for 30(a).

**36, ll. 14 the griffin** see the note for 30(a).

**37, ll. 15 the black eagle** Sir William Hamilton (1788–1856), philosopher, studied medicine at Edinburgh before attending Balliol College, Oxford, in 1807 as a Snell exhibitioner. Hamilton was a close friend of John Lockhart. Hamilton became an advocate in Edinburgh in 1813; he lost to John Wilson in the election for Professor of Moral Philosophy at the University of Edinburgh in 1820, but later was appointed Professor of Civil History. He began publishing articles on philosophy in the *Edinburgh Review* in 1829 after Macvey Napier became editor. For additional information about Hamilton, see the *Oxford DNB* article by A. Ryan.

**37, ll. 16 the stork [...] devoureth all manner of unclean things** James Wilson

(1795–1856), naturalist and zoologist, and brother to John Wilson (the 'leopard' of the 'Chaldee'). Wilson contributed a number of articles to *BEM*, including the series 'Sketches of Foreign Scenery and Manners' in the issues for June through September 1817; he also wrote zoology-related articles for the *Encyclopædia Britannica*. Wilson was a member of the Wernerian Society and later was a fellow of the Royal Society of Edinburgh. His later publications include *Illustrations of Zoology* (1831) and a series of natural history studies: *An Introduction to the Natural History of Quadrupeds and Whales* (1838), *An Introduction to the Natural History of Fishes* (1838), and *An Introduction to the Natural History of Birds* (1839). For additional information, see the *Oxford DNB* article by Yolanda Foote.

**37, II. 17 the hyæna […] riddle unto the vain man** see the note for 30(a).

**37, II. 18 the beagle and the slow-hound after their kind** unidentified. See also the notes for 28(d)–29(a) and 30(a).

**37, II. 21–22 a physician […] neither was there any gall within him** verses 21–22 refer to John Gordon (1786–1818), Edinburgh physician and lecturer on anatomy and physiology. Dr Gordon published an article, 'The Doctrines of Gall and Spurzheim', in the June 1815 *Edinburgh Review*, in which he discredited the phrenological theories of F. J. Gall and G. Spurzheim.

**38, III. 5** in the BL proof Hogg replaced 'farm' with 'field', so that the verse reads 'the Philistines will come into my field'. The Philistines were perennial enemies of the Israelites in the Old Testament.

**38, III. 8** in the BL proof Hogg replaced 'penny' with 'two shekels of the sanctuary' so that the verse reads: 'and the two shekels of the sanctuary which ye have of me'. This verse echoes Exodus 30. 13: 'This they shall give, every one that passeth among them that are numbered, half a shekel after the shekel of the sanctuary'. See also Numbers 3. 47.

**38, III. 14–19 a familiar spirit […] deliver some malefactors which he loved** verses 14–19 refer to Francis Jeffrey (1773–1850), advocate and editor of the *Edinburgh Review*, 'who at this very time had been defending some of the Kilmarnock Radicals, and fairly beat the Lord Advocate (now Lord Meadowbank) in the Court of Justiciary' (NLS, MS 4807, fols 42–43). Although Jeffrey had been editor of the *Edinburgh Review* for nearly fifteen years in October 1817, he did not participate in Constable's *Edinburgh Magazine*; Jeffrey continued to edit the *Review* until 1829. In 1830 Jeffrey was appointed Lord Advocate and also elected a Member of Parliament. For additional information about Jeffrey, see the *Oxford DNB* article by Michael Fry.

**38, III. 17 those which have command over the devils** that is, printer's devils, young apprentices whose responsibility it is to run errands for the printer.

**39, III. [21]** in the BL proof, verse 21 reads: 'And the first was an ugly spirit, which flew through the air, riding upon a long broom'. Hogg marked through this verse and replaced it with the following: 'and the first was an unclean spirit and [ILLEGIBLE] as the pestilence that walketh at noon day and the sword that passed between his feet was like the staff of a weaver's loom'. Verse 21 of the proof was deleted before publication, but Hogg's revised verse was not inserted. The verses were renumbered for publication. As Douglas Mack has suggested, the 'ugly spirit' probably refers to Henry Brougham (1778–1868), one of the founders and a major contributor to the *Edinburgh Review*. Brougham was an influential voice for the Whig political perspectives espoused by the *Review*. (For additional information about

Brougham, see the *Oxford DNB* article by Michael Lobban.) The phrase 'the staff of a weaver's loom' is probably a reference to the Radical politics of the time, led by the weavers in the west of Scotland. See also the note for 38, III. 14–19.

**39, III. 21 a cunning spirit […] full of strong ice** John Leslie (1766–1832), natural philosopher and professor of mathematics at the University of Edinburgh. Leslie made important discoveries in properties of heat and published *Experimental Enquiries into the Nature and Properties of Heat* in 1804. Leslie also experimented with a process that used the absorbency of oatmeal to freeze water. Leslie wrote for the *Edinburgh Review* on topics relating to mathematics and science. In the BL proof Hogg revised the second part of the verse to read: 'for when he becometh an hungered and asketh for bread lo he giveth to him water that is as hard as a piece of the nether millstone'. For additional information about Leslie, see the *Oxford DNB* article by Jack Morrell.

**39, III. 22 a little blind spirit […] one of the scoffers** John Playfair (1748–1819), son of a minister and was himself ordained a Presbyterian minister in 1770. However, his primary interests were in mathematics and natural philosophy, and he held professorships in both fields at the University of Edinburgh. Playfair wrote extensively on scientific topics for the *Edinburgh Review*. Among Playfair's publications are *Illustrations of the Huttonian Theory of the Earth* (1802) and *Analysis of the Volcanic Theory of the Earth,* which accounts for the reference to 'worshippers of fire'. For additional information about Playfair, see the *Oxford DNB* article by Jack Morrell.

**39, III. 23 no ear unto his outcry […] voice of his supplication** 'None of those connected the [*sic*] Edinburgh Review ever gave any assistance to Constable's magazine' (NLS, MS 4807, fols 42–43). The image is from Psalm 143. 1: 'Hear my prayer, O Lord, give ear to my supplications'.

**39, III. 26 a magician which is of my friends** Constable, too, sought assistance from Sir Walter Scott in the magazine competitions. Scott had occasionally published in Constable's *Edinburgh Review*, and Constable had been Scott's Edinburgh publisher for many of his extraordinarily-successful works of poetry and fiction. John Lockhart in his *Life of Scott* writes of Constable's response to these verses in the 'Chaldee': 'nothing nettled [Constable] so much as the passages in which he and Blackwood are represented entreating the support of Scott for their respective Magazines, and waved off by "the Great Magician" in the same identical phrases of contemptuous indifference. The description of Constable's visit to Abbotsford may be worth transcribing—for Sir David Wilkie, who was present when Scott read it, says he was almost choked with laughter, and he afterwards confessed that the Chaldean author had given a sufficiently accurate version of what really passed on the occasion' (III, 165n).

**39, III. 27** in the BL proof Hogg revised this verse to read: 'So he arose and came unto that great magician which hath his dwelling at the fords of the river Jordan as you pass by to the borders of the kingdom of the south'. In the BL proof this verse is numbered 28.

**40, III. 34 shook the dust from his feet** from Matthew 10. 14: 'And whosoever shall not receive you, nor hear your words, when ye depart out of that house or city, shake off the dust of your feet'. In the BL proof Hogg revised the last sentence of this verse to read: 'Verily, my gold is become dim and my most fine gold is perished'. This verse is numbered 35 in the BL proof.

**40, III. 36–44 the other beast** verses 36–44 refer to John Graham Dalyell (1775–1851). Dalyell was a person of varied interests; he was a lawyer, but his intellectual interests primarily lay in history and natural history. He published *Fragments of Scottish History* in 1798, edited a collection of sixteenth-century Scottish poetry (1801), and published several studies on natural history during his life. He was a member of the Society of Antiquaries of Scotland and the Highland Society of Scotland. He was severely injured as an infant in a fall and permanently lamed. Because of the defamatory nature of these verses, Dalyell sued William Blackwood for £5000 for damages and £500 for legal expenses, although the two parties agreed to a settlement in July 1818 in which Blackwood paid Dalyell £230. The legal summons, dated 10 November 1817, describes Dalyell's allegations against Blackwood:

> the said William Blackwood has committed a cruel, malicious, and wanton injury, in holding up, in a style of mockery and derision, the personal infirmities under which the said pursuer labours, impiously scoffing at what is the visitation of Heaven alone, and no fault of him the sufferer: That, regardless of those divine and moral precepts, teaching all mankind to succour and protect their fellows, afflicted by calamities, which, from the will of Providence, may speedily become their own, the said William Blackwood, not content with simple mockery [...] endeavours to deprive the pursuer of the means of subsistence, by bringing public contempt and obloquy upon him, in a calumnious charge of his being unfit for undertakings whereon his talents or industry may be exercised. (NLS, MS 4807, fols 48–49)

Hogg later claimed, though, in a letter to Thomas Pringle, that the 'author of that article, I can prove, knew not that such a man as J. Graham Dalziel existed and in fact he was no more alluded to in the part litigated than you were' (*Letters 1*, p. 378). These verses were a major factor in the decision to omit the 'Chaldee' sketch from the second edition of the October 1817 number. A 'Note from the Editor' in the November 1817 number addresses the omission: 'The Editor has learned with regret, that an Article in the First Edition of last Number, which was intended merely as a *jeu d'esprit*, has been construed so as to give offence to Individuals justly entitled to respect and regard; he has on that account withdrawn it in the Second Edition, and can only add, that if what has happened could have been anticipated, the Article in question certainly never would have appeared'. For additional information about Dalyell, see the *Oxford DNB* article by Kathleen Dalyell.

**40, III. 37** in the BL proof Hogg has revised the second part of this verse to read: 'spoiled: he was shapen in sin and brought forth in iniquity, his doings also are impure'. This verse is from Psalm 51. 5: 'Behold, I was shapen in iniquity; and in sin did my mother conceive me'.

**40, III. 42 sharper than any two edged sword** from Hebrews 4. 12: 'For the word of God is quick, and powerful, and sharper than any twoedged sword, piercing even to the dividing asunder of soul and spirit, and of the joints and marrow, and is a discerner of the thoughts and intents of the heart'.

**41, III. 47–48 another beast [...] disease was the murrain [...] Heu! heu!** verses 47–48 refer to Hugh Murray (1779–1846), who was an editor of Constable's *Scots Magazine* before Cleghorn and Pringle. Murray was a geographer and a fellow of the Royal Society of Edinburgh and the Royal

Geographical Society. He wrote extensively about the subject; his best-known work was the *Encyclopaedia of Geography* (1834). For additional information about Murray, see the *Oxford DNB* article by G. le G. Norgate, rev. Elizabeth Baigent.

**41, IV. 1 one which was his familiar friend** verses 1–4 refer to Macvey Napier (1776–1847), a close friend of Archibald Constable for many years. Napier was a regular contributor to the *Edinburgh Review* and edited for Constable a *Supplement* to the sixth edition of the *Encyclopaedia Britannica*. Napier taught conveyancing at the University of Edinburgh and in 1824 was appointed Professor. Napier later (1829) became editor of the *Edinburgh Review*, although he was much less successful than his predecessor, Francis Jeffrey. For additional information about Napier, see the *Oxford DNB* article by Joanne Shattock.

**41, IV. 6 another of his friends** verses 6–7 refer to Robert Jamieson (1772?–1844), who published *Popular Ballads and Songs* [...] *with Translations from the Antient Danish Language* (1806) and collaborated with Henry Weber and Sir Walter Scott on *Illustrations of Northern Antiquities* (1814). Scott acknowledged the importance of Jamieson's recognition of the connections between Scottish and Scandinavian balladry. Jamieson also worked in the Edinburgh General Register House from 1809 until 1843. For additional information about Jamieson, see the *Oxford DNB* article by T. W. Bayne, rev. Harriet Harvey Wood.

**42, IV. 8 a lean man** [...] **by the great pool to the north of the New City** verses 8–13 refer to Patrick Neill (1776–1851), noted Edinburgh printer, naturalist, and horticulturalist, who lived at Canonmills on the Water of Leith; his garden at Canonmills was well-known for its collection of unusual plant life. Neill was secretary of both the Wernerian Natural History Society and the Caledonian Horticultural Society, and his publications before the date of the 'Chaldee' include *A Tour through Orkney and Shetland* (1806) and a translation of *An Account of the Basalts of Saxony* (1814). In 1820 he designed the Princes Street Gardens in Edinburgh. Neill's later works include accounts of his travels in Europe and *The Flower, Fruit, and Kitchen Garden* (1840), which was published from his *Encyclopædia Britannica* article on 'Gardening'. For additional information about Neill, see the *Oxford DNB* article by B. D. Jackson, rev. Peter Osborne.

**42, IV. 17 four beasts** that is, Cleghorn, Pringle, Dalyell, and Murray. See 40–41, III. 35–52.

**42, IV. 18 one which teacheth in the schools of the young men** [...] **gray garment whereof one half his wife had weaved** James Gray (1770?–1830), classics teacher at Edinburgh High School, was a friend of Hogg's and a contributor to Hogg's periodical, *The Spy*. He was portrayed as the fifteenth bard in Hogg's *The Queen's Wake* (1813), and Gray was himself the author of two volumes of poetry. Hogg in his *Memoir* mentions Gray as having been considered 'the fittest person for a principal department' in a plan that Hogg and Pringle devised for a literary magazine—a plan, Hogg claims, that ultimately led to the establishment of *BEM* (p. 43). In 1820 Hogg married Margaret Phillips, the sister of Gray's first wife, Mary Phillips. Gray later became principal of Belfast Academy and then a chaplain for the East India Company. Gray's second wife, from 1808, was Mary Peacock (1767–1829); she was also an author and contributor to *The Spy*. For additional information about Gray, see Gillian Hughes's 'Notes on Contributors' in *The Spy* (S/SC, 2000), pp. 562–63, and the *Oxford DNB* article by Peter Jackson.

**42, IV. 19 Samuel** 'Samuel McCormick, Esq Advocate, then a Depute Advocate' (NLS, MS 4807, fols 42–43). Mackenzie adds: 'A cousin of Professor Wilson's, and at this time one of the Crown Counsel' (I, xxxi note).

**42, IV. 20 John, the brother of James** John Ballantyne (1774–1821), brother of the Edinburgh printer and business partner of Sir Walter Scott, James Ballantyne (1772–1833). John Ballantyne worked for a time for his brother before establishing his own short-lived publishing business. In 1816 John became literary agent for Sir Walter Scott and an auctioneer of books and art. He published *The Sale-Room*, a weekly periodical, for the first six months of 1817. (For additional information about Ballantyne, see the *Oxford DNB* article by Sharon Anne Ragaz.) This verse also echoes Mark 5. 37: 'And he suffered no man to follow him, save Peter, and James, and John the brother of James'.

**42, IV. 21 James, the young man [...] nibbleth the shoe-latchets of the mighty** verses 21–22 refer to James Grahame (1790–1842), author of *An Inquiry into the Principle of Population* (1816), in which he takes issues with the population theories of the English economist, Thomas Malthus. Grahame published a response to the 'Chaldee' in a series of five 'Letters to the Rev. Dr Thomas M'Crie, and the Rev. Mr Andrew Thomson' (1817) under the pseudonym 'Calvinus'. 'The shoe-latchets of the mighty' echoes Luke 3. 16: 'but one mightier than I cometh, the latchet of whose shoes I am not worthy to unloose'.

**43, IV. 23 George, the chief of the synagogue, a principal man** George Baird (1761–1840), a Church of Scotland minister, served the parish church of Dunkeld beginning in 1787, then a series of churches in Edinburgh: the New Greyfriars (1792), the New North Church (1799), and the High Church (1801). In 1792 he was also appointed Professor of Hebrew at the University of Edinburgh and in 1793 became Principal of the University. For additional information about Baird, see the *Oxford DNB* article by A. B. Grosart, rev. M. C. Curthoys.

**43, IV. 24 one David** David Bridges (1776–1840). With his father Bridges owned a clothing shop on High Street in Edinburgh. Bridges was acquainted with many of the leading artists of the time and maintained a collection of art in a room below the main shop. He is described by Lockhart in *Peter's Letters* as 'an active, intelligent, and warm-hearted fellow, who has a prodigious love for the Fine Arts, and lives on familiar terms with all the artists of Edinburgh' (II, 230). Bridges figures in several of Hogg's works; see, for example, 'If e'er you would be a brave fellow', pp. 162–63 in the present edition, and note for 163, l. 40.

**43, IV. 25 Andrew the chief physician, and Andrew his son** Andrew Duncan (1744–1828) and his son, Andrew (1773–1832), were both prominent physicians and medical teachers and writers in Edinburgh. Andrew the younger was a musician and contributor to the *Edinburgh Review*. For additional information about the Duncans, see the separate articles in the *Oxford DNB* by G. T. Bettany, the article on the elder Duncan revised by Lisa Rosner and the article on the younger Duncan revised by Brenda M. White.

**43, IV. 26 James the baker** 'James Baxter, Writer to the Signet' (NLS, MS 4807, fols 42–43). The word 'baxter' in Scots means 'baker'.

**43, IV. 27 Peter who raileth at his master** Patrick Gibson (1782?–1829), who was a pupil of Alexander Nasmyth's and prominent artist and writer about art; he was sometimes identified as 'Peter Gibson' in art exhibition catalogues of the time. Gibson contributed articles on art and design to the *Edinburgh Encyclopædia* and published 'A View of the Progress and Present State of the Art of Design in Britain' in the *Edinburgh Annual Register* for 1816, which was edited by John Lockhart. For additional information on Gibson, see the *Oxford DNB* article by J. M. Gray, rev. Mungo Campbell.

**43, IV. 28 Samuel, which is a mason** 'Samuel Anderson, high among the Freemasons of Scotland. He was a wine-merchant, but in Brougham's Chancellorship, received the lucrative appointment of Registrar of the English Court of Chancery' (Mackenzie, I, xxxi note).

**43, IV. 34 John the brother of Francis** 'John Jeffrey, younger brother of the critic', Francis Jeffrey (Mackenzie, I, xxxi note).

**43, IV. 34 man which offered Consolation** William Gillespie (1776–1825), author of *Consolation, with Other Poems* (1815). Gillespie, a Church of Scotland minister in the parish of Kells, was also a contributor to Constable's *Scots Magazine* and to Hogg's periodical, *The Spy*. For additional information about Gillespie see the *Oxford DNB* article by Edwin Cannan, rev. Rosemary Mitchell.

**43, IV. 35 seven young men** unidentified.

**43, IV. 39** in the BL proof this verse is numbered '34'. Hogg deleted this verse and inserted the following verses:

> 34 And the man that talked with me said What thinkest thou of this matter, and what shall be the end thereof? And I said my lord I cannot tell.

> 35 And he said tell them it not in Gath, nor publish it in the streets of Askelon, but the man who is *crafty* in counsel shall fall down before the enemy—nay is already fallen, and lo! there shall not be left unto him one that pisseth against the wall

> 36 But the women and the feeble of the land and the poor and the impotent shall remain with him and all that are shut up and left in Paran and he shall gnash his teeth upon them for the truth shall break forth as in open day and knowledge shall no more be hid from the simple.

Hogg's new verse 35 is derived from several biblical verses. See II Samuel 1. 20: 'Tell it not in Gath, publish it not in the streets of Askelon; lest the daughters of the Philistines rejoice, lest the daughters of the uncircumcised triumph; II Samuel 1. 19: 'how are the mighty fallen'; I Kings 16. 11: 'he left him not one that pisseth against a wall, neither of his kinsfolks, nor of his friends'. Hogg's new verse 36 is also derived from multiple sources. Paran was a wilderness south and southwest of Canaan—see, for example, Genesis 21. 21 and Numbers 13. 3; 'gnash his teeth upon them' echoes Psalm 112. 10; 'truth shall break forth' echoes Isaiah 58. 8: 'Then shall thy light break forth as morning'; and 'knowledge shall no more be hid from the simple' echoes Psalm 119. 130: 'The entrance of thy words giveth light; it giveth understanding unto the simple'.

**44, IV. 40** in the BL proof Hogg marked out 'I' in the opening line and inserted 'he', so that the revised line would read: 'And while he was yet speaking'.

**44, IV. 41 Cry. And I said, What shall I cry?** see the note for 30(b).

**44, IV. 41 ruled the nations with a rod of iron** see the note for 30(b).
**44, IV. 42 I fled into an inner chamber to hide myself [...] I wist not what it was** see the note for 30(b).

### The Boar

'The Boar' was not published in Hogg's lifetime. It is published in the present edition from Hogg's fair-copy manuscript that is preserved among the Blackwood papers in the National Library of Scotland as MS 4807, fols 44–47. The manuscript consists of two sheets, each measuring *c.* 38 cm x 23 cm, and each sheet folded to make two folios of *c.* 19 cm x 23 cm. The paper does not bear a watermark. Alan Lang Strout published 'The Boar' as part of his article 'James Hogg's "Chaldee Manuscript"', *PMLA*, 65 (September 1950), 695–718 (pp. 710–713).

The date of composition of 'The Boar' is uncertain. 'The Boar' immediately follows the 'Chaldee Manuscript' in the present edition because of the close affinity of this satirical sketch with the 'Chaldee'. 'The Boar' is written in the style of the 'Chaldee', employing the language of the Authorised Version of the Bible, as well as incorporating frequent biblical allusions. 'The Boar' clearly addresses the public outcry in response to the 'Chaldee', and Hogg in 'The Boar' gives credit to himself, the 'great boar of Lebanon', for the disarray within the Constable camp that resulted from the 'Chaldee' publication. It is likely, however, that 'The Boar' was written several months later than the 'Chaldee', for the work also seems to address conflicts that developed between Hogg and *BEM*'s two most influential contributors, John Wilson and, to a lesser degree, John Lockhart, in the early months of the new Maga.

Hogg's concerns about his role in *BEM* had surfaced as early as August 1817 as Blackwood struggled with the direction of his magazine; Hogg complained to Blackwood about being kept in the dark about Blackwood's efforts to re-cast the magazine: 'I regret much that you have told me so little of your plan; if the name is to change who is to be Editor &c' (*Letters 1*, p. 295). The October 1817 issue, too, signalled a new direction for Hogg's role with *BEM*, and Hogg metaphorically expressed his puzzlement with Maga's primary authors in 'The Hunt of Eildon', a story in *The Brownie of Bodsbeck; And Other Tales*, which was published by Blackwood in May 1818. Furthermore—and perhaps the immediate motivation for writing 'The Boar'—Hogg was upset by the series of articles about himself that began with 'Letter to Mr James Hogg', written by John Wilson under the pseudonym of Timothy Tickler, in the February 1818 issue of *BEM*. (For further discussion of the 'Tickler' letters controversy, see 'Letter to Timothy Tickler' in the present edition, p. 72, and notes.)

The present edition of 'The Boar' follows Hogg's manuscript, including occasional irregular spellings and punctuation, except that end punctuation has been silently added as required. The text is also emended as follows:
    46(d) stunned with] stunned with stunned with (manuscript).

**44(b) the boar of Lebanon** James Hogg. See 'Chaldee' note for 36, II. 13. In the first three verses of 'The Boar', Hogg describes the effect of the 'Chaldee' on Archibald Constable's magazine publishing business.
**44(b) the host of the enemy** host, in the sense of 'camp', is a common biblical term.
**44(b) contended with them [...] plucked off their hair** from Nehemiah 13.

25: 'And I contended with them, and cursed them, and smote certain of them, and plucked off their hair'.

**44(b) tarried at Jericho until their beards were grown** from II Samuel 10. 5: 'and the king said, Tarry at Jericho until your beards be grown, and then return'.

**44(c) dung had been laid upon the face of the ground** echoes Jeremiah 8. 2: 'they shall be for dung upon the face of the earth'.

**44(d) the man in the veil** a reference to the 'veiled editor' of *BEM*. See 'Chaldee' note for 36, II. 2.

**44(d) the leopard [...] woundeth whom he listeth even though they put their trust in him** John Wilson. See 'Chaldee' note for 36, II. 10. Wilson was the author of the 'Tickler' letters. Hogg claims to have seen the manuscripts of the letters, so he would have known Wilson was the author. See p. 74(b) in the present edition.

**44(d) sting in his tail** echoes Revelation 9. 10: 'And they had tails like unto scorpions, and there were stings in their tails'.

**44(d) ebony** William Blackwood.

**45(a) the gall of bitterness and the bond of iniquity** from Acts 8. 23: 'For I perceive that thou art in the gall of bitterness, and in the bond of iniquity'.

**45(a) if they throw unto him an acorn he will go over to the other side** Blackwood was concerned that Hogg would change his periodical allegiance to Archibald Constable, Blackwood's Edinburgh publishing competitor. Hogg had earlier been a contributor to Constable's *Scots Magazine*, and Constable had published some of Hogg's early book-length works, including *The Mountain Bard* (1807), *The Shepherd's Guide* (1807), and *The Forest Minstrel* (1810). Hogg wrote to Blackwood on 15 July 1818: 'I have been quizzed too much by your chaps already I will not so easily take again. I am writing for another Magazine with all my birr and intend having most excellent sport with it as the editors will not understand what one sentence of my celebrated allegories mean, till they bring the whole terror of Edin aristocracy on them' (*Letters 1*, p. 363). A week later, though, Hogg claims that he was merely referring to another satire on the Blackwood-Constable rivalry that he was writing, 'John Paterson's Mare', although he also reiterated his displeasure with his treatment by Wilson and Lockhart:

> Does it ever enter into your stupid head that I would write any thing against your work and my old friends. It would only be on consultation and a certainty that it would be advantageous to all parties if I did. At any rate I never accused you of quizzing me and I hope I never shall have occassion as for the two devils the thing is implanted in their very natures and I must bear it though I believe they have banished me their too much loved society it may make me angry for an hour or two at a time but shall never make me admire or love them the less The thing that I hinted at was that I might publish John Paterson's Mare and some strange rubs on another party which would not in the least be understood until they came to Edin. (*Letters 1*, p. 365)

'John Paterson's Mare' eventually was published as 'Annals of Sporting. No. I.–John Paterson's Mare' in the *Newcastle Magazine*, 4 (January 1825), 3–12.

**45(a) they that are not for me be against me** an expression that occurs several times in the gospels. See, for example, Matthew 12. 30 and Mark 9. 40.

**45(a) the man that was crafty** Archibald Constable. See 'Chaldee' note for

28(a–b).

45(a) **one that pisseth against the wall** from I Kings 16. 11: 'he left him not one that pisseth against a wall, neither of his kinsfolks, nor of his friends'.

45(b) **voice of their cry [...] woman in travail** see Jeremiah 13. 21: 'shall not sorrows take thee, as a woman in travail?'

45(b) **the beasts** James Cleghorn and Thomas Pringle, who became editors of Constable's *Scots Magazine* (renamed the *Edinburgh Magazine and Literary Miscellany*) after their failures with *BEM*. See 'Chaldee' note for 27(a).

45(c) **in a moment in the twinkling of an eye** a reference to I Corinthians 15. 51–52: 'We shall not all sleep, but we shall all be changed, In a moment, in the twinkling of an eye, at the last trump'.

45(c) **the mole that walketh in darkness** the identity of the mole is unclear, but this is probably a reference to Hogg himself. Hogg in 'The Boar' suggests that the mole has been unjustifiably excluded from the 'house' of Blackwood, but if the mole should decide to turn against Blackwood, the mole could significantly damage the 'house': 'his house is of *Wood* and if that mole but once breathe upon it he will shake it to its foundations as a tree is shaken by the winds of heaven' (see p. 46(d) and note). Hogg seems to imply that he could create the same disorder within the Blackwood's firm that he did within Constable's.

45(c) **pestilence that rageth at noon-day** echoes Psalm 91. 6: 'Nor for the pestilence that walketh in darkness; nor for the destruction that wasteth at noonday'.

45(d) **certain of the Amalekites and those of Ishmael** images of outcasts, suggesting that those who remained with Constable were outside the mainstream of the Edinburgh literati. The Amalekites were descendants of Amalek, the grandson of Esau (Genesis 36. 12). Esau had been exiled by God for the murder of his brother, Abel (Genesis 4). Ishmael was the son of Abraham by Hagar, the handmaid of Abraham's wife, Sarah. Sarah forced Abraham to 'cast away' Hagar and Ishmael after the birth of Sarah's son, Isaac (Genesis 21).

46(a) **the great physician** Francis Jeffrey. See 'Chaldee' note for 38, III. 14–19.

46(a) **gates of death** echoes Psalm 9. 13: 'thou that liftest me up from the gates of death'.

46(a) **a mark upon his forehead** from Revelation 14. 9–10: 'If any man worship the beast and his image, and receive his mark in his forehead, or in his hand, The same shall drink of the wine of the wrath of God'.

46(a) **the great horn** *The Edinburgh Review*. See 'Chaldee' note for 32, I. 17–18.

46(d) **darkness is in his name and folly is with him** echoes I Samuel 25. 25: 'Nabal is his name, and folly is with him'. 'Nabal' means 'fool'; Hogg, in effect, suggests that Blackwood is a fool.

46(d) **shake it to its foundations** a common biblical image. See II Samuel 22. 8 and Psalm 18. 7, for example.

47(a) **should have win its way** Hogg writes 'win' in the manuscript although 'won' would be the expected form in this context. Perhaps Hogg intends 'win' to be consistent with his imitation of the language of the Authorised Version of the Bible.

47(a) **voice of Jacob the son of Levi who came from the city that bordereth on the river of the west** in the Genesis story of Jacob and Levi (chapter 29), it is Jacob who is the father. Levi is one of Jacob's twelve sons, the third son by his wife, Leah. The names of Jacob's sons become the names of the twelve tribes of Israel, and Jacob's name eventually is changed to Israel. In these last four paragraphs of 'The Boar', Hogg probably is referring to John Lockhart, who was from Glasgow on the River Clyde–'the city that bordereth on the river of the west'. Lockhart was the son of Dr. John Lockhart, Church of Scotland minister and minister of the college kirk of Blackfriars in Glasgow from 1796. See also 'Chaldee' note for 36, II. 12.

**47(b) land of Tyre and Sidon where the merchants traffic with the men of a far country** the biblical cities of Tyre and Sidon were the principal port cities of ancient Phoenicia, located on the coast of modern Lebanon. Although the cities were more than twenty miles apart, they were often mentioned together in the Bible. Here Hogg seems to be referring to Glasgow.

**47(b) young man** Lockhart was only twenty-three years old when the 'Chaldee Manuscript' was published.

**47(b) attacted the old and the feeble the low and the vulgar** perhaps a particular reference to the personal attack on John Graham Dalzell, whose physical appearance and disabilities are lampooned in the 'Chaldee' (see 'Chaldee' note for 40, III. 36–44). However, Lockhart wrote two articles that also appeared in the October 1817 issue with the 'Chaldee': 'On the Cockney School of Poetry' (pp. 38–41), which attacked Leigh Hunt and his poem, *The Story of Rimini*, and the 'Letter to the Lord High Constable, from Mr Dinmont' (pp. 35–36), which, like the 'Chaldee', attacked Archibald Constable and his literary associates.

### A Letter to Charles Kirkpatrick Sharpe, Esq.
### On his Original Mode of Editing Church History

'A Letter to Charles Kirkpatrick Sharpe' was published in *Blackwood's Edinburgh Magazine*, 2 (December 1817), 305–09. Hogg's 'Letter to Sharpe' is the first of only two review essays Hogg published in *BEM*; the second, 'The Honourable Captain Napier and Ettrick Forest', appeared in the February 1823 number of *BEM* (pp. 114–37 of the present edition). The 'Letter to Sharpe' reviewed Sharpe's edition of *The Secret and True History of the Church of Scotland, from the Restoration to the Year 1678*, by the Reverend Mr James Kirkton (London: Longman; Edinburgh: John Ballantyne, 1817). Sharpe edits the text from a previously-unpublished manuscript then in his possession. Sharpe provides an introduction to Kirkton and Kirkton's text and also includes notes to the text. Hogg's article is signed with the pseudonymous initials 'M. M.', and Hogg's authorship is not otherwise indicated in the *BEM* text. However, Hogg's authorship is verified in the publisher's records (Strout, p. 33). The 'Letter to Sharpe' was not reprinted in Hogg's lifetime.

James Kirkton (*d.* 1699) was a Church of Scotland minister who served churches in Lanark and Mertoun before losing his charge in 1662 for failing to conform to Episcopal jurisdiction. He lived in England for several years, and in 1672 he was offered an indulgence at Carstairs, which he declined. In July 1674 Kirkton was declared a rebel for holding unlawful conventicles, but he avoided arrest for two years. He was finally arrested in 1676 but was soon rescued by his brother-in-law, Robert Baillie of Jerviswood. Kirkton fled to Holland, where he remained until after the institution of the Toleration Act of 1687. He returned to his ministry at Mertoun in 1690, and in 1691 became minister of the Tolbooth Church in Edinburgh, a position he held until his death in 1699. In addition to *A Secret and True History*, Kirkton published sermons, a treatise on baptism, and a life of the Ayrshire minister, John Welsh. For additional information on Kirkton, see the *Oxford DNB* article by Ralph Stewart.

Charles Kirkpatrick Sharpe (1781–1851) was an antiquary, artist, genealogist, and collector of Scottish antiquities. He attended Christ Church, Oxford (BA, 1802; MA, 1806), planning to enter the Church of England ministry, but he never pursued ordination upon completion of his Oxford degrees. Sharpe contributed to Sir Walter Scott's *Minstrelsy of the Scottish Border* and over the years developed a friendship with Scott. Scott writes of Sharpe in his *Journal*: 'He has infinite wit and a great turn for antiquarian lore as the publications of Kirkton etc. bear witness. His drawings are the most fanciful and droll imaginable—a mixture between Hogarth and some of those foreign masters who painted temptations of Saint Anthony and such grotesque subjects. As a poet he has not a very strong touch'—see *The Journal of Sir Walter Scott*, ed. by W. E. K. Anderson (Oxford: Oxford University Press, 1972), p. 2. Sharpe published a book of his own poetry, *Metrical Legends and other Poems* (1807), and he also edited *A Ballad Book* (1823). For additional information on Sharpe, see the *Oxford DNB* article by Patrick Cadell.

Sharpe had approached William Blackwood in 1815 about publishing the Kirkton volume. Sharpe and Blackwood clashed, however, over editorial control of the extensive notes that Sharpe included in the edition. Sharpe insisted that the publisher could not alter anything in his notes. Blackwood, on the other hand, was not willing to give up his publisher's prerogative to make editorial suggestions. Blackwood wrote to Sharpe:

You state as your *sine qua non* that you will not cancel a single line of these notes. Now, I hope you will pardon me for saying that if I understand you rightly this is so much *en cavalier* that I cannot without some explanation publish a work where I conceive myself to be so very differently treated from what I have always been by the authors with whom I have had the honour to be connected. I have always been accustomed to take an interest in the literary department of my business, and however trifling my suggestions may have been, I have had them considered and attended to by men of no small note. (Mrs. Oliphant, *Annals of a Publishing House*, 2 vols (Edinburgh: William Blackwood, 1897), I, 54)

Sharpe responded by insulting Blackwood with a suggestion of Blackwood's inferior social standing. Blackwood then ended the negotiations, writing to Sharpe that 'it was quite unnecessary for you to propose anew my publishing "Kirkton." I should never be able to duly appreciate the "distinctions of society" and the "punctilios," which really I was not aware of' (Oliphant, I, 54–55). It was probably this exchange that led to Sharpe's being parodied in the 'Chaldee Manuscript': 'But behold, while they were yet speaking, they heard a voice of one screeching at the gate, and the voice was a sharp voice, even like the voice of the unclean bird which buildeth its nest in the corner of the temple, and defileth the holy places. ¶But they opened not the door, neither answered they a word to the voice of its screaming. So the unclean thing flew away, neither could they find any trace of its going' (see 35, I. 62–63 in the present edition and notes).

As Peter Garside notes in his Introduction to *Confessions*, the publication of Kirkton's *History* was actually born in the fire of ideological opposition in contemporary Edinburgh. [...] The publication of Walter Scott's *Old Mortality* (1816), at the end of the preceding year, had triggered an intense debate over this period, with Thomas McCrie in the *Edinburgh Christian Instructor* attempting to vindicate the Presbyterian Covenanters against Scott's allegedly demeaning portrayal, and Scott himself through anonymous self-reviewal in the Tory *Quarterly Review* countering with fresh documentary evidence. Aware that McCrie might be contemplating an edition of Kirkton, from a manuscript in the Advocates' Library, Scott set out to pre-empt the situation by encouraging his friend Sharpe to undertake the work himself. (p. xxxvi)

Sharpe was a Tory and a member of the Church of England, so Sharpe's politics and theology were diametrically opposed to those of Kirkton and the Covenanters. Kirkton's *History* provides a sympathetic chronicle of the struggles of the Covenanters to 1678, but Sharpe's notes to Kirkton's text introduce sources that often provide conflicting perspectives from those of Kirkton and, in Hogg's opinion, deliberately provide unnecessarily disparaging views of the Covenanters. Even Walter Scott, whose political views were more closely-allied with those of Sharpe than Kirkton—and who was in part responsible for Sharpe's edition—thought Sharpe tended to overstep the bounds of decency in some of his historical investigations. Scott's assessment of Sharpe's character in his *Journal* applies to Sharpe's editing of Kirkton: '[Sharpe] is a very complete genealogist and has made many detections in Douglas [*Peerage of Scotland*] and other books on pedigree which our nobles would do well to suppress if they had an opportunity. Strange that a man should be curious after Scandal of centuries old' (*Journal*, p. 2).

Hogg had entered the covenanting debate with the publication of his review of Sharpe's edition of Kirkton, but Hogg's role in the debate would soon take on greater proportions. At the time of the publication of this review, Hogg was busily preparing for publication with William Blackwood *The Brownie of Bodsbeck* (1818), Hogg's sympathetic portrayal of the history of the Covenanters (see the note for 50(b) below). However, Garside also sees in Hogg's review of Sharpe a source for Hogg's narrative voices in *Confessions*. Hogg criticises Sharpe's editorial method and style, which pretend reasoned historical objectivity in contrast to the fanatical bias of Kirkton; the truth is, Hogg argues, Sharpe's annotations are 'a medley of base ribaldry, profane stuff, and blasphemous inuendos' in contrast to 'the manly narrative of honest Kirkton'. Garside writes: 'It is difficult not to sense some resemblance between this and the juxtaposition within *Confessions* of the editorial "objective" viewpoint, written from a modern North British standpoint, and the first-person, biblically-charged (yet vulnerable) voice which drives on Robert Wringhim's "Memoirs"' (p. xxxvii). Thus, *Confessions* can be seen as Hogg's most important comment on the Covenanting debate, a point effectively argued by Douglas Mack in his book, *Scottish Fiction and the British Empire* (Edinburgh: Edinburgh University Press, 2006), pp. 159–66.

Although Hogg disagreed with Sharpe's editorial practice in handling Kirkton's *History*, that disagreement did not become a barrier to a friendly relationship with Sharpe. Hogg soon (November 1818) applied to Sharpe for assistance with the engraver for his subscription edition of *The Queen's Wake* (*Letters 1*, p. 390), for which Sharpe also provided an illustration to 'The Witch of Fife'; Hogg acknowledges Sharpe's assistance in his *Memoir*: 'the *fifth edition* of the

"Queen's Wake," in royal octavo, with plates, was a plan concocted by Mr. Blackwood to bring me in a little money. He was assisted in this undertaking by Charles Sharpe, Esq., Mr. Walter Scott, and several other friends' (pp. 33–34).

The present edition publishes the *BEM* text without emendation.

**47**(c) **your edition** [...] **was announced** the work was announced in the April 1817 issue of *BEM* (p. 89) under 'Works Preparing for Publication'.

**48**(a) **intercommuned Whig** Covenanter, a supporter of the National Covenant of 1638 and Solemn League and Covenant of 1643. The Covenanters pledged to uphold Scottish Presbyterianism and opposed King Charles I's efforts to impose the English church's forms of worship on the Scots. Under the Solemn League and Covenant the Scottish Presbyterians agreed to support the English Parliament in opposition to King Charles I in return for the English adopting Presbyterianism. After the Restoration, Charles II restored the Episcopal form of government to the Scottish church and required ministers to accept an oath of allegiance to the king and the authority of the bishops in the church. Conventicles were outlawed, so that the Covenanters were 'intercommuned' if they failed to conform to the Episcopal jurisdiction re-imposed by the king. It is this period, when the Covenanters were outlawed for failing to adhere to the restrictions placed on the practice of their religion, that Kirkton covers in his *History.*

**48**(b) **the council** the Scottish Privy Council, which was the ruling arm of King Charles II in Scotland.

**48**(b) **higher degree of credit** [...] **raked up in a subsequent age** Walter Scott concludes the opening (preliminary) chapter of *The Tale of Old Mortality* by quoting John Hume's *Douglas: A Tragedy* and exclaiming 'Peace to [the] memory!' of both sides of the covenanting struggle: 'Let us think of them as the heroine of our only Scottish tragedy entreats her lord to think of her departed sire, "O, rake not up the ashes of our fathers! | Implacable resentment was their crime, | And grievous has the expiation been"'–see Walter Scott, *The Tale of Old Mortality*, ed. by Douglas Mack (Edinburgh: Edinburgh University Press, 1993), p. 14. Hogg echoes this sentiment again in *The Three Perils of Woman*, as Antony Hasler discusses in his Introduction to the S/SC edition of the novel (pp. xxiii–xxviii). Acknowledgment is made to Douglas Mack for calling this to the present editor's attention.

**49**(d) **Cameronian** follower of Richard Cameron (*d.* 1680), covenanting field preacher. Cameron, a native of Fife, attended St Andrews University. He was a schoolmaster and held some private chaplaincy posts before becoming licensed to preach by a group of ministers outside of the mainstream of the Church of Scotland. Cameron had a dedicated following of extremists, in spite of the violent attacks on the Covenanters by government forces. In June 1680 Cameron drew up what became know as the Sanquhar Declaration, which denounced the tyrannical Charles II and disavowed allegiance to him. A month later Cameron was hunted down and killed by government troops. (For additional information, see A. S. Wayne Pearce's article on Cameron in the *Oxford DNB.*)

**49**(d) **Donald Cargill** (*c.* 1627–81) preacher and covenanting leader. Cargill originally intended to practice law with his father, but after a religious conversion experience he attended the University of St Andrews to prepare for the ministry. Cargill's extreme religious and political views made it difficult for him to secure a call to a church, but finally in 1655 became minister of the Barony Church in Glasgow. After the Restoration, Cargill continued to oppose the monarchy and the Episcopal church in Scotland. He was banished from Glasgow parishes in 1662 and in 1674 was outlawed for unauthorised preaching. Cargill was wounded at the battle at Bothwell Bridge in 1679, but escaped to the Netherlands for a few months. He returned to Scotland later in 1679 and joined Richard Cameron in field preaching and leading the Covenanters. He was finally captured in 1682, tried for treason, and executed in Edinburgh. (For additional information, see John Callow's article on Cargill in the *Oxford DNB*.)

**49(d) Francis Macmillan** unidentified. Perhaps Hogg meant John Macmillan (1669–1753), who was ordained as a Church of Scotland minister in 1700. Macmillan's adherence to the principles of the covenanting movement resulted in his being dismissed from the Presbyterian church for his divisive behaviour, although he continued to minister to his loyal parishioners. In 1712, preaching before a large crowd of covenanting sympathisers, Macmillan went so far as to excommunicate the Queen and the Parliament, which 'caused a stir in Scotland as Macmillan consciously identified himself as a successor to former covenanting leaders, such as Donald Cargill' (see 'John Macmillan' by Derek B. Murray, *Oxford DNB*).

**50(b) set of men in the present day [...] caricature humble zeal** Hogg is probably including Sir Walter Scott, whose novel *The Tale of Old Mortality* had been published in December 1816. Hogg had taken issue with Scott's negative portrayal of the Covenanters in *Old Mortality*, as well as a picture of government forces that Hogg considered too sympathetic and false. At the time Hogg was writing the 'Letter to Sharpe', he was also preparing for publication with Blackwood *The Brownie of Bodsbeck; And Other Tales*. Hogg's *Brownie*, set in the time of Kirkton's *History*, is more closely aligned with the political sympathies of Kirkton than with Sharpe or Scott. In his *Anecdotes of Scott*, Hogg relates a visit with Scott in which Scott is critical of Hogg's *Brownie* as 'a false and unfair picture of the times and the existing characters altogether An exhaggerated and unfair picture!' Hogg replies to Scott:

'I dinna ken Mr Scott. It is the picture I hae been bred up in the belief o' sin' ever I was born and I had it frae them whom I was most bound to honour and believe. An' mair nor that there is not one single incident in the tale—not one—which I cannot prove from history to be literally and positively true. I was obliged sometimes to change the situations to make one part coalesce with another but in no one instance have I related a story of a cruelty or a murder which is not literally true. An' that's a great deal mair than you can say for your tale o' Auld Mortality. (pp. 50–51)

John Lockhart, too, initially expressed an opinion of Scott's *Old Mortality* that concurred with Hogg's assessment. In a letter to Jonathan Christie, Lockhart writes that *Old Mortality* is 'delightful [...] but I have, unfortunately, read too much of the history of that period to approve of the gross violations of historical truth which he has taken the liberty—often, I think, without gaining anything by it—to introduce. [...] Claverhouse's original letters I have seen— they are vulgar and bloody, without anything of the air of a polished man, far less of a sentimental cavalier in them'—see Andrew Lang, *Life and Letters of John Gibson Lockhart*, 2 vols (London: Nimmo, 1897), I, 114–15.

**50 (d) this refined, reasoning, and deistical generation** Hogg further develops his ideas on this subject in his sermon 'Deistical Reformers'. See *A Series of Lay Sermons on Good Principles and Good Breeding*, ed. by Gillian Hughes with Douglas S. Mack (S/SC, 1997), pp. 108–20.

**50 (d) rude forefathers of the hamlet** from line 16 of Thomas Gray's 'Elegy Written in a Country Churchyard': 'The rude forefathers of the hamlet sleep'.

**51 (a) not one hair of their heads shall fall to the ground** from I Kings 1. 52: 'And Solomon said, If he will shew himself a worthy man, there shall not an hair of him fall to the earth'.

**51 (c) revered and worthy old friend** unidentified and probably a fiction. In spite of the author's claims that the conversation 'is no fabricated speech, in order to discredit' Sharpe's work, it is likely that Hogg did fabricate the dialogue in order to provide a distancing voice to speak his harshest criticism.

**52 (b) But nothing can be more unfair [...] fanatically violent or ignorant** Hogg also defends the motives and behaviour of the majority of the Covenanters against the improper actions of a few in *The Brownie of Bodsbeck*: 'In like manner, because some of the Covenanters said violent and culpable things, and did worse, it is hard to blame the whole body for these; for, in the scattered prowling way in which they were driven to subsist, they had no controul over individuals'–see *The Brownie of Bodsbeck*, ed. by Douglas S. Mack (Edinburgh: Scottish Academic Press, 1976), p. 75.

**53 (a) Mr John Ballantyne** (1774–1821) was the Edinburgh publisher of *The Secret and True History*. See also the note for 42, IV. 20 in the present edition. Walter Scott was a major partner in Ballantyne's publishing firm.

**53 (b) Dainty Davie** David Williamson (*d.* 1706), covenanting minister. Sharpe's note relates Williamson's reputation for 'frequenting brothel-houses' and his having been married seven times (pp. 350–51). Sharpe quotes the *Memoirs of Captain John Creighton*:

> My first action [...] after being taken into the guards, was with a dozen gentlemen more to go in quest of Mr David Williamson, a noted covenanter, since made more famous in the book called the Scotch Presbyterian Eloquence. I had been assured that this Williamson did much frequent the house of my Lady Cherrytrees, (within ten miles of Edinburgh), but when I arrived first with my party about the house, the lady well knowing our errand, put Williamson to bed to her daughter, disguised in a woman's night-dress: When the troopers went to search in the young lady's room, her mother pretended that she was not well; and Williamson so managed the matter, that when the daughter raised herself a little in the bed to let the troopers see her, they did not discover him, and so went off disappointed; but the young lady proved with child, and Williamson, to take off the scandal, married her in some time after. (p. 349n)

'Dainty Davie' was a popular subject of the ballad tradition. The version that appeared in David Herd's *Ancient and Modern Scottish Songs, Heroic Ballads, etc.* follows; the Herd text includes this note: 'The following song was made upon Mess David Williamson, on his getting with child the Lady Cherrytree's daughter, while the soldiers were searching the house to apprehend him for a rebel'–2 vols (Glasgow: Ker & Richardson, 1869), II, 215.

O LEEZE me on your curly pow,
  Dainty DAVIE, dainty DAVIE;
Leeze me on your curly pow,
  Mine ain dainty DAVIE.

It was in and through the window broads,
  And a' the tirlie wirlies o'd;
The sweetest kiss that e'er I got,
  Was frae my dainty DAVIE.
*O leeze me on your curly pow, &c.*

It was down among my dady's pease,
  And underneath the cherry-trees;
O there he kist me as he pleas'd,
  For he was mine ain dear DAVIE.
*O leeze me on your curly pow, &c.*

When he was chas'd by a dragoon,
  Into my bed he was laid down;
I thought him wordy o' his room,
  And he's ay my dainty DAVIE.
*O leeze me on your curly pow, &c.*

Dainty Davie was also the subject of a Burns song (Kinsley 424).

**53(b) Ebenezer** in I Samuel 7. 12, Samuel set a stone as a memorial to mark the defeat of the Philistines by Israel; he called the stone Eben-ezer, the stone of help. 'Ebenezer' came to be used as a slang term for 'penis', and Sharpe gratuitously introduces this suggestive use of Ebenezer in his notes. Sharpe's note to Kirkton's mention of John Blackadder's having died in prison reads, in part: 'He had a son, Colonel Blackadder, a soldier in the Duke of Marlborough's army, who wrote his own Memoirs, which have been printed. He was as great a fanatic as his father, pretending that Heaven inspired him with means to cure himself of the tooth-ache [...] and in his epistolary correspondence, he tells his wife and another gentlewoman that he hath still his Ebenezer before him, which I dare say they were very glad to hear, considering the dangers of war' (pp. 361–62n).

**53(b) John Knox in the kiln-logie** Sharpe quotes Edinburgh town council records for 18 June 1563 regarding Eufame Dundas, who 'had spoken divers injurious and sclandarous wordis baith of doctrine and ministeris: and in especiall of Jhonne Knox, minister, sayand, that within few dayis past, the said Jhonne Knox was apprehendit and tane furth of ane killogye with ane commoun hure; and that he had bene ane commone harlot all his dayis' (p. 22n). A 'kiln-logie', or 'killogie', is a kiln, although the term is used variously to apply to different parts of a kiln, such as the covered space in front of a kiln or the space underneath the drying chamber of a kiln (*SND*).

**53(b) stories about servant lasses, ladies' petticoats** Sharpe, for example, quotes from Lord Fountainhall's manuscripts to counter charges Kirkton levels against Episcopal clergy: 'Mr John M'Queen, one of the ministers of Edinburgh, in Dec. 1683, having by trapane got a petycoat of Euphame Scott's, after Lady Eymouth, (and spous to Wynram of Eymouth, who is now broken, and she dead,) with whom he was deadly in love, tho' she hated him, he made thereof a wastecoat and drawers; for which he was suspended: but the Bishop of Edinburgh, Paterson, reponed him in Feb.

1684' (pp. 184–85n). Sharpe also notes that a 'Mr Duncan, a minister in Perthshire, is condemned to death by the Earl of Perth, as stewart of Crieff, for murdering an infant begotten by him in fornication with his servant maid' (p. 187n). He also relates a story of the Reverend Alexander Peden from *The Life and Prophecies of the Rev. Mr Alexander Peden*: 'When he was about to enter the ministry, a young woman fell to be with child in adultery, a servant in the house where he staid. When she found herself to be with child, she told the father thereof. He said, "I'll run for it, and go to Ireland. Father it upon Mr Peden; he has more to help thee and bring it up (he having a piece of heritage) than I have"' (pp. 264–65n).

53 (b) **fastidious in these matters to a fault** Hogg himself was often a victim of the 'fastidious' critics, especially William Blackwood himself, who was easily offended by Hogg's sexual innuendoes. For example, see the notes to 'The Brakens wi' Me', 'Dramas of Simple Life No. II', and 'The Marvellous Doctor' in the present edition.

54 (a) **Berwickshire and Northumberland** neighbouring counties on the northeast coast of Britain. Berwickshire is in Scotland and Northumberland in England.

54 (a) **best educated and instructed [...] highest sense of religion** John Knox initiated efforts to establish a national system of education in Scotland in order to insure the continued success of the Reformed Church in Scotland. Knox argued that people 'are born ignorant of all godliness' and, therefore, the nation's leadership 'must be most careful for the virtuous education and godly upbringing of the youth of this Realm'—see Knox, *John Knox's History of the Reformation in Scotland*, ed. by William Croft Dickinson, 2 vols (London: Thomas Nelson, 1949), II, 295. The Bible and the Church of Scotland's Catechism remained standard texts in the schools in Scotland into the nineteenth century. See also 'Examination of the School of Southside', pp. 146–52 in the present edition, and notes.

54 (b) **fed only on the crumbs that fell from his table** echoes Luke 16. 20–21: 'And there was a certain beggar named Lazarus, which was laid at [the rich man's] gate, full of sores, And desiring to be fed with the crumbs which fell from the rich man's table'.

54 (d) **as Burns says** the lines quoted are from Robert Burns's poem 'The Dumfries Volunteers', published in the *Edinburgh Courant*, 4 May 1795, and the *Dumfries Journal*, 5 May 1795. In the second line of the quoted stanza, the *BEM* article prints *soil* in place of the original *spoil* (Kinsley 484).

54 (d) **Your friend, M. M.** pseudonymous initials were often used to sign articles in *BEM*. The initials 'M. M.' probably refer to 'Mordecai Mullion', a fictitious name also used by John Wilson and John Lockhart.

### A Hebrew Melody

'A Hebrew Melody' is a love song that draws heavily on images from the biblical Song of Solomon. Hogg sent the song to William Blackwood on 5 January 1818: 'Along with Scott's and Laidlaw's contributions to your miscellany I also inclose my mite a little Hebrew Melody which was written for a London work but not yet published' (*Letters 1*, p. 323). Although Hogg was not aware of it, the song probably had already been published in the collection of eight 'Hebrew' poems by Hogg, *A Selection of German Hebrew Melodies* [*c*. 1817], pp. 15-23, that included harmonised musical scores. The songs of the *Hebrew Melodies*

may have been written as early as 1815, however, when Hogg was 'applied to
by a celebrated composer of music, in the name of a certain company in
London, to supply verses, suiting some ancient Hebrew Melodies, selected in
the synagogues of Germany' (*Memoir*, p. 51). Byron's *A Selection of Hebrew Melodies*
was also published in 1815, and Hogg was probably influenced by the popularity
of Byron's work; Hogg wrote to John Murray, Byron's publisher, on 7 May
1815: 'people are commending some of Lord Byron's melodies as incomparably
beautiful' (*Letters 1*, p. 249).

The title of the song in *Hebrew Melodies* is 'The Rose of Sharon'. 'A Hebrew
Melody' was published in *Blackwood's Edinburgh Magazine*, 2 (January 1818),
400, with only minor revisions, most of which can be attributed to editorial
preferences for punctuation rather than Hogg's rethinking of text. Hogg's
authorship is acknowledged in *BEM* with the by-line 'By the Ettrick Shepherd'.
The song was included in the 1822 *Poetical Works* (IV, 212–14) as 'The Rose of
Sharon' and there largely follows the *Hebrew Melodies* version.

The present edition follows the *BEM* printing without emendation.

**55, ll. 1–2 rose of the East [...] valley of Sharon** from Song of Solomon 2. 1:
'I am the rose of Sharon, and the lily of the valleys'. Sharon is a plain on the
Mediterranean coast of Israel south of Mt Carmel and north of Joppa.

**55, l. 3 Judah** the southern kingdom of the Israelites, expanded from the
home of the tribe of Judah and ruled by the descendants of Solomon.

**55, l. 8 For my heart it is sick for my love** from Song of Solomon 5. 8: 'if ye
find my beloved, that ye tell him, that I am sick of love'.

**55, ll. 11–12 the roes and the hinds [...] till she please** from Song of Solomon
2. 7: 'I charge you, O ye daughters of Jerusalem, by the roes, and by the
hinds of the field, that ye stir not up, nor awake my love, till he please'. See
also Song of Solomon 3. 5, 5. 8, and 8. 4.

**55, l. 16 Zion** another name for Jerusalem and sometimes used to refer to the
people. See Song of Solomon 3. 11.

**55, l. 22 Her teeth are the lambs on the hill** Song of Solomon 4. 2: 'Thy teeth
are like a flock of sheep that are even shorn'. See also Song of Solomon 6.
6.

**55, ll. 23–24 Her breasts two young roes [...] vallies at will** from Song of
Solomon 4. 5: 'Thy two breasts are like two young roes that are twins,
which feed among the lilies'.

**55, l. 27 tower of Damascus** Song of Solomon 7. 4: 'the tower of Lebanon
which looketh toward Damascus'. Damascus is the capital of present-day
Syria.

**55, l. 32 my bosom is ravished with love** echoes Song of Solomon 4. 9:
'Thou hast ravished my heart, my sister, my spouse'.

**56, ll. 34–36 couch on Amana [...] From Shinar and Hermon [...] mountains
of leopards** Song of Solomon 4. 8: 'look from the top of Amana, from the
top of Shenir and Hermon, from the lions' dens, from the mountains of the
leopards'. Amana is the northern ridge of the Antilibanus range of mountains;
Hermon is a mountain at the southern end of the range. Shenir is an
Amorite name for Mt Hermon.

**56, l. 37 Shulamite** a female character in the Song of Solomon. The name
possibly refers to an inhabitant of Shunem, but it might also be a feminine
form of Solomon. See Song of Solomon 6. 13.

**56, l. 40 the singing of birds is at hand** from Song of Solomon 2. 12: 'the time of the singing of birds is come'.

### The Ettrick Shepherd not the Author of the Poetic Mirror

In the notices 'To Correspondents' that appear on the reverse of the title page in the January 1818 number of *Blackwood's Edinburgh Magazine*, the editor announces that '"The Ettrick Shepherd not the Author of the Poetic Mirror," is under consideration'. The work was not published in *BEM*, however, and apparently was not published elsewhere in Hogg's lifetime. 'The Ettrick Shepherd not the Author of the Poetic Mirror' is included in the present edition because Hogg clearly intended the work for publication in *BEM*. Unfortunately, the full text of the work has not been preserved; the work is printed herein from the fragment of Hogg's manuscript that is preserved in the National Library of Scotland as MS 2245, fols 301–02. The manuscript consists of the last two pages of Hogg's work, numbered 5 and 6, on paper watermarked EVANS & SONS | 1814. Hogg signed the manuscript with the pseudonym 'J. P. Anderson'. 'The Ettrick Shepherd not the Author of the Poetic Mirror' was first published in the S/SC edition of Hogg's *Collected Letters* (*Letters 1*, 320–22); the annotations for the work in the present edition are indebted to Gillian Hughes's published annotations for *Letters 1*, as well as her unpublished advice.

Hogg's volume of poetic parodies, *The Poetic Mirror, or The Living Bards of Britain*, was published anonymously by Ballantyne in Edinburgh and Longman in London in October 1816, followed by a second edition in December 1816. In 1814 Hogg had proposed to publish a 'poetical repository', a semi-annual periodical that would include works from the leading poets of the age. Hogg explained his original plan in a letter to Robert Southey, 4 June 1814: 'now that the rage for politics is somewhat subsided and as people who have been used to read must still read something I propose in conjunction with some literary friends to establish a *poetical repository* in Edin. to be continued half-yearly price 5/ One part of it is to consist of original poetry and the remainder to be filled up with short reviews or characters of every *poetical* work published in the interim' (*Letters 1*, p. 181). Hogg's project did not proceed as he had hoped; he was disappointed by the contributions that he had received, as well as by the neglect of the project by some authors, such as Walter Scott. Hogg wrote in his *Memoir*:

> I began, with a heavy heart, to look over the pieces I had received, and lost all hope of the success of my project. They were, indeed, all very well; but I did not see that they possessed such merit as could give celebrity to any work; and after considering them well, I fancied that I could write a better poem than any that had been sent or would be sent to me, and this so completely in the style of each poet, that it should not be known but for his own production. It was this conceit that suggested to me the idea of "The Poetic Mirror, or Living Bards of Britain." I set to work with great glee, as the fancy had struck me, and in a few days I finished my imitations of Wordsworth and Lord Byron. (p. 40)

Hogg, then, wrote all of the poetic imitations in *The Poetic Mirror* except for 'Epistle to Mr R– S * * * *', which was written by Thomas Pringle and which had been sent to Hogg to be published in the 'poetical repository' according to Hogg's original intentions. Hogg, however, included Pringle's work in the *Poetic Mirror* as an imitation of Walter Scott's poetry. On the title page of *The Poetic Mirror* Hogg offers a subtle hint about the fabricated authorship of the poems with the quotation from Shakespeare's *The Winter's Tale* (IV. 4. 264–65): '*Mopsa.*– Is it true think you? | *Auti.*–Very true, and but a month old'. Yet, in the 'Advertisement' to the first edition of *The Poetic Mirror*, Hogg wears the mask of his original 'poetical repository' editorship, maintaining that the poems printed in *The Poetic Mirror* were collected from the 'Bards' themselves:

> A number of years have now elapsed since [the Editor] first conceived the idea of procuring something original from each of the principal living Bards of Britain, and publishing those together, judging that such a work, however small, could not fail of forming a curiosity in literature. On applying to them all personally, or by letter, he found that the greater part of them entered into his views with more cordiality than he had reason to expect; and, after many delays and disappointments, he is at last enabled to give this volume to the public. He regrets that there are many of the living Poets, whom he highly esteems, that have not yet complied with his request; but as he is almost certain of something from each of them being forthcoming, he hopes, at no distant period, to be able to lay before the world another volume, at least more diversified than the present. (pp. iii–iv)

'The Ettrick Shepherd not the Author of the Poetic Mirror' seems to be an effort by Hogg to further the sport of *The Poetic Mirror* and, as Gillian Hughes argues, to continue the 'deliberate mystification surrounding the publication of *The Poetic Mirror*' (*Letters 1*, p. 321n).

'The Ettrick Shepherd not the Author of the Poetic Mirror' is published in the present edition from the NLS manuscript without emendation.

**56(b) effect *as the production of Lord Byron,* [...] all the company** the surviving fragment of this manuscript opens as the fictitious author of 'The Ettrick Shepherd not the Author of the Poetic Mirror', 'J. P. Anderson | Corseknock by Carlisle', seems to conclude the story of the pretended authentication of 'The Guerilla' by the Edinburgh literati. Anderson's story echoes the story Hogg tells in his *Memoir* of his sport with the poem: 'I had got the poem transcribed, and gave it to Mr. Ballantyne to read, who did it ample justice. Indeed, he read it with extraordinary effect; so much so, that I was astonished at the poem myself, and before it was half done all pronounced it Byron's. Every one was deceived, except Mr. Ballantyne, who was not to be imposed on in that way; but he kept the secret until we got to the Bridge, and then he told me his mind' (pp. 40–41).

**56(b) Southey** Robert Southey (1774–1843), poet and historian, who became Poet Laureate in 1813. Southey's major poetical works include *Thalaba the Destroyer* (1801), *Madoc* (1805), *The Curse of Kehama* (1810), *Roderick, the Last of the Goths* (1814), and a translation of *Chronicle of the Cid* (1808). He wrote a popular *Life of Nelson* (1813), and he was also a major contributor to the *Quarterly Review*. Hogg had corresponded with Southey as early as 1811, and Southey had contributed a poem to Hogg's periodical *The Spy*. Hogg wrote to Southey on 4 June 1814 to request a poem for his 'repository', and Hogg notes in his *Memoir* that when he met Southey in Keswick in September 1814, Southey 'gave me, with the utmost readiness, a poem and a ballad of his own, for a work which I then projected' (pp. 65–66). In a letter to Hogg, 1 December 1814, Southey identifies the ballad as 'the Ballad of the Devil & the Bishop' (NLS, MS 2245, fols 7–8), but there is no mention of the other poem.

**56(c) Wordsworth [...] subsequent letter from that gentleman reclaiming it**
William Wordsworth (1770–1850). In his *Memoirs of a Literary Veteran*, 3 vols
(London: Richard Bentley, 1851), R. P. Gillies prints a letter from Wordsworth
to Gillies that suggests that Wordsworth sent Hogg a poem, 'Yarrow Visited',
for Hogg's proposed collection of poetry. However, Wordsworth made
extensive revisions to the earlier version that he had sent to Hogg, so he
requested through Gillies that Hogg not publish the original: 'You are a
most indulgent and good-natured critic, or I think you would hardly have
been so much pleased with "Yarrow Visited;" we think it heavier than my
things generally are, and nothing but a wish to show to Mr. Hogg that my
inclinations towards him and his proposed work were favourable, could
have induced me to part with it in that state. I have composed three new
stanzas in place of the three first, and another to be inserted before the two
last, and have made some alterations in other parts; therefore, when you
see Mr. Hogg, beg from me that he will not print the poem till he has read
the copy which I have added to Miss E. Wilson's MSS., as I scarcely doubt,
notwithstanding the bias of first impressions, that he will prefer it' (II, 148).
Hogg later wrote that he had 'often regretted' caricaturing Wordsworth in
*The Poetic Mirror* (*Memoir*, p. 68).

**56(c) Wilson** John Wilson. See also note to 40, II. 10. Hogg in his letter to
Byron, 3 June 1814, indicated that Wilson was among those poets 'of high
respect' who had 'already assented' to contribute to the project. Hogg also
notes that Wilson had agreed to be one of the editors, along with Hogg and
R. P. Gillies (*Letters 1*, p. 178).

**56(c–d) Mr Scott [...] cannot be supposed that he would be behind in such
a generous effort** Walter Scott was named along with Wilson and others in
Hogg's letter to Byron, 3 June 1814, as having agreed to contribute—see
note for 56(c) above. However, Hogg may have just assumed that Scott
would assist, but in fact Scott adamantly refused. Hogg knew that
contributions from Byron and/or Scott would be critical to the success of
his proposed 'poetical repository', so Hogg was not completely forthcoming
with Byron. Hogg wrote to Byron again on 30 July 1814 that he was
depending on Byron's 'generosity for less or more—So much indeed that till
I get it or am assured of it I will not venture the work to the press for I have
excused Mr. Scott for the first half year from a conviction that we both had
that your name in particular fairly ensured the sale of the first N°.' (*Letters 1*,
p. 191). Hogg confesses in his *Memoir* that he became very angry with Scott
for refusing to participate, and Hogg's tone suggests that even in 1832 the
resentment could be made to return:

> Mr. Walter Scott absolutely refused to furnish me with even one
> verse, which I took exceedingly ill, as it frustrated my whole plan.
> What occasioned it I do not know, as I accounted myself certain of
> his support from the beginning, and had never asked any thing of
> him in all my life that he refused. [...] He remained firm in his
> denial, which I thought very hard; so I left him in high dudgeon,
> sent him a very abusive letter, and would not speak to him again
> for many a day. I could not even endure to see him at a distance,
> I felt so degraded by the refusal; and I was, at that time, more
> disgusted with all mankind than I had ever been before, or have
> ever been since (p. 40).

**57(c) two volumes of dramas** Hogg's *Dramatic Tales*, 2 vols (London: Longman; Edinburgh: John Ballantyne, 1817). The authorship of *Dramatic Tales* is identified on the title page as 'by the author of "The Poetic Mirror"'.

## New Poetic Mirror

In the 'Advertisement' to the first edition of Hogg's anonymously-published collection of poetic parodies, *The Poetic Mirror, or The Living Bards of Britain* (Edinburgh: Ballantyne; London: Longman, 1816), Hogg notes that 'he hopes, at no distant period, to be able to lay before the world another volume, at least more diversified than the present' (p. iv). Hogg's second volume never appeared, however, although Hogg wrote several additional parodies in the same vein as those in *The Poetic Mirror*. Hogg published two of these parodies, or imitations, in the *Edinburgh Literary Journal* under the 'Poetic Mirror' title: 'A New Poetic Mirror. | *By the Ettrick Shepherd*. | No. I.–Mr W.W. | *Ode to a Highland Bee*', which appeared in the 5 September 1829, number (p. 199), and 'The New Poetic Mirror. | No. II.–MR T–. M–. | *By the Ettrick Shepherd*', which appeared in the number for 24 October 1829 (pp. 297–98). The two poems published in the present edition under the title 'New Poetic Mirror', '*Hamatory* Verses to a Cow' and 'To the Whore of Babylon', apparently were never published in Hogg's lifetime. The poems are included in the present edition because Hogg intended the works to be published in *Blackwood's Edinburgh Magazine*, and the manuscript of the 'New Poetic Mirror' is preserved among the Blackwood papers in the National Library of Scotland as MS 4805, fols 95–98. The manuscript consists of two sheets, each sheet measuring *c.* 22.5 cm x 37.4 cm and folded to make two folios of *c.* 22.5 cm x 18.7 cm. Hogg has numbered the pages [1]–7; '*Hamatory* Verses to a Cow' appears on pp. 1–3, and 'Whore of Babylon' appears on pp. 4–7. The paper is watermarked A MACGOUN | 1816.

Although the date of composition of the 'New Poetic Mirror' is uncertain, the poems appear to be much earlier than the publication dates of the 'New Poetic Mirror' works included in the *Edinburgh Literary Journal*. The watermark on the paper suggests an earlier date, as does the subject of the poems. The poems are purported to be by Leigh Hunt and parody Hunt's long poem, *The Story of Rimini*, which had been published in January 1816. The parodies also echo the themes of an essay by John Lockhart that appeared in the October 1817 number of *BEM* (vol. 2, pp. 38–41), 'On the Cockney School of Poetry'. It is possible that the 'New Poetic Mirror' poems were submitted to *BEM* as Hogg's intended contributions to what became a series of attacks on the 'Cockney School' in *BEM*. The placement of the poems in the present edition in early 1818, following 'The Ettrick Shepherd not the Author of the Poetic Mirror', therefore, is a reasonable, if uncertain, chronology.

Leigh Hunt (1784–1859), poet and critic, was editor of *The Examiner*, a reformist periodical that was established by his brother, John, in 1808. The Hunts' published liberal political views upset the government, and in late 1812 they were convicted of libelling the Prince of Wales. During his two years in prison Leigh Hunt wrote a great deal of poetry, including his most ambitious poetical work, *The Story of Rimini*. *Rimini* is based on a story from Dante's *Inferno* of an adulterous love affair between Francesca da Rimini and Paulo, the brother of Francesca's husband, Gianciotto Malatesta. The Tory *BEM*, through Lockhart's essay on the 'Cockney School', attacked the vulgarity of both the poem and the poet: 'The poetry of Mr Hunt is such as might be expected from the personal character and habits of its author. As a vulgar man is perpetually labouring to be genteel—in like manner the poetry of the man is always on a stretch to be grand' (p. 39). While acknowledging that *Rimini* 'possesses some tolerable passages' (p. 38), Lockhart writes that the poem as a whole is 'pretence, affectation, finery, and gaudiness' (p. 39). Lockhart also objects to the author's treatment of the sexual themes of the story: 'The author has voluntarily chosen—a subject not of simple seduction alone—one in which his mind seems absolutely to gloat over all the details of adultery and incest' (p. 40). Hogg, though, by choosing parody as a form for his attacks on Hunt, writes in a comic rather than a serious tone, and effectively renders Hunt's poem absurd by ridiculing Hunt's verse in Hunt's own words. Hogg's 'New Poetic Mirror' in large measure lifts Hunt's language directly from *Rimini* and artfully rearranges the borrowed lines to create the satire. Of the 140 total lines in the two poems of 'New Poetic Mirror', 107 lines have been taken verbatim, or substantially so, from *The Story of Rimini.* Hogg also ridicules the speech patterns of the Cockneys, such as adding an 'h' to words beginning with a vowel sound, dropping the 'h' from words beginning with an 'h', and changing the 'v' sound to 'w'.

For further discussion of *The Poetic Mirror* and Hogg's later parodies, including the manuscript poems of the 'New Poetic Mirror', see David Groves, *James Hogg: Poetic Mirrors* (Frankfurt: Peter Lang, 1990). In the notes that follow, the references to *The Story of Rimini; a Poem* are to the first edition (London: Murray; Edinburgh: Blackwood; Dublin: Cumming, 1816). The *Rimini* references include the canto number and line numbers followed by the page number.

The present edition follows the manuscript version of the 'New Poetic Mirror' without emendation.

**58, ll. 5–6 Thy tail of rural white [...] coronet of pearls** from *Rimini*, 1. 123–24 (p. 10): 'The dress of bridal white, and the dark curls | Bedding an airy coronet of pearls?'

**58, ll. 11–12 O hide me [...] bosom's fragrant sighs** from *Rimini*, 1. 121–22 (p. 10): 'What need I tell of lovely lips and eyes, | A clipsome waist, and bosom's balmy rise'.

**58, ll. 15–18 There *his* not [...] call thee his.** from *Rimini*, 1. 125–28 (p. 10):
>There's not in all that crowd one gallant being,
>Whom if his heart were whole, and rank agreeing,
>It would not fire to twice of what he is,
>To clasp her to his heart, and call her his.

**58, ll. 19-22 Thy *hardent* keen [...] the *hopen* grin** from *Rimini*, 1. 117–20 (p. 10):
>With that, a keen and quivering glance of tears
>Scarce moves her patient mouth, and disappears;
>A smile is underneath, and breaks away,
>And round she looks and breathes, as best befits the day.

**58, ll. 25–28 When I walk out [...] *houtlines* in the sun** from *Rimini*, 3. 504–07 (p. 72):
>One day,—'twas on a summer afternoon,
>When airs and gurgling brooks are best in tune,
>And grasshoppers are loud, and day-work done,
>And shades have heavy outlines in the sun.

**58, ll. 29–30 If thou art [...] bottom that I fear** from *Rimini*, 3. 529–30 (p. 73): 'Painfully clear those rising thoughts appeared, | With something dark at bottom that she feared'.

**58, ll. 31–32 When as I stroll [...] thick short grass,** from *Rimini*, 3. 253–54 (p. 57): 'And did he stroll into some lonely place, | Under the trees, upon the thick soft grass'.

**58, ll. 33–34 And hear thy voice [...] *hanthem* to the *wirgin*** from *Rimini*, 3. 498–99 (p. 72): 'Her gentle voice from out those shades emerging, | Singing the evening anthem to the Virgin'.

**58, ll. 35–38 I look *haround* me [...] my *'eart's* liberty** from *Rimini*, 3. 525–28 (p. 73):

> And looking round her with a new-born eye,
> As if some knowledge had been nigh,
> To taste of nature, primitive and free,
> And bask at ease in her heart's liberty.

**58–59, ll. 43–54 I cannot bear the loathed theme, to make [...] shall do to the last** from *Rimini*, 4. 2–15 (pp. 81–82):

> Should thus pursue a mournful theme, and make
> My very solace of distress partake.
> And I have longed sometimes, I must confess,
> To start at once from notes of wretchedness,
> And in a key would make you rise and dance,
> Strike up a blithe defiance to mischance.
> But work begun, an interest in it, shame
> At turning coward to the thoughts I frame,
> Necessity to keep firm face on sorrow,
> Some flattering, sweet-lipped question every morrow,
> And above all, the poet's task divine
> Of making tears themselves look up and shine,
> And turning to a charm the sorrow past,
> Have held me on, and shall do to the last.

**59, l. 56 under the sky-light glowing,** quoted from *Rimini*, 3. 574 (p. 76).

**59, ll. 57–58 And there [...] insects humming** from *Rimini*, 2. 202–03 (p. 36): 'Like a wild people at a stranger's coming; | Then hushing paths succeed, with insects humming'.

**59, ll. 59–62 With one permitted arm [...] touch together thrillingly!** from *Rimini*, 3. 591–94 (p. 77):

> And Paulo, by degrees, gently embraced
> With one permitted arm her lovely waist;
> And both their cheeks, like peaches on a tree,
> Leaned with a touch together, thrillingly.

**59, (title) Whore of Babylon** in the biblical book of Revelation, the Whore of Babylon is an allegorical figure representing immoral conduct. The image is from Revelation 17, especially verses 1–5: 'And there came one of the seven angels which had the seven vials, and talked with me, saying unto me, Come hither; I will shew unto thee the judgment of the great whore that sitteth upon many waters. [...] And upon her forehead was a name written, MYSTERY, BABYLON THE GREAT, THE MOTHER OF HARLOTS AND ABOMINATIONS OF THE EARTH'.

**59, ll. 1–2 Rich courtly figure [...] smiles and blushes** from *Rimini*, 1. 101–02 (p. 9): 'And all the listening looks, with nods and flushes, | Break round him into smiles and sparkling blushes'. The image of the 'courtly figure' of the

'Whore' is from Revelation 17. 4: 'And the woman was arrayed in purple and scarlet colour, and decked with gold and precious stones and pearls, having a golden cup in her hand full of abominations and filthiness of her fornication'.

**59, ll. 5–8 Never was nobler finish [...] smite across his heart** from *Rimini*, 1. 265–68 (p. 18):

> Never was nobler finish of fine sight;
> 'Twas like the coming of a shape of light;
> And every lovely gazer, with a start,
> Felt the quick pleasure smite across her heart.

**59, ll. 9–12 Pulls out his 'andkerchief [...] thy flowing air** from *Rimini*, 1. 277–81 (p. 19):

> Then for another and a deafening shout;
> And scarfs are waved, and flowers come fluttering out;
> And, shaken by the noise, the reeling air
> Sweeps with a giddy whirl among the fair,
> And whisks their garments, and their shining hair.

**59–60, ll. 17–28 Sweeter than snowy white [...] readable as open book!** from *Rimini*, 1. 286–97 (pp. 19–20):

> The rest in snowy white from the mid thigh:
> These catch the extrinsic and the common eye:
> But on his shape the gentler sight attends,
> Moves as he passes,—as he bends him, bends,—
> Watches his air, his gesture, and his face,
> And thinks it never saw such manly grace,
> So fine are his bare throat, and curls of black,—
> So lightsomely dropt in, his lordly back,—
> His thigh so fitted for the tilt or dance,
> So heaped with strength, and turned with elegance;
> But above all, so meaning is his look,
> Full, and as readable as open book.

**60, ll. 29–36 Yet there is nothing [...] blood can go** from *Rimini*, 3. 40–41, 46–51 (pp. 45, 46):

> Yet there was nothing in it one might call
> A stamp exclusive, or professional,—
> [...]
> A graceful nose was his, lightsomely brought
> Down from a forehead of clear-spirited thought;
> Wisdom looked sweet and inward from his eye;
> And round his mouth was sensibility:—
> It was a face, in short, seemed made to shew
> How far the genuine flesh and blood could go.

**60, ll. 41–48 Should we two meet [...] would be done divinely** from *Rimini*, 3. 127–30, 133–36 (pp. 50, 51):

> Was there a court-day, or a sparkling feast,
> Or better still,—in my ideas, at least,—
> A summer party to the greenwood shade,
> With lutes prepared, and cloth on herbage laid,
> [...]
> And made the time so exquisitely pass

With stories told with elbow on the grass,
Or touched the music in his turn so finely,
That all he did, they thought, was done divinely.

**60, ll. 50–58 The loose goats […] come creepingly** from *Rimini*, 3. 469, 472–75, 478–81 (pp. 70–71):

And goats with struggling horns and planted feet:
[…]
That shewed, in various scenes, the nymphs themselves;
Some by the water side on bowery shelves
Leaning at will,–some in the water sporting
With sides half swelling forth, and looks of courting,–
[…]
Some tying up their long moist hair,–some sleeping
Under the trees, with fauns and satyrs peeping,–
Or, sidelong-eyed, pretending not to see
The latter in the brakes come creepingly.

**60, ll. 61–62 There we should have […] bower-enshaded kisses** from *Rimini*, 3. 462–63 (p. 70): 'And lived with them in a long round of blisses, | Feasts, concerts, baths, and bower-enshaded kisses'.

**61, ll. 65–66 How would that look […] what I did,** from *Rimini*, 3. 601–02 (p. 77): 'That touch, at last, through every fibre slid; | And Paulo turned, scarce knowing what he did'.

**61, ll. 67–68 And sigh in whisper […] O yes–certainly!** from *Rimini*, 3. 583–84 (p. 76): 'A moment, as for breath, and then with free | And usual tone said, "O yes,–certainly."'

**61, ll. 69–72 I could not hold […] whate'er it is!!!** from *Rimini*, 3. 603–06 (p. 78):

Only he felt he could no more dissemble,
And kissed her, mouth to mouth, all in a tremble.
Sad were those hearts, and sweet was that long kiss:
Sacred be love from sight, whate'er it is.

**61, ll. 75–76 Thou could'st not chuse […] person than his brother.** from *Rimini*, 2. 40–41 (p. 27): 'And he might send and wed her by another,– | Of course, no less a person than his brother'.

### Further Anecdotes of the Shepherd's Dog

Hogg's 'Further Anecdotes of the Shepherd's Dog' was first published in *Blackwood's Edinburgh Magazine*, 2 (March 1818), 621–26. The sketch was written as a continuation of William Laidlaw's anecdote, 'Sagacity of a Shepherd's Dog', which had been published in the January 1818 number of *BEM*, vol. 2, pp. 417–21. Laidlaw wrote to William Blackwood on 5 January 1818, enclosing his article which, he said, 'will be a good introduction (if fit to be inserted) to a number of others from Hogg–for view of which he requested me to strike out a notice at the conclusion which would come better from him self afterwards' (NLS, MS 4003, fols 113–14). Laidlaw also enclosed with his letter Sir Walter Scott's article on gypsies and a letter from Hogg with which Hogg sends 'A Hebrew Melody' and a promise to do an article on the shepherd's dog for the next *BEM*: 'Now that Laidlaw has furnished one anecdote of the Shepherd's dog mine will follow better next month' (*Letters 1*, p. 323). Later, in an undated letter to Blackwood, Laidlaw again suggested that Hogg should furnish several dog anecdotes for *BEM*: 'I was extremely glad that you were pleased with the Preaching & the Dog—You will get some fine stories from Hog [sic] on that subject, & he will write them as fast as the A, B, C' (NLS, MS 4003, fols 125–26).

William Laidlaw (1779–1845) would have known Hogg's 'fine stories' of shepherds' dogs from a close friendship with Hogg, which at this time was of more than twenty-five years' standing. Hogg and Laidlaw had become friends when Hogg was a shepherd for William's father, James Laidlaw, a position Hogg held for ten years from 1790. William Laidlaw early on encouraged Hogg in his literary pursuits, and it was Laidlaw who made the connection between Hogg and Walter Scott when Scott was collecting ballads for his *Minstrelsy of the Scottish Border*. Hogg also included poems by Laidlaw in his 1810 collection, *The Forest Minstrel*. In 1817 Laidlaw became Scott's steward at Abbotsford, and Hogg encouraged William Blackwood to involve Laidlaw in Blackwood's magazine enterprises.

Hogg's 'Further Anecdotes of the Shepherd's Dog' concludes with the promise of a continuation of the anecdotes, a story about his dog Hector, 'when I have leisure' (p. 69(a) in the present edition). Hogg never published an article specifically following up 'Further Anecdotes'; however, six years later, in the February 1824 number of *BEM*, Hogg tells a story of Hector as an instalment of 'The Shepherd's Calendar' series: 'The Shepherd's Calendar. Class IV. Dogs', *BEM*, 15 (February 1824), 177–83. 'Further Anecdotes' was not reprinted in Hogg's lifetime as an independent sketch, but it was slightly revised and combined with 'Class IV. Dogs' to form a single story, 'The Shepherd's Dog', that was published in the second volume of Hogg's collection of stories and anecdotes, *The Shepherd's Calendar*, 2 vols (Edinburgh: Blackwood; London: Cadell, 1829), II, 293–326. 'The Shepherd's Dog' was reprinted in the 1836–37 *Tales and Sketches*, IV, 241–62, based on *The Shepherd's Calendar* version.

The editorial revisions for *The Shepherd's Calendar* publication, as well as the arrangement of texts, apparently were made by Hogg's nephew, Robert Hogg, at William Blackwood's request rather than by the author himself, although Hogg agreed to Robert's editorial authority; Hogg wrote to Blackwood that Robert had 'full liberty to prune as he likes and arrange as he likes' (*Letters 2*, p. 287). Robert eliminated the magazine-specific language of 'Further Anecdotes' and added two paragraphs at the beginning of the story that introduce the primary anecdote of Laidlaw's story. Robert also revised the end of 'Further Anecdotes' and the magazine beginning of 'Class IV. Dogs' to provide a clean transition to a unified story of 'The Shepherd's Dog'. Because 'Further Anecdotes of the Shepherd's Dog' was neither part of the original 'Shepherd's Calendar' series in *BEM* nor revised by Hogg's own hand for 'The Shepherd's Dog', Douglas Mack has not included it in the S/SC edition of *The Shepherd's Calendar* (1995). For a full discussion of Robert Hogg's role in editing *The Shepherd's Calendar*, see Douglas Mack's introduction to the S/SC edition.

The present edition follows the *BEM* printing without emendation.

**61**(c) ***Eltrieve-Lake*** Hogg's farm in Yarrow, which had been granted to Hogg in 1815 by the Duke of Buccleuch at a 'nominal' rent. For a full discussion of the history of Eltrive/Altrive and Hogg's connection to it, see Peter Garside, 'Hogg, Eltrive, and *Confessions*', *Studies in Hogg and his World*, 11 (2000), 5–24.

**61**(c) **former Number of your Miscellany** the January 1818 issue of *BEM*, which included William Laidlaw's 'Sagacity of a Shepherd's Dog'; Laidlaw's article was signed 'M'.

**61(c) John Hoy, was my uncle; that is, he was married to my mother's sister** Hoy was married to Agnes Laidlaw, younger sister of Hogg's mother, Margaret Laidlaw–see *Letters 1*, p. 330.

**62(b) *Nimble*, she of whom your Correspondent writes** Laidlaw's 'Sagacity of a Shepherd's Dog' focuses on an anecdote about Nimble, one of John Hoy's dogs. Hoy and his ewe-milkers were among the people who had assembled for the celebration of a 'Cameronian Sacrament' near Hoy's farm of Chapelhope. Rather than leave the worship service to gather the sheep, Hoy spoke instructions to his dog; those in attendance witnessed from a distance the extraordinary feat of Nimble's gathering the sheep from the hills and leading them into the 'bought' for milking.

**62(b) *the seventy-four*** the snow storms in the Scottish borders were especially heavy and frequent in January and February 1774. William John Napier in his book *A Treatise on Practical Store-Farming* (Edinburgh: Waugh and Innes, 1822), quotes Alexander Laidlaw's diary for 1774: 'There was a very severe storm of snow this year. All the sheep of this district were away in Annandale, or foddering; but I do not hear of very much loss, except by snow-mails' (p. 38).

**62(b) Chapelhope** located at the head of Loch of the Lowes, about four miles northwest of Ettrick. *The Brownie of Bodsbeck* (1818) is set in Chapelhope, and the shepherd of Chapelhope is named John Hoy.

**62(d) *The Middle*** Middle Hill is located about one mile west of Chapelhope.

**62(d) Ashiesteel** a farm on the Tweed, about four miles east of Innerleithen, formerly rented by Walter Scott before he moved to Abbotsford in 1811.

**63(c) on his way rejoicing** from Acts 8. 39: 'And when they were come up out of the water, the Spirit of the Lord caught away Philip, that the eunuch saw him no more; and he went on his way rejoicing'.

**64(c) shepherd for ten years on the same farm** Hogg wrote in his *Memoir*: 'At Whitsunday 1790, being still only in the eighteenth year of my age, I left Willenslee, and hired myself to Mr. Laidlaw of Black House, with whom I served as a shepherd for ten years' (p. 16). James Laidlaw of Blackhouse was the father of William Laidlaw. The Blackhouse farm was located on the Douglas Burn, which flows into Yarrow Water about a mile east of St Mary's Loch.

**64(c) the *short*, or *black-faced* breed** Michael J. H. Robson in *Sheep of the Borders* (Newcastleton: Robson, 1988) notes that the Blackface sheep, a hardy breed suited to the climate and terrain of the Borders, 'predominated in the upland Selkirkshire valleys of Yarrow and Ettrick, and were so identified with the area that they were given the old country name of "The Forest breed". This practice of giving the Blackface the name of the immediate locality, be it county–Tweeddale, Forest–or district–Tweedsmuir, Linton–suggests the antiquity of the link between breed and place' (p. 6). The introduction of the Cheviot breed (which were white faced and less hardy) into the Borders was a source of controversy among the shepherds and farmers. Hogg discusses the breeds of sheep in more detail in his *BEM* article, 'The Honourable Captain Napier and Ettrick Forest', pp. 96–137 of the present edition.

In *Familiar Anecdotes of Sir Walter Scott* Hogg tells an amusing story of his meeting with Sir Walter Scott at the farm of Ramseycleuch when Scott was collecting ballads for his *Minstrelsy of the Scottish Border*:

> During the sociality of the evening, the discourse ran very much on the different breeds of sheep, the everlasting drawback on the community of Ettrick Forest. The original black-faced forest breed being always denominated the *short sheep*, and the Cheviot breed the *long sheep*. The disputes at that time ran very high about the practicable profits of each. Mr. Scott, who had come into that remote district to visit a bard of Nature's own making and preserve what little fragments remained of the country's legendary lore, felt himself rather bored with the everlasting question of the long and short sheep. So, at length, putting on his most serious calculating face, he turned to Mr. Walter Brydon, and said, 'I am rather at a loss regarding the merits of this *very* important question. How long must a sheep actually measure to come under the denomination of *a long sheep?*'
>
> Mr. Brydon, who, in the simplicity of his heart, neither perceived the quiz nor the reproof, fell to answer with great sincerity, 'It's the woo', sir; it's the woo' that mak's the difference, the lang sheep hae the short woo' an' the short sheep hae the lang thing, an' these are just kind o' names we gie them, ye see'. (*Anecdotes of Scott*, pp. 38–39)

**64(c–d) lambs [...] that day taken from their dams** the lambs had just been weaned and separated from their mothers. It was important to keep the newly-weaned lambs separated from their mothers; were the lambs to reunite with their dams, they would return to nursing instead of grazing. In 'Dramas of Simple Life No. II' Hogg also includes an incident in which the 'lambs are come off and landit amang their mithers again'. See p. 221(a) in the present edition.

**65(b) the farm of Glen** about three and a half miles north of Blackhouse on the Quair Water in Traquair parish.

**65(b) the Black Cleuch** a ravine about two miles northwest of Blackhouse.

**66(a) place in Tweeddale, called Stanhope [...] fifteen miles** on a map Stanhope is about ten miles west of Blackhouse at the juncture of Stanhope Burn and the River Tweed; the terrain would have made Hogg's journey much longer. Tweeddale is another name for Peeblesshire.

**66(b) travel to yon sun [...] destined to do both the one and the other** an allusion to Hogg's poem *The Pilgrims of the Sun* (1815), which involves a journey to the sun.

**66(c) Manor Water** runs from near Dollar Law into the River Tweed about one mile southwest of Peebles. Manor Water is about half way between Stanhope and Blackhouse.

**67(a) outrageous ear for music** in 'The Honourable Captain Napier and Ettrick Forest', Hogg writes about the participation of the shepherds' dogs in worship and the dogs' 'most unequivocal organs of music' (p. 125(d) in the present edition).

**67(d) tax upon my master** Elaine Petrie explains in the notes to her edition of Hogg's *Scottish Pastorals* (Stirling: Stirling University Press, 1988):

> The 'Act for granting to His Majesty certain Duties on Dogs', 5 July 1796, was another tax aimed at property owners and was designed to help fund the war effort. The fees were: five shillings (a crown) per dog for owners with sporting dogs or with more than one dog of any kind; or three shillings per dog for people who owned a single non-

sporting dog and who were also eligible for the house, windows and light taxes; or a flat rate of fifteen pounds irrespective of the number of dogs. The fee, payable annually on 5 April was increased by ten per cent in 1797. (p. 47)

**69 (a) the renowned Hector, shall form the subject of another letter** Hogg had published a poem about his dog Hector ('A Shepherd's Address to His Auld Dog Hector') in the December 1805 issue of the *Scots Magazine*; the poem was reprinted in *The Mountain Bard* (1807) as 'The Author's Address to His Auld Dog Hector'. Hector died in 1808—see *Letters 1*, p. 98. Hogg did not 'have leisure' to publish 'another letter' on Hector until 1824, when he published a new instalment of 'The Shepherd's Calendar. Class IV. Dogs' in *BEM*, 15 (February 1824), 177–83.

# April 1818–March 1819 (Volumes 3–4)

## Sonnet to John Carnegie, Esq.

'Sonnet to John Carnegie' was published in *Blackwood's Edinburgh Magazine*, 3 (April 1818), 58, and has not been reprinted. The poem is signed 'J. H.' in *BEM*, and Hogg's authorship is noted in a review article in *BEM*, 'Poems by a Military Amateur', 5 (May 1819), 206–10. The article, attributed by Strout (p. 53) to Thomas Hamilton, reviews a fictitious collection of poetry by the fictitious writer Morgan Odoherty; Hamilton notes that Odoherty 'is not indeed what Mr Hogg elegantly terms Mr Carnegie—"The bard of tender tears and gentle sighs"' (p. 206). Hogg was in Edinburgh throughout most of March and April 1818, and the poem may have been the consequence of his interaction with the Blackwood's writers during this time. Carnegie has not been identified.

The poem is introduced in *BEM* with the following comment:

[We have received from Mr John Carnegie of Glasgow, a poem, entitled "Largo's Vale." It is, we fear, rather long for insertion in our Magazine, though we hope to find room for it soon. Meanwhile we publish with much pleasure the following beautiful Sonnet, from a distinguished pen, to the Bard of the Largs. EDITOR.]

Apparently the only poetry attributed to Carnegie in *BEM* is a seven-stanza excerpt from what was purported to be a verse-letter inviting the editors of *BEM* to a party at the home of Carnegie's brother at Ardgartan, Argyllshire. The verses supposedly are taken from a song to the tune of 'Fy let us a' to the wedding'. The verses appear as part of a footnote in the September 1819 'Tent' issue of *BEM*; the song is introduced as follows: 'We beg leave thus publicly to acknowledge our gratitude to Mr John Carnegie of Glasgow, for the very kind and handsome invitation which he sent us, to join a joyous party at Ardgartan, Argyllshire, the abode of his excellent brother the captain. Nothing but the distance prevented us from beating up the hospitable quarters' (p. 713).

Carnegie is the butt of further *BEM* jokes in the '"Luctus" on the Death of Sir Daniel Donnelly', published in the May 1820 number of *BEM* (vol. 7, pp. 186–205). Daniel Donnelly (1788–1820), popular Irish boxing champion, had died on 18 February 1820. The 'Luctus' is a collection of parodies and satirical poems and sketches, most of which take the life and death of Donnelly as the ostensible subject. One of these poems, 'Sorrow is Dry, *Being a New Song, by Dr James Scott*' (pp. 188–89), written by William Maginn, involves Carnegie in the satire on Donnelly's fame. The following excerpts are taken from the second and third verses of the seven-verse song:

> I took a turn along the street, to breathe the Trongate air,
> Carnegie's lass I chanced to meet, with a bag of lemons fair;
> Says I, "Gude Meg, ohon! ohon! you've heard of Dan's disaster—
> If I'm alive, I'll come at five, and feed upon your master—
> A glass or two no harm will do to either saint or sinner,
> And a bowl with friends will make amends for a so so sort of
>    dinner."
> [...]
> I found Carnegie in his nook, upon the old settee,
> And dark and dismal was his look, as black as black might be,
> Then suddenly the blood did fly, and leave his face so pale,
> That scarce I knew, in alter'd hue, the bard of Largo's vale.

The present edition reprints the *BEM* version without emendation.

**70, l. 1 Largo's Vale** Carnegie apparently was from Largs, a coastal town in North Ayrshire, eighteen miles southwest of Greenock. See l. 10.

### On Carmel's Brow

'On Carmel's Brow', like 'A Hebrew Melody' (see pp. 55–56 of the present edition and notes), was first published with musical score in Hogg's *A Selection of German Hebrew Melodies* [*c.* 1817], pp. 46–49. The song was published in *Blackwood's Edinburgh Magazine*, 3 (April 1818), 90, and Hogg's authorship was acknowledged with the by-line 'By the Ettrick Shepherd'. With the exception of line 33, there are only minor printing differences between the two versions. In *BEM* line 33 was revised to 'But who had seen that Prophet's eye' from 'But, o that prophet's vision'd eye' in *Hebrew Melodies*. The poem was reprinted in the 1822 *Poetical Works* (IV, 220–24), using the *Hebrew Melodies* version of line 33. 'On Carmel's Brow' primarily draws on images from the prophecies of Isaiah that look forward to a messiah who will redeem and restore an exiled Israel.

The present edition prints the *BEM* text without emendation.

**70, l. 1 Carmel's brow** Mt Carmel, a mountain in Canaan that projects into the Mediterranean and divides the regions of Sharon and Esdraelon.

**70, l. 3 Palestine** the land along the eastern coast of the Mediterranean Sea, the land of Israel.

**70, l. 5 old Seer** the prophet, probably Isaiah.

**71, ll. 14–16 By wave and waterfall [...] Deep unto deep did call** echoes Psalm 42. 7: 'Deep calleth unto deep at the noise of thy waterspouts: all thy waves and thy billows are gone over me'.

**71, l. 17 Kison's strand** Kishon, a brook that runs from Mt Tabor into the Mediterranean north of Mt Carmel.

**71, l. 17 Ephratah** another name for Bethlehem and the surrounding area.

**71, l. 20 Asherite** a descendant of Jacob's son Asher, one of the twelve tribes of Israel, or one who lives in the part of Canaan given to Asher. See Joshua 19. 24–31.

**71, l. 26 Jordan** the Jordan River, the principal river in Palestine.

**71, l. 29 vultures held their jubilee** echoes Isaiah 34. 15: 'there shall the vultures also be gathered'.

**71, l. 30 harp and cymbal** common biblical images of joy, praise, and celebration.

**71, l. 32 baleful satyr** from Isaiah 34. 14: 'The wild beasts of the desert shall also meet with the wild beasts of the island, and the satyr shall cry to his fellow'.

**71, l. 41 Bozrah** the principal city in northern Edom, a kingdom on the southeastern border of Judah traditionally associated with the descendants of Esau.

**71, ll. 45–48 Who's this [...] not with wine** from Isaiah 63. 1–2: 'Who is this that cometh from Edom, with dyed garments from Bozrah? this that is glorious in his apparel, traveling in the greatness of his strength? I that speak in righteousness, mighty to save. Wherefore art thou red in thine apparel, and thy garments like him that treadeth in the winefat?'

**71, l. 46 Edom** see note for line 41.

**72, ll. 51–52 The dwellers [...] praise to thee** from Isaiah 42. 11–12: 'let the inhabitants of the rock sing, let them shout from the top of the mountains. Let them give glory unto the Lord, and declare his praise in the islands'.

**72, l. 53 Tabor and Hermon** Mt Tabor is in the northeast of the Plain of Esdraelon. Mt Hermon overlooks the Bashan plateau and the Jordan valley west of Damascus. See Psalm 89. 12: 'Tabor and Hermon shall rejoice in thy name'.

**72, ll. 57–60 The happy child [...] in love unite** echoes Isaiah 11. 6: 'The wolf also shall dwell with the lamb, and the leopard shall lie down with the kid; and the calf and the young lion and the fatling together; and a little child shall lead them'.

**72, l. 61 Zion's hill** Jerusalem, or sections of it. See Psalm 2. 6: 'Yet have I set my king upon my holy hill of Zion'.

### Letter to Timothy Tickler

Hogg's 'Letter to Timothy Tickler' was never published in Hogg's lifetime. Hogg apparently intended the 'Letter' for *BEM* as a reply to a series of articles that were published in *BEM* over several issues from February to July 1818. The articles were in the form of letters to various authors and were signed with the pseudonym 'Timothy Tickler'. The first two of the *BEM* articles were addressed specifically to Hogg: 'Letter to Mr James Hogg', 2 (February 1818), 501–04, and 'Letters of Timothy Tickler to Various Literary Characters. Letter II.–To the Ettrick Shepherd', 2 (March 1818), 654–56. The Tickler letters to Hogg in *BEM* were published in response to a series of three articles, 'Life and Writings of James Hogg', that were written by Hogg's friend, James Gray, and published in Archibald Constable's *Edinburgh Magazine*, 2 (January through March 1818), 35–40, 122–29, 215–23.

Timothy Tickler was one of several fictional personae used by the *BEM* writers. Tickler was loosely based on Robert Sym, an Edinburgh Writer to the Signet and John Wilson's uncle. Hogg was on friendly terms with Sym, and in his 'Reminiscences of Former Days', Hogg writes fondly of visiting Sym at his Edinburgh home in George Square (*Memoir*, pp. 76–78). Although Sym is associated with the Tickler character in *BEM*, Sym probably never wrote anything ascribed to Tickler. John Wilson almost certainly was the author of both Tickler letters to Hogg, as well as other letters in the series.

Hogg's 'Letter to Timothy Tickler' is published in the present edition from the draft manuscript preserved among the James Hogg Papers in the Alexander

Turnbull Library of the National Library of New Zealand as MS-Papers-0042-08. The present edition publishes the 'Letter to Timothy Tickler' as Hogg had revised it for publication. The complete draft of Hogg's letter, including the portions that Hogg marked for deletion in the manuscript, is published in Gillian Hughes's S/SC edition of Hogg's letters (*Letters 1*, pp. 366–75). Acknowledgement is made to Dr. Hughes, whose notes to this letter, as well as her general advice, have been a major source of annotations for this work, even where not specifically acknowledged in the notes.

72(c) **attacting every body slap-dash name and surname** Hogg is the subject of the first two 'Tickler' letters in *BEM*; the third 'Tickler' letter, *BEM*, 3 (April 1818), 75–77, is addressed to Francis Jeffrey, editor of Constable's *Edinburgh Review*, a rival to *BEM*. Other articles in *BEM* that attacked authors by 'name and surname' include the series 'On the Cockney School of Poetry', the first of which was published in the October 1817 number of *BEM* (vol. 2, pp. 38–41). The 'Tickler' letters did not end the attacks on Hogg in *BEM*; in the August 1821 number of *BEM*, John Wilson published a rancorous article on Hogg in a review of Hogg's 'Memoir of the Author's Life' in the third edition of *The Mountain Bard* (1821). For details see 'Familiar Epistles to Christopher North, *From an Old Friend with a New Face*', *BEM*, 10 (August 1821), 43–52.

72(c) **my father** Robert Hogg (1729–1820).

72(d) **first begun, in public, to let fly your crackers at me** the first 'Tickler' letter in *BEM* was 'Letter to James Hogg', which was published in *BEM*, 2 (February 1818), 501–04.

72(d) **my sequestered shieling** Hogg signs this work from Altrive Lake, his farm in Yarrow.

72(d) **"nursing my wrath to keep it warm"** from line 12 of Robert Burns's poem 'Tam o' Shanter'—see Kinsley 321.

73(a) **smart puppy** perhaps a reference to John Lockhart, whom Hogg later refers to as 'a mischievous Oxford puppy, for whom I was terrified' (*Memoir*, p. 73).

73(a) **old malevolent, starched, erudite gentleman** this description fits the fictitious editor of *BEM*, 'Christopher North', although the adjective 'old' does not apply at this time to John Wilson, the person most associated with the North persona.

73(b) **fashoin [*sic*] of my clothes** the author of the first 'Tickler' letter to Hogg comments on Hogg's dress: 'I have seen you with my own eyes at a rout with top boots; and the flying Tailor of Ettrick, though like yourself a man of genius, never hits your shape, and leaves the tail of your coat infinitely too long' (p. 502).

73(b) **walked the parliament house** the Court of Session in Edinburgh convened here, so it would have been a place familiar to Sym, who was a Writer to the Signet.

73(c) **insinuated that when I was a shepherd I drank whisky like a fish** 'Tickler' in his first letter imagines Hogg as a weary Shepherd on a rainy night under the shelter of a rock, 'kept in life, not by the spirit of poetry, but of malt' (p. 504). The characterisation of Hogg as a heavy drinker continued in the *Noctes Ambrosianæ*. Hogg later complained that the portrayal of his character in the *Noctes* damaged his chances for a pension from the Royal Society of Literature, leading John Lockhart to write in the *Quarterly Review*:

'We may take liberty of adding [...] that a more worthy, modest, sober and loyal man does not exist in his Majesty's dominions than this distinguished poet, whom some of his waggish friends have taken up the absurd fancy of exhibiting in print as a sort of boozing buffoon'—see 'Lives of Uneducated Poets', *Quarterly Review*, 44 (January 1831), 52–82 (p. 82).

73(d) **from my youth upward** echoes Matthew 19. 20: 'All these things have I kept from my youth up'.

74(a) HOGG ON SHEEP Hogg published *The Shepherd's Guide; being a Treatise on the Diseases of Sheep* in 1807. As Gillian Hughes notes, 'Hogg on Sheep' was the wording on the paper label on the spine of the original issue of this work in boards (*Letters 1*, p. 374).

74(a) *The Pilgrims of the Sun* Hogg's book-length poem of this title was published in 1814.

74(a) **my inimitable witch and fairy ballads** Hogg is probably referring to the poems of *The Queen's Wake* (1813), especially 'The Witch of Fife' and 'Kilmeny'.

74(b) **"Nunquam sunt grati qui nocuêre salis"** proverbial: 'Those witticisms are never agreeable, which wound the feelings of any'—see *A Dictionary of Select and Popular Quotations, which are in daily use* (Philadephia: Claxton, Remsen & Haffelfinger, 1873), p. 181.

74(c) **Constable's Magazine** the *Edinburgh Magazine and Literary Miscellany*. When William Blackwood ceased publication of the *Edinburgh Monthly Magazine*, his original editors, James Cleghorn and Thomas Pringle, became editors of Constable's *Scots Magazine*, which Constable renamed the *Edinburgh Magazine and Literary Miscellany*. See 'Chaldee' note for 28(a–b).

74(d) **Mr Horace "O major tandem parcas insane minore"** from Horace's *Satires*, 2. 3. 326, translated by H. Rushton Fairclough: 'O greater one, spare, I pray, the lesser madman!' See Horace, *Satires, Epistles and Ars Poetica*, Loeb Classical Library (London: Heinemann, 1929), pp. 180–81.

75(b) **put a stop to the publication** the articles on Hogg in the *Edinburgh Magazine* were discontinued after the third instalment, which was published in the March 1818 number.

75(c) **differed [...] once about a certain epitaph** a reference to 'Epitaph on a Living Character', which was published in the second number of Hogg's periodical, *The Spy* (8 September 1810). The subject of this rather personal attack is Alexander Gibson Hunter, who was a partner in the bookselling business with Archibald Constable. See Hogg, *The Spy*, ed. by Gillian Hughes (S/SC, 2000), p. 19 and note, p. 576.

75(c) **invincible stupidity of Bob Miller** of the Edinburgh publishing firm Manners & Miller. Hogg approached Archibald Constable to publish *The Pilgrims of the Sun*, but Constable referred Hogg to Miller, promising to market the poem in all his outlets if Hogg would allow Miller to publish it. Hogg acceded to Constable's request, but Miller did not publish the poem within the agreed-upon time. When Hogg 'wrote to a friend to inquire the reason', the friend replied: 'Mr. Miller, I am privately informed, sent out your MS. among his blue-stockings for their verdict. They have condemned the poem as extravagant nonsense. Mr. Miller has rued his bargain, and will never publish the poem, unless he is sued at law' (*Memoir*, pp. 37–38).

75(d) **a tree will always be known by its fruit** echoes Matthew 12. 33: 'for the tree is known by his fruit'. See also Matthew 7. 16–20.

75(d)–76(a) **"Quantum quisque [...] habet et fidei"** from Juvenal's 'Satire III', ll. 143–44, translated by G. G. Ramsay: 'A man's word is believed in exact proportion to the amount of cash which he keeps in his strong box'—see *Juvenal and Persius*, Loeb Classical Library (London: Heinemann, 1928), pp. 42–43.

**76(a) "Quem simper […] habebo"** Hogg quotes part of a sentence from Virgil's *Aeneid*, Book 5, ll. 49–50; the full sentence reads: iamque dies, nisi fallor, adest, quem simper acerbum, | simper honoratum (sic di voluistis) habebo'. These lines are translated as: 'And now, if I err not, the day is at hand which I shall keep (such, O gods, was your will) ever as a day of grief, ever as a day of honour'—see Virgil, *Eclogues, Georgics, Aeneid I–VI*, trans. H. R. Fairclough, rev. G. P. Goold, Loeb Classical Library (Cambridge: Harvard University Press, 1999), pp. 474–75.

**76(a) letter to Mr. Jefferey** see note for 72(c).

**76(a) Mr. Grieve's liberary** probably John Grieve (1781–1836), a friend of Hogg's from Ettrick, who became a hatter in Edinburgh. Grieve was a faithful supporter of Hogg's literary efforts, and Hogg portrays him as the Fourteenth Bard in *The Queen's Wake*.

**76(c) Mr. Jamieson (not Robert […])** not identified, although Gillian Hughes (*Letters* 1, p. 375) reasonably suggests that Hogg here refers to John Jamieson (1759–1838), Edinburgh author best known for his *Etymological Dictionary of the Scottish Language* (1808). Robert Jamieson (1772?–1844), author and ballad collector, was known for his studies of Scandinavian and Scottish literature; see 'Chaldee' note for 41, IV. 6. However, it is also possibly a fictitious name. It is a common device of Hogg's to include within his own articles a voice of criticism that he attributes to another, often fictitious, voice. See, for example, 'A Letter to Charles Kirkpatrick Sharpe', pp. 51–54 in the present edition.

**77(a) outrageous Magazine in Prince-street** *Blackwood's Edinburgh Magazine*. William Blackwood's publishing firm was located at 17 Princes Street.

**77(a) I have given up writing for that work** Hogg's frustration and anger with the Blackwoodians over the Tickler letters led Hogg to cease publication with *BEM*. Except for 'Verses addressed to the Right Hon. Lady Anne Scott of Buccleuch', which was extracted from *The Brownie of Bodsbeck* in lieu of a review, Hogg did not publish in *BEM* from April 1818 until April 1819.

**77(a) New Series of the Scots Mag.** see note for 74(c).

**77(a) the Dominies magazine** Gillian Hughes suggests that this magazine is 'probably the *Literary and Statistical Magazine of Scotland*, published by Macreadie, Skelly, & Co. in Edinburgh between 1817 and 1820' (*Letters 1*, p. 375).

**77(a) new magazine set afoot at Lanark** probably the *Clydesdale Magazine*, which began publication in May 1818 and which published Hogg's story 'An Old Soldier's Tale' in the July 1818 number.

**77(b) continuation of the Chaldee Manuscript** in his *Memoir* Hogg notes that he had written a 'long continuation of the manuscript, which I have by me this day, in which I go over the painters, poets, lawyers, booksellers, magistrates, and ministers of Edinburgh, all in the same style' (p. 45). This 'Chaldee' continuation apparently was never published. For Hogg's additional 'Chaldee' material see 'The Boar' (pp. 44–47) and Appendix A in the present edition.

**77(b) another firm […] "the three brethren, Shadrach, Meshech, and Abednego"** the firm is not identified. In the biblical story from Daniel 3. 8–30, the

Chaldeans accused Shadrach, Meshach, and Abednego, who were Jews, of refusing to worship King Nebuchadnezzar's gods. The King ordered the three men cast into a 'burning fiery furnace'. However, the God of the Jews prevented the three men from coming to any harm. This story from Daniel is in keeping with Hogg's original intent of the 'Chaldee Manuscript' that was 'supposed to have been written by Daniel' (see p. 26 in the present edition).

# April 1819–March 1820 (Volumes 5–6)

### Letter from the Ettrick Shepherd, Enclosing a Letter from James Laidlaw

Hogg's 'Letter from the Ettrick Shepherd, Enclosing a Letter from James Laidlaw' was first published in *Blackwood's Edinburgh Magazine*, 6 (March 1820), 630–32, and was not reprinted in Hogg's lifetime. A fair copy manuscript of the first part of this work, the letter from the Ettrick Shepherd, is preserved in the National Library of Scotland as MS 4005, fols 152–53. The manuscript consists of a single sheet *c.* 22 cm x 37 cm folded to make two folios of *c.* 22 cm x 18.5 cm. The paper is watermarked BATH | 1817, and the printer's instruction 'Across the page' is written at the beginning of the letter. The manuscript letter is addressed to William Blackwood | 17 Princes Street | Edin*r*, and was folded and sealed for posting. The bottom half of fol. 153 has been torn away but has been preserved separately in the NLS as MS 4719, fol. 190; this separate portion is Hogg's note to Blackwood, offering both letters to Blackwood for publication: 'If you like you may give the callans the above to publish as a letter to the editor inclosing the other' (*Letters 2*, p. 9). The letter from Laidlaw is not preserved with the letter from Hogg, however.

As Hogg notes in his letter, James Laidlaw was Hogg's cousin, the son of Robert Laidlaw, who was a brother of Hogg's mother, Margaret Laidlaw. James Laidlaw was from Hopehouse, Selkirk, and immigrated to Canada in 1818. Laidlaw had six children; Mary, Andrew, James, and Walter immigrated to Canada with their father. Andrew was also accompanied by his wife, Agnes, and their son, James, who died shortly after arriving in Canada; Agnes gave birth to a daughter, Isobel, on the journey to North America. Robert, to whom the 'Letter from James Laidlaw' is addressed, and Robert's brother, William, remained in Scotland, although William and his wife, Mary Scott, immigrated to Illinois in 1836. The immigration of the Laidlaw family is documented in Donald Whyte's *A Dictionary of Scottish Emigrants to Canada before Confederation*, 2 vols (Ontario Genealogical Society, 1986; 1995), I, 157. The contemporary Canadian writer, Alice Munro, is a direct descendant of James Laidlaw and has written about the Laidlaw family and Hogg's connection with them. See Alice Munro, 'Changing Places', in *Writing Home*, ed. by Constance Rooke (Toronto: McClelland & Stewart, 1997), pp. 190–206, and *The View from Castle Rock: Stories* (New York: Alfred A. Knopf, 2006). Hogg's 'Letter' in *BEM* figures prominently in the early stories of *The View from Castle Rock*, and clearly Munro's title is taken from Hogg's anecdote of Laidlaw's visit to Edinburgh Castle (p. 78(d) in the present edition). Acknowledgement is made to Alice Munro, who graciously discussed the history of the Laidlaw family with the editor of the present edition.

It is not clear how Hogg acquired his cousin's letter, although it almost certainly circulated among family members for news of the Laidlaws' new life in Canada. Why Hogg decided to publish Laidlaw's letter in *BEM* is also not clear, although from Hogg's introductory letter it is obvious that Hogg was amused by his cousin's character, as well as Laidlaw's unique writing style. Perhaps Hogg was also capitalising on the popularity of writing about Scottish settlements in Canada in the early nineteenth century. Nearly seven years later (18 January 1827), a letter by James Laidlaw dated 8 January 1827 was published in a Canadian newspaper, *The Colonial Advocate*, ostensibly against Laidlaw's wishes. Ironically, in the letter Laidlaw complains of Hogg's unauthorised publication of his letter to his son, Robert. Laidlaw is irritated that his letter circulated throughout North America by way of *Blackwood's Magazine* even before he knew that the letter had been received by Robert. Laidlaw also takes the opportunity to return Hogg's insults by noting that 'Hogg poor man has spent most of his Life in coining Lies and if I read the Bible right I think it says that all Liares is to have there pairt in the Lake that Burns with fire and Brimston'. The idiosyncratic style and spelling of Laidlaw's *Colonial Advocate* letter serve to authenticate the *BEM* letter. The letter also provides additional background to the Laidlaw family's immigration and settlement.

very Dear Sir

I have taken upon me to write you a few Lines to Let you kno that the Scotts Bodys that Lives heare is all doing Tolaribley well for the things of this world but I am afraid that few of them thinks a bout what will Come of their Soul when Death there days doth End for they have found a thing they Call Whiskey and a great many of them dabbales and drinks at it till they make themselves worce than an ox or an ass for they Differ among them Selves and men that meets good freinds before they pairt is Like to cut one anothers throts Burns Speaks of the Barley Bree Sementing the qurall but the ra Bree hear is almost sure to mak a Qurall for since the Bodys turnd Lairds Every one is for being Master and they never consider that their Neighbour is as far up in the world as themselves, but AMerica is a good Contry for a poor man if he is able to work but is a Contry that is full of Rongs that is what I like it worst for for there is very few but will Cheat you if they can if I had known it to be what it is it Should never have seen me but times being bad in Scotland after the War and old Shepherds Like me being not Much thought of when we get old I thought of coming to America and there was an Advertisement in one of the Edinburgh News Papers in the year 1816 that ony Body that wished to go to Canada Goverment wold take them out free of Expence and they were to Write to a Mr Campble in Edinburgh so I Wrote Mr Campble telling him what famiely I had that I had five sons and told him there age and I wanted to know houw much land each of us ould get, so he wrote me that I was a very fit hand to go to America having so many sons and that I ould get Two hundred acers for my self and Like ways for Every one of my sons that was come of age but I could not get away as stock was so low and it could not be turnd into money but times was better in two years so I sold all that I had and came away 1818 and I had to come out on my own Expence for by this time there was no word of Bringing ony to Canada So I came to york and went through all there offices acording to acte of parlement I sopose and aye the other Dolor to pay but they ould give us only one Hundred

acers Each,—and that was to be drawn by Ballat if it was good Land we
were the better of it and if Bad we bid Haud with it if there Map said it
was capable of cultivation I belive the Cribblers in york ould tak the last
Shilling that a poor man has before they ould do any thing for him in the
way of getting land for in one of their offices they were crying it is five
and Sixpence five and Sixpence and only Marking Two or three words,
but I will pas them for they are an an avericeous Set. I am Realy feard
that the Deil get the must part of them if they do not bethink them
selves in time. I sopose that they never read the tenth commandment or
they ould not covet there niboures money—the folke hear is for geting a
Liberary and we have got Mr Leslees Catloge of Books for 1825 the
Nixt Catloge he prints he would do well to Let people kno the price of
his Books, but he got into the yankee fashin but when among us a Book
that he ould Like to have and knows the price he knows whither he can
purchas it or not and ould Send for it with some of his Nibours I never
saw a Catloge of Books in Scotland but the price was marked at the tail
of it, Now Sir be so good as not put me in your News papers or I will
stand a Chance of getting the Lake to keep where they put your Types
if you let theys fellos away without punishment ye should be whiped
with a road of Birks it would be well dune to take them and dip them
Twise or Thrise a day in the Lake this col'd wether it ould Cool them and
let them find that Douking in the Lake is no Joke, Now Mr Mcanzie I
ould not have taken this Liberty I hope that you will not take it ill I am
afraid that yov will not can read it as I am a very Bad Writer but I was
never at the School a quarter of a year in my Life.

Now Sir I cowld tell you Bits of Stories but I am afraid that you put
me in your Colonial Advicate I do not Like to be put in prent I once
wrot a bit of a letter to my Son Robert to Scotland and my friend Jas.
Hogg the poet put it in Blackwoods Magzine and had me through all
North America before I New that my letter was gone Home. Hogg poor
man has spent must of his Life in coining Lies and if I read the Bible
right I think it says that all Liares is to have there pairt in the Lake that
Burns with fire and Brimston But they find it a Loqarative trade for I
Belive that Hogg and Walter Scott has got more money for Lieing than
old Boston and the Erskins got for all the Sermons ever they Wrote but
the Greatst Blessings in this warld is set must Light by for people is
fonder of any Book than the Bible altho it is the greatest Blissing that
Ever the warld saw

Now my the Blessing of God rest on you and on all Loers of his name
is the sincer prayer of your Loving Contry man old
JAMES LAIDLAW
ESquising

The following notes to James Laidlaw's letter include documentation of Laidlaw's
description of settlement conditions from James Strachan's *A Visit to the Province
of Upper Canada in 1819* (Edinburgh: Oliver and Boyd; London: Longman,
1820), which was published in Scotland about the same time as Hogg's 'Letter'
to *BEM*. The present edition reprints the *BEM* version without emendation.

**78(a) Dear Christopher** Christopher North, the fictional editor of *BEM*. Hogg's
manuscript reads 'Dear Sir'.

**78(b) America** the manuscript reads 'the United States'. Laidlaw went to York in Upper Canada (now Toronto, Ontario), and settled in Esquesing when his land became available.

**78(b) approaching his sixtieth year** Laidlaw was born in 1763, so he was fifty-five years old when he emigrated from Scotland.

**78(b) sons had formed attachments at home** two of Laidlaw's sons, Robert–to whom the letter is addressed–and William, remained in Scotland. William eventually immigrated to Illinois (1836), but only after the death of his father.

**78(d) Walter Bryden** James Russell in *Reminiscences of Yarrow*, ed. by Professor Veitch, 2nd edn, preface by Campbell Fraser (Selkirk: George Lewis & Son, 1894), provides anecdotes of Cow Wat: 'An old man, familiarly termed "Cow Wat," alluding to the high respect in which [my father] was held, said to me one day, "Dr Russell was just a goddess among us;" a compliment not one whit the less that there was a slight confusion of the genders–as much so, as when, on another occasion, speaking of a little unbaptised granddaughter, he complained that they had had "an uncircumcised Philistine ower lang in the house"' (p. 15). Cow Wat is also mentioned in 'The Honourable Captain Napier and Ettrick Forest' (see p. 100(c) and note in the present edition). A different 'Wattie Bryden' is also a character in 'Tales and Anecdotes of the Pastoral Life. No. II' (see p. 14(b) and note in the present edition).

**78(d) Thomas Hogg, the celebrated flying Ettrick tailor** Hogg's cousin, who appears as 'Tam the tailor' in 'Tales and Anecdotes of the Pastoral Life. No. III' (see p. 21(a) of the present edition and note). Thomas Hogg's epithet is probably derived from one of Hogg's parodies of Wordsworth's poetry, 'The Flying Tailor', which was included in *The Poetic Mirror* (1816), pp. 155–70.

**79(a) the braid way that leads to destruction** a reference to Matthew 7. 13: 'Enter ye in at the strait gate: for wide is the gate, and broad is the way, that leadeth to destruction'.

**79(c) James Cunningham** probably either the father or son named James Cunningham, both of whom were tenants of Thirlestane farm in Ettrick and known to Hogg. Hogg had business dealings with Walter Cunningham, the older son and brother. See Gillian Hughes's notes to Walter Cunningham in *Letters 1*, pp. 453–54.

**79(c) Sandy o' Bowerhope** Alexander Laidlaw, of Bowerhope farm in Yarrow, and Hogg were friends from youth, and Laidlaw was one of Hogg's closest friends. Laidlaw was a source of farming information for William Napier's *A Treatise on Practical Store-Farming* (1822), which Hogg reviewed in the February 1823 number of *BEM*. See p. 115 of the present edition.

**79(c) Adie o' Aberlosk** Adam Bryden (1766–1850) of Aberlosk, Eskdalemuir. He also figures in 'Tales and Anecdotes of the Pastoral Life' Nos. II and III, in the May and June 1817 issues of *BEM* (pp. 6 and 19 of the present edition). See the note for 10(c).

**80(a) got Each of us one 100 acers** 'The Boards are permitted to give only 100 acres of land to any applicant' (Strachan, p. 53).

**80(a) Andrew and George Bell, from Eskdale** unidentified and not listed in Whyte's *Dictionary of Scottish Emigrants to Canada before Confederation*.

**80(a) 60,000 Acers for one Township** 'a township contains 66,000 acres'

(Strachan, p. 177).

80(b) **Eighteen Mounths to do our settling deuties in** 'The lands are granted with a condition not to be disposed of for three years, and no deed can be issued till the settling duties are performed; which duties are, to clear five acres upon each hundred granted, and the half of the road in front of the same' (Strachan, p. 55).

80(c) **him that Dwelt in the Bush** according to Exodus 3, God spoke to Moses from a burning bush to call Moses to deliver the children of Israel out of Egyptian captivity.

80(c) **mans thoughts are vanity** a reference to Psalm 94. 11: 'The Lord knoweth the thoughts of man, that they are vanity'.

80(c) **Wolfhope** William Laidlaw, James's son and Robert's brother, lived at Wolfhope in Ettrick parish.

80(d) **Wat was taken with the ague** 'The province has, indeed, got a reputation for fevers and agues; but with much the same truth as it has for savageness and cold' (Strachan, p. 182).

81(b) **King George** King George III (1738–1820), King of Great Britain from 1760, although his son was appointed regent in 1811 when the King's mental illness rendered him incapable of ruling.

81(c) **they pay no taxes, but Just a perfict trifell** 'The people of Upper Canada cannot be said to pay any taxes. The duties on articles of consumption are so trifling as not to be felt; and, being chiefly collected at Quebec, are scarcely known to one-tenth part of the inhabitants' (Strachan, pp. 135–36).

81(c) **they Save all infants […] fall from it tomorrow** in contrast to Laidlaw's Presbyterian doctrine that held that God 'elects' certain people for salvation and, once chosen by God, they cannot lose that salvation.

82(b) **John Riddel** unidentified, but Riddell was a common name in Ettrick and Yarrow.

82(b) **god of Jacob** Jacob was the son of Isaac and Rebekah and grandson of Abraham. 'The God of Abraham, of Isaac, and of Jacob' is a common biblical phrase expressing God's long-standing covenant relationship with God's people. See, for example, Exodus 3. 6.

# April 1820–December 1821 (Volumes 7–10)

### Account of a Coronation-Dinner at Edinburgh

'Account of a Coronation-Dinner at Edinburgh' was first published in *Blackwood's Edinburgh Magazine*, 10 (August 1821), 26–33, and the work has not been reprinted. In fact, this sketch of a fictional dinner to celebrate King George IV's coronation has not been identified previously as Hogg's. A. L. Strout, in his *Bibliography of Articles in Blackwood's Magazine 1817–1825*, suggests that the work is John Galt's. Strout cites a letter from Galt to William Blackwood dated 30 July 1821 in which Galt writes that he is sending the 'first part of the Coronation' (p. 83). However, the 'Coronation' to which Galt refers is a chapter in Galt's serialised novel, *The Steam-Boat*, which appeared in the second part of the double issue for August 1821 with 'Account of a Coronation-Dinner'. The correspondence between Hogg and Blackwood, however, suggests that the sketch is Hogg's, as does evidence within the sketch itself. Hogg apparently submitted the work to Blackwood under a different title, and the work was originally longer than the published version. Hogg wrote to Blackwood on 19 August 1821: 'if you publish *the Bagman* the song about the queen I am afraid will not do it must either be left out or some verses substituted' (*Letters 2*, p. 105). Blackwood answered Hogg on 23 August 1821, acknowledging that Blackwood revised the sketch beyond the omission of the song about the queen: 'You will see that we have changed the title of your article, and left out the song about the Queen, and likewise the speeches which were not equal to the rest of the article. I have credited your account 5 Guineas for it, and if you find it agreeable to continue your contributions I shall only say that you will be well paid for them' (NLS, MS 30,301, p. 200). As the annotations below indicate, there is internal evidence within the sketch that also supports the attribution to Hogg: for example, a manuscript in Hogg's hand of the song 'Carle, an' the King Come' is preserved in the National Library of Scotland (see the note for 90(a)), and Hogg's anecdote of Lockhart is apparently based on an actual event that Hogg later relates in his 'Reminiscences of Former Days' (see the note for 86(d)–87(a)).

The weeks leading up to King George IV's coronation found Hogg in financial difficulty, trying to stock his farm, and Hogg had written to Sir Walter Scott for financial assistance. Scott's proposed solution to Hogg's money woes, in part, included an invitation to Hogg to attend the coronation in London so that Hogg could earn money by writing about the events from a perspective that would appeal to Hogg's rural audience. Scott also wanted to obtain a pension for Hogg from the new Royal Society of Literature. (See Scott's letter of 1 July 1821 to Lord Montagu, *The Letters of Sir Walter Scott*, ed. by H. J. C. Grierson, 12 vols (London: Constable, 1932–37), VI, 487). For the sake of his farm Hogg could not miss St Boswell's Fair, which occurred the day before the coronation, so Hogg wrote to Scott on 5 July, declining the invitation: 'if I were to run off privately and leave the market and my farm half stocked I were judged mad beyond all hope of recovery. *I may not do it*! The thing is impossible. But as there is no man in his majesty's dominions admires his great talents for government and the energy and dignity of his administration so much as I do, I will write something at home' (*Letters 2*, p. 100). Hogg was interested in the prospect of a pension from the Society, however, but he was afraid that his presence in London might be a liability to the process. Furthermore, Hogg believed he had already written the requisite national poetry to secure the pension. Hogg's letter continues:

> If you were to procure me a pension from that society you talk of or any society; you will get it as well and better without me than with me. You may at least say this for me that there is not a more loyal bard in Britain and that I have written more loyal and national ditties well known among our peasantry than perhaps all the bards of Scotland put together. Either the song of *Scotia's Glens* or that entitled *Caledonia* recited by Mr. James Ballantyne would if well timed procure me a pension at once. It is such a pity that the coronation should have been at this juncture or that I had not thought of it sooner for much need have I to be in London. (*Letters 2*, p. 100)

After Hogg's decision not to go to London, Lockhart takes up Hogg's cause and entreats Hogg to participate actively and literarily in the Edinburgh coronation dinner. Lockhart wrote to Hogg on 13 July 1821: 'I assure you I think there is every chance of something being done for you by this new

Society. Write a real grand song for the Kings coronation dinner *here* & come in & sing it accompanied by yr friend Gow; and write another famous "Carle an the King come" & yr business is done. By all means come to the coronation dinner & shew yr face' (NLS, MS 2245, fols 58–59). Hogg apparently did not answer Lockhart's letter, but since Hogg was restocking his farm at the St Boswell's Fair, he would have had to turn down Lockhart's invitation to the Edinburgh coronation dinner as he turned down Scott's invitation for the London trip. A brief report in the *Caledonian Mercury* for 21 July 1821 notes that 'Gow's music enlivened the festivity with delightful airs', but apparently Gow's music did not include a 'grand song' for the king by Hogg. Although 'Account of a Coronation-Dinner' includes a song entitled 'Carle, an' the King Come', it seems that Hogg did not make a serious effort to prepare a performance version of the song until a year later when the King's visit to Edinburgh was imminent (see note for 90(a)).

Hogg was fond of the literary sport that typifies 'Account of a Coronation-Dinner'. Given what seemed to be at stake for Hogg, though, it is unclear why Hogg chose to write a satirical sketch of his literary friends rather than a serious tribute for the coronation. The sketch probably was, in part, a response to two sporting sketches in *BEM*, 'The True and Authentic Account of the Twelfth of August, 1819', and 'The Tent', published in the August 1819 and September 1819 numbers of *BEM*, respectively. The format of the 'Coronation-Dinner'–using a naïve narrator to provide a first-hand account of the events–may have been inspired by Lockhart's *Peter's Letters to His Kinsfolk* (1819), especially the account of the Burns Dinner in volume I (pp. 110–47), wherein the fictitious Peter Morris records his impressions of the speeches, toasts, songs, Scottish food, and participants of another grand public dinner. However, the kind of dinner described in 'Account of a Coronation-Dinner' was commonplace in Edinburgh society, and Hogg would have had a great deal of experience with such occasions. 'Coronation-Dinner' appears to be set specifically at Young's Tavern in the High Street of Edinburgh at a dinner of the Dilletanti Society, of which Hogg was a member. The connection to the Dilletanti Society is suggested in particular by the mention of the presence of the artists at the dinner; the Society was largely comprised of artists and those who were interested in art and literature. James Nasmyth, son of the Edinburgh artist Alexander Nasmyth, writes of his father's connection with the Dilletanti Society and includes a list of some of its prominent members:

> Its meetings were held every fortnight, on Thursday evenings, in a commodious tavern in the High Street. The members were chiefly artists, or men known for their love of art. Among them were Henry Raeburn, Hugh Williams (the Grecian), Andrew Geddes, William Thomson, John Shetkay, William Nicholson, William Allan, Alexander Nasmyth, the Rev. John Thomson of Duddingston, George Thomson, Sir Walter Scott, John Lockhart, Dr. Brewster, David Wilkie, Henry Cockburn, Francis Jeffrey, John A. Murray, Professor Wilson, John Ballantyne, James Ballantyne, James Hogg (the Ettrick Shepherd), and David Bridges, the secretary. The drinks were restricted to Edinburgh ale and whisky toddy.' (*James Nasmyth Engineer An Autobiography*, ed. by Samuel Smiles (London: John Murray, 1891), p. 35)

It seems, however, that Hogg's lighthearted satire in 'Coronation–Dinner' is directed more towards his Edinburgh literary associates than the artists of his acquaintance.

Apparently the manuscript of 'Account of a Coronation-Dinner' has not survived, so exactly what Blackwood omitted is not known. The 'song about the Queen' has not been identified, but because the circumstances surrounding the relationship between King George IV and Queen Caroline were controversial, it is reasonable to expect that the song would be controversial as well, especially for the Tory 'Maga'. The 'Coronation-Dinner' concludes, though, with a song in memory of George III, 'Our Good Auld Man', that apparently has not been published outside of this *BEM* sketch. The song is sung by 'an elderly gentleman with spectacles' who claims that the song was 'written by a gentleman in the company, who, he believed, had written more loyal and national songs that any bard now living, perhaps than all of them put together'. Hogg here underscores his contention, already expressed to Scott, that he deserves the Royal Society of Literature pension based on his previous body of work. Ironically, he does so in a fictional voice that describes Hogg in terms that would not have made him broadly identifiable.

Although 'Coronation-Dinner' is a fictitious occasion, it is likely that Hogg had in mind particular individuals in nearly all of his character descriptions in the sketch. The annotations that follow suggest identities for most of the characters in the sketch, but it has not been possible to identify with certainty all of the characters based on the brief descriptions and caricatures provided by Hogg within the story. Even D. M. Moir, a close Blackwood insider, was stumped by some of Hogg's characters; Moir wrote to Blackwood on 23 August 1821: 'The Coronation dinner is spiritedly written, though the characters in one or two instances fairly baffled my endeavours to find them out' (NLS, MS 4077, fols 194–95). Those characters that have not been identified are also noted below.

The present edition reprints 'Account of a Coronation-Dinner' without emendation.

**83, (title) John M'Indoe [...] William M'Ilhose** probably fictitious, although the *Glasgow Directory* for 1821 includes a John M'Indoe as owner of a 'Scotch cloth shop' at 323 High-street. There is no listing for M'Ilhose.

**83 (a) this boasted city** Edinburgh.

**83 (b) the appearance of this small eastern metropolis, which you despise [...] about the *men of genius here*, the only thing worth notice** the opening letter of Lockhart's *Peter's Letters to His Kinsfolk* describes a view of Edinburgh from Calton Hill, which leaves Peter Morris in 'a sort of stupor of admiration' (I, 12). Morris also claims, though, that his 'sole purpose, or nearly so, in coming to Scotland, was to see and converse with the illustrious men who live here' (I, 51). The narrator of 'Coronation-Dinner', a Glasgow businessman, also seems to be commenting on the rivalry between the two major Scottish cities–Edinburgh, the capital city, and Glasgow, at this time a thriving commercial centre.

**83 (c) Mr J–y [...] political French novel in MS. written by a lady** Francis Jeffrey, advocate and editor of the *Edinburgh Review*. Hogg refers to Jeffrey's admiration for the author and political activist, Madame de Staël (1766–1817), Baroness of Staël-Holstein. Her *salon* attracted important French political and intellectual figures; her social position and her political ideas led to periods of exile shortly after the Revolution and again under Napoleon's rule. Madame de Staël's works were frequently and, usually, favourably reviewed in the *Edinburgh Review*. (See, for example, the *Edinburgh Review* numbers for October 1807, April 1809, July 1813, and October 1813.) Her works include the novels *Delphine* (1802) and *Corinne* (1807) and her popular study of Germany and Romanticism, *De l'Allemagne*, which was first published by John Murray in London in 1813. Madame de Staël's posthumous publications include *Considérations sur les principaux événements de la Révolution française* (1818) and *Dix années d'exil* (1821). For additional information about de Staël, see the *Oxford DNB* article by Madelyn Gutwirth.

83 (c) **Sir W– S– [...] Saxon coins, and two Caledonian javelins** Sir Walter Scott. Scott was well known as a collector of antiquities.

83 (c) **Mr C– N– [...] song from Dr Scott** Christopher North, the fictitious editor of *BEM* and the *BEM* pseudonym usually associated with John Wilson. Dr. James Scott was a dentist, who became known as 'The Odontist' in *BEM*. Lockhart, especially, appropriated Scott's name for his mischievous satirical verse. Hogg was particularly taken with Lockhart's jokes at Dr Scott's expense. Hogg writes in 'Reminiscences of Former Days':

> Of all the practical jokes that ever Lockhart played off on the public in his thoughtless days, the most successful and ludicrous was that about Dr. Scott. He was a strange-looking, bald-headed, bluff little man, that practised as a dentist, both in Glasgow and Edinburgh, keeping a good house and hospitable table in both, and considered skilful; but for utter ignorance of every thing literary, he was not to be matched among a dozen street porters with ropes round their necks. [...] Well, at last this joke took so well, and went so far, that shortly after the appearance of "The Lament for Captain Patton," one of John Lockhart's best things, by-the-bye, but which was published in the doctor's name, he happened to take a trip to Liverpool in a steamboat, and had no sooner arrived there than he was recognised and hailed as Ebony's glorious Odontist! (*Memoir*, pp. 75–76)

In the September 1819 'Tent' issue of *BEM* (pp. *640–*641), the Ettrick Shepherd sings, although probably did not compose, 'L'Envoy; An Excellent New Song in Honour of Dr Scott', which is answered by 'Dr Scott's Farewell to Braemar'.

83 (c) **Mr – [...] Glasgow ice, and the Gorbals weaver's theory on the mean temperature of the globe** John Lockhart, a native of Glasgow, devotes a large portion of the third volume of *Peter's Letters to His Kinsfolk* to descriptions of Glasgow. 'Glasgow ice' may be a reference to cold Glasgow punch, for which Peter Morris provides a lengthy description and a recipe (III, 173–74, 226–28). Morris's conversation with 'the philosophical weaver' includes the weaver's analysis of the impact of the weather on agricultural and commercial interests (III, 209–10). The Gorbals is a working-class district in Glasgow south of the River Clyde.

83 (d) **P– W– [...] verses to the moon [...] Finlay** Professor Wilson. John Wilson was elected Professor of Moral Philosophy at the University of Edinburgh in 1820. John Finlay (1782–1810) was a friend of Wilson's and a classmate of Wilson's at Glasgow University. Finlay's publications include *Wallace, or, the Vale of Ellerslie, and other poems* (1802) and *Scottish Historical and Romantic Ballads* (1808). Wilson published 'Some Account of John Finlay, with Specimens of his Poetry' in the November 1817 number of *BEM* and additional poems in the February 1818 number. Moon images also feature

prominently in Wilson's own poetry, such as *The Isle of Palms* (1812); Hogg wrote an imitation of Wilson's poetry, 'Hymn to the Moon', which was published in Hogg's *Poetic Mirror* (1816). See also the notes for 'Elegy' in the present edition.

83 (d) **G– [...] German dialogue of Paisley manufacture** Robert Pearse Gillies (1789–1858) was a contributor to *BEM* and published numerous translations of works from the German. His publications in *BEM* include several articles in the series *Horae Germanicae* and *Horae Danicae* in 1819 and 1820, as well as a sonnet, 'On seeing a Spark fall from Mr Hogg's pipe', 5 (May 1819), 205. The character 'Kempferhausen', from 'The True and Authentic Account of the Twelfth of August', *BEM*, 5 (August 1819), 597–*613, and later the *Noctes Ambrosianæ*, is based on Gillies. The reference to 'Paisley manufacture' is probably a reference to John Wilson's role in making Gillies's character in *BEM*; Wilson was a native of Paisley.

83 (d) **E– S– on pretence of buying his wool** the Ettrick Shepherd. In the second 'Editor's Narrative' in Hogg's novel *The Private Memoirs and Confessions of a Justified Sinner* (1824), the editor comments: 'Mr. L–t introduced me to [Hogg] as a great wool-stapler, come to raise the price of that article' (*Confessions*, p. 170).

83 (d) **19th of July** the coronation of King George IV was 19 July 1821.

83 (d) **the great public dinner** *The Edinburgh Evening Courant* for 9 July 1821 announces a 'public dinner to celebrate His Majesty's Coronation' to be held at the Waterloo Hotel on 19 July with 'The Lord Provost in the Chair'. Tickets were available in advance (none at the door) from Mr Oman at Oman's tavern for £1-11-6. This is the dinner that Lockhart had advised Hogg to attend in his letter of 13 July 1821 to Hogg (see head-note above).

83 (d) **a celebrated tavern** probably Young's Tavern on High Street, Edinburgh, where the fortnightly meetings of the Dilletanti Society were held.

84 (a–b) **a jeweller [...] an artist** the characters mentioned in this section have not been identified.

84 (a) **a mercantile gentleman** probably Archibald Constable since the description in 'Coronation-Dinner' later suggests that the gentleman's political sympathies are more Whig than Tory. In this paragraph and the one that follows Hogg depicts what must have been a common scene in the Edinburgh bookshops of Hogg's time. In *Peter's Letters* Lockhart describes the 'great lounging book-shop[s]' (II, 186) in Edinburgh, including Constable's, Blackwood's, and Manners and Miller's. Lockhart writes of Constable:

> The importance of the Whigs in Edinburgh, and the Edinburgh Review, added to the great enterprize and extensive general business of Mr Constable, have, as might have been expected, rendered the shop of this bookseller by far the most busy scene in the Bibliopolic world of the North. [...] On entering, one sees a place by no means answering, either in point of dimensions, or in point of ornament, to the notion one might have been apt to form of the shop from which so many mighty works are every day issuing–a low dusky chamber, inhabited by a few clerks, and lined with an assortment of unbound books and stationery [...]. The Bookseller himself is seldom to be seen in this part of the premises; he prefers to sit in a chamber immediately above, where he can proceed in his own work without being disturbed by the incessant cackle of the young Whigs who lounge below; and

where few casual visitors are admitted to enter his presence, except the more important members of the great Whig corporation—Reviewers either in *esse*, or, at least, supposed to be so in *posse*—contributors to the Supplement of the Encyclopædia Britannica—and the more obscure editors and supporters of the innumerable and more obscure periodical works, of which Mr Constable is the publisher. (II, 174–75)

**84(c) two celebrated lawyers** Hogg probably is suggesting Francis Jeffrey (1773–1850), and Henry Cockburn (1779–1854), both of whom were 'celebrated lawyers', as well as close friends, political allies, and literary associates with Constable. See also the note for p. 313, l. 11.

**85(a) the Merchant of Venice** suggests the playful title that Constable apparently awarded himself. In his *Life of Scott* Lockhart tells of a dinner he attended with Sir Walter Scott and Archibald Constable. Lockhart writes: 'I had not in those days been much initiated in the private jokes of what is called, by way of excellence, *the trade*, and was puzzled when Scott, in the course of the dinner, said to Constable, "Will your Czarish Majesty do me the honour to take a glass of Champagne?" I asked the master of the feast for an explanation. "Oh!" said he, "are you so green as not to know that Constable long since dubbed himself *The Czar of Muscovy*, John Murray *The Emperor of the West*, and Longman and his string of partners *The Divan?*"' (III, 203). Later in the 'Coronation-Dinner' sketch, Hogg refers to this character as 'the Merchant of Venice, alias the Royal Merchant' (p. 91(c) of the present edition).

**85(b) taking a hearty pinch of snuff with one nostril** this also is reminiscent of the description of William Blackwood's use of snuff in the 'Chaldee Manuscript': 'And he took from under his girdle a gem of curious workmanship of silver, made by the hand of a cunning artificer, and overlaid within with pure gold; and he took from thence something in colour like unto the dust of the earth, or the ashes that remain in a furnace, and he snuffed it up like the east wind, and returned the gem again into its place' (see p. 29(c) of the present edition).

**86(a) Tod and Finlayson [...] Dugald's** probably fictitious, although these were common names in Glasgow. The *Glasgow Directory* for 1821 lists several Tods, Todds, and Finlaysons. A Robert Dougal is listed as a 'spirit dealer' at 410 Gallowgate.

**86(b) I was to give no names, that having become of late a most dangerous experiment** an article in *The Scotsman* for 23 June 1821 took Hogg to task for his forthright 'Memoir' that introduces the third edition of *The Mountain Bard* (1821):

But, tasking our nature so far as to hold it possible that the Shepherd might not see any thing unpardonable in offences committed anonymously, or under the fictitious name of Morris, or North and Company, the case was mightily altered when he came, *in propria persona*, to write a memoir of his own life. But there we find the worst of sins committed in the most insensate manner. A friend who has always been enthusiastic in his praise, and who would at any time have divided with him the only meal he could command in the world, is held up to general ridicule, gratuitously, and without aim or object, unless it be to shew, that James Hogg, the Ettrick Shepherd, could tell a ludicrous story. (p. 199)

**86(b) old man with long grey locks [...] often heard but seldom seen** probably a reference to the fictitious editor of *BEM*, who is described in *Peter's Letters* as 'an obscure man, almost continually confined to his apartment by rheumatism, whose labours extend to little more than correcting proof-sheets, and drawing up plans, which are mostly executed by other people' (II, 225–26).

**86(c) gentleman [...] young, sprightly, and whimsical; with hawk's eyes, and dark curled hair** John Gibson Lockhart. See also the note for 86(d)–87(a) below.

**86(c) country-looking man, well advanced in life, with red whiskers** James Hogg. John Wilson provides a lengthy description of Hogg's appearance in an unpublished manuscript that was originally part of his vicious essay 'On Hogg's Memoirs', which appeared in the same issue of *BEM* with 'Account of a Coronation-Dinner'. Wilson writes:

> Mr Hogg has favoured the public occasionally with descriptions of the personal appearance of some of his Friends. Why has he not given us a slight sketch of his own? We shall, in a few words, supply this deficiency. James, is a stout, not ill-put-together, common-place-looking man, according to his own confession, about 50 years of age. When you first see him, you do not perceive any distinct difference between him and any other Individual. There he is,–you discern that he is not his next-chair neighbour,–but you no sooner turn away your eyes from him, than you forget his form and presence, and feel that he has not left an Image. Neither do you attribute to him any precise period of life. He seems a man of whatever age you please to fix upon him. We have heard him computed at 35–and yet there would be no absurdity in running him up as high as threescore. It is not that his face, or person is insignificant: for he has enormous buck-teeth and good calves to his legs. But still there is something about him, God knows what, that utterly disconnects him with time and place. Thus, while you are in the dark about his age, you are equally so as to his profession. You would never take him for a Shepherd who had dozed thirty years of his life on the braes of Yarrow. He has, we think somewhat of the look of a grocer in a small Country Town who had made some money, and retired a few hundred yards into the Country, feeding his own pork & watching the growth of cabbages. Though he wears top-boots, they never make you think of a Horse–or if they do you wonder why any man can be addicted to riding in nankeen breeches. His coat does not seem single breasted, and yet there is something about it puzzling and unsatisfactory. It is also of a very doubtful colour. We believe he ties his neckcloth with a small knot curiously unfolded, and the ends hanging down about a foot-long. This gives him at times, rather a dressy effect, and we have heard him remembered in company, more than once by this apparently trifling circumstance. His hands, by the way, are rather kenspeckle–the fingers being brown & dumpy, and natted with reddish hair. In hot summer weather this gives them a sultry look–and when suddenly protruded to grab his toddy, his 'bunch of fives' at first sight is not a little startling. He is fond of a waiscoat [*sic*] with a large pattern and that the emblems

might not be injured, its length of flap is quite immoderate, and overladens unduly the breeches aforesaid. He sports this vest however only when dining out. A diamond or Scotch pebble set in a gold ring sparkles on his big little finger—and he sports a brooch in his unfrilled shirt, adorned with the hair of a Servant Lass in Ettrick Forest who died in a certain condition in the 89. When sitting he uniformly puts his feet into the first position, and his paws into his breeches pockets, his mouth being in general wide open, partly by choice, but chiefly from necessity. (NLS, MS 4887, fols 5–6)

**86(c) like quills upon the fretful porcupine** from *Hamlet* I. 5. 19–20: 'And each particular hair to stand on end | Like quills upon the fretful porcupine'.

**86(d)–87(a) The young gentleman [...] no in the least intentional** In Hogg's reminiscence of Lockhart, included in his 'Reminiscences of Former Days' in *Altrive Tales* (1832), Hogg gives the following characterisation of Lockhart:

I remember once, at a festival of the Dilletanti Society, that Lockhart was sitting next me, and charming my ear with some story of authorship. I have forgot what it was; but think it was about somebody reviewing his own book. On which I said the incident was such a capital one, that I would give a crown bowl of punch to ascertain if it were true.

"What?" said Bridges; "did any body ever hear the like of that? I hope you are not suspecting your young friend of telling you a falsehood?"

"Haud your tongue Davie, for ye ken naething about it," said I. "Could ye believe it, man, that that callant never tauld me the truth a' his days but aince, an' that was merely by chance, an' without the least intention on his part?" These blunt accusations diverted Lockhart greatly, and only encouraged him to farther tricks. (*Memoir*, p. 74)

**86(d) *Marriage*** a novel by Susan Ferrier (1782–1854), published by William Blackwood in 1818. Three years after 'Account of a Coronation-Dinner' (28 June 1824) Hogg writes to Blackwood of his admiration for Ferrier and her novels:

I should like much to address a song ode or sonnet to the authoress of Marriage &c and if I do it shall be to her as the sister of David Wilkie. Never was there such a painter as she is (if a she it be of which I have strong doubts) Sir W Scott's portraits are sometimes more strongly defined but they are not more unique and rarely or never so humourous. He can paint an individual well the hero of the story But can he paint a group like the family of the fairbairns? No I defy him or any *man* alive save David Wilkie as for *women* there's no saying what *they* can do when men and children are the objects. In short if the author of MARRIAGE and THE INHERITANCE be a woman I am in love with her and I authorise you to tell her so. (*Letters 2*, p. 202)

**87(a) Let every man ride the ford as he finds it** proverbial. See Colin Walker, *Scottish Proverbs* (Edinburgh: Birlinn, 2000), p. 171. Walker cites Sir Walter Scott's *Rob Roy*: 'Let ilka ane ruse the ford as they find it. | *Let each one speak of a thing as they find it*' (Walker's rendering in italics).

**87(b) young gentleman, tall, fair, and athletic** John Wilson. Wilson is described in *Peter's Letters* as 'a very robust athletic man, broad across the back—firm set upon his limbs—and having altogether very much of that sort of air which is inseparable from the consciousness of great bodily energies. [...] His hair is of the true Cicambrian yellow; his eyes are of the lightest, and at the same time of the clearest blue' (I, 130).

87 (c) ingenious gentleman [...] now so publicly known, that I dare not even describe him perhaps Hogg is satirising William Blackwood and the significance of John Wilson's influence on him. This character makes a lengthy speech towards the end of the dinner that concludes with a toast to the memory of King George III. See pp. 91–92.

87 (d) facetious little gentleman, with an Irish accent William Maginn (1794–1842), native of Cork, Ireland, became a regular contributor to *BEM* in 1819. He was known for his parodies and his fun-loving, but often reckless and mean-spirited, articles. He became the model for Morgan Odoherty in the *Noctes* and frequently contributed to that series.

87 (d) stout boardly gentleman perhaps Dr Scott, whom Hogg describes in 'Reminiscences of Former Days' as 'that queer fat body, Dr. Scott' (*Memoir*, p. 74). See also the note on 'Mr C– N–' for 83 (c).

88 (a) Campbell's house unidentified.

88 (a) a little fat Gibbon-faced scholar, with a treble voice [...] addicted to the ludicrous perhaps Charles Kirkpatrick Sharpe, antiquarian, artist, musician, and intellectual. Sharpe was editor of James Kirkton's *Secret and True History of the Church of Scotland*, which Hogg reviewed in the December 1817 number of *BEM* (see pp. 47–54 and notes in the present edition). Hogg attacked Sharpe for his focus on the scandalous in his notes to Kirkton's text. Sir Walter Scott in his journal writes that Sharpe 'was bred a clergyman but did not take orders owing I believe to a peculiar effeminacy of voice which must have been unpleasant in reading prayers'–see *The Journal of Sir Walter Scott*, ed. by W. E. K. Anderson (Oxford: Oxford University Press, 1972), p. 2. Sharpe's high-pitched voice is also satirised in the 'Chaldee Manuscript' (see 35, II. 62–63 and note in the present edition).

88 (a) a fellow of infinite wit and humour Hamlet remembers Yorick as 'a fellow of infinite jest, of most excellent fancy'–see *Hamlet*, V. 1. 180–81.

88 (b) tall elegant old gentleman probably Robert Sym, the uncle of John Wilson and the personality upon whom Timothy Tickler is based in *BEM*. Sym had been a contributor to Hogg's periodical, *The Spy*, and Hogg describes his first meeting with Sym in 'Reminiscences of Former Days':

> Judge of my astonishment, when I was admitted by a triple-bolted door into a grand house in George's Square, and introduced to its lord, an uncommonly fine-looking elderly gentleman, about seven feet high, and as straight as an arrow! His hair was whitish, his complexion had the freshness and ruddiness of youth, his looks and address full of kindness and benevolence; but whenever he stood straight up, (for he had always to stoop about half way when speaking to a common-sized man like me,) then you could not help perceiving a little of the haughty air of the determined and independent old aristocrat. [...] His reading, both ancient and modern, is boundless, his taste and perception acute beyond those of other men; his satire keen and biting; but at the same time his good-humour is altogether inexhaustible, save when ignited by coming in collision with Whig or Radical principles. (*Memoir*, p. 77)

**88(d) whaups, or tilliwhillies, withertyweeps, and bristlecocks** although Scottish himself, the narrator assumes these birds are rare because he has never heard these names. Hogg seems to be having a joke at the expense of the city merchant by using Scottish terms for common birds. 'Whaups, or tilliwhillies' are Scottish terms for curlews, 'withertyweeps' are lapwings, and 'bristlecocks' are turkey-cocks.

**89(a) the King's Anthem** Hogg published a version of 'The King's Anthem' ('God bless our lord the king') in the second series of *Jacobite Relics* (1821) – see *Jacobite Relics. Second Series*, ed. by Murray G. H. Pittock, (S/SC, 2003), pp. 50–52.

**89(b) set the circle in a roar of laughter** echoes *Hamlet* v. 1. 184–87: 'Where be your gibes now, your gambols, your songs, your flashes of merriment that were wont to set the table on a roar?'

**89(d) Whigs Leyden's bit auld sang– | 'My name is doughty Jock Elliot, | And wha dare meddle wi' me'** lines from the Border ballad 'Little Jock Elliott':

> And wha daur meddle wi' me,
> And wha daur meddle wi' me
> My name is little Jock Elliot
> And wha daur meddle wi' me.

Jock Elliot, a member of the family of Elliots of Liddesdale, became famous primarily for his having wounded the Earl of Bothwell, the future husband of Mary, Queen of Scots, and escaped Bothwell's pursuit. John Leyden (1775–1811), from Denholm, Roxburghshire, was an exceptional scholar of languages, a physician, and a poet. Leyden assisted Walter Scott in collecting ballads for the *Minstrelsy of the Scottish Border*, and for a short time he was editor of Constable's *Scots Magazine*. In his 'Memoirs' of John Leyden, Sir Walter Scott includes an anecdote from General John Malcolm that had originally been published in the *Edinburgh Annual Register* for 1811. Malcolm writes of visiting Leyden when Leyden was ill and reading him a letter containing news of the Borders:

> I read him a passage which described the conduct of our volunteers on a fire being kindled by mistake at one of the beacons. The letter mentioned that the moment the blaze, which was the signal of invasion, was seen, the mountaineers hastened to their rendezvous, and those of Liddesdale swam the Liddel River to reach it. They were assembled (though several of their houses were at a distance of six or seven miles) in two hours, and at break of day the party marched into the town of Hawick (at a distance of twenty miles from the place of assembly) to the Border tune of *'Wha dar meddle wi' me.'* Leyden's countenance became animated as I proceeded with this detail, and at its close he sprung from his sick-bed, and, with strange melody, and still stranger gesticulations, sung aloud, *'Wha dar meddle wi' me, wha dar meddle wi' me.'* Several of those who witnessed this scene looked at him as one that was raving in the delirium of a fever.

See *The Miscellaneous Prose Works of Sir Walter Scott*, 6 vols (Edinburgh: Cadell; London: Longman, 1827), IV, 214–15.

**89(d) welcome to our King to Scotland** King George IV did visit Scotland in August 1822, a year after the coronation.

**90(a) I'm never at a loss for a sang [...] patching up an auld ane** the song that the 'countryman' sings is 'an auld ane' that Hogg has rewritten for the occasion. This *BEM* publication of 'Carle, an the King come' is the only publication of this version of the song by Hogg. Hogg also includes a different version in the first series of *Jacobite Relics* (1819). In the notes to *Jacobite Relics*, Hogg writes that the song 'is reported to be as old as the time of the Commonwealth, though with different words'–see *Jacobite Relics. [First Series]*, ed. by Murray G. H. Pittock (S/SC, 2002), p. 209. Additionally, a manuscript in Hogg's hand of 'Carle, an the King Come', in a slightly revised version and subtitled 'A Song for the Month of August', is preserved in the National Library of Scotland as MS 1809, fols 79–80. The song is addressed to 'Neil Gow Esq | Gow & Son' and is postmarked 27 July 1822. A year after 'Account of a Coronation-Dinner' Hogg suddenly seems in a rush to publish a performance version of the song. The manuscript includes a note from Hogg to Gow:

> Please publish the above song in a sheet with the music and accompaniments without any delay for my sake. You will see I have written it both ways but you should be able to have out a small edition before the arrival of his Majesty but if you find that impracticable then print it the way as corrected namely "Carle since the king's come" [...] You will get a good enough set of the fine old air in the Jacobite Relics but be sure to put it on a good singing key and if possible get it introduced on the stage. As I will be in town I can easily effect that. I think your father has accompaniments to it somewhere. (*Letters 2*, p. 170)

The manuscript follows, with minor revisions, the version published in 'Account of a Coronation-Dinner'. More substantial revisions occur in the first four lines of stanza three,

> Many a brave and true heart
> Mourn'd our exiled Stuart;
> Then for their sakes we'll hail their son,
> Carle an' (since) the King('s) come,

and the last four lines of stanza six,

> Since yellow corn waves on the rigs
> And whigs are tories, tories whigs,
> We'll lilt, and dance our Scottish jigs
> Carle an' (since) the King('s) come

**91(c)** ***Wad ye ken what a Whig is?*** Hogg published 'Would you know what a Whig is' with music in his first series of *Jacobite Relics*, originally published in 1819–see *Jacobite Relics. [First Series]*, ed. by Murray G. H. Pittock (S/SC, 2002), p. 44. In his notes to the song in *Jacobite Relics*, Hogg called the song 'one of the most violent of all the party songs, bitter as they are. It was often sung by the Tory clubs in Scotland, at their festive meetings, during the late war, in detestation of those who deprecated the principles of Pitt' (p. 212). Hogg also published a new version of the song in *BEM*, 30 (August 1831), 415.

**91(d) celebrated whig minister, who was taken from Perthshire to London** unidentified.

**92(a) the seceder minister** a member of a dissenting group that broke from the mainline Presbyterian Church of Scotland in the 1730s in protest of patronage and in support of a congregation's right to call its own minister.

**92(b) our late venerable and beloved Sovereign [...] whose descent to the grave was long overshadowed by the darkest of human calamities** King George III, who died 29 January 1820, became so mentally deranged that his son was appointed regent in February 1811. The disease with which he was afflicted gradually rendered him blind and deaf.

**92(c) gentleman [...] written more loyal and national songs** clearly another reference to Hogg himself. In a letter to Sir Walter Scott, 5 July 1821, Hogg had written in similar terms: 'You may at least say this for me that there is not a more loyal bard in Britain and that I have written more loyal and national ditties well known among our peasantry than perhaps all the bards of Scotland put together' (*Letters 2*, p. 100). A decade later Hogg's opinion of his own importance had not changed, as he wrote in his introduction to 'The Highlander's Farewell' in his 1831 collection of *Songs*: 'It is a mercy that I live in a day when the genuine heir of the Stuarts fills their throne, else my head would only be a tenant at will of my shoulders. I have composed more national songs than all the bards of Britain put together. Many of them have never been published; more of them have been, under various names and pretences: but few of them shall ever be by me again' (p. 133).

**92(d) a most beautiful old air [...] Albyn's Anthology** *Albyn's Anthology; or, a Select Anthology of the Melodies and Vocal Poetry, Peculiar to Scotland and the Isles, Hitherto Unpublished*, ed. by Alexander Campbell, 2 vols (Edinburgh: Oliver & Boyd, 1816, 1818). Hogg published thirteen songs is this collection, five in the first volume and eight in the second volume. The specific tune referred to here is not identified.

**92(d) Our good auld man** apparently this song in memory of King George III was never published separately from 'Account of a Coronation-Dinner'.

**93(b) whig dinner, with Kelly in the chair, at the Black Bull** probably a reference to the Black Bull Inn in Argyle Street, Glasgow, since the narrator is from Glasgow. The Black Bull in Glasgow was also the station for coaches to Edinburgh. There were also two Black Bull inns or taverns in Edinburgh associated with Hogg and Blackwood's. Hogg sets part of the action of *Confessions* in a Black Bull tavern in a close off High Street. (See Peter Garside's note for 17(b), 'the Black Bull tavern', in the S/SC edition of *Confessions*, p. 218.) John Lockhart writes of a different Black Bull Inn, a popular stage-coach stop near the east end of Princes Street. Peter Morris in the first edition of *Peter's Letters* (1819) describes the Black Bull Inn: 'My evil genius, in the shape of an old drivelling turnpike-man, directed me to put up at the Black Bull, a crowded, noisy, shabby, uncomfortable inn, frequented by all manner of stage-coaches and their contents, as my ears were well taught before morning' (I, 4). This description resulted in legal action against Blackwood, and the passage was deleted from the second edition of *Peter's Letters*. 'Kelly' is unidentified.

# January 1822–December 1822 (Volumes 11–12)

## The Women Folk

'The Women Folk' was first published in *A Border Garland* (Nathaniel Gow and Son, [1819], pp. 6–7) with an 'Air' by Hogg; the *Border Garland* publication also includes an arrangement for piano forte. The song was reprinted untitled but with music in *Blackwood's Edinburgh Magazine*, 12 (December 1822), 705–06, where it is sung by the 'Hogg' character in the *Noctes Ambrosianæ No. VI*. The publication of 'The Women Folk' in *BEM* marks Hogg's first publication in the *Noctes*, as well as his first appearance as a character in the fictional dialogue, although Hogg had been a topic of discussion in earlier numbers of the *Noctes*. 'The Women Folk' was reprinted in the second issue of *No. of the Border Garland* (Edinburgh: Robert Purdie, [1828], pp. 31–33), and again in the 1831 *Songs* (pp. 65–67). There are only minor spelling and punctuation differences among the publications, all of which can be attributed to printers' preferences. The third stanza of 'The Women Folk' is sung by Sandy in 'Dramas of Simple Life No. II' (p. 239 of the present edition), and the same stanza is sung by Rob as 'Song XII' in 'The Bush Aboon Traquair', which was posthumously published in *Tales and Sketches by the Ettrick Shepherd*, 6 vols (Glasgow: Blackie, 1836–37), II, 275–338 (p. 326).

In the introduction to the work in *Songs*, Hogg writes that 'The Women Folk' 'is my own favourite humorous song, when forced to sing by ladies against my will, which too frequently happens; and, notwithstanding my wood-notes wild, it will never be sung by any so well again' (p. 65).

In *BEM* the first stanza of the song is published within the music; the music in the present edition is included in Appendix B. Otherwise, the present edition reprints the *BEM* version with the following emendation:

p. 95, l. 15 lo'ed] loe'd *BEM*.

# January 1823–December 1823 (Volumes 13–14)

## The Honourable Captain Napier and Ettrick Forest
### [Manuscript Version]

'The Honourable Captain Napier and Ettrick Forest' was published in *Blackwood's Edinburgh Magazine*, 13 (February 1823), 175–88, and was not reprinted in Hogg's lifetime. The subject of 'Captain Napier' is William John Napier's book, *A Treatise on Practical Store-Farming, As Applicable to the Mountainous Region of Etterick Forest, and the Pastoral District of Scotland in General* (Edinburgh: Waugh and Innes, 1822), and the essay is the second of only two review essays published by Hogg in *BEM* (see also 'A Letter to Charles Kirkpatrick Sharpe, Esq., On his Original Mode of Editing Church History' in the present edition, pp. 47–54). The article is signed '*An* Ettrick Shepherd' rather than '*The* Ettrick Shepherd' (emphasis added), but Hogg's authorship is verified through the correspondence between Hogg and William Blackwood, as well as the existence of a manuscript in Hogg's hand of an earlier version of the essay.

William John Napier (1786–1834) was the ninth Lord Napier of Merchistoun (Merchiston), inheriting the title on his father's death in 1823. In 1803 Napier began a successful career in the navy, serving on several ships, including the *Defence* in the British victory at Trafalgar. He left the navy in September 1815, married Elizabeth Cochrane-Johnstone in March 1816, and settled on the family property in Selkirkshire as a sheep farmer. Napier dedicated himself to improving the land and the farming methods in the region–to mixed reception in Ettrick and Yarrow–and the results of his work are the basis for his book, *A Treatise on Practical Store-Farming*. Napier returned to the sea in 1824, serving in South America and China; in 1833 he became chief superintendent of trade in China, a position he held unsuccessfully due to his inadequate experience. Napier died in Macau in 1834–see the *Oxford DNB* article on Napier by J. K.

Laughton, rev. Andrew Lambert.

Hogg considered himself the logical person to write this particular review for *BEM*, given both his connection to *BEM* as a writer and, more importantly, his personal experience as a shepherd in Ettrick for most of his life. By the time of this review Hogg had also published several works on sheep farming, including *The Shepherd's Guide* (1807) and a number of articles in the *Farmer's Magazine*. (For information about Hogg's publications in the *Farmer's Magazine*, see David Groves, 'James Hogg and the *Farmer's Magazine*', *Newsletter of the James Hogg Society*, 8 (May 1989), 20–21.) In spite of his qualifications, though, Hogg sought Captain Napier's approval of the article, either out of concern for his relationship with Napier or at Blackwood's insistence. No doubt Blackwood was anxious about what Hogg would write about Napier, given Hogg's fondness for literary sport, and Blackwood was certainly aware of Hogg's feelings about Napier's having cut off Hogg's boating privileges on St Mary's Loch (see notes for 105(b)). Hogg sent the article to Blackwood on 9 January 1823 after a final evening of revising the article in Napier's presence. Hogg's accompanying letter to Blackwood expressed his frustration with Napier, as well as with Blackwood himself:

> I have found the Captain so very capricious and thin skinned that at one time I took the resolution of suppressing the article altogether; and had it not been that every thing has seemed to combine against me ever appearing among my old friends in your Magazine again I certainly would not have spoiled my article so much for no man alive. He has revised it twice, and after spending the day and a part of the night here with me yesterday he authorised the publication of the article as it now stands. (*Letters 2*, p. 179)

Hogg had written Napier earlier (the letter is undated) offering to 'suppress' the article altogether since Napier apparently could not be satisfied with Hogg's sportive criticisms of both Napier and his wife. Hogg's offer to withdraw the article comes in response to a request from Napier to meet again about the article, an invitation that Hogg initially declines because of a conflicting engagement. Hogg then reminds Napier of the right of magazine writers to publish personal information about their subjects:

> but keep yourself perfectly at ease; for as the matter is but a seven or eight pounds article I will at once suppress it altogether. I little deserved you had been so thin skinned when I set about bringing your work, improvements, and markets into that notice which I deemed they deserved, and without some account of these the rest was of little avail. Before you be half the time before the public that I have been you will be better innured to such jokes If you think the reviewers and magazine makers have not a right to bring every circumstance of a man's life that is publicly known and any way connected with his work forward you are in a confounded mistake, and that you will find. Did I not now know that you were a real good fellow in the main, I would laugh at all such strictures, but as it is I will never give either you or my very highest favourite your Lady a moments pain or disgust for such a trifle. (*Letters 2*, p. 177)

The manuscript version printed herein is based on the incomplete manuscript preserved in the Alexander Turnbull Library of the National Library of New Zealand (James Hogg Papers, 0042-02, Item 9). The manuscript is described by Peter Garside as 'Copy text for the article under the same title in *Blackwood's*

*Edinburgh magazine*, 13 (February 1823), 175–88). Printer's marks passim. The final paragraph of the printed version is not in the manuscript. 5 single leaves (two smaller), plus one 4pp booklet, 25 x 20cm., irregularly paginated by Hogg to p. 10. WM: MACNAY PICKERING & CO; LONDON/ 1815'–see 'An annotated checklist of Hogg's literary manuscripts in the Alexander Turnbull Library, Wellington, New Zealand', *The Bibliotheck*, 20 (1995), 5–23 (pp. 8–9). The manuscript consists of the following pages: the first leaf, pages 1 and 2 of the manuscript, is complete; the second leaf is missing the top half, leaving the bottom half each of pages 3 and 4, although these pages are not numbered; the third leaf, consisting of pages 5 and 6, is complete. The manuscript lacks pages 7 and 8; the fifth leaf, pages 9 and 10, is complete. The final four pages of the extant manuscript are not numbered but apparently are pages 11–14 of the manuscript. The sixth leaf, pages 11 and 12, is torn at the top, affecting about six to eight lines on each page. The last leaf, pages 13 and 14, has a small tear in the upper-right-hand corner; the tear does not affect page 13, but there is a loss of a few words in the first line of text on page 14. There are minor textual revisions on the manuscript in Hogg's hand; also, the reviewer's voice is changed throughout the manuscript from the first-person plural editorial 'we' to the first-person singular 'I', although this change might have been made by an editor rather than by Hogg.

The manuscript version probably represents the original version that Hogg intended for publication in *BEM* before Captain Napier reviewed the manuscript and forced revisions upon Hogg. Because the manuscript version and the printed version represent distinct texts, the present edition publishes both versions. The manuscript version printed herein follows Hogg's manuscript, including Hogg's occasional idiosyncratic spellings; end punctuation has been added silently where Hogg normally would have expected the printer to add it. The extracts from Napier's *Treatise on Practical Store-Farming* are added to the present edition of the manuscript version following Hogg's manuscript instructions. The annotations to the manuscript version also address the differences between the manuscript and the printed text. The text is also emended as follows:

100(c) appear to have] appear to to have (manuscript)

**96(b) no Mr Weir [...] eclogues of Virgil, and the works of Aristotle** Mr Weir is unidentified. Virgil's *Eclogues* is a series of ten pastoral poems. The poems are not about a 'mode of pasturage', although occasionally there are hints of farming methods. In 'Eclogue I', for example, Meliboeus says: 'So these lands will still be yours, and large enough for you, though bare stones cover all, and the marsh chokes your pastures with slimy rushes. Still, no strange herbage shall try your breeding ewes, no baneful infection from a neighbour's flock shall harm them'–see Virgil, *Eclogues, Georgics, Aeneid I–VI*, trans. H. R. Fairclough, rev. G. P. Goold, Loeb Classical Library (Cambridge: Harvard University Press, 1999), p. 29. The reference to Aristotle probably includes Aristotle's *History of Animals*.

**96(d) Ambrose's** the tavern in Gabriel's Road that was a regular gathering place for the *BEM* writers. See note for 36. II. 1.

**96(d) contemporary journals [...] avoided the path itself** as mentioned in the head-note above, Hogg had been a contributor to Constable's *Farmer's Magazine*. Hogg was also interested in *BEM* including more works of agricultural interest. As early as 25 September 1817 Hogg had written to

Blackwood: 'I have been thinking of something to give the work a pastoral and agricultural turn' (*Letters 1*, p. 303). Blackwood did not take up the farming cause, however, until 1828, when he established the *Quarterly Journal of Agriculture*.

97(a) **beast** an allusion to the 'Chaldee Manuscript' in which the writers and editors for Blackwood's and Constable's magazines are denominated as beasts. See pp. 26–44 of the present edition.

97(a) **Indeed [...] enterprising spirit** this sentence is not in *BEM*.

97(a) **Lord Napier [...] Thirlstane and Howpasley** Captain Napier's father, Lord Napier, was the eighth Lord Napier of Merchistoun (see the *Oxford DNB* article by Robert Clyde). The first Lord Napier of Merchistoun was Archibald Napier (*c.* 1575–1645), the eldest son of John Napier the mathematician; however, the association of Napiers with the lands of Merchistoun goes back to the fifteenth century when Alexander Napier, provost of Edinburgh, was granted land by James I in payment of a loan. (See the *Oxford DNB* article on Archibald Napier by David Stevenson.) Napier was also descended from Sir William Scott (*c.* 1670–1725) of Thirlestane and his wife, Elizabeth, daughter of Margaret, Baroness Napier. Their son, Francis, became the third Lord Napier (For additional information about Scott, see the *Oxford DNB* article by S. M. Dunnigan.) Hogg published two poems about the Scotts, the 'ancient knights of Thirlestane' and ancestors of Lord Napier, in *The Mountain Bard* (Edinburgh: Constable, 1807): 'The Pedlar' (pp. 15–34), and 'Thirlestane. A Fragment' (pp. 117–27). (See also *The Mountain Bard*, ed. by Suzanne Gilbert (S/SC, 2007), pp. 26–36, 77–81.)

97(b) THE DEFENCE **at the glorious battle of Trafalgar** *HMS Defence* was a gun ship in the British navy. It was part of the fleet that defeated the French and Spanish navies at the Battle of Trafalgar on 21 October 1805. *The Defence* forced the surrender of the Spanish ship *San Ildefonso*.

97(b) **assisting in the capture [...] his paternal name** this portion of text is not in *BEM*.

97(c) **He was twice [...] royal navy** revised in *BEM*. See p. 115(d) in the present edition.

97(c) **when the country had no more need of his arm** Napier left the navy in September 1815 following the end of the Napoleonic wars.

97(d) **set a stout heart to a steep brae** proverbial, meaning to apply courage and determination to a difficult task. Colin Walker cites the proverb from 'Alexander Montgomerie's famous poem "The Cherrie and the Slae" first published in 1597': 'Sic gettis ay as settis ay stout stomakis to the bray'—see *Scottish Proverbs* (Edinburgh: Birlinn, 2000), p. 221. Hogg also uses a variation on the expression, '*set a stout heart to a strait brae*', in *A Tour in the Highlands in 1803* (Paisley: Alexander Gardner, 1888), p. 81.

98(a) **improvement of the roads** Hogg later writes: 'But the roads and bridges were never put into a complete state of repair, till the present Lord Napier settled in the country; and to his perseverance Ettrick Forest is indebted for the excellence of her roads, now laid out and finished in every practicable direction, as well as for many other valuable improvements. With an indomitable spirit of perseverance, he has persisted against much obloquy and vituperation, and from none more than the writer of this article. But, honour to whom honour is due, Lord Napier has effected wonders, and the late impervious Ettrick Forest may compare in the beauty and efficiency of her roads, with any mountain district in the united kingdom'—see 'Statistics of Selkirkshire', *Prize Essays and Transactions of the Highland Society of Scotland*, 3 (1832), 281–306 (p. 290).

**98(a) for in it […] intentions merited.** this portion of text is not in *BEM*.

**98(b) Michmoor** a mountain three miles southeast of Innerleithen on the border of Peebleshire and Selkirkshire, altitude 1865 feet.

**98(b) Bodsbeck-Law** a mountain seven miles northeast of Moffat on the border of Dumfriesshire and Selkirkshire, altitude 2173 feet.

**98(c) [MS BREAK]** this portion of missing text corresponds approximately in the printed text to the first twenty-four lines of p. 117 in the present edition.

**98(c) Annandale** the middle district of the three districts of Dumfriesshire.

**98(c) Birkhill-Path** a mountain pass, altitude 1080 feet, on the borders of Selkirkshire and Dumfriesshire about four miles southwest of St Mary's Loch.

**98(c) He absolutely compelled the men of Tweedale […] their county** Tweedale is the old name of Peebleshire. In *BEM* this language is softened to: 'He was obliged to force one through a part of the county of Tweedale, by subscription, which was, however, readily supported by several gentlemen of that district'.

**99(a) [MS BREAK]** this portion of missing text corresponds approximately in the printed text to p. 118, l. 13, through p. 119, l. 1, in the present edition.

**99(b) Cheviot breed of sheep […] black faced natives** the Cheviot sheep were introduced widely into the Borders in the second half of the eighteenth century. The Cheviots were white faced and were typically less hardy than the black-faced (or short) sheep, although their wool was longer and commanded a higher price. The author of the 'Eskdalemuir' section of *The Statistical Account of Scotland 1791–1799*, ed. by Sir John Sinclair, 20 vols (Edinburgh: W. Creech; repr. Wakefield: EP Publishing, 1978) addresses the inferiority of the Cheviot sheep in certain areas of Scotland:

> But the principal production of the parish is sheep, which are coming daily more into request. At the head of the parish, they are all the short kind; but lower down they are, for the most part, of the Cheviot breed. Some attempts were made to introduce them on the higher grounds, but without success. The general opinion of the farmers is, that the grounds are too wet and stormy; that the sudden changes hurt them more than the short sheep; and that death among the lambs is greater. (IV, 159)

See also the note for 64(c).

**99(b) Clydesdale** the valley of the River Clyde in South Lanarkshire.

**99(c) the Doddies** hornless cattle, but a term also applied to sheep in Scotland; here it is used derisively.

**99(c) St. Boswell's fair** St Boswell's is a village in Roxburghshire. The sheep fair was held on July 18.

**99(c) wedders** wethers, castrated rams.

**100(b) David Wilkie** (1785–1841), Scottish artist, a genre painter whom Hogg greatly admired. Hogg met Wilkie in 1817 at Bowhill, the Duke of Buccleuch's estate, where Wilkie was visiting along with Sir Walter Scott. Lockhart reports that on meeting Wilkie, Hogg said: 'Thank God for it. I did not know that you were so young a man' (*Life of Scott*, III, 139). Hogg wrote three sketches for *The Amulet* for 1830 (although they were not published) in recognition of

Wilkie: 'The Dorty Wean', 'The History of an Auld Naig', and 'David Wilkie'–
see *Contributions to Annuals and Gift-Books*, ed. by Janette Currie and Gillian
Hughes (S/SC, 2006), pp. 181–85. The opening line of 'The Dorty Wean'
expresses Hogg's admiration for Wilkie's talent and vision: 'I never see an
interesting and original figure or a group but I uniformly think to myself
"O if I had but David Wilkie here!"' (p. 181). Hogg frequently makes
reference to Wilkie in his works, such as in the 'Love Adventures of George
Cochrane' (*WET*, p. 214) and 'Trials of Temper' (p. 321 in the present
edition).

**100(c) Auld Watie Bryden** Walter Bryden, familiarly known as 'Cow Wat'.
See note for 85(d).

**100(c) like whited walls, and painted sepulchres full of rottenness within**
from Matthew 23. 27: 'Woe unto you, scribes and Pharisees, hypocrites!
for ye are like unto whited sepulchres, which indeed appear beautiful outward,
but are within full of dead men's bones, and of all uncleanness'.

**100(c) James Bryden** unidentified, but Bryden was a common name in Ettrick
and Yarrow. Hogg mentions a Jamie Bryden in the second part of 'Storms'
in 'The Shepherd's Calendar' series in *BEM*, 5 (May 1819), 214. See *The
Shepherd's Calendar*, ed. by Douglas S. Mack (S/SC, 1995), p. 17.

**100(d) horn of the unicorn** from Psalm 22. 21: 'Save me from the lion's
mouth: for thou hast heard me from the horns of the unicorns'.

**100(d) Old John Rieve [...] Grieve)** Hogg refers to a Mr Grieve, a farmer at
Craik, in *The Shepherd's Guide: Being a Practical Treatise on the Diseases of Sheep*
(Edinburgh: Constable; London: Murray, 1807), p. 129.

**101(a) their stink may come up into his nostrils** from Amos 4. 10: 'and I have
made the stink of your camps to come up unto your nostrils'.

**101(b) short ewe** also known as Blackface or Forest breed; the term 'short'
refers to the length of the wool. See note for 64(c).

**102(a) [MS BREAK]** this portion of missing text corresponds approximately in
the printed text to p. 122, l. 5, through p. 124, l. 16, in the present edition.

**102(b) So long has the round house [...] drink with his associates** this sentence
is not in *BEM*. It is likely that Captain Napier did not consider it appropriate
to include Mrs Napier in this joke. A 'round house' is a place to lock up
persons who have been arrested.

**102(b) These markets** the article on 'Ettrick' in the *New Statistical Account* describes
the Ettrick markets:

> Here there are four fairs held annually. One in the end of March for
> the sale of *grit ewes*; for the hiring of servants, and especially for the
> hiring of shepherds. Another held in the end of July, called the *lamb
> fair*, where wool and lambs are disposed of, and a great deal of other
> business transacted. The third is in the month of September, for the
> sale of *draft ewes* and small lambs, and for the purchasing of tups and
> fat sheep. This is the largest of the four, and is a very important
> market both for the seller and purchaser. [...] The fourth, called the
> Little fair, is held in November, and is principally for selling and
> purchasing fat sheep for *marts*. (III, 75–76)

Hogg uses the September fair at Thirlestane as the setting for the meeting
between the 'Editor' and 'James Hogg' in *Confessions of a Justified Sinner* (S/
SC, 2001), pp. 169–70.

**102(c) the Pastoral Club** established by Napier in 1818 to improve farming conditions in Ettrick and Yarrow, and most land-owners and farmers of Ettrick and Yarrow were members. The Rev. James Smith, author of the 'Ettrick' section of the *New Statistical Account*, quotes Alexander Laidlaw on the value of the Pastoral Club: 'The society not only stirs up a spirit of emulation among farmers in general, but serves also as a school where the young farmer will *see* the real and apparent properties of live stock pointed out by the judges, but also *hear* the relative advantages and disadvantages of almost every breed fearlessly discussed at the annual general meeting' (III, 71).

103(a) **the poor's rates** a legal assessment on the landowners to provide for the poor of the parish. In Scotland the kirk session and heritors had the authority to assess parishioners for the support of the poor, although parishes often were successful in raising money through church collections and voluntary contributions by the heritors, especially in the rural parishes. The process of voluntary contributions typically was preferred in Scotland to the compulsory assessments that were legal in Scotland and widely imposed in England. See Callum G. Brown, *Religion and Society in Scotland since 1707* (Edinburgh: Edinburgh University Press, 1997), pp. 69, 97.

103(a–b) **and once went so far [...] shall be the last** this section was omitted from *BEM*.

103(d) **accustomed rascals** revised to 'experienced tikes' in *BEM*.

104(b) **Accordingly, on the next Sunday [...] church in the kingdom** this section was omitted from *BEM*.

105(a) **[MS BREAK]** this portion of missing text corresponds approximately in the printed text to lines 13–23 on p. 127 in the present edition.

105(a) **Clavers** John Graham of Claverhouse—see note for 12(a). Hogg humourously compares the 'carnage' of the rabbits with the 'carnage' resulting from Claverhouse's attacks on the Covenanters. Also, as Douglas Mack pointed out, Hogg had a greyhound named Clavers. Hogg wrote to John Wallace on 25 November 1818: 'I have three as fine greyhounds as ever sprung to a hill; their names will amuse you Clavers, Burly, and Kettledrummle' (*Letters 1*, p. 393). All are named for characters in Walter Scott's *Old Mortality* (1816); Kettledrummle is fictitious, but Clavers and Burly (from John Balfour of Burley, one of the assassins of Archbishop Sharp) are named for historical persons.

105(b–d) **It will likewise be observed, [...] altogether untenable** this section omitted from *BEM*. Hogg had been upset with Lord Napier for depriving him of his boating privileges on St Mary's Loch, a personal slight that Hogg never completely forgot. Henry Scott Riddell in his biographical sketch of Hogg, 'James Hogg, the Ettrick Shepherd', *Hogg's Weekly Instructor,* 21 August 1847, pp. 403–09, sees this incident as illustrative of Hogg's character:

When he disliked, or disesteemed any one, he did not conceal his sentiments, but in general spoke out what he thought, in such a way of truth and simplicity, that however much the individual might regret the Shepherd's disapproval of him, yet he could scarcely feel offended. The Shepherd himself, when offended by anyone, entertained no bitterness of feeling towards him, although, at the same time, he maintained his plea with positive power. When the late Lord Napier destroyed from off the Lake of St Mary the boat and boat-house which Mr Ballantyne of Tinnis had put upon it, and which was ever

free to Hogg and his friends, the poet and his lordship corresponded
by letter on the subject, and the matter was somewhat made up;
nevertheless, nine or ten verses were inserted in the ballad of Mary
Scott, in the last edition of the "Queen's Wake," in consequence of
this procedure, which casts a reflection upon his lordship, though
evidently by a mind that entertained and cherished no malice. (p.
408)

It is not likely that Captain Napier wished to continue the public dispute
between Hogg and the Napier family, even if Hogg's language in this section
pretends to lay some blame upon Hogg as well. See also the notes to
105(b) and 105(c) below.

105(b) **"The Queen's Wake"** [...] RED WILL OF THIRLESTANE Hogg adds the
twenty-eight-line 'Red Will of Thirlestane' section to 'Mary Scott' in 'Night
the Third' of the fifth edition of *The Queen's Wake* (1819) in place of a four-
line stanza that had insulted the Napier character. Hogg wrote Napier that
in reading over *The Queen's Wake* for a new edition, 'the moment that my eye
came on [the stanza] I blotted it out, but in its place I could not refrain
having a joke upon you for though I regard you as a most noble fellow I
cannot help thinking there is something peculiar in your character' (*Letters 1*,
pp. 334–35). The letter includes a draft of the replacement verses, although
the verses were revised before they were published in *The Queen's Wake*–see
the S/SC edition of *The Queen's Wake*, pp. 321–22, ll. 708–35.

105(c) **He ne'er in all his restless life | Did unbecoming thing BUT ONE!**
from 'Mary Scott' in the fifth edition of *The Queen's Wake*–see the S/SC
edition, p. 322, ll. 734–35. Hogg writes in his introduction to 'I'll No Wake
wi' Annie' in *Songs*: 'Lord Napier never did so cruel a thing, not even on the
high seas, as the interdicting of me from sailing on that beloved lake, which
if I have not rendered classical, has not been my blame. But the credit will
be his own,–that is some comfort' (p. 224). See also notes to 105(a) and
105(b) above.

105(c) **something about the WATER COW of St. Mary's Loch** stories about
legendary water cows, water bulls, and water horses in the lochs of the
Borders and Highlands were common; the modern 'Loch Ness monster' is
the most enduring legend of this kind of beast. Hogg mentions the Water
Cow of St Mary's Loch in his poem 'Mess John': 'And deep, and long, from
out the lake, | The Water-Cow was heard to low' (see *The Mountain Bard*
(Edinburgh: Constable, 1807), p. 83). Hogg's notes to 'Mess John' introduce
the legend of the beast:

In some places of the Highlands of Scotland, the inhabitants are still
in continual terror of an imaginary being, called *The Water-Horse*. When
I was travelling over the extensive and dreary isle of Lewis, I had a
lad of Stornoway with me as a guide and interpreter. On leaving the
shores of Loch Rogg, in our way to Harries, we came to an inland
lake, called, I think, Loch Alladale; and, though our nearest road lay
alongside the shores of this loch, Malcolm absolutely refused to
accompany me by that way for fear of the *Water-Horse*, of which he
told many wonderful stories, swearing to the truth of them; and, in
particular, how his father had lately been very nigh taken by him, and
that he had succeeded in decoying one man to his destruction, a short
time previous to that. This spectre is likewise an inhabitant of Loch

Aven at the foot of Cairngorm, and of Loch Laggan, in the wilds
betwixt Lochaber and Badenoch. Somewhat of a similar nature seems
to have been *The Water-Cow*, which, in former times, haunted Saint
Mary's loch, of which some extremely fabulous stories are yet related;
and, though rather less terrible and malevolent than the Water-Horse,
yet, like him, she possessed the rare slight of turning herself into
whatever shape she pleased, and was likewise desirous of getting as
many dragged into the lake as possible. Andrew Moore, above-
mentioned, said, that, when he was a boy, his parents would not suffer
him to go to play near the loch for fear of her; and that he remembered
of seeing her once coming swimming towards him and his comrades
in the evening twilight, but they all fled, and she sunk before reaching
the side. A farmer of Bourhope once got a breed of her, which he kept
for many years, until they multiplied exceedingly; and he never had
any cattle throve so well, until once, on some outrage or disrespect on
the farmer's part towards them, the old dam came out of the lake
one pleasant March evening, and gave such a roar, until all the
surrounding hills shook again; upon which her progeny, nineteen in
number, followed her all quietly into the loch, and were never more
seen. (pp. 94–95)
(See also Hogg, *The Mountain Bard*, ed. by Suzanne Gilbert (S/SC, 2007), pp.
60, 66.) Sir Walter Scott also records a story of a highland Water Cow in his
*Journal* for 23 November 1827:
    Clanronald told us as an instance of highland credulity that a set of
    his highland kinsmen, Borradale and others, believing that the fabulous
    Water Cow inhabited a small lake near his house, resolved to drag
    the monster into day. With this view they bivouackd by the side of
    the lake in which they placed by way of night bait two small anchors
    such as belong to boats each baited with the carcase of a dog slain for
    the purpose. They expected the Water cow would gorge on this bait
    and were prepared to drag her ashore the next morning. When to
    their confusion of face the baits were found untouchd. It is something
    too late in the day for setting baits for Water Cows. (pp. 383–84)
**105(d) Alexander Laidlaw** (*d.* 1842), shepherd of Bowerhope farm in Yarrow
and one of Hogg's closest friends from their childhood.
**106(a–b) Eldinhope [...] Sundhope** the farms here discussed by Laidlaw and
Hogg were all located within a few miles of each other in the Yarrow and
Ettrick valleys.
**106(b) *(The additional sentence here)** in the *BEM* version, there is a paragraph
at this point that is not in the manuscript. See p. 128 of the present edition.
**106(b) essay by the Rev^d Dr Singers** Napier devotes about ten pages (pp. 63–
72) of his work to the opinions of Singers, who supported Napier's preference
for the Cheviot breed of sheep. The Reverend William Singers was minister
of Kirkpatrick in Dumfriesshire and an agricultural writer. He published
numerous farming articles, especially in *Prize Essays and Transactions of the
Highland Society*, and he was also author of a book, *General View of the Agriculture,
State of Property, and Improvements, in the Country of Dumfries* (1812).
**106(c) the Clyde** the river Clyde rises in southeast Lanarkshire and flows for
more than a hundred miles before opening into the Firth of Clyde west of
Glasgow.

**106(d)–107(a) There is another remarkable fact [...] say to this?** this paragraph was omitted from *BEM*.

**107(b) led farms** farms controlled by absentee owners.

**107(d) "rack-rent"** excessive rents that approach the value of a tenant's income from the farm. Although single quotes are called for here, the double quotes are retained as in *BEM*.

**110(d)–111(a) Let it not [...] shall be required** this portion of the quotation from Napier is not in *BEM*. Hogg's manuscript instructions, however, include this section.

**114(a) Messrs Balfour & Clark's best stile of printing** Andrew Balfour and James Clarke operated printing businesses in Edinburgh and worked together on a number of projects in the late 1810s and early 1820s. By 1824, however, James Clarke was working independently and printed Hogg's novel, *The Private Memoirs and Confessions of a Justified Sinner*. For further discussion of Balfour and Clarke, see Peter Garside's introduction to the S/SC edition of *Confessions* (2001), pp. lv–lxvi.

**114(a) the Black Douglas** Sir James Douglas (*d.* 1330), also known as the Good Sir James, was a soldier and one of King Robert the Bruce's most fierce and loyal military leaders. Besides fighting for the King, Douglas also directed some of his military activity towards recovering the family land in Ettrick that had been granted to Sir Robert Clifford by Edward I after the arrest and death of Douglas's father, Sir William. For additional information about Douglas, see the *Oxford DNB* article by A. A. M. Duncan.

### The Honourable Captain Napier and Ettrick Forest
### [*BEM* Version]

'The Honourable Captain Napier and Ettrick Forest' is a review essay of William John Napier's book, *A Treatise on Practical Store-Farming, As Applicable to the Mountainous Region of Etterick Forest, and the Pastoral District of Scotland in General* (Edinburgh: Waugh and Innes, 1822). It was published in *Blackwood's Edinburgh Magazine*, 13 (February 1823), 175–88, and was not reprinted in Hogg's lifetime. A manuscript of an earlier version is preserved in the Alexander Turnbull Library of the National Library of New Zealand. Because the manuscript and published versions represent distinct texts, the present edition includes both versions. For information about the composition and publication of 'The Honourable Captain Napier and Ettrick Forest', see the head-note to the annotations for the manuscript version. The annotations that follow address in full those points that are unique to the *BEM* version; for notes that are common to both *BEM* and the manuscript, the reader is directed to the appropriate reference in the manuscript version.

The text of the printed version follows the *BEM* publication with the following emendations:

118(d) a',] a,' *BEM*
126(a) overpowering] overpowing *BEM*

**115(a) no Mr Weir [...] Eclogues of Virgil, and the works of Aristotle** see the note for 96(b).

**115(b) Ambrose's** see the note for 96(d).

**115(c) contemporary journals [...] avoided the path itself** see the note for 96(d).

**115(c) beast** see the note for 97(a).

**115(d) Lord Napier [...] Thirlstane and Howpasley** see the note for 97(a).

**115(d) THE DEFENCE at the glorious battle of Trafalgar** see the note for 97(b).

**116(b) set a stout heart to a steep brae** see the note for 97(d).

**116(c) improvement of the roads** see the note for 98(a).

**116(d) Michmoor** see the note for 98(b).

**116(d) Bodsbeck-Law** see the note for 98(b).

**117(a) *wreaths* of snow** snowdrifts.

**117(c) the inhospitable Moors of Ale** Ale Water rises on Henwoodie Hill in Roberton Parish and joins the Teviot near Ancrum.

**117(c) the Eskdale district of Dumfries-shire** the eastern district of the three districts of Dumfriesshire.

**117(c) Annandale** see the note for 98(c).

**117(c) Birkhill-Path** see the note for 98(c).

**117(c) the county of Tweedale** the old name of Peeblesshire.

**117(d) The readiness [...] ages to come** this paragraph was added to the *BEM* version.

**118(b) hirsel** a flock of sheep.

**118(b) wauf hoggs** a hogg is a young sheep from the time it is weaned until its first shearing, a yearling; 'wauf' means stray or wandering.

**118(c) old Bonnety** a general term for a shepherd derived from the cap typically worn by shepherds. See also the note on 'blue bonnets' for 121(a).

**118(d) the rot** a disease of the liver in sheep caused by feeding on moist pasture-lands or the fluke-worm in the liver. Hogg discusses the rot at length in *The Shepherd's Guide* (Edinburgh: Archibald Constable; London: John Murray, 1807). Hogg attributes the cause of the rot to 'a sudden fall in condition' of the sheep (p. 127). Hogg recommends 'draining all the marsh and boggy land on the farm, except such of it as produces deer-hair and ling' (p. 155).

**118(d) stells** enclosures to shelter sheep on a hillside, usually circular and made of stone.

**119(a) Cheviot breed of sheep [...] black-faced natives** see the note for 99(b).

**119(a) Clydesdale** see the note for 99(b).

**119(b) *the doddies*** see the note for 99(c).

**119(b) St Boswell's fair** see the note for 99(c).

**119(b) stout wedders** see the note for 99(c). The manuscript reads 'short wedders'; the black-faced sheep were also known as 'short' sheep. The word 'stout' may be a misreading of 'short' by the typesetter.

**120(a) David Wilkie** see the note for 100(b).

**120(b) *Auld Watie Brydon* see the note** for 100(c).

**120(b) like whited walls, and painted sepulchres, full of rottenness within** see the note for 100(c).

**120(b) James Bryden** see the note for 100(c).

**120(c) horn of the unicorn** see the note for 100(d).

**120(c) Old John Rieve [...] Grieve)** see the note for 100(d). This sentence begins a new paragraph in the manuscript.

**120(d) their stink may come up into his nostrils** see the note for 101(a).

**121(a) "O be nae [...] shed their blood."** this sentence added to the *BEM* version.

**121(a) Will o' Phaup** William Laidlaw, Hogg's maternal grandfather. See the notes for 'A Last Adieu' and for 8(d).

**121(a) spare a wee bit remnant, to show the generations that are to come what has been afore them** echoes Ezekiel 6. 8, 9: 'Yet will I leave a remnant, that ye may have some that shall escape the sword among the nations. [...] And they that escape of you shall remember me among the nations whither they shall be carried captives'.

**121(a) blue bonnets and the cloutit shoon** see the notes for 1(c) and 142(d). Both terms are used figuratively by Will o' Phaup to refer to the Covenanters.

**121(b) short ewe** see the note for 101(b).

**122(a) Halcyon days** a period of calm and quiet.

**123(d) public markets** see the note on 'These markets' for 102(b).

**124(a) Lochmaben** a town in Dumfriesshire about nine miles northeast of Dumfries and about twenty-five miles southwest of Thirlestane.

**124(a) Wahabee Indian** a follower of the Muslim reformer Abd-el-Wahab (1691–1787), whose influence extended throughout much of Arabia and into India.

**124(b) ragged Black-Jock-man** a Black Jack or Jock is 'a black leather jerkin' (*SND*), but the specific reference is unidentified.

**124(b) round-house** a place to lock up persons who have been arrested.

**124(d) the Pastoral Club** see the note for 102(c).

**125(b) the poors' rates** see the note for 103(a).

**125(b) in as far as [...] must gradually diminish** this part of the sentence was added in *BEM*.

**126(c) But all the opposition [...] solemn part of the service** this paragraph was added to the *BEM* version.

**126(c) Etterick, as Mr Boston and the Captain spell it** Thomas Boston (1676–1732) was minister of the Ettrick parish kirk from 1707 until 1732. In his *Memoirs* (1776), for example, Boston uses the spelling 'Etterick' throughout. Ironincally, the 'Etterick' spelling is also used in Hogg's record of his 1802 Highland tour, first published in the *Scots Magazine*, although this spelling might have been editorial rather than authorial. See, for example, 'A Journey through the Highlands of Scotland', *Scots Magazine*, 64 (October 1802), 814.

**127(b) Mr Hogg's stories as if they were gospel** Napier quotes extensively from Hogg's 'Storms', which had been published in *BEM*, 5 (April and May 1819), 75–81, 210–16, and reprinted as part of 'The Shepherd's Calendar' in *Winter Evening Tales* (1820), II, 152–80. In the lines that follow in 'Captain Napier', Hogg introduces doubt about the accuracy of the 'Storms' essay, although in the 'Storms' essay itself Hogg writes that 'I shall, therefore, in order to give a true picture of the storm, merely relate what I saw, and shall in nothing exaggerate'—see *BEM*, 5 (April 1819), p. 77; also *WET*, p. 376, and *Shepherd's Calendar*, p. 5. Perhaps in the 'Captain Napier' article Hogg intends to suggest that he was not the author of the review of Napier's book. Napier, of course, already knew of Hogg's authorship; for the rest of the *BEM* readership, this subterfuge of authorship must have been merely for Hogg's delight in magazine sport.

**127(b) Beds of Esk [...] great thaw in February 1794** in 'Storms' Hogg writes of the devastation of the storm of 24 January 1794 and the ensuing thaw: 'The greater part of the rivers on which the storm was most deadly, run into the Solway Firth, on which there is a place called *the Beds of Esk*, where the tide throws out, and leaves whatsoever is carried into it by the rivers.

When the flood after the storm subsided, there were found on that place, and the shores adjacent, 1840 sheep, nine black cattle, three horses, two men, one woman, forty-five dogs, and one hundred and eighty hares, besides a number of meaner animals'—see *BEM*, 5 (April 1819), p. 77; also *WET*, p. 376, and *Shepherd's Calendar*, pp. 4–5. William Brown, the author of the 'Eskdalemuir' chapter of the *New Statistical Account*, describes the snow storm of late January 1794 as 'the most dreadful ever known in this place' (IV, 414).

**127(c) Clavers** see the note for 105(a).

**127(c) Alexander Laidlaw** see the note for 105(d).

**127(d)–128(b) Eldinhope [...] Woolee** the farms here discussed by Laidlaw and Hogg were all located within a few miles of each other in the Yarrow and Ettrick valleys.

**128(a–c) In stating the losses [...] affect his arguments** this paragraph was added to the *BEM* version.

**128(a) gimmers** female sheep between the first and second shearing (*SND*).

**128(b) Langholm fair** Langholm is a town in east Dumfriesshire at the confluence of the rivers Ewes and Esk about thirty miles east of Dumfries. The Langholm Summer Fair was one of the largest lamb fairs in Scotland and was normally held on the last Friday of July.

**128(c) essay by the Rev. Dr Singers** see the note for 106(b).

**128(d) the Clyde** see the note for 106(c).

**129(a)–130(a) There is another thing [...] the Yorkshire markets** these two paragraphs were added to the *BEM* version.

**129(a) farm of Thirlestane** Napier's farm in Ettrick. Napier includes a fold-out map of the farm opposite the title page of *A Treatise on Practical Store-Farming*; the map indicates the location of the stells, parks, houses, and other improvements to the land described in the book. The primary landmarks of the farm are present on modern Ordnance Survey maps: the farm extended along Ettrick Water in the south approximately from Ramseycleuch to Hopehouse, with the northeast border extending along Hopehouse Burn and Kings Grain to Berrybush Burn, the northern border along Berrybush Burn to west of Cowan's Croft, and then the western border encompassing Ward Law south to Ramseycleuch.

**130(b) led farms** see the note for 107(b).

**130(d) "rack-rent"** see the note for 107(d).

**136(d) Messrs Balfour and Clark's best style of printing** see the note for 114(a).

**136(d) the Black Douglas** see the note for 114(a).

**137(b–d) Now, Mr North [...] from your obedient** this concluding paragraph is not part of the draft manuscript and very likely was added by John Wilson. It is true, though, that Hogg, like many authors of his time, expected editorial assistance in punctuating his works for publication. Hogg's surviving manuscripts among the Blackwood papers typically either lack punctuation altogether or are inconsistently punctuated. Unfortunately, this concluding paragraph is an unnecessary distraction from the seriousness of Hogg's essay.

**137(c) Charlie's wain** or wagon, is a cluster of stars in the constellation Ursa Major, also known as the Big Dipper because of the dipper-shaped configuration of the stars.

137(d) AN ETTRICK SHEPHERD | *Buccleuch* | *Jan. 8th,* 1823 Hogg's letter to Blackwood the next day (9 January) is signed from Altrive Lake, Hogg's own farm leased from the Duke of Buccleuch. Perhaps Hogg signs the 'Captain Napier' review letter from 'Buccleuch' rather than 'Altrive Lake' to provide an extra measure of authority to the article by making the reader associate the article with the Duke of Buccleuch. The signature does not appear in the manuscript, however, so it is also possible that it is editorial.

## When the Kye Comes Hame

One of Hogg's personal favourites, 'When the Kye Comes Hame' was first published in Hogg's novel *The Three Perils of Man*, 3 vols (London: Longman, 1822), III, 17–22. It appeared untitled in *Blackwood's Edinburgh Magazine*, 13 (May 1823), 598, in the *Noctes Ambrosianæ No. VIII*, where it is sung by the 'Hogg' character. The *BEM* publication of the song also included the music; the tune, though not specified in *BEM*, is identified by Hogg in a letter to George Thomson as Hogg's variation on 'The Blathrie o't', with an additional chorus: 'I have written a wee trife [*sic*] that I like to hear sung exceedingly to the tune of "The Bladrie o't" to which I have subjoined a second part to suit my chorus I wish you would publish it for I think *it will take*' (*Letters 2*, p. 132). See Appendix B for the music from *BEM*.

Hogg's song appears in the *Noctes* in a dialogue primarily between the Odoherty and Hogg characters. The *Noctes* characters discuss the popular French songwriter, Pierre Jean de Béranger (1780–1857), and Odoherty sings Béranger's song , 'L'Ombre D'Anacreon'. The Hogg character, who does not understand French, questions Odoherty about the contents of the song and concludes that the song has been 'plunder't out o' my *Perils*' by Béranger. Hogg then sings what he calls 'the original'. Following Hogg's song, Odoherty compliments Hogg on his new song, but then Hogg attacks Odoherty and accuses him of not having read *The Three Perils of Man*, where the song first appeared, even though Odoherty supposedly had reviewed the novel five times. Tickler defends Odoherty by commenting that the song was so extensively revised and improved that Odoherty might reasonably mistake the song for a new one.

Tickler's comment about the revisions to the poem is to the point. 'When the Kye Comes Hame' was published in *The Three Perils of Man* under the title 'The Sweetest Thing the Best Thing'. The song was published untitled in *BEM* in May 1823 and was reprinted in *Songs* under the title 'When the Kye Comes Hame'; there are significant variations with each publication. There are at least two surviving manuscripts of the song, one of which pre-dates the first publication. The earlier manuscript, with the title 'When the kie comes hame', is included in a letter dated 14 December 1821 from Hogg to George Thomson, music collector and publisher, and is preserved in the British Library as Additional Manuscript 35,265, fols 98–99 (see *Letters 2*, pp. 131–33). A second manuscript is preserved in a letter to 'My dear Blakie' (correspondent unidentified) in the Edinburgh University Library, MS Dc. 4. 101–103 (see *Letters 2*, pp. 217–19); the letter is undated, but the paper is watermarked 1824, thus it was written after the *BEM* publication.

The version in the Thomson manuscript, which Thomson did not publish, consists of three verses only, with the following opening stanza:

Come rove with me come love with me
And laugh at noble men

> I'll tell ye of a secret rare
>   That courtiers dinna ken
> What is the greatest bliss
>   That the tongue of man can name
> 'Tis to meet a bonny lassie
>   When the kie comes hame[.]

In a note to Thomson following the song, Hogg writes: 'I dont like the first four lines but I had no other ready' (*Letters 2*, p. 133). Hogg revised the opening four lines for the first publication in *Three Perils*:

> Come tell me a' you shepherds
>   That love the tarry woo',
> And tell me a' you jolly boys
>   That whistle at the plow[.]

Apparently still not satisfied, Hogg revised the opening lines again for the *BEM* version, and the *BEM* version of the opening lines was used in later printings. The *Noctes* dialogue addresses the revision; Tickler says: 'The song is a good deal altered since [*Three Perils*], and much for the better. As it stands in the novel, if I recollect right, it begins with some trash about "Tarry woo'", and "whistling at the plow". The Standard-bearer might easily think the song a new one' (p. 599).

The *Three Perils* version consists of eight verses, although the 'horn mad' poet who sings the song claims there are sixteen. The poet first sings the verse beginning 'When the bluart bears a pearl', the fourth verse of the *BEM* version, in a discussion of which verse is the favourite among the poet's companions. After further discussion, the poet sings five verses of the song before his memory fails him. He then concludes by singing the last two verses, which he claims are verses fifteen and sixteen. The second and third verses of *Three Perils* correspond with the *BEM* version. The fourth verse of the *Three Perils* version is not included in *BEM*, although it is the same as the second verse of the Thomson manuscript. Verse five is the same in *BEM* and *Three Perils*, as are the last two verses, which in *BEM* are verses six and seven and in *Three Perils* verses fifteen and sixteen.

The 'Blakie' manuscript generally follows the *BEM* version through the first four verses. Verse five of *BEM* is omitted in 'Blakie'; the sixth verse of *BEM* becomes verse five in 'Blakie'. Verse six of 'Blakie' is not in earlier versions:

> Then since all nature joins
> In this love without alloy
> O wha wad prove a traitor
> To nature's dearst joy
> Or wha wad chuse a crown
> Wi' its perils and its fame
> And miss his bonny lassie
>   When the kye come hame[.]

The seventh (and final) verse of 'Blakie' is the same as the fourth verse of *Three Perils* and is not in *BEM* (see above). In the 'Blakie' manuscript the verses are numbered 1 through 7; as is common in Hogg's manuscripts, there is no punctuation. In a letter to Blakie, Hogg writes: 'You will see and feel that the song is much too long for singing and yet none of the verses can well be spared save the last, which I always leave out when singing it to ladies, and the anti-penult one when singing it to gentlemen only' (*Letters 2*, p. 219). It is certain that the 'Blakie' version was written after the *BEM* publication; it is almost certain that it was written before *Songs* was published. Both 'Blakie' and *BEM* use the same standard grammatical form of 'when the kye *come* hame'. Hogg explains his reversion to the popular form of 'when the kye *comes* hame' in an introductory note to the song in *Songs*: 'In the title and chorus of this favourite pastoral song, I choose rather to violate a rule in grammar, than a Scottish phrase so common, that when it is altered into the proper, every shepherd and shepherd's sweetheart account it nonsense. I was once singing it at a wedding with great glee the latter way, ("when the kye come hame,") when a tailor, scratching his head, said, "It was a terrible affectit way that!" I stood corrected, and have never sung it so again' (p. 51).

Hogg's *Songs* version contains further revisions. There are seven verses in *Songs*. The first four verses correspond to the first four verses in *BEM* and 'Blakie', although verse two has been extensively revised as follows:

> 'Tis not beneath the coronet,
>   Nor canopy of state,
> 'Tis not on couch of velvet,
>   Nor arbour of the great—
> 'Tis beneath the spreading birk,
>   In the glen without the name,
> Wi' a bonny, bonny lassie,
>   When the kye comes hame.
>   When the kye comes hame, &c.

The sixth and seventh verses of 'Blakie' have been reversed in *Songs*. The last verse is followed by the full chorus in *Songs*. In a note following the song in *Songs*, Hogg comments on the length as he does in the 'Blakie' version: 'It is too long to be sung from beginning to end; but only the second and antepenult verses can possibly be dispensed with, and these not very well neither' (p. 55); however, in *Songs* he does not connect the omissions to the gender of his audiences.

In *BEM* the first verse is included only within the music (see Appendix B for the music). The first verse is printed here without the music; otherwise, the present edition follows the *BEM* version with the following emendation.

  138, l. 19 fauldit] fouldit *BEM*

**138, ll. 18–19 When the bluart bears a pearl [...] fauldit up his ee** images of flowers whose blossoms close at night.

**138, l. 23 eye shines sae bright, the hale soul to beguile** echoes Luke 11. 34: 'The light of the body is the eye: therefore when thine eye is single, thy whole body also is full of light; but when thine eye is evil, thy body also is full of darkness'.

## A Scots Mummy

'A Scots Mummy' was first published in *Blackwood's Edinburgh Magazine*, 14 (August 1823), 188–90. The narrative was not reprinted as a separate story in Hogg's lifetime; however, Hogg includes a large portion of the work within the second 'Editor's Narrative' of his novel, *The Private Memoirs and Confessions of a Justified Sinner* (1824). In the novel Hogg omits the portion of the *BEM* story that sets the magazine context: the first nine paragraphs, the last five sentences of the fourteenth paragraph (p. 142(b) in the present edition), and the concluding paragraph. Otherwise, Hogg includes the sketch in *Confessions* with only minor printing changes and one additional editorial change, the insertion of '(Auld-Righ, *the King's burn,*)' following 'Mr Anderson of Eltreive' (p. 140(c)). For further discussion of the *BEM* story in the context of *Confessions*, see Peter Garside's Introduction to the S/SC edition of the novel (2001).

Hogg wrote to William Blackwood on 7 August 1823, enclosing 'A Scots Mummy': 'I send you in for Maga the particulars of a curious incident that has excited great interest here' (*Letters 2*, p. 193). Hogg sets a playful Maga context for the story. The early paragraphs suggest that 'Christopher North', the fictional editor of *BEM*, had requested that Hogg send a story about 'the boundless phenomena of nature'. Hogg complies with North's request and sends a story about the opening of the grave of a young suicide and the unusual preservation of the man's body. In the 'Yarrow' article in *The New Statistical Account of Scotland* (III, 29–58), James Russell corroborates Hogg's account of this 'phenomenon'. In commenting on the 'preservative quality' of the peat in the Yarrow district, Russell gives this example: 'There was a tradition of a suicide having been buried in a moss near Berrybush more than a century before; and, in digging the place a few years ago [Russell's article is dated 1833], the body was found entire, with a bonnet, coat, plaid, hose, &c. quite fresh' (p. 38). An article in *Chambers's Journal* for 1 May 1897 provides further evidence based on a former herd-boy to Hogg, John Burnett: 'I remember the year I went to Hogg a strange circumstance happened. Hogg had written a story about a stranger in these parts who had hanged himself over a hay-rick, about one hundred years ago, and was not therefore allowed to be buried in the churchyard but out in the moors at a place where three lairds' ground met. [...] One day, therefore, when John Burnett was in the farm-yard, Mr Hogg came down from the hills with some others, and gave Johnnie an old bonnet of the Glengarry sort and some pieces of woolen cloth to wash in the burn. Johnnie washed them, and on coming in was told that these were some of the clothes of the suicide' ('A Living Link with Scott, Hogg, and Wilson', pp. 280–82; acknowledgement is made to Gillian Hughes for this information). See also Douglas S. Mack, 'The Suicide's Grave in *Confessions of a Justified Sinner*', *Newsletter of the James Hogg Society*, 1 (1982), 8–11, and David Groves, 'James Hogg's *Confessions*: New Information', *Review of English Studies*, 40 (1991), 116–17.

The present edition reprints the *BEM* version of 'A Scots Mummy' without emendation. Acknowledgement is made to Peter Garside, whose thorough notes to the S/SC edition of *The Private Memoirs and Confessions of a Justified Sinner* have greatly informed the annotations for the present edition of 'A Scots Mummy'.

139 (a) **Sir Christopher North** the fictitious editor of *BEM* and a pseudonym most often associated with John Wilson.

139 (a) **Ambrose's** the tavern that is a common gathering place for the *Blackwood's* writers and the setting of the *Noctes Ambrosianæ*. See note for 36. II. 1.

139 (a) **what I would have called, had I been writing poetry, a moveless attitude** perhaps a reference to Hogg's *Queen Hynde*:

> For sure such beauty, such array,
> Such moveless eye of wild dismay,
> Such attitude was never given
> To being underneath the heaven. (Book First, ll. 498–501)

See *Queen Hynde*, ed. by Suzanne Gilbert and Douglas Mack (S/SC, 1998), p.

17.

**139(c) mair nor half seas ower** intoxicated.

**139(c) atween the heaven an' yirth** echoes Hamlet's words to Horatio: 'There are more things in heaven and earth, Horatio | Than are dreamt of in your philosophy' (*Hamlet* I. 5. 166–67).

**140(a) no phenomenons, if I understand that French word properly** in a letter to William Blackwood, 23 August [1823], D. M. Moir observes: 'Hogg is perfectly characteristic. It is curious that all these *French phenomenons* should occur about Selkirk and Yarrow, and no where else in the civilised world' (NLS, MS 4011, fols 85–86).

**140(b) On the top of a wild height, called Cowanscroft** the portion of the story reprinted in *Confessions* begins here—see p. 165 of the S/SC edition of the novel. Cowanscroft is a hill (1897 feet) about five miles southwest of Hogg's farm, Altrive, and between Altrive and Ettrick.

**140(b) lands of three proprietors meet all at one point** Hogg later in the story identifies the three proprietors as the Duke of Buccleuch, the Laird of Drummelzier, and Lord Napier (p. 141(d)), all of whom were major landholders in Yarrow and Ettrick. As Garside notes: 'Most obviously, Hogg is thinking of the division between the farms of Berrybush (acquired in the 18th century by the Buccleuch family from Scott of Harden), Riskinhope, and Thirlestane' (*Confessions*, p. 249). See also notes to 'Songs for the Duke of Buccleuch's Birth Day' and 'The Honourable Captain Napier and Ettrick Forest' in the present edition.

**140(c) Mr Anderson of Eltrieve** an Anderson family is associated with tenants of Eltrieve at least as early as the sixteenth century, and Andersons were tenants of Eltrieve in the eighteenth century, closely coinciding with the chronology of the novel. At a later point in *Confessions* (p. 171), after the section quoted from the *BEM* story, 'the Eltrive men' who intend to bury Wringhim are led on their mission by 'Mr. David Anderson', although the name of 'David' is not used in the *BEM* story. For a thorough discussion of the Andersons of Eltrieve see Peter Garside, 'Hogg, Eltrive, and *Confessions*', *Studies in Hogg and his World*, 11 (2000), 5–24, as well as Garside's notes and editorial essays in the S/SC edition of the novel.

**140(d) James Anderson, his master's son,** as Garside has argued, it is likely that the David and James Anderson who were tenants of Eltrieve were brothers rather than father and son.

**141(a) the Hart Loup** Hart's Leap, a pass between the Ettrick and Yarrow valleys which, according to *The New Statistical Account of Scotland*, was the site of a hunting excursion of James V: 'It retains the significant name of the *Hart's Leap*; the distance of the leap, being distinctly visible at the time when the ground was covered with snow, is still marked by two grey whinstones, twenty-eight feet apart, which are said to have been raised by the king and his followers' ('Selkirkshire', III, 44).

**141(a) Eldinhope** a farm in Yarrow that bordered on the Andersons' farm of Eltrieve.

**142(b) Well, you may [...] to come to yet** these four sentences were omitted from *Confessions*.

**142(b) auld fools an' young bairns [...] half done** proverbial: 'Fools and bairns should not see half-done work' (*ODEP*, p. 277).

**142(c) William Sheil and W. Sword** unidentified, although as Peter Garside has noted, Hogg is drawing on names common to Ettrick and Yarrow (*Confessions*, pp. 249–50). Hogg uses the name Jamie Sword in 'Tales and Anecdotes of the Pastoral Life. No. III', which was published in the June 1817 number of *BEM* (see p. 23(b) of the present edition).

**142(c) casting peats** that is, digging and cutting peat, normally to allow it to dry in the summer heat so it can be burned for fuel.

**142(d) broad blue bonnet** 'a man's flat-topped, round cap, without a snout' (*SND*), often used figuratively to refer to a Scotsman or a Covenanter or Presbyterian.

**143(c) flesh will now fall to dust.** echoes Genesis 3. 19: 'for dust thou art, and unto dust thou shalt return'. The portion of the story reprinted in *Confessions* ends here—see p. 169 of the S/SC edition of the novel.

**143(d) think of trying the experiment on yourself** the final paragraph of the *BEM* narrative is not included in *Confessions*. Although the tone of this suggestion that 'Christopher North' (John Wilson) should hang himself is playful here, there is no doubt that Hogg frequently was frustrated enough with Wilson's treatment of him that he must have wished for Wilson to 'try the experiment'. In the *Noctes Ambrosianæ* in *BEM* for June 1824, the 'Hogg' character says 'I'll be buried beside Yarrow mysell', to which 'Odoherty' replies: 'And dug up, no doubt, quite fresh and lovely, like this new hero of yours, one hundred summers hence. I hope you will take care to be buried in the top-boots, by the by—they will gratify the speculators of the year two thousand and two' (p. 715).

# January 1824–December 1824 (Volumes 15–16)

## The Left-Handed Fiddler

'The Left-Handed Fiddler' was first published in *Blackwood's Edinburgh Magazine*, 16 (November 1824), 528–29. The poem was reprinted in the *New Times* on 6 December 1824 (p. 3) from the *BEM* publication. John Stoddart, the editor of the *New Times*, wrote Hogg on 22 December 1824, praising the poem: 'the "left-handed Fiddler" which I inserted in my Paper of the 6th instant would alone suffice (independently of your numerous other productions) to stamp you as a Writer of rich & genuine humour' (NLS, MS 2225, fols 86–87). Stoddart also invited Hogg to publish occasionally in the *New Times*. Hogg, though, had sent Stoddart his only copy of a manuscript poem entitled 'Anti-Burgher', which Stoddart lost. Hogg apparently did not publish again with Stoddart, although Hogg attempted to use Stoddart's invitation as leverage with Blackwood. Hogg wrote Blackwood on 5 January 1825: 'I never had so many applications for communications in my life as this winter nor such liberal offers, among others amost [*sic*] pressing and flattering one from Dr Stoddart of The New Times!!! I have rejected all' (*Letters 2*, p. 220).

The present edition reprints the *BEM* version without emendation.

**144, l. 11 Lord \* \* \* \* \* \* \* \* \* \* \* \*** unidentified.

**144, l. 17 *ne-plus-ultra* of ludification** the highest point of deception or mockery.

**144, l. 18 Ned Irving of old Hatton Garden** Edward Irving (1792–1834), Church of Scotland minister, became minister of the small Scottish Church at Hatton Garden, London, in 1822. Within months his preaching eloquence had attracted hundreds to his church, including a large congregation of fashionable and influential people.

**144, l. 23 princely Jeffrey** Francis Jeffrey (1773–1850), critic, editor of the *Edinburgh Review*, and advocate, was highly regarded for his extraordinary rhetorical skills and his persuasive speeches in jury trials. Lockhart writes of Jeffrey in *Peter's Letters*: 'There is no speaker in Britain that deals out his illustrations with so princely a profusion, or heaps upon every image and every thought, that springs from an indefatigable intellect, so lavish a garniture of most exquisite and most apposite language' (II, 74).

**144, l. 28 wee black gown** Jeffrey was a short man so he would have needed a 'wee' gown. Lockhart in *Peter's Letters* writes that Jeffrey's 'stature is so low, that he might walk close under your chin or mine without ever catching the eye even for a moment' (I, 55).

**145, l. 45 Vice of the heteroclite** i.e., an anomaly.

**145, l. 65 Patriarch Jubal** Jubal is described in Genesis 4. 21 as 'the father of all such as handle the harp and organ'.

**146, l. 91 great MacTurk's emphatic curse** the 'fierce M'Turk' is a character in 'Dumlanrig', the 'Sixteenth Bard's Song' on the third night of *The Queen's Wake*. Douglas Mack's note to '144, l. 1418' in the S/SC edition of *The Queen's Wake* (2004, p. 437) suggests that 'fierce M'Turk' is 'an oblique reference to James M'Turk', a friend of Hogg's from his time as a shepherd in Dumfriesshire (1805–09). Hogg lived with M'Turk for a time at his Stenhouse farm before Hogg took a position at Locherben. M'Turk was also a subscriber to *The Queen's Wake*. (Mack's note acknowledges Gillian Hughes for providing information about M'Turk.) Perhaps the reference here, though, is to Captain MacTurk, a character in Sir Walter Scott's novel *St. Ronan's Well*, 3 vols (Edinburgh: Constable, 1824). Scott's MacTurk is 'a Highland lieutenant' given to strong drink and 'ready to fight with any one' (I, 75–76). His speech often included the expression 'cot tamn'. In the *New Times* printing of the poem, in the quotation from MacTurk, 'paaticularly' is standardised and the expletive is spelled out fully: 'The de'il particularly damn the dog!'

### Examination of the School of Southside. By Mr W. W

'Examination of the School of Southside' was first published in *Blackwood's Edinburgh Magazine*, 16 (December 1824), 653–57. A. L. Strout in *A Bibliography of Works in Blackwood's Magazine* (p. 126) speculates that the work is by R. F. St Barbe, although Strout acknowledges that there is no evidence to support the claim for St Barbe's authorship beyond the fact that St Barbe previously had published dramatic work in *BEM*. However, 'Examination' is identified as Hogg's in a letter from D. M. Moir to William Blackwood: 'Hogg's Examination, though whimsical and outré, is on the whole very good—but if it is intended for personal satire, it is too obscure for my optics, though I occasionally see visions of Duddingstone and Davie Bridges' (NLS, MS 4724, fols 66–67). Furthermore, the work is signed from Hogg's farm, 'Altrive'.

'Examination of the School of Southside' is in the style of—and perhaps is a continuation of—Hogg's *Poetic Mirror* (1816), a collection of parodies and imitations of works of major poets of the age, almost all of which were written by Hogg. *The Poetic Mirror* included imitations of William Wordsworth's poetry that were presented as extracts from Wordsworth's planned long poem, *The Recluse*, part of which had been published in 1814 as *The Excursion*. The 'Advertisement' to the first edition of *The Poetic Mirror* promised a second collection, which was never published; however, Hogg wrote additional poems under the title 'New Poetic Mirror', most of which were published in 1829 in the *Edinburgh Literary Journal*. Among the 'New Poetic Mirror' poems in the *ELJ* is one from 'Mr W. W.' that parodies Wordsworth's poetry: 'A New Poetic Mirror. | *By the Ettrick Shepherd*. | No. I.–Mr W.W. | *Ode to a Highland Bee*'. (See also the notes to the 'New Poetic Mirror' in the present edition.) Furthermore, David Groves suggests that the 'allusions to Timothy Tickler refer to a series of reviews of contemporary periodicals which appeared in *Blackwood's Magazine* in the form of "Letters of Timothy Tickler", and which supposedly originated from the village of Southside. It seems therefore that in the "Examination" poem the satirist is partly trying to convey what he imagined would have been William Wordsworth's response to the Tickler reviews and to *Blackwood's Magazine* in general'–David Groves, *James Hogg: Poetic Mirrors* (Frankfurt: Peter Lang, 1990), p. 188. See also 'Letter to Timothy Tickler', pp. 72–77 in the present edition, and notes.

'Examination of the School of Southside' was not reprinted in Hogg's lifetime. Most recently the work has been edited by David Groves and published in his edition of Hogg's *Poetic Mirrors*, pp. 187–97. The present edition reprints the *BEM* publication without emendation.

**146(title) Southside** the George Square, Edinburgh, residence of Robert Sym, upon whom the fictional *BEM* persona of Timothy Tickler is based. Hogg wrote in his *Memoir*: 'I first met that noble and genuine old Tory, the renowned Timothy Tickler, in his own hospitable mansion of South Side, *alias* George's Square' (p. 76). The 'Letter to James Hogg', which appeared in the February 1818 issue of *BEM* (pp. 501–04) was signed 'Timothy Tickler | Southside'.

**146, l. 1 Mr Strap** the name suggests a parody of Scottish schoolmasters, who regularly used corporal punishment as a method of discipline. This stereotyped portrayal of the schoolmaster was common in Scottish literature of the early nineteenth century. Sir Walter Scott's Jedediah Cleishbotham is probably the best known of these characters: 'cleish' is Scots for 'to whip or lash', hence 'whip bottom'. 'Mr Whackbairn' in *The Heart of Mid-Lothian* is another example. Mr Strap's character, however, does not conform to the caricature suggested by the name.

**146, ll. 10–11 Know they aught of the leading principles | Of our religion** the Scottish education system in the early nineteenth century in many respects still retained its historical connection with the Church of Scotland, often including the Bible and Catechism among the school texts.

**147, l. 38 Newton** Sir Isaac Newton (1642–1727), scientist and mathematician, best known for his theories of universal gravitation and dynamics.

**147, l. 39 Napier** John Napier (1550–1617), mathematician, whose most important achievement was the invention of logarithms; his mathematical study was published in *Mirifici logarithmorum canonis descriptio* (1614). Napier was also the author of a popular apocalyptic work, *Plaine Discovery of the Whole Revelation of Saint Iohn* (1593).

**147, l. 40 David Brewster** (1781–1868), scientist and author, whose work included important discoveries about the properties of light. Brewster occasionally wrote for *BEM* and figured in the 'Chaldee Manuscript'. See the 'Chaldee' note for 35, l. 54.

**148, l. 86 dost thou know who made thee** the minister is testing the boy's knowledge of the children's catechism for the Church of Scotland. The first question of the youth catechism is, '*Who is your Maker and Preserver?*', and the full answer is, 'The Almighty God, who made and preserves all things'–see the Rev. Andrew Thomson, *A Catechism for Young Persons*, 2nd edn (Edinburgh: William Blackwood, 1816). Hogg writes of his own schooling that he 'had the honour of standing at the head of a juvenile class, who read the Shorter Catechism and the Proverbs of Solomon' (*Memoir*, p. 12). The Church of Scotland catechism also figures importantly, if in a twisted way, in young Robert Wringhim's life in Hogg's *Confessions*–see the S/SC edition, p. 68 and notes, p. 227.

**149, l. 109 I have him on the hip** proverbial, meaning to have one at a disadvantage (*ODEP*, p. 374).

**149, ll. 116–17 which may your wisdom deem | The best book in the world?** the boy answers the minister's question with 'Blackwood's Magazine' (l. 118). David Groves argues that it is 'fitting' that the boy, whose name is Tickler, answer in this manner: 'Through these discussions between the minister and the boy and girl, the satirist is gently but firmly criticising *Blackwood's*, first for its tendency to puff itself at the expenses of other journals, and secondly for its reliance on a small clique of anonymous reviewers who were able to praise each other's works, and damn those of outsiders, all under the protective pseudonym of "Tickler". The boy and girl are probably meant to represent two *Blackwood's* critics who wrote under the name "Tickler", and who prudently refused to let their own actual identities be known'–see *James Hogg: Poetic Mirrors*, pp. 194–95.

**149, ll. 134–35 certain stage [...] good friend David's corner** David Bridges (see note for 43, IV. 24), along with his father, owned a clothing shop at the corner of High Street and Bank Street, Edinburgh. The shop was across the street from the site of executions in Edinburgh. The minister is suggesting that the boy is destined for a hanging because of his failure to learn and follow the precepts of his religion. David Bridges's proximity to the execution site also figures in Hogg's poem, 'If e'er you would be a brave fellow, young man'–see pp. 162–63 of the present edition and notes for 163, ll. 38, 40.

**150, l. 143 Mr Pringle's butler of the Yair** the butler is unidentified, but probably a character of Hogg's acquaintance or local reputation. Pringle was a common name in the regions of Selkirkshire and Roxburghshire, but 'Mr Pringle' in this work is likely either Alexander Pringle of Whytbank and Yair (1747–1827), or his son, also Alexander (1791–1857). The elder Pringle served in the East India Company, and in the 1780s repurchased the family's Yair land, which had been sold to the Duke of Buccleuch by the elder Pringle's father. The younger Alexander, an advocate and later Member of Parliament for Selkirkshire, travelled with Sir Walter Scott to Waterloo in 1815. Hogg knew both the elder and younger Pringles, and later (August 1828) Hogg writes of having dined at Yair as the guest of the younger Alexander, then Captain Pringle, on the occasion of the dissolution of the Selkirkshire Yeomanry (see *Letters 2*, pp. 303–06). Yair is on the River Tweed, about two and a half miles north of Selkirk.

**150, ll. 148–49 somewhat tall | Too for thy years** the young boy's height is a further association with the original 'Tickler'. Hogg wrote in his *Memoir* of his first meeting with Robert Sym: 'Judge of my astonishment, when I was admitted by a triple-bolted door into a grand house in George's Square, and introduced to its lord, an uncommonly fine-looking elderly gentleman, about seven feet high, and as straight as an arrow' (p. 77).

**150, l. 151 Duddingston** a village about one mile southeast of the Edinburgh city centre and south of Holyrood Park. The association of Tickler with Duddingston is not clear.

**150, ll. 158-61 "An' eh what a parish!"** the four lines of this verse are from a version of the traditional song, 'O What a Parish'—see *A North Countrie Garland*, ed. by James Maidment, rev. by Edmund Goldsmid (Edinburgh: Privately Printed, 1891), pp. 62-64. Little Dunkeld is a parish in Perthshire, south of Dunkeld and the River Tay.

**151, l. 192 My little Catechism** the girl in Strap's school answers her questions more to the minister's liking than does the boy—see note for 148, l. 86. The young person's catechism literally is 'little'; *A Catechism for Young Persons* is a thin pamphlet measuring *c.* 8.5 cm x 13.5 cm.

**151, l. 195 gem of the first water** that is, of the highest quality.

# January 1825–December 1825 (Volumes 17–18)

## Correspondence Between Mr James Hogg and Lord Byron

The 'Correspondence Between Mr James Hogg and Lord Byron' was never published in Hogg's lifetime and is published in the present edition from the *Blackwood's Edinburgh Magazine* proof preserved in the National Library of Scotland as MS 4808, fols 32-33. The 'Correspondence' includes an introductory statement from 'J. H.' to 'C. N.', a letter from Hogg to Byron, and a letter from Byron to Hogg. The letter from Byron to Hogg has been published previously from the NLS proof in *Byron's Letters and Journals*, ed. by Leslie Marchand, 12 vols (London: John Murray, 1973-82), IV, 84-86. The letter from Hogg to Byron has not been published. The correspondence between Hogg and Blackwood regarding the Byron letters casts doubt on the authenticity of the letters and suggests that Hogg may have authored the entire 'Correspondence' published herein in late 1824 or early 1825.

Apparently Hogg initiated a correspondence with Byron in June 1814. Hogg wrote to Byron on 3 June 1814 to ask Byron for a contribution to his proposed 'poetical repository'. Hogg's letter opens in terms that would suggest there was no previous connection: 'You will wonder at seeing a letter from the banks of Yarrow with the name of a stranger at the bottom of it, and you will wonder more I believe at the request that stranger makes of you' (*Letters 1*, p. 178). Hogg's poetry, though, was not unknown to Byron; Byron had written to Sir Walter Scott in September 1813, expressing his admiration for Hogg's poem, *The Queen's Wake* (see note for 154(d) below). The correspondence between Byron and Hogg seems to have been concentrated in the period 1814-16. Leslie Marchand's edition of *Byron's Letters and Journals* includes only two letters from Byron to Hogg, as well as a fragment of a third letter, although Hogg's extant letters suggest that there had been several more. Volume 1 of *The Collected Letters of James Hogg* includes nine letters from Hogg to Byron. (For further discussion of the Byron-Hogg relationship, see Gillian Hughes's 'Notes on Correspondents' in *Letters 1*, pp. 451-52.)

Byron had died on 19 April 1824, and William Blackwood knew, certainly, that the correspondence between Byron and Hogg was likely to stir a great deal of interest. Blackwood and Lockhart encouraged Hogg to publish the letters, as Hogg later reminded Blackwood: 'The Byron correspondence was a thing that you and Mr Lockhart pressed on me' (*Letters 2*, p. 222). The discussions regarding publication of Hogg's correspondence with Byron must have begun within a few weeks after Byron's death. The 'Shepherd' character in the *Noctes Ambrosianæ* for June 1824 comments: 'I have a gay hantle letters o' Byron's in my ain dask–I wonder what the trade would give a body for a sma' volume of his epistolary correspondence wi' his friends' (vol. 15, p. 710). Hogg cannot find his letters, however, as he writes to Blackwood on 28 June 1824: 'I am dreadfully vexed that I have been unable to light on Lord Byron's letters. How well they would have come in in the Noctes! I am sure they are well laid by somewhere for there were some of them that I had resolved never to part with to mortal flesh But perhaps they may be stolen for I have not seen them for several years' (*Letters 2*, p. 203). Eight years later, in the *Memoir* that prefaces *Altrive Tales*, Hogg writes further about the loss of the Byron letters, but he also addresses the character of the content of the letters:

> I may here mention, by way of advertising, that I have lost all Lord Byron's letters to me, on which I put a very high value; and which I know to have been stolen from me by some one or other of my tourist visitors, for I was so proud of these letters, that I would always be showing them to every body. It was exceedingly unkind, particularly as they never can be of use to any other person, for they have been so often and so eagerly read by many of my friends, that any single sentence out of any one of them could easily be detected. I had five letters of his of two sheets each, and one of three. They were indeed queer *harumscarum letters*, about women, and poetry, mountains, and authors, and blue-stockings; and what he sat down to write about was generally put in the postscript. They were all, however, extremely kind, save one, which was rather a satirical, bitter letter. I had been quizzing him about his approaching marriage [to Anna Isabella Millbanke], and assuring him that he was going to get himself into a confounded scrape. I wished she might prove both a good *mill* and a *bank* to him; but I much doubted they would not be such as he was calculating on. I think he felt that I was using too much freedom with him. (pp. 39–40)

The discussion of the Byron letters in the 1832 *Memoir* was not present in the version published in the 1821 *Mountain Bard*. It is likely, therefore, as Douglas Mack has suggested, that Hogg did not know that the letters were lost until he began to prepare the correspondence for publication.

In December 1824, however, the plan to publish the Hogg-Byron correspondence in *BEM* was moving forward, in spite of the fact that Hogg did not seem to have the letters. The *Noctes Ambrosianæ* for November 1824 included the 'Hogg' character's recollections of a fictitious meeting between Hogg and Byron in the Lake District, perhaps in part intended as an introduction to a later series of publications of the correspondence between the two poets, even if equally fictitious. Blackwood wrote to Hogg on 4 December 1824: 'You will laugh very heartily at your account of your interview with Byron and the Laker, which you will find in the Noctes. I anxiously hope you are preparing the correspondence. You should give the letters as near as you possibly can recollect them (NLS, MS 2245, fols 84–85). Blackwood's letter suggests that the Byron-Hogg correspondence was potentially interesting enough to the *BEM* readership that Blackwood was willing for Hogg to reconstruct the content.

Blackwood soon changed his mind, however, apparently at Lockhart's urging. Blackwood wrote to Hogg on 22 January 1825: 'I am more in doubt as to the propriety of both on your account & my own of inserting the Byron Correspondence we will have a crack about this whoever [*sic*] when you come to town which I hope will be very soon' (NLS, MS 30,308, pp. 43–44). As Gillian Hughes suggests, Lockhart undoubtedly raised concerns about the proprietary and copyright issues regarding Byron's letters (*Letters 2*, p. 245), but there must have been additional 'propriety' concerns as well, given Hogg's confession in the *Memoir* of 'using too much freedom' with Byron; the fact that Hogg was not in possession of most of the letters meant that he would be inventing the content. Hogg replies to Blackwood on 25 January 1825 that he thinks the 'Correspondence' 'would create a considerable sensation and if any questions are asked you can do nothing but refer the enquirers to me you have not a word to say on the matter' (*Letters 2*, p. 222). Lockhart must have been as concerned about the potential for Hogg's creating a 'considerable sensation' as he was about the copyright questions.

When Blackwood declined to publish the 'Correspondence', Hogg tried other avenues. On 28 March 1825 Hogg wrote to Aeneas Mackay, enclosing a song on Byron (see 'Ode for Music. On the Death of Lord Byron', pp. 257–59, and notes in the present edition), but Hogg also took the opportunity to explore Mackay's possible interest in the Byron correspondence: 'By the by what will you give me for a very curious and interesting literary correspondence with Lord Byron for the space of several years? I have at least five long letters of his on various subjects besides some short ones of no value and copies of seven of my own in answer to these. Several of his fill three sheets of his rambling and dashing hand. The originals I will not part with, having lost some of them already in a way not very fair, but I see no evil in publishing a genuine and original correspondence (*Letters 2*, pp. 227–28). Mackay's response apparently has not survived, but the letters did not get published. A year later, Hogg writes to Blackwood, complaining that he 'never saw again the Byron letters' (*Letters 2*, p. 243). Blackwood, justifiably, seems to have read Hogg's complaint about his not returning the letters as a renewal of his desire to have the letters published. Blackwood wrote to Hogg on 25 March 1826: 'As to the Byron Letters, I thought I had explained to you sufficiently why it could not have been safe to have published them in the magazine. Mr Lockhart was completely satisfied on this head, and I thought you had also been too' (NLS, MS 30,309, pp. 163–65). This seems to have ended Hogg's efforts to publish the letters with Blackwood, but it did not end Hogg's frustration with Blackwood for not returning Hogg's letters. Hogg wrote to Blackwood again on 12 September 1826: 'Speaking this way have you never seen any more of my letters to Lord Byron As for those in his name I care not a doit about them but the two to him I set a high value on as I know I never wrote any thing half so good in the epistolary stile' (*Letters 2*, p. 250). Although it is not certain that Hogg ever sent Blackwood any authentic letters, either Byron's or his own, it is clear that Hogg was pleased with his 'Correspondence' and desired to publish the letters, if only for their literary merit.

The present edition prints the 'Correspondence' from the NLS proof with the following emendations:

155(c) mine.] time. (proof)
157(c) *March*] *Maoch* (proof)

158(b) And] hnd (proof)
158(b) of ] o (proof)
158(b) Able's ] ble's (proof)
158(b) small] smallf (proof)
158(c) As for] for (proof)
159(a) stirring age] stirringage (proof)
159(a) probably] probable (proof)

**153(a) *To C. N. Esq.*** Christopher North, the fictional editor of *BEM*.

**153(a) Blue Stocking Club** apparently originated in the mid-eighteenth century in reference to gatherings of ladies and literary men at Mrs Montagu's house in London for the purpose of intellectual and literary discussions. The term came into general use and was often used disparagingly.

**153(b) Mr Murray** John Murray (1778–1843), Byron's London publisher. On 3 August 1814 Byron wrote to Murray to recommend that Murray consider publishing Hogg: 'I have a most amusing epistle from the Ettrick Bard Hogg—in which speaking of his bookseller—whom he denominates the "shabbiest" of the *trade*—for not "lifting his bills" he adds in so many words "G–d d–n him and them both" this is a pretty prelude to asking *you* to adopt him (the said Hogg) but this he wishes—and if you please you & I will talk it over […]. Seriously—I think Mr. Hogg would suit you very well—and surely he is a man of great powers and deserving of encouragement––I must knock out a tale for him—and *you* should at all events consider before you reject his suit'—see *Byron's Letters and Journals*, IV, 150–51. Byron renewed his recommendation of Hogg to Murray on several occasions.

**153(b) Mr Gillies** R. P. Gillies. See note for 35, l. 57.

**153(c) *Dean-Haugh, near Edinburgh, March 7ᵗʰ, 1812*** Hogg was living in Deanhaugh at the time this letter is dated, and he wrote *The Queen's Wake* while living there. R. P. Gillies in his *Memoirs of a Literary Veteran*, 3 vols (London: Richard Bentley, 1851) notes that Hogg 'tenanted a room at a suburban residence near Stockbridge. It was a weather-beaten, rather ghostly, solitary looking domicile, like an old farm-house in the country' (II, 121). The date of Hogg's letter, however, obviously is incorrect, and perhaps is part of Hogg's fiction. There are several references within the letter that are inconsistent with the year 1812. For example, see notes for 153(d), 154(a), and 156(c) below.

**153(d) Mr Scott read me the page in your letter to him** Byron wrote to Scott on 27 September 1813 expressing approval of Hogg's poem *The Queen's Wake* (apparently Byron's letter has not survived). In a letter from Scott to Byron, dated 6 November 1813, Scott wrote: 'The author of the Queen's Wake will be delighted with your approbation. He is a wonderful creature for his opportunities, which were far inferior to those of the generality of Scottish peasants'—*The Letters of Sir Walter Scott*, ed. by H. J. C. Grierson, 12 vols (London: Constable, 1932–37), III, 373. Scott read Byron's praise for *The Queen's Wake* to Hogg.

**154(a) it would have been regarded by the world as a review of his own** in his *Anecdotes of Scott* Hogg quotes Scott's reason for not reviewing *Queen Hynde*, which was published in December 1824: 'upon the whole I felt that we were so much of the same school that if I had given as favourable a review as I intended to have done that it would have been viewed in the light of having applauded my own works' (pp. 8–9). The similarity of these comments might suggest that Hogg authored the Byron letter in late 1824 or early 1825.

**154(c) "hitherto shalt thou come, but no farther"** from Job 38. 11; God speaks to Job in reference to God's command to the waves of the sea.

**154(c) Childe Harold [...] I wrote a review of it** the first two Cantos of Byron's long poem, *Childe Harold's Pilgrimage*, were first published by John Murray on 10 March 1812. In his *Memoir*, Hogg notes that he reviewed John Wilson's *Isle of Palms* and a number of other poetical works 'in a Scottish Review then going on in Edinburgh' (p. 32). Gillian Hughes in her notes to the *Memoir* suggests that Hogg is referring to '*The Scotish [sic] Review*, a quarterly periodical printed by D. Schaw and Son of the Lawnmarket, Edinburgh' (p. 231). David Groves has discussed the *Isle of Palms* review, as well as Hogg's relationship with *The Scotish Review* and other periodicals, in his article 'Four Unrecorded Book Reviews by the Ettrick Shepherd, 1811–1812', *Studies in Scottish Literature*, 25 (1990), 23–48.

**155(a) Campbell's numbers** Thomas Campbell (1777–1844), Scottish poet whose works include *The Pleasures of Hope* (1799) and *Gertrude of Wyoming* (1809).

**155(a) Moore's** Thomas Moore (1779–1852), Irish poet, best known for his popular series of songs, *Irish Melodies* (1808–34), and his oriental romance, *Lallah Rookh* (1817). Moore later edited *Byron's Letters and Journals* (London: John Murray, 1830). Sir Walter Scott in a *Journal* entry for December 12, 1825, records a meeting with Hogg in which they discussed Moore's songs:

> Hogg came to breakfast this morning, having taken and brought for his companion the Galashiels bard David Thompson as to a meeting of huzz Tividale poets. The honest grunter opines with a delightful naïveté that Moore's verses are far *owre* sweet–answerd by Thompson that Moore's ears or notes, I forget which, were finely strung. "They are far owre finely strung" replied He of the forest "for mine are just reeght"–It reminded me of Queen Bess when questioning Melville sharply and closely whether Queen [Mary was] taller than her and extracting an answer in the affirmative she replied "Then your Queen is too tall for I am just the proper height" (*The Journal of Sir Walter Scott*, ed. by W. E. K. Anderson (Oxford: Clarendon Press, 1972), pp. 34–35).

**155(a) Harmonicon** harmonica; also applied to musical glasses–glasses that contained water and were played by rubbing a finger on the glasses. A monthly musical journal entitled the *Harmonicon* was published from 1823 to 1833 and included several of Hogg's songs.

**155(c) Southey** Robert Southey. See note for 56(b).

**156(a) clean horn daft** an expression meaning 'very mad'.

**156(a) If you die a young man** Byron died at age thirty-six.

**156(c) steeps of Parnassus** a mountain in central Greece sacred to Apollo and home to the Muses.

**156(c) The Poetic Mirror; or, the Living Bards of Britain** see notes to 'Ettrick Shepherd not the Author of the Poetic Mirror' in the present edition. Hogg's original title for his proposed collection of his contemporary poets was the 'Edinburgh Poetical Repository', a title he was using in August 1814 (*Letters 1*, p. 242)–again, after the date of this letter to Byron.

**156(d) Mr Wilson** John Wilson. See note for 29(d).

**157(b) John Grieve** (1781–1836), Hogg's long-time friend, who operated a hatter's business in Edinburgh. Hogg frequently stayed with Grieve when he was in Edinburgh, especially during the 1810s.

**157(b) ndy sre[asaaen** this incorrect typesetting perhaps indicates that additional text was to have been inserted.

**157(b) Mrs Gray of Belfast** Mary Gray (1767–1829), neé Mary Peacock, was the second wife of Hogg's friend, James Gray. Mrs Gray was a poet and contributed to Hogg's periodical, *The Spy*. The Grays moved to Belfast in 1822, where they lived until 1826. See Gillian Hughes's 'Notes on Contributors' in *The Spy* (S/SC, 2000), p. 564.

**157(c) *Albany, March* 24** this date, too, is questionable. Byron apparently moved into Albany House in Piccadilly, London, four days later, as he notes in his journal on 28 March 1814: 'This night I got into my new apartments, rented of Lord Althorpe, on a lease of seven years'—see *Byron's Letters and Journals* (III, 255).

**158(a) Abel was a fine pastoral poet, and Cain a fine bloody poet** in the Genesis story of the brothers Cain and Abel, 'Abel was a keeper of sheep, but Cain was a tiller of the ground'. Cain killed Abel because God 'had respect' for Abel's offering of a sheep but not Cain's offering of the 'fruit of the ground'—see Genesis 4. 1–8.

**158(a) Pye** Henry James Pye (1745–1813) became poet laureate in 1790, a position he held until his death in 1813. Although Pye had the honour of the laureate title, he was not a well-respected poet.

**158(c) *A horse, a horse, my kingdom for a horse!*** from Shakespeare's *Richard III*, v. 4. 7.

**158(c) Tom Jones** the title character of Henry Fielding's novel, *The History of Tom Jones, A Foundling* (1749).

**158(d) Cibber's** Colley Cibber (1671–1757), actor, theatre manager, and popular playwright, but perhaps best known for his autobiography, *An Apology for the Life of Mr Colley Cibber, Comedian* (1740). He was named poet laureate in 1730.

**159(c) Phillupean namby** namby-pamby, a term for affected sentimentality derived from the name of Ambrose Philips (*d.* 1749), whose poetry was the subject of ridicule from more-accomplished poets, such as Alexander Pope.

**159(c) Mrs Baillie** Joanna Baillie (1762–1851), Scottish poet and playwright, whose works include *Poems* (1790), the three-volume *Plays on the Passions* (1798, 1802, 1812), *Miscellaneous Plays* (1804), and *Fugitive Verses* (1840).

**159(c) peat reek** whisky. Peat is used as a fuel in the grain drying process in whisky-making. The 'reek', or smoke, of the peat permeates the malt, giving the whisky a smoky flavour.

## Hymn to the Devil

'Hymn to the Devil' was first published in Hogg's novel *The Three Perils of Man; or, War, Women, and Witchcraft*, 3 vols (London: Longman, 1822), III, 26–29. It appeared in *Blackwood's Edinburgh Magazine*, 17 (March 1825), 367–69, as part of the *Noctes Ambrosianæ No. XIX*, where it is recited by the 'Shepherd' character. Although the poem was first published in *The Three Perils of Man*, the *Noctes* dialogue implies that the poem is new. The dialogue that introduces the poem rubs salt in Hogg's wounds from the poor sales and critical reception of *Queen Hynde*; both Hogg and Blackwood had expected better. North asks the

Shepherd: 'Have you written any poetry lately, James? The unparalleled success of Queen Hynde must have inspirited and inspired my dear Shepherd'. The Shepherd replies: 'Success! She's no had muckle o' that, man. Me and Wordsworth are aboon the age we live in—it's no worthy o' us; but wait a whyleock—wait only for a thousand years, or thereabouts, Mr North, and you'll see who will have speeled to the tap o' the tree'. North responds sarcastically to the Shepherd's sense of popularity and importance: 'Nay, James, you are by far too popular at present to be entitled to posthumous fame. You are second only to Byron'. Referring to the conclusion of *Queen Hynde*, North again asks the Shepherd: 'have you written anything since the Burning of Beregonium?' The Shepherd responds with an offer of an 'Ode to the Devil'. In the dialogue there is no mention of *The Three Perils of Man*.

The *BEM* version of 'Hymn to the Devil' follows the *Three Perils* version with only minor changes attributable to printer's preferences. The present edition prints the *BEM* version without emendation.

**159–60, ll. 1–25** 'Hymn to the Devil' was written within a few years of the end of the Napoleonic Wars. Douglas Mack suggests that these wars provide the context for the opening lines of the poem. As Hogg wrote in his sermon 'Soldiers': 'After the campaigns of Buonaparte, and the slaughter of so many millions among the most civilised nations on the face of the earth, and which ended so completely in smoke, I really thought there would never be any more wars in Europe, but that all would be settled by arbitration; and I have still a hope that, in this enlightened age, the days of battle and war are far hence'—see *Lay Sermons*, ed. by Gillian Hughes (S/SC, 1997), p. 41.

**159, l. 7 Javel** a low or worthless fellow; a rascal (*OED*).

**160, l. 14 gonfalons flee** 'gonfalons' are heraldic flags or standards; 'flee' is Scots for 'fly'.

**160, l. 24 dogs of havock** the military cry of 'havoc' was a signal to soldiers to pillage. The phrase 'dogs of havock' echoes the line in Shakespeare's *Julius Caesar*: 'Shall in these confines with a monarch's voice | Cry "havoc!" and let slip the dogs of war' (III. 1. 275–76).

**160, l. 42 sons of the abbot are lords of the Highlands** possibly a reference to 'The Abbot M'Kinnon', the concluding poem in *The Queen's Wake*—see *The Queen's Wake*, ed. by Douglas S. Mack (S/SC, 2004), pp. 151–59. In his introduction to *The Queen's Wake*, Douglas Mack writes: 'In Hogg's poem, the Abbot M'Kinnon is a deeply corrupt man who, in "his visioned sleep", is called to account by the spirit of Saint Columba, "the saint of the isle"' (p. xlvii).

**161, l. 59 Ave Mari** Latin, Hail Mary. In the Catholic Church 'Hail Mary' is a common set prayer to Mary, the mother of Jesus.

**161, l. 84 Prince of the Air** from Ephesians 2. 2: 'in times past ye walked according to the course of this world, according to the prince of the power of the air, the spirit that now worketh in the children of disobedience'.

**162, l. 99 rights divine** the concept of the divine right of kings—that kings were in power by the authority of God, which was granted in part through the ancestry of the kings, and that kings had absolute power and must not be opposed. After the Glorious Revolution of 1688, the power of the British government shifted from the monarchy to Parliament. Although the concept of the 'divine right' of the monarchy had greatly diminished by Hogg's time, nonetheless the Tories maintained a belief in a strong monarchy. In the lines that follow Hogg seems to associate the devil with Whig politics.

**162, l. 116 King of the Elements** the Devil.

### If E'er You Would Be a Brave Fellow

'If E'er You Would Be a Brave Fellow' was first published in *Blackwood's Edinburgh Magazine,* 17 (March 1825), 382–83, where it is sung by the 'Shepherd' character in the *Noctes Ambrosianæ No. XIX.* The song was reprinted in *Songs* (pp. 28–30) under the title 'The Noctes Sang'. In his introduction to the *Songs* version, Hogg writes that the song was written in Edinburgh to be sung at Ambrose's: 'I did not sing it till late at night, when we were all beginning to get merry; and the effect on the party was like electricity. It was encored I know not how oft, and Mr Gillies ruffed and screamed out so loud in approbation, that he fell from his chair, and brought an American gentleman down with him. [...] It has been always the first song at our jovial meetings ever since' (p. 28). R. P. Gillies gives a more detailed description of what was probably the occasion on which the song was written in 'Some Recollections of James Hogg', *Fraser's Magazine,* 20 (October 1839), 414–30 (pp. 428–29).

Hogg revised the work substantially for publication in *Songs.* The *Songs* version consists of three rather than four verses. In *Songs* Hogg preserves the first and fourth verses of *BEM* with minor revisions; he combines the first five lines of the second verse of *BEM* with the last five lines of the third verse to make a new second verse in *Songs.* The remaining ten lines of the *BEM* version are omitted in *Songs.*

The present edition reprints the *BEM* version without emendation.

**162 AIR,—***Whistle, and I'll come to ye, my Lad* Hogg claims in his introduction to the *Songs* version that the 'air is my own, and a very capital one. I believe it is preserved in the Noctes, and nowhere else' (p. 28). However, only the title of the air is given in the *Noctes*; the music is not published with the song. See Appendix B for the music to this tune from *The Scots Musical Museum.*

**162, l. 2 the Blue and the Yellow** *The Edinburgh Review*, whose covers were blue and yellow. *The Edinburgh Review* was aligned with Whig politics.

**162, l. 5 lads that get mellow** a reference to the *BEM* writers, who drink, converse, and write during their nights at Ambrose's Tavern.

**163, l. 10 auld Geordie Buchanan** George Buchanan (*c.* 1506–1582), classical scholar and Scottish historian, whose likeness was on the cover and title page of *Blackwood's Edinburgh Magazine.*

**163, l. 20 dadds wi' a docken** hits with something of little effect.

**163, l. 25** *puffing the Radical Papers* for the *BEM* writers, one could stoop no lower in literary circles than to praise the 'Radical Papers', such as *The Examiner*, established by John Hunt in 1808 and edited by John's brother, the poet Leigh Hunt. Leigh Hunt was the primary focus of a series of scathing articles in early numbers of *BEM*, 'On the Cockney School of Poetry'. *The Examiner* took strong positions in favour of Irish independence and Catholic emancipation, and the Hunts spent two years in prison (1813–15) for libels against the king.

**163, l. 33 Our King and his Throne** George IV (1762–1830) became king in 1820.

**163, l. 37 lecture** Hogg adds a note to the *Songs* version: 'A celebrated London professor was lecturing here then' (p. 30). The 'professor' is not identified.

**163, l. 38 cutty-mun** Hogg adds a note for 'cutty-mun' to the *Songs* version: 'an old Scottish tune of exceedingly quick and cramp time' (p. 30). The last three lines of the song suggest an execution by hanging.

**163, l. 40 General Director** a reference to David Bridges, who was known as the 'Director General' throughout the *Noctes Ambrosianæ*, a title he acquired in the September 1819 issue of *BEM*. The illustration between pp. 672 and 673 of the September issue, 'Pilgrimage to the Kirk of Shotts', is dedicated to Bridges: '*To DAVID BRIDGES JUN^R ESQUIRE, Secretary, Treasurer & Croupier to the Dilettanti Society of Edinburgh, and Director General of the Fine Arts in Scotland: THIS PRINT is, with his gracious permission, Dedicated, by his affectionate Admirer. | Hugh Mullion | Provision Warehouse | N° 1. Grass Market.* Bridges and his father owned a clothing shop on the corner of High Street and Bank Street, a short distance from the High Street site of executions in Edinburgh, hence the note in *BEM* for 'General Director'. The younger Bridges was an art collector and maintained a collection of prominent artists' work on a lower level of his shop. See also 'Chaldee' note for 43, IV. 24.

### The Laird o' Lamington

'The Laird o' Lamington' was published with music in *Blackwood's Edinburgh Magazine*, 17 (May 1825), 620, where it is sung by the 'Hogg' character in the *Noctes Ambrosianæ No. XX*. The song was first published in *No. of the Border Garland* (Edinburgh: Nathaniel Gow and Son, [1819], pp. 18–19) with an 'Air' by Hogg; this earlier *Border Garland* edition also includes an arrangement for piano forte. However, the song was omitted from Hogg's second version of *The Border Garland* (Robert Purdie, 1828).

Lamington is a village in Lanarkshire, about twelve miles southeast of Lanark on the river Clyde. The 'lairds' of Lamington are descendants of William Baillie of Hoprig, who was knighted and granted the barony of Lamington by David II in 1368. Apparently the laird of Hogg's song is a fictitious character, although a 'laird of Lamington' also is a character in the traditional ballad, 'Katherine Jaffray' (Child 221), or 'Janfarie' as it appears in the third edition of Scott's *Minstrelsy of the Scottish Border*. As Scott notes in the introduction to the ballad, 'The Ballad was published in the first edition of this work, under the title of "The Laird of Laminton." It is now given in a more perfect state, from several recited copies'—see *Minstrelsy of the Scottish Border*, 3rd edn, 3 vols (London: Longman; Edinburgh: Constable, 1806) II, 336. Scott changes the Laird of Laminton to Lord Lauderdale in the 'Katherine Janfarie' ballad; the ballad apparently also influenced 'Lady Heron's Song' ('Lochinvar') in Scott's *Marmion*. However, it seems that Hogg's song owes nothing to the traditional ballad beyond the title character. Hogg's song is a drinking song and in the *Noctes* follows a lengthy discussion of the politics of the day, which ends with a toast to Henry Brougham.

In *BEM* the first stanza is printed with the music; the present edition prints the text of the entire song, but otherwise the text is printed herein without emendation. See Appendix B for the music.

**164, l. 5 Canty war ye o'er your kale** that is, the laird merrily spends his time (and money) on his food and drink.

**164, l. 11 falls in bagnio** visits a brothel.

**164, l. 19 drinks to drauck his dust** drinks to soak his dryness, quench his thirst.

## Some Passages in the Life of Colonel Cloud

'Some Passages in the Life of Colonel Cloud' was first published in *Blackwood's Edinburgh Magazine*, 18 (July 1825), 32–40, and the *BEM* publication of the story is the only appearance of the work in Hogg's lifetime. It is not clear when the story was written or exactly when Hogg sent the story to Blackwood, but Blackwood sent the story to D. M. Moir on 2 June 1825 for Moir's opinion: 'As you are my magazines Apollo, I send you also an affair of Hogg's. It is meant to be a satire on that fellow Brown who was the Editor of Constable's Magazine. I saw this whenever I began to read it, but no one will perceive the end or aim of the affair, and if they did such a creature is not worth satirizing' (NLS, Acc. 9856, no. 39). Moir replied, in an undated letter, expressing his pleasure in the story and advising Blackwood to publish it:

> I return you Hoggs "Passages of Colonel Cloud," which have entertained me very much in the perusal. It is one of the most natural and naive things that the Shepherd has written. Unless Hogg might be bothered about it I would advise you to publish it. To those who know the hero it will be capital fun, and to those who do not see what it is about, it will afford a pleasing riddle: for as Gray remarks in one of his Letters 'we are ever most apt to be pleased when the subject a little transcends our comprehension.' Till the moment I read the paper I always imagined Brown to have been a half-pay Captain. The Dogs and the Fishing are admirable. (NLS, MS 4724, fols 188–90)

The subject of Hogg's satirical sketch is James Browne (1793–1841), who at the time the story was published was editor of Archibald Constable's new version of the *Scots Magazine*, the *Edinburgh Magazine and Literary Miscellany*, a position he held from 1821 to 1826. Browne, a native of Perthshire, attended St Andrews University in preparation for the ministry, although he never served a parish church. He had positions as a tutor in a family in Europe and as a teacher at Perth Academy before turning to the law, which he also never practiced. Browne was an occasional contributor to the *Edinburgh Review*, and in 1827 he became editor of an Edinburgh newspaper, the *Caledonian Mercury*. He was also the author of a successful four-volume *History of the Highlands and the Highland Clans* (1835–38). In 1832 Browne published a blistering response to Hogg's 'Memoir' that prefaced the volume of *Altrive Tales*: *The "Life" of the Ettrick Shepherd Anatomized; in a Series of Strictures on the Autobiography of James Hogg, Prefixed to the First Volume of the "Altrive Tales."* By An Old Dissector (Edinburgh: William Hunter, 1832). (For additional information about Browne, see the *Oxford DNB* article by T. F. Henderson, rev. G. Martin Murphy. For further discussion of Hogg's connection with Browne, see David Groves, 'The Genesis of "Gil-Martin": James Hogg, "Colonel Cloud", and "The Madman in the Mercury"', *Notes and Queries*, 52 (December 2005), 467–69. Acknowledgement is made to David Groves, whose research has in part informed the present editor's notes to 'Colonel Cloud'.)

The correspondence between Hogg and Blackwood indicates that Hogg had also intended 'Colonel Cloud' to be part of a series and collection of stories, *Lives of Eminent Men*, that Hogg had hoped Blackwood would publish. Hogg proposed two additional stories to Blackwood for this collection within months following the publication of 'Colonel Cloud': 'Some Remarkable Passages in the Life of An Edinburgh Baillie' and 'The Adventures of Colonel Peter Aston'. Blackwood also sent these stories to Moir for review, and Moir advised against their publication in *BEM* and as a collection. Hogg persisted in trying to find a publisher for the collection, even though Blackwood was not interested in Hogg's 'Eminent Men' series. As late as 1828 Hogg still hoped to publish a collection of stories that would include 'Colonel Cloud'. Hogg wrote to Allan Cunningham on 17 October 1828 to request Cunningham's assistance with finding a London publisher for the collection, although he insisted that Blackwood should not know of it:

> I have a M. S. work by me for these several years which Blackwood objected to or at least wished it delayed two years ago till better times I know and am sure it will sell and if you could find me a London publisher for it I would like excessively well that it should come out ere ever Blackwood was aware It is "Singular Passages in the lives of eminent men" By the Ettrick Shepherd These are An Edin^r Baillie, Col. Peter Aston, Sir Simon Brodie, Col. Cloud, and Mr Alexander M,Corkindale They are all fabulous stories founded on historical facts and would make two small volumes. (*Letters 2*, p. 312)

Hogg was never successful with this publishing venture; however, the 'Edinburgh Baillie', 'Colonel Aston', and 'Simon Brodie' stories were later published as part of a collection of stories, *Tales of the Wars of Montrose* (1835), all of which focus on the civil war of 1644–45 and the history leading up to it. Clearly, 'Colonel Cloud' did not fit this collection as it was finally published, although Hogg's original plan for the collection did not limit the stories to a specific historical context. (For further discussion of the development of the *Montrose* volume, see Gillian Hughes's Introduction to *Tales of the Wars of Montrose* (S/SC, 1996).) Much earlier than the proposed *Lives of Eminent Men*, however, Hogg had considered writing another series of sketches about interesting people he met on his Highland journeys, as he notes in a letter of 1 June 1816 to Mrs. Alexander Bald of Alloa: 'When I began this journal of my tour to you I intended to give you likewise an account of all the curious charact [*eol*] that I had met with which I am certain would have amused you but on beginning to think them over I find the subject would take a volume' (*Letters 1*, p. 278). The story of 'Colonel Cloud' would have better suited this proposed collection about 'curious characters', and the place names cited in the story generally are places Hogg visited over the course of his Highland tours within the first two decades of the nineteenth century. Hogg was on one of these Highland tours in June 1816 when he wrote Mrs Bald; 'Colonel Cloud' is set during this 1816 tour. Like the 'Tales and Anecdotes of the Pastoral Life' stories, Hogg seems to develop the fictitious 'Colonel Cloud' story by combining real places and characters with fictitious ones.

'Some Passages in the Life of Colonel Cloud' is reprinted from the *BEM* text without emendation.

**166 (title) Mrs A—r—y** probably Mrs Abercromby. Mary Anne Abercromby (*d.* 1821), was the wife of Sir Ralph Abercromby (1734–1801) of Tullibody, Alloa. She became Baroness Abercromby after the death of her husband. Although apparently there is no extant correspondence between Hogg and Mrs Abercromby, Hogg probably knew her through his connections with Alloa, where Hogg was a prominent member of the Shakespeare Club (see notes to 'The Shakspeare Club of Alloa' in the present edition).

**166(b) Glen-Lyon** a glen in western Perthshire that carries the River Lyon from Loch Lyon into the River Tay near Aberfeldy. Hogg had been in Glen Lyon in June 1816 at the time the story is set.

**166(c) Mr Robertson** perhaps James Robertson, who was Hogg's Edinburgh publisher of the first thirteen issues of *The Spy*. Hogg describes Robertson in his *Memoir* as 'a kind-hearted, confused body, who loved a joke and a dram. He sent for me every day about one o'clock, to consult about the publication; and then we uniformly went down to a dark house in the Cowgate, where we drank whisky and ate rolls with a number of printers, the dirtiest and leanest-looking men I had ever seen' (p. 25). For further information on Hogg and Robertson, see Gillian Hughes's Introduction to *The Spy* (S/SC, 2000), pp. xx–xxv.

**166(d) quizzing-glass** a monocle.

**167(a) Captain Harper** unidentified.

**167(b) Turf Coffee-room** the Turf Coffee House was located in St Andrews Street, Edinburgh.

**168(a) Major Campbell** perhaps Hogg is referring to Angus Campbell, who was tacksman of Ensay and factor to Macleod of Harris. Hogg visited Ensay—a small island in the Sound of Harris, southwest of the Isle of Lewis in the Outer Hebrides—on his 1803 Highland journey. See 'Hogg in the Hebrides in 1803', ed by Hans de Groot, *Studies in Hogg and his World*, 13 (2002), 143–80 (p. 151) and notes, pp. 172–73.

**168(b) Dr. M'Leod** probably Dr William Macleod (1749/1750–1811) of Luskinder, whom Hogg visited on his Highland journey of 1803—see 'Hogg in the Hebrides in 1803', pp. 145–48 and note, p. 167. Hogg had signed a failed lease agreement with Macleod in 1803 for a farm on Harris—see *Letters 1*, pp. 43–45.

**168(b) Scalpa** Scalpay is an island in the Outer Hebrides at the entrance of Loch Tarbert. Hogg apparently is referring to the laird or tacksman of Scalpay, who is unidentified.

**168(c) Tarbet** a small town in Dunbartonshire on the west shore of Loch Lomond, about 2 miles east of Arrochar.

**168(c) Greenock** a port city on the Forth of Clyde in Renfrewshire.

**168(c) Cowal** a peninsula in southeastern Argyll between Loch Fyne and Loch Long.

**168(d) Bute** an island in the Firth of Clyde, just south of Cowal.

**168(d) Tontine** a hotel in the heart of Greenock. Hogg in his *Memoir* writes that he first met John Galt at a supper at the Tontine in 1804 (p. 72), although Hans de Groot has argued that the meeting probably took place in 1803—see 'When did Hogg meet John Galt?', *Studies in Hogg and his World*, 8 (1997), 75–76.

**169(a) Charles' Street** Hogg's friend John Grieve lived at 6 Charles Street in Edinburgh for a few years in the 1810s. Hogg stayed with Grieve when he was in Edinburgh. See *Letters 1*, pp. 334–36.

**169(b) Rothsay** Rothesay, the principal town on the Isle of Bute.

**169(b) Mr M'Neill** unidentified.

**169(b) Loch-Fine** Loch Fyne, a sea loch that opens off the Firth of Clyde and extends into Argyllshire past Inverary.

**169(b) Clyde** the river Clyde rises in southeast Lanarkshire and flows for more than a hundred miles before opening into the Firth of Clyde west of Glasgow.

**169(c) Major Cameron** unidentified, but Hogg records in his 1803 Highland journey that his party was joined by 'a Captain Cameron' near Inverlochy Castle—see *A Tour in the Highlands in 1803* (Paisley: Alexander Gardner, 1888), p. 43.

**169(c) Coalpepper** apparently fictitious, but 'Coalpepper' is probably derived from 'Coupar'. Browne's father was a manufacturer in Coupar Angus. Hogg perhaps is suggesting that Browne had a fiery temperament.

**170(a) Right and Wrong Club** Hogg was one of the founders and the croupier of this club, which had a short life in late 1814. Hogg notes that the club 'was established one night, in a frolic, at a jovial dinner party [...]. The chief principle of the club was, that whatever any of its members should assert, the whole were bound to support the same, whether *right or wrong*' (*Memoir*, p. 47). R. P. Gillies was also a founder and the president of the club; see Gillies's *Memoirs of a Literary Veteran*, 3 vols (London: Bentley, 1851), II, 195–97.

**170(a) *sang froid*** French, literally 'cold blood'. The expression means 'composure', especially under difficult circumstances.

**170(b) Norman M'Leod** unidentified.

**170(d) Mr Gildas, or Gillies** R. P. Gillies. See also note for 35, I. 57.

**171(c) M'Millan, of Millburgh** unidentified.

**171(c) Wood of Culloch-More** Culloch lies about five miles southeast of Crieff in Perthshire.

**172(a–b) various breeds of dogs [...] their names [...] either German or classical** Hogg later provides the names of the dogs. See p. 178(a–b) and notes.

**172(c) Deputy-Adjutant-General, under the Emperor of Austria** the Emperor of Austria at the time Hogg's story is set was Francis II (1768–1835), who had been Holy Roman Emperor until 1804. He became Emperor of Austria in 1804 as Francis (Franz) I and held the title until his death in 1835. Austria joined with Great Britain in the war against France in 1813.

**172(d) the Almanack** *The Edinburgh Almanack, and Imperial Register*, an annual publication that included a calendar and important public information. Although Hogg could not find 'staff-officers' of the Emperor of Austria in the *Almanack*, information about the Emperor himself was listed.

**173(a) *in statu quo*** Latin for 'in the same state'.

**173(a) engaged to be at Alloa on the 23d of April [...] Glen-Lyon early in May.** Hogg was in Alloa, a port town on the River Forth in Clackmannanshire, in April 1816 for the annual Shakespeare Festival, which Hogg attended regularly (see notes for the 'Shakspeare Club of Alloa' in the present edition). Hogg also wrote to Mrs Bald from Meggernie Castle in Glen Lyon on 1 June 1816 and describes his Highland travels after leaving the Balds at the conclusion of the Shakespeare Festival. See *Letters 1*, pp. 277–78.

**173(a) Athol** Atholl, a district in northern Perthshire north of the River Almond.

**173(a) Mr Forbes** *The Post-Office Annual Directory* for Edinburgh for 1816–17 lists Peter Forbes and Company, wine and spirit merchants at Adam Square.

**173(b) Mr Laing's shop** probably the bookshop of William Laing and his son, David, located at 49 South Bridge, Edinburgh.

**173(d) Crief** Crieff, a town in southern Perthshire about twelve miles west of

Perth.

**173(d) Glen-Orchay** Glen Orchy, the glen in Argyll that carries the river Orchy from Bridge of Orchy to Loch Awe.

**174(a) annual festival [...] anniversary of Shakespeare** see note for 173(a). The Shakespeare festival in Alloa was established in 1804, and Hogg wrote his 'Ode' on Shakespeare for the 1815 festival.

**174(a) the Devon** the River Devon rises in the Ochil Hills in Perthshire and empties into the River Forth at Cambus.

**174(b) M'Isaac** apparently a merchant in Alloa on whom Hogg relied for fish hooks. In a letter of 1 June 1816 to Mrs Alexander Bald, Hogg sends a message to her husband that in the next ten days 'it will be as good [...] that M,Isaac have a stock of fish-hooks' (*Letters 1*, p. 278).

**174(b) Mr Bald** Mr Alexander Bald, merchant in Alloa and friend of Hogg's. See notes to the 'Shakspeare Club of Alloa' in the present edition.

**174(d) The mason word is a humbug** the Scottish Freemasons had private methods of recognition known only to the members. Hogg is suggesting that the society of fly-fishers is a more exclusive society than even that of the Freemasons.

**175(c) village of Cambus** two miles west of Alloa in Clackmannanshire.

**176(a) Glen-Almond** the glen that carries the River Almond from near Loch Tay to near Perth.

**176(a) Amberlee** unidentified. Perhaps Hogg intends Amulree, a hamlet in Perthshire about ten miles northeast of Crieff.

**176(a) Kinnaird** at the time the story is set, the estate of Chalmers Izett in Athol. Izett had been a partner with Hogg's friend John Grieve in the hatter business in Edinburgh. Izett's wife, Eliza, was a close friend and adviser of Hogg's. Hogg writes in his *Memoir* that she 'had taken an early interest in my fortunes, which no circumstance has ever abated. I depended much on her advice and good taste; and had I attended more to her friendly remonstrances, it would have been much better for me' (p. 34). Hogg's poem *Mador of the Moor* (1816), which he says was begun while visiting Kinnaird, is partly set in the area around Kinnaird. See *Mador of the Moor*, ed. by James E. Barcus (S/SC, 2005).

**176(b) Dunira** an estate two miles northwest of Comrie in Perthshire and at one time home to Henry Dundas, first Viscount Melville (1742–1811). Dunira is the setting of 'Kilmeny' in *The Queen's Wake*.

**176(c) Strath-Tay** a valley in Perthshire that carries the River Tay from Loch Tay to the Firth of Tay.

**176(c) Appin and Lorn** regions in Argyllshire along the eastern shores of Loch Linnhe and the Firth of Lorn. This territory is associated with the legendary Gaelic warrior Fingal, whose exploits were recorded in the poetry of his son, Ossian. Hogg's poem *Queen Hynde* (1824) is set in this territory. See *Queen Hynde*, ed. by Suzanne Gilbert and Douglas S. Mack (S/SC, 1998).

**176(d) Ossian and Fingal** see the note for 176(c).

**177(d) Glen-Sheagy** unidentified and perhaps fictitious. Hogg also uses variations on this place name, Sheagy More and Strone of Sheavy, later in the story.

**178(a–b) Penelope [...] Hector and Cressida** these dogs are named for prominent characters in the stories about the Trojan War. Penelope was the faithful wife of Odysseus; Hector was a noble warrior and son of Priam, the Trojan king; in medieval and Renaissance literature, Cressida was the daughter of the traitor Calchas and had an ill-fated relationship with Troilus, another son of King Priam.

178(a) **Wolga** the largest river system in Europe, the Volga River rises in the Valday Hills northwest of Moscow and empties into the Caspian Sea near Astrakhan.

178(b) **Hungarian dog Eugene** probably named for Prince Eugene of Savoy (1663–1736), military leader under emperor Leopold I. He defeated the Turks to end their power in Hungary and fought with Malborough at Blenheim and successive campaigns.

178(b) **Archduke John** a reference to the Archduke John of Austria (1782– 1859), brother of Francis I, the Emperor of Austria. See note for 172(c).

178(b) **Sobieski, the great blood-hound from the forest of Poland** John III Sobieski (1624–96) became king of Poland in 1674. Hogg is perhaps also making reference to the impostor John Sobieski Stolberg Stuart (1795?– 1872). He and his brother, Charles Edward Stuart (1799?–1880), pretended to be the heirs of another 'pretender', Prince Charles Edward Stuart. Their real names were John and Charles Allen, sons of Thomas Gatehouse Allen. They became well known in Edinburgh and were present for King George IV's visit to Edinburgh in 1822. For additional information about these brothers, see the *Oxford DNB* article by K. D. Reynolds.

178(b) **Do I hear with my ears, and understand with my heart?** echoes Isaiah 6. 10: 'lest they see with their eyes, and hear with their ears, and understand with their heart, and convert, and be healed'.

179(a) *Lord, what is man* from Psalm 8. 4 'What is man, that thou art mindful of him?'

179(a) **a manufacturer** James Browne's father was a manufacturer at Coupar Angus.

180(b) **There's the rub** echoes *Hamlet* III. 1. 67.

### There's Naught Sae Sweet in this Poor Life

'There's Naught Sae Sweet in this Poor Life' was published in *Blackwood's Edinburgh Magazine*, 18 (September 1825), 391–92, and was the only publication of the song in Hogg's lifetime. The song appears in the *Noctes Ambrosianæ No. XXI*, where it is sung by the 'Hogg' character; however, there is no further corroboration of Hogg's authorship. The song is a sentimental but playful celebration of the companionship of the *Blackwood's* writers in their nights of conversation and drink at Ambrose's Tavern. Hogg did not like his role in this *Noctes*, however, as he wrote to Blackwood on 1 September 1825: 'the former part of the NOCTES is very good my part abominable' (*Letters 2*, p. 237). The song is based on Robert Burns's song 'Auld lang syne' (Kinsley 240) and is sung to that tune by Hogg.

The text of the song for the present edition is based on the *BEM* version and has been extracted from the context of the *Noctes* in which it was published. The song is not printed in a standard verse format, but the verses are interspersed with *Noctes* dialogue. After singing the first verse, the Hogg character calls on his companions to join him in the chorus. As Hogg begins the second verse, his singing is interrupted by Odoherty, who questions Hogg's lyrics. After an exchange between Odoherty and Hogg, Hogg continues the song without interruption. The song in the context of the *Noctes* dialogue follows:

## HOGG.

Some people's intellects are sairly malshackered by age.–(*Sings.*)
Air–*Auld langsyne.*

There's nought sae sweet in this poor life
  As knittin' soul to soul;
And what maist close may bind that knot?
  The glass and bowl!
    The glass and bowl, my boys
    The glass and bowl;
    So let us call, for this is out
    Anither bowl.

Chorus–ye neerdoweels, chorus.

Chorus.

The glass and bowl, &c.

We never paddled in the burn,
Nor pull'd the gowan droll–

## ODOHERTY.

The gowan droll! What is there droll about a gowan? The gowan fine,
you mean.

## HOGG.

Sir Morgan Odoherty, if ye be Sir Morgan, ye'll hae the goodness to mak
sangs for yersell, and no for me. It was, nae doubt, "gowans fine," in
Burns, for he wanted it for a rhyme to "Auld langsyne." Now I want it to
rhyme to "bowl," a word far different. And besides, the gowan is a droll-
like sort of crater as ye wad see in a field.

## ODOHERTY.

I beg your pardon–Proceed, Shepherd.

## HOGG.

We never dabbled in the burn,
  Nor pull'd the gowan droll,
But often has the sun's return
  Surprised our bowl.
Chorus.–Our glass and bowl, my boys,
    Our glass and bowl;
    So let us call, as this is out–
    Another bowl.

The final three verses follow without a break.

**180, Air –*Auld Langsyne*** see Appendix B for the music.
**180, ll. 10–11 dabbled in the burn, | Nor pull'd the gowan droll** The third
  and fourth stanzas of Burns's 'Auld Langsyne', to which Odoherty refers
  when he interrupts Hogg's singing, are as follows:
    We twa hae run about the braes,
      And pou'd the gowans fine;
    But we've wander'd mony a weary fitt,
      Sin auld lang syne.
      For auld, &c.
    We twa hae paidl'd in the burn,
      Frae morning sun till dine;
    But seas between us braid hae roar'd,

Sin auld lang syne.
    For auld, &c.  (Kinsley 240)

**181, l. 20 hooted mony a whiggish wretch** 'hoot' is to discredit or dismiss
with contempt. A regular pastime of the Tory Blackwoodians in their nights
at Ambrose's was to attack the rival Whigs.

### The Brakens Wi' Me

'The Brakens wi' Me' was first published in *Blackwood's Edinburgh Magazine*, 18
(December 1825), 753–54. It appears in the *Noctes Ambrosianæ No. XXIII*, where
it is sung by the 'Shepherd' character; the *BEM* publication includes music.
The song was reprinted in *Select and Rare Scotish Melodies* (London: Goulding
and D'Almaine, 1829), pp. 45–50, and again in *Songs* (1831), pp. 17–19, both
times under the title 'Gang to the Brakens wi' Me'. The *Scotish Melodies* version
includes a musical arrangement by Henry Bishop, although Hogg noted in
*Songs* that Bishop 'ruined the simplicity of my favourite air, which I deemed a
masterpiece' (p. 17).

A letter from William Blackwood to Hogg, 19 November 1825, indicates
that the *BEM* publication omitted a portion of the song from Hogg's original:

> Your song will be one of the most popular you have ever written. I wish
> I had seen you again before you left town, in order that you might have
> altered the part of it which referred to Bankers, bonds, Bills &c which are
> so foreign to pastoral feelings—for a country lass to talk of her lover
> *drawing on her at sight*, is either most unnatural for what can she know
> about drawing bills?—or it is what those who accuse you of coarseness
> could call not decent. It would not have done to have altered any thing
> except you had seen it yourself, and therefore we thought it the safest
> course to omit what would have prevented the song from being a general
> favourite—it is besides now of a good singing length (NLS, MS 30,308, p.
> 161).

Apparently Hogg's original manuscript has not been preserved, and Hogg did
not restore the omitted *BEM* stanza to later publications.

The song was revised, however, for the *Scotish Melodies* publication. The last
four lines of stanza two in *BEM* are omitted and replaced by the first four lines
of stanza three; the last four lines of stanza three of *BEM* are omitted. Stanza
four of *BEM* becomes stanza three in *Scotish Melodies*, and the following new
stanza is added to *Scotish Melodies* as stanza four. This new stanza hints at the
kind of sexual innuendo that Blackwood would have found objectionable:

> She turn'd her around, and said, smiling,
>     While the tear in her blue ee shone clear,
> You're welcome, kind sir, to your mailing,
>     For O, you have valued it dear.
> Gae make out the deed, do not linger,
>     Let the parson endorse the decree,
> And then for a wave o' your finger
>     I'll gang to the brakens wi' thee.

The *Scotish Melodies* version is the version used in *Songs*.

In *BEM* the first stanza is printed with the music; the present edition prints
the text of the entire song, but otherwise the text is printed herein without
emendation. See Appendix B for the music.

**181,** *Air–Driving the Steers* Hogg also uses his 'favourite air' for his 'Scottish Ode (for Music) | On the death of Lord Byron', which apparently was never published. Hogg sent the Byron 'Ode' to William Baynes and Sons in March or April 1825. Hogg referred Baynes to Captain Simon Fraser's *Airs and Melodies Peculiar to the Highlands of Scotland and the Isles* (1816, p. 57) for the music to this Gaelic air, 'Ioman nan gamhna'. See also *Letters 2*, pp. 229–32, as well as the notes for 'Ode for Music. On the Death of Lord Byron' in the present edition.

# January 1826–December 1826 (Volumes 19–20)

## Songs for the Duke of Buccleuch's Birth Day

'Songs for the Duke of Buccleuch's Birth Day' consists of two songs, 'Rejoice, Ye Wan and Wilder'd Glens' and 'Wat o' Buccleuch', as well as an introductory *Noctes* dialogue that Hogg had originally intended for publication with the songs. The two songs were published for the first time in *Blackwood's Edinburgh Magazine*, 19 (February 1826), 217–19, where they are sung by the 'Shepherd' character in the *Noctes Ambrosianæ No. XXIV*; apparently neither song was reprinted in Hogg's lifetime. However, as Blackwood wrote to Hogg, 'Christopher did not take the Forest dialogue, but he liked the songs' (NLS, MS 30,309, pp. 163–65). The omission of the introductory dialogue disappointed Hogg and, Hogg suggested, diminished the effect of the songs. Hogg wrote to Blackwood on 19 March 1826: 'I was chagrined that the Forest dialogue I sent was not inserted in the Noctes not for any intrinsic merit that it had for it had none but then it gave a *truth* a *locality* to Ambrose's which without such a native touch that ideal meeting never can possess' (*Letters 2*, p. 243). The present edition publishes the 'Forest dialogue' for the first time with the songs, thus restoring the text of 'Songs for the Duke of Buccleuch's Birth day' to Hogg's original intent.

The songs were written for the occasion of the nineteenth birthday of Walter, the fifth Duke of Buccleuch, on 25 November 1825. Walter Francis Montagu-Douglas-Scott (1806–1884) was the son of Charles William Henry Montagu-Scott, the fourth Duke of Buccleuch, and Harriet Katherine Townshend. It was Walter's father, Charles, who had granted Hogg the lease of Altrive farm in 1815. Walter served as host to King George IV in 1822 and twenty years later to Victoria and Albert. He married Lady Charlotte Anne Thynne in 1829. Walter's positions later included president of the Highland Agricultural Society and of the Society of Antiquaries, and he was lord privy seal under Robert Peel. For additional information, see the *Oxford DNB* article by K. D. Reynolds.

The present edition publishes 'Songs for the Duke of Buccleuch's Birth Day' from the manuscript preserved in the National Library of Scotland as MS 4854, fols 29–30. The manuscript consists of a single sheet measuring *c.* 31 cm x 37 cm, folded in the centre to make two folios measuring *c.* 31 cm x 18.5 cm. The paper bears no watermark. A line is drawn through the dialogue as an instruction to the printer to omit this text. The *BEM* publication of the two songs follows the manuscript except to add punctuation as Hogg would have expected. The present edition follows the manuscript without emendation except to add silently end punctuation within the prose dialogue where necessary.

**183(a) duke of Buccleuch's birth day** 25 November 1825.

**183(a) Mitchell** the landlord of what is now the County Inn, Selkirk—see Michaela Reid, *The Forest Club 1788–2000: The History of a Border Dining and Coursing Club Associated with Sir Walter Scott* (Kelso: The Forest Club, 2003), p. 35.

**183(b) Tailor o' Yarrowford** probably Thomas Hogg, Hogg's cousin, who appears as 'Tam the tailor' in 'Tales and Anecdotes of the Pastoral Life. No. III' (p. 21(a) in the present edition) and as 'the celebrated flying Ettrick tailor' in 'Letter from the Ettrick Shepherd, Enclosing a Letter from James Laidlaw' (p. 78(d) in the present edition).

**183(c) Mount-Benger Law** a mountain (1781 feet) just north of Hogg's farm of Mountbenger.

**183(d) Wattie Henderson [...] Geordie Scott** Henderson is unidentified; George Scott is probably a butcher from Selkirk from whom Hogg bought beef—see Norah Parr, *James Hogg at Home* (Dollar: Douglas S. Mack, 1980), pp. 73–74.

**183(d) crock-siller** 'crock' is an old ewe past bearing; 'siller' is money.

**183(d) Falkirk tryste** Falkirk is a town in southeast Stirlingshire. In Hogg's time major cattle markets, or trysts, were held twice yearly, in September and October, at Stenhousemuir. The 'Falkirk tryste' was known especially as a market for Highland cattle.

**184(a) Tam Anderson** probably Thomas Anderson (*d.* 1835), who was Provost of Selkirk.

**184(a) Joseph Hume** probably a reference to Joseph Hume (1777–1855), a native of Montrose and who at this time was a Member of Parliament. Hume has been described as a 'dull but dogged orator'—see the article on Hume in the *Oxford DNB* by V. E. Chancellor. Hume's long-windedness is referenced again in the *Noctes Ambrosianæ* for June 1826 in the dialogue that introduces Hogg's poem 'Meg o' Marley'—see the notes for 'Meg o' Marley' in the present edition.

**184(b) Mr Ambrose** the owner of Ambrose's Tavern in Gabriel's Road, where the *BEM* writers gathered for the *Noctes Ambrosianæ*. See the note for 36, ll. 1.

**184(c) Better twa laugh than ane greet** perhaps a variation on the proverb, 'better two skaiths than one sorrow' (*ODEP*, p. 56).

**184(d) Davie Tamson the poet o' Galashiels** David Thomson, weaver and poet from Galashiels. Scott writes in his *Journal* for 12 December 1825: 'Hogg came to breakfast this morning, having taken and brought for his companion the Galashiels bard David Thompson as to a meeting of huzz Tividale poets' (pp. 34–35). In his *Life of Scott* Lockhart writes about Scott's attendance at the annual festival at Galashiels 'when their Deacon and Convener for the year entered on his office' (VII, 93). Thomson usually sent Scott a verse invitation on the occasion, and Scott and his family were escorted to the festival by a procession of weavers. Hogg often accompanied Scott to the festival and, as Lockhart wrote, 'many of Hogg's best ballads were produced for the first time amidst the cheers of the men of Ganderscleuch' (VII, 96).

**185(b) Air—*Killiecrankie*** see Appendix B for the music.

**185(b) dowie dells o' Yarrow** James Russell in *Reminiscences of Yarrow*, ed. by Professor Veitch, 2nd edn, preface by Campbell Fraser (Selkirk: George

Lewis & Son, 1894), describes the 'dowie dells': "The Dowie Dens of Yarrow" have been known to fame from days of yore. Forming part of a royal forest, and furnishing many adventures of the chase,—lying near the Scottish border, and frequently involved in feudal strife,—embracing in their annals many doughty deeds of arms and stirring scenes of love,—it is not wonderful that they have given birth to legends and ballads in abundance. The deep gloom of the densely wooded district was sufficient to suggest the name' (p. 209). The *New Statistical Account* provides additional details:

> There is a piece of ground lying to the west of Yarrow Kirk, which appears to have been the scene of slaughter and sepulchre. From time immemorial it was a low waste moor till twenty-five years ago, when formed into a number of cultivated enclosures. [...] The real tradition simply bears, that here a deadly feud was settled by dint of arms; the upright stones mark the place where the two lords or leaders fell, and the bodies of their followers were thrown into a marshy pool, called the *Dead* Lake, in the adjoining haugh. It is probable that this is the location of "the Dowie Dens of Yarrow." One cannot easily, however, unravel the details, or fix the date of the event which the old ballad describes. (III, 46–47)

Sir Walter Scott claims that the first publication of 'The Dowie Dens of Yarrow' was in his *Minstrelsy of the Scottish Border*—see 3rd edn, 3 vols (London: Longman; Edinburgh: Constable, 1806), II, 354–60. Scott describes the ballad as 'a very great favourite among the inhabitants of Ettrick Forest' (II, 354), so it certainly would have been familiar to Hogg. In his effort to 'unravel the details', Scott offers two stories about the ballad's subjects. One story, which includes an account of the unusual preservation of the victim's body, suggests 'that the hero of the ballad might have been identified with John Scott, sixth son of the laird of Harden, murdered in Ettrick Forest by his kinsmen, the Scotts of Gilmanscleugh [...]. This appeared the more probable, as the common people always affirm, that this young man was treacherously slain, and that, in evidence thereof, his body remained uncorrupted for many years; so that even the roses on his shoes seemed as fresh as when he was first laid in the family vault at Hassendean' (II, 355). The second story suggests that the ballad is about a duel 'betwixt John Scott of Tushielaw and his brother-in-law Walter Scott, third son of Robert of Thirlestane, in which the latter was slain' (II, 355). Scott also notes that the victim was an ancestor of Lord Napier.

**185(d) For gloaming far too early** Hogg's note indicates that this line refers to the deaths of the Duke and Duchess of Buccleuch. Charles William Henry Montagu-Scott, the fourth Duke, had died in 1819, and Harriet Catherine Townshend, the Duchess, had died in 1814.

**186(a) Air–*Thurot's defeat*** see Appendix B for the music.

**187(a) Douglas and Stuart** like the Scotts of Buccleuch, the Douglases and Stuarts were prominent Border families. Branches of the three families were connected by marriage. Sir Walter Scott of Branxholm and Buccleuch (1549–74) married Lady Margaret Douglas, the daughter of David Douglas, the seventh Earl of Angus. Their son, Walter (1565?–1611), was the first Lord Scott of Buccleuch. Following the death of her husband, Lady Margaret married Francis Stewart (1562–1612), the first Earl of Bothwell. See 'Walter Scott of Buccleuch' and 'Francis Stewart' by Rob Macpherson, *Oxford DNB*.

**187 (a) Scotts wha kept order** for the balance of the poem, 'Wat o' Buccleuch' celebrates the historical significance of the Scotts of Buccleuch for the Borders.

**187 (c) Of reif and of rattle** that is, robbery by force and violence.

**187 (d) The Wats** include, among others, the Border chieftan, Sir Walter Scott of Buccleuch (c. 1490–1552), and Walter Scott, first Lord Scott of Buccleuch (1565?–1611), a Border reiver, who conducted numerous raids across the English border.

**188 (a) chief of Buccleuch** young Walter has taken his place as head of the Buccleuch family.

### The Great Muckle Village of Balmaquhapple

'The Great Muckle Village of Balmaquhapple' was first published in *Blackwood's Edinburgh Magazine*, 19 (June 1826), 739–40, and the song appears in the *Noctes Ambrosianæ No. XXVI.* 'North' calls upon 'Beelzebub' to 'read the bit of paper you have in your fist', to which the Shepherd replies: 'They're my ain verses too—Whisht—whisht'. Although the music is not printed in the *Noctes,* Hogg indicates that it is to be sung to the air of 'Soger Laddie' (see Appendix B). The song was reprinted with minor revisions in *Songs* (pp. 41–44) under the title 'The Village of Balmaquhapple' and includes the framing dialogue from the *Noctes.* In a note to the *Songs* edition, Hogg writes: 'I cannot conceive what could induce me to write a song like this. It must undoubtedly have some allusion to circumstances which I have quite forgot' (p. 44). The song is in the spirit of Robert Burns's kirk satires, such as 'Holy Willie's Prayer'.

The present edition reprints the *BEM* version with the following emendations:
189, l. 17 "There's] There's *BEM*
189, l. 25 "There] There *BEM*
189, l. 33 "But] But *BEM*
189, l. 40  Balmaquhapple."] Balmaquhapple. *BEM*

**188, l. 1 Balmaquhapple** apparently fictitious.

**188, l. 6 Saint Andrew, the god o' the Fife folks** St Andrew is the patron saint of Scotland. One of the original twelve disciples of Jesus, Andrew was martyred on a saltire. According to tradition, relics of Andrew were taken to the coast of Fife, where the town of St Andrews was established.

**188, l. 11 auld thief** Satan.

**189, l. 17 elder** in the Presbyterian Church of Scotland, an elected church officer who is a member of the Session that oversees the governance of the local church.

**189, l. 27 deacon** in the Presbyterian Church of Scotland, an elected officer responsible for the temporal affairs of the church.

### Meg o' Marley

'Meg o' Marley' is a playful song that presents a favourite theme of Hogg's: the bewitching character of a beautiful woman. The song was first published in *Blackwood's Edinburgh Magazine*, 19 (June 1826), 756, where it is sung by the 'Shepherd' character to conclude the *Noctes Ambrosianæ No. XXVI.* The song follows North's offer to bring the Shepherd into Parliament, to which the Shepherd replies: 'I wadna swap ane o' my ain bit wee sangs wi' the langest-wunded speech that has been "hear'd, hear'd," this Session'. At the conclusion of the song, North agrees that 'Meg o' Marley' is 'well worth Joseph Hume's

four hours' speech, and forty-seven resolutions' (p. 756)—see also the note for
184(a). 'Meg o' Marley' was reprinted in *Songs* (pp. 100–02) with only minor
revisions to the *BEM* publication; the *Songs* publication includes the *Noctes*
dialogue that sets the context of the song. Hogg did not indicate a tune for this
song.

The present edition reprints the *BEM* version without emendation.

**189, l. 1 Marley glen** apparently fictitious.

**189, l. 5 stown the Bangor frae the clerk** 'Bangor' is a hymn tune used in the
Church of Scotland; the 'clerk' is the Session Clerk, who would have been
second only to the minister in authority in the local church and who frequently
served as precentor during worship services. The song describes a series of
characters who have been distracted from their responsibilities by Meg's
beauty, including the Session Clerk and the minister.

**189, l. 7 minister's fa'en through the text** 'fa through' is 'to make a botch of,
to mismanage, bungle' (*SND*).

**190, l. 13 tailor's fa'en out-ower the bed** echoes Burns's song 'The Taylor fell
thro' the bed, &c' (Kinsley 286).

**190, l. 19 curse an' ban** 'ban' also means 'to curse'; the expression means 'to
curse vigorously' (*SND*).

## My Bonny Mary

'My Bonny Mary' appears in *Blackwood's Edinburgh Magazine*, 20 (July 1826),
93–94, in the *Noctes Ambrosianæ No. XXVII* and is sung by the 'Shepherd' character.
The song was a favourite of Hogg's, and the reception in the *Noctes* was
exceptionally positive. Tickler responds to the Shepherd's singing: 'Equal to
anything of Burns"; and North adds: 'Not a better in all George Thomson's
collection [...] and there's no end to your genius' (p. 94). 'My Bonny Mary' was
sent to Blackwood together with 'O Weel Befa' the Maiden Gay', which was
also published in *Noctes No. XXVII* (see p. 192 in the present edition). When
Hogg sent the poems to Blackwood, he included a note to 'C. N.' [Christopher
North]: 'Last night we were at Ambrose's you asked me for one or two pastoral
love songs. I send you them An edition of the one was once published I know
not where or when but not at all I believe as it is here. That however does not
hinder me from singing it if called on for it' (*Letters 2*, p. 247). Both songs, in
fact, had been published previously in different versions, but William Blackwood
was pleased to have them for *BEM*. On 24 June 1826 Blackwood wrote to
Hogg: 'On Saturday I had the pleasure of receiving your two capital Songs
just in time for the Noctes. They are really good and I am sure will be much
liked. They enliven the Noctes, and I hope you will send some more very
soon. I have credited your acct with two Guineas for them' (NLS, MS 30,309,
fols 229–30).

The date of composition of 'My Bonny Mary' is uncertain, but in the
introduction to the work in *Songs* Hogg refers to it as 'one of the songs of my
youth' (p. 103). 'My Bonny Mary' was first published in *The Forest Minstrel*
(1810) under the title 'Bonny Mary'. (See Hogg, *The Forest Minstrel*, ed. by P. D.
Garside and Richard D. Jackson, with musical notation by Peter Horsfall (S/
SC 2006), pp. 51–53.) The song was revised and reprinted in Hogg's 1822
*Poetical Works* (IV, 341–44) under the title 'Bonnie Mary'; among other revisions
in *Poetical Works*, the order of the stanzas beginning 'Oft has the lark' and

'When Phoebus mounts' was reversed. The order of verses in *Poetical Works* was maintained in *BEM*, but the poem underwent additional major revisions for *BEM*. Of special significance, the second verse of *BEM* was added for this version, and the setting of the poem was shifted from Scaur Water and the Lowther Hills to Yarrow Water and Mountbenger, probably to update the poet's own residence in 1826 at Mount Benger from the Dumfriesshire locations where Hogg was a shepherd from 1805 to 1809 when the poem likely was written.

The *BEM* version of 'My Bonny Mary' was printed from a fair-copy manuscript, a part of which is preserved in the National Library of Scotland as MS 4017, fol. 141. The surviving manuscript fragment is a single sheet measuring *c.* 31 cm x 19 cm; the paper does not have a watermark. The sheet is addressed to 'William Blackwood Esqr | 17 Princes Street' and has been folded for posting. The manuscript includes only the last three stanzas of the poem; the last two stanzas of the manuscript are numbered 6 and 7, although there are eight stanzas in the published version. The stanzas are not numbered in any of the published versions. As is common in Hogg's poetry manuscripts, the manuscript contains no punctuation.

There is no tune included for this song in the present edition. Hogg notes in the Preface to *The Forest Minstrel* that the air for 'Bonny Mary' had been deemed unsuitable 'to some excellent judges' so that the he leaves the choice for an appropriate tune 'to the discernment of the singer' (S/SC, p. 7). The reader is referred to the S/SC edition of *The Forest Minstrel* for an appropriate tune (p. 51), as well as a full discussion of alternative music choices (pp. 253–56).

The text for the present edition is the *BEM* printing without emendation.

**190, l. 1 Yarrow** Yarrow Water, which runs between St Mary's Loch and Selkirk.

**191, l. 17 Benger's haughty head** Mountbenger Law (1781 feet) overlooks the Yarrow valley.

**191, l. 21 Brownhill cheek** probably a reference Brown Rig, a hill between the Yarrow and Ettrick valleys and about five miles south southwest of Hogg's farm of Mount Benger. On the map of Captain Napier's property included in his book *A Treatise on Practical Story-Farming* (1822), Brown Rig forms the northeast boundary of Napier's property.

**191, l. 25 Phoebus** 'the light'. In Greek mythology Phoebus Apollo was, among other things, the god of light and therefore associated with the sun.

## O Weel Befa' the Maiden Gay

'O Weel Befa' the Maiden Gay' was published in *Blackwood's Edinburgh Magazine*, 20 (July 1826), 108; it is the second of two love songs sung by the 'Shepherd' character in the *Noctes Ambrosianæ No. XXVII.* (See notes to 'My Bonny Mary' in the present edition for correspondence regarding these two songs.) 'O Weel Befa' the Maiden Gay' apparently was written in September 1814 while Hogg was visiting John Wilson at his home at Elleray in the Lake District. Hogg discusses the circumstances of the composition of the poem in his introduction to the work in *Songs*: 'Mr Wilson and I had a Queen's Wake every wet day–a fair set-to who should write the best poem between breakfast and dinner, and, if I am any judge, these friendly competitions produced several of our best poems, if not the best ever written on the same subjects before' (p. 117).

'O Weel Befa' the Maiden Gay' was first published as the concluding song in Hogg's dramatic poem, 'The Haunted Glen', which was included in the two-volume collection of the author's *Dramatic Tales* (Edinburgh: Ballantyne; London: Longman, 1817), II, 269–70. It was reprinted in the 1822 *Poetical Works* (II, 227–28), also as the final song of 'The Haunted Glen', with only minor changes attributable to the printer's preferences. Hogg revised the poem for the *BEM* publication, however, and what Hogg published in *BEM* is a very different work. The *BEM* version consists of four ten-line verses instead of the three ten-line verses of 'The Haunted Glen'. The opening verses of both versions are essentially the same, although the first line of the song in 'The Haunted Glen' is 'O weel befa' the guileless heart'. The third (and final) verse of 'The Haunted Glen' version became the second verse of *BEM*. The third verse of *BEM* is new in this version. The second verse of 'The Haunted Glen' was slightly revised and became the fourth (and final) verse of *BEM*. Hogg further revised 'The Haunted Glen' version for publication with music in the *Musical Bijou* for 1830—see Hogg's *Contributions to Annuals and Gift-Books*, ed. by Janette Currie and Gillian Hughes (S/SC, 2006), p. 154. The work was also published as 'Song. By the Ettrick Shepherd' in the February 1830 issue of the *Monthly Musical and Literary Magazine*—see Gillian Hughes, 'Hogg and the *Monthly Musical and Literary Magazine*', *Studies in Hogg and his World*, 15 (2004), 120–25.

'O Weel Befa' the Maiden Gay' was published again in Hogg's *Songs* based on the *BEM* version with only minor revisions, including the substitution of 'wons' for 'smiles' in the final line. The *Songs* version also omits the first 'sae' in line 6, although apparently this is a printer's error. The song was published a second time in *BEM*, 29 (March 1831), 546–47, and again sung by the 'Shepherd' character in the *Noctes*. This second publication of the song was in the context of a notice about the publication of Hogg's 1831 collection of *Songs,* which was not otherwise reviewed in *BEM*, and as such was probably an editorial selection rather than a submission by Hogg. The Shepherd introduces the song by saying 'Noo, I'll sing you a bit sang, out o' the colleckshun'. The 1831 *Noctes* reprints the song from the *Songs* collection, including the revised last line, but the *Noctes* version also restores 'sae' in line 6 so that the line correctly reads 'aye sae kind'.

The present edition prints the *BEM* version of 1826 without emendation.

**192, l. 3 the bonny May** in a footnote to Canto Second of *Mador of the Moor* Hogg writes: 'A May, in old Scottish ballads and romances, denotes a young lady, or a maiden somewhat above the lower class'—see *Mador of the Moor*, ed. by James E. Barcus (S/SC, 2005), p. 33.

**192, l. 7 blooming asphodel** a flower of the lily family, and in classical literature associated with Persephone, Queen of the Underworld.

**192, l. 25 dear thing of blame** a reference to the biblical Eve, who, according to the Genesis story, was responsible for bringing sin into the world as a consequence of her disobedience to God (see Genesis 3).

**193, l. 32 hinny in the haw** honey in the hawthorn.

## A Pastoral Love Scene

'A Pastoral Love Scene' was written for *Blackwood's Edinburgh Magazine* but was not published in *BEM* and apparently was never published in its original form in Hogg's lifetime. Hogg revised the drama into a story, entitled 'Katie Cheyne', and sent it to Alan Cunningham in the spring 1828 for publication in Cunningham's annual, *The Anniversary* (for 1829). Hogg's revisions were substantial, and he clearly paid special attention to the demands of the annuals market, particularly by editing out the drama's sexual suggestiveness and providing a happier ending by eliminating the violent death of the main character. 'Katie Cheyne' was held over by Cunningham for a second number of *The Anniversary*, which was never published, but the story was published instead in *Sharpe's London Magazine*, 1 (August 1829), 56–63. The 'Katie Cheyne' version was reprinted in the posthumously-published *Tales and Sketches*, 6 vols (Glasgow: Blackie, 1836–37), III, 171–82; 'Katie Cheyne' is also published in James Hogg, *Contributions to Annuals and Gift-Books*, ed. by Janette Currie and Gillian Hughes (S/SC, 2006), pp. 108–19. A fair-copy manuscript of 'A Pastoral Love Scene' is preserved in the Mitchell Library, Glasgow, as MS 308865 and likely represents the version Hogg intended for publication in *BEM*. The manuscript version of 'A Pastoral Love Scene' is significantly different from what was eventually published as 'Katie Cheyne' and, therefore, constitutes a different text. The Mitchell Library manuscript serves as the copy text for the present edition.

'A Pastoral Love Scene' was the first of what Hogg intended as a series of three pastoral dramas that he wanted to publish in three separate numbers of *BEM*. Hogg wrote to Blackwood on 26 July 1826: 'The dramas of simple life I have written off hand–I have not so much as got leisure to read them over Tell me if they will suit Maga or what they will require–' (*Letters 2*, pp. 248–49). The first drama, 'A Pastoral Love Scene', did not 'suit' Blackwood, and he later wrote Hogg that it was 'really not a piece that is worthy of you' (NLS, MS 30,309, pp. 385–87). In September Hogg was still encouraging Blackwood to publish all three dramas: 'I know at least I suspect the first number of my Dramas to be inferior but you *must* publish it that's absolute for both the second and third number are a great deal happier I would send them both were it not for the dread of never seeing them again. On second thoughts I think I will send the second only you are to swear by all the holy saints and martyrs not to lose it' (*Letters 2*, p. 250). Hogg adds a note to the end of this letter, reiterating his requirement that all the dramas be published individually: 'I forgot to mention that if you publish the dramas as is likely you must cancel the first title and make them thus "Dramas of simple life" and publish only one No. at a time please put the proper direction on Roberts letter' (*Letters 2*, p. 251). Blackwood liked the second of the dramas and agreed to publish it with some revision, but Hogg would not publish it without the first drama. The disposition of the proposed third drama is not known and apparently has not survived. (The second of Hogg's dramas is published in the present edition as 'Dramas of Simple Life No. II'; see pp. 209–53 and notes.) Hogg persisted in his efforts to publish the dramas in *BEM*, writing again to Blackwood in August 1827 and January 1828 (see *Letters 2*, p. 276 and p. 282) before giving up on Blackwood and eventually sending the story to Cunningham.

The Mitchell Library manuscript consists of four sheets measuring *c.* 31 cm x 38 cm, each folded to make two folios measuring *c.* 31 cm x 19 cm; the manuscript has been bound for library preservation. Hogg has written on the recto and verso of each folio except the verso of the last folio, and he has numbered the pages [1]–15. The paper does not have a watermark. The original title of the work in manuscript was 'Pastoral Love Scenes, or Dramas of Simple Life | by the Ettrick Shepherd | Drama First', but Hogg marked through the 's' in 'Scenes', the subtitle, and 'Drama First', and then added 'A' to the beginning, leaving 'A Pastoral Love Scene' as the title. As is typical of Hogg's manuscripts, there are inconsistencies in punctuation and idiosyncrasies in spelling. The present edition follows the manuscript except that end punctuation and the marking of quotations within quotations are made consistent for the convenience of the reader.

'A Pastoral Love Scene' was edited from the Mitchell Library manuscript by Janette Currie for *Studies in Hogg and his World*, 11 (2000), 87–121; acknowledgement is made to Dr. Currie, whose research has been an important source for the present edition. For further information about the role of 'A Pastoral Love Scene' in the textual history of 'Katie Cheyne', see James Hogg, *Contributions to Annuals and Gift-Books*, ed. by Janette Currie and Gillian Hughes, (S/SC, 2006), pp. 307–09.

**194(a) there's a mote gaen into ane o' them** echoes Matthew 7. 3: 'And why beholdest thou the mote that is in thy brother's eye, but considerest not the beam that is in thine own eye?'

**196(a) Lammas** August 1, one of the Scottish quarter days celebrating the first fruits of harvest.

**196(d) Cowhally** apparently fictitious, as are the names and places of the story as a whole.

**197(a) Blow lowne a wee** calm down, make less noise or fuss.

**198(a) unmeet to clean the shoes of the heir of Cowhally** echoes Mark 1. 7: 'There cometh one mightier than I after me, the latchet of whose shoes I am not worthy to stoop down and unloose'.

**200(c) Eye for eye [...] head for head** echoes Leviticus 24. 20: 'Breach for breach, eye for eye, tooth for tooth: as he hath caused a blemish in a man, so shall it be done to him again'.

**201(d) chimlaw brace** a mantelpiece.

**202(c–d) O weels me on my cozy plaid** although Duncan tells Matilda that this song is 'auld', apparently it is an original of Hogg's. It is entitled 'The Shepherd's Plaid' in 'Katie Cheyne'.

**202(d) *gladie*** in the manuscript the word 'shadie' is written beside '*gladie*' as if Hogg were considering a revision. There are no additional markings to suggest that Hogg in fact decided to replace '*gladie*'. In 'Katie Cheyne' the entire line is revised to 'And better for a ladie'—see *Contributions to Annuals and Gift-Books*, p. 116.

**204(d) claymazee** this word seems to be Hogg's invention, perhaps derived from 'clishmaclaver' (gossip) or 'clamersum' (noisily discontented).

**206(a) state of Egyptian bondage** that is, a kind of servitude like the Israelites experienced in Egypt after the death of Joseph. See Exodus 1. 13–14: 'And the Egyptians made the children of Israel to serve with rigour: And they made their lives bitter with hard bondage, in mortar, and in brick, and in all manner of service in the field: all their service, wherein they made them serve, was with rigour'.

**206(c) drivelling snivelling tune of St Pauls** a hymn tune that apparently Hogg had grown weary of from hearing too much of it on Sundays. In the sketch on 'Dogs' in *The Shepherd's Calendar*, pp. 57–67, Hogg tells the story of his father's having been given the responsibility of precentor in the Ettrick Church:

Now, my father could have sung several of the old church tunes middling well, in his own family circle; but it so happened, that, when mounted in the desk, he never could command the starting notes of any but one (St Paul's) [...]. The minister giving out psalms four times in the course of every day's service, consequently, the congregation were treated with St Paul's, in the morning, at great length, thrice in the course of the service, and then once again at the close. Nothing but St Paul's. And, it being of itself a monotonous tune, nothing could exceed the monotony that prevailed in the primitive church of Ettrick. (pp. 60–61)

**206(d) come away ben** an expression meaning 'come inside', an invitation to the inner part or 'best room' of the house.

**209(b) duffle hero** 'duffle' is probably derived from a sense of 'duff', meaning 'worthless' or 'counterfeit', similar to Scots 'dowf' or 'duffie'. Clearly Hutchison is insulting Duncan's foolish bravado.

## Dramas of Simple Life No. II

'Dramas of Simple Life No. II' is published for the first time in the present edition. It is published from the incomplete fair-copy manuscript that is preserved among the James Hogg Papers in the Alexander Turnbull Library, Wellington, New Zealand, as MS-Papers-0042-06. The manuscript consists of two parts. The main part of the manuscript is entitled 'Dramas of Simple Life | N II by the Ettrick Shepherd' and is described by Peter Garside as a 'combination of 4pp booklets and single sheets, 31 x 19cm., irregularly paginated'; there is no watermark on the paper, and page 31 of this manuscript is missing. The second part of the manuscript is described by Professor Garside as '[t]wo single leaves, 31x19cm., headed "This to follow the song Bush aboon Traquair"'; there is also no watermark on this separate part. See P. D. Garside, 'An annotated checklist of Hogg's literary manuscripts in the Alexander Turnbull Library, Wellington, New Zealand', *The Bibliotheck*, 20 (1995), 5–23 (p. 22).

'Dramas of Simple Life No. II' is the second of what Hogg had proposed as a three-drama series for publication in *BEM* (for more discussion of the series as a whole, see the notes to 'A Pastoral Love Scene' in the present edition). Hogg apparently sent this second drama to Blackwood on 12 September 1826: 'I know at least I suspect the first number of my Dramas to be inferior but you *must* publish it that's absolute for both the second and third number are a great deal happier I would send them both were it not for the dread of never seeing them again. On second thoughts I think I will send the second only you are to swear by all the holy saints and martyrs not to lose it' (*Letters 2*, p. 250). Blackwood did not want to publish the first of the dramas, 'A Pastoral Love Scene', but he liked the second drama and agreed to publish it if Hogg would revise it. Blackwood wrote to Hogg on 23 September 1826: 'I like this No. II of your Dramas very much though some parts occasionally "border on the confines of coarseness"—You should however add another scene to it in order to finish the story. I therefore return it to you and I entreat of you to send it back finished by next week's Carrier' (NLS, MS 30,309, pp. 385–87). Hogg complied with Blackwood's request and promptly prepared the additional scene; he sent the revised text to Blackwood on 5 October but reiterated his condition of publication: 'I have added another scene to the little drama you liked but they can only appear in a work where the whole series appears'. In this same letter he also underscored his frustration with writing for *BEM*: 'I have told you a thousand times it was vain in me attempting to write for you I have thrown away more time in attempting it than all other literary avocations put together' (*Letters 2*, p. 253).

Hogg's 'Dramas of Simple Life No. II' was not published in *BEM*, presumably because Blackwood refused to publish the first drama and, thus, Hogg refused to allow the second one to stand on its own. Nearly a year later, however, Hogg and Blackwood seem to have reconsidered the dramas. Hogg wrote to Blackwood on 11 August 1827: 'I have literally nothing finished save a pastoral drama with songs of which you once approved but which I refused you out of some pet' (*Letters 2*, p. 276). Blackwood must have requested further revisions for matters of taste, for Hogg wrote Blackwood again on 5 January 1828: 'The Pastoral drama is in Roberts hands for you but he suspects you will object to some small part of it on the *old score*. May the deil take the indelicacy of both your mind and his!' (*Letters 2*, p. 282). 'Dramas of Simple Life No. II' still did not find its way into *BEM*. At some point—and possibly much later—Hogg significantly revised and enlarged the drama at least twice. The revised drama was not published until after Hogg's death. It appeared as 'The Bush Aboon Traquair' in the first printing of *Tales and Sketches*, 6 vols (Glasgow: Blackie, 1836–37), II, 275–338, although in later printings of *Tales and Sketches* it was replaced by other stories. A manuscript of an earlier version of 'The Bush Aboon Traquair' is also preserved among the James Hogg Papers in the Alexander Turnbull Library, Wellington, New Zealand, as MS-Papers-0042-06. The manuscript is described by Garside in his 'checklist' in *The Bibliotheck*: '"The Bush Aboon Traquair/ or/ The Natural Philosophers/ A Pastoral drama/ With Songs/ By the Ettrick Shepherd". Fair copy in booklet with stiff marbled covers, 22 x 19cm., paginated [1]–70, no WM. Eventually printed in *Tales and sketches, by the Ettrick Shepherd*, 6 vols (Glasgow, 1837), II, 275–338' (p. 22). The Turnbull manuscript appears to be a 'transition' stage in the development of the drama between 'Dramas of Simple Life' and the published version of 'Bush'. An incomplete manuscript for the printed version of 'Bush' is preserved in the National Library of Scotland as MS 1869, fols 1–52. For further discussion, see Philip Lodge, '*The Bush Aboon Traquair*: the First Version Rediscovered', *Papers given at the Second James Hogg Society Conference (Edinburgh 1985)*, ed. by Gillian Hughes, Association for Scottish Literary Studies Occasional Papers 8 (Aberdeen: ASLS, 1988), pp. 68–78.

The present edition follows the idiosyncratic and sometimes inconsistent spelling and punctuation of Hogg's manuscript. However, for the convenience of the reader the designation of speaking voices has been regularised by following Hogg's most common practice of italicising the speaker's name followed by a dash. The present edition also regularises the printing of scenes and stage directions. Unless otherwise noted, the songs in 'Dramas of Simple Life No. II' are originals by Hogg and are republished only in 'The Bush aboon Traquair'. The present text includes the following emendations:

   209(title) No. II] N II (MS)
   210(d) steal either] steal ? either (MS)
   238(a) they're caught] the're caught (MS)
   241(d) think ye] think (MS)
   245(a) (*snapping his fingers*)] (*snapping is fingers*) (MS)

**209(d) (title)** the title in the manuscript is 'Pastoral Love Scenes | or | Dramas of Simple Life N II'. The first part of the title has been lined out, leaving the title as in the present edition.

**210(a) Minnyive** apparently based on Moniaive, a town in Dumfriesshire about sixteen miles northwest of Dumfries. This place name is usually spelled 'Minnyhive' within the 'Drama'. 'Minny' or 'minnie' is 'an affectionate term for a mother' (*SND*), and 'hive' is a haven.

**210(a) fruit maele o' the original transgression** 'maele' is a spot or blemish. The 'original transgression' according to Genesis was that Adam and Eve disobeyed God by eating the fruit in the Garden of Eden that had been forbidden them. See Genesis 3. 1–7.

**210(b) primary curse** in Genesis 3. 16, for Eve's disobedience, God says he 'will greatly multiply thy sorrow and thy conception; in sorrow thou shalt bring forth children; and thy desire shall be to thy husband, and he shall rule over thee'.

**210(c) minny Eve** mother Eve. The Goodwife is playing ironically on the name of the town, Minnyhive.

**211(c) waking a' night wi' his new spained lambs** the newly-weaned lambs needed to learn to graze so that they could survive independently of their mothers. The shepherds had to watch the lambs through the night to prevent them from returning to their mothers. Often someone would sit with the shepherd during this time to watch the lambs or to prevent his falling asleep and neglecting the lambs. The subject of a shepherd and a young woman sitting together all night in an isolated spot provided a good subject for love literature. See also 'I'll No Wake wi' Annie' in the present edition, p. 311.

**212(c) Air MAID THAT TENDS THE GOATS** see Appendix B for the music.

**212(c) By a bush on yonder brae** a version of this song was written by Hogg much earlier than the composition of 'Dramas of Simple Life No. II'. The poem was published in the *Edinburgh Magazine*, 21 (January 1803), 52–53, but Hogg included this poem, among others, in a letter to Walter Scott in September 1802 (see *Letters 1*, 20–28). The song was revised for publication in *The Forest Minstrel* (1810), pp. 194–96, and revised again for 'Dramas II'. The first and last stanzas are similar across the different versions, and the middle stanzas are different for each version. The 'Dramas II' version was published with only minor revisions as Song I in 'A Bush aboon Traquair' (pp. 279–80). Hogg consistently identifies the tune as 'Maid that Tends the Goats'. For a full discussion of the textual history of 'By a Bush', see Peter Garside, 'Editing *The Forest Minstrel*: The Case of "By a Bush"', *Studies in Hogg and his World*, 13 (2002), 72–94. See also *The Forest Minstrel* (S/SC, 2006), pp. 354–55.

**212(c) airy Benger rises** Hogg provides a note to this in his letter to Scott: 'Mount Benger is a large high hill on the north side of the Yarrow' (*Letters 1*, p. 26).

**212(d) Yarrow [...] bonny sister stream** Yarrow Water, which runs between St Mary's Loch and Selkirk, and its 'sister stream', Ettrick Water, which runs between Capel Fell in southwest Selkirkshire and Selkirk. The two streams join near Selkirk.

**213(a) Yarrow's Flower could ne'er outvie** that is, Mary is even more beautiful than the legendary 'Yarrow's Flower'. John Buchan in *Sir Walter Scott* (London: Cassell, 1932), writes that the Scotts of Harden 'produced such figures of

ballad and folk story as Auld Wat of Harden, who in 1567 married Mary
Scott, the "Flower of Yarrow"' (p. 21).

**213(a) Meet thy titty** 'titty' is sister; this is a reference to the convergence of
the sister streams, Yarrow and Ettrick, that meet near Selkirk. See the note
for 212(d) above.

**213(c) tint the airts** that is, lost his sense of direction.

**214(b) sic a day** such ado.

**215(a) pair o' gloves on your wedding day** a gift of gloves was a traditional
gift from newlyweds to close friends. Hogg writes to Margaret Phillips on
10 April 1820 in anticipation of their wedding: 'I must trust to you for a few
gloves favours and such like trifles which I neither know nor care aught
about' (*Letters 2*, p. 23).

**216(d) clad score** a clad, or cled, score is twenty-one and is normally used is
reference to sheep.

**217(c) O weels me on my shepherd lad** this verse was published as 'Song II' in
'The Bush aboon Traquair' (p. 287).

**217(d) Dinna count afore your host** Henny seems to misapply the proverb:
'he that reckons without his host must reckon again' (*ODEP*, p. 667).

**218(a) great battle [...] sun has aince mair stood still ower the valley of
Jehoshaphat** Sandy combines two biblical stories. Joshua commanded the
sun to stand still as the Israelites prevailed in battle at Gibeon, north of
Jerusalem between Jerusalem and Bethel: 'Sun, stand thou still upon Gibeon;
and thou, Moon, in the valley of Ajalon. And the sun stood still, and the
moon stayed, until the people had avenged themselves upon their enemies'
(Joshua 10. 12–13). The Valley of Jehoshaphat is a valley east of Jerusalem
between Jerusalem and the Mount of Olives, where God sat in judgment
on the enemies of Israel: 'Let the heathen be wakened, and come up to the
valley of Jehoshaphat; for there will I sit to judge all the heathen round
about' (Joel 3. 12). Sandy, of course, is complaining about the apparent
length of the day because he is impatiently waiting for Mary to 'wake' with
him through the night. Geordie Cochrane in 'The Love Adventures of Mr
George Cochrane' makes the same complaint for similar reasons–see *WET*,
p. 176.

**218(b)–219(c) The day-beam's unco laith to gang** an earlier version of this
song was published in No. 14 of *The Spy*–see *The Spy*, ed. by Gillian Hughes
(S/SC, 2000), pp. 151–52. The 'Dramas' version has minor revisions
throughout, and the first four lines are completely new. The song is included
in 'The Bush aboon Traquair' as Song III (pp. 289–90), although the fourth
stanza of the 'Dramas' version is omitted from the 'Bush' version.

**220(d) utter profusion** part of Hogg's humorous characterisation of Rob, the
'philosopher', is that Rob is prone to use long words, which are either
nonsense words or legitimate words used incorrectly.

**222(a) douf an' dowie** both words mean sad or dispirited.

**222(c) the fourth an' the seventh** the fourth commandment is 'Remember the
sabbath day, to keep it holy' (Exodus 20. 8) and the seventh commandment
is 'Thou shalt not commit adultery' (Exodus 20. 14).

**223(c) eild crock ewes** yeld (barren) old ewes, barren because they are too old
to bear young. The expression is also used disparagingly of women. The
Goodman uses 'auld crock ewe' in reference to the Goodwife; see p. 236(a).

**223(d)–224(a) Dinna look sae high lassie** this song is included as 'Song IV' in

'The Bush aboon Traquair' (p. 299).

**225(a) 'Oho! the devil!'** echoes the proverb 'Talk of the devil, and he is sure to appear' (*ODEP*, p. 804).

**225(c) trouble o' the M,Gregors** unidentified.

**226(c) some trees are planted in dry soil** echoes the parable of the sower. See Mark 4. 1–9.

**227(a) Nearest the heart nearest the mouth** proverbial (*ODEP*, p. 557).

**230(d)–231(c) When'er I try the word to say** this song is reprinted as Song VIII in 'The Bush aboon Traquair' (p. 314). (There is a 'Song VII' in 'Bush', but there is no 'Song V' or 'Song VI'). This song is repeated in 'Dramas of Simple Life No. II', p. 249 (see the note for 249(a–c) below).

**232(d)–233(b) Hey for Sandy Don** the song is included in 'The Bush aboon Traquair' as 'Song IX' (pp. 316–17). The first stanza of this song is a revised version of 'Came ye o'er frae France', published by Hogg in his first series of Jacobite songs (1819). See James Hogg, *The Jacobite Relics of Scotland [First Series]*, ed. by Murray G. H. Pittock (S/SC, 2002), pp. 87–88.

**234(d) "the flowers of the Forest are a' wed away!"** a line from the popular poem 'The Flowers of the Forest', by Jean Elliot (1727–1805).

**234(d)–235(a) scene to act this night [...] winna believe what's gaun on** a playful echo of the portents of nature on the night King Duncan is murdered in *Macbeth*, especially Lennox's speech in Act 2:

> The night has been unruly. Where we lay
> Our chimneys were blown down, and, as they say,
> Lamentings heard i'th' air, strange screams of death,
> And prophesying with accents terrible
> Of dire combustion and confused events
> New-hatched to th' woeful time. The obscure bird
> Clamoured the livelong night. Some say the earth
> Was feverous and did shake. (II. 3. 53–59)

**235(b) Some love it is like a novelle** this song is published as Song X in 'The Bush Aboon Traquair' (p. 319).

**236(a) put out o' my seven senses** a variation on the expression 'scared out of my seven senses' (see, for example, Sir Walter Scott, *Rob Roy*, London: Dent, 1906, p. 325). *Brewer's Dictionary of Phrase and Fable* (rev. Ivor H. Evans, New York: Harper & Row, 1970) defines 'seven senses': 'According to ancient teaching the soul of man, or his "inward holy body" is compounded of seven properties which are under the influence of the seven planets. Fire animates, earth gives the sense of feeling, water gives speech, air gives taste, mist gives sight, flowers give hearing, the south wind gives smelling. Hence the seven senses are animation, feeling, speech, taste, sight, hearing, and smelling' (p. 985).

**237(b) brocket cow** coloured with black and white stripes or spots

**237(c) sit down here** the manuscript reads 'sit down between my feet', but Hogg has marked through 'between my feet, presumably because he knew it would be too suggestive for Blackwood.

**238(a) have her on the hip** see the note for 149, l. 109.

**238(b) By the Gordons** 'the regiment raised by the fourth Duke of Gordon in 1794' (*SND*) at the Duke's expense and in response to the French Revolution. The regiment was stationed for a time in Kent and was reviewed by King George III in London.

**238(c) deil a bit** an expression meaning 'not at all'.

**239(a) confusion of Babylon** Genesis 11. 1–9 tells the story of the division of speech: 'Therefore its name is called Babel because the Lord did there confuse the language of all the earth' (v. 9).

**239(c) THE WOMEN FOCKS** Hogg's song was first published in *A Border Garland* (Nathaniel Gow and Son, [1819]), pp. 6–7, and reprinted in *BEM*, 12 (December 1822), 705–06. The 'stave' sung by Sandy and Rob corresponds with the third stanza and chorus in the *BEM* version (see pp. 102–03 in the present edition and notes). This stanza is also included in 'The Bush aboon Traquair' as 'Song XII' (p. 326), although the chorus is not reprinted in 'Bush'.

**240(b–c) Whoever has bow'd at Beauty's dear shrine** this song is published in 'The Bush aboon Traquair' as 'Song XIII' (p. 327).

**242(a) snipelting** Hogg has Girzy use this word twice in this line; however, it seems to be a nonce word of Hogg's.

**242(b) sight that's good for sair een** a Scots variation on the expression 'sight for sore eyes' (*ODEP*, p. 732).

**242(c) rule over you–an' we'll do it wi' a rod of iron too** echoes Revelation 12. 5; see the note for 30(b).

**244(a) I have *her* on the hip** see p. 238(a) and note.

**244(c) [MS BREAK]** p. 31 of the Turnbull manuscript is missing.

**245(a) the James Watt** a steamboat, named after James Watt (1736–1819), the scientist and inventor best known for his improvements to the steam engine.

**245(b) When I was a young man striking at the studdy** this song is published as 'Song XIV' of 'The Bush aboon Traquair' (p. 335).

**245(c) There's nae fools to an old fool!** a Scottish variation on the proverb 'No fool to the old fool' (*ODEP*, p. 276).

**247(a–b) Thou bonny bush aboon Traquair** this song was published as 'Song XV' in 'The Bush aboon Traquair' (p. 336).

**248(a) the witch of Fife** Hogg's witch of Fife first appeared as the subject of the 'Eighth Bard's Song' in *The Queen's Wake*; he there notes that the 'Witch of Fife' was 'founded on popular traditions' (see *The Queen's Wake*, ed. by Douglas S. Mack (S/SC, 2004), p. 179 and notes). The Witch of Fife was also the subject of one of Hogg's songs in the previously-unpublished 'Songs for the Baloon' (see pp. 346–48 of the present edition and notes). This song was published as 'Song Third' in 'Dr David Dale's Account of a Grand Aerial Voyage', *Edinburgh Literary Journal*, 23 January 1830, p. 53. The *ELJ* song was also reprinted in *Songs* (pp. 235–36) as 'The Witch o' Fife'. Henny at this point is being tossed in a blanket; in Hogg' poems, the witches take journeys by air.

**248(b) How will that do think ye?** *Scene closes* both the Turnbull manuscript version and the published version of 'The Bush Aboon Traquair' end here.

**248(b) *Enter Mr Pom and Mr Murphy*** Blackwood had requested an additional scene, but the entrance of these new characters at this point in the story is awkward. Hogg must have realized this, though. In the Turnbull manuscript of 'Bush', a revised scene between Pom and Murphy is the third scene of Act I; however, the scene has been marked through for deletion in the manuscript. In the published version of 'The Bush Aboon Traquair', this scene with Murphy has been eliminated and Pompey is introduced in a new scene with the Goodwife at the end of Act I. The scene in which Pompey attempts to teach Ann lessons of 'seduction' was revised and is part of Act II, Scene I in both the Turnbull manuscript and the published version of 'The Bush Aboon Traquair'.

**249(a) Gin you meet a bonny lassie** these two lines of verse are the first two lines of what became 'Song VII' of 'The Bush aboon Traquair' (p. 308). These two lines appear at the end of a manuscript leaf. The song beginning 'Wheneer I try the word to say' (see note for 249(a–c) below) begins a manuscript leaf. It is likely that there was additional text that has not been preserved. In addition to the remainder of 'Gin you meet a bonny lassie', the surviving text lacks a clear transition from the scene between Pom and Murphy and the scene that follows with Mary, Ann, and Girzy. In the Turnbull manuscript of 'Bush', the song concludes the scene between Pom and Murphy; the rest of the song is as follows:

> But gin you meet a dirty hussie
> Fie gae rub her owr wi' strae
> Be sure you dinna quit the grip
> Of ilka joy while you are young
> Before old age your vitals rip
> And lay you twafauld owr a rung.

What follows in the Turnbull manuscript of 'Bush' is a revised version of the scene in the kitchen that begins on p. 216 in the present edition.

**249(a) [MS BREAK]** an undetermined number of pages is missing in the manuscript.

**249(a–c) Wheneer I try the word to say** this song is sung by Sandy as a soliloquy earlier in the drama (pp. 248–49). When the song appears in the earlier place in the manuscript, it is written as a fair copy with only one word changed in the manuscript. However, at the second instance of this song in the manuscript, Hogg makes substantial changes to the song to arrive at what is essentially the same song as that on pp. 248–49. Hogg marks through the first, second, fourth, fifth, and sixth lines of the first stanza and writes new lyrics above each deleted line. He changes only one word in the second stanza; in the third stanza, he makes revisions to the fifth line and writes a new seventh line. Hogg's intent here is not clear. Perhaps he misremembered lines of the preceding version, or perhaps he began with a new direction and then changed his mind. Because the song follows a missing segment of the manuscript, it is possible that the song is intended to be mocking or ironic.

**253(c) a mark to ken you by** an ironic echo of Genesis 4. 15: 'And the Lord set a mark on Cain, lest any finding him should kill him'. God exiled Cain after Cain killed his brother, Abel. God put a mark on Cain to protect him in his exile.

### I Lookit East–I Lookit West

'I Lookit East–I Lookit West' appeared in *Blackwood's Edinburgh Magazine*, 20 (October 1826), 622–23, as the first of three of Hogg's songs sung by the 'Shepherd' character in the *Noctes Ambrosianæ No. XXVIII*. On 23 September 1826 William Blackwood wrote to Hogg that the songs in this number 'are admirable particularly "I lookit east I lookit west"' (NLS, MS 30,309, pp. 385–87). At the conclusion of the song in the *Noctes*, 'North' comments: 'Very touching, James, indeed. You are a tragic poet after Aristotle's own heart–for well you know how to purge the soul by pity and terror' (p. 623).

'I Lookit East–I Lookit West' was written for the occasion of the dinner instituting the Caledonian Asylum in London. The Royal Caledonian Asylum was founded in 1815 to provide support and education for children of Scottish military personnel and of indigent Scots living in London; John Galt was its founding secretary. In a note to this work in *Songs* (1831), Hogg comments on the origin of the song: 'It was written many years ago, at the joint request of Mr Galt and some other literary friends, for singing at the first meeting of some benevolent society in London, the denomination of which I have forgot; but it was for the purpose of relieving the wives and families of Scottish soldiers who had fallen in our sanguine wars abroad. The song was well received, having been sung by professional singers to the Scottish air of "The Birks of Invermay"' (pp. 39–40). The song was issued in a special printing for the occasion: 'SONG, | BY THE ETTRICK SHEPHERD, | *Sung at the Institutory Dinner of the CALEDONIAN ASYLUM, at the Fremasons' Tavern, Saturday, March 4th,* 1815; | HIS ROYAL HIGHNESS THE DUKE OF YORK AND ALBANY, | IN THE CHAIR'. A copy of the separate printing is preserved in the Perth Museum as National Register of Archives, 1492/150. The song was also published in the *Edinburgh Evening Courant* on 13 March 1815 in an article reporting on the occasion for which the song was written. The *Edinburgh Evening Courant* identifies the singer as 'Master Millar, a pupil of Mr Addison'. (For a full discussion of the newspaper context of this and related works, see Gillian Hughes's article, 'James Hogg, and Edinburgh's Triumph over Napoleon', *Scottish Studies Review*, 4 (Spring 2003), 98–111. The editor of the present edition is indebted to Dr Hughes, who discovered the separate printing and the newspaper publication of the song.)

The song was next published with minor revisions in Hogg's 1822 *Poetical Works* (IV, 316–18) under the title 'The Soldier's Widow'. (A different poem, also entitled 'The Soldier's Widow', had been published in Hogg's 1810 collection, *The Forest Minstrel*.) The song was substantially revised for publication in *BEM*. The song was printed again in *Songs* as 'I Lookit East, I Lookit West'; the text of the *Songs* version is based on the *BEM* version and includes the framing dialogue from the *Noctes*.

A manuscript of 'I Lookit East–I Lookit West' is preserved in the British Library as Additional MS 35,265, fol. 340, part of a collection of letters and manuscripts sent to the song collector and publisher George Thomson. The manuscript is not dated and no accompanying letter is preserved with the manuscript, although the title in the manuscript–'Song for the Aniversary [*sic*] of The Caledonian Assylum' [*sic*]–suggests that this version is later than the *Edinburgh Evening Courant* version. The manuscript differs in wording from the newspaper version throughout the song, but the main revision is in the combining of two stanzas. In the manuscript the last four lines of stanza four and the last four lines of stanza five have been marked out, thus combining the first four lines of each stanza (with additional revisions) into a single stanza:

> The breeze scarce on the aspin stirred
>   Scarce bore aside the falling dew
> I thought I heard a bonny bird
>   Singin amid the air so blue
> O Sweet as breaks the dawning hue
>   Of sun-beam thro' the wavy rain

                    Fell on my soul the music new
                      Of hope and pity was the strain[.]
Apparently the Thomson version was never published.

The manuscript, the *Edinburgh Evening Courant*, and the *Poetical Works* versions open with the following stanza that is not in the *BEM* version or the *Songs* version:

                    The flag waved o'er the castle wa',
                      The hind came lilting o'er the lea,
                    Loud joy rang thro' the lighted ha',
                      An' ilka ane was blithe but me;
                        For, ah! my heart had tint its glee,
                    Although the wars had worn away—
                      The breast, that used my stay to be,
                    Was lying cauld in foreign clay.

The present edition reprints the *BEM* version without emendation.

**254, l. 39 The widow and the fatherless** there are numerous biblical mandates to attend to the needs of 'the widow and the fatherless'. See Psalm 146. 9 and James 1. 27, for example.

## Tam Nelson

'Tam Nelson' was first published in *The Scots Magazine* (April 1814, p. 296) as 'Tam Wilson'. The song was published in *Blackwood's Edinburgh Magazine*, 20 (October 1826), 623. 'Tam Nelson' was submitted to William Blackwood under its original title, 'Tam Wilson', but Blackwood changed the character's name without explanation. Blackwood wrote to Hogg on 23 September 1826 that his songs are 'admirable particularly "I lookit east I lookit west" and Tam whom you will see we have called Nelson is most humourous' (NLS, MS 30,309, p. 386). Gillian Hughes suggests that the subject of the poem is based on a former tenant of Altrive, Thomas Wilson, to whom Hogg referred in a letter to the Duchess of Buccleuch of 7 March 1813 as 'a mean fellow named Wilson' (*Letters 1*, p. 132). Wilson seems to have died in the summer of 1814, so he would have been alive when the poem was first published but deceased when Hogg recycled the poem in *BEM*. Perhaps Blackwood changed Wilson's name to keep from appearing to insult the memory of the late tenant. See also *Letters 1*, p. 187.

'Tam Nelson' is the second of three of Hogg's songs in the *Noctes Ambrosianæ No. XXVIII* and is sung by the 'Shepherd' character. This humorous song follows immediately the serious song 'I Lookit East—I Lookit West', which elicited from North the comment that Hogg is 'a tragic poet after Aristotle's own heart' (p. 623). In 'Tam Nelson' the Shepherd demonstrates that he knows not only how 'to purge the soul by pity and terror', but also 'by a' sorts o' odd humours too' (p. 623).

The *BEM* version contains extensive minor revisions in terms of punctuation. There are several substitutions of English words for Scots, such as *good* for *gude* in line 2, *soulless* for *sauless* in line 8, and *living* for *leevin* in line 26; there are also substitutions of Scots words for English, such as *dee't* for *died* in line 17 and *donsy* for *useless* in line 19. In the *BEM* version Hogg changes *catch* to *psalm* in line 33, and in the last line he makes the expletive clear by printing *For d—n him* instead of *For — him*.

The present edition prints the *BEM* version without emendation.

### There's Some Souls 'ill Yammer and Cheep

'There's Some Souls 'ill Yammer and Cheep' was published untitled in *Blackwood's Edinburgh Magazine*, 20 (October 1826), 630–31, and the *BEM* publication is the only edition of the song in Hogg's lifetime. It is the third of three songs sung by the 'Shepherd' character in the *Noctes Ambrosianæ No. XXVIII* and follows 'I Lookit East–I Lookit West' and 'Tam Nelson'. Blackwood's contributors' book indicates that Hogg was paid one guinea for 1¾ pages in the *Noctes*, although the specific contributions are not identified. The Shepherd introduces the song in the *Noctes* as 'a sort o' nonsensical sang', and at the conclusion of the Shepherd's singing, North calls the song 'a queer, bold, independent, soul-speaking thing'. Hogg does not indicate a tune for this song.

The present edition reprints the *BEM* text without emendation.

**256, l. 2 win'le strae** windlestrae, 'a tall, thin, withered stalk of grass' (*SND*).
**256, l. 7 ne'er fash their noddle** pay no heed, not be troubled by.
**256, ll. 9–10 some wi' big scars on their face, | Point out a prin scart on a frien'** echoes Matthew 7. 3, 4: 'And why beholdest thou the mote that is in thy brother's eye, but considerest not the beam that is in thine own eye? Or how wilt thou say to thy brother, Let me pull out the mote out of thine eye; and, behold, a beam is in thine own eye?' See also Luke 6. 41.
**256, l. 11 black as sweeps** that is, chimney sweeps.

## January 1827–December 1827 (Volumes 21–22)
### Ode for Music. On the Death of Lord Byron

'Ode for Music. On the Death of Lord Byron' was first published in *Blackwood's Edinburgh Magazine*, 21 (May 1827), 520–21. The poem was published in *BEM* from a fair-copy manuscript that is preserved among the Blackwood papers in the National Library of Scotland as MS 4805, fols 1–2. The manuscript consists of a single sheet *c.* 38 cm x 32 cm, folded to *c.* 19 cm x 32 cm; the poem is written on the recto and verso of fol. 1 and the recto of fol. 2. The paper is watermarked with a shield device and dated 1825.

Hogg sent the Byron 'Ode' to Blackwood in a letter dated 5 April 1827: 'I could not light upon an unpublished song which these pieces are the one new written the Ode I wrote when the Bard died' (*Letters 2*, p. 261). Blackwood then sent the 'Ode for Music' to D. M. Moir for Moir's opinion, and Moir responded, in a letter postmarked 20 April 1827, with his typically qualified praise of Hogg's work: 'Hoggs Ode on Byron is striking, and with a little more infusion of feeling would have been admirable; it rather dazzles with its metre than delights with it imagery' (NLS, MS 4020, fols 17–18).

Although the poem was not published in *BEM* until 1827, it was written in late 1824 or early 1825 and sent to Blackwood only after Hogg failed to find a publisher for the poem elsewhere. Hogg had written to Aeneas Mackay on 28 March 1825, in response to a request from 'Mr Baynes' for a poem, promising Mackay two versions of the Byron 'Ode': 'You shall have one song for Scotland and another for England on the loss of our great national poet Byron but the air for the former I must either compose or select myself the latter I hope you will put into good hands' (*Letters 2*, pp 227–28). Hogg sent the 'Scottish Ode (for Music) | On the death of Lord Byron' to William Baynes and Sons in March or April 1825. The manuscript for this poem has also been preserved in the National Library of Scotland (MS 3581, fols 139–40) and is published in *Letters 2*, pp. 229–31. There are only minor differences between the texts of the Baynes version and the *BEM* version throughout most of the song, although the Baynes version is specifically prepared for musical performance. However, the *BEM* version adds twelve lines between the last two choruses; these lines correspond to lines 85–96 in the *BEM* version.

For additional information about Hogg's admiration for and relationship with Byron, see 'Correspondence with Byron' (pp. 153–59 in the present edition) and notes, as well as 'Notes on Correspondents' in *Letters 1* (pp. 451–52). The present edition follows the *BEM* printing without emendation.

**257, ll. 1–2 Dee's winding waters [...] Forests of Marr** the River Dee rises in the Cairngorms and flows for over ninety miles into the North Sea near Aberdeen. Byron was taken by his mother to live in the Dee Valley in her native Aberdeenshire when he was a youth. The phrase 'Dee's winding waters' also echoes Byron's love song, 'When I rov'd, a young Highlander, o'er the dark heath', which is in part a remembrance of '*Dee's* rushing tide' (l. 19)—see *Lord Byron: The Complete Poetical Works*, ed. by Jerome J. McGann, 7 vols (Oxford: Clarendon Press, 1980–93), I, 47–48. The Dee in part winds through the Forest of Mar, which is just west of Braemar in the western part of the ancient district of Mar.

**257, l. 3 glens of the Gordons** Byron's mother was Catherine Gordon, daughter of George Gordon, the laird of Gight in Aberdeenshire. Byron was named George Gordon Byron for his mother's family.

**257, l. 4 dark Loch-na-Gaur** a mountain in Aberdeenshire. Hogg is echoing the image of 'dark Loch na Garr', which concludes each stanza of Byron's poem 'Lachin Y Gair'—see *Byron: Poetical Works*, I, 103–04.

**257, ll. 7–8 sweet seraphs [...] fiends of the air** images of seraphs and fiends are common in Byron's poetry, as are images of conflict in general. Here, though, Hogg sees the representatives of both heaven and hell united in their despair at the 'fall of a bard'. Gillian Hughes suggests that Hogg here perhaps is also alluding to 'Byron's Immortality; or the Vision of Childe Harold', a poem and print published in London by G. Hunt—see *Letters 2*, p. 232.

**258, l. 51 Grey Shade of Selma** Hogg associates Byron with Ossian (see l. 57), the ancient Gaelic poet and son of the legendary Fingal. Selma was the capital and castle of Fingal's land. Byron's own poetry was influenced by the popular but controversial 'Ossianic' poetry of the eighteenth-century poet, James Macpherson. For references to Macpherson's influence, see under 'MacPherson' in the index to *Byron: Poetical Works*, VII, 348. Hogg's epic poem *Queen Hynde* (1824) is also set in Ossian's Selma—see *Queen Hynde*, ed. by Suzanne Gilbert and Douglas S. Mack (S/SC 1998), pp. 218, 239.

**258, l. 55 fallen at Freedom's holy shrine** Byron sailed from Italy to Greece in July 1823 to fight for Greece in the war for independence from Turkey. Byron invested a great deal of his personal fortune in the war, and in December 1823 he joined Prince Mavrocordatos at Missolonghi, where he took command of several hundred Suliote soldiers. Byron suffered a debilitating seizure in February 1824 and died 19 April 1824 in Missolonghi at age 36.

**258, l. 60 Father of pity** echoes Psalm 103. 13: 'Like as a father pitieth his children, so the Lord pitieth them that fear him'.

**258, ll. 61–62 never from erring being [...] Beyond what his heavenly bounty gave** echoes I Corinthians 10. 13: 'but God is faithful, who will not suffer you to be tempted above that ye are able; but will with the temptation also make a way to escape, that ye may be able to bear it'. However, given the following lines (63–64), 'And never was given [...] without an alloy', Hogg perhaps also hints at a higher responsibility for Byron as poet as suggested by Luke 12. 48: 'For unto whomsoever much is given, of him shall be much required; and to whom men have committed much, of him they will ask the more'.

**259, l. 102 heaven and earth** *Heaven and Earth* is the title of a controversial dramatic poem by Byron, first published in the 1 January 1823 issue of *The Liberal*. Hogg here also is perhaps echoing Revelation 21. 1: 'And I saw a new heaven and a new earth: for the first heaven and the first earth were passed away; and there was no more sea'.

### Hogg on Women!!!

'Hogg on Women!!!' is published in the present edition from a fair-copy manuscript preserved in the National Library of Scotland as MS 1809, fols 86–87. The manuscript consists of a single sheet measuring *c*. 22.5 cm x 37.5 cm, folded to make two folios. The paper bears a date-only watermark of 1826. Although Hogg apparently intended the poem for publication in *BEM*, the poem was not published there and apparently was never published in Hogg's lifetime in the version represented in the NLS manuscript.

Hogg wrote to Blackwood on 5 April 1827, sending him the 'Ode for Music. On the Death of Lord Byron' and one additional work: 'I could not light upon an unpublished song which these pieces are the one new written the Ode I wrote when the Bard died' (*Letters 2*, p. 261). Hogg's letter suggests that he is sending a second poem, and given the date of 6 April 1827 on the manuscript of 'Hogg on Women!!!', it is likely, although not certain, that Hogg sent the poem to Blackwood with the Byron 'Ode'. The Byron 'Ode' was published in the May 1827 number of *BEM*; however, Blackwood wrote to Hogg on 25 May 1827, returning 'the Verses on Women' (NLS, MS 30,310, pp. 128A–30).

'Hogg on Women!!!' was revised for publication in *The Bijou; or, Annual of Literature and the Arts* for 1829, pp. 93–96—see James Hogg, *Contributions to Annuals and Gift-Books*, ed. by Janette Currie and Gillian Hughes (S/SC, 2006), pp. 30–32, and notes. The poem also appears as part of Hogg's long poem, *Love's Legacy*, corresponding approximately to lines 172–281 of Canto Third in the version eventually published in *Fraser's Magazine*, 10 (December 1834), 639–644. (These lines appear in Canto Second in the manuscript of *Love's Legacy* preserved in the Alexander Turnbull Library of the National Library of New Zealand, James Hogg Papers, MS 0042-07, Item 74). The date of composition of *Love's Legacy* is uncertain, so it is not possible to tell whether 'Hogg on Women!!!' was incorporated into or extracted from the longer work. Hogg wrote to Blackwood about *Love's Legacy* on 12 February 1828, which would suggest that the poem was complete at that time, although Hogg despaired of publishing the poem: 'I have likewise apoem [*sic*] about the length of The Pleasures of Memory. Entitled LOVE'S LEGACY or A FAREWELL GIFT but after my grievious dissapointment with Queen Hynde neither dare I offer it to the public' (*Letters 2*, p. 287); *Queen Hynde* had been published in December 1824. Selections from 'Hogg on Women!!!' were also quoted in a revised arrangement, along with additional lines from *Love's Legacy*, in 'A Letter about Men and Women', which was published in *BEM*, 26 (August 1829), 245–50 (pp. 246–47). In 'A Letter about Men and Women', however, Hogg pretends the poem is 'all off-hand' (p. 246) and does not acknowledge its earlier composition. For more information about *Love's Legacy*, see David Groves's edition of the poem in *Altrive Chapbooks*, 5 (September 1988), 1–53, as well as his article '"This Thrilling Tempest of the Soul": An Introduction to *Love's Legacy*', *Newsletter of the James Hogg Society*, 7 (1988), 10–17.

The present edition follows the manuscript of 'Hogg on Women!!!' without emendation, including Hogg's punctuation and occasional idiosyncratic spellings.

**260, l. 28 David Haggart with a Blair** David Haggart was executed in Edinburgh on 18 July 1821 for the murder of Thomas Morrin, a jailer in Dumfries. The highly-popular *Life of David Haggart* was published in 1821 after Haggart's execution. Blair is probably Hugh Blair (1718–1800), a prominent Church of Scotland minister, academician, and author. Blair's positions included minister of St Giles's Kirk in Edinburgh and Professor of Rhetoric and Belles-Lettres at the University of Edinburgh. Blair's *Sermons* (1777–1801) which extended to five volumes, were also immensely popular.

**260, l. 29 Hunt with Southey** Leigh Hunt (1784–1859), poet and editor of *The Examiner*. Hunt and the 'Cockney School' were frequently the objects of ridicule in *BEM*. See Hogg's parody of Hunt's poetry, 'New Poetic Mirror' (pp. 57–61 in the present edition) and notes. On the other hand, Hogg admired the poetry of Robert Southey (1774–1843), and Hogg and Southey were good friends. Southey became poet laureate in 1813; see note for 15(c). Hogg probably also intends a contrast in politics as well since both writers were also well known for their political alliances, Southey as a Tory and Hunt as a Radical.

**260, l. 30 lord of Buchan with a Scott** David Steuart Erskine (1776–1829), the eleventh Earl of Buchan, and founder of the Society of Antiquaries in Scotland. Erskine was a strong supporter of the Whig party and political reform. Although the 'Scott' is not specified, the prominent Scotts of Hogg's association, Sir Walter Scott and the Scotts of Buccleuch, were staunch Tories whose politics stood in stark contrast to those of the Earl. Sir Walter Scott was probably intended by Hogg, however. In *Anecdotes of Scott* Hogg tells the story of a gathering at Abbotsford where the talk turned to 'the Earl of Buchan's ornamental improvements at Dryburgh and among other things of the collossal statue of Wallace which I rather liked and admired but which Sir Walter perfectly abhorred he said these very words. "If I live to see the day when the men of Scotland like the children of Israel shall every one do that which is right in his own eyes *which I am certain either I or my successors will see* I have settled in my own mind long ago what I shall do first. I'll go down and blow up the statue of Wallace with gun powder. Yes I shall blow it up in such stile that there shall not be one fragment of it left! the horrible monster!"' (p. 71; see also p. 15).

**260, l. 31 Jeffery** Francis Jeffrey (1773–1850), advocate and editor of the *Edinburgh Review*. Jeffrey was highly regarded for his rhetorical skills as an advocate, as well as his courtroom presence. Hogg also uses Jeffrey as a standard of judgment in his poem 'The Left-Handed Fiddler'—see p. 144, ll. 23–32, in the present edition. On the other hand tailors were often the subject of Hogg's derision.

**260, l. 33 Peter Rob'son** Patrick (Peter) Robertson (1794–1855), Edinburgh advocate and friend of John Wilson. Robertson was a well-respected and effective advocate; he was later to become dean of the Faculty of Advocates and in 1843 replaced Lord Meadowbank as a lord of session. He had a reputation for his 'convivial and social qualities' and his 'wit and humour'; 'in sheer power of ridicule he was without a rival among his contemporaries' (G. F. R. Barker, rev. H. J. Spencer, *Oxford DNB*). In *Anecdotes of Scott* Hogg relates an occasion with Robertson that 'made Sir Walter laugh as he had been tickled'—see p. 27 and note, p. 106.

**260, l. 34 Doctor Brown with Doctor Browne** 'Doctor Brown' is probably the Reverend Dr William Brown (1764–1835), minister of the parish of Eskdalemuir and author of the 'Eskdalemuir' chapter in *The Statistical Account of Scotland*. Hogg wrote a letter of introduction for Robert Chambers to Brown in May 1826 (*Letters 2*, p, 246). Douglas Mack discusses William Brown and Eskdalemuir in his 'Historical and Geographical Note' to the paperback edition of *The Three Perils of Woman*, ed. by Antony Hasler and Douglas S. Mack (S/SC, 2002), p. 424. 'Doctor Browne' is probably Dr James Browne (1793–1841), who became editor of the *Caledonian Mercury*, an Edinburgh newspaper, in 1827. Browne is the subject of a playful satire, 'Some Passages in the Life of Colonel Cloud', which was published in the July 1825 number of *BEM*—see pp. 166–80 in the present edition and notes. Hogg contrasts the admirable Dr William Brown with the inept Dr James Browne.

**261, ll. 66–68 moral poet [...] woman is at heart a rake** Alexander Pope (1688–1744). Lines 67–68 are from Pope's 'Epistle II To a Lady. Of the Characters of Women': 'Men, some to Bus'ness, some to Pleasure take; | But ev'ry Woman is at heart a Rake' (ll. 215–16)—see *Epistles to Several Persons (Moral Essays)*, ed. by F. W. Bateson (London: Methuen; New Haven: Yale, 1951), p. 65.

### The Marvellous Doctor

'The Marvellous Doctor' was first published in *Blackwood's Edinburgh Magazine*, 22 (September 1827), 349–61. The story was reprinted in a revised version in *The Shepherd's Calendar*, 2 vols (Edinburgh: Blackwood, 1829), II, 108–49, although it was not part of the original *Shepherd's Calendar* series in *BEM*. The story was reprinted again based on the *Shepherd's Calendar* version in the posthumously-published *Tales and Sketches*, 6 vols (Glasgow: Blackie, 1836–37), IV, 145–73.

Apparently the manuscript of 'The Marvellous Doctor' has not survived, although the correspondence leading to the publication of the story makes one regret that Hogg's original is not available. Hogg sent the manuscript to William Blackwood in May 1827. Blackwood wrote to Hogg on 25 May 1827 after he had read Hogg's story: 'I have laughed prodigiously at your Doctor, but the fun I fear is too strong for delicate folks to tolerate. I shall however keep him safe and if I find that I cannot venture to give it a place I will return it carefully to you' (NLS, MS 30,310, pp. 128A–30). Hogg did not want his clever story to fall victim either to Blackwood's fastidiousness or his carelessness, so Hogg wrote back to Blackwood on 28 May 1827, suggesting that Hogg's nephew, Robert Hogg, revise the story to suit Blackwood's 'taste':

> I should be very sorry to have *The Marvellous Doctor* rejected as I am
> sure it will afford great amusement to many of your readers and to The
> professor not the least who knows the ground-work of the story. But as
> I never pretend to depend on my own taste in matters of modern delicacy
> if you have any suspicions on that head send the M. S. to Robert merely
> mentioning the division or divisions of the narrative about which you
> are scrupulous and you may depend on him that his slight alterations
> will completely obliterate any appearance of indelicacy. (*Letters 2*, p. 266)

A month later Blackwood wrote to Hogg, agreeing with both the merit of the
work and Hogg's advice to send the story to Robert for revision: 'The Wonderful
Doctor contains much that is excellent, but it will require pruning which your
Nephew and I will manage' (NLS, MS 30,310, pp. 173–74).

Robert returned the edited story to Blackwood in early July: 'I return the
Marvellous Doctor, having looked over his history and made alterations as
you suggested. The three last adventures it appeared to me impossible to
retain, and I have struck them out, leaving only some of the intermediate
remarks connected in such a way as to bring the thing to a feasible conclusion.
The two stories which remain have I think no positive indelicacy, and are very
absurd and amusing' (NLS, MS 4719, fols 200–01). Apparently Blackwood did
not keep Hogg informed of the action on the manuscript, so on 11 August
1827 Hogg wrote to Blackwood, reminding him that he still had the story:
'You have still likewise the Marvellous Doctor with all his train of marvellous
appendages which I hope you and Robert will make the best thing of the
whole' (*Letters 2*, p. 276). Robert's revisions generally satisfied Blackwood, as
well as D. M. Moir, who frequently served as a reader for Blackwood. Moir
had seen Hogg's original version, which he agreed was offensive; Blackwood
sent Moir the final version even before he sent it to Hogg. Moir generally
approved of the revised version, though, and he wrote to Blackwood on 24
August 1827: Hogg [*sic*] Doctor has I observed undergone a most judicious
curtailment; he is really a much more respectable personage with [*sic*] old
Aunty and the Ram, and after all there is a good deal to admire there is still
much to fault' (NLS, MS 4020, fols 35–36). The next day Blackwood finally
wrote to Hogg, echoing Moir's sentiments about the omission of 'Aunt Cricky'
but approving of the final story as a whole: 'By the No which I send with this
you will see that your Nephew has managed very judiciously with the Marvellous
Doctor. [...] Even as it now is John Cay and some of our squeamish friends
will rather be startled with your bold pictures. However there is quite enough
of good stuff in it to please generally' (NLS, MS 30,310, pp. 261–63).

'The Marvellous Doctor' was further edited by Robert for publication in
*The Shepherd's Calendar*. As Douglas Mack discusses in his introduction to the S/
SC edition of *The Shepherd's Calendar*, Robert was given the task of selecting
and editing material for the two-volume collection published by Blackwood.
Hogg was unhappy with Robert's revisions to the stories in general and to
'The Marvellous Doctor' in particular; he wrote to Blackwood on 10 March
1829: 'Robert has in several instances spoiled the effect of the tales at the
close by winding them too abruptly up The Marvellous Doctor is quite ruined
for though previously shortened one half to suit Maga that was no reason the
other half should now have been withheld' (*Letters 2*, p. 328). The additional
revisions to the story were extensive; Robin MacLachlan notes in his edition

of 'The Marvellous Doctor' that there are at least 120 'substantive changes' in the *Shepherd's Calendar* version—see *Altrive Chapbooks* (James Hogg Society, 1986), 75–97 (p. 94).

The present edition prints the *BEM* version without emendation.

**262(d) my parents lived in the old manse of Ettrick** probably a reference to the cottage of Ettrickhall, next to the Ettrick parish kirk, where Hogg lived until he was six years old.

**262(d) my mother** Hogg's mother, Margaret Laidlaw Hogg. See 'A Last Adieu', pp. 18–19 in the present edition, and notes.

**264(b) the Queen of that country** Maria Amalia of Saxony (1724–60) was married to Charles III of Spain when Charles became King of Spain in 1759.

**265(a) Don Felix de Valdez** apparently fictitious.

**266(a) young King, Charles the Third** (1716–88), was king of Spain from 1759 to his death in 1788.

**266(c) The Prado** the National Museum of Painting and Sculpture in Madrid. The Prado was built during the reign of Charles III.

**278(a) The bull perceiving one of his favourite mates thus distempered** in the *Noctes Ambrosianæ No. XLVIII*, published in the April 1830 number of *BEM* (vol. 27, pp. 659–94), the 'Shepherd' character tells a story of his being charged by a bull that had mistaken his 'B sharp for anither Bonassus challengin' him to single combat'. The Shepherd stripped off his clothes, and stood before the Bonassus 'as naked as the day I was born—and sic is the awe, sir, wi' which a human being, *in puris naturalibus*, inspires the maddest of the brute creation, (I had tried it ance before on a mastiff,) that he was a' at aince, in a single moment, stricken o' a heap, just the very same as if the butcher had sunk the head o' an aix intill his harn-pan'. With the bull in this weakened condition, the Shepherd 'mounted him' and roused the bull until 'he feenally recovered his cloots, and, as if inspired wi' a new speerit, aff like lichtin' to the mountains' (p. 670). John Wilson was the author of this *Noctes*, and perhaps this 'bull' story was part of the 'ground-work' of 'The Marvellous Doctor' that Hogg references in his letter to Blackwood of 28 May 1827, quoted above. For discussion of this *Noctes* episode in the broader context of John Wilson's writing about Hogg's physicality, see Ian Duncan, 'Hogg's Body', *Studies in Hogg and his World*, 9 (1998), 1–15.

**281(b) Family Compact** an alliance between the ruling Bourbon families of Spain and France in opposition to Great Britain during the Seven Years War. The Family Compact was agreed upon in 1761, after the death of the Queen, so Hogg's timeline is slightly off. Hogg apparently is making a political statement here, however, suggesting that the Spanish nobility must have been under a spell in order to align with the French against the British.

**282(c) Many of his relations were still more marvellous** Hogg's nephew, Robert, edited out of the manuscript an unknown number of episodes because of the 'indelicacy' of the stories.

**282(d) Johnie Faa's seduction of the Earl of Cassillis's lady** from the traditional ballad, 'Johnny Faa and the Earl of Cassillis' Lady', a version of 'The Gypsy Laddie' (Child 200). In a story set in the first half of the seventeenth century, Lady Jean, the wife of John Kennedy (1601/07–1668), the sixth Earl of Cassillis, allegedly was led away from her husband under a spell cast by Johnny Faa, or Faw, a gypsy. Gypsy Fa families also figure in 'Geordie Fa's

Dirge' (see *Scottish Pastorals*, ed. by Elaine Petrie (Stirling: Stirling University Press, 1988), pp. 1–2, 38–42), and 'A Genuine Border Story', ed. by Gillian Hughes, *Studies in Hogg and his World*, 3 (1992), pp. 95–145.

**282 (d) Hector Kennedy's seduction of three brides** unidentified, but possibly connected to the story of 'Johnny Faa and the Earl of Cassillis' Lady'. The Kennedy family, originally from Carrick in southwest Scotland, held the title of Earl of Cassillis throughout the sixteenth and seventeenth centuries. It is also possible that the Hector Kennedy story was a traditional regional story Hogg heard from his family, for the name Kennedy figures in gypsy stories from Hogg's native Ettrick. In 'Notices Concerning the Scottish Gypsies', an article in the April 1817 issue of *BEM* (*Edinburgh Monthly Magazine*), the authors, Sir Walter Scott and Thomas Pringle, include 'an interesting communication' from Hogg in which Hogg provides anecdotes of the Ettrick gypsies. In particular, Hogg notes that his grandfather, Will of Phaup, for many years provided shelter for gypsies, until he had a combative encounter with a gypsy named Ellic Kennedy (vol. 1, pp. 52–53).

**283 (a) Sophy Sloan, who left Kirkhope** unidentified and possibly a local story. Similarly, though, in 'The Brownie of the Black Haggs' Hogg tells a story about Lady Wheelhope, who 'eloped after' Merodach as if she were 'in a state of derangement, or rather under some evil influence, over which she had no control'. 'The Brownie of the Black Haggs' was published in *BEM* a year after 'The Marvellous Doctor', 24 (October 1828), 489–96; see *The Shepherd's Calendar*, (S/SC, 1995), pp. 242–55, and notes, pp. 276–77. Kirkhope is a parish on Ettrick Water near Ettrickbridge in Selkirkshire.

**283 (a) water of Milk** a stream in southeast Dumfriesshire that flows from about seven miles northwest of Langholm into the Annan southwest of Ecclefechan.

**283 (c) Eustace's *Pharmacopœia*** apparently fictitious.

### Ane Pastorale of the Rocke

'Ane Pastorale of the Rocke' was published in *Blackwood's Edinburgh Magazine*, 22 (December 1827), 675–84; the work was not reprinted in Hogg's lifetime. Hogg began writing 'Ane Pastoral' in the summer of 1827, but he delayed completing the work because of the shooting season. Hogg wrote to Blackwood on 11 August 1827, the day before the opening of the season: 'I have been trying all I could to finish "Ane Pastorale of the Rocke" for you but on looking at the ominous date of this you must percieve that it is sticked for the present The moors! the moors! nothing else can at present be thought of' (*Letters 2*, p. 276). Blackwood replied to Hogg on 25 August, eager to receive Hogg's finished poem: 'I hope you have now had enough of the Moors and have got home again, for I am very impatient to have "Ane Pastoral of the Rocke" and to hear that you are doing something for next Noctes which are to take such a high flight' (NLS, MS 30,310, pp. 261–63). Hogg finally sent Blackwood the manuscript with an undated letter, probably sometime in November; the published poem is end-dated 14 November 1827: 'I send you the pastoral begun before Lammas and only taken up again this week owing to the bad weather Retain either of the names you choose Perhaps the original one is the best' (*Letters 2*, p. 278).

'Ane Pastorale of the Rocke' is written in the mock-antique Scots Hogg had employed in several other works written for *BEM*, such as 'The Perilis of

Wemyng' (August 1827), that were later collected for *A Queer Book* (1832). In his 'Introduction' to the Stirling / South Carolina edition of *A Queer Book* (1995), Peter Garside comments on the effectiveness of Hogg's 'beloved ancient stile' (p. xvi), which Garside describes as 'a combination of ballad phraseology, the rhetoric of the late medieval Scottish "makars", such as Robert Henryson, and more modern idiomatic expression' (p. xv): Hogg

> found freedom to mix different genres, combining pathos with dark humour, physical and spiritual levels of experience, the supernatural and the satirical, sometimes creating a kind of "magic realism" not dissimilar to that now seen in postmodern fiction. Through word play, allegory, and the camouflage provided by "antiquity", he could also be more daring in sexual terms than in any other contemporary public mode, and so discovered a means of circumventing, if only for brief moments, the incipient prudishness of the later 1820s. (p. xvi)

The playful language is also especially suited to Hogg's satire on a favourite subject of the Tory *BEM* writers, Whig politics. The style of 'Ane Pastoral of the Rocke' is reminiscent of Robert Henryson's *Morall Fabillis of Esope* and other medieval beast fables; the poem uses animal characters to depict—and satirise—human behaviour, concluding in an explicit 'moral'. In 'Ane Pastorale' the 'Egil' rules the Scottish bird kingdom, but he is challenged by the upstart raven. The eagle and the raven seem loosely to represent Tories and Whigs, respectively; although both birds are subjects of Hogg's satire, ultimately the poem leads to a negative statement about the rise of Whigs, the 'mildewe of the commonwelthe' (l. 590). The controversial political debates of 1827 centred on Catholic Emancipation and the Corn Laws; *BEM* regularly published articles about both issues throughout 1827. Adding to the controversies were the circumstances surrounding King George IV's appointment of George Canning (1770–1827) as Prime Minister in April 1827 after Lord Liverpool became incapacitated. Although Canning had run afoul of the King by supporting Queen Caroline against the government in 1820, Canning's political circumstances changed dramatically over the next few years so that he was fortunately positioned at the time of Liverpool's resignation. However, Canning was a liberal Tory and supporter of Catholic Emancipation, and his liberal ideologies angered such prominent Tory leaders as the Duke of Wellington and Robert Peel, who resigned rather than serve in Canning's administration. Canning then formed a coalition government that included several Whig leaders. Hogg concludes his poem by echoing Samuel Johnson's assertion that the first Whig was the devil (see note for p. 298, ll. 593–94). Hogg later went so far as to suggest that 'Whig ascendancy' was even responsible for Sir Walter Scott's death: 'The real truth I believe is that the Whig ascendancy in the British cabinet killed Sir Walter. Yes. It affected his brain and killed him. From that period forth he lost all hope of the prosperity and ascendancy of the British empire. Nay he not only lost hope of the success of the empire but that of every individual pertaining to it and I am sorry to see and to feel his prediction but too well verified' (*Anecdotes of Scott*, pp. 18–19).

The present edition reprints the *BEM* text without emendation.

**284, l. 36 golde of Ophir** Ophir is an ancient city, apparently in southwest Arabia, that was a trade link between India and the West and known for its gold. There are several biblical references to the 'gold of Ophir', such as I Kings 9. 28: 'And they came to Ophir, and fetched from thence gold, four hundred and twenty talents, and brought it to King Solomon'.

**285, l. 72 graite Mogulle** a European term for the Emperor of Delhi, whose empire included most of Hindustan.

**285, l. 78 Gilborachis** unidentified.

**286, ll. 101–02 Egillis yelloch broke [...] from rocke to rocke** reminiscent of Scott's description of Loch Skene in the Introduction to Canto Second in *Marmion*:

> And my black Palmer's choice had been
> Some ruder and more savage scene;
> Like that which frowns round dark Loch-skene.
> There eagles scream from isle to shore;
> Down all the rocks the torrents roar;
> O'er the black wave incessant driven,
> Dark mists infect the summer heaven (ll. 247–53)

In his *Anecdotes of Scott*, Hogg describes a visit to Loch Skene and the Grey Mare's Tail with Scott and William Laidlaw. Hogg wrote that he was 'disappointed in never seeing some incident in [Scott's] subsequent works laid in a scene resembling the rugged solitude around Loch-Skene, for I never saw him survey any with so much attention' (p. 42).

**288, l. 189 Goode Lorde, how lowe the grait are hurlilt** echoes II Samuel 1. 19: 'The beauty of Israel is slain upon the high places: how are the mighty fallen'! See also II Samuel 1. 25.

**288, l. 202 baisse-born Kytis** a kite is a bird of prey, but the term is also used figuratively as a term of contempt.

**288, l. 210 Cooternebbe** the coot or cooter.

**289, ll. 231–32 she spoke hir counsellis deipe,– | Which wyffis are ne'er disposit to keipe** an echo of Burns's 'Tam o' Shanter':

> Ah, gentle dames! it gars me greet,
> To think how mony counsels sweet,
> How mony lengthen'd sage advices,
> The husband frae the wife despises! (Kinsley 321, ll. 33–36).

**290, l. 270 Ill pycke the eyne out of thyne haffat** an echo of the ballad 'The Twa Corbies': 'And I'll pike out his bonny blue een'. See Walter Scott, *Minstrelsy of the Scottish Border*, 3rd edn, 3 vols (London: Longman; Edinburgh: Constable, 1806), II, 206.

**291, l. 310 my old gutchere left the arke** 'gutcher' is literally 'grandfather' but here used in the sense of ancestor. In the biblical story of Noah and the flood, as the water subsided after the rain ended, Noah 'sent forth a raven, which went forth to and fro, until the waters were dried up from off the earth' (Genesis 8. 7).

**292, l. 356 Baykel lake** perhaps Lake Baikal in southern Siberia near the city of Irkutsk, which is the world's deepest lake and entirely surrounded by mountains.

**292, l. 362 Ben-hope, Ben-alder, and Loch-skeine** Ben Hope, a mountain (3040 feet) ten miles southwest of Tongue in North Sutherland. Ben Alder is a mountain (3757 feet) on the west short of Loch Ericht in Inverness-shire. Loch Skene is in Dumfriesshire, about five miles southwest of St Mary's Loch. Ben Hope to Loch Skene covers almost the whole length of Scotland.

**298, ll. 593–94 Maister Sauthan [...] Whigge accursit** Hogg here echoes

Samuel Johnson's assertion that 'the Devil was the first Whig'—see *Boswell's Life of Johnson*, ed. by George Birkbeck Hill, rev. L. F. Powell, 6 vols (Oxford: Clarendon Press, 1946), III, 326. Hogg perhaps also was influenced by Byron's poem, 'The Vision of Judgment':

> The very cherubs huddled altogether,
>> Like birds when soars the falcon; and they felt
> A tingling to the tip of every feather,
>> And form's a circle like Orion's belt
> Around their poor old charge; who scarce knew whither
>> His guards had led him, though they gently dealt
> With royal manes (for by many stories,
>> And true, we learn the angels are Tories.)

See *Lord Byron: The Complete Poetical Works*, ed. by Jerome J. McGann, 7 vols (Oxford: Clarendon Press, 1980–93), VI, 320.

**298, l. 597 With oder Whiggis we shalle haif funne** Hogg published at least two additional 'pastoralis' that addressed contemporary political issues with particular focus on Catholic Emancipation. 'Will and Sandy' was published in *BEM*, 25 (June 1829), 748–51, and 'The Last Stork', which was originally titled in manuscript 'Ane pastoral of the Swamp', appeared in *BEM*, 27 (February 1830), 217–22. Both works were reprinted in *A Queer Book* (1832)—see pp. 175–188 and notes in the S/SC edition.

# January 1828–December 1828 (Volumes 23–24)

## Trials of Temper

'Trials of Temper', a humorous story of mistaken identity among potential lovers, was first published in *Blackwood's Edinburgh Magazine*, 23 (January 1828), 40–47. On 29 December 1827 William Blackwood wrote to Hogg: 'I send you Maga which you will find a capital No. and your Trials of Temper not the least amusing article in it. The Moralitas is one of the prettiest pieces you ever wrote' (NLS, MS 2245, fols 110–11). The *BEM* publication of 'Trials of Temper' was the only publication of the work in Hogg's lifetime. The story was reprinted in a later issue of the 1836–37 *Tales and Sketches* (II, 319–31), largely based on the *BEM* text, although portions of several paragraphs were omitted, as was the concluding poem, 'Moralitas'. (As Peter Garside and Gillian Hughes have argued, the editing of texts in later issues of *Tales and Sketches* was probably driven by space considerations. See 'James Hogg's Tales and Sketches and the Glasgow Number Trade', Cardiff Corvey Articles, 14 (Summer 2005) <http://www.cf.ac.uk/encap/corvey/articles/cc14_n02.html> [accessed 12 November 2005].)

The present edition follows the *BEM* publication with the following emendation:

299(d) lacs] Iacs *BEM*

**299(c) Galashiels gray-cloth** coarse woollen cloth made in Galashiels, a manufacturing town on the Gala Water in Selkirkshire.

**299(c) Kilmarnock bonnets** broad, flat woollen bonnets of blue, black, or red (*SND*).

**299(c) pirnie caps** woolen nightcaps, especially those made in Kilmarnock, originally striped (*SND*).

**299(d) Mahometans** Muhammadans, followers of or believers in Muhammad.

**299(d) thousand lacs of rupees** a 'lac' of rupees is one hundred thousand rupees.

**300(a) Nabob** a term originally applied to a Muslim provincial official or a provincial ruler in India, it came to be applied in Britain to people who earned large fortunes in business in India.

**300(b) Kashmere** Kashmir, a native state in the north of India, now properly known as Jammu and Kashmir.

**300(d) Fort William** a British fort in the Indian city of Calcutta. The walled forts of the British East India Company protected the major factories in the company's territories. See also the note for 309(b) below.

**304(d) Ganges** the longest river in India, sacred to the Hindus.

**304(d) meeting all the lines at Musselburgh** a town just east of Edinburgh at the mouth of the River Esk, Musselburgh is known for golf links, horse racing, fishing, the Royal Society of Archers' annual archery competition, and cloth and netting industries. Prince Charles Edward Stewart marched his troops through Musselburgh on the way to Prestonpans, and the Battle of Pinkie (1547) took place near Musselburgh. Walter Scott was frequently in Musselburgh in his role as quartermaster of the Edinburgh Light Horse. However, the meaning of 'meeting all the lines' has not been identified.

**304(d)–305(a) Ethiopian cannot change his skin, nor the leopard his spots** from Jeremiah 13. 23: 'Can the Ethiopian change his skin, or the leopard his spots? then may ye also do good, that are accustomed to do evil'.

**305(b) with all his infirmities on his head** echoes *Hamlet* I. 5. 78–79: 'No reck'ning made, but sent to my account | With all my imperfections on my head'.

**305(d) patience of Job** proverbial, from the story of the title character in the biblical book of Job. See *ODEP*, p. 613.

**308(a) He drank tops and bottoms** that is, he drank every drop, or drank to the dregs. The *OED* gives this example: 'The labourers who board the steamers inquire anxiously for "tops and bottoms"–that is, everything that has been left undrunk in the passengers glasses'.

**308(c) Mr David Wilkie** (1785–1841), Scottish genre painter whom Hogg greatly admired. See note for 100(b).

**309(b) Presidency** in India one of the divisions of the British East India Company's territory; each division originally was governed by a President. The East India Company was granted a Royal Charter in 1600, which gave the company almost exclusive trade privileges with India. By 1689 the Company had gained political rule over three large territories, or Presidencies: Bengal, Madras, and Bombay. The company was dissolved in 1858.

**309(c) seven senses** see the note for 236(a).

**310(b) Esculapius** in Greek mythology, the god of medicine or the healing arts.

**310(d) Moralitas** this concluding poem serves the purpose of delivering the 'moral' of the story, and apparently Hogg intended the story as a modern-day fable. The term 'moralitas' is the title given by Robert Henryson to the concluding sections of his fables in which he expresses the moral. See Robert Henryson, *The Morall Fabillis of Esope the Phrygian*, in *Poems*, ed. by Charles Elliott, 2nd edn (Oxford: Clarendon Press, 1974), pp. 1–89.

**311(b) fruit of the forbidden tree [...] primal sin** in the biblical story, Adam and Eve were forbidden to eat the fruit of the 'tree of the knowledge of good and evil' in the garden of Eden. Adam and Eve disobeyed God and ate the fruit; this was the 'primal sin', and as the Genesis story explains, the cause of 'woman's woe'. See Genesis 2–3.

## I'll No Wake Wi' Annie

'I'll No Wake Wi' Annie' was published with music in *Blackwood's Edinburgh Magazine*, 23 (January 1828), 113–14; the song is sung by the 'Shepherd' character in a lengthy opening soliloquy in *Noctes Ambrosianæ No. XXXV*, although there is no specific contextual purpose for this particular song. 'I'll No Wake Wi' Annie' was first published in Hogg's *No. of the Border Garland* (Nathaniel Gow, [1819], pp. 2–3. In the *Border Garland*, the music is identified as an 'Air, by James Hogg'. In addition to the voice line, which is reprinted in *BEM*, the *Border Garland* edition includes an arrangement for the piano forte. The song was reprinted in Hogg's second version of *The Border Garland* (Robert Purdie, [1828], pp. 25–27), and again in *Songs* (pp. 224–27). The *BEM* version follows the first *Border Garland* version with minor punctuation differences attributable to printer's preferences. The second *Border Garland* and *Songs* versions, too, have only minor revisions, although each chorus is written out with each stanza in *Songs*.

Hogg writes of the circumstances of the composition of the song in his introduction to the work in *Songs*: 'I composed this pastoral ballad, as well as the air to which it is sung, whilst sailing one lovely day on St Mary's Loch; a pastime in which, above all others, I delighted, and of which I am now most shamefully deprived. Lord Napier never did so cruel a thing, not even on the high seas, as the interdicting of me from sailing on that beloved lake, which if I have not rendered classical, has not been my blame. But the credit will be his own,—that is some comfort' (p. 224). (For more on Hogg's relationship with Napier, see 'The Honourable Captain Napier and Ettrick Forest', pp. 96–137 of the present edition, and notes; see also Hogg, *The Queen's Wake*, ed. by Douglas S. Mack (S/SC, 2004), pp. 453–54.)

In *BEM* the first stanza is printed with the music; the present edition prints the text of the entire song, but otherwise the text is printed herein without emendation. See Appendix B for the music.

**312, l. 3 wake the ewes** to watch over or tend the ewes during the night. See also p. 211(c) and note.

## In Embro Town They Made a Law

'In Embro Town They Made a Law' was published in *Blackwood's Edinburgh Magazine*, 23 (May 1828), 782; the song was not reprinted in Hogg's lifetime. The song is the first of three songs sung by the 'Shepherd' character in the *Noctes Ambrosianæ No. XXXVI*; the other two songs are 'Chalk! Chalk!' and 'Good Night and Joy Be Wi' You A''. Blackwood's contributors' book lists 'pieces from Hogg' and others for the May 1828 *Noctes*, but specific contributions by Hogg and the other writers are not identified and no payment amount is specified (NLS, MS 30,659). Hogg's authorship is not otherwise indicated.

The song appears in the *Noctes* in the context of a celebration of Christopher North's seventy-third birthday. Macrabin has proposed a toast to North; the Shepherd sings 'In Embro Town' to give North time to think of a response to the toast. The song is based on Robert Burns's song, 'Act Sedurunt of the

Session—A Scots Ballad' (Kinsley 436). Hogg's version is a playful attack on the Whigs by the Tory *BEM* 'judges', who are holding court in Ambrose's 'spence', where the characters have their fill of food and liquor. Hogg has expanded Burns's version and has replaced Burns's transgressing 'standing pr-cks' in the third line with 'Kit and his lads' (see note below).

The present edition reprints the *BEM* version with the following emendation: 314, l. 24 threshin'.] threshin. *BEM*

**313, TUNE**—*O'er the muir amang the heather* see Appendix B for the tune from the *Scots Musical Museum*. Burns's 'Act Sedurunt' is also set to the tune of 'O'er the muir amang the heather'.

**313, l. 1 Embro** 'A familiar form of *Edinburgh*' (*SND*). The word appears as 'Edinburgh' in the Kinsley edition but 'Embrugh' in Burns's *Merry Muses of Caledonia* (Kinsley 436n).

**313, l. 2 Court o' Session** the supreme civil tribunal of Scotland, established by an Act of Parliament in 1532 (*OED*).

**313, l. 3 Kit and his lads were fautors a'** a reference to Christopher North, the fictional editor of *BEM*, and the *BEM* writers. A 'fautor' is a 'wrongdoer, a defaulter, esp. against Church discipline' (*SND*).

**313, l. 5 Decreet** a decree, the judgment of a civil court.

**313, l. 6 Act sederunt** the *OED* refers to the *Encyclopaedia Britannica* from 1875: 'Act of Sederunt, in *Scotch Law*, an ordinance for regulating the forms of procedure before the Court of Session, passed by the Judges in virtue of a power conferred by an Act of the Scotch Parliament, 1540'.

**313, l. 11 Cobrun to blaw, and Jamffrey to craw** Henry Cockburn (1779–1854), advocate and author, was a Whig politician and close friend of Francis Jeffrey (1773–1850), lawyer and editor of the *Edinburgh Review* from its beginnings to 1829. Jeffrey was also an important voice for Whig politics in Scotland, both through the *Review* and in his own person. Both Cockburn and Jeffrey had reputations as exceptionally persuasive advocates.

**314, l. 19 vif auld man** the fictional Christopher North, whose seventy-third birthday is the occasion of the song.

## Chalk! Chalk!

'Chalk! Chalk!' was first published in *Blackwood's Edinburgh Magazine*, 23 (May 1828), 794; it is the second of three songs sung by the 'Shepherd' character in the *Noctes Ambosianæ No XXXVI*, appearing between 'In Embro Town' and 'Good Night and Joy'. The publisher's records indicate 'pieces from Hogg' and others in this *Noctes*, although the specific contributions by Hogg and the other writers are not identified. Hogg's authorship is not otherwise indicated and, as discussed below, the style of the poem raises doubts about Hogg's authorship. Although Hogg does not indicate a tune for this song, 'Chalk! Chalk!' is patterned on Sir Walter Scott's song, 'Blue Bonnets over the Border', from his novel *The Monastery*, 3 vols (Edinburgh: Constable; London: Longman, 1820), II, 322–23. (Acknowledgement is made to Gillian Hughes, who noted the connection of 'Chalk! Chalk!' to Scott's poem.)

'Chalk! Chalk!' is a satirical piece primarily aimed at Henry Colburn (1784/5–1855), who operated a successful London publishing firm in the first half of the nineteenth century. Colburn established his publishing business in 1807, focusing largely on fiction. Beginning in 1814 and continuing over several years, however, Colburn founded or had an interest in several literary magazines. Colburn was a partner with Frederic Shoberl in the *New Monthly Magazine* (est. 1814), which included Alaric Watts and Thomas Campbell among its editors. Colburn founded the *Literary Gazette* in 1817 and *John Bull* in 1820. He also was a partner in *The Athenaeum* (1828). In the 1820s Colburn published popular 'silver fork' novels by such writers as Robert Plumer Ward and Thomas Henry Lister, as well as several scandalous memoirs; some of these publications are addressed in the second stanza of 'Chalk! Chalk!'—see Peter Garside's article on Colburn in the *Oxford DNB*.

'Chalk! Chalk!' was not William Blackwood's first attack on Henry Colburn, however. As early as 1819, Blackwood and Colburn had exchanged criticisms of one another's publications. Colburn apparently had taken issue with comments in John Wilson's brief review of John Snart's *Thesaurus of Horror*, *BEM*, 5 (June 1819), 334–47. Wilson concluded his article with a gratuitous criticism of Colburn: 'It may seem invidious to mention names; but we seriously beseech Mr Colburn to consider what he is about, and that he will infallibly get the character of a most notorious quack, if he suffers any more of his poor patients to suffer premature interment, during a syncope, like Dr Polidori' (p. 347). On 18 August 1819 Blackwood wrote to Colburn, responding to Colburn's concerns: 'The Editor of my Magazine felt so disgusted at the barefaced plagiarisms and imitations of some of our articles by Mr Watts or others in your magazine he could not believe but what you must be aware of them. [...] The publication of the vampire and D Polidori have been spoken of in the way that they deserve your name never has been introduced but as a publisher, and if any of your publications have been roughly treated, they perhaps deserved to be so treated. This however is not my affair, but the Editors, as I never on any occasion interfere with them' (NLS, MS 30,001, fols 159–60).

John Lockhart, who was editor of the *Quarterly Review* at this time, was the primary author of the *Noctes* in which 'Chalk! Chalk!' appears. The first number of the *Quarterly Review* for which Lockhart was fully responsible as editor included an article by William Stewart Rose, 'Novels of Fashionable Life', which reviewed (less than favourably) three of Colburn's social novels—see *Quarterly Review*, 33 (March 1826), 474–90. It is not unreasonable to suggest that Lockhart had a large hand in 'Chalk! Chalk!', perhaps contributing details of Colburn's publications. In fact, the style and content are more characteristic of John Lockhart's poetry than Hogg's, so it is possible that the song is entirely by Lockhart. The song is included here because there is no clear evidence to contradict the attribution within the text.

The *BEM* publication is the only appearance of the poem in Hogg's lifetime. The present edition reprints the *BEM* version without emendation.

**314, l. 3 Cockneys** a term of disparagement used by *BEM* writers to refer to certain London writers in the early nineteenth century. Leigh Hunt was the primary focus of criticism, but John Keats and William Hazlitt were also included in the group. Beginning with the October 1817 issue and continuing sporadically over several years, *BEM* published a series of articles 'On the Cockney School of Poetry', as well as a number of other works attacking Hunt and others associated with him. See also the notes for the 'New Poetic Mirror' in the present edition.

**314, ll. 4, 10 Hampstead hills and the Battersea border [...] Hounslow to Holborn** districts in the greater London area. Hounslow is southwest of central London, and Holborn is in central London. Fellow 'Cockney' poets Leigh Hunt and John Keats were neighbours in Hampstead, a district northwest of the city. Battersea is a London district on the south bank of the Thames.

**314, l. 5 Chalk! chalk! puffing-men [...] cheaper for Colburn** As Peter Garside notes in his *Oxford DNB* article on Colburn: 'Colburn's barely disguised manipulation of [his] journals, and others, for his own purposes soon helped gain him an adverse reputation for "puffing" his own books'. Hogg expressed his personal disdain for 'puffing' in a letter to Blackwood, 25 January 1825: 'I had forgot to mention to you that I was afraid terrified for high praise in Maga because our connection considered it would have been taken for *puffing* a thing of all things that I detest and one that I think has ought but a good effect' (*Letters 2*, p. 221).

**314, l. 8 new-farrant hum** new-fashioned humbug or hoax.

**314, l. 11 "GRANBY" and "NORMANBY"** *Granby* is a novel about high-society life written by Thomas Henry Lister (1800–1842) and published by Colburn in 1826. Lister was also the author of *Herbert Lacy* (1828) and *The Life and Administration of Edward, first Earl of Clarendon* (1837–38). In the 1830s Lister was a frequent contributor to the *Edinburgh Review*. (For additional information about Lister, see the *Oxford DNB* article by Donald Hawes.) *Granby* was reviewed favourably in the February 1826 number of the *Edinburgh Review*; the novel was treated less kindly, however, in the *Quarterly Review*. In an article entitled 'Novels of Fashionable Life' (March 1826), William Stewart Rose discusses three 'fashionable' novels, all of which were published by Colburn: *Tremaine*, by Robert Plumer Ward (see note for 314, l. 19); *Matilda*, by the marquess of Normanby; and *Granby*. Rose is dismissive of *Granby*, asserting that the novel 'would claim more room in this Article, did it not very much resemble Matilda; from the root of which it has evidently sprung' (p. 488). *Matilda* (1825) was written by Constantine Henry Phipps (1797–1863), marquess of Normanby. Normanby was an author and politician, who served as a Member of Parliament off and on from 1818 to 1830. Normanby published one other 'fashionable' novel with Colburn, *Yes and No* (1828). For additional information about Normanby, see the *Oxford DNB* article by Richard Davenport-Hines.

**314, l. 14 "HARRIETTE WILSON"** Wilson (1786–1845?) was mistress of several prominent men in the early nineteenth century, including Lord Craven, the marquess of Lorne, Lord Ponsonby, Lord Brougham, and the Prince Regent. Wilson published an account of her affairs in a four-volume work, *Memoirs of Harriette Wilson, Written by Herself* (1825). As she was writing the book she let it be known that she would omit names of her lovers for payment of £200 each—see the *Oxford DNB* article by K. D. Reynolds.

**314, l. 14 "CLUB-LAND, A STORY,"** probably a reference to Charles Marsh's *The Clubs of London: with anecdotes of their members, sketches of character, and conversation*, which was published in 1828 by Henry Colburn. Tickler comments in the *Noctes* in which 'Chalk! Chalk!' appears: 'What a vile system this is, of encouraging all the broken down *roués* of Boulogne and Dieppe to write their recollections of the Societies they were, in their better days, suffered to contaminate in town! I venture to say, that Harriette Wilson is nothing to the inditers of these "Clubs of London," "Drafts on Lafitte," "Anecdotes of the Beefsteaks," and so forth;–these escape valves of the bitterness of the black-balled and the ejected!' (p. 789).

**314, l. 17 WRIGHT'S IN THE COLONNADE! SOHO HOLDS EADY!** unidentified.

**314, l. 19 BUY BOBBY WARD'S DE VERE** Robert Plumer Ward (1765–1846), politician and author, practiced law and published a history of international law in 1795. Ward was a supporter of William Pitt and in 1802 became a Member of Parliament. Ward held a variety of political posts over the next two decades and became a novelist after retiring from politics. His first novel, *Tremaine, or, The Man of Refinement*, was published by Colburn in 1825 and was the primary focus of Rose's article in the *Quarterly*. His second novel, *De Vere, or, The Man of Independence*, was published by Colburn in four volumes in 1827. *De Vere* apparently was based on the politicians in Ward's own experience, such as William Pitt and George Canning—see the *Oxford DNB* article by Clive Towse.

**314, l. 20 shool out the ready!** shovel out the cash.

## Good Night and Joy Be Wi' You A'

'Good Night and Joy' was published in *Blackwood's Edinburgh Magazine*, 23 (May 1828), 802, and is Hogg's third song in the *Noctes Ambrosianae No. XXXVI.* The 'Shepherd' character sings the song to close out an all-night conversation at Ambrose's Tavern; as the Shepherd says, 'Nae harm, my dear lads, in partin' wi' a bit bonny sang o' my ain'. Hogg's version of this traditional parting song was first published with music as the concluding song in R. A. Smith's six-volume collection of Scottish songs, *The Scottish Minstrel: A Selection from the Vocal Melodies of Scotland Ancient and Modern Arranged for the Piano Forte* (Edinburgh: Robt Purdie [1821–24], VI, 104). The song was also reprinted as the concluding work in Hogg's collection of *Songs* (1831); the *Songs* version is based on the version in *The Scottish Minstrel.*

Although there are differences in printing preferences and minor word revisions throughout the song, the most significant revision for the *BEM* version is in the first verse, which adapts the song to the end of the night (at Ambrose's) rather than the end of the year. The first verse of *The Scottish Minstrel* version follows:

> The year is wearin' to the wane,
>     An' day is fadin' west awa';
> Loud raves the torrent an' the rain,
>     An' dark the cloud comes down the shaw.
> But let the tempest tout an' blaw,
> Upon his loudest winter horn,
>     Good night an' joy be wi' you a',
> We'll maybe meet again the morn.

The present edition reprints the *BEM* version without emendation.

## A Strange Secret. Related in a Letter from the Ettrick Shepherd

'A Strange Secret' was first published in *Blackwood's Edinburgh Magazine*, 23 (June 1828), 822–26. The story in its original form was never reprinted, but 'A Strange Secret' was revised and greatly expanded for inclusion in the two-volume edition of *The Shepherd's Calendar* (1829), II, 49–107. At the conclusion of the story in *BEM,* Hogg leaves open the possibility for the story to be continued in a later number of *BEM* by having the narrator acknowledge that he had requested additional information about the events in the narrative and that 'if it be of such a nature as to suit publicity, I shall send it you as soon as it arrives' (p. 323 of the present edition). The continuation never appeared in the magazine, however. Furthermore, the revisions to the *BEM* part of the story were almost certainly made by Hogg's nephew, Robert Hogg, who had been charged by Hogg and Blackwood with preparing the texts for the book publication of *The Shepherd's Calendar*. For a full discussion of the publication history of *The Shepherd's Calendar* and Robert Hogg's role in it, see Douglas Mack's Introduction to the S/SC edition of *The Shepherd's Calendar* (1995).

It is not clear why the continuation was not published in *BEM*, although it is likely the result of a combination of factors. The length of the continuation probably was an issue—it is three times longer than the original part. It is possible that Blackwood regarded the second part as either inferior to or inconsistent with the first part. It is also possible that Hogg simply took too long to complete the continuation. Hogg wrote to Blackwood on 15 July 1828—apparently in reply to a request from Blackwood to send the conclusion of 'A Strange Secret'—informing Blackwood that the completion of the story was several months away: 'Send ye the hinder end o' the highland correspondence! Lord help ye! Ye winna see the end o't for a towmont [a year] or at least no afore the end o December' (*Letters 2*, p. 297). The delay in completing the story perhaps also meant that the timing of the publication of *The Shepherd's Calendar* rendered it impractical to publish the work in *BEM* and in book form in such close proximity. Finally, it is also possible that Hogg never wrote a continuation and that the conclusion of the story as it appeared in *The Shepherd's Calendar* was a fabrication of Robert Hogg's from what Hogg intended to be another story altogether.

The origin of 'A Strange Secret' is not known. Gillian Hughes suggests a possible link between 'A Strange Secret' and an unidentified series of stories referred to as the 'M,Corkindale letters' in Hogg's correspondence with Blackwood (see *Letters 2*, p. 299). Hogg had included the 'M,Corkindale letters' among the works he had hoped to publish in a collection to be known as 'Some passages in the lives of eminent men'—a series of stories Hogg had begun at least as early as 1825 (see notes to 'Some Passages in the Life Colonel Cloud' in the present edition). Hogg wrote to Blackwood on 1 September 1825 about the possible joint publication with Longman of London of 'two small works about Martinmass about 7/6 each "The Shepherd's Callander" and "Some passages in the lives of eminent men"' (*Letters 2*, p. 236). Blackwood was not interested in the 'eminent men' stories, and three years later Hogg was still seeking a publisher. On 17 October 1828 Hogg wrote Alan Cunningham to request his assistance in finding a London publisher for his 'eminent men' stories, and he noted that he would like the work to 'come out ere ever Blackwood was aware'. It is in the letter to Cunningham that Hogg first mentions 'M,Corkindale' among the 'eminent men' stories: 'These are An Edin^r Baillie, Col. Peter Aston, Sir Simon Brodie, Col. Cloud, and Mr Alexander M,Corkindale They are all fabulous stories founded on historical facts and would make two small volumes' (*Letters 2*, p. 312). The other stories Hogg mentions for this series eventually were reworked for publication in *Tales of the Wars of Montrose* (1835); the 'M,Corkindale letters', however, do not appear in the *Montrose* volume and are not known to have been published elsewhere. (For a thorough discussion of the development of the stories in *Tales of the Wars of Montrose*, see Gillian Hughes's Introduction to the S/SC edition (1996)). A letter from Hogg to Blackwood, though, implies that the 'M,Corkindale letters' were included in the 1829 *Shepherd's Calendar*. Hogg wrote to Blackwood on 10 March 1829 expressing surprise at seeing two stories in *The Shepherd's Calendar* that were intended for *BEM*: 'You know that I sent you both Nancy Chisholm and M,Corkingdale avowedly for the Magazine without once adverting to the need there might [*sic*] for inserting them elsewhere and as I recieved no hint that they would be taken for the Calendar' (*Letters 2*, p. 328). As Hughes notes, there is no story in *The Shepherd's Calendar* with a M,Corkindale character, and as the narrator of 'A Strange Secret' comments, the second part of the story was 'thrown' into a narrative from 'a series of letters of different dates, and many of them at long intervals from each other' (p. 324). The character 'Sandy MacTavish' in 'A Strange Secret', then, might have begun as 'Alexander M,Corkindale', and the entire second part of 'A Strange Secret' might have been extracted by Robert—with Blackwood's blessing—from a different work and reconstructed to fit Hogg's original story. (See also Gillian Hughes's notes to Hogg's letter of 10 March 1829 (*Letters 2*, p. 330)).

Like most of the stories that ended up in the *Montrose* volume, 'A Strange Secret' has a particular historical setting, although the story is not necessarily based on clearly-identifiable historical characters. The story is set in the years around 1803, when Britain was under threat of invasion by Napoleon, but there are also historical associations with the Jacobite rebellion of 1745. The story centres on the disappearance of the son of the sister of an unnamed Earl, the search for the child among the Catholic clergy, and the eventual restoration of the child—now a soldier—to his 'legitimate' position as a 'Protestant Earl' (p. 345). 'A Strange Secret' was probably influenced by two similar plot lines in Walter Scott's novel *The Antiquary*—the restoration of the Earl of Glenallan's son to his biological father and rightful position, and the raising of a militia to prepare for war with the French. Also, like 'Colonel Cloud', many of the places named in the story are associated with places Hogg visited on his Highland tours.

Douglas Mack did not include 'A Strange Secret' in the S/SC edition of *The Shepherd's Calendar* because the story was not originally part of *The Shepherd's Calendar* series in *BEM*. The present edition publishes the first part of the story from the *BEM* version and the second part from the 1829 *Shepherd's Calendar* version. The notes that follow address the major revisions of the *BEM* text—almost certainly made by Hogg's nephew, Robert—for publication in *The Shepherd's Calendar*. The present edition regularises the spelling of *shieling*; silently corrects the omission of quotation marks at one point, and makes the following emendations:

316(d) seat] speat *BEM*.
320(a) frock he] frock she *BEM*

**315(d) YESTERDAY** revised to 'SOME years ago' in *Shepherd's Calendar* (II, 49).
**315(d) Thomas Henderson** apparently fictitious.
**315(d)–316(a) It is not deserving […] fresh in my memory** revised in *Shepherd's Calendar* to: 'His story, as a whole, was one of very deep interest to himself, no doubt, but of very little to me, as it would be to the world at large if it were repeated; but as one will rarely listen to even the most common-place individual without hearing something to reward the attention bestowed

upon him, so there was one incident in this man Henderson's life which excited my curiosity very much. I shall give it nearly in his own words:—' (II, 49).

316(b) **"Pray, what was that [...]. But it was this** this section omitted from *Shepherd's Calendar* (II, 50), and what follows in this paragraph is combined with the preceding paragraph.

316(c) **Lady Julia** a name Hogg also uses in a later story, 'A Horrible Instance of the Effects of Clanship', *BEM*, 28 (October 1829), 680–87. A revised version of the 'Clanship' story, 'Julia M,Kenzie', was published in Hogg's *Tales of the Wars of Montrose* (1835)—see the S/SC edition (1996), ed. by Gillian Hughes, pp. 138–53. 'Julia M,Kenzie' is set in 1645.

316(d) **Aberduchra** unidentified and perhaps fictitious.

317(b) **Beinny-Veol** perhaps Hogg intends Beinn Bheiol, a mountain (3393 feet) in Badenoch, just west of Loch Ericht.

317(b) **Glen-Ellich** unidentified.

318(a) **sounds of mental agony** revised to 'sounds of agony' in *Shepherd's Calendar* (II, 53).

318(b) **L—d J—s** presumably 'Lord Jesus'. This oath was omitted from the *Shepherd's Calendar* publication.

318(d) **cheek for chowe** a Scottish variation on the expression 'cheek by jowl', meaning 'side by side' (see *ODEP*, p. 117).

320(a) **Billy** 'Fellow in general, lad as opposed to lass, the word taking its peculiar complexion of affection, contempt or ridicule from its context' *SND*.

320(d) **what the misery is to** revised to 'what it is to' in *Shepherd's Calendar* (II, 59).

320(d)–321(a) **she opened her gown, and laid the remnant on** revised to 'she placed the relic in' in *Shepherd's Calendar* (II, 59).

321(a) **Lewie** Douglas Mack suggests that Lewie is probably intended to invoke the song 'Lewis Gordon'. The song is based on Lord Lewis Gordon (*c.* 1725-54) of Banffshire, who was lord lieutenant of Aberdeen and Banff for Prince Charles Edward Stewart in the Jacobite uprising of 1745 (*Oxford DNB*, Murray G. H. Pittock). The song was included in the second series of Hogg's *Jacobite Relics*. See *Jacobite Relics. Second Series*, ed. by Murray G. H. Pittock (S/SC, 2003), pp. 81–82, 298, and notes, pp. 503–04. The Gordons also figure prominently in Hogg's story, 'Some Remarkable Passages in the Life of An Edinburgh Baillie', in *Tales of the Wars of Montrose*. See pp. 1–98 in the S/SC edition and notes.

321(b) **imp o' darkness** revised to 'imp' in *Shepherd's Calendar* (II, 59).

321(d) **Neck butt, neck ben [...] mix my bread** a variation on the rhyme from the traditional story 'Jack the Giant-Killer':

> Fee, fi, fo, fum!
> I smell the blood of an Englishman!
> Be he alive or be he dead,
> I'll grind his bones to make me bread!

322(a) **plash for plash** literally 'splash for splash'. In *The Shepherd's Calendar* Hogg writes of some of the sayings of his grandfather, Will o' Phaup, one of which is 'one plash more, quo' Will o' Phaup'. According to Hogg this saying originated in the drunken Will's search for a drunken friend after they had both fallen off a horse into a river while riding home from Moffat one very dark night. See pp. 105–06 of the S/SC edition. (Acknowledgement is made to Douglas Mack for the reference to this anecdote.)

**322(b) Good G—! what a fate has been mine!** replaced by 'Then, after a short pause, he continued' in *Shepherd's Calendar* (II, 62).

**322(d) great loss** revised to 'great pity' in *Shepherd's Calendar* (II, 62).

**322(d) or unmarried** revised to 'or that she was not married' in *Shepherd's Calendar* (II, 62).

**323(a) the danger is […] disclose them** revised to 'but then it is almost certain either that he will not dare, or that he will not choose, to disclose them' (II, 63).

**323(a) Having twice met […] it arrives** this paragraph was omitted from the *Shepherd's Calendar* version (II, 63).

**323(b) MOUNT BENGER** Hogg's farm in Yarrow. The *BEM* version ends here. The remainder of the story in the present edition is the continuation of 'A Strange Secret' from *The Shepherd's Calendar*, II, 63–107.

**324(a) Innismore** unidentified.

**324(b) the time when the French were all to be killed in Lochaber […] raising the militia soldiers** a reference to the threatened invasion of Britain by Napoleon in 1803. Lochaber is a district in the south of Inverness-shire, largely bounded by the rivers Leven and Lochy and the lochs Lochy, Leven, and Laggan; it includes the town of Fort William. In his song 'Donald McDonald', Hogg imagines the invasion of the Highlands by Buonaparte and the Highland response to it:

> If Buonapart land at Fort-William,
>> Auld Europe nae langer shall grane;
> I laugh, whan I think how we'll gall him
>> Wi' bullet, wi' steel, an' wi' stane:
> Wi' rocks o' the Nevis an' Gairy
>> We'll rattle him aff frae the shore;
> Or lull him asleep in a cairney,
>> An' sing him *Lochaber no more!*

See Hogg, *The Forest Minstrel*, ed. by P. D. Garside and Richard D. Jackson (S/SC, 2006), p. 178, and notes, pp. 348–52. Hogg in his *Memoir* claims that the song was composed in '1800, on the threatened invasion by Buonaparte' and first sung 'to a party of social friends at the Crown Tavern, Edinburgh' (p. 20). Peter Garside has convincingly argued, however, that the song was composed in 1803 (*Forest Minstrel,* pp. 348–52), and in his *Tour in the Highlands in 1803* (Paisley: Alexander Gardner, 1888) Hogg writes that he first sang the song in public at 'the house of Auchtertyre, inhabited by Donald Macdonald, Esquire, of Barrisdale. […] It was here that I first ventured to sing my song of Donald Macdonald, which hath since become so popular, and although afraid to venture it I could not forbear, it was so appropriate, Barrisdale being one of the goodliest and boldest looking men anywhere to be met with. It was so highly applauded here that I sung it very often during the rest of my journey' (p. 68). In John Galt's novel *Annals of the Parish*, ed. by James Kinsley (London: Oxford University Press, 1967), Galt has his minister narrator, Micah Balwhidder, devote his account of 1803 to the threat of the French invasion and the raising of a militia. The chapter ends by noting that the local poet, Colin Mavis, 'made a song for this occasion, that was very mightily thought of, having in it a nerve of valiant genius, that kindled the very souls of those that heard it' (p. 182). In addition to Hogg's 'Donald Macdonald', there are several instances of songs devoted to the subject appearing in the newspapers and published as broadsides.

**324(c) Clunie side of the river** in the 1803 Highland tour Hogg writes of crossing Glen Loyn and then after 'a most fatiguing march' crossing Loch Cluny at the head of the loch and passing the isolated 'house of Cluny' (*A Tour in the Highlands in 1803*, p. 53). It is the following day that Hogg says he first sang 'Donald Macdonald'. Loch Cluny, or Cluanie, is in the Lochaber district about twelve miles west of Fort Augustus. There is also a Loch of Clunie in Perthshire between Dunkeld and Blairgowrie and just south of the Forest of Clunie.

**324(c) Bogle of Glastulochan** unidentified. In his notes to 'The Pedlar' in *The Mountain Bard*, Hogg tells the story of the '*Bogle of Bell's Lakes*', which, according to Hogg, was widely known throughout 'the south of Scotland' to have haunted the neighbourhood around Yarrow Kirk and Bell's Lakes. See *The Mountain Bard*, ed. by Suzanne Gilbert (S/SC, 2007), pp. 34–35, 249–50.

**325(b) the Spean** the River Spean rises in Loch Laggan and flows through Glen Spean and Spean Bridge into the River Lochy.

**326(c) island of Illismore** unidentified, but perhaps Hogg intends Lismore, an island in the lower waters of Loch Linnhe. The narrator's boat would have passed Lismore on the sail from Glasgow to Fort William.

**330(d) Correi-beg of Glen-Anam** unidentified and perhaps fictitious. A 'correi' or 'corrie' is a hollow in a hillside or between hills (*SND*); 'Anam' is a Gaelic word meaning 'soul' or 'mind' (*GED*). In 'A Strange Secret' Elspeth Cowan uses the word 'anam' to mean 'wraith' (p. 338(a)).

**330(d) wounded birds eyed me with strange, unearthly looks […] some enchantment in this case** for additional stories from Hogg of enchanted birds, see Hogg's Note X in *The Queen's Wake* (S/SC 2004), pp. 182–84, and Douglas Mack's notes to Hogg's note, p. 444; see also Hogg's story 'The Hunt of Eildon' in *The Brownie of Bodsbeck*, 2 vols (Edinburgh: Blackwood, 1818), II, 231–346.

**331(a) creature said, in Gaelic. […] not be expected that a ptarmigan should have spoken English** the ptarmigan, typically an Arctic bird, is found in Scotland only in the high mountains of the Highlands; therefore, if it were to speak, it would likely speak Gaelic rather than English.

**332(d) skein-ochil** a short-bladed Highland dagger, so named because it is typically concealed in the sleeve near the arm pit–from Gaelic 'sgian' or 'sgeine' (knife) and 'achlais' (arm pit) (*GED*).

**335(a) Ochon, ochon!** 'Alas, alas!', an exclamation of lament.

**336(a) Glen-Caolas** unidentified. 'Caolas' is a Gaelic word for 'channel firth, inlet, kyle' (*GED*) and is commonly found in Highland place names, especially in the Western Isles. Caolas is also a settlement at the eastern end of Tiree, and there is a village called Caol in Lochaber just to the north of Fort William.

**336(b) pass of Bally-keurach** unidentified.

**337(b) Averile** April.

**338(a) *anam*** see the note to 330(d).

**339(d) *Cheas gear*** cut ear, from *chluas gearr*. Acknowledgement is made to Beth Frieden and Wilson McLeod for providing the appropriate Gaelic form of Hogg's expression. Later in the story (p. 340(b)) Hogg identifies the pony's distinguishing mark as 'cropped ears'.

**341 (a) Abertarf** Abertarf, a parish in Inverness-shire, primarily on the northwest side of Loch Ness. The Tarf is a small river that enters Loch Ness near Fort Augustus.

**341 (b) Arisaig** a peninsula, the western point of South Morar and south of Mallaig on Loch nan Uamh, a port for boat traffic to the western islands. Supposedly it was near here that Prince Charles Edward Stuart arrived in mainland Scotland in July 1745 and departed from Scotland just over a year later after the defeat of the Jacobites. Hogg visited Arisaig on his 1804 Highland journey and writes about the Stuart connection: 'we came to the very creek where the unfortunate Prince Charles Stewart first landed on the mainland of Scotland in the year 1745. Yea, the people told us a thing of much importance, that we even stepped out upon the very same rock which he stepped out upon, and shewed us the cottage where he and his few companions lodged that night' ('A Journey through the Highlands and Western Isles, in the Summer of 1804', *Scots Magazine*, 70 (December 1808), 891).

**341 (b) Tobermory** a settlement on the Isle of Mull on the north side of Tobermory Bay.

**341 (d) the Shannon** Ireland's longest river, the River Shannon rises in Cuilcagh Mountain in County Cavan and empties into the Atlantic Ocean near Limerick.

**341 (d) Limerick** a city in the County of Limerick at the head of the Shannon, about fifty miles north of Cork.

**341 (d) Greenock** a port town on the Firth of Clyde in Renfrewshire.

**342 (c) Clare side of the river** County Clare, on the west coast of Ireland. Clare is north of the Shannon estuary and Limerick.

**343 (d) the Deveron** the River Deveron rises in the Ladder Hills in Moray and flows through Huntly and into the Moray Firth between Banff and Macduff.

**345 (d) Buchan or Mar** districts of Aberdeenshire. Buchan is in the north, bounded by the rivers Deveron and Ythan; Mar is in the west, bounded by the rivers Don and Dee.

### Songs for the Baloon

Hogg wrote the 'Songs for the Baloon' for a proposed special series of the *Noctes Ambrosianæ* in which the *Noctes* characters travel across Scotland in a hot-air balloon. Hogg was enthusiastic about the plan because it would provide numerous opportunities for publishing his songs in *Blackwood's Edinburgh Magazine*–songs that he could write effortlessly. Hogg wrote to William Blackwood on 11 August 1827: 'I approve highly of the Baloon Noctes I wish the inimitable author to send us over the highlands and by all means over the scenes he has himself visited else they are sure to be wrong described and bring us home again by a steam boat through the kyles of Sky and sound of Mull. It is the grandest conception ever was formed in embrio and must at least occupy three Noctes's Such songs are indeed well adapted for my stile' (*Letters 2*, p. 276).

More than a year later the *Noctes* still had not been written, and on 8 October 1828 Hogg wrote to Blackwood to ask him to return the songs, along with some other works that Blackwood would not publish. Blackwood wrote back to Hogg that John Wilson 'still intends to use' the songs (NLS, MS 30,311, pp. 71–73); Blackwood did not return the songs as Hogg requested, but neither did Wilson write the *Noctes*. Hogg, frustrated with Wilson and Blackwood, eventually wrote his own balloon tale for his balloon songs, which he sent to *BEM* for publication but which Blackwood rejected, presumably because Wilson still had an interest in the project. Hogg wrote to Blackwood on 4 January 1830: 'I cannot help laughing at your most unfair and disingenious excuse for not publishing *any* of *my* pieces on pretence that they will interfere with something that Mr Wilson may write but which he never will write and I am sure *he* at least has more generosity than to keep back an acknowledged good article of mine on any such selfish pretence' (*Letters 2*, p. 368). In the same letter Hogg indicated that he had sent the tale with poems to Henry Glassford Bell, editor of *The Edinburgh Literary Journal; or, Weekly Register of Criticism and Belles Lettres*. *ELJ* published Hogg's work as 'Dr David Dale's Account of a Grand Aerial Voyage' in the issue for 23 January 1830, pp. 50–54.

Ballooning was a timely topic in Scotland in the late-eighteenth and early-nineteenth centuries. James 'Balloon' Tytler (1745–1804) made the first balloon ascent in Great Britain on 27 August 1784 in Edinburgh, but six weeks later, in front of a large crowd of paying customers at Comely Gardens, Tytler unfortunately crashed his balloon. The well-known and popular Italian balloonist, Vincenzo Lunardi, visited Edinburgh in 1785, the same year that the first successful balloon crossing of the English Channel took place. By the time of the proposed 'Balloon Noctes', there were widespread opportunities for the general public not only to witness ballooning, but also to take balloon rides. See L. T. C. Rolt, *The Balloonists: The History of the First Aeronauts* (Phoenix Mill: Sutton, 2006); repr. of *The Aeronauts* (1966).

The present edition publishes 'Songs for the Baloon' from the manuscript preserved among the Blackwood papers in the National Library of Scotland as MS 4805, fols 101–02. The manuscript consists of a single sheet measuring *c.* 27 cm x 37.4 cm, folded to make two folios measuring *c.* 27 cm x 18.7 cm. The watermark is obscured, although the date appears to be 1826. The present edition follows Hogg's manuscript without emendation, including Hogg's irregular punctuation and occasional idiosyncratic spelling. The songs were revised for publication in Hogg's *ELJ* balloon tale, as the annotations that follow indicate. However, it is reasonable to assume that the songs were revised for the balloon tale that Hogg submitted to Blackwood since Hogg wrote Blackwood that he 'transferred' the work to Bell for *ELJ* (*Letters 2*, p. 368).

**346, (title) Song First** was first published as 'Song Third' in Hogg's 'Dr David Dale's Account of a Grand Aerial Voyage', *Edinburgh Literary Journal*, 23 January 1830, p. 53. The song was revised from the manuscript for *ELJ*. The *ELJ* version consists of a single sixteen-line song, and the last eight lines (the second stanza of the manuscript) were revised to read:

> Away again o'er the mountain and main
>> To sing at the morning's rosy yet,
> An' water my mane at its fountain clear—
>> But I see her yet! I see her yet!
> Away, thou bonny witch o' Fife,
>> On the foam of the air to heave an' flit,
> An' little reck thou of a poet's life,
>> For he sees thee yet! he sees thee yet!

The song was reprinted in *Songs* (pp. 235–36) as 'The Witch o' Fife'. The *Songs* version consists of two stanzas, not numbered, but the text is based on the *ELJ* version. Hogg had previously used 'Witch of Fife' as the title subject of the 'Eighth Bard's Song' in *The Queen's Wake*, and there he notes that the 'Witch of Fife' was one of several events and characters 'founded on popular traditions' (see *The Queen's Wake*, ed. by Douglas S. Mack (S/SC, 2004), p. 179 and notes, p. 443). The exploits of the witches in *The Queen's Wake* version include a flight to Carlisle:

> And we flew owr hill, and we flew owr dale,
> And we flew owr firth and sea,
> Until we cam to merry Carlisle,
> Quhar we lightit on the lea. (pp. 44–45, ll. 765–68)

**346, ll. 5, 7 gowden wain [...] the Bear** the golden wain, or wagon, is a reference to the stars that make up the constellation 'Charles's Wain', also known as Ursa Major, or Great Bear. See also 137(c) and note.

**346, (title) Song Second** was first published as 'Song Second' in Hogg's 'Dr David Dale's Account of a Grand Aerial Voyage', *Edinburgh Literary Journal*, 23 January 1830, p. 52. The song was revised from the manuscript for publication in *ELJ*; there were minor revisions to the first stanza, but the second stanza was more extensively revised, as follows:

> Yet still thou bear'st a human face,
> Of calm and ghostly dignity;
> Some emblem there I fain would trace
> Of Him that made both thee and me.
> Fareweel, thou bonny Lady Moon,
> For there's neither stop nor stay for me;
> But when this mortal life is done,
> I will take a jaunt and visit thee.

The song was reprinted in *Songs* (pp. 233–34) as 'The Moon', with only minor revisions to the *ELJ* version. *Songs* also reprints the Shepherd's introductory comments from *ELJ*.

**346, l. 5 Ben-Lommond** Ben Lomond (3192 feet), a mountain in Stirlingshire to the east of Loch Lomond.

**346, l. 7 grampian range** see note for 17, l. 36.

**347, (title) Song Third** was first published as 'Song Fourth' in 'Dr David Dale's Account of a Grand Aerial Voyage', *Edinburgh Literary Journal*, 23 January 1830, p. 53. The song was revised from the manuscript for the *ELJ* publication. Most significantly, Hogg omits the first stanza of the manuscript version in *ELJ*; he also changes 'Sir Robert's pencil' (l. 9) to 'an angel's pencil', and 'George Laidlaw's snuggest shed' (l. 18) to 'Glengarry's snuggest bed'.

**347, l. 7 grey-haired pilgrim of the Sun** Hogg published a book-length poem, *Pilgrims of the Sun*, in 1815. The 'grey-haired pilgrim'-author would have been nearly 57 years old when he wrote to Blackwood about the 'Baloon Noctes'.

**347, l. 9 Sir Robert's pencil** Sir Robert Ker Porter (1777–1842), a well-known painter and author and brother of novelist Jane Porter. Although born in Durham, Porter grew up in Edinburgh. Porter achieved widespread recognition among the artistic community even as a teenager for his paintings based on biblical subjects. Later he turned to large-scale depictions of military subjects. Porter traveled extensively in the early 1800s and in 1809 published a two-volume travel account with his own illustrations, *Travelling Sketches in Russia and Sweden during the Years 1805–1808*. Perhaps the work that attracted

Hogg's attention was Porter's two-volume illustrated travel work, *Travels in Georgia, Persia, Armenia, Ancient Babylonia, 1817–1820* (1821). The illustrations for this work included striking drawings of the scenery in his travels. For additional information about Porter, see the *Oxford DNB* article by Thomas Seccombe, rev. Raymond Lister.

**347, l. 13 Loch-Awe** located in Argyllshire, the longest lake in Scotland.

**347, l. 15 Cruachan's clefted height** Ben Cruachan, a mountain (3694 feet) of four ridges, situated at the northern end of Loch Awe, between Loch Awe and Loch Eltive, in Argyllshire.

**347, l. 16 Mount-Benger** Hogg's farm in Yarrow that he leased from the Duke of Buccleuch from 1821 to 1830.

**347, l. 19 George Laidlaw** probably the brother of Hogg's friend, William Laidlaw. Hogg worked as a shepherd to William and George's father at Blackhouse from 1790 to 1800.

**347, l. 21 Ben Nevis** the highest mountain in Great Britain (4406 feet), located in Inverness-shire, about seven miles southeast of Fort William.

**347, (title) Song Fourth** was first published as 'Song First' in 'Dr David Dale's Account of a Grand Aerial Voyage', *Edinburgh Literary Journal*, 23 January 1830, p. 52. The *ELJ* version follows the manuscript version with minor revisions except for the last line, which in *ELJ* reads: 'Hech wow! that's a serious thought! *Amen!*' 'Song Fourth' perhaps functions as a metaphor for Hogg's earlier poetic achievements, his 'dreams' and 'Journies sublime' that have lifted him 'aboon' the 'tempest' of the earth.

**348, l. 13 Gillan-an-dhu** unidentified, but Hogg uses a similar refrain in 'The Harper's Song' in Canto I, line 283 of *Mador of the Moor*: '*Sing Ho! Ro! Gillan of Allanhu!*'. James Barcus suggests that the *Mador* line is 'perhaps an echo of "Roderigh Vich Alpine dhu, ho! iero!", the chorus in the "Boat Song" in Canto II of *The Lady of the Lake*' (*Mador of the Moor*, ed. by James E. Barcus (S/SC, 2005), pp. 23, 114).

**348, (title) verses to the Comet in 1811** was first published as 'A Night Piece' in the *Poetical Register*, 8 (1810–11), 90–91. It was reprinted in *Edinburgh Magazine*, 5 (July 1819), 30, and reprinted again in Hogg's 1822 *Poetical Works* (II, 241–44). The verses in the 'Baloon' manuscript correspond (with only minor revisions) to verses seven through ten of the original twelve-verse poem.

**348, l. 4 the Wain** see note for 346, ll. 5, 7.

**348, l. 12 Like foam-bells on a tranquil sea!** Hogg also uses this image in the Conclusion to *The Queen's Wake*: 'Light as the fumes of fervid wine, | Or foam-bells floating on the brine' (ll. 42–43). See *The Queen's Wake*, ed. by Douglas S. Mack (S/SC, 2004), p. 164.

## The Stuarts of Appin

'The Stuarts of Appin' was first published in *Blackwood's Edinburgh Magazine*, 24 (October 1828), 535–36, where it is sung by the 'Shepherd' character in the *Noctes Ambrosianæ No. XXXVIII*. In the *Noctes*, the Shepherd says he had written two songs for the dinner celebrating the appointment of General David Stewart of Garth to the 'government of St Lucie': 'The ane on Garth himsel' I'll sing anither time.–But here's the ane ca'd the "Stuarts o' Appin"' (p. 535). The second song has not been identified.

David Stewart of Garth (1772–1829) was descended from a Jacobite family and one of his grandfathers was killed at Culloden. Stewart himself had a distinguished military career, much of it with the 42nd Highlanders, the Black Watch, and included assignments in the West Indies, Gibraltar, Egypt, and Maida. Stewart was the author of *Sketches of the Character, Manners, and Present State of the Highlanders of Scotland: With Details of the Military Service of Highland Regiments* (1822), and as founder of the Celtic Society of Edinburgh did much to support Highland culture. He was a friend of Sir Walter Scott's and assisted Scott in the preparations for King George IV's visit to Scotland in 1822. Stewart was named governor of St Lucia in 1828 but died less than a year after taking up the post (*Oxford DNB*, E. M. Lloyd, rev. Roger T. Stearn). It was Stewart of Garth who had initiated the project on behalf of the Highland Society of London that became Hogg's *Jacobite Relics* (1819, 1821). Although the project resulted in the publication of two volumes of Jacobite and Whig songs, there was a dispute between Hogg and the Society over Hogg's payment for the edition. Hogg claimed that 'Col. Steuart with all his goodness and kind intentions has misled me' (*Letters 2*, p. 133), and Stewart accused Hogg of providing an unsatisfactory collection. For a full discussion of the relationship between Garth and Hogg regarding the *Jacobite Relics*, see Murray Pittock's introductions to the S/SC editions: *The Jacobite Relics of Scotland [First Series]* (2002) and *Second Series* (2003).

Appin is a region of Argyllshire on the east shore of Loch Linnhe between Benderloch and Loch Leven. The Appin Stewarts were descended from Alexander Stewart (*c.* 1214–83), Steward of Scotland (1246–83), through John Stewart of Lorne. Dugald Stewart, son of John of Lorne, became the first Appin chief in 1493. The Stewarts of Appin were loyal Jacobites, and as Bruce Lenman has noted, 'This pattern of smallish clans, often with very young chiefs, was common in the Jacobite ranks. At Killiecrankie the Stewarts of Appin were led by their chief, Robert Stewart, a mere lad who had hurried from college to join the force being assembled by his guardian, John Stewart of Ardsheal, Tutor of Appin'—see *The Jacobite Risings in Britain 1689–1746* (London: Eyre Methuen, 1980), pp. 46–47. The Appin Stewarts suffered heavy losses at Culloden. One of the best-known stories of the Stewarts of Appin is the 'Appin Murder'. In May 1752, Colin Campbell of Glenure, factor for forfeited Stewart lands, was murdered. James Stewart, also known as James of the Glen, was arrested, convicted, and hanged for the crime, although apparently he was not the guilty party. Robert Louis Stevenson based his novel, *Kidnapped*, on the Appin Murder, and one of the main characters, Alan Breck, is a Stewart of Appin.

Hogg sent 'The Stuarts of Appin' to Blackwood on 6 August 1828 (*Letters 2*, p. 300), although he had written to Blackwood on 1 August that the song was ready: 'I have a series of M,Corkindale letters a grand Coronach and a calander all ready for you' (*Letters 2*, p. 299). A fair-copy manuscript of 'The Stuarts of Appin' is preserved in the Dunedin Public Libraries, Dunedin, New Zealand. The manuscript bears an 1827 watermark. There are minor revisions of the manuscript in Hogg's hand; these revisions result in the text that was ultimately published in *BEM*. A second manuscript, consisting of only the first, fifth, and sixth stanzas, is preserved in the National Library of Scotland as Acc. 10,001. This manuscript is an autograph presentation to Mrs Mary Ann Hughes, dated 27 July 1828. 'The Stuarts of Appin' was reprinted in *Songs* (pp. 59–62) based on the *BEM* publication, and as Hogg notes in his introduction to the *Songs* version, it was 'set to a fine warlike air, by Peter M'Leod, Esq.' (p. 59).

Hogg later wrote to M'Leod that John Thomson 'altered the accompaniments more into the coronach stile' (NLS, MS 2208, fols 39–40). The song was reprinted in *The Harmonicon* (October 1832) as 'The Stuarts of Alpin' [*sic*], where the reviewer comments on the melody: 'This is a most characteristic air, and ought to charm every son of Caledonia, for it is full of Gaelic reminiscences, and we can indulge imagination to the length of fancying some of the musical phrases to be such as Fingal himself would recognize were he permitted to "revisit the glimpses of the moon"' (p. 231).

The text of the present edition follows the *BEM* version without emendation.

**349, ll. 5–6 Ossian [...] Selma, and reign of Fingal** see note for 258, l. 51.

**349, l. 9 Oh-hon, an Rei** 'Alas for the king'. Hogg provides a note for this in the *Songs* publication, as well as in the Dunedin and NLS manuscripts mentioned in the head-note above; however, Hogg's note does not appear in *BEM*. The expression is written as 'Oh-hon, an Righ' in *Songs*.

**349, l. 13 the Sassenach** the English, from the Gaelic for 'Saxon'. The term is also used traditionally in the Highlands to refer to Lowland Scots.

**349, l. 14 the Campbells** in Argyll, the Campbells were among the strongest of the clans, and because they were staunch Whigs, they were at times in conflict with the Jacobite Stewarts. However, the conflicts of Highland clans with the Campbells were often motivated by personal rather than political circumstances, which Michael Lynch has described as 'a loose pan-Celtic alliance held together by hatred of the Campbells'—see *Scotland: A New History* (London: Pimlico, 1992), p. 275.

**349, l. 15 Glenorchy** Glen Orchy carries the River Orchy from Loch Tulla to Loch Awe in Argyllshire. Glen Orchy is part of the traditional land of clan Campbell.

**349, l. 15 Lorn** a district in Argyllshire bordered by Loch Leven, Loch Awe, Loch Linnhe, and Rannoch Moor. Lorn was a seat of the Stewarts before being overtaken by the Campbells.

**349, l. 16 one of the STUARTS held claim on the crown** the Stuart claimants on the Crown included James Francis Edward (Stuart) (1688–1766), also known as James VIII and III and the Old Pretender, and Charles Edward (Stuart) (1720–88), also known as the Young Pretender and Bonnie Prince Charlie. James's claim to the throne came as the son of the exiled King James VII and II. Charles's claim came as the eldest son of the Old Pretender. For additional information see the *Oxford DNB* articles, 'James Francis Edward' by Edward Gregg, and 'Charles Edward' by Murray G. H. Pittock.

**349, l. 19 Whig efforts** included the Oath of Abjuration, which required public officials and clergy to pledge loyalty to the British monarchy and repudiate the claim of the Stuarts to the Crown, and the Riot Act of 1715, which granted powers to civil authorities to disperse crowds of more than twelve people.

**349, ll. 23–31 year of the Graham [...] Inverlochy [...] Appin** the Stuarts of Appin fought with James Graham, the first marquess of Montrose, in 1645 against the marquess of Argyll's army at Inverlochy. Argyll was soundly defeated by Montrose, losing perhaps half his army.

**349, l. 28 peaks of Cruachin** Ben Cruachan; see note for 347, l. 15. Cruachan, too, traditionally is part of Clan Campbell's territory. 'Cruachan' is also the battle cry of the Campbells.

**349, l. 35 Culloden** near Inverness and the site (Drummossie Muir) of the devastating defeat of the Jacobites by the Hanoverian army in 1746.

**349, ll. 36–37 Glen-creran, Glen-duror, Ardshiel [...] conquered were never** Glen Creran carries the River Creran from near Beinn Fhionnlaidh into Loch Creran. Glen Duror carries the River Duror into Loch Linnhe at Cuil Bay. The Ardsheal Peninsula lies just northeast of Cuil Bay within Loch Linnhe. These land features, all of which are in Appin, symbolise the heroic Highland claim never to have been conquered–a claim whose loss must now be lamented. For additional references to this image in Hogg's poetry, see the note for 16, ll. 39–40.

**349, l. 41 Clan-Chattan** closely allied to the Mackintoshes, Clan Chattan recognized the Mackintosh Chief as their chief.

**349, l. 41 Seaforth** the Mackenzie clan, whose chiefs were the Earls of Seaforth. Kenneth Mackenzie, the fourth Earl of Seaforth, supported the exiled King James in the Revolution of 1688 and died in exile. However, Bruce Lenman writes: 'Things were never quite what they seemed to be in the Highlands. Seaforth, the chief of Clan Mackenzie, was nominally for King James in the Revolution of 1688, but when he faced a significant Williamite force at Inverness he sent word to the Williamite command that though honour compelled him to make Jacobite gestures, he would make sure they were ineffective'–see *The Jacobite Clans of the Great Glen* (London: Methuen, 1984), p. 50. Kenneth's son, William, became the fifth Earl. William raised an army to support the Earl of Mar and the Jacobites in 1715. He retired to France after losses at the battle of Sheriffmuir.

**349, ll. 42–43 Clan-Ranald [...] Glenco [...] Clan-Donnachie** Ranald and Glenco are branches of the MacDonalds, each clan with its own chief. Hogg refers to the 'four clans of M'Donald' in 'The Adventures of Captain John Lochy, Written by Himself'–see *Altrive Tales,* ed. by Gillian Hughes (S/SC, 2005), p. 142. The other two MacDonald clans are Keppoch (see note for 349, l. 44) and Glengarry. Clan Donnachie, or Clan Duncan, is also known as Clan Robertson.

**349, l. 44 bold Keppoch, the loved of Lochaber** Coll MacDonald of Keppoch had attempted to settle old conflicts with the Mackintosh Chief, but his efforts were refused and Coll was imprisoned for a time. Following his release, he refused to submit to Mackintosh's authority and pay rent. In July 1688 Mackintosh gathered an army to attack Keppoch, but the MacDonalds at Lochaber surprised and defeated the Mackintosh army. In 1690 the MacDonalds and Mackintoshes reached a peaceful agreement. See George Eyre-Todd, *The Highland Clans of Scotland: Their History and Traditions,* 2 vols (London: Heath Cranton, 1923), II, 265–66. Alexander MacDonald of Keppoch, Coll's son, was killed at Culloden. According to John L. Roberts, the MacDonalds apparently had been 'reluctant' to respond to orders to attack the Hanoverian soldiers: 'Alexander MacDonald of Keppoch seems to have broken the impasse. Yelling out in frustration, "*Mo Dhia, an do threig clan mo chinnidh mi?*" (My God, have the children of my clan forsaken me?), he rushed forward alone, brandishing his pistol and broadsword, to be hit almost immediately by a musket ball which shattered his right arm'. MacDonald's clan followed their chief, but he soon received a fatal chest wound. See *The Jacobite Wars: Scotland and the Military Campaigns of 1715 and 1745* (Edinburgh: Polygon at Edinburgh, 2002), p. 173.

**350, l. 46 dogs of the south** presumably the Hanoverian soldiers. The final story of Hogg's novel, *The Three Perils of Woman* (1823), concludes with a powerful and poignant account of the aftermath of Culloden in which the narrative voice asks: 'Is there human sorrow on record like this that winded up the devastations of the Highlands'—see Hogg, *The Three Perils of Woman*, ed. by David Groves, Antony Hasler, and Douglas S. Mack (S/SC, 1995), p. 407.

## John Nicholson's Daughter

'John Nicholson's Daughter' was published in *Blackwood's Edinburgh Magazine*, 24 (December 1828), 688. The song is sung by the 'Shepherd' character in the *Noctes Ambrosianæ No. XL*. 'North' comments at the conclusion of the song: 'Bravo! You have sent that song to our friend Pringle's Friendship Offering—haven't you James?' The Shepherd replies: 'I hae—and anither ['The Minstrel's Boy'] as gude, or better' (p. 688). The song was published in the annual, *Friendship's Offering*, for 1829 (pp. 263–64) under the title 'Auld Joe Nicholson's Bonnie Nannie. A Scotch Sang'; the annual would have appeared late in 1828 in time for the Christmas market. There are only minor differences between the two versions, attributable to printers' preferences. The song was reprinted in *Songs* (pp. 268–70) under the title 'Auld Joe Nicholson's Nanny', again with only minor differences. In the introduction to the *Songs* version, Hogg writes that since its initial publication the song has become 'a favourite, and has been very often copied', but that he has 'refused all applications to have it set to music, having composed an air for it myself, which I am conscious I will prefer to any other, however much better it may be' (p. 268). Although Hogg refused 'to have it set to music', a version of the song, entitled 'Niddity Noddity Nannie, A Ballad in the Scotch Style, was published (undated) in London by Mori & Lavenn with music by 'J. Blewit' (BL, H.1650.gg(16))—possibly unbeknownst to Hogg. Apparently Hogg's 'air' was never published and has not survived; the present edition, therefore, does not include music. For additional information about the annual context and publishing history of this song, see *Contributions to Annuals and Gift-Books*, ed. by Janette Currie and Gillian Hughes (S/SC 2006), pp. 123–24, and notes, pp. 311, 388.

The present edition reprints the *BEM* version without emendation.

# Glossary

This Glossary is intended as a convenient guide to the Scots of Hogg's publications in *Blackwood's Edinburgh Magazine*. Those wishing to make an in-depth study of Hogg's Scots should consult *The Concise Scots Dictionary*, ed. by Mairi Robinson (Aberdeen: Aberdeen University Press, 1985), *The Scottish National Dictionary*, ed. by William Grant and David Murison, 10 vols (Edinburgh: Scottish National Dictionary Association, 1931–76), and the online *Dictionary of the Scots Language* at www.dsl.ac.uk/dsl/. This Glossary deals with single words; where it is useful to discuss the meaning of a phrase, this is done in the Notes. In using the Glossary, it should be remembered that in Scots the suffix *-it* is the equivalent of the English *-ed*. In Hogg's mock-antique Scots, *quh-* stands for *wh-*, plurals are often given as *-is* rather than *-s*, *y* is frequently used for *i*, *ai* for *a*, and *ei* for *ee*; for words normally ending in a consonant, Hogg often doubles the consonant and adds a final *e*. Words that appear unfamiliar only because of Hogg's 'ancient' spelling, such as *myndis* (minds) and *grimme* (grim), are generally not included in the Glossary.

*a':* all
*aboon:* above
*abreed:* abroad, scattered
*ae:* one
*aff:* off
*afore:* before
*aft:* often
*agroof:* face downwards, prone
*ahint:* behind
*aige:* age
*aigh: interjection* expressing surprise
*aigit:* aged
*aik:* oak
*ain:* (one's) own
*aince:* once
*airches:* takes aim
*airts:* points of the compass
*aith:* oath
*alaike:* alack
*alane:* alone
*alang, alangis:* along, alongst
*als:* as
*amaist:* almost
*amang, 'mang:* among, in or into the midst of
*an, an':* and

*ance:* once
*ane:* one; a certain person, someone
*aneath:* under, below, beneath
*anither:* another
*arles:* earnest money
*arychte:* aright
*asklent(e):* aslant; aside, astray; askew
*a-swoomin:* a-swimming
*a' thegither:* altogether, nothing but
*atween:* between
*auld:* old
*aumorous(e):* amorous
*aumrie:* a cupboard, pantry
*ava:* at all
*aw:* I; all
*awa:* away
*awthegither:* see *a'thegither*
*ay, aye:* always, continually; yes
*ayont:* beyond

*bainstelis:* banstickle, the stickleback
*bairn, bairnie:* a child
*bait:* bit
*baith:* both
*ban:* swear, utter curses

*bane:* bane, bone
*bang (up):* rise hastily, raise
*barleyfummil:* an ill-tempered person (from drunkenness)
*baughlesse:* weak, timid
*bauk:* a wooden beam, rafter
*bauld:* bold
*bawbee:* a coin originally worth six pennies Scots or a halfpenny sterling
*be:* be; by
*beckin:* bowing, moving up and down
*befa':* befall
*begoud(e):* began
*beildy:* sheltered, cosy
*ben:* inside; in towards the inner part of a home; the inner room
*bendit:* cocked, ready for firing
*benty-necks:* weaklings
*bever:* shake, tremble
*bichel:* a bundle
*bicker:* beaker, a drinking vessel, especially of wood
*bide:* to remain; to endure
*bien:* cosy, comfortable, in good condition
*big:* to build; to make a nest
*bik:* bick, bitch
*billy:* a friend, comrade; a fellow, lad
*birky:* consisting mainly of birches
*birl:* revolve rapidly, whirl round
*bit:* (with omission of 'of') indicates smallness, endearment, or contempt; a small piece of ground, a spot; (with 'the') the same place
*bittern:* a species of bird, similar to a heron
*blate:* bashful, timid
*blaw:* blow
*blee:* colour, hue
*bleer'd:* bleared
*blithe:* joyous, cheerful
*bloterit:* soiled, tarnished, stained
*blouse:* to look fresh and plump
*blousterous, blousteryng:* boasting
*bluart:* blewart; one of several blue

plants: the harebell, the cornflower, the germander speedwell
*blude:* blood
*blychtyng:* blighting
*bob:* bob, move up and down; dance
*boddle:* a small copper coin worth two pence Scots
*bode:* bode, portend; a greeting, hence a visit
*bonis:* bones
*bonnie, bonny:* beautiful, pretty
*boordlye:* boardly, burly, stalwart
*borelesse:* without an opening
*borelis:* bore-holes
*boud:* behove
*bouet:* a lantern
*brae:* a bank or stretch of ground rising fairly steeply; a hillside
*brag:* brag; a defiant note; a challenge
*braid:* broad
*braifit:* braved
*brak:* broke
*braken:* bracken
*branglement:* confusion, disturbance
*brangler:* wrangler, brawler
*branx:* branks, bridle or halter; *figuratively* under control, cut down to size
*braw:* brave, fine, splendid
*braxy:* intestinal disease of sheep, food made from sheep that died of braxy
*braye:* harsh cry
*bree:* the eyebrow; the brow, forehead
*breeks:* trousers
*breery:* briery
*brik(ke):* break; to curdle in the process of churning; (with 'on') begin to use
*brikfast:* breakfast
*brisket:* breast
*brither:* brother
*brock:* badger, a contemptuous term for a person
*brocket:* having black and white

stripes or spots
*brode:* a brood, to brood; broad
*broderhood:* brotherhood
*broket:* see *brocket*
*broolzie:* brulzie, broil, a quarrel, commotion
*broose:* a race at a country wedding from the church or the bride's home to the bridegroom's home
*broostal:* hard exertion
*brose:* a dish of oat- or pease-meal mixed with boiling water or milk, with salt and butter added
*broxy:* see *braxy*
*brychte:* bright
*bryde:* a bird
*brykke:* see *brik*
*brykkis:* see *breeks*
*bught:* a sheepfold; specifically a small inner fold for milking ewes
*buller:* a bubble
*bullit-heedit:* bullet-headed
*bumm:* make a droning or humming sound
*bummil:* blunderer; a person who reads, sings, or plays badly
*bund:* bound
*bunn:* a cake
*burde:* a bird
*burn:* a brook, stream
*burn-brae:* a slope at the bottom of which a stream runs
*burstit:* burst
*butt:* the kitchen or outer room
*byke:* a dwelling, a habitation
*byrnis:* the scorched stems of heather remaining after the small twigs are burnt
*byzzing:* buzzing, fizzing

*ca':* call
*cadger:* an itinerant dealer, an ill-tempered person
*cairn:* a pyramid of loose stones as a boundary marker or other landmark
*callan(t):* an associate; a youth, fellow

*cam:* came
*cann:* can, a container
*canna:* cannot
*cannie, canny:* cautious, prudent; favourable, lucky; gentle, pleasant, kind *in the negative* unnatural, supernatural
*cantrip:* a spell, charm; a trick, piece of mischief
*canty:* lively, cheerful
*carcage:* carcass, corpse
*carle:* a man, a fellow
*carlin:* woman, a witch
*cassa:* a cobbled street or pavement
*cauffe:* a calf
*cauld, cauldness:* cold
*cauldrife:* cold; cold in manner, indifferent
*caup:* a (wooden) cup or bowl
*certy:* certes, assuredly; (with 'my') expressing surprise or interest
*chayerman:* chairman
*cheat:* cheat; deception
*cheike:* the cheek (of the face)
*cheild:* see *chiel*
*cheite, chete:* see *cheat*
*chiel, chield:* a young man, a fellow; child
*clacker:* chatterer, gossiper
*claes:* clothes
*clap:* clap; pat affectionately; flop (down)
*clatter:* noisy idle chatter, gossip
*cleuch:* a gorge, ravine; a cliff, crag
*clink:* money
*cloddit:* pelted
*clog:* a log or block of wood
*clout:* to patch with a metal plate or cloth; to hit; a cloth
*clouts:* clothes
*clud:* cloud
*cockilit:* unsteady, easily knocked over
*colde:* could
*collapis:* collapse
*comberance:* a hindrance or encumbrance, annoyance
*consaivit:* conceived

*coof:* a fool

*coontry:* country

*cooternebbe:* also coulter-nibbit, having a long sharp nose

*corbye:* the raven

*corky:* a feather-brained person

*coronach:* a funeral lament or outcry; a dirge

*cot:* a cottage

*cottar:* a tenant occupying a cottage with or without land attached

*coudna, couldna:* could not

*coured:* crouched, cowered

*couthie:* agreeable, friendly

*crabbit:* crabbed; in a bad temper, cross

*crack:* boast, brag

*craig:* a rock, a cliff

*craw:* the crow, the rook; to crow

*cremationis:* creation's

*crompilit:* crumpled, bent, crooked

*croose, crouse:* bold, courageous; confident; arrogant, proud

*crooseness:* boldness

*cutty-mun:* the name of a dance

*dabbe:* to peck

*dadd:* to strike

*dae:* do, done

*daffin:* fun, foolish behaviour

*daft:* foolish, stupid, lacking intelligence

*daille:* dale

*dainteths:* dainties

*dang:* struck with heavy blows; drove, dashed (with violence)

*darena, darna:* dare not

*day:* see *dae*

*decreet:* decreed; judgment of a court or judge

*dee:* die

*deil, de'il:* devil

*deil-be-lickit:* devil a bit, absolutely nothing; (also used as an expletive)

*demore:* demure

*deray:* disturbance, noise

*deuk:* duke

*didna:* did not

*dight:* wipe, rub

*dikelouper:* a person of immoral habits

*din:* din; a dingy colour

*ding:* to knock, beat, or strike; drive out

*dink:* neat, dainty; prim

*dinna:* do not

*dirt:* contemptuous term for a person

*disna:* does not

*dispyte:* despite

*dizzened:* dizened, dressed in finery (often used contemptuously)

*dockan, docken:* dock, the plant

*doddie:* a hornless sheep

*doit:* something of little value; act foolishly; be crazed, enfeebled, or confused in mind

*doitrified:* stupefied, senseless

*dole:* grief, pain

*dompe:* thump, beat

*donsy:* an unfortunate, luckless person

*douce:* pleasant, comfortable

*douf:* spiritless, melancholy

*doukit:* ducked; drenched, soaked

*doun:* doon; down

*doup:* the buttocks

*douss:* thrash

*dovering:* dozing off

*dowie, dowy:* sad, dismal; dull, dispirited

*downa:* dare not

*drabbis:* spots, stains

*dram:* a small drink of liquour

*drap:* a drop of; to drop

*drappit:* dropped

*drauck:* to quench; drench, soak

*dree:* endure, suffer

*drog:* drug

*droukit:* drenched, soaked

*drouth:* dry, thirsty; also addicted to drinking

*droyten:* drucken, drunken

*drumble:* mud raised when water is disturbed

*dudds:* ragged clothes; *figuratively,* a
  dull, spiritless person
*duddy:* ragged, tattered
*dumfoundered:* bewildered
*dwalls:* dwells
*dychte:* wipe or rub clean or dry
*dysse:* a ledge on a hillside, cliff

*ear':* early
*ee, e'e, een, eine:* eye, eyes
*e'e bree:* eyebrow
*e'en:* even
*een-hole:* eye socket
*egil:* eagle
*eild:* yeld; barren
*eile:* eel
*eire:* ear
*eiry:* ghostly, gloomy, melancholy
*eithlye:* easily
*eldrich:* weird, ghostly, strange,
  earthly
*eldron:* elder
*ell:* a measure of length common in
  tailoring; the Scottish ell was
  about 36–37 inches; the *ellwand*
  is a measuring stick one ell long.
*ellis:* else
*Embro:* Edinburgh
*eneuch:* enough
*enew:* a sufficient number
*e'now:* at the present time
*ernyng:* yearning
*extericks:* hysterics

*fa':* to fall; to befall, usually with
  another word, such as 'shame'
*factor:* a person appointed to
  manage property for its
  proprietor
*fae:* foe
*faice:* face
*fain:* fain; loving, affectionate
*faite:* fate
*fallow:* fellow; also, the young of an
  animal especially one still
  dependent on its mother
*fand:* found; infatuated
*fankit:* entangled
*farrant:* of a certain disposition,
  specified by an adjective
  preceding, such as 'new-farrant'
*farrest:* farthest
*fash:* to trouble, annoy, anger,
  inconvenience
*fauld:* fold, a pen
*fauldit:* folded, enclosed
*fautor:* faulter, wrongdoer
*fauts:* faults
*fawn:* fallen
*feck:* a large amount
*feckless:* ineffective, weak,
  incompetent
*feiste:* feast
*feite:* feet
*felit:* felt
*fell(e):* fierce, ruthless; severe,
  grievous; hill, especially rocky
  and precipitous; a tract of hill-
  moor; very much, extremely,
  greatly; *of the weather* severe,
  inclement
*fende:* sustain existence
*ferce, ferse:* fierce, intense
*ferly:* to wonder, marvel
*feughten:* fought
*fike:* see *fyke*
*firth, frith:* a wide inlet of the sea
*flaip:* a dull, heavy, unbroken fall
*flapper:* bird; something that moves
  in a loose, unsteady, flapping
  way
*flee:* fly
*fleech:* coax, entreat; use cajoling or
  flattering words
*flegh:* a scare; a kick or blow
*fley:* to frighten, scare
*fliting:* see *flyting*
*flunkies:* servants, lackeys
*flyting:* scolding, quarreling,
  employing abusive language
*focks:* folks
*forbeirs:* ancestors
*forbye:* besides
*fore-fit:* forefoot
*fore-foughen:* worn out from exertion
*forgie:* forgive
*forret:* forward

*fors:* to force; to cause to happen

*fou:* full; drunk

*fouks:* folks

*frae:* from

*fraimit:* framed, made

*freat:* a superstitious belief

*freens:* friends

*fu':* full

*fuffing:* puffing, panting

*fyke:* a state of uneasiness, restlessness; to fidget

*gab(be):* speech, conversation, chatter

*gabbillying, gabbling:* uttering with rapidity inarticulate sounds

*gae:* go; gave; see also *gie*

*gaffawing:* guffawing

*gaite:* see *gate*

*gallant:* gallant; to flirt

*gane:* gone

*gang:* go

*gar:* to cause (something to be done)

*garrat:* garret

*gart:* caused

*gat:* got

*gate:* way, manner

*gaudy:* dashing

*gaun, gawn:* going

*gaupus:* stare open-mouthed

*gay:* gay; very; considerable (quantity)

*gayan, gay an, gayen:* very

*geeyt:* moved to one side; raised

*gerse, gersy:* grass; grassy

*gie, gi'e:* give

*giglet:* one acting or speaking in a silly or foolish way

*gill:* one fourth of a mutchkin, almost three quarters of the imperial gill

*gimmer:* a year-old ewe; a ewe between its first and second shearing

*gin:* if, whether

*girdlefu:* a combination of 'girdle', an iron plate used for baking, and 'fu', full

*glaikit:* foolish, stupid, irresponsible

*glamour:* enchantment

*gleed:* a live coal or peat, an ember

*glen:* a valley or hollow, chiefly one traversed by a stream or river, and frequently narrow and steep-sided

*gliff:* a short time; a sudden fright, scare

*glime:* take a sidelong glance

*gloaming:* evening twilight, dusk

*glofe:* see *gliff*

*gloom:* frown, scowl

*glowrin':* staring; scowling

*gluthering:* gurgling, spluttering

*goadman:* a person who drives oxen or horses with a goad

*gode:* good

*godewyffe:* goodwife, the mistress of a house

*gomeral, gomral:* a fool; foolish

*goodemanne:* goodman, the head of a household

*gorbel(l)yng:* making a noise like a turkey-cock; gobbling

*gowan:* the daisy

*gowd:* gold

*gowk:* a fool, simpleton, lout

*grains:* prongs

*graite:* great

*gran(n)e:* groan, groaning; complaining

*gree:* the prize, pre-eminence

*greet:* weep, cry, lament

*greine:* green

*grenit:* longed or yearned (for)

*grew:* a greyhound

*griene:* to long or yearn (for)

*grit:* great

*groulle:* to growl

*grousy:* dismal, horrible

*grummil:* to grumble

*grund:* ground, the bottom or lowest part

*gude:* good; God

*gudeman:* see *goodemanne*

*guide:* treat, use, handle

*gullot:* gullet; a narrow, deep channel or rocky inlet

*gurr:* a growl, snarl

*gutchere:* a grandfather

*gyte:* mad, insane; love-sick

*ha' clay:* a kind of clay used for whitening doorsteps

*hadna:* had not

*hae, ha'e:* have

*haena:* have not

*haffat, haffets:* halfhede; the side of the head, side-lock of hair

*haggies:* haggis, the traditional Scottish dish of sheep offal, oatmeal, etc.

*haill(e):* whole, complete; the whole of

*haillucket:* also hallock, hallockit, etc.: foolish, good-for-nothing; irresponsible

*hald:* had

*hale:* sound, in a healthy state; whole

*hallershaker:* hallanshaker, a beggar, vagabond

*hame:* home

*hap:* cover, surround, so as to shelter or conceal

*happing:* wrapping up in a garment (such as a plaid)

*harl:* drag (violently or roughly), pull

*harrigalds, harrigillis:* the viscera of an animal, entrails of a fowl, the pluck

*haud:* hold

*hauffe:* half

*hauld:* hold; *of fish* hide, lurk under stones, shelter

*haver:* to talk in a foolish or trivial way; *as a plural noun* foolish talk, nonsense, gossip

*haw:* haw, hawthorn (-berry)

*hawkit:* spotted or streaked with white; white-faced

*hech, hegh:* interjection expressing surprise or contempt

*hedis:* heads

*heid(e):* head

*heire:* hear

*heirskep:* inheritance

*helms:* helmets

*helsome:* wholesome, health-giving

*heuch:* a steep side of a hill

*hewe, hewis:* hue: colour, appearance of, complexion; outcry, clamour

*hie:* hasten, proceed quickly

*Hieland:* Highland

*himsel:* himself

*hind:* a youth, a stripling; a farm-servant; hind, a female deer

*hing:* hang

*hinney, hinny:* term of endearment; honey

*hinny moons:* honey moons

*hirsel:* a flock of sheep, the number of sheep looked after by one shepherd or on a small farm

*hofis:* hoofs

*hogg:* a young sheep from the time of its weaning to its first shearing

*hoggit:* hogshead, a large cask

*hoord:* hoard

*hoot:* expressing dissent, incredulity, impatience, annoyance, remonstrance, or dismissal of another's opinion; *hoot na:* a strong negative

*hope:* a small enclosed upland valley

*horning:* an outlaw or rebel

*houghis:* thighs

*hout:* see *hoot*

*howdin:* bobbing up and down

*howdy:* a midwife, an untrained sick-nurse; also a woman who lays out the dead

*howe:* a depression or hollow

*howke:* to dig into; to scoop out the inside of

*humple backit:* hunchbacked

*hunder:* hundred

*hurdies:* the buttocks

*huzzy: slightly disparaging* a woman; a servant girl

*hynd-wynd:* directly

*ilk, ilka:* each, every

*ill-faur'd:* unpleasant
*illwillie:* unfriendly, hostile
*inklin:* inclination
*intil, intill:* into
*inwith:* inwards, inside
*isna:* is not
*ither:* other
*itsel(l):* itself

*jaloused:* suspected
*jaunderin:* talking idly, foolishly, or jokingly
*jaunders:* idle or foolish talk
*jaw:* pour abruptly, splash
*jockis:* joke's
*joe:* a sweetheart
*jouk:* dodge, evasion
*jybe:* gibe

*kail, kale:* cabbage
*kail yard:* cabbage garden
*keek:* to peep
*kembe:* comb
*ken(ne):* to make known; to know; knowledge, acquaintance, comprehension, insight
*kie:* see *kye*
*kilted:* tucked up
*kimmer:* a girl, lass
*kintry:* country
*kip:* a jutting point on a hill
*kirk:* church
*kirk-stile:* a stile or narrow entrance to a churchyard, sometimes used as a meeting place
*kirn:* a churn; to churn
*kist:* a chest, a trunk
*kivering:* covering
*knap:* the kneecap
*kneveller:* a sharp blow, a punch
*knevillin:* pounding, pummeling
*knowe:* knoll, a hill or rising ground
*kye:* cows

*laigh, laigher:* low, lower
*laike-a-day, lak-a-daisy:* alas!
*lair:* a place where animals lie down, a fold or enclosure; a mire
*laird:* the landlord of an estate

*laith:* loath
*lammie, lammis:* lamb, lambs
*lane:* lone, alone
*lanesome:* lonesome
*lang:* long
*langsyne:* long since; old times
*lauchin:* laughing
*lave:* the rest, remainder
*laverock, lavrock:* the skylark
*law:* a rounded, conical hill
*lea:* lea, ground left untilled
*leal:* loyal, faithful to one's allegiance or duties; *of a woman:* chaste, pure
*leddy:* lady
*lee:* a lie; to lie
*leears:* liars
*leel:* see *leal*
*lee-lang:* livelong
*leeve, leevin':* to live, living
*leglin:* lade-gallon, a wooden bucket used as a milk pail
*leire:* learning
*leister:* a pronged spear used for salmon fishing
*lentrin:* Lent
*leughen:* laughed
*lickerish:* like
*lift:* lift; sky
*liker:* something like; *added as an intensifier*
*liket:* liked
*lilt:* sing in a low clear voice with a sweet tone and light cheerful rhythm
*limmer:* a rascal
*lingit:* long, lanky
*linn:* a waterfall or pool below a waterfall; a deep, narrow gorge
*lippen:* trust, depend on
*list:* listen
*loch-leech:* the leech
*loke:* a small quantity, a bundle or handful; look
*loon, loun, lowne:* a fellow of the lower orders, one of the riffraff; a rogue, scoundrel, worthless person

*loot:* let

*loup:* any natural bend or configuration, such as the winding of a river in its valley

*love-blink:* a loving or amorous glance

*lowe:* a flame, fire; also *low; a lowe,* on fire

*lown(e): of the wind* lowered, calm; *of a place* sheltered, snug; see also *loon*

*lucken:* having a compact head as in a bud

*lucky:* a familiar form of address to an elderly woman

*lugs:* ears

*lum:* a chimney

*ly:* to lie

*lychte:* light

*lyffe:* life

*mae:* more

*maele:* a stain

*maike:* make; likeness

*mailing:* a tenant farm

*mair:* more

*mairgin:* margin

*maist:* most

*mak:* make

*mare:* chief magistrate, mayor

*maun:* must

*maunna:* must not

*mazelled:* confused, stupefied

*meide:* a reward

*melle:* mix, mingle

*meltith:* a meal

*mense:* to do honour to, credit; common sense

*menselesse:* unmannerly, objectionable in behaviour

*merkat:* market

*messe:* to take food

*mids:* the middle, midst

*mim:* prim, restrained

*min':* mind; remember

*mirk:* darkness, night, twilight

*mither:* mother

*mochte:* may

*mockryffe:* scornful, mocking

*moderis:* mother's

*molde:* the form or shape of an animal body

*mony:* many

*mools:* earth, soil

*mootit:* moulted; worn away, shabby

*morefulis:* moor fowl's

*moste:* must; most

*mou:* mouth

*moudiwort:* the mole

*moul':* see *mools*

*moustenit:* perfumed with musk

*muckle:* great, big; much

*muffis:* muffs; tufts of feathers around the head or legs of a bird

*muir:* moor

*mumis, mums:* murmurs

*mumpis:* whisper; mere suggestion (of something)

*mutchkin:* a Scots measure equal to one-fourth of a pint

*mymmis:* mimicry

*myneviris:* minivers, a kind of fur used as a lining and trimming in ceremonial costumes

*myrgeon:* a mocking or grotesque movement of the body or face

*mysel(l):* myself

*na:* no, not

*nabb:* a person of importance or prestige

*nae:* no, not, not any

*naebody:* nobody

*naething:* nothing

*naig:* nag, a horse

*nane:* none

*neb:* a nose; the beak of a bird

*needfu':* needful

*needna:* need not

*neide:* need

*neiste:* next

*neuk:* nook

*new-drappit:* new-born

*new-farrant:* see *farrant*

*new spained:* see *spained*

*nibbit:* nibbie, a walking stick
*nieve:* a fist
*no:* no, not
*nonedaye:* noonday
*noo:* now
*nouther:* neither
*nycheris:* sniggers

*o':* of
*od: God (a mild oath)*
*oder:* other
*ony:* any
*othis:* oaths
*ou:* oh!
*outbye:* away from, distant
*outher:* either
*outower:* outwards and over; over the top of; over to the other side of; across
*ower, owre:* over
*owrance:* mastery, control

*paddockis:* frogs
*pairt(e):* part
*pat:* put; pot
*pawkie, pawky:* shrewd, lively
*penn:* pen
*percit:* pierced, penetrated; seen
*persaife:* perceive
*pingle:* an effort, struggle; a labour with little result
*pit:* put
*plack:* a small copper coin, usually worth four pennies Scots; money in general; *in the negative,* nothing of any value
*plash:* a splash
*plishy-plashy:* tasteless drink
*plookye:* spotty, covered with growths or pimples
*ply:* work hard and perseveringly
*pookyng:* plucking; grab at
*powney, pownie:* pony, a riding horse
*pree:* to try by tasting
*presynkis:* precincts, environs, the region lying immediately around a place
*prie:* pry, a species of grass
*prin:* a metal pin; as a symbol of

something of very little value
*proprate:* appropriate
*pu:* to pull
*punds:* pounds
*pyatte:* the magpie
*pylis:* piles

*quat:* quit, give up
*quean:* a woman, usually a young unmarried one

*raffe:* abundance
*raid:* settled with
*raikit:* raked
*raillie:* a woman's short-sleeved front-bodice, worn on dress occasions
*rair(e):* to roar; a roar
*rangkling:* rankling, festering
*rannle-bauks:* a bar across a chimney from which a pot could be suspended; a roof beam or rafter
*rape:* rope, the ropes securing thatch on a roof
*raw:* a row, a line
*reaming:* frothy; the froth on top of ale; full to the brim
*rearding:* reirding, roaring, making a loud noise
*rechit:* reached
*redd:* to disentangle, to remove
*reed-wood:* stark staring mad
*reek:* smoke
*reif(e):* plunder; to rob
*reiste:* roost
*reyne:* rain (on)
*rigg:* a ridge of high ground; a piece of land planted with a crop
*rin:* to run
*rit:* scratch, score; mark with a shallow furrow as a guide in ploughing, draining
*rive:* tear, rip
*roudess:* a coarse, ill-natured woman
*routh:* abundance, abundant, well-endowed
*row(e), rowl:* roll; to wrap up or envelope in

*rowntre:* rowan, the mountain ash
*rowt:* low loudly; bellow
*ruffe:* a wading bird of which the male of the species has a large ruff
*runt:* contemptuous term for an ill-natured old woman
*ryffe:* rife, abundant

*sae:* so
*saft:* soft
*sair, sairly:* sore, sorely; causing physical or mental pain or distress; surely
*sal, sall:* shall
*sanctis:* saints
*sang:* song
*sanna:* shall not
*sant:* saint
*sauf:* save
*saul:* soul
*saut:* salt(y)
*scart:* a scratch; to scratch, claw
*scraugh:* to utter a shrill cry; to shriek
*screeded:* composed quickly
*seile:* the seal
*senis:* sense
*sennins:* sinews
*ser':* serve
*seuch:* a drainage trench
*sey(e):* to try, test; say
*shakel:* shackle
*shaugle:* shuffle, walk clumsily
*shaw:* a small natural wood, a thicket
*shedding:* a pen for separating sheep
*sheine:* bright
*shekilis:* shackles
*sheuk:* shook
*shieling:* high or remote summer pasture with a shepherd's hut; the hut itself
*sho:* she
*sholde:* should
*shool:* to shovel
*shoon:* shoes
*shouldna:* should not

*shyviris:* splinters
*sic, siccan, sickan:* such
*sickerly:* certainly, safely
*siller:* silver; money in general
*simmer:* summer
*sin':* since
*sindrie:* apart
*sinsyne:* since then
*sittled:* settled
*skaille:* scatter, disperse, spread about
*skaithe:* damage, harm
*skeel:* skill
*skelping:* naughty
*skeugh:* skew, slant
*skiff:* to move lightly, glide
*skreide:* a shrill or screeching noise
*skreime:* scream
*skulduddery:* skulduggery
*slaken:* diminish, decrease
*sleeperyheadit:* sleepy headed, *figuratively,* stupid
*sleike:* sleek
*sleive:* sleeve
*sma':* small
*smeddum:* spirit, energy, vigorous resourcefulness
*smiddy:* smithy
*smoor:* to choke, suffocate, especially by being buried in a snowdrift
*snap:* a small piece, scrap (of food)
*snaw:* snow
*snirting:* sniggering
*snood:* to bind (one's hair) with a band
*snool:* to humiliate, subdue, reprove
*sock:* a ploughshare
*sonsy:* comely, attractive; buxom
*sorges:* surges
*soun':* sound, soundly
*spained:* speaned, weaned; *new spained:* newly weaned
*speer, spier:* to ask, inquire
*splore:* a fuss
*splunting:* wooing or courting
*spurring:* scratching around
*stamocke:* stomach
*stane:* stone

*stane-clod:* a stone's throw

*stapple:* staple, a principal commodity

*starn:* stars

*stave:* a stanza or verse of a song or poem; a walking stick, a staff; to stave

*steghing:* steching, stuffing oneself with food

*steike:* close, shut up

*steipe:* steep; to steep, soak; in the process of being soaked, *figuratively* to become intoxicated

*stell:* an open enclosure of walling used as a shelter for sheep; to fix in a stare of astonishment

*sternies, sterns:* stars

*stickit:* come to a premature halt in a trade or profession

*stiddy:* a blacksmith's anvil

*stirlis:* nostrils

*stottin:* staggering, stuttering, stammering

*stounde:* a pang, twinge

*stoup:* a flagon, tankard, mug

*stour(e):* a disturbance

*stown:* stolen

*strae:* straw

*strang:* strong

*streek:* stretch; to go at full speed

*streuk:* struck

*studdy:* stithy, an anvil

*suckumm:* succumb

*suddled:* soiled, dirty

*sude:* should

*suple:* supple

*swairf, swarf:* to faint

*swattle:* drink greedily or noisily

*swee:* to sway, swing

*swelsh:* swale, a wet hollow

*swith:* quickly; *interjection,* be gone, speed away

*swone:* to swoon

*sybow:* the spring onion (contemptuous)

*syne:* since, ago

*tae:* toe; to; one (of two)

*tagonist:* antagonist

*taigling:* entangling, confusing

*tak:* take

*tap:* a tuft of hair, feathers; a bird's nest

*tat:* that

*tattering:* ragged

*tauld:* told

*tawpy:* a giddy, scatterbrained, untidy, awkward, or careless person

*tent:* pay attention to, observe

*thack:* thatch

*thae:* those

*thaime:* theme

*the-day:* today

*thegether, thegither:* together

*the-morn:* tomorrow

*themsel(l)s:* themselves

*thole:* to suffer, have to bear, be subjected to; endure with patience, tolerance

*thou's:* thou shall

*thrangin:* crowding

*thrapple:* the throat

*thraw:* to twist, turn; to throw

*thraward:* perverse, contrary

*tid:* favourable time, opportunity; mood

*tikabed:* tike-o-bed, a mattress

*tike:* dog; an ill-mannered person (usually contemptuous)

*till:* till; to (a person, thing, or place)

*tinckell:* tinkle

*tine:* to lose, suffer the loss, destruction or disappearance of, cease to have or enjoy

*tint:* lost

*tither:* the other (of two)

*titty:* sister, girl

*tocher:* a dowry

*tombelit:* tumbled

*toth:* coarse grass which grows on ground manured by sheep or cattle

*toulde:* told

*tout(s):* to trumpet; speak loudly; also a dismissive *interjection towzye:* dishevelled, tangled

*trammis:* legs

*trews:* trousers

*trig:* neat in figure, dress

*troth(e):* truth; *interjection* indeed!, upon my word!

*trow:* believe

*tuke:* took

*tup:* a ram

*twa, twae:* two

*twall:* twelve

*unca, unco:* very; extraordinary; uncanny

*unnaimit:* unnamed

*uppittings:* accommodations

*vif:* lively

*vizies:* looks at attentively, inspects

*wa':* wall

*wad:* would

*wadna:* would not

*wae:* woe

*waefu':* woeful

*waif(e):* the wave

*wailit:* chose, picked out

*wake:* to watch over during the night

*wale:* wale; choice

*wals:* was

*wan:* wan; see also *win, won*

*war:* were, worse

*warena, warna:* were not

*wark:* work

*warld:* world

*warly:* warily, cautiously

*warrand, warrant:* warrant; vouch for the truth of; defend; guarantee

*warrandice:* guarantee, surety for

*wasna:* was not

*wat:* wet; know

*water-craw:* water blackbird

*wauf:* strayed, wandering

*waukin:* awake

*waur:* worse; see also *war*

*weary:* weary; sad, miserable; depressing, dispirited; *weary fa':* an expression of exasperation, 'confound', 'the devil take'

*wedder:* a wether

*wee (a wee):* small, tiny; a small measure, quantity, or degree of some thing or of time, distance etc.

*weel:* well; weal, welfare

*weet:* to know; wet

*weetless:* unknowing, unsuspecting

*weil:* an eddy

*weir:* war, things warlike

*welkin:* the apparent vault of heaven; the sky

*well-ee:* a place in a bog from which a spring rises

*wemyng:* women

*we's:* we shall

*westlan:* westland, western

*wha:* who

*whan:* when

*whaten:* what

*whaup:* the curlew

*wheel:* wheel; spin; turn

*wheen:* a quantity, an indefinite number

*whew:* whistle

*whiles:* times

*whilk:* which

*whipper-in:* a huntsman's assistant who brings stray hounds into the pack

*whisht: interjection,* be quiet!

*whushe:* whish, a rushing noise

*wi':* with

*wight:* person (frequently with contempt or pity)

*wilder'd:* pathless, wild, a place where one might lose one's way

*win:* win; earn; to make or find one's way

*win'le, windle:* a bundle of straw

*winna:* will not

*witching:* bewitching, enchanting

*wite:* blame; the person or thing to blame

*witters:* barbs

*wizen:* throat

*wizzened:* shrivelled, dried up

*won:* see *win*

*wot:* know, knew

*wraith:* an apparition of a living person, usually taken as an omen of death; a ghost

*wrang:* wrong

*wreath:* a drift of snow

*wud:* would

*wul-cat:* wild cat

*wychte:* see *wight*

*wyffe:* wife; a woman

*wyte:* see *wite*

*yammer:* howl, lament, cry out in distress; whine, whimper; grumble, complain

*yaud:* an old mare or horse, especially a worn-out horse

*yaup:* to cry shrilly, scream

*yellper:* yelper, an animal that yelps or makes a shrill cry

*yer:* your

*yerk:* a blow, a hard knock; to hammer; (with 'off') to rattle off, to perform in a lively way

*yermit:* hermit; a solitary dwelling

*yerthe:* earth

*ye's:* ye, you

*yestreen:* yesterday evening

*yett:* gate

*yirb:* herb

*yirth(e):* see *yerthe*

*yocke:* yoke

*yont:* beyond, on the other side; yonder; see also *ayont*

*yooldaye:* screaming, whining

*yoursel:* yourself

*yout(e):* shout, roar, yell

*youtheid:* youth, young people

*yowle:* howl, wail

*yukit:* itchy